Expert PL/SQL Practices

for Oracle Developers and DBAs

John Beresniewicz, Adrian Billington, Martin Büchi,
Melanie Caffrey, Ron Crisco, Lewis Cunningham,
Dominic Delmolino, Sue Harper, Torben Holm,
Connor McDonald, Arup Nanda, Stephan Petit,
Michael Rosenblum, Robyn Sands, Riyaj Shamsudeen

Expert PL/SQL Practices: for Oracle Developers and DBAs

ISBN-13 (pbk): 978-1-4302-3485-2

ISBN-13 (electronic): 978-1-4302-3486-9

President and Publisher: Paul Manning
Lead Editor: Jonathan Gennick
Technical Reviewers: Chris Beck, Mike Gangler, Toon Koppelaars
Editorial Board: Steve Anglin, Mark Beckner, Ewan Buckingham, Gary Cornell, Jonathan Gennick, Jonathan Hassell, Michelle Lowman, James Markham, Matthew Moodie, Jeff Olson, Jeffrey Pepper, Frank Pohlmann, Douglas Pundick, Ben Renow-Clarke, Dominic Shakeshaft, Matt Wade, Tom Welsh
Coordinating Editor: Corbin Collins
Copy Editor: Mary Behr
Production Support: Patrick Cunningham
Indexer: SPI Global
Artist: SPI Global
Cover Designer: Anna Ishchenko

Distributed to the book trade worldwide by Springer Science+Business Media, LLC., 233 Spring Street, 6th Floor, New York, NY 10013. Phone 1-800-SPRINGER, fax (201) 348-4505, e-mail orders-ny@springer-sbm.com, or visit www.springeronline.com.

For information on translations, please e-mail rights@apress.com, or visit www.apress.com.

Apress and friends of ED books may be purchased in bulk for academic, corporate, or promotional use. eBook versions and licenses are also available for most titles. For more information, reference our Special Bulk Sales–eBook Licensing web page at www.apress.com/bulk-sales.

Contents at a Glance

Contents

About the Authors

John Beresniewicz is a consulting member of the technical staff at Oracle headquarters in Redwood Shores, CA. He joined Oracle in 2002 to work on Enterprise Manager in the database performance area and has played significant role in the design of Diagnostic and Tuning packs, Real Application Testing, Support Workbench, and Exadata. He has been a frequent speaker on database performance and PL/SQL programming over many years at Oracle Openworld and other conferences. He is co-author of *Oracle Built-in Packages* (O'Reilly & Associates, 1998) with Steven Feuerstein and is a founding member of the OakTable network.

Adrian Billington is a consultant in application design, development, and performance tuning who has been working with Oracle databases since 1999. He is the man behind `www.oracle-developer.net`, a web site full of SQL and PL/SQL features, utilities, and techniques for Oracle developers. Adrian is also an Oracle ACE and a member of the OakTable Network. He lives in the UK with his wife Anji and three children Georgia, Oliver, and Isabella.

Martin Büchi has worked since 2004 as Lead Software Architect for Avaloq, a provider of a standardized banking software built on the Oracle RDBMS with 11 million lines of PL/SQL code. Together with two colleagues he defines the system architecture and reviews the designs and code of 170 full-time PL/SQL developers, looking for simplicity, efficiency, and robustness. Martin regularly speaks at Oracle conferences. In 2009 he was named PL/SQL Developer of the Year by *Oracle Magazine*. Before getting into the Oracle database, Martin worked in object-oriented systems, formal methods, and approximate record matching. He holds an MSc from the Swiss Federal Institute of Technology and a PhD from the Turku Center for Computer Science in Finland. In his spare time, Martin enjoys various outdoor sports with his family.

Melanie Caffrey is a Senior Development Manager for Oracle Corporation, providing front-end and back-end Oracle solutions for the business needs of various clients. She is co-author of several technical publications including *Oracle Web Application Programming for PL/SQL Developers, Oracle DBA Interactive Workbook,* and *Oracle Database Administration: The Complete Video Course,* all published by Prentice Hall. She has instructed students in Columbia University's Computer Technology and Applications program in New York City, teaching advanced Oracle database administration and PL/SQL development. She is a frequent Oracle conference speaker.

Ron Crisco has been a software designer, developer, and project leader for 28 years and has worked with Oracle databases for 21 years. He works at Method R Corporation, designing and developing software, managing software products (like Method R Profiler, MR Tools, and MR Trace), consulting, and teaching courses. His specialty is simplifying complex work, which is especially valuable in helping the people around him accomplish extraordinary things.

▨**Lewis Cunningham** has been working in IT for over 20 years and has worked with Oracle databases since 1993. His specialties are application design, database design, and coding of high volume, VLDB databases. He is currently a Senior Database Architect at a financial services company in St Petersburg, FL working on very large, high transaction rate analytical databases and applications. He spends an inordinate amount of time keeping up with current technology and trends and speaking at user groups and doing webinars. Lewis is also an Oracle ACE Director and Oracle Certified Professional. He has written several articles for the Oracle Technology Network and maintains an Oracle technology blog at http://it.toolbox.com/blogs/oracle-guide. Lewis has written two books: *EnterpriseDB: The Definitive Reference* (Rampant Techpress, 2007) and *SQL DML: The SQL Starter Series* (CreateSpace, 2008). He lives in Florida with his wife and two sons. You can contact him at lewisc@databasewisdom.com.

▨**Dominic Delmolino** is the Lead Oracle and Database Technologist for Agilex Technologies, a consulting firm specializing in assisting government and private enterprises to realize the value of their information. Dominic has over 24 years of database experience, including more than 20 years as an Oracle Database Engineering and Development professional. He is a member of the Oak Table Network and regularly presents at conferences, seminars, and user group meetings in Europe and the US. He also maintains www.oraclemusings.com, a site focused on database coding and design practices related to database application development. Dominic holds a Bachelor of Science degree in computer science from Cornell University, Ithaca, NY.

▨**Sue Harper** is a Product Manager for Oracle SQL Developer and SQL Developer Data Modeler in the Database Development Tools group. She has been at Oracle since 1992 and is currently based in London. Sue is a regular contributor to magazines, maintains a technical blog, and speaks at many conferences around the world. She has authored the technical book *Oracle SQL Developer 2.1* (Packt Publishing, 2009) When not at work, Sue is a keen walker and photographer. Sue takes time out to work with a charity in the slums of New Delhi, where she works with the women and children.

▨**Torben Holm** has been in the computer business as a developer since 1987. He has been working with Oracle since 1992; his first four years as system analyst and application developer (Oracle 7 and Forms 4.0/Reports 2.0 and DBA), then two years as developer (Oracle6/7, Forms 3.0 and RPT, and DBA). He spent several years working for Oracle Denmark in the Premium Services group as a Senior Principal Consultant performing application development and DBA tasks. He also worked as an instructor in PL/SQL, SQL, and DBA courses. Torben now works for Miracle A/S (www.miracleas.dk) as a consultant with a focus in application development (PLSQL, mod_plsql, Forms, ADF) and database administration. He has been at Miracle A/S 10 years. He is an Oracle Certified Developer and a member of OakTable.net.

▨**Connor McDonald** has worked with Oracle since the early 1990s, cutting his teeth on Oracle versions 6.0.36 and 7.0.12. Over the past 11 years, Connor has worked with systems in Australia, the U.K., Southeast Asia, Western Europe, and the United States. He has come to realize that although the systems and methodologies around the world are very diverse, there tend to be two common themes in the development of systems running on Oracle: either to steer away from the Oracle-specific functions or to use them in a haphazard or less-than-optimal fashion. It was this observation that led to the creation of a personal hints and tips web site (www.oracledba.co.uk) and more presenting on the Oracle speaker circuit in an endeavor to improve the perception and usage of PL/SQL in the industry.

▓**Arup Nanda** has been an Oracle DBA since 1993, which has exposed him to all facets of database administration, from modeling to disaster recovery. He currently leads the global DBA team at Starwood Hotels, the parent of chains such as Sheraton and Westin, in White Plains, NY. He serves as a contributing editor of *SELECT Journal*, the publication of Independent Oracle Users Group (IOUG); speaks at many Oracle Technology events such as Oracle World and local user groups such as New York Oracle User Group; and has written many articles for both print publications such as *Oracle Magazine* and online publications such as *Oracle Technology Network*. Arup has coauthored two books: *Oracle Privacy Security Auditing* (Rampant, 2003) and *Oracle PL/SQL for DBAs* (O'Reilly, 2005). Recognizing his professional accomplishments and contributions to user community, Oracle chose him as the DBA of the Year in 2003. Arup lives in Danbury, Connecticut, with his wife Anindita and son Anish. He can be reached at arup@proligence.com.

▓**Stephan Petit** began his career in 1995 at CERN, the European Laboratory for Particle Physics, located in Geneva, Switzerland. He is now in charge of a team of software engineers and students delivering applications and tools to the laboratory and beyond. One of these tools is the Engineering and Equipment Data Management System, also known as the CERN EDMS. Projects like CERN's Large Hadron Collider (LHC) have a lifetime of 40 years or more. The EDMS is the digital engineering memory of the laboratory. More than a million documents relating to more than a million pieces of equipment are stored in the EDMS, which is also used as CERN's Product Lifecycle Management (PLM) and Asset Tracking system. EDMS is based almost entirely on PL/SQL and is intended to have a lifetime at least as long as the LHC.

Stephan and his team have been polishing coding conventions and best practices in PL/SQL in order to meet their very interesting mix of challenges: maintainability over decades, reliability, efficient error handling, scalability, and reusability of the modules. These challenges are compounded by the frequent rotation of team members, most of whom are students only temporarily at CERN. The oldest piece of code was written in 1995 and is still in use — with success! Apart from polishing PL/SQL, Stephan also enjoys being on stage from time to time as rock band singer at the CERN's rock & roll summer festival and as actor in various plays.

▓**Michael Rosenblum** is a Software Architect/Development DBA at Dulcian, Inc. where he is responsible for system tuning and application architecture. Michael supports Dulcian developers by writing complex PL/SQL routines and researching new features. He is the co-author of *PL/SQL for Dummies* (Wiley Press, 2006) and author of a number of database-related articles (IOUG Select Journal, ODTUG Tech Journal). Michael is an Oracle ACE, a frequent presenter at various regional and national Oracle user group conferences (Oracle OpenWorld, ODTUG, IOUG Collaborate, RMOUG, NYOUG, etc), and winner of the ODTUG Kaleidoscope 2009 Best Speaker Award. In his native Ukraine, he received the scholarship of the President of Ukraine, a Master of Science degree in Information Systems, and a diploma with honors from the Kiev National University of Economics.

▓**Robyn Sands** is a Software Engineer for Cisco Systems, where she designs and develops embedded Oracle database products for Cisco customers. She has been working with Oracle since 1996 and has extensive experience in application development, large system implementations, and performance measurement. Robyn began her work career in industrial and quality engineering, and she has combined her prior education and experience with her love of data by searching for new ways to build database systems with consistent performance and minimal maintenance requirements. She is a member of the OakTable Network and a coauthor of two books on Oracle: *Expert Oracle Practices* and *Pro Oracle SQL* (both Apress, 2010). Robyn occasionally posts random blog entries at http://adhdocddba.blogspot.com.

▓**Riyaj Shamsudeen** is the Principal Database Administrator and President of OraInternals, a performance/recovery/EBS11i consulting company. He specializes in real application clusters, performance tuning, and database internals. He also frequently blogs about these technology areas in his blog `http://orainternals.wordpress.com`. He is also a regular presenter in many international conferences such as HOTSOS, COLLABORATE, RMOUG, SIOUG, UKOUG, etc. He is a proud member of OakTable Network. He has over 16 years of experience using Oracle technology products and over 15 years as an Oracle/Oracle applications database administrator.

About the Technical Reviewers

Chris Beck has a degree in computer science from Rutgers University and has been working with multiple DBMS's for more than 20 years. He has spent the last 16 years as an Oracle employee where he is currently a Master Principal Technologist focusing on core database technologies. He is a co-inventor of two US Patents on software methodologies that were the basis for what is now known as Oracle Application Express. Chris has reviewed other Oracle books including *Expert One-On-One* (Peer Information Inc., 2001) and *Expert Oracle Database Architecture* (Apress, 2005), both by Tom Kyte and is himself the co-author of two books, *Beginning Oracle Programming* (Wrox Press, 2005) and *Mastering Oracle PL/SQL* (Apress, 2005). He resides in Northern Virginia with his wife Marta and four children; when not spending time with them, he can usually be found wasting time playing video games or watching Series A football.

Mike Gangler is a Database Specialist and Infrastructure Architect with over 30 years of data processing industry experience, primarily as a Database Technical Lead, Systems Analyst, and DBA on large corporate Information Systems projects. As a past President of the Detroit Oracle Users Group and Ann Arbor Oracle User groups, and charter member of the Board of Directors of the International Oracle Users Group, Mike has attained worldwide recognition as an accomplished and Certified Oracle DBA and relational database expert.

Toon Koppelaars is a long-time Oracle technology user, having used the Oracle database and tools software since 1987 (Oracle version 4). During this time, he has been involved in application development and database administration. He is an ACE Director (database development) and frequent speaker at Oracle-related events. He's also the declarer of "The Helsinki Declaration (IT version)" which describes a database-centric approach to modern application development. Together with Lex de Haan, Toon has co-authored *Applied Mathematics for Database Professionals* (Apress, 2007).

Introduction

Rarely do I take the opportunity to introduce a book that I've helped create. Normally I am content with my place in the background where book editors rightfully belong. I make an exception this time because the content in this book brings back so many memories from own experiences as a developer in days gone by.

Expert PL/SQL Practices is about wielding PL/SQL effectively. It's not a book about syntax. It's a book about how to apply syntax and features along with good development practices to create applications that are reliable and scalable—and maintainable over the long term.

With any tool, one of the first things to know is when to wield it. Riyaj Shamsudeen deftly tackles the question of when to use PL/SQL in his opening chapter *Do Not Use!* I put that chapter first in the book because of personal experience: My best-ever performance optimization success came in the late 1990s when I replaced a stack of procedural code on a client PC with a single SQL statement, taking a job from over 36 hours to just a couple of minutes. PL/SQL was not the culprit, but the lesson I learned then is that a set-based approach—when one is possible—is often preferable to writing procedural code.

Michael Rosenblum follows with an excellent chapter on dynamic SQL, showing how to write code when you don't know the SQL statements until runtime. He reminded me of a time at Dow Chemical in the early 1990s when I wrote a data-loading application for a medical record system using Rdb's Extended Dynamic Cursor feature set. I still remember that as one of the most fun applications that I ever developed.

Dominic Delmolino tackles parallel processing with PL/SQL. He covers the benefits that you can achieve as well as the candidate workloads. Just be careful, okay? One of my biggest-ever blunders as a DBA was when I once unthinkingly set a degree of parallelism on a key application table in order to make a single report run faster. It was as if the Enter key was connected to my telephone, because my phone rang within about a minute of my change. The manager on the other end of the line was most unpleased. Needless to say, I decided then that implementing parallelism deserved just a tad bit more thought than I had been giving it. Dominic's chapter will help you avoid such embarrassment.

Several chapters in the book cover code hygiene and good programming practices. Stephan Petit presents a set of useful naming and coding conventions. Torben Holm covers PL/SQL Warnings and conditional compilation. Lewis Cunningham presents a thought-provoking chapter on code analysis and the importance of truly understanding the code that you write and how it gets used. Robyn Sands helps you think about flexibility and good design in her chapter on evolutionary data modeling. Melanie Caffrey tours the various cursor types available, helping you to make the right choice of cursor for any given situation.

Other chapters relate to debugging and troubleshooting. Sue Harper covers PL/SQL unit testing, especially the supporting feature set that is now built into SQL Developer. (I remember writing unit test scripts on paper back in the day). Save yourself the embarrassment of regression bugs. Automated unit tests make it easy and convenient to verify that you've not broken two new things while fixing one.

John Beresniewicz follows with a chapter on contract-oriented programming. A key part of John's approach is the use of asserts to validate conditions that should be true at various points within your code. I first learned of the assert technique while doing PowerBuilder programming back in the Stone Age. I've always been happy to see John promote the technique in relation to PL/SQL.

Arup Nanda helps you get control over dependencies and invalidations. Dependency issues can be a source of seemingly random, difficult-to-repeat application errors. Arup shows how to get control over what must inevitably happen, so that you aren't caught out by unexpected errors.

We could hardly leave performance and scalability out of the picture. Ron Crisco talks about profiling your code to find the greatest opportunities for optimization. Adrian Billington talks about the performance aspects of invoking PL/SQL from within SQL statements. Connor McDonald covers the tremendous performance advantages available from bulk SQL operations.

An unusual aspect of scalability not often thought about is that of application size and the number of developers. Is PL/SQL suited for large-scale development involving dozens, perhaps hundreds of programmers? Martin Büchi shows that PL/SQL is very much up to the task in his chapter on PL/SQL programming in the large by recounting his success with an 11-million line application maintained by over 170 developers.

You can probably tell that I'm excited about this book. The authors are top notch. Each has written on an aspect of PL/SQL that they are passionate and especially knowledgeable about. If you're past the point of learning syntax, then sit down, read this book, and step up your game in delivering applications using the full power of PL/SQL and Oracle Database.

Jonathan Gennick
Assistant Editorial Director, Apress

CHAPTER 1

Do Not Use

By Riyaj Shamsudeen

Congratulations on buying this book. PL/SQL is a great tool to have in your toolbox; however, you should understand that use of PL/SQL is not suitable for all scenarios. This chapter will teach you when to code your application in PL/SQL, how to write scalable code, and, more importantly, when not to code programs in PL/SQL. Abuse of some PL/SQL constructs leads to unscalable code. In this chapter, I will review various cases in which the misuse of PL/SQL was unsuitable and lead to an unscalable application.

PL/SQL AND SQL

SQL is a set processing language and SQL statements scale better if the statements are written with set level thinking in mind. PL/SQL is a procedural language and SQL statements can be embedded in PL/SQL code.

SQL statements are executed in the SQL executor (more commonly known as the SQL engine). PL/SQL code is executed by the PL/SQL engine. The power of PL/SQL emanates from the ability to combine the procedural abilities of PL/SQL with the set processing abilities of SQL.

Row-by-Row Processing

In a typical row-by-row processing program, code opens a cursor, loops through the rows retrieved from the cursor, and processes those rows. This type of loop-based processing construct is highly discouraged as it leads to unscalable code. Listing 1-1 shows an example of a program using the construct.

Listing 1-1. Row-by-Row Processing

```
DECLARE
  CURSOR c1 IS
    SELECT prod_id, cust_id, time_id, amount_sold
    FROM sales
```

1

```
     WHERE amount_sold > 100;
   c1_rec c1%rowtype;
   l_cust_first_name customers.cust_first_name%TYPE;
   l_cust_lasT_name customers.cust_last_name%TYPE;
BEGIN
   FOR c1_rec IN c1
   LOOP
      -- Query customer details
      SELECT cust_first_name, cust_last_name
      INTO l_cust_first_name, l_cust_last_name
      FROM customers
      WHERE cust_id=c1_rec.cust_id;
      --
      -- Insert in to target table
      --
      INSERT INTO top_sales_customers (
        prod_id, cust_id, time_id, cust_first_name, cust_last_name,amount_sold
        )
        VALUES
        (
          c1_rec.prod_id,
          c1_rec.cust_id,
          c1_rec.time_id,
          l_cust_first_name,
          l_cust_last_name,
          c1_rec.amount_sold
        );
   END LOOP;
   COMMIT;
END;
/
```

PL/SQL procedure successfully completed.

Elapsed: 00:00:10.93

In Listing 1-1, the program declares a cursor c1, and opens the cursor implicitly using cursor–for-loop syntax. For each row retrieved from the cursor c1, the program queries the customers table to populate first_name and last_name to variables. A row is subsequently inserted in to the top_sales_customers table.

There is a problem with the coding practice exemplified in Listing1-1. Even if the SQL statements called in the loop are highly optimized, program execution can consume a huge amount of time. Imagine that the SQL statement querying the customers table consumes an elapsed time of 0.1 seconds, and that the INSERT statement consumes an elapsed time of 0.1 seconds, giving a total elapsed time of 0.2 seconds per loop execution. If cursor c1 retrieves 100,000 rows, then the total elapsed time for this program will be 100,000 multiplied by 0.2 seconds: 20,000 seconds or 5.5 hours approximately. Optimizing this program construct is not easy. Tom Kyte termed this type of processing as *slow-by-slow processing* for obvious reasons.

▓ **Note** Examples in this chapter use SH schema, one of the example schemas supplied by Oracle Corporation. To install the example schemas, Oracle-provided software can be used. You can download it from `http://download.oracle.com/otn/solaris/oracle11g/R2/solaris.sparc64_11gR2_examples.zip` for 11gR2 Solaris platform. Refer to the Readme document in the unzipped software directories for installation instructions. Zip files for other platforms and versions are also available from Oracle's web site.

There is another inherent issue with the code in Listing 1-1. SQL statements are called from PL/SQL in a loop, so the execution will switch back and forth between the PL/SQL engine and the SQL engine. This switch between two environments is known as a *context switch*. Context switches increase elapsed time of your programs and introduce unnecessary CPU overhead. You should reduce the number of context switches by eliminating or reducing the switching between these two environments.

You should generally avoid row-by-row processing. Better coding practice would be to convert the program from Listing 1-1 into a SQL statement. Listing 1-2 rewrites the code, avoiding PL/SQL entirely.

Listing 1-2. Row-by-Row Processing Rewritten

```
--
-- Insert in to target table
--
INSERT
INTO top_sales_customers
  (
    prod_id,
    cust_id,
    time_id,
    cust_first_name,
    cust_last_name,
    amount_sold
  )
SELECT s.prod_id,
  s.cust_id,
  s.time_id,
  c.cust_first_name,
  c.cust_last_name,
  s.amount_sold
FROM sales s,
     customers c
WHERE s.cust_id     = c.cust_id and
s.amount_sold> 100;

135669 rows created.

Elapsed: 00:00:00.26
```

The code in Listing 1-2, in addition to resolving the shortcomings of the row-by-row processing, has a few more advantages. Parallel execution can be used to tune the rewritten SQL statement. With the use of multiple parallel execution processes, you can decrease the elapsed time of execution sharply. Furthermore, code becomes concise and readable.

▓ **Note** If you rewrite the PL/SQL loop code to a join, you need to consider duplicates. If there are duplicates in the customers table for the same cust_id columns, then the rewritten SQL statement will retrieve more rows then intended. However, in this specific example, there is a primary key on cust_id column in the customers table, so there is no danger of duplicates with an equality predicate on cust_id column.

Nested Row-by-Row Processing

You can nest cursors in PL/SQL language. It is a common coding practice to retrieve values from one cursor, feed those values to another cursor, feed the values from second level cursor to third level cursor, and so on. But the performance issues with a loop-based code increase if the cursors are deeply nested. The number of SQL executions increases sharply due to nesting of cursors, leading to a longer program runtime.

In Listing 1-3, cursors c1, c2, and c3 are nested. Cursor c1 is the top level cursor and retrieves rows from the table t1; cursor c2 is opened, passing the values from cursor c1; cursor c3 is opened, passing the values from cursor c2. An UPDATE statement is executed for every row retrieved from cursor c3. Even if the UPDATE statement is optimized to execute in 0.01 seconds, performance of the program suffers due to the deeply nested cursor. Say that cursors c1, c2, and c3 retrieve 20, 50, and 100 rows, respectively. The code then loops through 100,000 rows, and the total elapsed time of the program exceeds 1,000 seconds. Tuning this type of program usually leads to a complete rewrite.

Listing 1-3. Row-by-Row Processing with Nested Cursors

```
DECLARE
  CURSOR c1 AS
    SELECT n1 FROM t1;
  CURSOR c2 (p_n1) AS
    SELECT n1, n2 FROM t2 WHERE n1=p_n1;
  CURSOR c3 (p_n1, p_n2) AS
    SELECT text FROM t3 WHERE n1=p_n1 AND n2=p_n2;
BEGIN
  FOR c1_rec IN c1
  LOOP
    FOR c2_rec IN c2 (c1_rec.n1)
    LOOP
      FOR c3_rec IN c3(c2_rec.n1, c2_rec.n2)
      LOOP
        -- execute some sql here;
        UPDATE … SET ..where n1=c3_rec.n1 AND n2=c3_rec.n2;
      EXCEPTION
      WHEN no_data_found THEN
```

```
      INSERT into… END;
    END LOOP;
  END LOOP;
 END LOOP;
COMMIT;
END;
/
```

Another problem with the code in the Listing 1-3 is that an UPDATE statement is executed. If the UPDATE statement results in a no_data_found exception, then an INSERT statement is executed. It is possible to offload this type of processing from PL/SQL to the SQL engine using a MERGE statement.

Conceptually, the three loops in Listing 1-3 represent an equi-join between the tables t1,t2, and t3. In Listing 1-4, the logic is rewritten as a SQL statement with an alias of t. The combination of UPDATE and INSERT logic is replaced by a MERGE statement. MERGE syntax provides the ability to update a row if it exists and insert a row if it does not exist.

Listing 1-4. Row-by-Row Processing Rewritten Using MERGE Statement

```
MERGE INTO fact1 USING
(SELECT DISTINCT c3.n1,c3.n2
 FROM t1, t2, t3
 WHERE t1.n1     = t2.n1
 AND t2.n1       = t3.n1
 AND t2.n2       = t3.n2
) t
ON (fact1.n1=t.n1 AND fact1.n2=t.n2)
WHEN matched THEN
  UPDATE SET .. WHEN NOT matched THEN
  INSERT .. ;
  COMMIT;
```

Do not write code with deeply nested cursors in PL/SQL language. Review it to see if you can write such code in SQL instead.

Lookup Queries

Lookup queries are generally used to populate some variable or to perform data validation. Executing lookup queries in a loop causes performance issues.

In the Listing 1-5, the highlighted query retrieves the country_name using a lookup query. For every row from the cursor c1, a query to fetch the country_name is executed. As the number of rows retrieved from the cursor c1 increases, executions of the lookup query also increases, leading to a poorly performing code.

Listing 1-5. Lookup Queries, a Modified Copy of Listing 1-1

```
DECLARE
  CURSOR c1 IS
    SELECT prod_id, cust_id, time_id, amount_sold
    FROM sales
    WHERE amount_sold > 100;
```

```
   l_cust_first_name customers.cust_first_name%TYPE;
   l_cust_last_name customers.cust_last_name%TYPE;
   l_Country_id countries.country_id%TYPE;
   l_country_name countries.country_name%TYPE;
BEGIN
 FOR c1_rec IN c1
 LOOP
   -- Query customer details
   SELECT cust_first_name, cust_last_name, country_id
   INTO l_cust_first_name, l_cust_last_name, l_country_id
   FROM customers
   WHERE cust_id=c1_rec.cust_id;

   -- Query to get country_name
   SELECT country_name
   INTO l_country_name
   FROM countries WHERE country_id=l_country_id;
   --
   -- Insert in to target table
   --
   INSERT
   INTO top_sales_customers
      (
        prod_id, cust_id, time_id, cust_first_name,
        cust_last_name, amount_sold, country_name
      )
      VALUES
      (
        c1_rec.prod_id, c1_rec.cust_id, c1_rec.time_id, l_cust_first_name,
        l_cust_last_name, c1_rec.amount_sold, l_country_name
      );
 END LOOP;
COMMIT;
END;
/
PL/SQL procedure successfully completed.
Elapsed: 00:00:16.18
```

The example in Listing 1-5 is simplistic. The lookup query for the country_name can be rewritten as a join in the main cursor c1 itself. As a first step, you should modify the lookup query into a join. In a real world application, this type of rewrite is not always possible, though.

If you can't rewrite the code to reduce the executions of a lookup query, then you have another option. You can define an associative array to cache the results of the lookup query and reuse the array in later executions, thus effectively reducing the executions of the lookup query.

Listing 1-6 illustrates the array-caching technique. Instead of executing the query to retrieve the country_name for every row from the cursor c1, a key-value pair, (country_id, country_name) in this example) is stored in an associative array named l_country_names. An associative array is similar to an index in that any given value can be accessed using a key value.

Before executing the lookup query, an existence test is performed for an element matching the country_id key value using an EXISTS operator. If an element exists in the array, then the country_name is retrieved from that array without executing the lookup query. If not, then the lookup query is executed and a new element added to the array.

You should also understand that this technique is suitable for statements with few distinct values for the key. In this example, the number of executions of the lookup query will be *probably* much lower as the number of unique values of country_id column is lower. Using the example schema, the maximum number of executions for the lookup query will be 23 as there are only 23 distinct values for the country_id column.

Listing 1-6. Lookup Queries with Associative Arrays

```
DECLARE
  CURSOR c1
  IS
    SELECT prod_id, cust_id, time_id, amount_sold
    FROM sales WHERE amount_sold > 100;
    l_country_names country_names_type;
    l_Country_id countries.country_id%TYPE;
    l_country_name countries.country_name%TYPE;
    l_cust_first_name customers.cust_first_name%TYPE;
    l_cust_lasT_name customers.cust_last_name%TYPE;
    TYPE country_names_type IS
    TABLE OF VARCHAR2(40) INDEX BY pls_integer;
    l_country_names country_names_type;
BEGIN
  FOR c1_rec IN c1 LOOP
  -- Query customer details
  SELECT cust_first_name, cust_last_name, country_id
  INTO l_cust_first_name, l_cust_last_name, l_country_id
  FROM customers
  WHERE cust_id=c1_rec.cust_id;
  -- Check array first before executing a SQL statement

  IF ( l_country_names.EXISTS(l_country_id)) THEN
    l_country_name := l_country_names(l_country_id);
  ELSE
    SELECT country_name INTO l_country_name
    FROM countries
    WHERE country_id                 = l_country_id;
  -- Store in the array for further reuse
    l_country_names(l_country_id) := l_country_name;
  END IF;
  --
  -- Insert in to target table
  --
  INSERT
  INTO top_sales_customers
    (
      prod_id, cust_id, time_id, cust_first_name,
      cust_last_name, amount_sold, country_name
    )
```

```
      VALUES
      (
        c1_rec.prod_id, c1_rec.cust_id, c1_rec.time_id, l_cust_first_name,
        l_cust_last_name, c1_rec.amount_sold, l_country_name
      );
END LOOP;
COMMIT;
END;
/
PL/SQL procedure successfully completed.

Elapsed: 00:00:10.89
```

▓ **Note** Associative arrays are allocated in the Program Global Area (PGA) of the dedicated server process in the database server. If there are thousands of connections caching intermediate results in the array, then there will be a noticeable increase in memory usage. You should measure memory usage increase per process and design the database server to accommodate memory increase.

Array-based techniques can be used to eliminate unnecessary work in other scenarios, too. For example, executions of costly function calls can be reduced via this technique by storing the function results in an associative array. (The "Excessive Function Calls" section later in this chapter discusses another technique to reduce the number of executions.)

▓ **Note** Storing the function results in an associative array will work only if the function is a deterministic function, meaning that for a given set of input(s), the function will always return the same output.

Excessive Access to DUAL

It is not uncommon for code to access the DUAL table excessively. You should avoid overusing DUAL table access. Accessing DUAL from PL/SQL causes context switching, which hurts performance. This section reviews some common reasons for accessing DUAL excessively and discusses mitigation plans.

Arithmetics with Date

There is no reason to access DUAL table to perform arithmetic operations or DATE manipulations, as most operations can be performed using PL/SQL language constructs. Even SYSDATE can be accessed directly in PL/SQL without accessing SQL engine. In Listing 1-7, the highlighted SQL statement is calculating the UNIX epoch time (epoch time is defined as number of seconds elapsed from January 1, 1970 Midnight) using a SELECT.. from DUAL syntax. While access to the DUAL table is fast, execution of the statement still results in a context switch between the SQL and PL/SQL engines.

Listing 1-7. Excessive Access to DUAL—Arithmetics

```
DECLARE
  l_epoch INTEGER;
BEGIN
  SELECT ((SYSDATE-TO_DATE('01-JAN-1970 00:00:00', 'DD-MON-YYYY HH24:MI:SS'))
          * 24 *60 *60 )
  INTO l_epoch
  FROM DUAL;
  dbms_output.put_line(l_epoch);
END;
```

You can avoid the unnecessary access to DUAL table by performing the arithmetic calculation using PL/SQL constructs like this:

```
l_epoch := (SYSDATE- TO_DATE('01-JAN-1970 00:00:00', 'DD-MON-YYYY HH24:MI:SS'))
          * 24 *60 *60 ;
```

There's simply no need to invoke SQL to execute numeric operations. Simply do the work from PL/SQL. Your code will be easier to read, and it will perform better.

Excessive access to query the current date or timestamp is another reason for increased access to DUAL table. Consider coding a call to SYSDATE in the SQL statement directly instead of selecting SYSDATE into a variable and then passing that value back to the SQL engine. If you need to access the column value after inserting a row, then use returning clause to fetch the column value. If you need to access SYSDATE in PL/SQL itself, use PL/SQL construct to fetch the current date in to a variable.

Access to Sequences

Another common reason for unnecessary access to DUAL table is to retrieve the next value from a sequence. Listing 1-8 shows a code fragment selecting the next value from cust_id_seq in to a variable and then inserting into customers table using that variable.

Listing 1-8. Excessive Access to DUAL— Sequences

```
DECLARE
  l_cust_id NUMBER;
BEGIN
  FOR c1 in (SELECT cust_first_name, cust_last_name FROM customers
             WHERE cust_marital_status!='married')
  LOOP
    SELECT cust_hist_id_seq.nextval INTO l_cust_id FROM dual;
    INSERT INTO customers_hist
      (cust_hist_id, first_name, last_name )
    VALUES
      (l_cust_id, c1.cust_first_name, c1.cust_last_name)
      ;
  END LOOP;
END;
/
```

9

```
PL/SQL procedure successfully completed.
```

```
Elapsed: 00:00:01.89
```

A better approach is to avoid retrieving the value to a variable and retrieve the value from the sequence directly in the INSERT statement itself. The following code fragment illustrates an INSERT statement inserting rows into customers using a sequence-generated value. With this coding practice, you can avoid accessing the DUAL table, and thus avoid context switches between the engines.

```
Insert into customers (cust_id, ...)
Values (cust_id_seq.nextval,...);
```

Better yet, rewrite the PL/SQL block as a SQL statement. For example, the following rewritten statement completes in 0.2 seconds compared to a run time of 1.89 seconds with PL/SQL loop-based processing:

```
INSERT INTO customers_hist
SELECT
   cust_hist_id_seq.nextval, cust_first_name, cust_last_name
FROM customers
WHERE cust_marital_status!='married';
```

```
23819 rows created.
Elapsed: 00:00:00.20
```

Populating Master-Detail Rows

Another common reason for excessive access to DUAL table is to insert rows into tables involved in a master-detail relationship. Typically, in this coding practice, the primary key value for the master table is fetched from the sequence into a local variable. Then that local variable is used while inserting into master *and* detail tables. The reason this approach developed is that the primary key value of the master table is needed while inserting into the detail table(s).

A new SQL feature introduced in Oracle Database version 9i provides a better solution by allowing you to return the values from an inserted row. You can retrieve the key value from a newly-inserted master row by using the DML RETURNING clause. Then you can use that key value while inserting in to the detail table. For example:

```
INSERT INTO customers (cust_id, ...)
VALUES (cust_id_seq.nextval,...)
RETURNING cust_id into l_cust_id;
...
INSERT INTO customer_transactions (cust_id, ...)
VALUES (l_cust_id,...)
...
```

Excessive Function Calls

It is important to recognize that well designed applications will use functions, procedures, and packages. This section is not a discussion about those well designed programs using modular code practices. Rather, this section is specifically directed towards the coding practice of calling functions unnecessarily.

Unnecessary Function Execution

Executing a function call usually means that a different part of the instruction set must be loaded into the CPU. The execution jumps from one part of instruction to another part of instruction. This execution jump adds to performance issues because it entails a dumping and refilling of the instruction pipeline. The result is additional CPU usage.

By avoiding unnecessary function execution, you avoid unneeded flushing and refilling of the instruction pipeline, thus minimizing demands upon your CPU. Again, I am not arguing against modular coding practices. I argue only against excessive and unnecessary execution of function calls. I can best explain by example.

In Listing 1-9, log_entry is a debug function and is called for every validation. But that function itself has a check for v_debug, and messages are inserted only if the debug flag is set to true. Imagine a program with hundreds of such complex business validations performed in a loop. Essentially, the log_entry function will be called millions of times unnecessarily even if the v_debug flag is set to false.

Listing 1-9. Unnecessary Function Calls

```
create table log_table ( message_seq number, message varchar2(512));
create sequence message_id_seq;

DECLARE
 l_debug BOOLEAN := FALSE;
 r1 integer;
 FUNCTION log_entry( v_message IN VARCHAR2, v_debug in boolean)
  RETURN number
  IS
  BEGIN
    IF(v_debug) THEN
      INSERT INTO log_table
        (message_seq, MESSAGE)
        VALUES
        (message_id_seq.nextval, v_message
        );
    END IF;
    return 0;
  END;
BEGIN
 FOR c1 IN (
        SELECT s.prod_id, s.cust_id,s.time_id,
               c.cust_first_name, c.cust_last_name,
               s.amount_sold
        FROM sales s,
            customers c
        WHERE s.cust_id     = c.cust_id and
        s.amount_sold> 100)
   LOOP
     IF c1.cust_first_name IS NOT NULL THEN
       r1 := log_entry ('first_name is not null ', l_debug );
     END IF;
```

```
      IF c1.cust_last_name IS NOT NULL THEN
        r1 := log_entry ('Last_name is not null ', l_debug);
      END IF;
   END LOOP;
END;
/

PL/SQL procedure successfully completed.
Elapsed: 00:00:00.54
```

The code in Listing 1-9 can be rewritten to call the log_entry function only if the variable l_debug flag is set to true. This rewrite reduces unnecessary executions of log_entry function. The rewritten program completes in 0.43 seconds. The performance improvement will be noticeable with higher number of executions.

```
...
IF first_name IS NULL AND l_debug=TRUE THEN
  log_entry('first_name is null ');
END IF;
...
/
PL/SQL procedure successfully completed.
Elapsed: 00:00:00.43
```

For a better approach, consider the conditional compilation constructs to avoid the execution of this code fragment completely. In Listing 1-10, the highlighted code uses $IF-$THEN construct with a conditional variable $debug_on. If the conditional variable debug_on is true, then the code block is executed. In a production environment, debug_on variable will be FALSE, eliminating function execution. Note that the elapsed time of the program reduces further to 0.34 seconds.

Listing 1-10. Avoiding Unnecessary Function Calls with Conditional Compilation

```
DECLARE
  l_debug BOOLEAN := FALSE;
  r1 integer;
  FUNCTION log_entry( v_message IN VARCHAR2, v_debug in boolean)
   RETURN number
   IS
   BEGIN
     IF(v_debug) THEN
       INSERT INTO log_table
         (message_seq, MESSAGE)
         VALUES
         (message_id_seq.nextval, v_message
         );
     END IF;
     return 0;
  END;
```

```
BEGIN
 FOR c1 IN (  .
        SELECT s.prod_id, s.cust_id,s.time_id,
               c.cust_first_name, c.cust_last_name,
               s.amount_sold
        FROM sales s,
            customers c
        WHERE s.cust_id     = c.cust_id and
            s.amount_sold> 100)
  LOOP
   $IF $$debug_on $THEN
    IF c1.cust_first_name IS NOT NULL  THEN
      r1 := log_entry ('first_name is not null ', l_debug );
    END IF;
    IF c1.cust_last_name IS NOT NULL    THEN
      r1 := log_entry ('Last_name is not null ', l_debug);
    END IF;
   $END
    null;
  END LOOP;
END;
/
PL/SQL procedure successfully completed.
Elapsed: 00:00:00.34
```

The problem of invoking functions unnecessarily tends to occur frequently in programs copied from another template program and then modified. Watch for this problem. If a function doesn't need to be called, avoid calling it.

INTERPRETED VS. NATIVE COMPILATION

PL/SQL code, by default, executes as an interpreted code. During PL/SQL compilation, code is converted to an intermediate format and stored in the data dictionary. At execution time, that intermediate code is executed by the engine.

Oracle Database version 9i introduces a new feature known as native compilation. PL/SQL code is compiled into machine instruction and stored as a shared library. Excessive function execution might have less impact with native compilation as modern compilers can inline the subroutine and avoid the instruction jump.

Costly Function Calls

If the execution of a function consumes a few seconds of elapsed time, then calling that function in a loop will result in poorly performing code. You should optimize frequently executed functions to run as efficiently as possible.

In Listing 1-11, if the function calculate_epoch is called in a loop millions of times. Even if the execution of that function consumes just 0.01 seconds, one million executions of that function call will result in an elapsed time of 2.7 hours. One option to resolve this performance issue is to optimize the function to execute in a few milliseconds, but that much optimization is not always possible.

Listing 1-11. Costly Function Calls

```
CREATE OR REPLACE FUNCTION calculate_epoch (d in date)
 RETURN NUMBER DETERMINISTIC IS
 l_epoch number;
BEGIN
 l_epoch := (d - TO_DATE('01-JAN-1970 00:00:00', 'DD-MON-YYYY HH24:MI:SS'))
        * 24 *60 *60 ;
 RETURN l_epoch;
END calculate_epoch;
/

SELECT  /*+ cardinality (10) */ max( calculate_epoch (s.time_id))  epoch
FROM sales s
 WHERE s.amount_sold> 100 and
      calculate_epoch (s.time_id) between 1000000000 and 1100000000;

    EPOCH
----------
1009756800

Elapsed: 00:00:01.39
```

Another option is to pre-store the results of the function execution, thus avoiding function execution in a query. You can do this by employing a function-based index. In Listing 1-12, a function-based index on the function calculate_epoch is created. Performance of the SQL statement improves from 1.39 seconds to 0.06 seconds.

Listing 1-12. Costly Function Call with Function-Based Index

```
CREATE INDEX compute_epoch_fbi ON sales
(calculate_epoch(time_id))
Parallel (degree 4);

SELECT  /*+ cardinality (10) */ max( calculate_epoch (s.time_id))  epoch
FROM sales s
 WHERE s.amount_sold> 100 and
      calculate_epoch (s.time_id) between 1000000000 and 1100000000;
    EPOCH
----------
1009756800

Elapsed: 00:00:00.06
```

You should also understand that function-based indexes have a cost. INSERT statements and UPDATE statements (that update the time_id column) will incur the cost of calling the function and maintaining the index. Carefully weigh the cost of function execution in DML operations against the cost of function execution in SELECT statement to choose the cheaper option.

⬛ **Note** From Oracle Database version 11g onwards, you can create a virtual column, and then create an index on that virtual column. The effect of an indexed virtual column is the same as that of a function-based index. An advantage of virtual columns over function-based index is that you can partition the table using a virtual column, which is not possible with the use of just function based indexes.

The function result_cache, available from Oracle Database version 11g, is another option to tune the execution of costly PL/SQL functions. Results from function execution are remembered in the result cache allocated in the Shared Global Area (SGA) of an instance. Repeated execution of a function with the same parameter will fetch the results from the function cache without repeatedly executing the function. Listing 1-13 shows an example of functions utilizing result_cache to improve performance: the SQL statement completes in 0.81 seconds.

Listing 1-13. Functions with Result_cache

```
DROP INDEX compute_epoch_fbi;
CREATE OR REPLACE FUNCTION calculate_epoch (d in date)
 RETURN NUMBER  DETERMINISTIC RESULT_CACHE IS
 l_epoch number;
BEGIN
 l_epoch := (d - TO_DATE('01-JAN-1970 00:00:00', 'DD-MON-YYYY HH24:MI:SS'))
        * 24 *60 *60 ;
 RETURN l_epoch;
END calculate_epoch;
/

SELECT  /*+ cardinality (10) */ max( calculate_epoch (s.time_id))  epoch
FROM sales s
 WHERE s.amount_sold> 100 and
       calculate_epoch (s.time_id) between 1000000000 and 1100000000;

     EPOCH
----------
1009756800

Elapsed: 00:00:00.81
```

In summary, excessive function execution leads to performance issues. If you can't reduce or eliminate function execution, you may be able to employ function-based indexes or result_cache as a short term fix in order to minimize the impact from function invocation.

Database Link Calls

Excessive database link-based calls can affect application performance. Accessing a remote table or modifying a remote table over a database link within a loop is not a scalable approach. For each access to a remote table, several SQL*Net packets are exchanged between the databases involved in the database link. If the databases are located in geographically separated datacenters or, worse, across the globe, then the waits for SQL*Net traffic will result in program performance issues.

In Listing 1-14, for every row returned from the cursor, the customer table in the remote database is accessed. Let's assume that the round trip network call takes 100ms, so 1 million round trip calls will take 27 hours approximately to complete. A response time of 100ms between the databases located in different parts of the country is not uncommon.

Listing 1-14. Excessive Database Link Calls

```
DECLARE
  V_customer_name VARCHAR2(32);
BEGIN
  ...
  FOR c1 IN (SELECT …)
  LOOP
    ...
    SELECT customer_name
    INTO v_customer_name
    FROM customers@remotedb
    WHERE account_id = c1.account_id;
    ...
  END LOOP;
END;
```

Judicial use of materialized views can be used to reduce network round trip calls during program execution. In the case of Listing 1-14, the customer table can be created as a materialized view. Refresh the materialized view before program execution and access that materialized view in the program. Materializing the table locally reduces the number of SQL*Net round trip calls. Of course, as an Application Designer, you need to compare the cost of materializing the whole table versus the cost of accessing a remote table in a loop, and choose an optimal solution.

Rewriting the program as a SQL statement with a join to a remote table is another option. The query optimizer in Oracle Database can optimize such statements so as to reduce the SQL*Net trip overhead. For this technique to work, you should rewrite the program so that SQL statement is executed once and probably not in a loop.

Materializing the data locally or rewriting the code as a SQL statement with a remote join are the initial steps to tune the program in Listing 1-14. However, if you are unable to do even these things, there is a workaround. As an interim measure, you can convert the program to use a multi-process architecture. For example, process #1 will process the customers in the range of 1 to 100,000, process #2 will process the customers in the range of 100,001 to 200,000, and so on. Apply this logic to the example program by creating 10 processes, and you can reduce the total run time of the program to 2.7 hours approximately. Use of `DBMS_PARALLEL_EXECUTE` is another option to consider for splitting the code in to parallel processing.

Excessive Use of Triggers

Triggers are usually written in PL/SQL, although you can write trigger code in Java as well. Excessive triggers are not ideal for performance reasons. Row changes are performed in the SQL engine and triggers are executed in the PL/SQL engine. Once again, you encounter the dreaded context-switch problem.

In some cases, triggers are unavoidable. For example, complex business validation in a trigger can't be avoided. In those scenarios, you should write that type of complex validation in PL/SQL code. You should avoid overusing triggers for simple validation. For example, use check constraints rather than a trigger to check the list of valid values for a column.

Further, avoid using multiple triggers for the same trigger action. Instead of writing two different triggers for the same action, you should combine them into one so as to minimize the number of context switches.

Excessive Commits

It is a not uncommon to see commits after every row inserted or modified (or deleted) in a PL/SQL loop. The coding practice of committing after every row will lead to slower program execution. Frequent commits generate more redo, require Log Writer to flush the contents of log buffer to log file frequently, can lead to data integrity issues, and consume more resources. The PL/SQL engine is optimized to reduce the effect of frequent commits, but there is no substitute for a well written code when it comes to reducing commits.

You should commit only at the completion of a business transaction. If you commit earlier than your business transaction boundary, you can encounter data integrity issues. If you must commit to improve restartability, consider batch commits. For example, rather than commit after each row, it's better to do batch commit every 1000 or 5000 rows (the choice of batch size depends upon your application). Fewer commits will reduce the elapsed time of the program. Furthermore, fewer commits from the application will also improve the performance of the database.

Excessive Parsing

Don't use dynamic SQL statements in a PL/SQL loop as doing so will induce excessive parsing issues. Instead, reduce amount of hard parsing through the use of bind variables.

In Listing 1-15, the customers table is accessed to retrieve customer details, passing cust_id from cursor c1. A SQL statement with literal values is constructed and then executed using the native dynamic SQL EXECUTE IMMEDIATE construct. The problem is that for every unique row retrieved from cursor c1, a new SQL statement is constructed and sent to the SQL engine for execution.

Statements that don't exist in the shared pool when you execute them will incur a hard parse. Excessive hard parsing stresses the library cache, thereby reducing the application's scalability and concurrency. As the number of rows returned from cursor c1 increases, the number of hard parses will increase linearly. This program might work in a development database with a small number of rows to process, but the approach could very well become a problem in a production environment.

Listing 1-15. Excessive Parsing

```
DECLARE
  ...
BEGIN
 FOR c1_rec IN c1
 LOOP
  -- Query customer details
  EXECUTE IMMEDIATE
   'SELECT cust_first_name, cust_last_name, country_id
    FROM customers
    WHERE cust_id= ' || c1_rec.cust_id  INTO l_cust_first_name, l_cust_last_name,↵
 l_country_id;
  ...
 END LOOP;
COMMIT;
END;
/
```

You should reduce hard parses as much as possible. Dynamic SQL statements in a loop tend to increase the effect of hard parse and the effect is amplified if the concurrency of execution increases.

Summary

This chapter reviewed various scenarios in which the use of few PL/SQL constructs was not appropriate. Keeping in mind that SQL is a set language and PL/SQL is a procedural language, the following recommendations should be considered as guidelines while designing a program:

- Solve query problems using SQL. Think in terms of sets! It's easier to tune queries written in SQL than to tune, say, PL/SQL programs having nested loops to essentially execute queries using row-at-a-time processing.

- If you must code your program in PL/SQL, try offloading work to the SQL engine as much as possible. This becomes more and more important with new technologies such as Exadata. Smart scan facilities available in an Exadata database machine can offload work to the storage nodes and improve the performance of a program written in SQL. PL/SQL constructs do not gain such benefits from Exadata database machines (at least not as of version 11gR2).

- Use bulk processing facilities available in PL/SQL if you must use loop-based processing. Reduce unnecessary work in PL/SQL such as unnecessary execution of functions or excessive access to DUAL by using the techniques discussed in this chapter.

- Use single-row, loop-based processing only as a last resort.

Indeed, use PL/SQL for all your data and business processing. Use Java or other language for presentation logic and user validation. You can write highly scalable PL/SQL language programs using the techniques outlined in this chapter.

CHAPTER 2

Dynamic SQL:
Handling the Unknown

By Michael Rosenblum

For the past ten years, I have attended a number of Oracle conferences all over the United States. Time after time, I have listened to presenters talking about building systems "better, faster, cheaper" But when these same people come down off the stage and discuss the same issues with you one-on-one, the message is much less optimistic. The often cited 75% failure rate of all major IT projects is still a reality. Adding in the cases of "failures declared successes" (i.e. nobody was brave enough to admit the wrongdoing), it becomes even more clear that there is a crisis in our contemporary software development process.

For the purposes of this chapter, I will assume that we live in a slightly better universe where there is no corporate political in-fighting, system architects know what they are doing, and developers at least have an idea what OTN means. Even in this improved world, there are the some risks inherent in the systems development process that cannot be avoided:

- It is challenging to clearly state the requirements of a system that is expected to be built.

- It is difficult to build a system that actually meets all of the stated requirements.

- It is very difficult to build a system that does not require numerous changes within a short period of time.

- It is impossible to build a system that will not be obsolete sooner or later.

If the last bullet can be considered common knowledge, many of my colleagues would strongly disagree with the first three. However, in reality, there will never be 100% perfect analysis, 100% complete set of requirements, 100% adequate hardware that will never need to be upgraded, etc. In the IT industry, we need to accept the fact that, at any time, we must expect the unexpected.

▨ **Developer's Credo**   The focus of the whole development process should be shifted from what we know to what we don't know.

Unfortunately, there are many things that you don't know:

- What elements are involved? For example, the system requires a quarterly reporting mechanism, but there are no quarterly summary tables.

- How should you proceed? The DBA's nightmare: How to make sure that a global search screen performs adequately if it contains dozens of potential criteria from different tables?

- Can you proceed at all? For each restriction, you usually have at least one workaround or "backdoor." But what if the location of that backdoor changes in the next release or version update?

Fortunately, there are different ways of answering these (and similar) questions. This chapter will discuss how a feature called *Dynamic SQL* can help solve some of the problems mentioned previously and how you can avoid some of the major pitfalls that contribute to system failure and obsolescence.

The Hero

The concept of Dynamic SQL is reasonably straightforward. This feature allows you to build your code (both SQL and PL/SQL) *as text* and *process it at runtime*—nothing more and nothing less. Dynamic SQL provides the ability of a program to write another program while it is being executed. That said, it is critical to understand the potential implications and possibilities introduced by such a feature. These issues will be discussed in this chapter.

▨ **Note**   By "process" I mean the entire chain of events required to fire a program in any programming language—parse/execute/[fetch] (the last step is optional). A detailed discussion of this topic is beyond the scope of this chapter, but knowing the basics of each of the steps is crucial to proper usage of Dynamic SQL.

It is important to recognize that there are different ways of doing Dynamic SQL that should be discussed:

- Native Dynamic SQL

- Dynamic Cursors

- DBMS_SQL package

There are many good reference materials that explain the syntactic aspects of each of these ways, both online and in the published press. The purpose of this book is to demonstrate best practices rather than providing a reference guide, but it is useful to emphasize the key points of each kind of Dynamic SQL as a common ground for further discussion.

▓ **Technical Note #1**   Although the term "Dynamic SQL" was accepted by the whole Oracle community, it is not 100% complete, since it covers building both SQL statements **and PL/SQL blocks**. But "Dynamic SQL **and PL/SQL**" sounds too clumsy, so Dynamic SQL will be used throughout.

▓ **Technical Note #2**   As of this writing, both Oracle 10g and 11g are more or less equally in use. The examples used here are10g-compatible, unless the described feature exists only in 11g (such cases will be mentioned explicitly).

Native Dynamic SQL

About 95% of all implementations using any variation of Dynamic SQL are covered by one of the following variations of the EXECUTE IMMEDIATE command:

```
DECLARE
   v_variable_tx VARCHAR2(<Length>)|CLOB;
BEGIN
   v_variable_tx:='whatever_you_want';
   EXECUTE IMMEDIATE v_variable_tx [additional options];
END;
```

or

```
BEGIN
   EXECUTE IMMEDIATE 'whatever_you_want' [additional options];
END;
```

or

```
BEGIN
   EXECUTE IMMEDIATE 'whatever_you_want1'||'whatever_you_want2'||… [additional options];
END;
```

Up to and including Oracle 10g, the overall length of the code that could be processed by EXECUTE IMMEDIATE (including the concatenation result) was 32KB (larger code sets were handled by DBMS_SQL package). Starting with 11g, a CLOB can be passed as an input parameter. A good question for architects might be why anyone would try to dynamically process more than 32KB using a single statement, but from my experience such cases do indeed exist.

Native Dynamic SQL Example #1

The specific syntax details would require another 30 pages of explanation, but since this book is written for more experienced users, it is fair to expect that the reader knows how to use documentation. Instead of going into PL/SQL in depth, it is much more efficient to provide a quintessential example of **why** Dynamic SQL is needed. To that end, assume the following requirements:

- The system is expected to have many lookup fields with associated LOV (list of values) lookup tables that are likely to be extended later in the process. Instead of building each of these LOVs separately, there should be a centralized solution to handle everything.

- All LOVs should comply with the same format, namely two columns (ID/DISPLAY) where the first one is a lookup and the second one is text.

These requirements are a perfect fit for using Dynamic SQL: repeated patterns of runtime-defined operations where some may not be known at the moment of initial coding. The following code is useful in this situation:

```
CREATE TYPE lov_t IS OBJECT (id_nr NUMBER, display_tx VARCHAR2(256));

CREATE TYPE lov_tt AS TABLE OF lov_t;

CREATE FUNCTION f_getlov_tt  (
        i_table_tx    VARCHAR2,
        i_id_tx        VARCHAR2,
        i_display_tx VARCHAR2,
        i_order_nr    VARCHAR2,
        i_limit_nr    NUMBER:=100)
RETURN lov_tt
IS
    v_out_tt lov_tt := lov_tt();
    v_sql_tx VARCHAR2(32767);
BEGIN
    v_sql_tx:='SELECT lov_item_t '||
                'FROM (SELECT lov_t(' ||
                            dbms_assert.simple_sql_name(i_id_tx)||', '||
                        dbms_assert.simple_sql_name(i_display_tx)||') lov_item_t '||
                    ' FROM '||dbms_assert.simple_sql_name(i_table_tx)||
                        ' order by '||dbms_assert.simple_sql_name(i_order_nr)||
                ')' ||
              ' WHERE ROWNUM <= :limit';
    EXECUTE IMMEDIATE v_sql_tx BULK COLLECT INTO v_out_tt USING i_limit_nr;
    RETURN v_out_tt;
END;

SELECT * FROM TABLE(CAST(f_getlov_tt(:1,:2,:3,:4,:5) AS lov_tt))
```

This example includes all of the core syntax elements of dynamic SQL:

- The code to be executed is represented as string PL/SQL variable.

- Additional parameters are passed in or out of the statement using bind variables. Bind variables are logical placeholders and linked to actual parameters at the execution step.

- Bind variables are used for values and not structural elements. This is why table and column names are concatenated to the statement.

- The DBMS_ASSERT package helps prevent code injections (since you have to use concatenation) by enforcing the rule that table and column names are "simple SQL names" (no spaces, no separation symbols, etc.)

- Since the SQL statement has an output, the output is returned to PL/SQL variable of matching type (Native Dynamic SQL allows user-defined datatypes, including collections).

The last statement in the example (the SELECT statement invoking F_GETLOV_TT) is what should be given to front end developers. It is the only piece of information they need to integrate into the application. Everything else can be handled by database developers, including tuning, grants, special processing logic, etc. For each of these items, there is a single point of modification and a single point of control. This "single-point" concept is one of the most critical features in helping to minimize future development/debugging/audit efforts.

Native Dynamic SQL Example #2

Example #1 is targeted at developers building new systems. Example #2 is for those maintaining existing systems.

At some point Oracle decided to change the default behavior when dropping function-based indexes: all PL/SQL objects referencing a table that owned such an index were automatically invalidated. As expected, this change wreaked havoc in a lot of batch routines. As a result, Oracle came up with a workaround via setting a trace event. The routine to drop any function-based index took the following form:

```
CREATE PROCEDURE p_dropFBIndex (i_index_tx VARCHAR2) is
BEGIN
    EXECUTE IMMEDIATE
        'ALTER SESSION SET EVENTS ''10624 trace name context forever, level 12''';
    EXECUTE IMMEDIATE 'drop index '||i_index_tx;
    EXECUTE IMMEDIATE
        'ALTER SESSION SET EVENTS ''10624 trace name context off''';
END;
```

This example illustrates another key element of Dynamic SQL. You are not limited by just DML. Any valid PL/SQL anonymous block or SQL statement, including DDL or ALTER SESSION, can be executed during runtime operations. As a result, DBAs no longer need their favorite scripts-generating-scripts-generating-scripts since all of these cases can be handled directly in the database.

Dynamic Cursors

The idea of dynamic cursors is similar to that of executing dynamic SQL. But instead of running an entire statement, you open a cursor and pass a SELECT statement as a parameter. For example:

```
DECLARE
    v_cur SYS_REFCURSOR;
    v_sql_tx VARCHAR2(<length>)|CLOB:='valid_SQL_query';
    v_rec ...<record type>;
         or
    v_tt ...<record collection>;
BEGIN
    OPEN v_cur FOR v_sql_tx [<additional parameters>];

    FETCH v_cur INTO v_rec;
          or
    FETCH v_cur BULK COLLECT INTO v_tt [<limit N>];

    CLOSE v_cur;
END;
```

From my previous experience, there are two cases when dynamic cursors may come in handy. Both examples follow.

Dynamic Cursors Example #1

The first case of using dynamic cursors has to do with environments using a lot of variables of type REF CURSOR as communication mechanisms between different layers of applications. Unfortunately, in most cases, such variables are created from the middle-tier layer and developed usually with a very little involvement of database-side experts. I have seen too many cases where the business case was 100% valid, but the implementation by solving a direct functional problem created a maintenance, debugging, and even a security nightmare!

The right way to fix this is to push the process of building REF CURSORs down to the database where all created logic is much easier to control (although, it will still be the responsibility of middle-tier developers to correctly close all opened cursors; otherwise the system will be prone to "cursor leaking"). On a basic level the wrapper function should look as follows:

```
CREATE FUNCTION f_getRefCursor_REF (i_type_tx VARCHAR2)
RETURN SYS_REFCURSOR
IS
  v_out_ref SYS_REFCURSOR;
  v_sql_tx VARCHAR2(32767);
BEGIN
    if i_type_tx = 'A' then
        v_sql_tx:=<some code to build query A>;
    elsif i_type_tx = 'B' then
        v_sql_tx:=<some other code to build query B>;
  ...
```

```
    END IF;
    OPEN v_out_ref FOR v_sql_tx;
    RETURN v_out_ref;
END;
```

Life becomes slightly more interesting when the task is not just to build and execute the query, but also pass some bind variables into it. There are different ways of solving this problem. The simplest one is to create a package with a number of global variables and the corresponding functions to return them. As a result, the whole process of getting the correct result consists of setting all of the appropriate variables and immediately calling F_GETREFCURSOR_REF in the same session. However, the solution I've just described is not perfect, since the middle-tier often talks to the database in a purely stateless way. In that case, it's impossible to use PL/SQL package variables.

▓ **Note** By stateless implementation of the middle-tier, I mean an environment where each database call gets a separate database session (even in the context of the same logical operation). This session could be either selected from the existing connection pool or opened on the fly, but in practical terms, all session-level resources should be considered "lost" between two calls, since there is no way of ensuring that the following call would hit the same session as the preceding one.

Still, Oracle provides enough additional options to overcome even that restriction using either object collections or XMLType (the latter is even more flexible). Of course, either of these methods requires some non-trivial changes to queries (as shown in the following example), but the outcome is a 100% abstract query-builder.

```
CREATE FUNCTION f_getRefCursor_ref
        (i_type_tx VARCHAR2:='EMP',
        i_param_xml XMLTYPE:= XMLTYPE(
                '<param col1_tx="DEPTNO" value1_tx="20" col2_tx="ENAME" value2_tx="KING"/>')
        )
RETURN SYS_REFCURSOR
IS
    v_out_ref SYS_REFCURSOR;
    v_sql_tx VARCHAR2(32767);
BEGIN
    IF i_type_tx = 'EMP' THEN
        SELECT
            'WITH param AS  ('||
            '    SELECT   TO_NUMBER(EXTRACTVALUE (in_xml, ''/param/@value1_tx'')) value1, '||
            '                      EXTRACTVALUE (in_xml, ''/param/@value2_tx'') value2 '||
            '    FROM (SELECT :1 in_xml FROM DUAL) '||
            '                            ) '||
            ' SELECT count(*)'||
            ' FROM scott.emp, '||
            '             param '||
            ' WHERE emp.'|| dbms_assert.simple_sql_name(
                                    EXTRACTVALUE (i_param_xml, '/param/@col1_tx')
                                        )||'=param.value1 '||
```

```
                'OR emp.'|| dbms_assert.simple_sql_name(
                                    EXTRACTVALUE (i_param_xml, '/param/@col2_tx')
                                    )||'=param.value2'
            INTO v_sql_tx  FROM DUAL;

      ELSIF i_type_tx = 'B' THEN
          v_sql_tx:='<queryB>';
    ...
      END IF;
      OPEN v_out_ref FOR v_sql_tx USING i_param_xml;
      RETURN v_out_ref;
END;
```

In this example, the parameters of a single XML variable represent a group of pairs where, in each group, the first parameter defines what columns should be filtered (EMP.DEPTNO and EMP.ENAME) and the second one sets the value of this filter (20 and KING). Columns (COL1_TX and COL2_TX) are evaluated when the query is being built since they are structural elements, while values are passed into the created query as a single input parameter of XMLType. Although the resulting syntax looks slightly convoluted, the example above proves that it's possible to put all database-related system elements where they belong, namely in the database.

Dynamic Cursors Example #2

Another case of effective utilization of dynamic cursors becomes self-evident if we accept the major limitation of EXECUTE IMMEDIATE. It is a single PARSE/EXECUTE/FETCH sequence of events that cannot be stopped or paused. As a result, in cases of multi-row fetching via BULK COLLECT, there is always a serious risk of trying to load too many elements into the output collection. Of course, this risk can be mitigated by adding WHERE ROWNUM <=:1, as shown in the initial example. But this option is also not perfect because it does not allow continuation of reading from the same source. Dynamic cursors can solve this problem.

For this example, assume that you need to write a module that would read the first N values from the table and stop if it does not reach the middle of the alphabet or continue until the end otherwise. The solution would look as follows:

```
CREATE FUNCTION f_getlov_tt  (
        i_table_tx    VARCHAR2,
        i_id_tx        VARCHAR2,
        i_display_tx VARCHAR2,
        i_order_nr    VARCHAR2,
        i_limit_nr     NUMBER:=50)
RETURN lov_tt
IS
    v_out1_tt lov_tt := lov_tt();
    v_out2_tt lov_tt := lov_tt();
    v_sql_tx VARCHAR2(32767);
    v_cur SYS_REFCURSOR;
BEGIN
    v_sql_tx:='SELECT lov_t(' ||
                        dbms_assert.simple_sql_name(i_id_tx)||','||
                dbms_assert.simple_sql_name(i_display_tx)||')'||
```

```
     ' FROM '||dbms_assert.simple_sql_name(i_table_tx)||
     ' ORDER BY '||dbms_assert.simple_sql_name(i_order_nr);

  OPEN v_cur FOR v_sql_tx;
  FETCH v_cur BULK COLLECT INTO v_out1_tt LIMIT i_limit_nr;
  IF v_out1_tt.count=i_limit_nr AND UPPER(v_out1_tt(i_limit_nr).display_tx)>'N' then
       FETCH v_cur BULK COLLECT INTO v_out2_tt;
       SELECT v_out1_tt MULTISET UNION v_out2_tt INTO v_out1_tt FROM DUAL;
  END IF;
  CLOSE v_cur;

  RETURN v_out1_tt;
END;
```

This implementation allows the program to fetch the first group of records (V_OUT1_TT), stop, and apply logical rules in the middle of fetching data from an already opened cursor: the second group of records (V_OUT2_TT) will be populated only if the defined rules succeed, but it will be populated from the same query by just continuation of fetching at no additional cost. That "stop-and-go" is what makes such an example valuable.

DBMS_SQL

The DBMS_SQL built-in package was the original incarnation of the dynamic SQL idea. Despite rumors of its potential abandonment, the package continues to evolve from one version of the RDBMS to another. Evidently, there is a very good reason to keep DBMS_SQL around since it provides the lowest possible level of control on the execution of runtime-defined statements. You can parse, execute, fetch, define output, and process bind variables as independent commands at will. Of course, the costs of this granularity are performance (but Oracle continues to close this gap) and complexity. Usually, the rule of thumb is that unless you know that you can't avoid DBMS_SQL, don't use it.

Following are some cases in which there are no other options but to use DBMS_SQL:

- You need to exceed the 32K restriction of EXECUTE IMMEDIATE (in Oracle 10g and below).

- You have an unknown number or type of input/output parameters (in all versions).

- You need granular control over the process (in all versions, but in 11g there are additional possibilities).

The first case is pretty straightforward. You either hit the limit or you don't. However, the latter two are much more interesting from the development point of view. What follows in this section is an illustration of what is doable by having low-level access to the system logic.

In every environment that heavily uses REF CURSOR variables, sooner or later someone asks the question: How do I know what exact query is being passed by such-and-such cursor variable? Up to Oracle 11g, the answer was either in the source code or at DBA-level SGA examination of v$-views. But starting with Oracle 11g, it became possible to bi-directionally convert DBMS_SQL cursors and REF CURSORs. This feature allows the following solution to exist:

```
CREATE PROCEDURE p_explainCursor (io_ref_cur IN OUT SYS_REFCURSOR)
IS
    v_cur      INTEGER := dbms_sql.open_cursor;
    v_cols_nr NUMBER := 0;
    v_cols_tt dbms_sql.desc_tab;
BEGIN
    v_cur:=dbms_sql.to_cursor_number(io_ref_cur);
    dbms_sql.describe_columns (v_cur, v_cols_nr, v_cols_tt);
    FOR i IN 1 .. v_cols_nr LOOP
        dbms_output.put_line(v_cols_tt (i).col_name);
    END LOOP;
    io_ref_cur:=dbms_sql.to_refcursor(v_cur);
END;

SQL> DECLARE
  2    v_tx VARCHAR2(256):='SELECT * FROM dept';
  3    v_cur SYS_REFCURSOR;
  4  BEGIN
  5    OPEN v_cur FOR v_tx;
  6    p_explainCursor(v_cur);
  7    CLOSE v_cur;
  8  END;
  9  /
DEPTNO
DNAME
LOC
PL/SQL procedure successfully completed.
SQL>
```

This example utilizes the procedure DBMS_SQL.DESCRIBE_COLUMNS that takes any opened cursor and analyzes its structure. In the case of a cursor opened for a SQL query, the information includes the number of columns in the output, the column names, and the column datatypes etc. That brings us back to the concept of managing the UNKNOWN. We take something that we don't know and, by applying the appropriate tools, we convert the raw material of potentially useful information into solid data that can be used to solve real business needs.

Sample of Dynamic Thinking

After the formal introduction of the hero of this chapter, it now makes sense to show a "gold standard" case of the appropriate application of dynamic thinking. The example in this section comes from an actual production problem and perfectly illustrates the conceptual level of problem currently faced by senior database developers. From the very beginning, the task was challenging.

- There were about 100 tables in a hierarchical structure describing a person: Customer A has phone B, confirmed by reference person C, who has an address D, etc.

- The whole customer with related child data occasionally has to be cloned.

- All tables have a single-column synthetic primary key generated from the shared sequence (OBJECT_SEQ); all tables are linked by foreign keys.

- The data model changes reasonably often, so hardcoding is not allowed. Requests must be processed on the spot so there is no way to disable constraints or use any other data transformation workarounds.

What is involved in the cloning process in this case? It is clear that cloning the root element (customer) will require some hardcoding, but everything else conceptually represents a hierarchical walk down the dependency tree. The process of cloning definitely requires some kind of fast-access storage (associative array in this case) that will keep the information about old/new pairs (find the new ID using the old ID). Also, a nested table data type is needed to keep a list of primary keys to be passed to the next level. As a result, the following types are created in addition to the declaration of a main procedure:

```
CREATE PACKAGE clone_pkg
IS
    TYPE pair_tt IS TABLE OF NUMBER INDEX BY BINARY_INTEGER;
    v_Pair_t pair_tt;

    PROCEDURE p_clone (in_table_tx VARCHAR2, in_pk_tx VARCHAR2, in_id NUMBER);
END;

CREATE TYPE id_tt IS TABLE OF NUMBER;
```

Note that the second type (ID_TT) should be created as database object because it will be actively used in SQL. The first type (PAIR_TT) is needed only in the context of PL/SQL code to store old/new values; that is why I created it in the package (CLONE_PKG) and immediately made a variable of this type.

Since I am trying to identify potential patterns, I will ignore the root procedure that would clone the customer (because it will be different from everything else). Also, I will ignore the first level down (phones belonging to customer) since it covers only a sub-case (multiple children of a single parent). Let's start two levels down and figure out how to clone reference people confirming existing phone number (assuming that new phones already were created). Logically, the flow of actions is the following:

1. Find all references confirming all existing phones.

    a. Existing phones are passed as a collection of phone IDs (V_OLDPHONE_TT).

    b. All detected references are loaded into staging PL/SQL collection (V_ROWS_TT).

2. Process each detected reference.

    c. Store all detected reference IDs (V_PARENT_TT) that will be used further down the hierarchical tree.

    d. Retrieve a new ID from the sequence and record old/new pair in the global package variable.

    e. In the staging collection (V_ROWS_TT), substitute the primary key (reference ID) and foreign key (phone ID) with new values.

3. Spin through the staging collection and insert new rows to the reference table.

The code to accomplish these steps is as follows:

```
DECLARE
    TYPE rows_tt IS TABLE of REF%ROWTYPE;
    v_rows_tt rows_tt;
    v_new_id NUMBER;
    v_parent_tt id_tt:=id_tt();
BEGIN
    SELECT * BULK COLLECT INTO v_rows_tt
    FROM REF t WHERE PHONE_ID in
        (SELECT column_value FROM TABLE (CAST (v_oldPhone_tt AS id_tt)));

    FOR i IN v_rows_tt.first..v_rows_tt.last LOOP
      v_parent_tt.extend;
      v_parent_tt(v_parent_tt.last):=v_rows_tt(i).REF_ID;

      SELECT object_Seq.nextval INTO v_new_id FROM DUAL;
      clone_pkg.v_Pair_t(v_rows_tt(i).REF_ID):=v_new_id;

      v_rows_tt(i).REF_ID :=v_new_id;
      v_rows_tt(i).PHONE_ID:=clone_pkg.v_Pair_t(v_rows_tt(i).PHONE_ID);
    END LOOP;

    FORALL i IN v_rows_tt.first..v_rows_tt.last
       INSERT INTO REF VALUES v_rows_tt(i);
END;
```

Interestingly enough, if you closely examine the created code, it becomes clear that it contains three kinds of elements:

- An incoming list of parent primary keys (V_OLDPHONE_TT).

- A main logical process.

- Functional identifiers that define objects the process should be applied to (marked bold):

    - child table name (REF).

    - primary key column name of the child table (REF_ID).

    - foreign key column name of the child table (PHONE_ID).

Technically, I am trying to build a module that has structural parameters (table names, column names) and data parameters (parent IDs), which is a perfect case of utilizing Dynamic SQL because it can handle both of these kinds.

Since each level of hierarchy could be completely represented by examining foreign key relationships, it is obvious that the Oracle data dictionary may be used to walk down through the parent-child tree (for now, I will assume that there are no circular dependencies in the system). The idea is very straightforward: take a table name as input and return a list of its children (with corresponding child primary key column and foreign key column pointing to the parent). Although the following code does not contain any dynamic SQL, it is useful enough to be shown (also extract from CLONE_PKG):

```
TYPE list_rec IS RECORD
        (table_tx VARCHAR2(50), fk_tx VARCHAR2(50), pk_tx VARCHAR2(50));
TYPE list_rec_tt IS TABLE OF list_rec;

FUNCTION f_getChildrenRec (in_tablename_tx VARCHAR2)
RETURN list_rec_tt
IS
    v_out_tt list_rec_tt;
BEGIN
    SELECT fk_tab.table_name, fk_tab.column_name fk_tx, pk_tab.column_name pk_tx
    BULK COLLECT INTO v_Out_tt
    FROM
        (SELECT ucc.column_name, uc.table_name
         FROM user_cons_columns ucc,
             user_constraints uc
         WHERE ucc.constraint_name = uc.constraint_name
         AND   constraint_type = 'P') pk_tab,
        (SELECT ucc.column_name, uc.table_name
         FROM    user_cons_columns ucc,
                (SELECT constraint_name, table_name
                 FROM user_constraints
                 WHERE r_constraint_name = (SELECT constraint_name
                                            FROM user_constraints
                                            WHERE table_name = in_tablename_tx
                                            AND constraint_type = 'P'
                                            )
                ) uc
         WHERE ucc.constraint_name = uc.constraint_name ) fk_tab
    WHERE pk_tab.table_name = fk_tab.table_name;
    RETURN v_out_tt;
END;
```

Now I have all of the pieces of information necessary to build generic processing module that would call itself recursively until it reaches the end of the parent-child chains, as shown next. As defined, the module will take as input a collection of parent primary key IDs and a single object of type CLONE_PKG.LIST_REC that will describe the parent-child link to be processed.

```
PROCEDURE p_process (in_list_rec clone_pkg.list_rec, in_parent_list id_tt)
IS
    v_execute_tx VARCHAR2(32767);
BEGIN
    v_execute_tx:=
        'DECLARE '||
        '   TYPE rows_tt IS TABLE OF '||in_list_rec.table_tx||'%rowtype;'||
        '   v_rows_tt rows_tt;'||
        '   v_new_id number;'||
        '   v_list clone_pkg.list_rec_tt;'||
        '   v_parent_list id_tt:=id_tt();'||
        'BEGIN '||
        '   SELECT * BULK COLLECT INTO v_rows_tt '||
        '   FROM '||in_list_rec.table_tx||' t WHERE '||in_list_rec.fk_tx||
        '      IN (SELECT column_value FROM TABLE (CAST (:1 as id_tt)));'||
```

```
'        IF v_rows_tt.count()=0 THEN RETURN; END IF;'||
'        FOR i IN v_rows_tt.first..v_rows_tt.last LOOP '||
'           SELECT object_Seq.nextval INTO v_new_id FROM DUAL;'||
'           v_parent_list.extend;'||
'           v_parent_list(v_parent_list.last):=v_rows_tt(i).'||in_list_rec.pk_tx||';'||
'           clone_pkg.v_Pair_t(v_rows_tt(i).'||in_list_rec.pk_tx||'):=v_new_id;'||
'           v_rows_tt(i).'||in_list_rec.pk_tx||':=v_new_id;'||
'           v_rows_tt(i).'||in_list_rec.fk_tx||
'                 :=clone_pkg.v_Pair_t(v_rows_tt(i).'||in_list_rec.fk_tx||');'||
'        END LOOP;'||
'        FORALL i IN v_rows_tt.first..v_rows_tt.last '||
'        INSERT INTO '||in_list_rec.table_tx||' VALUES v_rows_tt(i);'||
'        v_list:=clone_pkg.f_getchildrenRec('''||in_list_rec.table_tx||''');'||
'        IF v_list.count()=0 THEN RETURN; END IF;'||
'        FOR l IN v_list.first..v_list.last LOOP '||
'           clone_pkg.p_process(v_list(l),v_parent_list);'||
'        END LOOP;'||
'END;';
    EXECUTE IMMEDIATE v_execute_tx USING in_parent_list;
END;
```

The last piece needed is an entry point that will take a root object and clone it. To start the whole process, you need to know the starting table, its primary key column and the primary key of the root element to be cloned.

```
PROCEDURE p_clone (in_table_tx VARCHAR2, in_pk_tx VARCHAR2, in_id NUMBER)
IS
    v_new_id NUMBER;
    PROCEDURE p_processRoot is
        v_sql_tx VARCHAR2(32767);
    BEGIN
      v_sql_tx:=
      'DECLARE '||
      '   v_row '||in_table_tx||'%ROWTYPE; '||
      '   v_listDirectChildren_t clone_pkg.list_rec_tt; '||
      '   v_parent_list id_tt:=id_tt(); '||
      '   v_old_id NUMBER:=:1; '||
      '   v_new_id NUMBER:=:2; '||
      'BEGIN '||
      '  SELECT * INTO v_row FROM '||in_table_tx||
      '     WHERE '||in_pk_tx||'=v_old_id;'||
      '     v_row.'||in_pk_tx||':=v_new_id;'||
      '     clone_pkg.v_Pair_t(v_old_id):=v_new_id;'||
      '     v_parent_list.extend;'||
      '     v_parent_list(v_parent_list.last):=v_old_id;'||
      '     INSERT INTO '||in_table_tx||' VALUES v_row;'||
      '     v_listDirectChildren_t:=clone_pkg.f_getChildrenRec(:3);'||
      '     FOR i IN v_listDirectChildren_t.first..v_listDirectChildren_t.last'||
      '     LOOP'||
      '         clone_pkg.p_process(v_listDirectChildren_t(i),v_parent_list); '||
      '      END LOOP;'||
      'END; ';
```

```
        EXECUTE IMMEDIATE v_sql_tx USING in_id,v_new_id,UPPER(in_table_tx);
    END;
BEGIN
    clone_pkg.v_Pair_t.delete;
    SELECT object_seq.nextval INTO v_new_id FROM DUAL;
    p_processRoot;
END;
```

The only step left is to assemble all of these pieces into a single package to create a completely generic cloning module. (A complete set of code snippets is available for download at this book's catalog page at Apress.com).

Why is the preceding example considered a "gold standard"? Mainly because the example is based upon the analysis of repeated patterns in the code that could be made generic. Recognizing these patterns is one of the key skills in becoming very efficient in applying Dynamic SQL to solving day-to-day problems.

Security Issues

From the security point of view, "handling the unknown" has to do with a bit of healthy paranoia. Any good developer should assume that if something *could* be misused, there is a good chance that it eventually *will* be misused. Also, very often, the consequences of "pilot errors" are more devastating than any imaginable intentional attack, which leads to the conclusion that a system should not only be protected against criminals, but against any unfortunate combinations of events.

In terms of using Dynamic SQL, the abovementioned concept should be translated into the following idea: under no circumstances should it be possible to generate any code on the fly that was not intended to be generated. Considering that code consists of both structural elements (tables, columns etc) and data, the following rules apply:

- Structural elements cannot be passed instead of data.

- Only allowed structural elements can be passed.

The solution that satisfies both of these conditions can be implemented by following just two rules:

- When an application user inputs pure data elements (such as values of columns, etc.), these values must be passed to the dynamic SQL using bind variables. No value concatenation to structural parts of the code should be allowed.

- When the whole structure of the code has to be changed as a result of actions made by application user, such actions must be limited to known repository elements. The overall system security should be enforced by the following separation of roles:

  - Regular users have no ability to alter the repository.

  - People who can change the repository are specially assigned administrators.

  - No administrators can also have the role of regular user.

It's very easy to explain the first rule. Because bind variables are evaluated only after the structure of the query is resolved, an unexpected value (like famous 'NULL OR 1=1') cannot impact anything at all, as shown here:

```
SQL> DECLARE
  2      v_tx VARCHAR2(256):='NULL OR 1=1';
  3      v_count_nr NUMBER:=0;
  4  BEGIN
  5      EXECUTE IMMEDIATE 'SELECT count(*) FROM emp WHERE ename = :1'
  6      INTO v_count_nr USING v_tx ;
  7      dbms_output.put_line('Bind: '||v_count_nr);
  8
  9      EXECUTE IMMEDIATE 'select count(*) FROM emp WHERE ename = '||v_tx
 10      INTO v_count_nr;
 11      dbms_output.put_line('Inject: '||v_count_nr);
 12  END;
 13  /
Bind: 0
Inject: 14
PL/SQL procedure successfully completed.
SQL>
```

The second rule implying the usage of a repository may go against the grain for the majority of contemporary developers, but it provides a unique opportunity for role separation between people who enter available options and people who really use them. Another advantage of such a repository-based solution is deployment cost. Since all required changes could be handled by DML against repository tables, there is no stoppage of service and no downtime. These considerations can sometimes be real project-savers as evidenced by the following real world example.

Once upon a time there was a classical 3-tier IT system that usually took about 4-6 hours of downtime to deploy even the smallest change to the front end (plus at least a day of preparations). Requests for new modules were coming in at least twice a week. These requests were very simple, such as take a small number of inputs, fire the associated routine, and report the results. Unfortunately, each request originally had to be coded separately as a new screen and deployed via the regular mechanism. As a result, there was always a group of unhappy people in the company made up of either users who could not get the needed data on time or the maintenance team who had to go through the pains of bringing the whole system down to add just a simple screen several times each week.

Applying the concept of handling the unknown to the problem should make the available alternatives more visible. Let's split the information into two groups:

- Known:

    - Each screen has to be deployed to the web.

    - Each screen is based on a single request.

    - Each request takes up to five simple parameters.

    - Each request returns a summary in textual form.

- Unknown:

    - Header information (name of the screen, remarks, names of parameters)

    - Data type of parameters (including nullability and possible format masks)

    - Formatting of the summary

By articulating the problem in the proposed structure, the format of the proposed solution is now clear:

- Each screen is represented by a single row in the repository with the following set of properties:
    - A generic name (header of the pop-up screen)
    - Up to 5 parameters, each including:
        - Header
        - Mandatory/not mandatory identification
        - Data type (NUMBER/DATE/TEXT/LOV)
        - Optional conversion expression (e.g. default date format in the UI since everything on the Web is text-based)
        - Value list name (for LOV datatypes)
    - Name of corresponding function in the following format:
        - Order (and count) of input parameters must match the order of on-screen parameters
        - Function should return a CLOB
- All CLOBs returned by registered functions must be fully formatted HTML pages, immediately available for display in the front end.
- All activities in the repository are accessible only by administrators and not visible to end users.

As a result, from the system point of view, the logical flow of actions now becomes very simple.

1. The user sees the list of available modules from the repository and selects one.

2. The front end application reads the repository and builds a pop-up screen on the fly with appropriate input fields and mandatory indicators. If the data type of the input field is a value list, the utility requests the generic LOV mechanism to provide existing ID/DISPLAY pairs.

3. The user enters whatever is needed and presses SUBMIT. The front end fires the main (umbrella) procedure by passing a repository ID of the module being used and all user-entered values into it.

4. The umbrella procedure builds a real function call, passes the entered values, and returns the generated CLOB to the front end (already formatted as HTML).

5. The front end displays the generated HTML.

Now all teams will be happy, since it will take only seconds from the moment any new module was declared production-ready to the moment when it is accessible from the front end. There is no downtime and no deployment—just one new function to be copied and one INSERT statement to register the function in the repository.

To illustrate how all of these "miracles" look, the preparatory part of the example is to build a function that satisfies all of the formatting requirements, to create a repository table, and to register the function in the repository:

```
CREATE FUNCTION f_getEmp_CL (i_job_tx VARCHAR2, i_hiredate_dt DATE)
RETURN CLOB
IS
    v_out_cl CLOB;
    PROCEDURE p_add(pi_tx VARCHAR2) IS
    BEGIN
        dbms_lob.writeappend(v_out_cl,length(pi_tx),pi_tx);
    END;
BEGIN
    dbms_lob.createtemporary(v_out_cl,true,dbms_lob.call);
    p_add('<html><table>');
    FOR c IN (SELECT '<tr>'||'<td>'||empno||'</td>'||'<td>'||ename||'</td>'||'</tr>' row_tx
                     FROM emp
                     WHERE job = i_job_tx
                     AND hiredate >= NVL(i_hiredate_dt,add_months(sysdate,-36))
                     )
    LOOP
        p_add(c.row_tx);
    END LOOP;
    p_add('</table></html>');
    RETURN v_out_cl;
END;

CREATE TABLE t_extra_ui
(id_nr                NUMBER PRIMARY KEY,
 displayName_tx VARCHAR2(256),
 function_tx          VARCHAR2(50),
 v1_label_tx          VARCHAR2(100),
 v1_type_tx           VARCHAR2(50),
 v1_required_yn  VARCHAR2(1),
 v1_lov_tx            VARCHAR2(50),
 v1_convert_tx     VARCHAR2(50),
...  - and 4 more groups of the same structure);

INSERT INTO t_extra_ui ( id_nr,displayName_tx,function_tx,
                     v1_label_tx, v1_type_tx, v1_required_yn, v1_lov_tx, v1_convert_tx,
                     v2_label_tx, v2_type_tx, v2_required_yn, v2_lov_tx, v2_convert_tx )
VALUES (100, 'Filter Employees', 'f_getEmp_cl',
        'Job','TEXT','Y',null,null,
        'Hire Date','DATE','N',null,'TO_DATE(:2,''YYYYMMDD'')');
```

This example includes a function that generates a list of employees with defined job titles and were hired after a defined date (or at least three years ago if such date was not provided). Dynamic SQL allows the assembly of all of these pieces in the following umbrella function

```
CREATE FUNCTION f_umbrella_cl (i_id_nr NUMBER,
                               v1_tx VARCHAR2:=null,...,v5_tx VARCHAR2:=null)
RETURN CLOB
IS
    v_out_cl CLOB;
    v_sql_tx VARCHAR2(32767);
    v_rec t_extra_ui%ROWTYPE;
BEGIN
    SELECT * INTO v_rec FROM t_extra_ui WHERE id_nr=i_id_nr;

    IF v_rec.v1_label_tx IS NOT NULL THEN
        v_sql_tx:=nvl(v_rec.v1_convert_tx,':1');
    END IF;
     ...
    IF v_rec.v5_label_tx IS NOT NULL THEN
        v_sql_tx:=v_sql_tx||','||nvl(v_rec.v5_convert_tx,':5');
    END IF;

    v_sql_tx:='BEGIN :out:='||v_rec.function_tx||'('||v_sql_tx||'); END;';

    IF v5_tx IS NOT NULL THEN
        EXECUTE IMMEDIATE v_sql_tx USING OUT v_out_cl, v1_tx,…,v5_tx;
     ...
    ELSIF v1_tx IS NOT NULL THEN
        EXECUTE IMMEDIATE v_sql_tx USING OUT v_out_cl, v1_tx;
    ELSE
        EXECUTE IMMEDIATE v_sql_tx USING OUT v_out_cl;
    END IF;

    RETURN v_out_cl;
END;
```

This function is the crux of the proposed solution, since it is the only part of the existing code visible outside of the database. From a code injection point of view, everything is completely safe, even allowing user-defined input to influence structural elements of the underlying calls. But all of these structural elements are declared in the repository table and the application user can only communicate to the system something like "run routine #N" (where N is selected from the value list) without any way of controlling how #N transforms into F_GETEMP_CL. This allows the system to be flexible enough without creating a security breach.

Overall, the biggest security risk nowadays is laziness. Everyone knows what should be done and how to write protected code, but not all development environments enforce enough discipline to make this a reality. Oracle provides enough options to keep all of the doors and windows safely locked.

Performance and Resource Utilization

In addition to security risks, there is one more bogeyman that prevents people from effectively using Dynamic SQL: it is considered too costly performance-wise. The problem is that this statement is never completed: costly in comparison to what? It is true that running the same statement directly is faster than wrapping it into an EXECUTE IMMEDIATE command. But this is like comparing apples to oranges.

It is absolutely irrelevant how much time it takes for an individual task to run, because the only critical thing to be tuned is the overall performance of the module.

Take another look at the example from the previous section using Dynamic SQL to work with the repository. Of course this leads to some overhead, namely pre-formatting results as HTML, using an umbrella module, dynamic calls to underlying functions, etc. Each of these elements decreases the speed of request processing compared to a screen built by hand. But the key question remains: Does anyone notice the slowdown? The answer is "No," because all of the listed "overhead" causes, at most, a millisecond of time, which is negligible compared to the total processing time.

This means that the actual factor to be evaluated is whether or not it is worthwhile to pay the price of using Dynamic SQL. Each time, the answer will depend upon detailed analysis of the specific business cases. There will be some instances where the price is acceptable (such as the one just reviewed) and other cases where the price will be too steep. The following example illustrates such a case.

Anti-Patterns

Occasionally end users ask for a multi-select option in the application. Usually it means that there should be an operation to be performed against an undefined list of elements. Since the length of the list is not known, it is very tempting to use a text string as communication mechanism, as in the following process:

1. Front-end code concatenates all selected IDs as a comma-separated string.

2. This string is passed to the PL/SQL function.

3. PL/SQL function utilizes Dynamic SQL to build the IN-clause.

The following is the necessary PL/SQL function for last step of the process:

```
CREATE FUNCTION f_getSumSal_nr (i_empno_tx VARCHAR2)
RETURN NUMBER
IS
    v_out_nr NUMBER:=0;
    v_sql_tx VARCHAR2(2000);
BEGIN
    IF i_empno_tx IS NOT NULL THEN
        v_sql_tx:='SELECT sum(sal) FROM emp WHERE empno IN ('||i_empno_tx||')';
        EXECUTE IMMEDIATE v_sql_tx INTO v_out_nr;
    END IF;
    RETURN v_out_nr;
END;
```

Unfortunately, this seemingly clean solution has a number of drawbacks that usually surface only after the application has been deployed to production for some time. Here are a few:

*   There is a restriction on the total number of objects that can be passed: 32K/(lenth_of_id+1) or 4K/(lenth_of_id+1) depending upon whether the function is used in PL/SQL only or as a part of SQL statement. Converting the whole module to CLOB instead of VARCHAR2 is very expensive because of the CLOB overhead, especially on the physical I/O.

*   If the list of values is not just made up of IDs, but some kind of text, this poses the question of having the correct number of quotes in the text.

- Because of the unknown number of items in the list, it's possible to get different Explain Plans. Also, this code will be very susceptible to changes in column-level statistics.

- It's not secure (passing `SELECT empno FROM emp` will immediately provide a different level of data access), but making this module injection-proof would require very nontrivial string parsing.

Overall, from my experience, the effect of Dynamic SQL in this case is negative. The alternative option will look like this:

```
CREATE TYPE id_tt IS TABLE OF NUMBER;

CREATE FUNCTION f_getSumSal_nr (i_tt id_tt)
RETURN NUMBER IS
    v_out_nr NUMBER:=0;
BEGIN
    IF i_tt IS NOT NULL AND i_tt.count>0 THEN
        SELECT sum(sal) INTO v_out_nr
        FROM emp
        WHERE empno IN (SELECT t.column_value FROM TABLE(CAST(i_tt as id_tt)) t);
    END IF;
    RETURN v_out_nr;
END;
```

This solution uses an object collection to pass the list. The overhead of such a collection is well compensated for by firing regular instead of Dynamic SQL and by not worrying about the data length/data structure.

Comparing Implementations of Dynamic SQL

Since there are different implementations of Dynamic SQL, what type of Dynamic SQL would be more efficient? The next real-life story illustrates why you need to know about DBMS_SQL package. The task started as a request from end users to be able to upload CSV-files based on a number of predefined templates to the system. Here are some of the requirements and characteristics of the system:

- The file prefix defines the template type. Column headers map directly to table columns (if the header is not registered, it will be ignored).

- One row of the file represents one logical group of from 1 to N rows. For example, one row could include both action and correction records (you can think of it as sale transaction and cancellation transaction—linked, but separate).

- Group-level validation must be supported. Rules are applicable to the whole set of rows rather than to each insert.

The original implementation of the solution was straightforward: read a row, build an INSERT statement as a text string using headers, fire the EXECUTE IMMEDIATE command. But with real volumes of data (10k+ rows in a single file), DBAs started to complain that the CPU workload became too high. Also, early-adopters were complaining that the performance of the module was significantly worse compared with the original estimates (and worsened with increased file sizes). After detailed database tracing, it became clear that all of the extra time spent was the result of parsing INSERT statements.

Keep in mind the following information about parsing:

- EXECUTE IMMEDIATE without bind variables: N hard parses for N calls

- EXECUTE IMMEDIATE with bind variables:

  - 10g and below: one hard parse + N-1 soft parse for N calls

  - 11: one hard parse only if the same statement is being executed over and over again. This is an internal optimization (invisible) and it doesn't work if there is more than one type of call.

- DBMS_SQL with separation of parsing and execution stage: only one hard parse for each type of call because DBMS_SQL allows storage of a parsed statement and reusing it multiple times.

Because the majority of templates included multiple types of INSERT statements, Oracle 11g unfortunately would not help at all in this case. However, switching from EXECUTE IMMEDIATE to DBMS_SQL sounded promising and I made the appropriate changes.

The first step was to prepare INSERT statements, assign each one its own DBMS_SQL cursor (already parsed), and store these cursors in the associative array for future access as shown here:

```
DECLARE
    TYPE integer_tt IS TABLE OF integer;
    v_cur_tt integer_tt;
    ...
BEGIN
    ...
    FOR r IN v_groupRow_tt.first..v_groupRow_tt.last LOOP
        v_cur_tt(r):=dbms_sql.open_cursor;
        FOR c IN c_cols(v_groupRow_tt(r)) LOOP
            FOR i IN v_header_tt.first..v_header_tt.last LOOP
                IF v_header_tt(i).text=c.name_tx THEN
                    v_col_tt(i):=c;
                    v_columnRow_tt(r||'|'||v_col_tt(i).name_tx):=v_col_tt(i).viewcol_tx;
                    v_col_tx:=v_col_tx||','||v_col_tt(i).viewcol_tx;
                    v_val_tx:=v_val_tx||',:'||v_col_tt(i).viewcol_tx;
                END IF;
            END LOOP;
        END LOOP;
        v_sql_tx:='INSERT INTO '||v_map_rec.view_tx||
                  '('||v_col_tx||') VALUES('||v_val_tx||')';
        dbms_sql.parse(v_cur_tt(r),v_sql_tx,dbms_sql.native);
    END LOOP;
```

Now it is only necessary to spin through all of the rows of the uploaded file, find the appropriate row type (from the array) and bind variables, and fire the INSERT statement.

```
    FOR i IN 2..v_row_tt.count LOOP -- first row is a header
        FOR r IN v_groupRow_tt.first..v_groupRow_tt.last LOOP
            FOR c IN v_col_tt.first..v_col_tt.last LOOP
                IF v_columnRow_tt.exists(r||'|'||v_col_tt(c).name_tx)THEN
                    dbms_sql.bind_variable
                        (v_cur_tt(r),':'||v_col_tt(c).viewcol_tx, v_data_tt(c).text);
```

```
            END IF;
        END LOOP;
        v_nr:=dbms_sql.execute(v_cur_tt(r));
      END LOOP;
    END LOOP;
    ...
END;
```

Imagine my surprise when the total processing time for a set of 60,000 rows dropped by a factor of 50! This definitely made the users happy.

This example perfectly illustrates the complexity of system tuning. It can't simply be narrowed down to low-level technical analysis, but must always include a global vision of what is expected to happen. Only this approach to performance optimization can guarantee that the selected options will be valid here and now. There is just no such thing as a general best approach—only special cases.

Object Dependencies

The third major concern (after security and performance) when using Dynamic SQL is based on the fact that converting a hardcoded solution into a dynamic one causes Oracle to lose track of object dependencies between different database objects. This argument is very hard to dispute since there is a significant piece of "free" information automatically collected at the compilation state that is just not there anymore. The real question remains: What exactly is the impact of not having such information about the system development process?

Negative Effects

It is clear that less available data is not good. But in a lot of cases, it's possible to get the same information from slightly different sources. Let's examine what options are available. The following are some negative effects from losing the record of object dependencies in your code.

There is No Dependency Path to Follow Up

The only clean way to be able to document object dependencies is to use repository-based solutions with one (and only one) way of generating code from them. Also, I strongly recommended that you model a repository in a similar way to that of Oracle's data dictionary. It is nice to have tables, columns, and PL/SQL objects explicitly referenced and not hidden deep in the text. Now the whole dependency problem is limited to comparing the Oracle data dictionary with your own, which should not be a big problem.

The requirement to use a single method of code generation is also critical because this provides 100% predictability. Since there is one and only one way of transforming a repository into code, everything follows the same pattern and it is impossible to encounter unexpected dependencies.

There is No Way to Determine Exactly What Will be Executed

Since many parameters are either user-entered or constructed on the fly, it's very difficult to predict possible syntax errors without actually encountering them. This problem is much more difficult to solve, but the concept of *samplers* can be very efficient. Here are some approaches you can take to get a grip on what exactly will be executed:

- Generate all possible (or as many as possible) permutations of the code to be executed and create PL/SQL modules with that code. This approach can help to identify any initial code problems.

- Record all dependencies and keep a simple module that references the same set of objects.

- If the sample becomes invalid, this is an indication of code problems.

Positive Effects

Any feature (including losing object dependencies) can be used in a good way. A few examples follow showing how the lack of dependency information can actually work to your advantage.

You Can Reference Objects Not Yet in the Database

If you have a separate generated procedure for each month (i.e. the year and the month are parts of the procedure name), it's easier to create a universal wrapper instead of writing a huge case statement. The following is an example of such a wrapper:

```
CREATE PROCEDURE p_runMonthly(i_dt date)
is
    v_sql_tx VARCHAR2(256):='BEGIN p_run_'||to_char(i_dt,'YYYYMM')||'; END;';
BEGIN
    EXECUTE IMMEDIATE v_sql_tx;
END;
```

Even better, this universal caller does not require any maintenance when you have to add yet another table to the list of existing ones. Of course, one could argue about the safety of building the logic on uniform naming patterns, but I have seen implementations of this type too often. Each time, creating a new object causes significant stress for the personnel involved, unless all references are wrapped into Dynamic SQL.

Insulate Your Code from Invalidated Dependencies

Sometimes having dependencies is not a good thing for a number of reasons:

- *Code generators*: If you wrap a call to the generated modules into Dynamic SQL, you can refresh these modules without invalidating all dependencies. This can be critical when using JDBC connections to the database, since they are significantly less forgiving (in comparison to Net8 calls).

- *Remote objects*: Since your maintenance cycle may not be the same as that of other teams involved in your project, there is a chance that you could reference objects via database links while they are inaccessible or invalid. In that case, the only safe way out is to wrap all remote calls into dynamic SQL.

- *Logical loops*: Even though it is very difficult, you could create a case where a chain of object references cycles itself. In that case, the only solution is to make one step a Dynamic SQL module.

Summary

Overall, the material covered in this chapter shows that you should not be scared to depart from the tried and tested ways of server-side application development. Of course, there will still be a reasonable learning curve and hidden traps, but the gains from applying more advanced techniques (such as Dynamic SQL) are enormous and include the following:

- Developers can achieve better code flexibility and sustainability.

- Architects can build solutions requiring higher level of abstractions, including repositories and code generators.

- Administrators can get more detailed control over existing systems and improve code manageability.

All of these positive effects ultimately lead to the conclusion that it is possible to build contemporary IT projects "better, faster, cheaper" (and now I promise to repeat the same story even off-stage!). You just need to have the right tools and accept the fact that unless you handle the unknown, it will handle you—against your will.

CHAPTER 3

PL/SQL and Parallel Processing

by Dominic Delmolino

Imagine if you went to the grocery store and only one person was allowed in at a time. Everyone else had to wait outside in a long line until each individual completed their trip before entering the store. Even worse, image if you were only allowed to buy one item while inside the store. If you needed multiple items, you were required to get back in line outside of the store for each one.

This example of one-at-a-time activity is called *serial processing*, and while it's possible to speed this activity up, perhaps by giving each shopper roller skates so they move through the store faster, or by allowing them to take a cart inside and pick out multiple items, it's still constrained by the design of only letting one person shop at a time.

Thank goodness most stores use *parallel processing*—the ability to let more than one activity happen at the same time. By allowing many people to shop at the same time, stores process many more orders in every given day. As long as each shopper is buying a different item, their activities are unique and independent—which makes them perfect for parallel processing. In fact, there are only a few times where this activity needs to serialize—usually when two or more people want to buy the same item off of a shelf. At that point the shoppers need to *coordinate* their activities by negotiating who gets the item.

Parallel processing activities are common in nature and society; we've all see armies of insects and schools of fish divide and conquer amazingly large tasks. Large data processing tasks are becoming more common as the cost of collecting and storing information keeps getting less and less expensive. As companies start to accumulate vast amounts of data, they are turning to parallel processing options as ways to analyze and deal with data across many processors and machines. A parallel programming technique called MapReduce has gained popularity as a method for generically building programs that can run in parallel. In this chapter, you'll explore these divide and conquer techniques and apply them to database activities using PL/SQL. By the end of this chapter, you'll be able to write your own parallel MapReduce programs using PL/SQL and parallel pipelined functions. But first let's dive into the history of parallel processing.

Why Parallel Processing?

In a word: speed. All of us want things to go faster, jobs to complete more quickly, to get answers on demand. And while computers have been getting faster and faster, doubling their number of circuits, increasing their clock speeds, and adding more and more on-chip capabilities, we're still not satisfied. As we encounter physical limitations on how fast individual processors can be, we start to look for other ways to speed up our programs.

It would be nice if computers could automatically figure out ways to divide problems into smaller parts and run procedures on those smaller parts in parallel. There has been significant research in automatic identification of parallelism, but it turns out that it's really hard for computers to understand where opportunities for parallelism can be applied. Attempts have been made to write compliers that can take high-level programming languages and generate explicitly parallel instruction streams for CPUs, but there hasn't been much success in this area, leaving us with the need to manually design parallel processing strategies on our own.

The good news is that when properly implemented, parallel processing techniques provide us with several benefits beyond simple speedup, including the following:

- Better system utilization in that all processors within a multi-processor system can be applied to a task.

- Removal of an all-or-nothing procedure, allowing for partial completion in case some sub-tasks fail.

- Ability to handle larger and larger data sets in a fixed amount of time, as opposed to simply speeding up a fixed data set into a smaller amount of time.

It turns out that these benefits are often worth the overhead and hard work required to design and implement parallel procedures.

Laws Affecting Parallel Processing

Techniques (or *algorithms*) for solving problems with computers are studied and codified by computer scientists, often in resulting in so-called *laws of computing*. Several of these laws have interacted with trends in computer architecture and data growth over the past few years to influence our thinking about parallel processing.

- Moore's Law (1965) states that the number of transistors that can fit on an integrated circuit doubles every two years and has implied that the speed and performance of computer microprocessors doubles as well. From the mid 1980's to approximately 2004, this *speedup* remained fairly true as processor frequency scaling kept pace. However, power consumption started to become a problem, leading to *multi-core* processors which require parallelism to take full advantage of the law.

- Amdahl's Law (1967) states that the speedup of a program using multiple processors in parallel computing is limited by the time needed for the sequential fraction of the program. Amdahl's Law had a chilling effect on parallel processing since it states that programs could not be any faster than the speed of their sequential component. This implies a limit on the amount of speedup you can gain by parallelizing your programs, often getting programs that are only 10 to 20 times faster than their serial counterparts.

- Gustafson's Law (1988) states that problems with very large, repetitive datasets can be efficiently parallelized, almost embarrassingly so (problems that have extremely small serial components and are easy to divide into small, independent units are formally called *embarrassingly parallel*).

Tension between these laws met up with one other industry trend in the mid 2000's—the rise of so-called "Big Data."

The Rise of Big Data

Up until roughly 2007, data growth remained fairly steady and linear. However, as technology has made it easier to capture, store, and send information, there has been an acceleration in the data growth curve. In 2011, the world will generate ten times the amount of data generated in 2006. Much of this data is actually machine generated, as the cost of sensors and data capture from web-based activities has come down. Where we once might have referred to gigabytes of data as being immense, we now look at terabytes, petabytes, and exabytes of data.

Awash in this sea of data, we start to see that attempting to put this data to work in a serial fashion just isn't feasible. With only 86,400 seconds in a day, we have to achieve extreme speeds to process this kind of data if we process one bit at time. Amdahl's Law, designed to predict the speedup of fixed problems sizes and serial portions ranging from 5 to 10%, simply doesn't provide a framework for dealing with problem sizes this large that are growing at this new rate. Ten to twenty times speedups just aren't enough; we need to look beyond serial speedup at ways to handle larger and larger data sets. Gustafson's Law, which includes the idea that people would like solve ever larger problems within a relatively fixed time, coupled with the decline in processor frequency speedups in 2004, has led to the renewed interest in parallel programming.

Parallel vs. Distributed Processing

At this point, you may be wondering about how to achieve parallel processing in a database environment. You may have had exposure to some of the newer data processing frameworks that use many inexpensive individual computers networked together to perform data analysis tasks in a way that sounds like parallel processing. After all, our examples from nature seem like perfect matches for this kind of architecture.

These kinds of environments are usually classified as distributed computing environments, which are distinguished by a lack of access to a shared memory area and consequently the need to communicate via message passing over some kind of network. In a distributed environment, there is significant overhead due to the need for systems to coordinate their activities over this slow (compared to local processing speed) network. Also, in distributed systems, it's assumed that each process can only see a portion of the data—none of the processes has access to the entire data set. This limits the applicability of distributed algorithms. They work well when the data is already distributed among the nodes, or if the data set is so large that the overhead tasks of splitting and distributing the data (including the inter-node communication overhead) are minuscule when compared to the overall data set size. Even so, there is significant overlap between parallel and distributed processing. A parallel system may be described as a tightly coupled distributed system, while a distributed system may be described as a loosely coupled parallel system.

The good news is that most distributed algorithms are easily translated to parallel procedures, so if you come across a distributed procedure that sounds promising, you should be able to modify it to run on a parallel architecture.

Parallel Hardware Architectures

There are several kinds of hardware architectures that may be suitable for parallel processing. It's also useful to understand which architectural features make a system less suitable for the requirements of a parallel procedure.

- *Single computer, single processor, single core*: As a base case, this kind of computer is rarely encountered, but it's useful to note that a single core, single processor, isolated computer can only do one thing at a time. There is no way to implement a parallel procedure on such a system.

- *Single computer, single processor, multi-core*: If the system exposes the multiple cores as separate processors to the operating system, then it's possible to exploit those cores in parallel. Generally, these cores share access to a high-speed memory cache on the chip and therefore can easily share coordination information.

- *Single computer, multi-processor, single or multi-core*: Often called symmetric multiprocessing systems (SMP), these kinds of computers have been the mainstay of open systems. These systems have processors that may not share a local high-speed memory, but all of them share access to the main computer memory through a memory bus. This shared memory access enables the processors to coordinate their activities. In some of these systems, the processors are grouped together on processor boards including a large amount of memory. If that memory is shared across processor boards, such access may be *non-uniform*, resulting in uneven memory access times.

- *Clustered systems of SMP computers*: Clustered systems usually employ some kind of high-speed dedicated system interconnection network to facilitate communication between the computer nodes. These kinds of computer clusters may or may not share access to disks. When they share access to disks, they are called *shared everything* architectures. When they don't, they are called *shared nothing* architectures and more closely resemble distributed systems. In some variants of clusters, the high-speed interconnect actually enables remote access to the memory of each individual computer node from all other nodes. While such remote memory access is much slower than local memory access, it is much faster than using the disk subsystem to transfer information between nodes. Oracle Real Application Clustering technology using Cache Fusion has taken advantage of this capability since version 9.

- *Distributed or networked systems of SMP computers*: This architecture has limited shared resources as each computer is designed to be independent. While this architecture has more fault tolerance than a clustered set of systems, it relies on message passing for activity coordination and is much more suitable for distributed algorithms.

Identify Your Goals

Now that you have a basic understanding of what parallel processing, how it differs from distributed processing, and what underlying computer architectures may be available to support parallel procedures, you'll need to understand your problem set and what you are trying to achieve with parallel procedures. One of the first things you should consider is whether or not you are trying to speed up an existing process or deal with varying size data sets of an ever increasing nature.

Speedup

Speedup is the concept of taking a process that runs in a serial fashion, modifying it to run in parallel, and assessing how much faster it runs. It is defined as the ratio of the time to run serially vs. the time to run in parallel.

```
SpeedUp = Time to Run Serially / Time to Run in Parallel
```

Ideally, you'd like your parallelization effort to be as efficient as possible. As an example, if you write your parallel process to use five processors instead of one, you'd expect to see the process finish in $1/5^{th}$ the time of the serial process. Unfortunately, there are overheads associated with partitioning the data set and tasks into pieces that can be processed by the parallel procedures, as well as activities to assemble the result. These tasks add to the time required by the parallel procedure, resulting in speedups that are not 100% efficient with regard to the number of processors applied to the problem. If those tasks represent 10% of the serial runtime, then the maximum possible speedup is only 10 times. This is the basis of Amdahl's Law.

Scaling Up

Scaling up is the concept of processing larger and larger tasks within a relatively constant time window. It can be defined as the ratio of the task size that can be handled within a time window for the parallel process vs. the serial process.

```
Scale = Size of Overall Task Accomplished in Parallel / Size of Task Accomplished in Serial
```

Ideally, you'd like to be able to increase the size of the task you want to process with every addition of a processor. As an example, if you write a parallel procedure that can perform 100 task items with four processors, you'd like that procedure to be able to perform 125 task items if you add a fifth processor. 100% scalability would mean that there is no decrease in the incremental number of task items you can accomplish when adding every new processor or computing node; this typically only applies when the incremental set of task items is purely independent of all other task items. If that's not the case, you'll achieve somewhat less than 100% scalability. However, there are many instances where task item independence is possible, and you should challenge yourself to identify those cases. This is particularly useful when considering how to design your system to handle an increase in the order of magnitude for the data it needs to process. Thinking about how to process a multifold increase in dataset sizes within a reasonably fixed amount of time will force you to consider ways to parallelize your processing. This is the basis of Gustafson's Law.

Degree of Parallelism

When taking a serial task and splitting into parallel task items, you can make decisions about how many task items you'd like to have running at the same time. This level of concurrency is called the *degree of parallelism* and is often referred to by the acronym DOP.

You'd think that it would be a good idea to simply set the DOP to the number of parallel task items; for example, if you can divide a serial process into 12 tasks, you'd like to run all 12 at once. However, there may be situations where you'd like to only run three tasks at a time in four batches, perhaps to reduce the resource consumption of the system while the parallel task is running. You should carefully consider how busy you want your system to be when handling parallel tasks. If you decide to set the DOP to less than the number of task items, the remaining items will wait—a situation known as *parallel queuing*.

Candidate Workloads for Parallel Processing

Now that you've got a handle on what your goals are for particular processes (speed up or scaling up), it's time to look at what kinds of workload you are dealing with and what will be the overall system impact of converting them to parallel processes.

It's important to understand that converting any serial process to a parallel process increases the resource consumption of your system during the time that the parallel processes are running. This is easy to picture in your mind if you use the example of the grocery store from the introduction. If you image a store that only allows one person in at a time, you can see that for any given time period, the store isn't very busy. But if you allow shoppers to shop in parallel, you can see that the store is much more busy during a specific time window. Another way to look at this is by measuring something like the CPU utilization of your system while the serial process is running and multiply that by the degree of parallelism you're considering for your tasks; you'll need to make sure that you have enough CPU to handle your desired parallel workload. This is particularly important when considering introducing parallelism into an already running system.

Parallelism and OLTP

Online transaction processing systems are usually characterized by high-volume, high-concurrency, short transactions that perform minimal amounts of work. These work units are typically independent, such as orders placed by individual customers. For the most part, customers' activities are independent from each other and therefore can run in parallel.

While not strictly parallel processing in that you're not taking a large task and breaking it down into smaller independent task units, OLTP activity does achieve higher system resource utilization by allowing multiple tasks to run concurrently at the same time. Well designed OLTP systems fully utilize all CPUs and CPU cores on SMP and clustered database servers, leaving little excess idle CPU. However, you may be tempted to further break down individual OLTP transactions into sub-tasks that can be parallelized.

For example, let's say you have an online shopping web site and some of your customers buy from you in bulk; perhaps they act as wholesalers. These customers may have shopping carts that contain thousands of items—many more than the average casual consumer. Processing the items in these carts (perhaps to calculate the taxable nature of each item) may take longer than you'd like; you want the experience to be similar to the ones for your casual customers. If possible, you may want to process the cart items in parallel, perhaps with a small degree of parallelism into order to make the cart "feel" like it's 4-5 times smaller than it really is. This is certainly possible, but you'll need to be careful not to swamp your system with extra concurrent workload. Examine your system's CPU utilization to see if you can handle the extra concurrency associated with your parallel algorithm. It may be possible to engage a small degree of parallelism for extra large carts.

Parallelism and Non-OLTP Workloads

Non-OLTP workloads like large reports, statistical analysis (perhaps to measure something like customer churn), or period full-scale data processing activities (like producing a periodic invoice for every customer or mass-mailing specific customers) generally lend themselves well to parallel processing activities.

These kinds of activities may include examining large amounts of data in parallel to identify particular items for processing, building interim summary results, or updating batches of rows. They also may perform activities like transforming large amounts of data in parallel. Generally these kinds of activities are run on system or time windows specifically set aside for this kind of processing, so that there is plenty of CPU available. You'll know that these systems are ripe for parallel exploitation if the serial job takes a long time to run, but the system's overall CPU utilization remains low or shows that very few of the available processors are actually being used.

The MapReduce Programming Model

MapReduce is a programming model for processing large data sets in parallel. The programming model is simple in that primitives are defined in such a way as to process *chunks* of data in an independent fashion, leading to the ability to process those chunks in parallel. The model begins by "sharding" or splitting the data into sets that are passed to map functions. A *map* function typically takes a set of input data and produces sets of key/value pairs which can then be handed to a set of *reduce* functions which perform aggregation of the mapped lists. The model has become popular due to its generic primitives, which have been used to perform a wide variety of tasks related to text scanning and filtering.

Many new database systems support MapReduce primitives as a way to perform large-scale aggregation and filtering tasks. If you're familiar with the paradigm, I'll take you through how to implement it in PL/SQL over the next few pages.

Before Looking to PL/SQL

It's often good to remember that the database can automatically parallelize many SQL DML and DDL operations without requiring any special PL/SQL programming. You may want to examine these options before attempting to manually parallelize your procedures to see if the automatic parallelism gives you the benefit you're looking for. You'll exploit some of the architectural underpinnings of the automatic parallelism in the examples, but first it might be useful for you to become familiar with what's available. Oracle calls this architecture *parallel execution* and it can be applied to several different kinds of operations.

- *Parallel Query*: Large queries involving scans across full tables and partitions can have those scans performed in parallel, including table scans, index fast full scans, and partitioned index range scans. Join methods such as nested loops, sort merge joins, hash joins, and star transformations can also be parallelized. Aggregation and set processing methods including `GROUP BY`, `NOT IN`, `UNION`, `UNION ALL`, `CUBE`, and `ROLLUP` can be parallelized, too.

- *Parallel DML*: `INSERT AS SELECT`, `UPDATE`, `DELETE`, and `MERGE` operations all can be performed in parallel, including the ability to insert into multiple tables with a single DML statement.

- *Parallel DDL*: `CREATE TABLE AS SELECT`, `CREATE INDEX`, `REBUILD INDEX`, `REBUILD INDEX PARTITION`, and `MOVE`, `SPLIT`, or `COALESCE PARTITION` can all be run in parallel.

As always, you should spend the time to make sure your serial operation is as efficient as possible before looking to parallel alternatives. While parallel execution may result in faster execution time, you should be wary of the efficiencies associated with speedup and scaling up, as covered earlier in this chapter. Since most parallelization techniques are less than 100% efficient, you'll be introducing extra resource consumption into your system, so you'll want to make sure that the extra consumption is worth the benefits. This is especially important for systems that tend to run near 100% utilization; you may want to see if you can recoup the overhead of parallelization by running more efficient serial-type operations.

Processes Available for Parallel Activities

Now that you've decided to try to implement a parallel process in PL/SQL, it's useful to understand your execution options. Since the database enables concurrent activity to occur through sessions that usually map to individual connections and operating system processes, you'll need to become familiar with which operating system processes can support your procedure. There are three options available.

- *Parallel Execution Servers*: These processes are sometimes called parallel query slaves and are automatically configured by the database to support parallel execution of SQL statements. Generally set by the parameters `parallel_min_servers` and `parallel_max_servers` to set up a pool of operating system processes for each database instance.

- *Job Queue Processes*: Using the `DBMS_JOB` or `DBMS_SCHEDULER` package, you can submit PL/SQL routines to be run by server job queue processes in an asynchronous manner. While there is no guarantee how many processes will be available at any time, the maximum number is controlled by the `job_queue_processes` parameter.

- *User Session Processes*: By manually creating your own operating system processes that establish connections to the database, you can create your own parallel processing support framework. You would need to control the degree of parallelism and task management outside of the database or by using database data structures.

In this chapter, you're only going to examine the use of the *parallel execution servers (through the use of parallel pipelined functions)* to support your parallel PL/SQL routines.

Using Parallel Execution Servers for MapReduce

So far you've seen that Oracle (specifically the Enterprise Edition) has several different options for parallel operations against tables, specifically in the areas of parallel query, where table data is divided among parallel execution servers for filtering, joining, and sorts. While that option appears attractive, how can you use it with PL/SQL?

The answer lies in the ability for the database to treat a PL/SQL function that returns values as a pseudo-table; this ability is called PL/SQL *pipelined functions* and first appeared Oracle 9i. Prior to Oracle9i, it was possible to CAST a PL/SQL function as a collection type and select from it, but that process required instantiating the entire result set in memory prior to returning any data from it. The memory needed for holding the full result set made it infeasible for the large problems you're considering for parallelization. The answer to that issue is the pipelined function.

Pipelined Table Functions

A pipelined table function enables you to use PL/SQL to generate data in a programmatic fashion, specifying what you want in each row and enabling the database to select from your function just like any other table. You do this by declaring the structure of your record using a database object type or a PL/SQL record type, and then creating a collection type that describes a "table" of your records

For your MapReduce example, you'll define a key/value pair record and then a collection type that describes a list of such records, like so:

```
create or replace package map_reduce_type as
  type key_value_pair is record (
    key_item    varchar2(32),
    value_item  number
  );
  type key_value_pairs is table of key_value_pair;
end map_reduce_type;
/
```

The particular problem you're going to try to solve using your parallel pipelined functions will be to count the occurrences of letters in a list of strings. For your list of strings, you'll use the over 100,000 column names within a standard installation of the Oracle database; from that list you'll try to determine which letter is the most popular.

In a MapReduce model, you'd begin by breaking down each string into its component letters, and "emitting" a list of letters in each string with a count of 1 (your Map function). Once you have the letters mapped, you'll hand them to a Reduce function to count them up. Let's dive into the example and see how this works:

Start by declaring your Map function, indicating that it will return a list of key/value pairs using a pipelined function. Your function will take one input parameter: a string to break up into its individual letters. Here's the code:

```
create or replace package map_letter_count as
  function result_set (p_input in varchar2)
    return map_reduce_type.key_value_pairs pipelined;
end map_letter_count;
/
```

Your function simply takes the input string, goes through it character by character and "pipes" the output as a row for each letter with a value of one, like so:

```
create or replace package body map_letter_count as

  function result_set (p_input in varchar2)
    return map_reduce_type.key_value_pairs pipelined is

    l_key_value_pair map_reduce_type.key_value_pair;

  begin

    for i in 1..length(p_input) loop

      l_key_value_pair.key_item := substr(p_input,i,1);
      l_key_value_pair.value_item := 1;

      pipe row(l_key_value_pair);

    end loop;
```

```
        return;

    end result_set;

end map_letter_count;
/
```

Now you can retrieve the results from this function by using it in a SELECT statement and casting it as a table.

```
select * from table(
map_letter_count.result_set('Hello, world!')
);
```

```
KEY_ITEM                          VALUE_ITEM
-------------------------------   ----------------------
H                                 1
e                                 1
l                                 1
l                                 1
o                                 1
,                                 1
                                  1
w                                 1
o                                 1
r                                 1
l                                 1
d                                 1
!                                 1
```

```
13 rows selected
```

So far you've seen how to use a pipelined function to take an input parameter and turn it into a list of MapReduce key/value pairs using the "pipe row" construct. This is nice, but right now your function is limited to a single string. Let's see how to extend it to handle a large set of strings.

To do that, you can modify your Map function to take as input a list of strings or documents in the form of a data cursor, like so:

```
create or replace package map_letter_count as
  function result_set (p_documents in sys_refcursor)
    return map_reduce_type.key_value_pairs pipelined;
end map_letter_count;
/
```

To set up your list of strings, create a documents table based on DBA_TAB_COLUMNS; to keep your testing manageable, limit it to 10 rows.

```
create table documents
as
select rownum doc_id, column_name text
from dba_tab_columns
where rownum <= 10;
```

Now your Map function will go through each document in turn to perform its mapping function.

```
create or replace package body map_letter_count as

  function result_set (p_documents in sys_refcursor)
    return map_reduce_type.key_value_pairs pipelined is

    type document_type is record (
      doc_id number,
      text    varchar2(4000)
    );
    l_document        document_type;
    l_key_value_pair map_reduce_type.key_value_pair;

    begin

      fetch p_documents into l_document;
      loop
        exit when p_documents%notfound;

        for i in 1..length(l_document.text) loop

          l_key_value_pair.key_item := substr(l_document.text,i,1);
          l_key_value_pair.value_item := 1;

          pipe row(l_key_value_pair);

        end loop;

        fetch p_documents into l_document;

      end loop;

      return;

    end result_set;

end map_letter_count;
/
```

Now selecting from your Map function returns the mapped keys and values for all of the documents in the table.

```
select * from table(
map_letter_count.result_set(
cursor(select doc_id, text from documents)
)
);
KEY_ITEM                         VALUE_ITEM
------------------------------   ---------------------
D                                1
                                 1
O                                1
B                                1
```

```
J                           1
#                           1
O                           1
R                           1
D                           1
E                           1
R                           1
#                           1
C                           1
…snip…
O                           1
L                           1
U                           1
D                           1
P                           1
R                           1
I                           1
O                           1
R                           1
I                           1
T                           1
Y                           1
S                           1
T                           1
A                           1
T                           1
E                           1

63 rows selected
```

Running this against the entire data set produces over 1 million rows.

```
drop table documents;
create table documents
as
select rownum doc_id, column_name text from dba_tab_columns;

select count(*)
from
(
select * from table(
map_letter_count.result_set(
cursor(select doc_id, text from documents)
)
)
);

COUNT(*)
----------------------
1132707
```

However, this entire process has been run serially.

```
select * from v$pq_sesstat;
```

STATISTIC	LAST_QUERY	SESSION_TOTAL
Queries Parallelized	0	0
DML Parallelized	0	0
DDL Parallelized	0	0
DFO Trees	0	0
Server Threads	0	0
Allocation Height	0	0
Allocation Width	0	0
Local Msgs Sent	0	0
Distr Msgs Sent	0	0
Local Msgs Recv'd	0	0
Distr Msgs Recv'd	0	0

```
11 rows selected
```

Trying to force it to run in parallel doesn't work, as you can see:

```
select count(*)
from
(
select /*+ parallel */ * from table(
map_letter_count.result_set(
cursor(select doc_id, text from documents)
)
)
);
```

```
COUNT(*)
----------------------
1132707
```

```
select * from v$pq_sesstat;
```

STATISTIC	LAST_QUERY	SESSION_TOTAL
Queries Parallelized	0	0
DML Parallelized	0	0
DDL Parallelized	0	0
DFO Trees	0	0
Server Threads	0	0
Allocation Height	0	0
Allocation Width	0	0
Local Msgs Sent	0	0
Distr Msgs Sent	0	0
Local Msgs Recv'd	0	0
Distr Msgs Recv'd	0	0

So now that you have your Map function, how do you get it to run in parallel using PL/SQL pipelined functions? The answer is the PARALLEL_ENABLE construct on the function declaration.

```
create or replace package map_letter_count as
  function result_set (p_documents in sys_refcursor)
    return map_reduce_type.key_value_pairs pipelined
      parallel_enable (partition p_documents by any);
end map_letter_count;
/
```

PARALLEL_ENABLE tells Oracle that the PL/SQL function can be run in parallel against chunks of data. In order to provide those chunks to the parallel instances of the function, you need to define a data set in the form of a cursor (here, you use a generic sys_refcursor). You tell the database to "shard" or "split" the data by using the PARTITION option for the PARALLEL_ENABLE parameter. The BY ANY clause tells the database that you don't care how the data is split up, just to pick reasonably equal sized subsets of the data.

You then modify your Map function to retrieve each item from its assigned subset (by FETCHING from the cursor) and the process each item into the target key/value pair.

```
create or replace package body map_letter_count as

  function result_set (p_documents in sys_refcursor)
    return map_reduce_type.key_value_pairs pipelined
    parallel_enable (partition p_documents by any) is

    type document_type is record (
      doc_id number,
      text    varchar2(4000)
    );
    l_document        document_type;
    l_key_value_pair map_reduce_type.key_value_pair;

  begin

    fetch p_documents into l_document;
    loop
      exit when p_documents%notfound;

      for i in 1..length(l_document.text) loop

        l_key_value_pair.key_item := substr(l_document.text,i,1);
        l_key_value_pair.value_item := 1;

        pipe row(l_key_value_pair);

      end loop;

      fetch p_documents into l_document;

    end loop;

    return;
```

```
        end result_set;

end map_letter_count;
/
```

Now when you tell the server to run this function in parallel, you see that it starts up several instances of the function to perform the map function.

```
select count(*)
from
(
select /*+ parallel */ * from table(
map_letter_count.result_set(
cursor(select doc_id, text from documents)
)
)
);
```

```
COUNT(*)
----------------------
1132707
```

STATISTIC	LAST_QUERY	SESSION_TOTAL
Queries Parallelized	1	1
DML Parallelized	0	0
DDL Parallelized	0	0
DFO Trees	1	1
Server Threads	2	0
Allocation Height	2	0
Allocation Width	1	0
Local Msgs Sent	56	56
Distr Msgs Sent	0	0
Local Msgs Recv'd	56	56
Distr Msgs Recv'd	0	0

```
11 rows selected
```

Now that you've completed your Map function, let's talk about the Reduce function. As explained earlier, Reduce functions typically take the results of Map functions and "reduce" them down using aggregation primitives. In your case, you're going to have your Reduce function go through the Map results and sum up the number of occurrences of each letter. You're also going to introduce a subtle error in your function in order to highlight an aspect of the MapReduce programming model and how to address it with PL/SQL parallel pipelined function options. You'll start with your function definition, and since you want the Reducers to run in parallel, you'll use the PARALLEL_ENABLE option and have it partition the results of the Map function just like before.

```
create or replace package reduce_letter_count is
  function result_set (p_key_value_pairs in sys_refcursor)
    return map_reduce_type.key_value_pairs pipelined
      parallel_enable (partition p_key_value_pairs by any);
end reduce_letter_count;
/
```

The definition of your Reduce function is pretty simple, since we know that Reducers always work on key/value pairs from Map functions. Your Reduce code will be simple as well. You'll just process the results from the Map function one-by-one, adding up the values and emitting a result when you switch to new letters. Here is the code:

```
create or replace package body reduce_letter_count as

  function result_set (p_key_value_pairs in sys_refcursor)
    return map_reduce_type.key_value_pairs pipelined
      parallel_enable (partition p_key_value_pairs by any) is

    l_in1_key_value_pair map_reduce_type.key_value_pair;
    l_out_key_value_pair map_reduce_type.key_value_pair;

  begin

    fetch p_key_value_pairs into l_in1_key_value_pair;
    l_out_key_value_pair.key_item := l_in1_key_value_pair.key_item;
    l_out_key_value_pair.value_item := 0;

    loop
      exit when p_key_value_pairs%notfound;

      if l_out_key_value_pair.key_item = l_in1_key_value_pair.key_item
      then

        l_out_key_value_pair.value_item :=
          l_out_key_value_pair.value_item +
          l_in1_key_value_pair.value_item;

      else

        pipe row(l_out_key_value_pair);

        l_out_key_value_pair.key_item := l_in1_key_value_pair.key_item;
        l_out_key_value_pair.value_item := 1;

      end if;

      fetch p_key_value_pairs into l_in1_key_value_pair;

    end loop;

    pipe row(l_out_key_value_pair);

    return;

  end result_set;

end reduce_letter_count;
/
```

Now, to test your Reduce function, you'll go back and define a single map that works against only one string.

```
create or replace package single_map_letter_count as
  function result_set (p_input in varchar2)
    return map_reduce_type.key_value_pairs pipelined;
end single_map_letter_count;
/

create or replace package body single_map_letter_count as

  function result_set (p_input in varchar2)
    return map_reduce_type.key_value_pairs pipelined is

    l_key_value_pair map_reduce_type.key_value_pair;

    begin

      for i in 1..length(p_input) loop

        l_key_value_pair.key_item := substr(p_input,i,1);
        l_key_value_pair.value_item := 1;

        pipe row(l_key_value_pair);

      end loop;

      return;

    end result_set;

end single_map_letter_count;
/
```

Now test your Reduce function by using it to reduce the results from a single map, like so:

```
select * from table(
reduce_letter_count.result_set(
cursor(select * from table(
single_map_letter_count.result_set('Hello, world!')
))))
order by key_item;
```

```
KEY_ITEM                       VALUE_ITEM
------------------------------ ----------------------
                               1
!                              1
,                              1
H                              1
d                              1
e                              1
l                              2
```

l	1
o	1
o	1
r	1
w	1

`12 rows selected`

That doesn't look right! You have two rows each for the letters 'l' and 'o'. What could have gone wrong?

Let's look at the Reduce code and pay particular attention to any assumptions you may have made in coding it up. Right away you should see that you had assumed that the data handed to the Reduce function was coming in sorted or clustered such that like letters would appear one after another from the Map output. However, the PARTITION … BY ANY option you used specifically told the server that you didn't care which letters went to which Reducer and you also didn't tell the server that you wanted the data sets sent to the Reducers in a such a way as to make sure that the items would come in clustered or sorted.

How can you tell Oracle that you want like letters sent to the same Reducers?

By replacing the generic sys_refcursor with information about columns in the cursor (in this case, the actual key/value pairs), you now have several ways to distribute rows to your parallel function instances. The full syntax for specifying the distribution is as follows:

```
{[ORDER | CLUSTER] BY column_list}
PARALLEL_ENABLE({PARTITION p BY [ANY | (HASH | RANGE) column_list]} )
```

Using these keywords, *partitioning* refers to the method used to divide the rows among the parallel function instances, while the *ordering* and *clustering* options refer to how the rows are pushed or "streamed" into each parallel function instance. You should be aware that specifying more control over the distribution and ordering/clustering of the rows adds overhead to your process and reduces both your speedup and scale up. Here are some descriptions and examples of these options:

- ORDERING vs. CLUSTERING: These options refer to how data is delivered to each parallel instance after it has been partitioned or divided. They're probably best explained by an example.

  Assume your function is going to work on the following subset of data values from a dataset:

  5,4,5,6,8,3,2,3,4,5,6,1,2,4,6

  Clustering would deliver the values in such a way that equivalent values would come in directly one after another, but not necessarily sorted

  6,6,6,3,3,8,1,4,4,4,5,5,5,2,2

  whereas ordering would deliver the values completely sorted

  1,2,2,3,3,4,4,4,5,5,5,6,6,6,8

  Both of these options add overhead to the process, as they are performed prior to the parallel function instance receiving data. Ordering the set takes more time than clustering like values.

- PARTITION BY ANY: As stated earlier, this method simply provides each parallel function instance with a random set of rows from the source set. Each function instance gets roughly the same number of rows, but they can't make any assumptions about the rows they're receiving.

  Technically, you can specify that you'd like those rows CLUSTERED (or grouped) by particular column values, or even that you'd like the entire set of data allocated to each parallel function to be completely ORDERED. However, since you don't know which rows are going to which function instance, these options are of limited value. With a random distribution of rows, you would not be able to assume that your clustering would contain all values that match the cluster, and while you could ask for the rows to be ordered, you would not know if you were missing any rows that were assigned to other parallel instances.

- PARTITION BY HASH: This method hashes the values from the columns you list to create subsets of data to be portioned out to the parallel function instances. Since values hash consistently, individual values from the master data set will essentially be grouped together and sent to each function instance. It's possible that multiple values will be sent to an instance, and they may not be adjacent values, but you can rely on the fact that each function instance will receive the full set of equivalent values. Basically, this is like using the CLUSTERING option when dividing up the data. One or more complete value clusters will be sent to each function instance. This method provides a relatively even distribution of data to each function, while also making sure that specific data values remain together.

  After the data has been divided, it can be further CLUSTERED or ORDERED for consumption by the parallel function.

- PARTITION BY RANGE: This method sorts the data before dividing it among the parallel function instances. This is like using the ORDERED option for portioning out the data. It ensures that data values will be grouped together for each function, and that functions will only deal with adjacent data values. The risk here is that if your data has any extremely skewed distributions, you will have unbalanced parallelism—some of the parallel function instances will have a lot more work to do than others. Like the PARTITION BY HASH option, the data can be further CLUSTERED or ORDERED for consumption by the parallel function.

In looking over these options, you see that you want to make sure all maps for a particular letter are sent to the same reduce function (you'll use a PARTITION BY RANGE for that), and that you want the letters grouped together when being processed. For that you'll use ORDERING or CLUSTERING. First, you'll set up the PARTITION BY RANGE and demonstrate that it isn't sufficient by itself. To do that, you need to replace your SYS_REFCURSOR with a strongly typed cursor that gives the database information about the items in the data set that can be used to distinguish which items can be used to distribute the data. You'll do that by declaring a typed ref cursor in your types package that describes a cursor made of key/value pairs.

```
create or replace package map_reduce_type as
  type key_value_pair is record (
    key_item    varchar2(32),
    value_item  number
  );
  type key_value_pairs is table of key_value_pair;
  type key_value_pair_cursor is ref cursor
```

```
        return key_value_pair;
end map_reduce_type;
/
```

Now you'll update the declaration of your Reduce function to indicate that the input key/value pairs should be divided into ranges which will be consumed by your Reduce function.

```
create or replace package reduce_letter_count is

  function result_set
     (p_key_value_pairs in map_reduce_type.key_value_pair_cursor)
    return map_reduce_type.key_value_pairs pipelined
      parallel_enable (
        partition p_key_value_pairs by range(key_item)
        );

end reduce_letter_count;
/

create or replace package body reduce_letter_count as

  function result_set
     (p_key_value_pairs in map_reduce_type.key_value_pair_cursor)
    return map_reduce_type.key_value_pairs pipelined
      parallel_enable (
        partition p_key_value_pairs by range(key_item)
        ) is

    l_in1_key_value_pair map_reduce_type.key_value_pair;
    l_out_key_value_pair map_reduce_type.key_value_pair;

  begin

      fetch p_key_value_pairs into l_in1_key_value_pair;
      l_out_key_value_pair.key_item := l_in1_key_value_pair.key_item;
      l_out_key_value_pair.value_item := 0;

      loop
        exit when p_key_value_pairs%notfound;

        if l_out_key_value_pair.key_item = l_in1_key_value_pair.key_item
        then

          l_out_key_value_pair.value_item :=
            l_out_key_value_pair.value_item +
            l_in1_key_value_pair.value_item;

        else

          pipe row(l_out_key_value_pair);
```

```
        l_out_key_value_pair.key_item := l_in1_key_value_pair.key_item;
        l_out_key_value_pair.value_item := 1;

    end if;

    fetch p_key_value_pairs into l_in1_key_value_pair;

  end loop;

  pipe row(l_out_key_value_pair);

  return;

 end result_set;

end reduce_letter_count;
/
```

Let's try it!

```
select * from table(
reduce_letter_count.result_set(
cursor(select * from table(
single_map_letter_count.result_set('Hello, world!')
))))
order by key_item;
```

KEY_ITEM	VALUE_ITEM
	1
!	1
,	1
H	1
d	1
e	1
l	2
l	1
o	1
o	1
r	1
w	1

```
12 rows selected
```

Now, even though you've distributed the map results appropriately, you still haven't made sure that the results are sent in any particular order to the reducers. To make that happen, you need to add the ORDERING or CLUSTERING option. Let's use the ORDERING option since that's the easiest to understand; I'll let you try the CLUSTERING option on your own.

```
create or replace package reduce_letter_count is

  function result_set
      (p_key_value_pairs in map_reduce_type.key_value_pair_cursor)
    return map_reduce_type.key_value_pairs pipelined
      parallel_enable (
        partition p_key_value_pairs by range(key_item))
        order p_key_value_pairs by (key_item);

end reduce_letter_count;
/
create or replace package body reduce_letter_count as

  function result_set
      (p_key_value_pairs in map_reduce_type.key_value_pair_cursor)
    return map_reduce_type.key_value_pairs pipelined
      parallel_enable (
        partition p_key_value_pairs by range(key_item))
        order p_key_value_pairs by (key_item)
        is

    l_in1_key_value_pair map_reduce_type.key_value_pair;
    l_out_key_value_pair map_reduce_type.key_value_pair;

  begin

    fetch p_key_value_pairs into l_in1_key_value_pair;
    l_out_key_value_pair.key_item := l_in1_key_value_pair.key_item;
    l_out_key_value_pair.value_item := 0;

    loop
      exit when p_key_value_pairs%notfound;

      if l_out_key_value_pair.key_item = l_in1_key_value_pair.key_item
      then

        l_out_key_value_pair.value_item :=
          l_out_key_value_pair.value_item +
          l_in1_key_value_pair.value_item;

      else

        pipe row(l_out_key_value_pair);

        l_out_key_value_pair.key_item := l_in1_key_value_pair.key_item;
        l_out_key_value_pair.value_item := 1;

      end if;

      fetch p_key_value_pairs into l_in1_key_value_pair;
```

```
      end loop;

      pipe row(l_out_key_value_pair);

      return;

   end result_set;

end reduce_letter_count;
/

select * from table(
reduce_letter_count.result_set(
cursor(select * from table(
single_map_letter_count.result_set('Hello, world!')
))))
order by key_item;
```

```
KEY_ITEM                        VALUE_ITEM
------------------------------  ----------------------
                                1
!                               1
,                               1
H                               1
d                               1
e                               1
l                               3
o                               2
r                               1
w                               1

10 rows selected
```

Success! Now, let's try it against your 100,000 strings and their resulting 1.1 million key/value map pairs.

```
drop table documents;
create table documents
as
select rownum doc_id, column_name text from dba_tab_columns;

select /*+ parallel */ * from table(
reduce_letter_count.result_set(
cursor(select /*+ parallel */ * from table(
map_letter_count.result_set(cursor(select * from documents))
))))
order by key_item;
KEY_ITEM                        VALUE_ITEM
------------------------------  ----------------------
                                11
#                               2522
$                               457
```

67

-	4
0	2104
1	1755
2	1679
3	993
4	798
5	536
6	348
7	254
8	241
9	225
A	83113
B	20226
C	44506
D	47611
E	131562
F	13999
G	19681
H	12801
I	72349
J	4564
K	6081
L	47635
M	45084
N	71110
O	64789
P	40780
Q	4763
R	64882
S	66557
T	94510
U	33837
V	10060
W	10161
X	7168
Y	16269
Z	2083
_	84576
a	1
b	1
c	1
e	5
g	1
i	2
j	1
l	1
m	1
n	1
o	1
p	1
r	2
s	1

```
t                              1
u                              1
v                              1
```

`58 rows selected`

It works! Timing tests showed that I was able to achieve parallel speedup relative to the number of CPUs on my server as the database ran the steps in parallel. From here on out, you should be able to use this technique to write your own parallel MapReduce functions in PL/SQL or take existing MapReduce algorithms and convert them to run against your Oracle database.

Guidance

Just because you have the ability to write parallel MapReduce algorithms in PL/SQL doesn't always mean you should use them. In many cases, it would take less code to accomplish the same result (including using parallelism) in a single SQL statement. Your entire example could be written as follows:

```
select     /*+ parallel */
           letter key_item,
           count(*) value_item
from
(
select     substr(d.text,c.i,1) letter
from       documents d,
           (select level i from dual connect by level <= 30) c
)
where      letter is not null
group by   letter
order by   letter;
```

The point is that not all solutions require implementation in terms of programming primitives like MapReduce. The real value in understanding this approach comes when you are trying to move back and forth from other parallel programming environments. By understanding how to implement a parallel algorithm in PL/SQL you can more easily translate concepts from other languages and systems.

Parallel Pipelined Table Functions Summary

You've seen how you can write PL/SQL functions that act like tables, producing rows programmatically and how these functions can be invoked in a parallel fashion. It's important to note that these functions can pass data to other PL/SQL table functions that can also be run in parallel, building a chain of parallel transformations and operations on data, similar to many MapReduce cycles.

Summary

Oracle provides many different ways to use PL/SQL to implement parallel programming algorithms. However, as noted, careful consideration must be given to whether or not parallel constructs will provide you with the benefit you're looking for. Parallel options *always* consume more system resources than their serial counterparts, but in situations where you have available capacity, they provide ways to both speed up long-running activities or give you an ability to handle very large data sets. These capabilities may also serve you well when translating parallel algorithms from other systems.

As of 11gR2, the parallel pipelined table functions provide you with the most flexible and mature method for dividing up work among independent processors and across clusters in a clustered database environment. The DBMS_PARALLEL_EXECUTE framework new in 11gR2 is also an intriguing option that Standard Edition users can take advantage of for a higher degree of programmatic control—at the cost of flexibility with regard to dividing and sorting data for parallelization.

CHAPTER 4

Warnings and
Conditional Compilation

by Torben Holm

When Oracle implemented Java in the RDBMS kernel, it was thought to be the end of PL/SQL. However, in version 10.2, Oracle rewrote the PL/SQL compiler and implemented various new features, proving that there is a future for PL/SQL. This chapter will cover two features that were first seen in Oracle 10.2: PL/SQL warnings and PL/SQL conditional compilation.

PL/SQL Warnings

In Oracle 10.2, Oracle implemented PL/SQL warnings. The feature gives the ability to compile PL/SQL and get warnings if some of the code implements poor practices or conflicts with reserved words or Oracle functions. Prior to Oracle 10.2, your PL/SQL would sometimes compile—only to throw errors at runtime. The purpose of PL/SQL warnings is to warn of potential mistakes at compile time when they are easier to fix, thereby ensuring that code being applied to the database is as robust and optimal as possible.

Basics

Before you start looking at what you gain from the PL/SQL warnings, first look at some basic aspects of the feature. By default, PL/SQL warnings are disabled. PL/SQL warnings can be enabled at the system, session, or procedure level. PL/SQL warnings are divided into three categories:

> **Severe:** These are warnings about code that contains a conflict with functions in SYS.STANDARD or SQL functions.

> **Performance:** These are warnings about code that may have a performance impact, such as the use of wrong data types in queries and the lack of use of NOCOPY compile directive when appropriate.

> **Informational:** These are warnings relating to code that does no harm and/or may even be removed.

When you create or compile a stored procedure, it inherits the settings in the session you are running by default. The PL/SQL warning level is determined by the value of the parameter `plsql_warnings`. You can show the current parameter value as follows:

```
SQL@V112> show parameter plsql_warnings

NAME                                TYPE        VALUE
----------------------------------- ----------- ------------------------------
plsql_warnings                      string      DISABLE:ALL

The default value is DISABLE:ALL
```

If you are not allowed to execute a SHOW PARAMETER command, the value of `plsql_warnings` can be examined with the following query:

```
SQL@V112> SELECT DBMS_WARNING.GET_WARNING_SETTING_STRING FROM DUAL;

GET_WARNING_SETTING_STRING
----------------------------------------------------------------
DISABLE:ALL
```

To enable all warnings for the current session, execute the following:

```
SQL@V112> alter session set plsql_warnings='ENABLE:ALL';

Session altered.
```

■ **Note** In most cases, you need the ALTER SESSION privilege to alter your session parameters. This is not the case when it comes to altering the `plsql_warnings` parameter.

Furthermore, the `plsql_warnings` string is not case sensitive.

To enable severe and performance warnings and disable informational warnings in one go, execute the following statement:

```
SQL@V112> alter session set plsql_warnings='ENABLE:SEVERE,ENABLE:PERFORMANCE,
DISABLE:INFORMATIONAL';

Session altered.
```

The parameter setting is not cumulative. If you first set `plsql_warnings` to ENABLE:SEVERE and afterwards ENABLE:PERFORMANCE, then only warnings regarding performance is enabled.

Should you want to set the parameter from within PL/SQL, you can do so by calling DBMS_WARNINGS.SETWARNING_SETTING_STRING. Enabling only setting one will disable others. This example will enable severe warnings only and at the session level:

```
SQL@V112> EXEC DBMS_WARNING.SET_WARNING_SETTING_STRING('ENABLE:SEVERE', 'SESSION');

PL/SQL procedure successfully completed.
```

Enabling warnings does not affect execution time, but it may affect compilation time a bit. Should you compile a procedure 1,000 times, you'd find the difference between compiling with warnings and compiling without warnings will be about one second in favor of the one not having warnings enabled.

If a procedure is compiled and compilation warnings occur, the procedure can still be executed. The warnings are there to give you a heads-up that you might have a problem in your code. But the compiler doesn't know everything. Not all warnings are problems. You are always free to execute your code.

■ **Tip** If you want to examine what type of warnings you can get and you have access to the Oracle binaries on the database server, you can examine the file `$ORACLE_HOME/plsql/mesg/plw<LANG>.msg`. This file contains the all the warning messages.

Using Warnings

Let's have a look at some examples. First, create a simple table called T1 with a column named KEY of type VARCHAR2 and a column called VALUE of VARCHAR2. Assume that the column KEY, although defined as VARCHAR2, only contains numbers. Sadly, you will sometimes see this approach in real-world production systems. Here is the code to create the table:

```
SQL@V112> CREATE TABLE T1 (
2 KEY VARCHAR2(10) CONSTRAINT PK_T1 PRIMARY KEY,
3 VALUE VARCHAR2(10))
4 /
```

Table Created.

Now, load the table with test data.

```
SQL@V112> insert into t1 select rownum, substr(text,1,10) from all_source where rownum <
10000;
```

9999 rows created.

Now enable severe and performance PL/SQL warnings.

```
SQL@V112> alter session set plsql_warnings='ENABLE:SEVERE, ENABLE:PERFORMANCE';
```

Session altered.

Next, create a function that will return the VALUE for a given key.

```
SQL@V112> CREATE OR REPLACE FUNCTION GET_T1_KEY (P_KEY NUMBER) RETURN VARCHAR2 IS
2   l_value T1.VALUE%TYPE;
3 BEGIN
4     SELECT VALUE INTO l_value FROM T1 WHERE KEY = P_KEY;
5     RETURN l_value;
6     EXCEPTIONS
7     WHEN NO_ROWS_FOUND THEN
```

73

```
8      RETURN 'No value found';
9  END;
10 /
```

```
SP2-0804 Procedure created with compilation warnings.
```

The procedure compiles with warnings. To show the warnings in SQL*Plus, simply do a show error, like so:

```
SQL@V112> show err
LINE/COL ERROR
-------- ------------------------------------------------------------------
1/1      PLW-05018: unit GET_T1_KEY omitted optional AUTHID clause;
         default value DEFINER used

4/45     PLW-07204: conversion away from column type may result in
         sub-optimal query plan
```

■ **Note** If you examine ATTRIBUTE and MESSAGE_NUMBER in the USER_ERRORS table, you'll see that ATTRIBUTE holds either ERROR or WARNING and the error/warning number is in MESSAGE_NUMBER column.

Even though the function is compiled with warnings, you will still be able to execute it.

```
SQL@V112> var txt varchar2(10);
SQL@V112> exec :txt := GET_T1_KEY(1);

PL/SQL procedure successfully completed.

Elapsed: 00:00:00.14
```

Whether or not the KEY column should or should not be changed to NUMBER is not the question for now. In this case, you need to change the function. So change the P_KEY parameter to VARCHAR2 and get rid of warning PLW-05018 by adding AUTHID DEFINER to the function. Here's the new version of the function:

```
SQL@V112> CREATE OR REPLACE FUNCTION GET_T1_KEY (P_KEY VARCHAR2) RETURN VARCHAR2
2  AUTHID DEFINER
3  IS
4    L_value T1.VALUE%TYPE;
5  BEGIN
6    SELECT VALUE INTO l_value FROM T1 WHERE KEY = P_KEY;
7    RETURN l_value;
8    EXCEPTIONS
9    WHEN NO_ROWS_FOUND THEN
10     RETURN 'No value found';
11 END;
12 /

Function created
```

This new version of the function is created without errors or warnings. Notice that it executes faster (twice as fast, in this case) now that the correct data type is being used and the function uses the index to look up the key. Here's an example execution:

```
SQL@V112> exec :txt := GET_T1_KEY('1');

PL/SQL procedure successfully completed.

Elapsed: 00:00:00.07
SQL@V112>
```

The PLW-7204 warning tells you that when selecting from the table T1, Oracle will have to do data type conversion. When using the parameter values, Oracle will have to do a data type conversion because the parameter data type is NUMBER and the data type for the column is VARCHAR2. When Oracle does a data type conversion (such as to_number, to_char, to_date, etc.), it may happen that indexes, if such exist on the queried column, will be ignored. That ignoring of indexes accounts for the time variance between the preceding two examples.

You could do a profiling of the code to examine where the code uses more time in the first example compared to the second, but because the code is simple, you'll just examine what happens by looking at the SELECT statement. Start by setting AUTOTRACE ON for the session and then use the KEY value correctly—as a character—according to the data type of the column in the table.

```
SQL@V112> select value from T1 where key = '1';

VALUE
----------
package ST

Elapsed: 00:00:00.01
SQL@V112>
```

Examining the execution plan shows that the index PK_T1 is used.

```
---------------------------------------------------------------------------------
| Id  | Operation                    | Name  | Rows  | Bytes | Cost (%CPU)| Time     |
---------------------------------------------------------------------------------
|   0 | SELECT STATEMENT             |       |     1 |    14 |     1   (0)| 00:00:01 |
|   1 |  TABLE ACCESS BY INDEX ROWID | T1    |     1 |    14 |     1   (0)| 00:00:01 |
|*  2 |   INDEX UNIQUE SCAN          | PK_T1 |     1 |       |     1   (0)| 00:00:01 |
---------------------------------------------------------------------------------

Predicate Information (identified by operation id):
---------------------------------------------------

   2 - access("KEY"='1')
```

In the next example, the KEY value is not correctly used according to the data type of the column in the table, but it would have been used in the first place, had I ignored the warning.

```
SQL@V112> select value from t1 where key = 1;

VALUE
----------
package ST

Elapsed: 00:00:00.20
```

The execution plan for the statement now shows that the index is not used and that Oracle does a full table scan. Notice the filter in the Predicate Information; Oracle has added a TO_NUMBER to the KEY column, and therefore the index is not being used. Should there be characters in the KEY column, as the definition allows, the function would have failed with an ORA-01722: invalid number. Here is the plan output:

```
-------------------------------------------------------------------------
| Id  | Operation        | Name | Rows  | Bytes | Cost (%CPU)| Time      |
-------------------------------------------------------------------------
|   0 | SELECT STATEMENT |      |     1 |    14 |     2   (0)| 00:00:01  |
|*  1 |  TABLE ACCESS FULL| T1  |     1 |    14 |     2   (0)| 00:00:01  |
-------------------------------------------------------------------------

Predicate Information (identified by operation id):
---------------------------------------------------

   1 - filter(TO_NUMBER("KEY")=1)

SQL@V112>
```

As you see in this example, the correct defined function is approximately 20 times faster than the function with the parameter with the wrong data type. If warnings had not been enabled, you might not have noticed the wrong parameter data type and therefore not corrected the function. As you might notice, you can't at first distinguish whether a warning is an informational, performance, or severe warning. The way to determine the warning's category is to execute the `dbms_warning.get_category` function, like so:

```
SQL@V112> SELECT DBMS_WARNING.GET_CATEGORY(7204) FROM DUAL;
    DBMS_WARNING.GET_CATEGORY(7204)
    ------------------------------------------------------------------------
    PERFORMANCE
```

As you work with warnings, you'll learn that severe warnings are in the range 5000 to 5999, informational are in the range 6000 to 6249, and performance in the range 7000 to 7249. Once you know the ranges, it becomes easy to classify the warnings by their numbers.

Promoting Warnings to Errors

As stated earlier, even though your functions or procedures are compiled with warnings, you are still able to execute them. If you want to ensure that stored procedures with specific warnings do not make it to you production system, you can promote these warnings to become errors.

The following code is what it looks like to compile the GET_T1_KEY function with the parameter as a NUMBER. Notice the warning that is generated.

```
SQL@V112> CREATE OR REPLACE FUNCTION GET_T1_KEY (P_KEY NUMBER) RETURN VARCHAR2
2  AUTHID DEFINER
3  IS
4     L_value T1.VALUE%TYPE;
5  BEGIN
6     SELECT VALUE INTO l_value FROM T1 WHERE KEY = P_KEY;
7     RETURN l_value;
8  EXCEPTIONS
9  WHEN NO_ROWS_FOUND THEN
10    RETURN 'No value found';
11 END;
12 /
```

SP2-0806: Function created with compilation warnings

```
SQL@V112> show err
```

LINE/COL ERROR
-------- --
6/49   PLW-07204: conversion away from column type may result in
         sub-optimal query plan

To ensure that this kind of code is not being deployed—at least not without errors—you can promote this warning to become an error. First, alter the session disabling all warnings (I do it in this example to concentrate on the warning I want to promote). In the same statement, promote the PLW-07204 warning to become an error instead of a warning, like so:

```
SQL@V112> alter session set plsql_warnings='DISABLE:ALL, ERROR:7204';
```

Session altered.

Then recompile the GET_T1_KEY function.

```
SQL@V112> alter function GET_T1_KEY compile;
```

Warning: Function altered with compilation errors.

```
SQL@V112> show err
Errors for FUNCTION GET_T1_KEY:
```

LINE/COL ERROR
-------- --
6/45   PLS-07204: conversion away from column type may result in
         sub-optimal query plan

Now try to execute the function. It will result in errors.

```
SQL@V112> exec :txt := get_t1_key(1);
BEGIN :txt := get_t1_key(1); END;

            *
ERROR at line 1:
ORA-06550: line 1, column 13:
```

```
PLS-00905: object ACME.GET_T1_KEY is invalid
ORA-06550: line 1, column 7:
PL/SQL: Statement ignored
```

Notice that PLW-07204 became PLS-07204. The warning is now an error, and you are unable to execute the function. To be able to execute the function, you will have to get rid of the error by changing the parameter type to VARCHAR2.

If you have an existing application with PL/SQL, and you enable warnings and recompile the PL/SQL code, you will probably get many warnings. Even though it feels good not to get any warnings, it may still, for one reason or another, be impossible to get rid of all of the warnings. Should warnings exist that you can't get rid of, you are free to ignore them.

■ **Caution** It can be tempting to make the elimination of all warnings a hard and fast goal. Non-technical managers especially can fall prey to that temptation, because they often don't understand the subtle difference between a warning and an error. Remember that warning messages come from a machine attempting to interpret your code against someone else's set of best practices. Warnings thus point to code that deserves to be examined more closely. However, sometimes you really do need to perform a certain action, and it would be a *worst practice* indeed to allow a compiler to coerce you into blindly following someone else's best practice.

Another small issue with warnings is that they clutter the USER_ERRORS view. Warnings are logged in the same view as errors. That may be annoying if you are used to checking whether the USER_ERRORS view is empty as a way to see whether you have errors in a give piece of PL/SQL code that you have just compiled. You can't eliminate this minor irritation. You must live with it, but it's a small price to pay for the value returned by the warnings feature.

Ignoring Warnings

You may want to ignore specific warnings for some reason. In the next example, all warnings are enabled. But one of the warnings can't be removed by changing the code, as the warning regards a column name conflicting with a reserved word, and you want to ignore this specific informational warning. To enable all warnings, set `plsql_warnings` to ENABLE:ALL, like so:

```
SQL@V112> alter session set plsql_warnings='ENABLE:ALL';
```

Next, create the following version of the GET_T1_KEY function:

```
SQL@V112>CREATE OR REPLACE FUNCTION GET_T1_KEY (P_KEY NUMBER) RETURN VARCHAR2
2    AUTHID DEFINER
3    IS
4        l_value T1.VALUE%TYPE;
5        l_1 NUMBER :=1;
6        l_2 NUMBER :=2;
7    BEGIN
8        IF l_1 = l_2 THEN
9            SELECT VALUE INTO l_value FROM T1 WHERE KEY = P_KEY;
10           RETURN l_value;
```

```
11      END IF;
12   END;
13   /
```

SP2-0806: Function created with compilation warnings

```
SQL@V112> show err
Errors for FUNCTION GET_T1_KEY:
```

```
0/0      PLW-06010: keyword "VALUE" used as a defined name
1/1      PLW-05005: subprogram GET_T1_KEY returns without value at line 11
9/11     PLW-06002: Unreachable code
9/51     PLW-07204: conversion away from column type may result in
         sub-optimal query plan
```

Let's look at the warnings one at a time.

- PLW-06010: A PL/SQL or SQL word has been used as a defined name. This is legal but not recommended. Reserved words can be examined in the V$RESERVED_WORDS view.

- PLW-05005: Oracle discovers that you never enter the IF statement and therefore will not return a value from the function.

- PLW-06002: Again, Oracle discovers that you never enter the IF statement and therefore will have unreachable code. Unreachable code does no harm as such, but this could indicate inappropriate code. Having too much unreachable code will take up memory when you execute PL/SQL.

- PLW-07204: Well, you know what do with that by now.

So, fix the code and get rid of the warnings. Let's say that for some reason, you're unable to change the column name VALUE, which is the cause for PLW-06010; for example, your application might be old, with too much code to be fixed if you change the column name.

The first thing to do is to prepare the session.

```
SQL@V112> alter session set plsql_warnings='ENABLE:ALL, ERROR:7204, DISABLE:6010';
```

In this case, all warnings are enabled, warning 7204 is still promoted to be an error, and warning 6010 is disabled. The function can now be reapplied and compiled without errors or warnings.

If you want to examine the PL/SQL warnings that a stored procedure has been compiled with, you can issue the following query:

```
SQL@V112> col plsql_warnings for a40
SQL@V112> SELECT NAME, PLSQL_WARNINGS FROM USER_PLSQL_OBJECT_SETTINGS;
```

```
NAME                              PLSQL_WARNINGS
------------------------------    ----------------------------------------
GET_T1_KEY                        ENABLE:ALL,DISABLE: 6010,ERROR: 7204
```

These results show the PLSQL_WARNINGS parameter value that was in effect when GET_T1_KEY was compiled.

Compilation and Warnings

Whenever you create or recompile stored procedures, they inherit the settings from the current session. So should you by accident compile a stored procedure in a session where warnings have not been set up, the stored procedure will just compile and settings will be lost. If your database is configured with system wide warnings (ALTER SYSTEM SET PLSQL_WARNINGS='ENABLE:ALL, ERROR:7204') and some of them have been promoted to be an error, the result may be more troublesome, as the recompiled procedure will fail. To recompile a procedure with its current settings, execute the following:

```
SQL@V112> ALTER FUNCTION GET_T1_KEY COMPILE REUSE SETTINGS;

Function Compiled.
```

Instead of having to execute an ALTER SESSION each time you want to compile a stored procedure with specific PL/SQL warnings, you can specify the warning setting at compile time.

```
SQL@V112> ALTER FUNCTION GET_T1_KEY COMPILE PLSQL_WARNINGS='ENABLE:ALL,
DISABLE:6010,ERROR: 7204';

Function Compiled.
```

If you have common warning settings for all stored procedures, you could add a login trigger to set PLSQL_WARNINGS at log in time. It's not uncommon that developers share the same database user to develop an application. In this case, the trigger could be quite simple and limited to that user only.

The trigger should, in this case, fire after login to the ACME schema. What the trigger does is an ALTER SESSION and thereby set the PLSQL_WARNINGS parameter.

Create the trigger connected as SYS.

```
SQL@V112> CREATE OR REPLACE TRIGGER dev_logon_trigger
  2   AFTER LOGON ON ACME.SCHEMA
  3   BEGIN
  4     EXECUTE IMMEDIATE q'"ALTER SESSION SET
PLSQL_WARNINGS='ENABLE:SEVERE,ENABLE:PERFORMANCE,ERROR:7204'"';
  5   END;
  6   /

Trigger created.
```

Then connect as the Acme user.

```
SQL@V112> conn ACME/acme
Connected.
```

Check that the parameter has been set.

```
SQL@V112> SELECT DBMS_WARNING.GET_WARNING_SETTING_STRING FROM DUAL;

GET_WARNING_SETTING_STRING
-----------------------------------------------------------------------
DISABLE:INFORMATIONAL,ENABLE:PERFORMANCE,ENABLE:SEVERE,ERROR:  7204
```

If your application has many stored procedures and they have different settings, it may be a good idea to build a framework that will help you remember their individual settings and can be used for recompilation (see the small framework example in the upcoming section "Conditional Compilation").

If you want to compile all stored procedures in a schema with the DBMS_UTILITY.COMPILE_SCHEMA procedure, you should be aware that the parameter reuse_settings is by default set to FALSE. The following is the description of the DBMS_UTILITY.COMPILE_SCHEMA procedure:

```
PROCEDURE COMPILE_SCHEMA
Argument Name                 Type                     In/Out Default?
----------------------------- ------------------------ ------ --------
SCHEMA                        VARCHAR2                 IN
COMPILE_ALL                   BOOLEAN                  IN     DEFAULT
REUSE_SETTINGS                BOOLEAN                  IN     DEFAULT
```

If you don't apply the reuse_settings parameter and set it to TRUE, all compiled packages will lose any warning settings. Therefore, when executing DBMS_UTILITY.COMPILE_SCHEMA, remember to set reuse_settings to TRUE, like so:

```
SQL@V112> exec DBMS_UTILITY.COMPILE_SCHEMA (schema=>'ACME', reuse_settings=>true);

PL/SQL procedure successfully completed.
```

■ **Caution**   You should use caution if setting `plsql_warnings` on the SYSTEM level. Even though you can't compile SYS with DBMS_UTILITY.COMPILE_SCHEMA, you can still compile individual packages. Setting `plsql_warnings` at SYSTEM level, and then compiling just a few packages may result in hundreds of warnings or, should you have promoted some warnings to errors, in errors being thrown.

As SYS or SYSTEM you can run the utility utlrp (@?/rdbms/admin/utlrp), that will compile all invalid stored procedures. Utlrp calls UTL_RECOMP.RECOMP_PARALLEL to compile stored procedures in parallel. When doing this, warnings promoted to errors or warnings that are ignored get striped off, as you shall see in the following example. This is a bug.

First, set session `plsql_warnings`

```
SQL@V112> alter session set plsql_warnings='Enable:all, ERROR:7204, DISABLE:6010';

Session altered.
```

and compile a selected function.

```
SQL@V112> alter function GET_T1_KEY compile;

Warning: Function altered with compilation errors.
```

Next, take a look on the function settings.

```
SQL@V112> SELECT NAME, PLSQL_WARNINGS FROM USER_PLSQL_OBJECT_SETTINGS WHERE NAME =↵
'GET_T1_KEY';

NAME                        PLSQL_WARNINGS
--------------------------- ----------------------------------------------------------------
------------------------------------
GET_T1_KEY                  ENABLE:ALL,DISABLE:  6010,ERROR:  7204
```

Now, connect as SYS

```
SQL@V112> conn / as sysdba
Connected.
```

and execute the recompilation, either by calling `utlrp.sql` or as here by executing UTL_RECOMP.RECOMP_PARALLEL directly.

```
SQL@V112> exec utl_recomp.recomp_parallel(1,'ACME');

PL/SQL procedure successfully completed.
```

Now reconnect

```
SQL@V112> conn ACME/ACME
Connected.
```

and examine the object settings.

```
SQL@V112> SELECT NAME, PLSQL_WARNINGS FROM USER_PLSQL_OBJECT_SETTINGS
WHERE NAME = 'GET_T1_KEY';

NAME                        PLSQL_WARNINGS
--------------------------- ----------------------------------------------------------------
------------------------------------
GET_T1_KEY                  ENABLE:ALL

ACME@V112>
```

Notice that specific warning settings have been removed; this must be a bug. It's not a disaster, as everything still works, but it's irritating because you now don't know if special warnings were set up.

If you export and import schemas using exp and imp, any stored code will be imported with the exported settings.

Final Words on Warnings

Other types of warnings you might encounter are warnings for not using the NOCOPY compiler directive when you will benefit from that. In Oracle 11g, there is a new, very useful warning for situations in which the exception WHEN OTHERS does not result in either RAISE or RAISE_APPLICATION_ERROR. I have personally spent hours wondering why I did not get an error in certain situations, just to experience that somebody did a WHEN OTHERS THEN NULL.

Conditional Compilation

Conditional compilation is not related to PL/SQL warnings, but it was implemented at the same time as PL/SQL warnings. Conditional compilation is done by preprocessing the source code, as you might know from other coding languages. In short, it gives you the ability to turn code on or off at compilation time, without having to edit the code. This could be turning on or off debug options or enabling code that has to do with this or that version of Oracle or perhaps two different editions of your application, such as a Standard Edition and Enterprise Edition.

■ **Note** Conditional compilation has been back-ported to Oracle 10.1.0.4 and 9.2.0.6 and can be enabled by setting the `parameter _conditional_compilation`.

Basics

Conditional compilation consists of a small number of directives. The directives starts with a $ (Dollar) sign. You use the directives to control the flow in the program or raise errors.

The system defined directives are: $IF, $THEN, $ELSIF, $ELSE and $END. You can raise your own compilation errors with the directive $ERROR ... $END. You can inquire on static Boolean expressions or static constants. Besides creating your own inquire variables, Oracle has a few you can inquire, which you will see later.

The easiest way to get started with conditional compilation is to start with an example. This example will show you how to enable logging of timing information for a stored procedure, which measures how long it takes to run the procedure and when the procedure was running. The following is the example code (the lines are numbered for later reference):

```
1 CREATE OR REPLACE PROCEDURE LEVEL2 AS
2 $IF $$TIMING_ON $THEN
3 $ELSIF NOT $$TIMING_ON $THEN
4 $ELSE
5     $ERROR ' The PLSQL_CCFLAG TIMING_ON, Must be set to either FALSE or TRUE before
compileing procedure ' || $$PLSQL_UNIT||'.'
6     $END
7 $END
8 $IF $$TIMING_ON $THEN
9     L_start_time TIMESTAMP;
10 $END
11 BEGIN
12 DBMS_APPLICATION_INFO.SET_MODULE($$PLSQL_UNIT, 'RUN');
13 $IF $$TIMING_ON $THEN
14     L_START_TIME:=CURRENT_TIMESTAMP;
15 $END
16 -- ------------------------------------------------
17 -- Application logic is left out
18 -- ------------------------------------------------
19 $IF $$TIMING_ON $THEN
20     LOGIT (P_PG=>$$PLSQL_UNIT, P_START_TIME=>l_start_time, P_STOP_TIME=>CURRENT_TIMESTAMP);
```

```
21 $END
22 DBMS_APPLICATION_INFO.SET_MODULE(NULL,NULL);
23 END LEVEL2;
24 /
```

The following is an explanation of the listing:

- Line 2-7: If the inquiry variable $$TIMING_ON is not set at compile time (in other words, it's neither FALSE nor TRUE), then an error will be thrown, telling the name of the stored procedure and line where the error occurred. Notice that you are allowed to have empty statements—an $IF … $THEN without any action.

- Line 8: If the inquiry variable $$TIMING_ON equals to TRUE, then you declare the variable l_start_time. Notice that the $END has no $IF as in PL/SQL END IF; and no semicolon.

- Line 12: Here you call DBMS_APPLICATION_INFO.SET_MODULE procedure, which will set the MODULE column in the V$SESSION view; you use the Oracle inquiry variable $$PLSQL_UNIT to hold the name of the stored procedure or, in case it is referenced in a PACKAGE, the name of the package. In prior Oracle versions, you would have had to create a function that executed the OWA_UTIL.WHO_CALLED_ME procedure that returns the name of the caller, then call that function to get the name. Calling the DBMS_APPLICATION_INFO.SET_MODULE is very helpful if you need to query V$SESSION to locate you session or if you are using Extended Trace in order to start tracing when the procedure starts.

■ **Note** If you are using SQL*Developer to develop your stored procedures, you can modify the template holding the CREATE PROCEDURE/FUNCTION template to include call to DBMS_APPLICATION_INFO.SET_MODULE($$PLSQL _UNIT, '<action>'), to ensure that it is always included. This is done from the menu Tools ➤ Preferences ➤ Database:SQL Code Editor Templates.

- Line 13: If the inquiry variable $$TIMING_ON equals TRUE, then register the start timestamp in the variable l_start_time.

- Line 16-18: This would be the PL/SQL code.

- Line 19: If the inquiry variable $$TIMING_ON equals TRUE, then call the LOGIT procedure in line 20. The LOGIT procedure is the logging procedure that will log timing information. The procedure is not described here as it isn't important.

- Line 22: Clear the DBMS_APPLICATION_INFO call.

Before the procedure is added to the database, the compiler flag TIMING_ON needs to be set. You can set that flag either at the system, session, or program level. In this example, it's set at the session level. Before you set the flag, try to add the code to the database to provoke the $ERROR error (assume that the code is saved in a file called level2.sql).

```
SQL@V112> @level2
```

Warning: Procedure created with compilation errors.

Do a show error to reveal the error, like so:

```
SQL@V102> show error
```

Errors for PROCEDURE LEVEL2:

```
LINE/COL ERROR
-------- ------------------------------------------------------------
5/4      PLS-00179: $ERROR:  The PLSQL_CCFLAG TIMING_ON, Must be set to
         either FALSE or TRUE before compileing procedure LEVEL2.
```

Now set the flag, like so:

```
SQL@V112> ALTER SESSION SET plsql_ccflags='TIMING_ON:TRUE';
```

The data type of the plsql_ccflags is either a Boolean static expression, PLS_INTEGER static expression, or VARCHAR2 static expression, depending on what you assign to it. Notice that setting plsql_ccflags will not enforce recompilation of any code; an ALTER PROCEDURE … COMPILE would have to be issued.

```
SQL@V102> ALTER PROCEDURE LEVEL2 COMPILE;
```

Procedure altered.

■ **Note**   Remember that every stored procedure that is compiled after the session plsql_ccflags has been set will inherit the plsql_ccflags setting.

To examine what plsql_ccflags was set to during a stored procedure compilation, execute the following query:

```
SQL@V102> col plsql_ccflags for a80 wrap
SQL@V102> select NAME, PLSQL_CCFLAGS FROM USER_PLSQL_OBJECT_SETTINGS;
```

```
NAME                          PLSQL_CCFLAGS
----------------------------- -------------------------------------------
LEVEL1
LEVEL2                        TIMING_ON:TRUE
LOGIT
...
```

As shown in the example below, if you have more than one plsql_ccflag set at a time, they must be separated by commas. The plsql_ccflag value is case insensitive.

```
SQL@V112> ALTER SESSION SET plsql_ccflags='TIMING_ON:TRUE,Standard:True';
```

What Part of the Code is Running?

In the simple procedure just shown in the "Basics" section, it's easy to get the overview of what code is actually running whether the TIMING_ON flag is set to TRUE or FALSE. The USER_SOURCE view reveals all the code in the stored procedure. The conditional compilation code you create may be very complex, so to see what code is actually compiled or not, you should call the DBMS_PREPROCESSOR.PRINT_POST_PROCESSED_SOURCE procedure. This procedure generates the code that is actually compiled (remember to set serveroutput on).

```
SQL@V112> CALL DBMS_PREPROCESSOR.PRINT_POST_PROCESSED_SOURCE('PROCEDURE', 'ACME','LEVEL2');
PROCEDURE LEVEL2 AS
L_start_time TIMESTAMP;
BEGIN
DBMS_APPLICATION_INFO.SET_MODULE( 'LEVEL2'            , 'RUN');
L_start_time:=CURRENT_TIMESTAMP;
-- -------------------------------------------------
-- Application logic is left out
-- -------------------------------------------------
LOGIT (P_PG=> 'LEVEL2'         , P_START_TIME=>l_start_time, P_STOP_TIME=>CURRENT_TIMESTAMP);
DBMS_APPLICATION_INFO.SET_MODULE(NULL,NULL);
END LEVEL2;

Call completed.
```

The code presented is without any of the formatting you may have applied to the code. Database objects in code that are not present in the preprocessed code will not be visible in the USER_DEPENDENCIES view. Wrapped code remains wrapped and you can't unwrap code using this procedure. (You can read more about dependencies in Chapter 15.)

If you want to process the pre-processed code yourself, you can call the DBMS_PREPROCESSOR.GET_POST_PROCESSED_SOURCE function, which will return a table of VARCHAR2 containing the code. The reason that formatting is lost it is because the package uses DBMS_OUTPUT.PUT_LINE. The PUT_LINE procedure removes leading spaces. If you create a procedure like the one below, adding a line number (or any character) to the left of the code will ensure that formatting is not lost. The following procedure—PRINT_SOURCE—will print the preprocessed code with formatting and line numbers, based on the parameters given:

```
SQL@V112> CREATE OR REPLACE PROCEDURE PRINT_SOURCE (P_OBJECT_TYPE VARCHAR2, P_SCHEMA_NAME↵
    VARCHAR2, P_OBJECT_NAME VARCHAR2)  IS
2   l_source_lines DBMS_PREPROCESSOR.source_lines_t;
3  BEGIN
4    l_source_lines := DBMS_PREPROCESSOR.GET_POST_PROCESSED_SOURCE(P_OBJECT_TYPE,
P_SCHEMA_NAME, P_OBJECT_NAME);
5    FOR I IN l_source_lines.FIRST .. l_source_lines.LAST LOOP
6       IF TRIM(SUBSTR(l_source_lines (i),1, length(l_source_lines (i))-1)) IS NOT NULL
THEN
7          DBMS_OUTPUT.PUT_LINE(RPAD(I,4, ' ')||REPLACE(l_source_lines(i), CHR(10),''));
8       END IF;
9    END LOOP;
10  END;
11  /
```

Executing the procedure with the given parameters results in the following output:

```
SQL@V112> set serveroutput on
SQL@V112> exec PRINT_SOURCE ('PROCEDURE','ACME','LEVEL2');


1    PROCEDURE LEVEL2 AS
8       l_start_time TIMESTAMP;
10   BEGIN
11   DBMS_APPLICATION_INFO.SET_MODULE( 'LEVEL2'              , 'RUN');
13      l_start_time:=CURRENT_TIMESTAMP;
15   -- ------------------------------------------------
16   -- Application logic is left out
17   -- ------------------------------------------------
19      LOGIT (P_PG=> 'LEVEL2'        , P_START_TIME=> l_start_time,↵
     P_STOP_TIME=>CURRENT_TIMESTAMP);
21   DBMS_APPLICATION_INFO.SET_MODULE(NULL,NULL);
22   END LEVEL2;
```

Benefits of Preprocessing Code

One of the benefits you gain by excluding code with preprocessed code is that the amount of memory used by the executing code may be reduced, thus less memory is used in the shared pool. Suppose, for example, that the procedure LEVEL2 was coded as follows:

```
SQL@V112> CREATE OR REPLACE PROCEDURE LEVEL2 (TIMING_ON BOOLEAN := FALSE) AS
2   l_start_time TIMESTAMP;
3   BEGIN
4   DBMS_APPLICATION_INFO.SET_MODULE('LEVEL2' ,NULL);
5      IF TIMING_ON THEN
6         l_start_time:=CURRENT_TIMESTAMP;
7      END IF;
8      -- ------------------------------------------------
9   -- Application logic is left out
10  -- ------------------------------------------------
11  IF TIMING_ON THEN
12     LOGIT (P_PG=>'LEVEL2', P_START_TIME=>l_start_time,
    P_STOP_TIME=>CURRENT_TIMESTAMP);
13  END IF;
14  DBMS_APPLICATION_INFO.SET_MODULE(NULL,NULL);
15  END LEVEL2;
16  /
```

This example shows how you might code a normal stored procedure, in which you would enable some timing measurements. The view USER_OBJECT_SIZE will show an estimate of how much memory in bytes a given program will require. However, you can't see how much memory the program requires at runtime, as runtime memory usage is dependent on how you write the code, whether you do bulk collects, and other such things. The following is the memory usage estimation for LEVEL2:

```
SQL@V112> SELECT * FROM USER_OBJECT_SIZE WHERE NAME = 'LEVEL2';

NAME           TYPE           SOURCE_SIZE PARSED_SIZE  CODE_SIZE ERROR_SIZE
-------------- -------------- ----------- ----------- ---------- ----------
LEVEL2         PROCEDURE              521         996        510          0
```

The column SOURCE_SIZE shows the size of the source code for the given procedure. Source code must fit in memory during compilation. PARSED_SIZE is how much memory the given program requires when other programs that are compiled reference it. CODE_SIZE is the amount of memory that the program requires in order to execute— as a start. And finally, the column ERROR_SIZE is the number of bytes in memory for error messages during compilation. In this case, ERROR_SIZE is 0 because no errors occurred during compilation.

Suppose you create the same procedure, but let a PL/SQL compiler flag control the timing measurement call, so that the code looks like this:

```
SQL@V112> CREATE OR REPLACE PROCEDURE LEVEL2 AS
2   $IF $$TIMING_ON $THEN
3     l_start_time TIMESTAMP;
4   $END
5   BEGIN
6   DBMS_APPLICATION_INFO.SET_MODULE($$PLSQL_UNIT ,NULL);
7     $IF $$TIMING_ON $THEN
8       l_start_time:=CURRENT_TIMESTAMP;
9     $END
10    -- ------------------------------------------------
11    -- Application logic is left out
12    -- ------------------------------------------------
13    $IF $$TIMING_ON $THEN
14      LOGIT (P_PG=>$$PLSQL_UNIT, P_START_TIME=>l_start_time,
P_STOP_TIME=>CURRENT_TIMESTAMP);
15    $END
16  DBMS_APPLICATION_INFO.SET_MODULE(NULL,NULL);
17  END LEVEL2;
18  /
Procedure created.
```

Setting the PL/SQL flag TIMING_ON to FALSE results in the following code sizes:

```
SQL@V112> SELECT * FROM USER_OBJECT_SIZE WHERE NAME = 'LEVEL2';

NAME           TYPE           SOURCE_SIZE PARSED_SIZE  CODE_SIZE ERROR_SIZE
-------------- -------------- ----------- ----------- ---------- ----------
LEVEL2         PROCEDURE              530         857        364          0
```

The SOURCE_SIZE is almost the same size as in the first example, even though $IF constructions have been added to control definition and reference of the variable l_start_time. The first example also has the parameter parsing in the code, so there's not much difference there either. But the PARSED_SIZE and CODE_SIZE values have both been reduced.

Now let's look at the case when timing is enabled. Compiling the procedure LEVEL2 with the compiler flag TIMING_ON set to TRUE gives the following result:

```
SQL@V112> SELECT * FROM USER_OBJECT_SIZE WHERE NAME = 'LEVEL2';

NAME          TYPE          SOURCE_SIZE PARSED_SIZE  CODE_SIZE ERROR_SIZE
------------- ------------- ----------- ----------- ---------- ----------
LEVEL2        PROCEDURE             530         917        478          0
```

Compared to the code that was compiled with TIMING_ON set to FALSE, the SOURCE_SIZE does not differ, but the PARSED_SIZE and CODE_SIZE values have been increased slightly. This is because of the call to the procedure LOGIT.

Now take a look now at the size of the original LEVEL2 procedure, this one with TIMING_ON set to TRUE.

```
SQL@V102> select * from USER_OBJECT_SIZE WHERE NAME = 'LEVEL2';

NAME          TYPE          SOURCE_SIZE PARSED_SIZE  CODE_SIZE ERROR_SIZE
------------- ------------- ----------- ----------- ---------- ----------
LEVEL2        PROCEDURE             730         917        497          0
```

The SOURCE_SIZE is larger than the LEVEL2 procedure without conditional compilation, but the PARSED_SIZE and CODE_SIZE are the same, or nearly so, as the limited LEVEL2 with conditional compilation. This is because the conditional compilation code is stripped during the compilation. Thus, you can see that using conditional compilation results in a bigger footprint in source and during compilation (and also during automatic recompilation triggered by dependencies). If Oracle executes an automatic recompilation, the REUSE SETTINGS compile option is used.

So, without conditional compilation, you get this:

```
SQL@V102> exec level2

Elapsed: 00:00:20.60
```

And with conditional compilation (TIMING_ON set to TRUE), you get this:

```
SQL@V102> exec level2

Elapsed: 00:00:20.49
```

Here the difference is only a matter of fragments of seconds. Such a small period of time is an inconsequential price to pay in return for the benefits of conditional compilation.

Invalidations

Objects dependent on other objects may be invalidated if the objects they dependent on change or get invalidated for some reason. Let's expand this idea a bit by creating a LEVEL1 procedure that calls the LEVEL2 procedure. The first example is running in Oracle 10.2.

```
SQL@V102> CREATE OR REPLACE PROCEDURE LEVEL1 AS
2  BEGIN
3    LEVEL2;
4  END;
5  /
Procedure created.
```

When you have to compile a procedure at a lower level, Oracle will invalidate the procedure at the higher level if dependencies exists and thereby force an automatic recompilation the next time the higher level procedure is called—if it's not compiled manually beforehand, that is.

After creating the LEVEL1 procedure, recompile the LEVEL2 procedure.

```
SQL@V102> ALTER PROCEDURE LEVEL2 COMPILE REUSE SETTINGS;

Procedure altered.
```

Then examine the STATUS of the procedures.

```
SQL@V102> SELECT OBJECT_NAME, STATUS FROM USER_OBJECTS WHERE OBJECT_NAME IN↵
  ('LEVEL1','LEVEL2');

OBJECT_NAME                 STATUS
--------------------------- -------
LEVEL1                      INVALID
LEVEL2                      VALID
```

Executing the LEVEL1 procedure will enforce a recompilation and validate the procedure.

```
SQL@V102> exec LEVEL1

PL/SQL procedure successfully completed.

SQL@V102> SELECT OBJECT_NAME, STATUS FROM USER_OBJECTS WHERE OBJECT_NAME IN↵
  ('LEVEL1','LEVEL2');

OBJECT_NAME                 STATUS
--------------------------- -------
LEVEL1                      VALID
LEVEL2                      VALID
```

The LEVEL1 procedure has been dynamically recompiled and is now valid again. This has nothing to do with conditional compilation—that's just how it works.

■ **Caution**   Having hundreds of stored procedures calling one another in a system and then making a recompilation either on purpose or indirectly of a procedure may be a disaster. Let me emphasize this with a true story. In a company with hundreds of concurrent users, a manual update of a table had gone wrong—a column was set to a wrong value. So the Database Administrator created a copy of the table with a SELECT AS OF TIMESTAMP. So far, everything was fine. Then he renamed the original table and quickly renamed the copy of the table to the original name. Well, Oracle will notice such a swapping of names, should there be any dependencies. In this case, this table was referenced by a low level procedure, which went invalid, causing all procedures that relied on this procedure to go invalid as well. This made almost all user sessions line up for recompilation of the code. The database had to be restarted, as nobody could work on the system. After the restart, the system worked as usual.

In Oracle 11g, Oracle has loosened the rules for invalidation of dependent objects. If you don't change the footprint of the parameter of a procedure, Oracle will not force an invalidation of dependent objects, whether it encounters procedures in packages or stand-alone procedures. If you rerun the preceding example involving LEVEL1 and LEVEL2 in Oracle 11g rather than Oracle 10g, the result will look like the following:

```
SQL@V112> SELECT OBJECT_NAME, STATUS FROM USER_OBJECTS WHERE OBJECT_NAME IN↵
  ('LEVEL1','LEVEL2');

OBJECT_NAME                  STATUS
---------------------------- -------
LEVEL1                       VALID
LEVEL2                       VALID

SQL@V112> ALTER PROCEDURE LEVEL2 COMPILE REUSE SETTINGS;

Procedure altered.

SQL@V112> SELECT OBJECT_NAME, STATUS FROM USER_OBJECTS WHERE OBJECT_NAME IN↵
  ('LEVEL1','LEVEL2');

OBJECT_NAME                  STATUS
---------------------------- -------
LEVEL1                       VALID
LEVEL2                       VALID

SQL@V112>
```

Notice that both procedures end up as valid. Because you are in Oracle 11g and because your procedure footprints have not changed, Oracle does not force a recompile.

Controlling Compilation

Having different plsql_ccflags for each procedure—and thus a large number of compiler flags—may be confusing. Even though you may execute an ALTER PROCEDURE <procedure name> COMPILE REUSE SETTINGS, at some point you may accidently compile a procedure without having set the appropriate compiler flags. And if you don't check in your conditional compilation code whether a ccflag is set, your code may compile with the "wrong" setting. A way to avoid this could be to build a small framework that controls the recompilation, as in the following example:

```
SQL@V112> CREATE TABLE CC_FLAGS (
2  OWNER         VARCHAR2(30),
3  OBJECT_TYPE   VARCHAR2(30),
4  OBJECT_NAME   VARCHAR2(30),
5  CCFLAGS       VARCHAR2(4000));

  Table Created.
```

Add the rows with information for each procedure.

```
SQL@V112> INSERT INTO CC_FLAGS (OWNER, OBJECT_TYPE, OBJECT_NAME, CCFLAGS) VALUES('ACME' ,↲
'PROCEDURE', 'LEVEL2', 'TIMING_ON:FALSE');
```

1 Row created.

```
SQL@V112> INSERT INTO CC_FLAGS (OWNER, OBJECT_TYPE, OBJECT_NAME, CCFLAGS) VALUES('ACME' ,↲
'PROCEDURE', 'LEVEL1', '');
```

1 Row created.

```
SQL@V112> COMMIT;
```

Commit complete.

```
SQL@V112> BEGIN
2  FOR I IN (SELECT * FROM CC_FLAGS) LOOP
3    EXECUTE IMMEDIATE 'ALTER ' ||I.OBJECT_TYPE||' '||I.OWNER||'.'||I.OBJECT_NAME||' COMPILE
PLSQL_CCFLAGS='''||I.CCFLAGS||'''';
4 END LOOP;
5 END;
6 /
```

PL/SQL procedure successfully completed.

So after running this anonymous PL/SQL block, the procedures are compiled with their settings. This could (or should) perhaps be a stored procedure, perhaps even with parameters to control whether one or all should be compiled; if so, don't put that procedure in the CC_FLAGS table or you will end up in a deadlock situation when the running procedure tries to compile itself.

Compiling a stored procedure with special plsql_ccflags by hand would look like the following example:

```
SQL@V112> ALTER PROCEDURE SPECIAL1 COMPILE PLSQL_CCFLAGS='SPECIAL_ONE:42';
```

Procedure altered.

In your development environment, you could use this framework and from it generate deployment scripts. If some stored procedure after deployment needs to be compiled with special flags, say you need to debug a procedure, it can be done as shown.

When creating deployment scripts, I ensure that I set the PLSQL_CCFLAGS, PLSQL_WARNINGS before I add stored procedures; should there be different flags and warnings, I set them before each stored procedure, as shown in the following code:

```
…
ALTER SESSION SET PLSQL_CCFLAGS='TIMING_ON:FLASE';
ALTER SESSION SET PLSQL_WARNINGS='ENABLE:SEVERE,ENABLE_PERFORMANCE,ERROR:7204';
@@ GET_T1_KEY
ALTER SESSION SET PLSQL_WARNINGS='ENABLE:SEVERE,ENABLE:PERFORMANCE';
@@ SET_T1_KEY
…
```

Inquiry Variables

So far, I've been talking about the plsql_ccflags parameter and conditional compilations. You can use conditional compilations without having to set the plsql_ccflags parameter. You do that by querying your own package constants or those defined by Oracle. Let's work through an example.

First, you create a PACKAGE specification holding a constant named TIMING_ON set to the value FALSE.

```
SQL@V112> CREATE OR REPLACE PACKAGE TIMING AS
2      TIMING_ON CONSTANT BOOLEAN := FALSE;
3  END;
4  /
```

Then you recreate the stored procedure referencing the PACKAGE constant.

```
TIMING.TIMING_ON
```

```
SQL@V112> CREATE OR REPLACE PROCEDURE LEVEL2 AS
2  $IF TIMING.TIMING_ON $THEN
3     L_START_TIME TIMESTAMP;
4  $END
5  BEGIN
6  DBMS_APPLICATION_INFO.SET_MODULE($$PLSQL_UNIT ,NULL);
7  $IF TIMING.TIMING_ON $THEN
8     L_START_TIME:=CURRENT_TIMESTAMP;
9  $END
10 -- -----------------------------------------------
11 -- Application logic is left out
12 -- -----------------------------------------------
13 $IF TIMING.TIMING_ON $THEN
14    LOGIT (P_PG=>$$PLSQL_UNIT, P_START_TIME=>L_START_TIME, P_STOP_TIME=>CURRENT_TIMESTAMP);
15 $END
16 DBMS_APPLICATION_INFO.SET_MODULE(NULL,NULL);
17 END LEVEL2;
18 /
```

```
Procedure created.
```

Calling the DBMS_PREPROCESSOR.PRINT_POST_PROCESSED_SOURCE shows you that the code has been preprocessed with TIMING_ON = FALSE, as expected.

```
SQL@V112> CALL DBMS_PREPROCESSOR.PRINT_POST_PROCESSED_SOURCE('PROCEDURE', 'SCOTT','LEVEL2');
PROCEDURE LEVEL2 AS
BEGIN
DBMS_APPLICATION_INFO.SET_MODULE( 'LEVEL2'    ,NULL);
-- -----------------------------------------------
-- Application logic is left out
-- -----------------------------------------------
DBMS_APPLICATION_INFO.SET_MODULE(NULL,NULL);
END LEVEL2;

Call completed.
```

Changing the PACKAGE constant to TRUE will set all stored procedures that reference this package to an invalid state. Hence, they all need to be recompiled.

```
SQL@V112> CREATE OR REPLACE PACKAGE TIMING AS
2      TIMING_ON CONSTANT BOOLEAN := TRUE;
3  END;
4  /

SQL@V112> SELECT OBJECT_NAME, STATUS FROM USER_OBJECTS WHERE OBJECT_NAME IN↵
 ('TIMING','LEVEL1','LEVEL2');

OBJECT_NAME                      STATUS
------------------------------   -------
TIMING                           VALID
LEVEL1                           INVALID
LEVEL2                           INVALID
```

After the recompilation of the code, it will match the TIMING_ON value. In this case, you have enabled timing measurements in all dependent stored procedures. Bear in mind the warning that I gave previously regarding recompiling all your code in a production environment.

Final Words on Conditional Compilation

Oracle offers a number of enquiry variables. Besides the $$PLSQL_UNIT enquiry variable, the $$PLSQL_LINE is becoming one of my favorites because it can be used for debugging.

- $$PLSQL_CCFLAGS hold the current PLSQL_CCFLAGS.

- $$PLSQL_WARNINGS holds the current plsql_warnings setting.

- $$PLSQL_OPTIMIZE_LEVEL holds the PLSQL_OPTIMIZE_LEVEL parameter value.

- $$PLSQL_LINE holds the line number where the $$PLSQL_LINE variable is located.

- $$PLSCOPE_SETTING holds the current value of the session PLSCOPE_SETTINGS parameter.

- $$PLSQL_CODE_TYPE holds the current value of the parameter plsql_code_type. Either NATIVE or INTERPRETED.

- $$NLS_LENGTH_SEMANTICS holds the NLS lengths semantics is BYTE or CHAR.

As a "normal" user , you're not able to execute the command show parameter <parameter> to show the value of the parameters such as plsql_ccflags or plsql_warnings. Therefore, these enquiry variables may come in handy. Create a script with an anonymous PL/SQL block and execute the script to show the value of inquiry variables in the current session, like so:

```
set serveroutput on
BEGIN
  dbms_output.put_line('PLSQL Unit     : ' ||$$PLSQL_UNIT);
  dbms_output.put_line('PLSQL CCFLAGS  : ' ||$$PLSQL_CCFLAGS);
  dbms_output.put_line('PLSQL Warnings : ' ||$$PLSQL_Warnings);
  dbms_output.put_line('Optimize Level : ' ||$$PLSQL_OPTIMIZE_LEVEL);
  dbms_output.put_line('Line: ' ||$$PLSQL_LINE);
```

```
  dbms_output.put_line('PLSCOPE setting: ' ||$$PLSCOPE_SETTING);
  dbms_output.put_line('PLSQL code type: ' ||$$PLSQL_CODE_TYPE);
  dbms_output.put_line('NLS length semantics: ' ||$$NLS_LENGTH_SEMANTICS);
 END;
/
```

Execute the script to see the value of the inquiry variables.

```
SQL@V112> @plsql_inqvar.sql
PLSQL Unit    :
PLSQL CCFLAGS : TIMING_ON:TRUE
PLSQL Warnings : DISABLE:INFORMATIONAL,ENABLE:PERFORMANCE,ENABLE:SEVERE,ERROR:  7204
Optimize Level: 2
Line          : 6
PLSCOPE setting:
PLSQL code type: INTERPRETED
NLS length semantics: BYTE

PL/SQL procedure successfully completed.
```

With this small script you are able to see the current value of the inquiry variables. The $$PLSQL_UNIT inquiry variable is empty, as its value is being queried from an anonymous block.

■ **Note** The PL/SQL inquiry variables are evaluated and translated at compilation time, so having this in a stored procedure would require a recompilation of the procedure if any of the flags have changed, in order to show the correct value.

You could issue the following command to show the current value of $$PLSQL_CCFLAGS:

```
SQL@V112> exec dbms_output.put_line($$PLSQL_CCFLAGS);
```

```
TIMING_ON:TRUE
```

One common use of conditional compilation is to enable specific code, depending on the Oracle version; in other words, to define variables as either NUMBER or BINARY_FLOAT, like so:

```
...
$IF DBMS_DB_VERSION.VERSION >=11 $THEN
   VAR BINARY_FLOAT;
$ELSE
  VAR NUMBER;
$END;
...
```

In the Package specification of DBMS_DB_VERSION, there are a number of Boolean "version" constants that can be used to include or exclude code.

```
...
$IF DBMS_DB_VERSION.VER_LE_11_2 $THEN
  ...
$ELSE
  ...
$END
...
```

Putting it a bit to the extreme you can make parameters to stored procedures conditional as shown in the example here.

```
SQL@V112> CREATE PROCEDURE EXTREME (P_PARAM VARCHAR2 $IF $$INQ_FLAG $THEN , P_PARAM2 VARCHAR2
$END) IS
  2    BEGIN
  3      NULL;
  4    END;
  5  /
```

So depending on the $INQ_FLAG you would have either one or two parameters - it can be done, but not advisable.

Summary

In this chapter, you learned what you may gain from enabling warnings. You looked into how to enable warnings at the session, system, or procedure level. You have explored how to either promote warnings to become errors or how to ignore them by disabling them. You saw that PL/SQL warnings would certainly help you to make your code perform better and make it more robust. It will, though, give you an extra administrative task, especially if you have too many exceptions for which warnings should be enabled, disabled, or promoted to be errors.

▓ **Note** You will not necessarily have to enable PL/SQL warnings on your production system if your code is checked in the development environment.

In looking at conditional compilation, you saw that using conditional compilation can limit the size of memory used by PL/SQL by only enabling logging or debugging information when required. You also saw that by using conditional compilation and setting a flag and performing a recompile, you were able to enable or disable code without having to edit the code. Conditional compilation is widely used in languages such as C++. Now you can have it as part of your PL/SQL toolbox, too.

CHAPTER 5

PL/SQL Unit Testing

by Sue Harper

Any developer accessing the Oracle Database uses SQL whether running SQL reports and queries developed personally or provided by another developer. While it may not be true to say that every developer runs and uses PL/SQL when working with the Oracle Database, the number is no doubt very high as any procedural access to the Oracle Database is best done using PL/SQL. As a developer, if you create and work with PL/SQL, you should be debugging and testing the PL/SQL to ensure accurate and efficient code.

In this chapter, you'll look at PL/SQL unit testing: what is meant by unit testing, why it's important in the development lifecycle, and how to build tests. There are a few tools and utilities available to help you build tests. It doesn't matter which you use. What does matter is that you get into the habit of building and running tests against your code. I use Oracle SQL Developer to do any testing and so that is the tool I'll use to illustrate an approach to building and running PL/SQL unit tests.

Why Test Your Code?

Software and application developers all write code; some write better code than others, but everyone tries to write code that does what it is meant to do and hopes it does that well. That is hardly a vote of confidence for writing good code! Not only is it essential your code is accurate and performs well, it is also important to know that it is robust and able to stand the test of time. This means that the code should perform in the same way, producing the same results over time regardless of changes made to the environment around it.

How can you guarantee this? Perhaps you can't because you can't be 100 percent certain of all the changes that may happen in the future, but if you write regression tests that can be run whenever you want or need to, then you can determine whether a program unit performs as expected and continues to do so. The more tests you write, with more variations, the closer you get to ensuring that the program units are robust and still working as intended.

It is crucial that not only do you know that your code is working today, but also that you can *prove* that it works—and that at any time in the future you can prove the same results. Depending on the requirements of the program unit, your code may have to support a range of scenarios or use cases, and you should be able to test a wide range of use cases. If you can show numerically that you have tested a broad spectrum of these use cases and rerun these test cases, you come closer to empirically proving that the code is robust. If you are able to rerun tests at any time and once again verify the results, you can quickly determine the points of failure and address them.

Without regression tests, you can't know if your code is working or when it stopped working. Even the best code may be unreliable, but you can't prove it one way or the other.

What Is Unit Testing?

Often used by the Java and Agile development communities, *unit testing* is a generic term for writing small repeatable tests where you are testing a "unit of work" or an area of responsibility. Writing unit tests is common in the Java development community where the developers write tests as they write their code. Many in the Java community use JUnit, a development framework for writing unit tests. Most serious Java developers will write unit tests alongside the code they're developing. Some even write tests before they start to write the code. They know the input types the code is expecting and they know the expected outcomes or expected results, so they can build up the tests before they begin. The general thinking in the Java world is "write a little, test a little, write a little, test a little..." and it is wise advice.

While PL/SQL developers have been developing PL/SQL program units for years, creating paper-based tests or using SQL*Plus, there are very few unit test frameworks available that support building up suites of tests to support and test the code. Some developers do build regression tests but without a framework, building unit tests costs time and it's hard to justify the extra time to management, so most have not ventured into this territory. When presenting on this topic at conferences and training events, the norm is that one or two people in the audience are writing unit tests for their PL/SQL regression testing.

As PL/SQL developers, you should see unit tests as part of the development cycle, part of the set of deliverables. Write your unit tests while writing the PL/SQL code and store the tests with the program units. You should be able to run and rerun tests at any point to verify the code still works as required and desired.

Debugging or Testing?

What's the difference between debugging a piece of code and building a unit test for it? This is not an either/or situation: you do need to debug your code to make sure it is doing what it needs to do or to find out why it is not doing what you thought it should do. However, if you want to consider differences, then one difference is the repeatability. If you have written a PL/SQL program unit and want to verify that it's doing what you want it to do, once it has compiled successfully, you can then instrument the code to verify the status at various points in the code, what the variable values are, which procedures call which procedure, and so on. You can pass in various sets of parameters and verify that the outcome is correct. However, if in a month's time you want to verify the same, you have to run through the same process. Martin Fowler, author of many books on agile development, refactoring, and extreme programming sums it up perfectly:

> *Whenever you are tempted to type something into a print statement or a debugger expression, write it as a test instead.*

When Should You Build Tests?

Consider the lifecycle of your PL/SQL code. You have a problem to solve and you know what the code needs to do. You either write the code using paper and pen, text editor, or graphical SQL development tool with a more sophisticated editor. Once you have written the PL/SQL, you compile it to verify that the syntax is correct. If the code compiles successfully, you can then execute it against the schema in the

Oracle Database. It may be that the code works as required immediately and the outcome is successful. If not, you need to debug the code to determine where the problem arises. This edit/compile/run/edit/compile/debug/compile/run cycle can continue until you are satisfied with the program unit and you are ready to ship the code.

Many advocates of unit testing say that you should write your tests before you start to write the code, and that you should see this as part of the complete process. The idea is that you already know what the outcome of your code should be and you know the results, so you can build the tests to suit the results, then you write the code to ensure the test passes! I think it is a combination of writing and planning and building tests, so I urge you see writing tests as part of the process, whether you start writing the code and then add a few tests and then fine tune the code and tests at the same time.

Tools for Building Unit Tests

There are a limited number of tools on the market for writing PL/SQL unit tests; as a result, many users have written their own testing mechanisms. I have listed three of the more popular options here; each have much to recommend them. If you are new to the world of testing, it is worth investing some time researching what is available.

utPLSQL: Working with Command Line Code

utPLSQL is possibly the earliest known unit test framework available for PL/SQL unit testing. Written by Steven Feuerstein, it has been available for some years. It is an open source PL/SQL testing framework for building unit tests. You install utPLSQL by running a script that installs all necessary tables, packages, procedures, and other objects required for the tests. You create and build all your tests in SQL*Plus or from the command line, so there is no tool or additional client required. utPLSQL is hosted on Sourceforge, `http://utplsql.sourceforge.net`, and has a wide variety of resources, documentation, and examples on how to install the software, build tests, and make good use of the framework.

Quest Code Tester for Oracle

Quest Code Tester for Oracle is a commercial product for defining and running tests. You can build tests for single programs or packages, and you can build individual tests or suites. The great advantage you gain by using a product like this is that you can build tests and then rerun them whenever needed, thus supporting the argument that you need to build up a full regression suite of tests for your project.

The Code Tester differs from other products in that it allows you to describe the expected behavior of your PL/SQL program units and store that in a repository. The tool then generates test code based on these definitions. It provides a set of possible expected outcomes based on the code you provide, which you can accept and include or exclude. This code generation is a useful and powerful feature in the tool. As you start building up the tests, you can use the Quick Build option to add test cases to your tests.

Code Tester is an independent product (not integrated into any editing environment), allowing you to build up and run tests independently of your development environment. The downside is that you need to take your code into a separate PL/SQL environment to debug it, if required. However, you can run the tests from Quest's Toad for Oracle and switch from the product to the Code Tester to do further work.

Oracle SQL Developer

Oracle SQL Developer is a free product that supports PL/SQL unit testing. Oracle SQL Developer unit testing was first introduced in SQL Developer 2.0 and already provides much of what the other tools on the market offer; supported by an Oracle Repository, it allows users to build and save tests. Anyone with access can run the tests and you can run the tests and suites from the command line and so incorporate them into the general build process. Oracle SQL Developer provides a set of reports that can be run at any time to review the test results. It also allows you gather code coverage statistics so that you can determine how much of the written code is tested.

■ **Note**   Oracle SQL Developer 3.0 is available as a free download from the Oracle Technology Network at

`www.oracle.com/technetwork/developer-tools/sql-developer`.

The best way to see how to incorporate unit tests into your development life cycle is to review a few examples. The rest of the chapter uses Oracle SQL Developer 3.0 to build unit tests to demonstrate the power of creating unit tests to improve your code; all instructions are related to the product.

Preparing and Maintaining the Unit Test Environment

Oracle SQL Developer uses a central repository where all users with access can store unit tests, share, and reuse them. Before you can start creating tests, you need to create the unit test repository using the repository wizard. The wizard creates the repository by granting all the required privileges to a repository owner and runs the scripts to create the objects that make up the repository.

Before you can run the wizard, you need to identify or create a user who will own and administrate the unit test repository. It is best to create a new user for this, so that only your unit test information is stored here. You need only create and grant the user basic connection privileges, as shown in the following example, as the wizard grants all additional privileges required:

```
CREATE USER repos_owner IDENTIFIED BY repos_owner;
GRANT CREATE SESSION to repos_owner;
```

You also need access to SYS while running the repository wizard. Use SQL Developer to create database connections for both SYS and the new user.

To create a connection, ensure you have the Connections navigator open, select the Connections node, right-click to invoke the context menu, and select New Connection; this invokes the dialog shown in Figure 5-1.

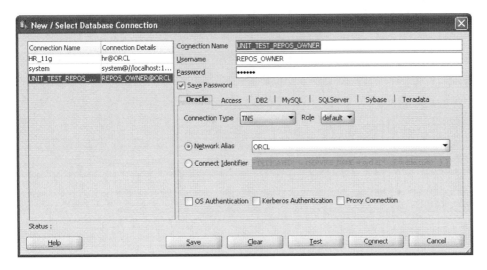

Figure 5-1. Create or update database connection

Creating the Unit Test Repository

To create the repository, select Tools ➤ Unit Test ➤ Select Current Repository, as shown in Figure 5-2. This invokes a connection dialog and selects the database connection—in this case for the new user created. If there is no repository present, the Oracle SQL Developer repository wizard will prompt you to create a new repository for the selected connection.

Figure 5-2. Create or select a Unit Test Repository

You can have a number of repositories in a single instance, so the wizard needs to verify whether the unit testing roles required by the users of the new repository already exist within the instance. If the roles are available, there's no need to rebuild them. If not, the required roles must be created. Once you have started the process, the wizard prompts you for each of the sets of requirements through a series of dialogs. In each case, the wizard displays the syntax, so you can review this and decide whether to proceed or not. You will also be prompted for the SYS password at this stage.

Initially, the wizard verifies whether the repository owner has the correct privileges; if not, the following privileges are granted:

```
GRANT CONNECT, RESOURCE, CREATE VIEW TO "REPOS_OWNER";
```

After this, the wizard grants the user access to the following required roles:

```
GRANT SELECT ON dba_roles TO repos_owner;
GRANT SELECT ON dba_role_privs TO repos_owner;
```

Finally, if the unit test roles are not available, the wizard displays the following syntax to create the roles and grant the rest of the required privileges:

```
CREATE ROLE ut_repo_administrator;
CREATE ROLE ut_repo_user;
GRANT CREATE PUBLIC SYNONYM,DROP PUBLIC SYNONYM TO ut_repo_administrator;
GRANT SELECT ON dba_role_privs TO ut_repo_user;
GRANT SELECT ON dba_role_privs TO ut_repo_administrator;
GRANT SELECT ON dba_roles TO ut_repo_administrator;
GRANT SELECT ON dba_roles TO ut_repo_user;
GRANT SELECT ON dba_tab_privs TO ut_repo_administrator;
GRANT SELECT ON dba_tab_privs TO ut_repo_user;
GRANT EXECUTE ON dbms_lock TO ut_repo_administrator;
GRANT EXECUTE ON dbms_lock TO ut_repo_user;
GRANT ut_repo_user TO ut_repo_administrator WITH ADMIN OPTION;
GRANT ut_repo_administrator TO "REPOS_OWNER" WITH ADMIN OPTION;
```

Accept each dialog in turn to grant access and create the repository. Once created, you can select the repository by using Tools ➤ Unit Test ➤ Select Current Repository.

Maintaining the Unit Test Repository

Once the repository has been built, browse the Unit Test navigator by selecting the View ➤ Unit Tests menu. This opens a navigator where you can do the following:

- Browse the unit test library.
- Create reusable lookup values.
- Run reports to review all the test runs.
- Build unit test suites.
- Create unit tests and unit test implementations.

You can now maintain your repository using the Unit Test menu, as shown in Figure 5-3.

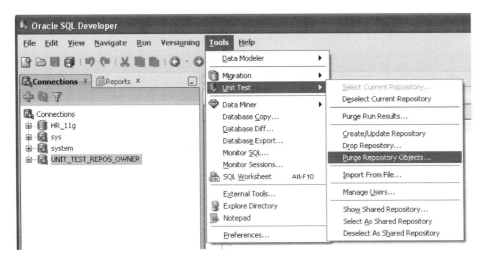

Figure 5-3. Managing unit tests

SQL Developer 3.0 provides the option to purge your run results. Depending on how often you run your tests, especially initially as you get to know the tool, you can end up with many run results, so having the ability to purge all results is very useful. There is a further option, which you will find in the context menu for the results, that allows you to delete sets of results between different dates.

■ **Caution**   There is a difference between Purge Run Results, which deletes the results of all the tests run, and Purge Repository Objects, which also deletes the tests themselves!

Importing Tests

Once you have a set of tests, you can export them to a file and place them under version control as a backup or include them with the rest of your project deliverables. Exporting tests to file also allows you to import them into other unit test repositories (more on importing and exporting tests later).

Building Unit Tests

Let's start by building a unit test for a small piece of PL/SQL code. I have removed any interesting code from the body because I want to focus on the parameter input and building the test, so the example code in Listing 5-1 is just a skeleton of a procedure, which expects a parameter. Using the example, you see how to create a test, the components of the test, and how to run the test; by extending the example, you see how to extend the test capabilities.

Listing 5-1. Skeleton Code for a Unit Test

```
CREATE OR REPLACE PROCEDURE simple_parameter
 (p_x in NUMBER)
 AS
BEGIN
   NULL;
   -- Add PL/SQL code to do something useful here
END simple_parameter;
```

Many procedures expect input parameters, so it is important to write a test where you can pass in a range of parameters or values and ensure they all produce the correct outcome. By writing a unit test, you can supply a wide variety of test values, and change and increase these over time.

To create the procedure, open a new SQL Worksheet and execute the code. For these examples, I use a separate database user from that of the repository owner called repos_user. Be sure the procedure compiles and that you can run it. Once you have a successfully compiled procedure, you are ready to begin.

Using the Unit Test Wizard

The easiest way to start creating unit tests is directly from a procedure or function listing in the Connections navigator. Open the Connections navigator in SQL Developer, expand the connection you created for your user, and find the PL/SQL program unit you want to test. For this example, after you have executed the code to create the procedure, expand the Procedures node.

Find and select the correct procedure, right-click to invoke the context menu, and select Create Unit Test. This invokes the Unit Test Wizard that you use to create all your tests. The wizard walks you through the various stages of the test in the order in which they are executed when you run the test. Because you are working with a PL/SQL skeleton, which only expects a single parameter and does nothing more, there are no additional setup or validations required, so you can accept the default test name, SIMPLE_PARAMETER, select the "Create with single Dummy implementation" option, and click Finish.

You have now created your first test. Select the View ➤ Unit Test menu to invoke the Unit Test navigator, expand the Tests node, and select your test. You can now review the full structure of the test and the test components.

Creating the First Implementation

An Oracle SQL Developer Unit Test comprises one or more implementations. If you expand your test, you'll see the first implementation created by the Unit Test wizard. You can create any number of implementations for a unit test, each with its own parameter set and expected outcome. Using the Unit Test wizard, you can start by creating a single implementation or seed the test with multiple implementations. For either situation, you can continue to add implementations after the test wizard has completed. Simply right-click on the test name and select Add Implementation from the context menu. The single default implementation expects one value for each of the input parameters, which you can add as you create the implementation in the wizard, or after the wizard completes. In Figure 5-4, the input parameter in the Test Implementation 1 section is null and waiting to be populated.

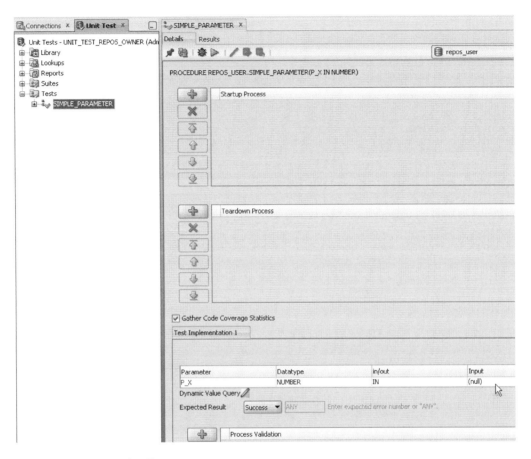

Figure 5-4. Unit test details

Using Figure 5-4, the next section reviews the constituent parts of the unit test, as laid out in the Details tab.

Adding Startup and Teardown Processes

One of the main advantages of building unit tests is that you can run them and rerun them. You can't test your procedure manually in quite the same way. This is particularly true if you have a procedure that changes the value of the data, possibly inserting rows into a table or updating records in a table; running and rerunning it will continually change the data. You need to be able to reset the environment or data back to the starting point before you run the code again. The purpose of the startup process is to take stock of the current situation; for example, you make a backup copy of the table and the data at the point before the test executes the procedure. You can then run the test, and hence the procedure, allowing it to do the updates as designed, and then run the teardown process. The teardown process is designed to reset or restore the status, such as returning the table and the data to the same state it was in before the procedure was executed.

The procedure in this example doesn't update or affect any data, so there is no need for either the startup or the teardown processes, thus they are empty. If you only have a single test, you may have startup and teardowns before and after the test run. You can add multiple startup and teardown processes to a unit test. You can also add a number of tests to a test suite. In this case, it is possible to move all the startup and teardown processes to the top level, so that you prepare the environment by running all the startup processes before the suite starts. Then you run the suite of tests and the teardown processes return the situation to normal at the end. This depends on the procedures themselves, what you are developing, and the impact one test may have on the next.

Collecting Code Coverage Statistics

Collecting the code coverage numbers is a good idea, especially as the number of procedures or functions in a project grows. You can ascertain how much of the code there is and how much of it you are testing. You may well have a test that is 100 percent successful, but if it only tests 10 percent of the procedure, then you can hardly call it a useful test. All code coverage statistics gathered are available in the Test Runs and Suite Runs code coverage reports, which you will find in the Reports node in the Unit Test navigator.

Specifying Parameters

Use the parameter grid in the Test Implementation section to add or update the input parameters the procedures or functions expect. You can either add these input values as you progress through the steps of the Unit Test Wizard or manually in the details tab, just before you run the test. The wizard creates the parameter listing, deriving these from the input parameters listed in the procedure or function.

Figure 5-5 shows the parameter page of the Unit Test wizard. Here you see that you can have either a static input value or a Dynamic Value Query. With the Dynamic Value Query—instead of a hardcoded value—you can use or query a table of values. The unit test queries the table and passes the results back to the procedure, using each value or set of values in turn as the input parameter(s) for the procedure. Adding a single value, as this example does, to verify that the test is working is a useful way to start, but you are not taking advantage of the power of automating your tests. Again, emphasizing the advantage of building unit tests, not only can you automate the process, but you can also pass in a wider set of test values for a single test run using the Dynamic Value Query. Moreover, by using a table of values, you can change and update the values in the table and hence pass a different set of values to the test without having to update the test.

The *expected result* of the execution of the procedure may be success or failure and you can test for either outcome. In this example, you expect an outcome of success. If you are testing for a failure, then the expected outcome is failure and you can add in the failure or error number here. In this case, when you run the test and you hit the expected the error, the test has succeeded and the final report will return a success!

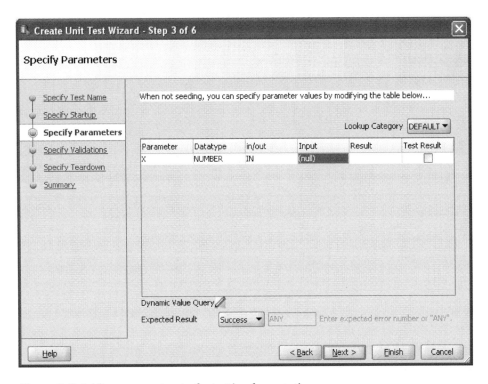

Figure 5-5. Adding parameters to the test implementation

Adding Process Validation

The last section of the test details page is the process validation. The execution of the procedure generally results in a change of status, whether you are updating records in a table or calculating a value. In these situations, you can provide a validation of the expected result. Figure 5-6 provides a list of possible process validation types. For example, if you are updating a column value in a table, you might want to verify that none of the values is above a certain amount. You can verify this by writing a select statement against the table and using the "Query returns no rows" option. In the case where you pass in a set of parameters, allowing the procedure to be run multiple times for each parameter(s), you may want to verify that every run of the procedure passes the required condition.

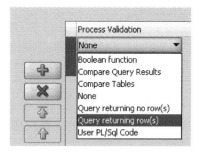

Figure 5-6. Selecting process validations

Saving Tests

Once you have run the Unit Test wizard, the test and its implementation(s) are saved to the Unit Test Repository. Any changes you make, such as changing the input parameter or switching from a static to dynamic query value, need to be saved to the repository before running the test. If you make a change and then try running the test, SQL Developer prompts you to save these changes.

Debugging and Running Tests

You can run tests in two ways: either from the command line or using the Unit Test Details window shown in Figure 5-7. To run tests from inside the tool, click the green run button or use F9.

Figure 5-7. Running a test

The test results are sent to the Results tab; you can review them there initially and then later in the test reports.

I find it useful to debug the test before running it, as this throws up any issues you might overlook before you run the test. For example, if you forget to add any input parameters, this is flagged in the debug window, as shown in Figure 5-8.

Figure 5-8. Debug window

Broadening the Scope of the Tests

Another advantage of building unit tests is that having built a single test, you can easily extend it to test a wide variety of input parameters. You can do this by running the same test implementation and just manually changing the input value; alternatively, you can create new implementations for each of the values you want to test. If you only need to test a few cases, then adding a few more implementations to the test is fine, but if the values you want to test vary over time or if you want to test a long set of values, then manually adding implementations is not a practical approach. Oracle SQL Developer's unit tests accept parameter values from a static list of values and from a dynamic query. You can use any of the following mechanisms to add input parameters:

- A static list of lookup values, using the drop-down list to populate each test implementation you create.

- A static list of lookup values to seed the implementations dynamically based on the permutations of available values.

- A dynamic query to populate a single implementation, using each of the values returned by the query as input parameters.

The next sections show examples of each of these and how they can add value to your tests.

Creating Lookup Values

Use a static list of lookup values when you have a small known set of data or if you have a standard set of values that you can use in many different tests. Typically, you test a range of values, including a few extreme values and the middle ground. So you might test high values, low values, and mid-range values in a set of numbers; or extreme length strings; or turn of the century dates. In each case, consider the edge case in addition to the set of expected values.

To see this static value list in action, you can create a set of lookup values to use with the same procedure, simple_parameter, used in the earlier example. This procedure expects a number as an input parameter, so you need to create a static list of numbers. To create the lookup values, expand the Lookups node in the Unit Test navigator. You can create a new lookup category or use the existing DEFAULT category. For this example, I recommend you create a new category, as it is easy to see the impact of using a list other than the default category. With the new category selected, right-click to invoke the context menu, click Add Datatype, and select Number from the DataType drop-down list in the dialog. You can now add a list of numbers. There is an example of a set of values in Figure 5-9. Once you have added the values, save the changes.

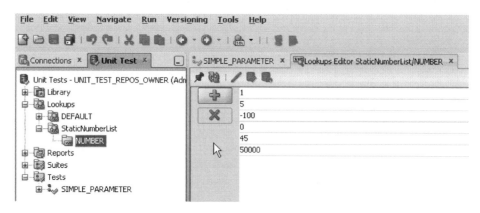

Figure 5-9. Adding static lookup values

Before you can use the new static list, you need to ensure that SQL Developer is aware of your list and to make sure this is the default used to input parameters for new implementations. To do this, you need to set the Unit Test parameter preference. Select the Tools ➤ Preferences menu and then click Unit Test Parameters to reveal the option for setting the configuration used in lookups. Using the drop-down list, select the new category. There is no need to do the step if you added the static values to the DEFAULT category, as this is displayed in the list by default. The preference is useful for those situations when you have many different categories. Select the category and close the preference dialog.

You can now return to the test you created, select the test, and right-click to select Add Implementation. Expand the test and select the new implementation to display the detail in the test screen. Using the Lookup Category drop-down list, change the value to display your new lookup category. You can now run and rerun the implementation using the static list to populate the parameter input values, as shown in Figure 5-10.

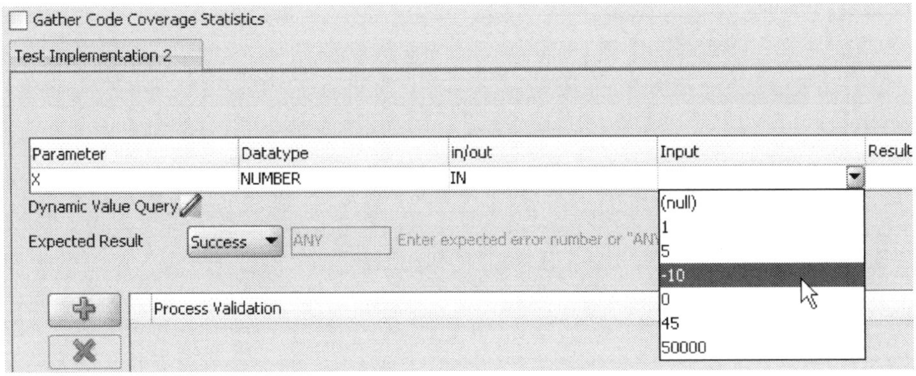

Figure 5-10. Using a static drop-down list

Seeding Test Implementations

You have seen that you can manually change the input parameters by either entering them or selecting them from a static drop-down list. You can also use the static list to seed multiple implementations in a test.

To learn this approach, you need to create a new test for your procedure. Select the Tests node in the Unit Test navigator, right-click to invoke the context menu, and select Create Test. This invokes the Unit Test wizard a stage earlier than you saw previously and is an alternative approach to creating a test. Select the connection and procedure you worked with earlier. Provide a new test name and select "Seed/Create implementations using lookup values." You can click Finish at the point or skip through the steps to review the Specify Parameters screen. Note that you can't modify or add any parameters here, but you should see the name of the lookup you created displayed in the lookup category; the wizard creates a new implementation using the values in the lookup. Finish the wizard and expand the new test. Notice that there are as many implementations created as there are values in your lookup.

To see the real impact of this, return to your procedure, add another input parameter such as p_y IN NUMBER, and compile the code. Your procedure now looks as follows:

```
CREATE OR REPLACE PROCEDURE simple_parameter
(
 p_x IN NUMBER,
 p_y IN NUMBER
)
 AS
BEGIN
   NULL;
   -- Add PL/SQL code to do something useful here
END simple_parameter;
```

Return to the Unit Test navigator and follow the same process you have just completed: create a new test, select "Seed/Create implementations using lookup values" and finish the Unit Test wizard. When you expand the new test, notice that the lookup list has been used to populate both parameters, so instead of 6 implementations created, as happened with the single parameter, there are now 6 x 6 implementations created. The advantage here is that you can test a vast range of values using a small static list of values.

When you run the unit test, each implementation is run. To run the test with all the implementations, select the test in the Unit Test navigator and use the right-click context menu to run the test. Switch to the Results tab to see the outcome, as shown in Figure 5-11. Notice how the input parameters used are combinations of the static values created in the lookup list.

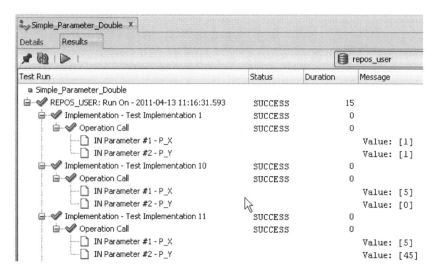

Figure 5-11. Reviewing seeded implementation results

Creating a Dynamic Query

Using a static lookup list to seed multiple implementations is a useful way of expanding the scope of what you test. However, the dynamic query mentioned earlier offers even greater flexibility. Using a query to provide the values that populate an implementation means that the set of values can change, increasing or decreasing over time.

To create a dynamic query, you need to have a table of values against which you run the query. For example, create the table and data as follows:

```
CREATE TABLE double_param_val
(p_val1 NUMBER(2),
p_val2 Number(5));

INSERT INTO double_param_val VALUES (2, 0);
INSERT INTO double_param_val VALUES (99, 20000);
INSERT INTO double_param_val values (0, 99999);
```

Once you have created the table, you can add a new implementation to the test. Instead of using the static list or manually adding a parameter, select the Dynamic Value Query option. This opens a dialog with a sample query, "select ? as P_X, ? as P_Y from ? where ?". Rewrite the query to query the new table of values as follows "select p_val1 as P_X, p_val2 as P_Y from double_param_val;" then save and run the test. Notice that you only need a single implementation for the dynamic query, even though the table itself may hold a number of values. Each value or set of values is passed to the procedure in turn. When you run the test, a full set of results, displaying an implementation for each set of input values, is displayed in the Results tab.

The advantage of using dynamic queries is that the values in the table can change, and you can continue to add and update them to test further options without having to add extra implementations. Compare this to the static lookup values where an implementation is created for each value in the list. If you want to test additional values, you have to add additional implementations.

Supporting Unit Test Features

SQL Developer also provides a number of additional features that support creating and running unit tests. A few of these are addressed in the following sections.

Running Reports

Once you have created and started running your unit tests, you can run the reports created for all the tests run. The reports include the following:

- User Test Runs: A report of all users who have run tests.

- Code Coverage: Reports of the code coverage in suites run and code coverage in individual tests. The coverage reports include the total number of lines and the number of lines covered by the test.

- Test Implementation Runs: Reports for the implementations run in a test and in a suite.

Figure 5-12 illustrates a set of all tests run. By selecting a single report, you can see the run details and code coverage.

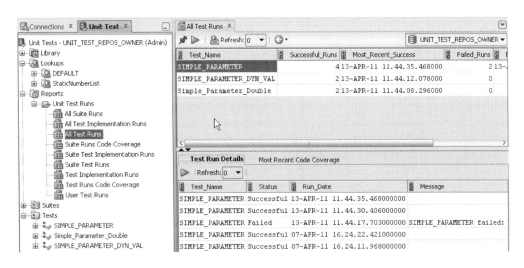

Figure 5-12. Running test reports

■ **Caution**   The reports query the results in the Unit Test repository, so purging test run results also purges them from the reports.

Creating a Library of Components

I have talked about the strength of unit tests being about repeatability. If you can build up a set of reusable components, you start building up a resource for putting together more tests. You can use the Library node as the starting point and create a selection of components in the library, but it is much easier to build up the components as you are creating your tests.

Still keeping to the most basic of PL/SQL programs, use the next example to build a test and create a set of library components at the same time. Use the following code, which creates two tables, one with data, as well as a procedure:

```
CREATE TABLE cities
  (city_id NUMBER(4,0),
   city VARCHAR2(30),
   country_abrv VARCHAR2(2)
  ) ;

CREATE OR REPLACE  PROCEDURE insert_cities (
    city_id NUMBER,
    city        VARCHAR2,
    country_abrv VARCHAR2)
  IS
  BEGIN
    INSERT INTO cities (city_id, city,country_abrv)
    VALUES (city_id, city, country_abrv);
  END;
/

CREATE TABLE places
  (
    location_id NUMBER(4,0),
    city VARCHAR2(30),
    country_id  CHAR(2)
  ) ;

INSERT INTO places  VALUES (1000,'Roma','IT');
INSERT INTO places  VALUES (1100,'Venice','IT');
INSERT INTO places  VALUES (1200,'Tokyo','JP');
INSERT INTO places  VALUES (1300,'Hiroshima','JP');
INSERT INTO places  VALUES (1400,'Southlake','US');
INSERT INTO places  VALUES (1500,'South San Francisco','US');
INSERT INTO places  VALUES (1600,'South Brunswick','US');
INSERT INTO places  VALUES (1700,'Seattle','US');
INSERT INTO places  VALUES (1800,'Toronto','CA');
INSERT INTO places  VALUES (1900,'Whitehorse','CA');
```

Create a new unit test for the procedure insert_cities. You can either do this from the Connection navigator (select the procedure, right-click for the Context menu, and select Create Unit Test) or from the Unit Test menu (select Tests ➤ Create Test from the Context menu). Once you have the wizard open, give the test a name and select "Create with single Dummy implementation."

In the startup process, you have a choice: you can leave the startup empty, insert the records, and then delete the inserted records on teardown, or you can copy the existing table, insert the rows with the procedure and then restore the state in the teardown. In this example, add a new startup and select "Table or Row copy" from the drop-down list. This invokes a new dialog. Browse to find and select the table you want to copy (in this case CITIES) and click OK to return the Startup Process dialog. If you are just building the unit test without also adding the code to the library, you would just continue through the wizard, but you are building up a library of components, so add a name to the Publish to Library field, as shown in Figure 5-13, and click Publish.

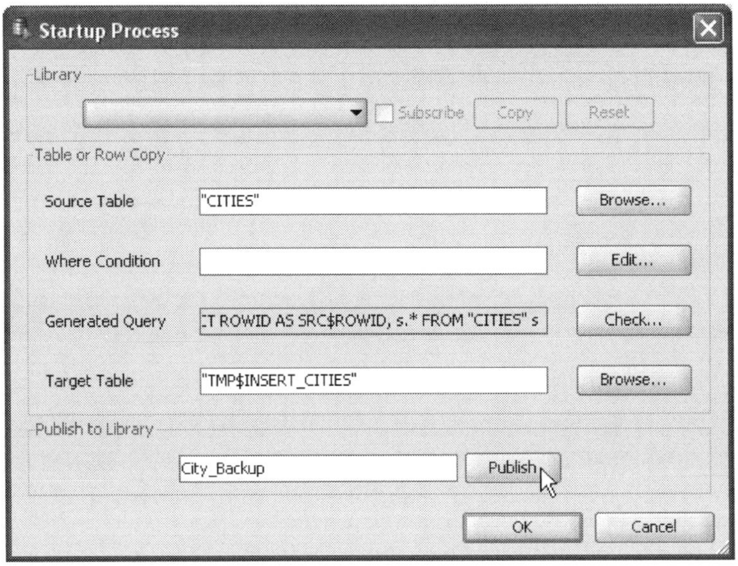

Figure 5-13. Creating a library Component

After you publish the component, the dialog changes and you can no longer edit the values. This remains true while you have the Subscribe checkbox selected. While the unit test remains subscribed to this library component, any changes made to the component are reflected in the tests that consume it. Once you have built up a set of components, you can select them from the library using this same dialog. If the library component does most of what you need, but not everything, you can create a copy and then modify it. The modifications are used by the test you are working on and don't affect any other test using the library component.

When you have published the startup to the library, continue to the next page of the wizard. You have already seen the different choices available for working with parameters, so select the Dynamic Value Query as this parameter option also provides the opportunity of saving the detail to the Library as a component. Add the following query:

```
SELECT LOCATION_ID AS CITY_ID,  CITY AS CITY,  COUNTRY_ID AS COUNTRY_ABRV
FROM PLACES
```

In order to publish the query to the library, enter a name in the Publish to Library field and click Publish as before. Continue to the Process Validation screen and add a new process validation. In this example, you need to check to see if the rows are inserted into the table. There are different approaches to doing this, one way is to query the updated table. Select **Query returning row**(s) from the drop-down list when you add the new process validation. Enter the following code:

```
SELECT CITY FROM CITIES WHERE  CITY_ID IN
(SELECT  LOCATION_ID FROM PLACES);
```

When you have entered the query, give the new process validation a name and publish it to the library. Figure 5-14 shows the dialog after the details are published to the library.

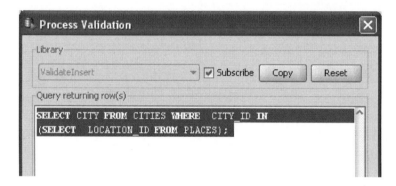

Figure 5-14. Adding process validations

The final stage of the wizard is the teardown process. In the startup process, you copied the table to a temporary table, so now you need to reverse the process and restore the table. An alternative approach to resetting the environment might be to delete the records inserted. Select Table or Row Restore from the drop-down list. The wizard populates the field in the teardown process with the details based on the startup process decisions you made. You can also publish this final component to the library. Complete the wizard by reviewing the summary page and click Finish to close the dialog.

Now that that test is complete, you can run it and review the results. The CITIES test table should remain empty because your test inserts the new records and then restores the table. Your validation process verifies that the records in the PLACES tables were inserted into the CITIES. If you want to test that the procedure is actually doing the inserts, just delete the startup and teardown processes, rerun the tests, and query the CITIES table. You should see the new records inserted.

Review the library components by expanding the Library node in the Unit Test navigator, as shown in Figure 5-15. Each of the component areas now has a reusable piece of code. You can edit and update these components; any changes you make are reflected in any tests consuming them.

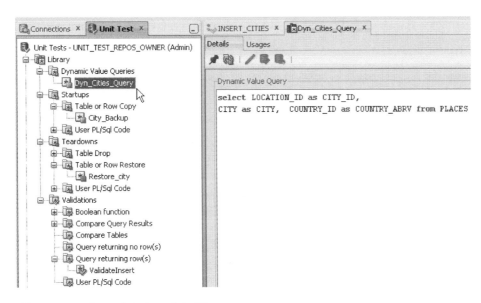

Figure 5-15. Expanded view of the library

Exporting, Importing, and Synchronizing Tests

You can share your tests with other users through the Unit Test Repository. This means that any users who have access to the Unit Test Repository can see the tests and run them. Not only can other users see the tests, everyone who has access can run the tests against the database connections of their choice. In other words, where it makes sense, you might run a test in the development environment and in a separate bug-testing environment. An alternative to this is to export the tests and share them on a central server. Other users can then import the tests.

When you initially create a test for a procedure, the procedure owner details are stored in the test details. You can see this in the Unit Test Details screen shown in Figure 5-16, which lists the fully qualified procedure name.

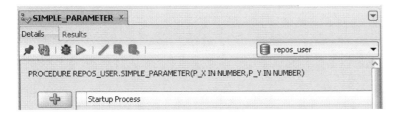

Figure 5-16. Showing the unit test details

The procedure name is also visible in the XML file created when you export tests. If you export and import the unit test, either you need to import it into a database with the same user and procedure or you need to point the test to the correct procedure in a new schema. So for the situation where you want to test the same procedure in different databases against different users and for different repositories, you can do so by exporting and then importing the test.

To export a test, simply right-click the test and select Export to File. For importing tests, you need to use the main Tools ➤ Unit Test menu and select Import from File.

Once you have imported the test, you may need to synchronise it with the new environment. Synchronizing tests is not only useful when moving tests to a different environment, but also if the procedures or functions you are working with in your own scenario change. For example, you may add or update the input parameters. There are a few alternatives as to why you might need to perform a synchronization.

- The procedure the test executes has the same parameters but in a different order.

- The procedure has different parameters from the one for which the test was originally built.

- The procedure exists in a schema different from that for which it was originally created.

To do the synchronization, select the test, right-click and select Synchronize Test. You can now browse to select the correct procedure, as shown in Figure 5-17.

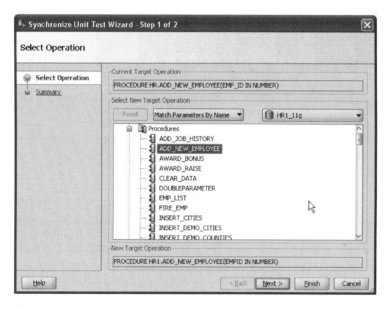

Figure 5-17. Synchronizing a unit test

Where the test requires changes, they are listed in the summary screen, as shown in Figure 5-18. In this example, the procedure needs to point to the procedure in the new schema and there is a change in the input parameter.

■ **Tip**   After you have synchronized a test, make sure you refresh the test details to reflect the changes. You may need to update any dynamic queries to match the new parameter changes.

```
Synchronize Unit Test Summary
-----------------------------------------------------------------
The current target operation signature is:
      PROCEDURE HR.ADD_NEW_EMPLOYEE(EMP_ID IN NUMBER)
-----------------------------------------------------------------
The new target operation signature is:
      PROCEDURE HR1.ADD_NEW_EMPLOYEE(EMPID IN NUMBER)
-----------------------------------------------------------------
The test will be modified as follows:
      1. The name of the schema containing the target operation with be changed.
      2. The source connection name will be changed.
      3. The following current target operation arguments will be deleted:
         EMP_ID
      4. The following new target operation arguments will be added:
         EMPID
-----------------------------------------------------------------
```

Figure 5–18. Synchronize unit test summary

Building Suites

Ultimately, you want to build up a suite of regression tests that you can run outside of the SQL Developer environment. To create a suite of tests, select the Suites node, invoke the Context menu, and select Create Suite. You can select and add as many tests to the suite as you like. The useful thing about a suite is that you only need to select the suite to run it, and you can move all the startup and teardown processes to the top level and then have them execute at the start of the testing. You can review the suite results in the reports in the same way you can review the reports for individual tests.

Running Tests from the Command Line

Once you have built your tests or suite of tests, you can run them from the command line and ultimately include them into your build process. To run SQL Developer Unit Tests from the command line, start a command line session and navigate to the \sqldeveloper\sqldeveloper\bin directory.

To get help and details about the unit test command line commands, enter ututil at the command prompt, without any additional parameters. The tool will return the three available command options: to run, import, or export unit tests. To see the parameters each of these expects, enter the command query

```
ututil -exp ?
```

Once you know the expected parameters, you can enter the complete command, for example:

```
D:\Builds\SQL Dev\3.0\3.0.04.34\sqldeveloper\sqldeveloper\bin>ututil -exp -test
-name SIMPLE_PARAMETER -repo UNIT_TEST_30 -file d:\working\myexptest.xml
```

You can build the full command to run, export, or import tests, as shown in Figure 5 -19, into your batch files and schedule them to run if and when you need them.

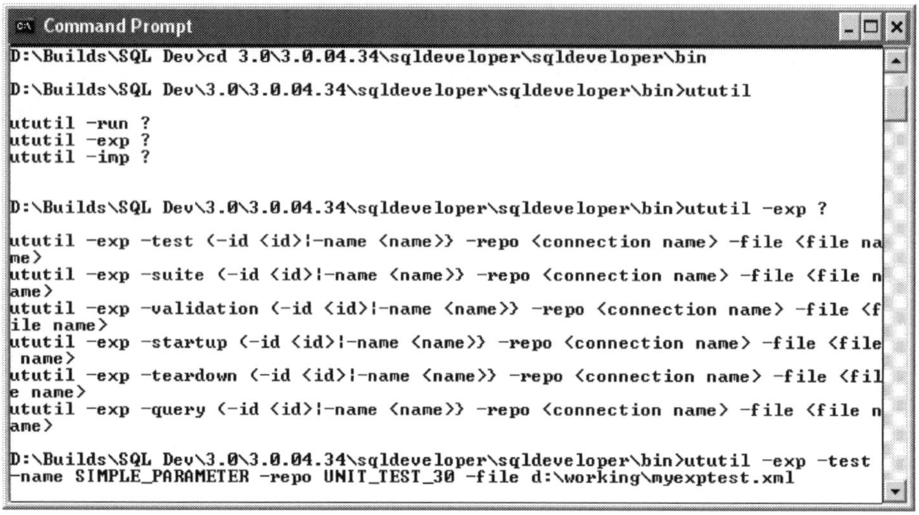

Figure 5-19. Exporting a unit test from the command line

The results of the test runs are written to the repository as before, so you can review the reports in the Tests or Suites sections.

Summary

Unit testing is key to building applications. Java developers have been building unit tests as part of their development process for some years now, while PL/SQL developers have been slower to make this a formal part of the development process. Unit tests can form part of a regression suite of tests and run from the command line to support a batch process. This chapter reviewed the reasons why you should build unit tests as well as when and why you need to see them as part of the full PL/SQL development cycle. Using Oracle SQL Developer 3.0 as a basis for the examples, the concepts of preparing the test environment through adding startup processes and resetting the environment through teardown process were introduced. Procedures and functions typically expect one or more input parameters, and so one section addressed the different options available for providing static or dynamic input parameters and the importance of validating the test process and outcome. Automating the testing process through running tests from the command line means that tests and test suites can be incorporated into the general application build cycle. By introducing unit testing and illustrating the advantages gained by using a testing framework, I hope you will be able to build tests quickly and easily, and develop robust code as part of your development cycle.

Bulk SQL Operations

by Connor McDonald

This chapter is about the bulk SQL operations available in PL/SQL. Bulk operations in PL/SQL enable you to manipulate and process many rows at once, rather than one row at a time. In this chapter, you'll learn about bulk fetching and bulk binding. Bulk fetching refers to the ability to retrieve a set of rows from the database into PL/SQL structures with a single call, rather than making a call to the database for each row to be retrieved. Bulk binding lets you perform the converse: to take those sets of rows stored in PL/SQL structures and save them to the database in an efficient manner.

You'll see the tremendous performance benefits possible with bulk SQL operations. To achieve these benefits requires a little extra complexity in your code, especially in the area of error handling, but I'll show you how to manage that complexity so that you will achieve performance benefits without compromising the manageability of your code.

The Hardware Store

My journey toward the benefit of bulk operations began at the hardware store—not the computer hardware store, but the DIY-style store where you purchase tools, fixings, paint and the like to perform handyman projects and maintenance on the family home.

I *love* the hardware store. Of course, being an Information Technology professional, my knowledge about anything that remotely resembles manual labor is pretty much zero. So every time I arrive at the cash register to pay for a new tool or a new tin of paint, within about 5 seconds I am back in the aisles to pick up an accompanying item; for example, a new tin of paint is not much use without a paint brush! By the time I actually have all of the tools required to perform the job at hand, I've probably been back and forth to the cash register six or seven times, each trip accompanied by an increasing level of profanity from the person at the till. There's a term of endearment my wife came up with when she observed me doing this—picking up a single item at a time— and that term is *idiot*. She's right; I should just grab a trolley, collect *all* of the items I need, and pay for them all at once!

And that's the great hypocrisy. For some strange reason, the same IT professionals that apply simple common sense to tackling "challenges" like going to the hardware store, struggle to apply that same common sense when it comes to working with the database. Much like the hardware store, if you are going to pick up a number of items (of data), it makes a lot more sense to use the coding equivalent of a trolley to collect that data.

Throughout this chapter, I'll often refer back to and expand upon this metaphor of purchasing items from the hardware store because it's useful for the sake of building examples, but also to reinforce the fact that everything discussed in this chapter is still merely a reflection of the common sense principles we use in our everyday lives away from technology.

Setting for the Examples in this Chapter

All of the examples in this chapter are downloadable from the book's catalog page on the Apress website, and each example is annotated with the appropriate file name. For each example, you will see an initial call to a script, like so:

```
@@bulk_setup.sql [populate | empty]
```

This creates a table representing the "hardware store" that all of the examples will use.

```
SQL> desc HARDWARE
 Name                            Null?    Type
 ------------------------------- -------- -------------
 AISLE                                    NUMBER(5)
 ITEM                                     NUMBER(12)
 DESCR                                    CHAR(50)
```

The table is created empty unless the 'populate' keyword is passed, upon which 1,000,000 rows will be added to the table via the following SQL:

```
SQL> insert /*+ APPEND */ into  HARDWARE
  2  select trunc(rownum/1000)+1 aisle,
  3         rownum item,
  4         'Description '||rownum descr
  5  from
  6    ( select 1 from dual connect by level <= 1000),
  7    ( select 1 from dual connect by level <= 1000);

1000000 rows created.
```

The script drops and recreates the table so that examples should run on your database with similar results to what you see in this chapter. Obviously with so many variants in terms of hardware platform and software versions, your mileage may vary, but the examples have all been run on the most common defaults, namely 8k block size residing within an ASSM tablespace.

▩ **Tip**   The trick of using DUAL to generate an arbitrary number of rows dates back to a post by Mikito Harakiri on the `asktom.oracle.com` site many years ago. Since then, it has almost become the de facto standard in demos on newsgroups, books, and the like for quickly synthesizing data. When pushed to extremes, care must be taken in order not to excessively consume memory. Refer to `http://blog.tanelpoder.com/2008/06/08/generating-lots-of-rows-using-connect-by-safely/` for details.

Bulk Operations in PL/SQL

Bulk processing in Oracle pre-dates PL/SQL, just via a different name, namely *array processing*. For as a long as I have worked with Oracle (circa version 6 in the early 1990s), the concept of array processing has been available. Rather than fetch a single row of data from the database, a *set* of rows is fetched into a buffer, and that buffer is passed back to the client as an array. Similarly, rather than modify or create a single row of data in the database, a buffer with an array of rows is populated and passed to the database. Application programmers could do array processing natively via OCI, or many of the popular Oracle tools of the time (such as Forms) would transparently take care of the task. You will soon see the performance and scalability benefits of such a strategy.

Presumably the PL/SQL team at Oracle faced a nomenclature problem in version 8.1 when they introduced native array processing. By that stage, the term "array" was already entrenched in PL/SQL, referring to the INDEX BY array data structure, and perhaps from this conflict, the term "bulk" arose. In fact, array processing in PL/SQL pre-dates even version 8.1; it was available via the DBMS_SQL package way back in Oracle 7. An example of PL/SQL array processing from version 7 is presented next (I will not step through the code in detail, since I'll be covering simpler mechanisms shortly).

The following example (`bulk_dbms_sql_array.sql`) shows how to perform array processing in version 8.0 and below. It fetches 500 rows at a time from the HARDWARE table.

```
SQL> set serverout on
SQL> declare
  2     l_cursor    int  := dbms_sql.open_cursor;
  3     l_num_row   dbms_sql.number_table;
  4     l_exec      int;
  5     l_fetched_rows    int;
  6  begin
  7    dbms_sql.parse(
  8            l_cursor,
  9            'select item from hardware where item <= 1200',
 10            dbms_sql.native);
 11    dbms_sql.define_array(l_cursor,1,l_num_row,500,1);
 12    l_exec := dbms_sql.execute(l_cursor);
 13    loop
 14        l_fetched_rows := dbms_sql.fetch_rows(l_cursor);
 15        dbms_sql.column_value(l_cursor, 1, l_num_row);
 16        dbms_output.put_line('Fetched '||l_fetched_rows||' rows');
 17        exit when l_fetched_rows < 500;
 18    end loop;
 19    dbms_sql.close_cursor(l_cursor);
 20  end;
 21  /
Fetched 500 rows
Fetched 500 rows
Fetched 200 rows

PL/SQL procedure successfully completed.
```

Sadly, even a decade after they were introduced, the bulk operations in PL/SQL are still an underused feature in modern PL/SQL-centric applications. Many a production PL/SQL program still processes data from the database in a row-by-row fashion. In particular, because most of my work is in the tuning arena, my primary motivation for the use of collections is that it encourages the developer to think more in terms of sets, rather than rows. While there is no functional reason that should prohibit developers from processing resultsets one row at a time, from an efficiency and performance perspective, it is generally bad news.

Similarly, criticism is often aimed at PL/SQL in terms of performance, but the most common cause of this is row-at-a-time processing rather than anything inherent in the PL/SQL engine. PL/SQL is not alone in misplaced criticism of this kind. Developers not taking advantage of host-based arrays in Pro*C led Oracle to add a PREFETCH compiler option, which converts the runtime Pro*C code into array fetching even though the developer has coded it in a conventional row-at-a-time manner. Similarly, ODP.NET defaults to array processing for most queries via its FetchSize parameter.

Getting Started with BULK Fetch

One of the great things about transitioning your code to take advantage of bulk operations in PL/SQL, is that it's easy to do and has a direct mapping to your existing code. Before bulk operations arrived in version 8.1, you could use one of the following three constructs to retrieve a row of data in PL/SQL

1. Implicit Cursor

A standard SQL query (SELECT-INTO) is used to retrieve a single row of data, or columns from that single row from a table into target variables. If no rows are retrieved or more than a single row is retrieved, an exception is raised. Here's an example (bulk_implicit_1.sql):

```
SQL> declare
  2     l_descr hardware.descr%type;
  3  begin
  4     select descr
  5     into   l_descr
  6     from   hardware
  7     where  aisle = 1
  8     and    item = 1;
  9  end;
 10  /

PL/SQL procedure successfully completed.
```

2. Explicit Fetch Calls

A cursor is explicitly defined within the PL/SQL declaration section. The cursor is then opened and fetched from, typically within a loop until the available rows are exhausted, at which point the cursor is closed. Here's an example (bulk_explicit_1.sql):

```
SQL> declare
  2     cursor c_tool_list is
  3        select descr
  4        from   hardware
  5        where  aisle = 1
  6        and    item between 1 and 500;
  7
  8     l_descr hardware.descr%type;
```

```
 9  begin
10    open c_tool_list;
11    loop
12      fetch c_tool_list into l_descr;
13      exit when c_tool_list%notfound;
14    end loop;
15    close c_tool_list;
16  end;
17  /
```

PL/SQL procedure successfully completed.

3. Implicit Fetch Calls

The third type is a hybrid between the two approaches. A FOR loop takes care of the cursor management, the cursor being either explicitly defined in advance or the directly coded within the FOR-loop itself. Here's an example (bulk_implicit_fetch_1.sql):

```
SQL> begin
  2    for i in (
  3      select descr
  4      from   hardware
  5      where  aisle = 1
  6      and    item between 1 and 500 )
  7    loop
  8      <processing code for each row>
  9    end loop;
 10  end;
 11  /
```

PL/SQL procedure successfully completed.

Converting each of those constructs to a bulk collection model is easy and straightforward. The following are the three bulk processing constructs that are the analogs of the non-bulk constructs just shown.

1. Implicit Cursor BULK Mode

A standard SQL query (SELECT-INTO) can now be used to retrieve multiple rows of data into a collection type simply by adding the BULK COLLECT keywords. Here's an example (bulk_implicit_2.sql):

```
SQL> declare
  2    type t_descr_list is table of hardware.descr%type;
  3    l_descr_list t_descr_list;
  4  begin
  5    select descr
  6    bulk collect
  7    into   l_descr_list
  8    from   hardware
  9    where  aisle = 1
 10    and    item between 1 and 100;
```

```
11   end;
12   /
```

PL/SQL procedure successfully completed.

2. Explicit Fetch Calls BULK Mode

The only changes required are to define a collection type to hold the results and to add the BULK COLLECT clause to the FETCH command. All of the rows in the cursor resultset will be fetched into the collection type variable in a single call. Here's an example (bulk_explicit_2.sql):

```
SQL> declare
  2    cursor c_tool_list is
  3      select descr
  4      from   hardware
  5      where  aisle = 1
  6      and    item between 1 and 500;
  7
  8    type t_descr_list is table of c_tool_list%rowtype;
  9    l_descr_list t_descr_list;
 10
 11  begin
 12    open c_tool_list;
 13    fetch c_tool_list bulk collect into l_descr_list;
 14    close c_tool_list;
 15  end;
 16  /
```

PL/SQL procedure successfully completed.

3. Implicit Fetch Calls BULK mode

Things gets even easier when converting the hybrid approach to bulk collect because there are *no* code changes to make. One of the best features to arrive in Oracle 10g was the "automatic bulk collect" enhancement for FOR loops. Because a FOR loop on a cursor will, by definition, fetch *all* of the rows in the cursor (unless an explicit EXIT command is present within the loop), the PL/SQL compiler can safely employ a bulk collect optimization to retrieve those rows as efficiently as possible. You will automatically get this optimization if you are on at least version 10 of Oracle, and the database parameter plsql_optimize_level is set to at least 2 (the default). The following example (bulk_implicit_fetch_2.sql) shows the database optimization level followed by a FOR loop that is automatically implemented for you using the bulk processing features:

```
SQL> select banner from v$version where rownum = 1;

BANNER
----------------------------------------------------------------------------
Oracle Database 11g Enterprise Edition Release 11.2.0.2.0 - 64bit Production

SQL> select value from v$parameter where name = 'plsql_optimize_level';
```

```
VALUE
-------------------------------------------------------------------------
2

SQL> begin
  2     for i in (
  3        select descr
  4        from   hardware
  5        where  aisle = 1
  6        and    item between 1 and 500 )
  7     loop
  8        null;
  9     end loop;
 10  end;
 11  /

PL/SQL procedure successfully completed.
```

It's not immediately apparent that bulk collection is taking place in the previous code. You'll soon see how you can verify that the code is indeed fetching multiple rows with a single call.

Three Collection-Style Datatypes

The final three examples in the preceding section are retrieving their rows in a nested table datatype. Since Oracle 8.1, there are three collection-style datatypes into which rows can be fetched into in bulk fashion.

- Varray

- Nested table

- Associative array

Deciding on what collection types to use typically will come down to which suits your application most. The types are not mutually exclusive. As well as collections being passed between PL/SQL programs, you may also be passing these collections back and forth between PL/SQL and your 3GL-based applications residing away from the database server. Many of the popular 3GL technologies used to communicate with Oracle databases have simple and effective interfaces to PL/SQL routines which take *associative arrays* as parameters, but not necessarily *varray* or *nested tables*.

For example,

- Within JDBC, the methods `setPlsqlIndexTable` and `registerIndexTableOutParameter` are available for passing data to and from the database via PL/SQL associative arrays.

- Within Pro*C, host arrays in C can be directly mapped to associative arrays in PL/SQL parameters.

- Within ODP.NET, Oracle parameters can be directly mapped to associative arrays, namely, `Param1.CollectionType = OracleCollectionType.PLSQLAssociativeArray;`

By comparison, if you head down the "object" path by creating user defined types comprising varrays and/or nested tables, then interacting with PL/SQL via these same 3GL's can start to get more complicated. Translation utilities are required, such as the Object Type Translator for Pro*C or custom metadata mapping for ODP.Net. For this reason, it may well be the case that associative arrays are the best choice if you have a strong interaction between your 3GL application code and PL/SQL. Alternatively, given the industry's current obsession with Service Oriented Architecture (SOA) where the data exchange medium is XML, it may be easier for 3GL applications to pass XML into the PL/SQL and use the facilities within the XMLTYPE datatype to cast the incoming XML into an PL/SQL object type. Here is example of such a translation (bulk_xml_to_obj.sql):

```
SQL> create or replace
  2  type COMING_FROM_XML as object
  3     ( COL1 int,
  4        COL2 int)
  5  /

Type created.

SQL> declare
  2     source_xml xmltype;
  3     target_obj coming_from_xml;
  4  begin
  5     source_xml :=
  6        xmltype('<DEMO>
  7                    <COL1>10</COL1>
  8                    <COL2>20</COL2>
  9                 </DEMO>');
 10
 11     source_xml.toObject(target_obj);
 12  end;
 13  /

PL/SQL procedure successfully completed.
```

Conversely, if your application is PL/SQL centric (Oracle's own Application Express is a perfect example of this), then perhaps using nested table and varray types are a better option, due to expansive ranges of set operators available on variables of these data types. See Chapter 5 of *The Object-Relational Developer's Guide* for details on the various set operations you can perform on nested table types.

Of course, you are free to mix and match. 3GL's can pass data to your PL/SQL via associative arrays, and then you could cast these arrays into more flexible object types within the PL/SQL for ongoing processing.

Why should I bother?

As you have just seen, converting row-by-row fetch calls into code that uses bulk collection requires just a few extra lines of code. So why should you bother with these extra few lines? The hardware store metaphor suggests that processing rows in bulk is all about efficiency, so let's compare the results between making many trips to the hardware store (the HARDWARE table) to pick up every item and just a single trip with a suitably large trolley (the nested table). The following code example (bulk_collect_perf_test_1.sql) compares the response time of a row-by-row code and its bulk collect equivalent:

```
SQL> declare
  2     cursor c_tool_list is
  3       select descr d1
  4       from   hardware;
  5
  6     l_descr hardware.descr%type;
  7  begin
  8     open c_tool_list;
  9     loop
 10       fetch c_tool_list into l_descr;
 11       exit when c_tool_list%notfound;
 12     end loop;
 13     close c_tool_list;
 14  end;
 15  /
```

PL/SQL procedure successfully completed.

Elapsed: 00:00:21.39

```
SQL> declare
  2     cursor c_tool_list is
  3       select descr d2
  4       from   hardware;
  5
  6     type t_descr_list is table of c_tool_list%rowtype;
  7     l_descr_list t_descr_list;
  8
  9  begin
 10     open c_tool_list;
 11     fetch c_tool_list bulk collect into l_descr_list;
 12     close c_tool_list;
 13  end;
 14  /
```

PL/SQL procedure successfully completed.

Elapsed: 00:00:02.20

It's 10 times faster, just by reducing the number of trips made to the database for data. Moreover, if the previous example is repeated with a session trace enabled, you'll get some interesting results from the resulting trace data. Now let's enable session tracing and re-run the demo:

```
SQL> alter session set sql_trace = true;
SQL> [repeat demo]
SQL> alter session set sql_trace = false;
```

Within the formatted trace file, if you search for column alias "D1", you will locate the SQL query that was subject to single row fetch calls.

```
SELECT DESCR D1
FROM   HARDWARE
```

call	count	cpu	elapsed	disk	query	current	rows
Parse	1	0.00	0.00	0	1	0	0
Execute	1	0.00	0.00	0	0	0	0
Fetch	1000001	8.17	8.15	0	1000010	0	1000000
total	1000003	8.17	8.15	0	1000011	0	1000000

And further along in the trace file, you will find the query containing the D2 alias, which was fetched from using bulk fetch:

```
SELECT DESCR D2
FROM   HARDWARE
```

call	count	cpu	elapsed	disk	query	current	rows
Parse	1	0.00	0.00	0	1	0	0
Execute	1	0.00	0.00	0	0	0	0
Fetch	1	1.85	2.08	0	9001	0	1000000
total	3	1.85	2.09	0	9002	0	1000000

Notice that along with reduction in elapsed time, there has been a marked reduction in CPU consumption as well. With bulk collect, not only are you are getting increased performance in your applications, their CPU footprint will shrink as well, which makes them more scalable.

■ **Tip** See Chapter 21 of the *Performance Tuning Manual* in the Oracle 11.2 database documentation for details on how to generate session trace files and format them with tkprof.

Returning briefly to the question of which collection type to use, all appear to be equivalent in terms of bulk collection performance. The following demo (`bulk_which_collection_type.sql`) ran virtually identically for each of the three collection types:

```
SQL> set timing on
SQL> declare
  2      type t_va is varray(1000) of number;
  3      type t_nt is table of number;
  4      type t_aa is table of number index by pls_integer;
  5
  6      va t_va;
  7      nt t_nt;
  8      aa t_aa;
  9  begin
 10      for i in 1 .. 10000 loop
```

```
11
12      select rownum
13      --
14      -- Comment in the collection type you want to test
15      --
16      bulk collect into va
17      --bulk collect into nt
18      --bulk collect into aa
19
20      from dual
21      connect by level <= 1000 ;
22    end loop;
23  end;
24  /
```

PL/SQL procedure successfully completed.

Monitoring Bulk Collect Overheads

Before you leap into converting all of your PL/SQL cursors to using bulk collect operations, it's important to be aware of one significant impact that bulk collect will have on your database session. As mentioned at the start of the chapter, array processing is about retrieving data into a *buffer*. That buffer has to be held somewhere, and that somewhere is in your session's memory. In Oracle parlance, your session's memory is the session's User Global Area (UGA). Depending on how your database has been configured, the session UGA will be held either privately for the connected session in the Process Global Area (PGA) or it will be sharable across processes in the System Global Area (SGA). A discussion on the pros and cons of Oracle's dedicated versus shared server architecture is beyond the scope of this book; just know that PL/SQL collections will consume session memory, which can easily become an important consideration if you either have large collections or large numbers of concurrent sessions in your database.

For the examples that follow, the most common configuration will be assumed, namely dedicated server connections, and thus the memory consumption focus will be on the PGA. Let's explore the memory consumption as larger and larger collection sizes are used for bulk collect. I'll also introduce the LIMIT clause, which can be used on the BULK COLLECT statement.

■ **Note** The example that follows intersperses text with code. You can find the entirety of the code in the file named bulk_collect_memory.sql.

First, I'll reconnect to reset the session level statistics (including PGA consumption).

```
SQL> connect
Enter user-name: *****
Enter password:  *****

SQL> set serverout on
SQL> declare
```

```
 2    type t_row_list is table of hardware.descr%type;
 3    l_rows t_row_list;
 4
 5    l_pga_ceiling  number(10);
 6
```

Next, I'll define an array of different fetch sizes that will be used to retrieve a set of rows from the HARDWARE table. So in the first iteration, 5 rows will be fetched, then 10 rows, then 50 rows, and so forth.

```
 7    type t_fetch_size is table of pls_integer;
 8    l_fetch_sizes t_fetch_size := t_fetch_sizes(5,10,50,100,500,1000,10000,100000,1000000);
 9
10    rc        sys_refcursor;
11  begin
12    select value
13    into   l_pga_ceiling
14    from   v$mystat m, v$statname s
15    where  s.statistic# = m.statistic#
16    and    s.name = 'session pga memory max';
17
18    dbms_output.put_line('Initial PGA: '||l_pga_ceiling);
19
20    for i in 1 .. l_fetch_sizes.count
21    loop
```

For each of the fetch sizes, I'll use the LIMIT clause to fetch a set of the rows from the table.

```
22      open rc for select descr from hardware;
23      loop
24        fetch rc bulk collect into l_rows limit l_fetch_sizes(i);
25        exit when rc%notfound;
26      end loop;
27      close rc;
28
```

Then, having performed the fetch, I'll capture the session level PGA statistics to see if the fetch has had an impact on the memory being consumed by the session on the database server. Here's the code to do that:

```
29      select value
30      into   l_pga_ceiling
31      from   v$mystat m, v$statname s
32      where  s.statistic# = m.statistic#
33      and    s.name = 'session pga memory max';
34
35      dbms_output.put_line('Fetch size: '||l_fetch_sizes(i));
36      dbms_output.put_line('- PGA Max: '||l_pga_ceiling);
37
38    end loop;
39
40  end;
41  /
Initial PGA: 3175904
```

```
Fetch size: 5
- PGA Max: 3175904
Fetch size: 10
- PGA Max: 3175904
Fetch size: 50
- PGA Max: 3241440
Fetch size: 100
- PGA Max: 3306976
Fetch size: 500
- PGA Max: 3306976
Fetch size: 1000
- PGA Max: 3372512
Fetch size: 10000
- PGA Max: 4224480
Fetch size: 100000
- PGA Max: 12482016
Fetch size: 1000000
- PGA Max: 95122912

PL/SQL procedure successfully completed.
```

Once the fetch sizes exceed 1,000 rows, the PGA consumption grows from 3MB up to 95MB when bulk collecting the entire set of 1,000,000 rows in a single fetch call. If you have hundreds of sessions all consuming hundreds of megabytes of memory, then that certainly is a scalability threat. Unless you have stock options in a memory chip company, massive bulk collect sizes are probably a bad idea. For this reason, it is recommended you never issue a FETCH BULK COLLECT on a resultset without a LIMIT clause when you do not know ahead of time the size (or approximate size) of the resultset.

Taken to extremes, a runaway collection could exhaust all of the memory on your server and possibly crash it. For example, the demo below attempts to bulk collect one billion rows into a PL/SQL collection; it hung my laptop in the process (which is why you will not find a script for this demo in the download catalog for this book!)

```
SQL> declare
  2     type t_huge_set is table of number;
  3     l_the_server_slaminator t_huge_set;
  4  begin
  5     select rownum
  6     bulk collect into l_the_server_slaminator
  7     from
  8       ( select level from dual connect by level <= 1000 ),
  9       ( select level from dual connect by level <= 1000 ),
 10       ( select level from dual connect by level <= 1000 );
 11  end;
 12  /

ERROR at line 1:
ORA-04030: out of process memory when trying to allocate 16396 bytes
```

■ **Tip** You may be thinking that the database initialization parameter `pga_aggregate_target` will insulate your system from such problems. This is not correct. This parameter only applies to memory allocations that the database can adjust internally as required, such as memory for sorting or hashing. If you ask for 100GB of PGA for PL/SQL collection memory, the database will try to honor that request, no matter how much trouble that may cause.

So on the surface, it would appear a compromise between performance and the memory consumption is required when using bulk operations. Let's explore that issue by taking advantage of the automatic bulk collect optimization with implicit cursor loops, when `plsql_optimize_level` is set to 2 or higher (which is the default from 10g onwards anyway). I'll reconnect to reset the session level statistics, and then fetch all 1,000,000 rows from the HARDWARE table, which is equivalent to the last iteration of the previous example that consumed 95 megabytes of PGA. The following example (`bulk_collect_perf_test_2.sql`) demonstrates the fetch of 1,000,000 rows using the automatic bulk collect optimization:

```
SQL> connect
Enter user-name: *****
Enter password:  *****
SQL> alter session set plsql_optimize_level = 2;

Session altered.

SQL> begin
  2     for i in (
  3        select descr d3
  4        from   hardware )
  5     loop
  6        null;
  7     end loop;
  8  end;
  9  /

PL/SQL procedure successfully completed.

Elapsed: 00:00:01.78
```

Notice that performance is just as good as when the full bulk collect example. By examining a session trace, it's possible to determine what the bulk collect fetch size is for automatic bulk collect. The following is the trace output from the previous PL/SQL block:

```
SELECT DESCR D3
FROM   HARDWARE
```

call	count	cpu	elapsed	disk	query	current	rows
Parse	1	0.00	0.00	0	1	0	0
Execute	1	0.00	0.00	0	0	0	0

```
Fetch     10001     1.03       1.13          0       18907          0     1000000
-------   ------   --------   ----------   ----------   ----------   ----------   ----------
total     10003     1.03       1.14          0       18908          0     1000000
```

1,000,000 rows fetched via 10,001 fetch calls suggests a fetch size of 100 rows. Although 10,000 fetch calls have been issued instead of 1, the performance is about the same. There are diminishing returns once your fetch array sizes get above the number of rows in a database block, so it's common for a fetch size of around 100 to be the sweet spot. Rather than carefully benchmarking every piece of code to determine the optimal bulk collect size, simply refactoring cursor loops just to take advantage of the automatic bulk collect optimization in the compiler is going to be close to optimal anyway

Refactoring Code to Use Bulk Collect

So far, converting your code to use bulk collect almost sounds too good to be true. Very simple code changes (or even none, if you are already using implicit fetch cursor loops) lead to tremendous performance improvements. However, there are a few pitfalls you need to guard against when refactoring your code

No Exception Raised

A conventional implicit cursor will raise the no_data_found exception if there are no rows in the resultset, and your application may depend upon this to take reparative actions. In the following example (bulk_ndf_1.sql), no_data_found is used to indicate that the query predicates are not valid:

```
SQL> set serverout on
SQL> declare
  2      l_descr hardware.descr%type;
  3  begin
  4      select descr
  5      into    l_descr
  6      from    hardware
  7      where   aisle = 0
  8      and     item = 0;
  9      dbms_output.put_line('Item was found');
 10  exception
 11      when no_data_found then
 12          dbms_output.put_line('Invalid item specified');
 13  end;
 14  /
Invalid item specified

PL/SQL procedure successfully completed.
```

However, when this example is converted to use bulk collect (without appropriate care), a bug is introduced into the code. Execute the following version (bulk_ndf_2.sql) and check the results on your own system:

```
SQL> set serverout on
SQL> declare
  2      type t_descr_list is table of hardware.descr%type;
  3      l_descr_list t_descr_list;
```

```
 4  begin
 5    select descr
 6    bulk collect
 7    into   l_descr_list
 8    from   hardware
 9    where  aisle = 0
10    and    item = 0;
11    dbms_output.put_line('Item was found');
12  exception
13    when no_data_found then
14      dbms_output.put_line('Invalid item specified');
15  end;
16  /
Item was found   <==== wrong !
```

PL/SQL procedure successfully completed.

The procedure runs successfully but returns the wrong result! This is because a bulk collect fetch call will *not* raise the no_data_found exception. You can interpret that lack of an exception as PL/SQL saying that it has successfully populated the target array with all of the available rows (in this case, none). The target array is indeed initialized even though it contains no data. This end result is subtly different to the target array not being initialized at all

The following example (`bulk_ndf_3.sql`) shows there is an important difference between a bulk collect returning no rows into a collection versus a collection not being used within a bulk collect call at all:

```
SQL> set serverout on
SQL> declare
  2    type t_descr_list is table of hardware.descr%type;
  3    l_descr_list t_descr_list;
  4  begin
  5    select descr
  6    bulk collect
  7    into   l_descr_list
  8    from   hardware
  9    where  aisle = 0
 10    and    item = 0;
 11    dbms_output.put_line(l_descr_list.count||' rows found');
 12  end;
 13  /
0 rows found
```

PL/SQL procedure successfully completed.

Comment out the SELECT statement and execute the same code again. The bulk collect never runs. Thus, the target array is never initialized. That lack of initialization leads to an error. For example, `bulk_ndf_4.sql` now crashes when attempting to reference the content of the collection.

```
SQL> declare
  2    type t_descr_list is table of hardware.descr%type;
  3    l_descr_list t_descr_list;
  4  begin
  5  --  select descr
```

```
 6  --   bulk collect
 7  --   into   l_descr_list
 8  --   from   hardware
 9  --   where  aisle = 0
10  --   and    item = 0;
11       dbms_output.put_line(l_descr_list.count||' rows found');
12  end;
13  /
declare
*
ERROR at line 1:
ORA-06531: Reference to uninitialized collection
ORA-06512: at line 11
```

Knowing that bulk collect operations initialize target arrays even when no rows are returned allows you to refactor existing code without too much difficulty. Simply check the number of records in the array and explicitly raise the no_data_found exception to keep the rest of the code working as previously. For example, the following code (bulk_ndf_5.sql) adds a conditional check to raise no_data_found when the collection is empty:

```
SQL> set serverout on
SQL> declare
 2     type t_descr_list is table of hardware.descr%type;
 3     l_descr_list t_descr_list;
 4  begin
 5     select descr
 6     bulk collect
 7     into   l_descr_list
 8     from   hardware
 9     where  aisle = 0
10     and    item = 0;
11
12     if l_descr_list.count = 0 then
13        raise no_data_found;
14     end if;
15
16     dbms_output.put_line('Item was found');
17  exception
18     when no_data_found then
19        dbms_output.put_line('Invalid item specified');
20  end;
21  /
Invalid item specified

PL/SQL procedure successfully completed.
```

Exiting a Loop

When fetching within a cursor loop with the conventional row-at-a-time mechanism, it is implicit when there are no more rows left in the result set. You issue a fetch call; if it fails, you're done. Things are slightly more complicated than that when you fetch in bulk—a fetch call may retrieve sufficient rows to fill the array, or it may retrieve no rows, or it may receive some rows but not enough to completely fill the array. This leads to a common program mistake when using the LIMIT clause.

First, here again is the row-at-a-time code (bulk_limit_exit_1.sql) as presented earlier in the chapter:

```
SQL> set serverout on
SQL> declare
  2    cursor c_tool_list is
  3      select descr
  4      from   hardware
  5      where  aisle = 1
  6      and    item between 1 and 25;
  7
  8    l_descr hardware.descr%type;
  9  begin
 10    open c_tool_list;
 11    loop
 12      fetch c_tool_list into l_descr;
 13      exit when c_tool_list%notfound;
 14      dbms_output.put_line('Fetched '||l_descr);
 15    end loop;
 16    close c_tool_list;
 17  end;
 18  /
Fetched Description 1
Fetched Description 2
Fetched Description 3
[snip]
Fetched Description 23
Fetched Description 24
Fetched Description 25

PL/SQL procedure successfully completed.
```

Note that 25 rows were fetched and displayed on the screen. Now the code is converted to bulk collect with the LIMIT clause in what appears to be the intuitive way, but as it turns out, the wrong way. Here is the incorrect solution (bulk_limit_exit_2.sql) and its output:

```
SQL> set serverout on
SQL> declare
  2    cursor c_tool_list is
  3      select descr
  4      from   hardware
  5      where  aisle = 1
  6      and    item between 1 and 25;
  7
  8    type t_descr_list is table of c_tool_list%rowtype;
  9    l_descr_list t_descr_list;
 10
 11  begin
 12    open c_tool_list;
 13    loop
 14      fetch c_tool_list
```

```
15        bulk collect into l_descr_list limit 10;
16        exit when c_tool_list%notfound;
17
18        for i in 1 .. l_descr_list.count loop
19          dbms_output.put_line('Fetched '||l_descr_list(i).descr);
20        end loop;
21      end loop;
22
23      close c_tool_list;
24    end;
25    /
Fetched Description 1
Fetched Description 2
Fetched Description 3
[snip]
Fetched Description 18
Fetched Description 19
Fetched Description 20

PL/SQL procedure successfully completed.
```

Notice that the cursor loop has been exited prematurely: 25 rows (exactly like the row-at-a-time example) should have been output, but the code stopped after 20. The problem lies with line 16: exit when c_tool_list%notfound. 10 rows per fetch call are being requested with the LIMIT clause. On the third pass through the loop, there are only 5 rows left to be fetched. Because all of the rows are now fetched, the %NOTFOUND attribute becomes true and the loop exits *without* processing those remaining 5 rows in the array.

The solution is simple, either defer the checking of the cursor attribute until after processing any rows found in the fetch array or change the exit condition to be <array>.count = 0 (which would also mean one extra iteration through the fetch loop).

The following is an example of the first solution in which the code defers checking of the cursor attribute until *after* processing any rows in the array (bulk_limit_exit_3.sql):

```
SQL> set serverout on
SQL> declare
  2    cursor c_tool_list is
  3      select descr
  4      from   hardware
  5      where  aisle = 1
  6      and    item between 1 and 25;
  7
  8    type t_descr_list is table of c_tool_list%rowtype;
  9    l_descr_list t_descr_list;
 10
 11  begin
 12    open c_tool_list;
 13    loop
 14      fetch c_tool_list
 15      bulk collect into l_descr_list limit 10;
 16
```

Note that because it is possible that there are no rows fetched, you cannot make any assumptions that there are rows in the array. All processing must be mindful of that fact and must honor the value from the array's count attribute, or you may get errors due to illegal references to array indexes. In the following code, the use of `l_descr_list.count` ensures that the loop will not even be entered if there are no entries in the array:

```
17      for i in 1 .. l_descr_list.count loop
18        dbms_output.put_line('Fetched '||l_descr_list(i).descr);
19      end loop;
20      exit when c_tool_list%notfound;
21    end loop;
22
23    close c_tool_list;
24  end;
25  /
Fetched Description 1
Fetched Description 2
Fetched Description 3
[snip]
Fetched Description 23
Fetched Description 24
Fetched Description 25

PL/SQL procedure successfully completed.
```

Over Bulking

It's rare but sometimes bulking up is *not* the appropriate way to retrieve way data from the database. Returning to the hardware store metaphor, consider the case where I drive down the store with only a few dollars in my pocket. I'll only be able to buy things until I run out of cash which, with only a few dollars, will not be much. Let's say I blindly follow the advice of always getting a trolley (a.k.a. bulk collect) to hold my items until I get to the cash register. What will be the result ?

- It will take time to initially get a shopping trolley from the front of the store.

- My trolley gets loaded with just a couple of items and then I have to stop—I've gone over my spending limit.

- I pay for my items.

- It takes more time to unload the items from the trolley into a bag, and then return the trolley back to the front of the store.

It is the same in database terms. If you know in advance that there may be some circumstance where you are not going to process an entire array of fetched rows, then going to the effort of trying to fetch them might actually hurt your performance rather than improve it. A very common cause of this is when processing a resultset that may need to prematurely exit. Consider the following example (`bulk_early_exit_1.sql`). First, I define a cursor to fetch some rows from the HARDWARE table, like so:

```
SQL> set timing on
SQL> declare
  2     cursor c_might_exit_early is
  3        select aisle, item
  4        from   hardware
  5        where  item between 400000 and 400050
  6           or  descr like '%10000%';
  7     begin
```

With the data in the HARDWARE table, this cursor will return 72 rows. The implicit fetch construct has been used in order to automatically get the bulk collect fetch size of 100 rows. However, the cursor is called c_might_exit_early for a reason.

```
  8     for i in c_might_exit_early
  9     loop
 10        if c_might_exit_early%rowcount = 40 then
 11           exit;
 12        end if;
```

Once 40 rows have been fetched, the cursor loop will be exited. Of course, a `rownum <= 40` predicate could have been added to the SQL defining the cursor, but in a real world scenario, the condition is likely to be more complicated. For example, with each row being fetched, it could be passed to a web service that may return a flag indicating that no more rows should be sent to it. The key thing here is that there is a likelihood that the cursor loop may be prematurely exited with a condition that can't be easily folded back into the cursor SQL statement.

```
 13     end loop;
 14  end;
 15  /
```

PL/SQL procedure successfully completed.

Elapsed: 00:00:00.38

The routine ran reasonably quickly, but 0.38 seconds seems sluggish for only 40 rows, and this is due to the automatic bulk collect. The code actually did the work of retrieving all of the 72 rows, because the first fetch call tried to retrieve 100 rows. The PL/SQL compiler did not know that the cursor processing may end prematurely. A session trace confirms that all 72 rows were retrieved.

```
SELECT AISLE, ITEM
FROM
 HARDWARE WHERE ITEM BETWEEN 400000 AND 400050 OR DESCR LIKE '%10000%'
```

call	count	cpu	elapsed	disk	query	current	rows
Parse	1	0.00	0.00	0	0	0	0
Execute	1	0.00	0.00	0	0	0	0
Fetch	1	0.17	0.17	0	10100	0	72
total	3	0.17	0.17	0	10100	0	72

It is the responsibility of the developer to recognize these types of situations and code accordingly; the PL/SQL compiler is not a mind reader. In the previous example, it turns out to be more efficient to not use bulk collect at all. For example (bulk_early_exit_2.sql) is the same routine coded in a more traditional row-by-row method.

```
SQL> set timing on
SQL> declare
  2     cursor c_might_exit_early is
  3       select aisle, item
  4       from   hardware
  5       where  item between 400000 and 400050
  6         or    descr like '%10000%';
  7     l_row c_might_exit_early%rowtype;
  8  begin
  9     open c_might_exit_early;
 10     loop
 11       fetch c_might_exit_early
 12       into l_row;
 13       exit when c_might_exit_early%notfound;
 14
 15       if c_might_exit_early%rowcount = 40 then
 16           exit;
 17       end if;
 18
 19     end loop;
 20     close c_might_exit_early;
 21  end;
 22  /
```

PL/SQL procedure successfully completed.

Elapsed: 00:00:00.17

Even with the overhead of 40 individual fetch calls, the performance is twice as good. The reason for this is that the SQL in this example has been crafted so that the last few rows are hard to find; that is, they are likely to be near the high water mark of the table. So while this is a slightly artificial example, it does demonstrate that you can't just assume the bulk collect will always yield benefits. For this particular example, savvy developers will realize that with some extra coding, you can have the best of both worlds by explicitly nominating the fetch size rather than leaving it to the PL/SQL compiler.

The following example comes from bulk_early_exit_3.sql; it explicitly nominates a fetch size as a compromise between row-by-row fetches and the automatic bulk collect fetch size of 100:

```
SQL> set timing on
SQL> declare
  2     cursor c_might_exit_early is
  3       select aisle, item
  4       from   hardware
  5       where  item between 400000 and 400050
  6         or    descr like '%10000%';
  7     type t_rows is table of c_might_exit_early%rowtype;
  8     l_rows t_rows;
  9
 10     l_row_cnt pls_integer := 0;
```

```
11
12  begin
13    open c_might_exit_early;
14    <<cursor_loop>>
15    loop
16      fetch c_might_exit_early
```

Obviously, for this demo, it's known that processing will stop after 40 rows, and thus a fetch size of 40 would be optimal. However, I've chosen a fetch size of 20 to reflect a real-world scenario where it's not known precisely when the processing would prematurely terminate, so a developer would opt for a compromise between getting good value from each fetch call and not fetching an excessive amount of rows that may not ultimately be required.

```
17        bulk collect into l_rows limit 20;
18
19        for i in 1 .. l_rows.count
20        loop
21          l_row_cnt := l_row_cnt + 1;
22          if l_row_cnt = 40 then
23            exit cursor_loop;
24          end if;
25        end loop;
26
27        exit when c_might_exit_early%notfound;
28      end loop;
29      close c_might_exit_early;
30    end;
31  /
```

PL/SQL procedure successfully completed.

Elapsed: 00:00:00.09

For this example, the turnaround time has been reduced from 0.38 seconds down to 0.09 seconds just by applying some of my own intelligence into the code rather than relying on the PL/SQL compiler's.

Bulk Binding

Fetching data in bulk using BULK COLLECT completes half the picture of optimizing the interaction between PL/SQL and the database. The other half is the ability to *manipulate* data dispatched from PL/SQL to database tables as efficiently as possible. Every time a PL/SQL program needs to insert, update, or delete data within the database, in most circumstances, it's best to achieve that in a single trip to the database. For some application requirements (for example, update attributes for a known primary key), the modification will be for a single row. However, when the requirement is to touch multiple rows in the database, PL/SQL can still perform that job in a single trip. This is known as "bulk binding," and just like bulk collect, is all about moving from a metaphor of row processing to set processing (via a PL/SQL collection).

■ **Note**   My wife generously offered to extend the metaphor by observing: "Is bulk bind the part of the chapter where you take all the junk you didn't need and should not have bought back to the hardware store?" If that helps your understanding of bulk bind, then so be it.

It's a common misconception that if the application requirement is modification of a single row, then bulk binding must not be appropriate. However, part of the art of writing efficient PL/SQL is the ability to recognize when what appears to be single-row process is perhaps not. For example, consider a web page that displays a tabular list of the employees, where each employee's details can be updated by the operator. While it's true that from the operator's viewpoint, each employee is being updated in isolation from all of the others, this is not a justification to map this a series of single row update SQL statements, called either directly or within a PL/SQL block.

The set of altered records can be stored in an array and passed down to a PL/SQL program in a single call and the appropriate bulk binding performed. Always be on the lookout for parts of your application that might benefit from such an approach.

Getting Started with Bulk Bind

Like bulk collect, converting existing conventional DML code into its bulk bind DML equivalent is easy and straightforward. In conventional DML, it's common to have a variable populated with values, and that variable is used within a DML statement. The following example (`bulk_bind_1.sql`) demonstrates a simple insert with PL/SQL variables repeated 100 times with a FOR loop:

```
SQL> declare
  2     l_row hardware%rowtype;
  3  begin
  4     for i in 1 .. 100 loop
  5        l_row.aisle := 1;
  6        l_row.item  := i;
  7        insert into hardware values l_row;
  8     end loop;
  9  end;
 10  /

PL/SQL procedure successfully completed.
```

In bulk bind DML, there is still a variable populated with values, but the variable is now an array, and DML is deferred until the array is filled with the values that will be used for the bulk binding. The FORALL keyword indicates that this is a bulk bind DML. For example (`bulk_bind_2.sql`) is equivalent to the row-at-a-time insert example above, but inserts 100 rows with a single call rather than 100:

```
SQL> declare
  2     type t_row_list is table of hardware%rowtype;
  3     l_row t_row_list := t_row_list();
  4  begin
  5     for i in 1 .. 100 loop
  6        l_row.extend;
  7        l_row(i).aisle := 1;
```

```
 8        l_row(i).item  := i;
 9     end loop;
10
11     forall i in 1 .. 100
12        insert into hardware values l_row(i);
13   end;
14   /

PL/SQL procedure successfully completed.
```

▓ **Note** Although FORALL seems to suggest some sort of loop processing, it is a single call to the database to perform the DML. This is easily confirmed with a session level trace.

```
INSERT INTO HARDWARE
VALUES  (:B1 ,:B2 ,:B3 ,:B4 )
```

call	count	cpu	elapsed	disk	query	current	rows
Parse	1	0.00	0.00	0	0	0	0
Execute	1	0.00	0.00	0	1	6	100
Fetch	0	0.00	0.00	0	0	0	0
total	2	0.00	0.00	0	1	6	100

Measuring Bulk Binding Performance

As with bulk collect, the motivation for bulk binding is performance, which can be quantified with simple benchmarks. I will start with a simple PL/SQL program that inserts a large number of rows into a table via single row inserts. The following example (bulk_insert_conventional.sql) adds 100,000 rows to the HARDWARE table, one row at a time:

```
SQL> set timing on
SQL> declare
  2    l_now date := sysdate;
  3  begin
  4   for i in 1 .. 100000 loop
  5     insert into HARDWARE
  6     values (i/1000, i, to_char(i), l_now);
  7   end loop;
  8  end;
  9  /

PL/SQL procedure successfully completed.

Elapsed: 00:00:04.52
```

145

Before moving into the bulk binding version, it's worth nothing that Oracle insertion performance, even single row at a time, is exceptional. But the database can do better. Let's move on to the bulk binding version (`bulk_insert_bind.sql`) and insert those 100,000 rows with a single call.

```
SQL> set timing on
SQL> declare
  2     l_now date := sysdate;
  3
```

A nested table type is defined to hold the array of records to be inserted.

```
  4     type t_rows is table of hardware%rowtype;
  5
  6     l_rows t_rows := t_rows();
  7   begin
```

And now instead of inserting the rows directly, the array is filled with the row values to be used.

```
  8     l_rows.extend(100000);
  9     for i in 1 .. 100000 loop
 10       l_rows(i).aisle := i/1000;
 11       l_rows(i).item := i;
 12       l_rows(i).descr := to_char(i);
 13       l_rows(i).stocked := l_now;
 14     end loop;
```

Finally, the FORALL syntax is used to load the records into the database in a single call.

```
 15
 16     forall i in 1 .. 100000
 17       insert into hardware values l_rows(i);
 18
 19   end;
 20   /

PL/SQL procedure successfully completed.

Elapsed: 00:00:00.31
```

From 4.52 seconds down to just 0.31 seconds! Just like bulk collect, migrating your code to a bulk bind approach for modifying sets of data gives dramatic performance improvements. But there are other not-so-obvious benefits occurring here as well. Every time you commence a new DML statement, undo structures must be allocated by the database to ensure that the DML statement can be rolled back if required, either due to error or explicit request. Using bulk binding issues less DML calls, which means less stress on your undo infrastructure. The following example (`bulk_bind_undo.sql`) examines the session level statistics to compare the undo required when using a row-by-row insert versus a bulk bind on insert:

```
SQL> set serverout on
SQL> declare
  2     type t_row_list is table of hardware.descr%type
  3         index by pls_integer;
  4     l_rows t_row_list;
  5
  6     l_stat1 int;
```

```
 7    l_stat2 int;
 8    l_stat3 int;
 9
10  begin
11    select value
12    into    l_stat1
13    from    v$mystat m, v$statname s
14    where   s.statistic# = m.statistic#
15    and     s.name = 'undo change vector size';
16
17    for i in 1 .. 1000 loop
18       l_rows(i) := rpad('x',50);
19       insert into hardware ( descr )  values ( l_rows(i) );
20    end loop;
21
22    select value
23    into    l_stat2
24    from    v$mystat m, v$statname s
25    where   s.statistic# = m.statistic#
26    and     s.name = 'undo change vector size';
27
28    forall i in 1 .. l_rows.count
29       insert into hardware ( descr )  values ( l_rows(i) );
30
31    select value
32    into    l_stat3
33    from    v$mystat m, v$statname s
34    where   s.statistic# = m.statistic#
35    and     s.name = 'undo change vector size';
36
37    dbms_output.put_line('Row at a time: '||(l_stat2-l_stat1));
38    dbms_output.put_line('Bulk bind:     '||(l_stat3-l_stat2));
39
40  end;
41  /
Row at a time: 64556
Bulk bind:     3296

PL/SQL procedure successfully completed.
```

So bulk bind gives a lot less undo. Similarly, those undo structures need to be protected by redo log entries so that the database instance is recoverable. If the previous example is repeated, but instead collects the redo size statistic instead of the undo change vector size (bulk_bind_redo.sql) then the output also shows a reduction in redo.

```
Row at a time: 295448
Bulk bind:     69552

PL/SQL procedure successfully completed.
```

■ **Tip**   When producing examples for benchmarking, you need to ensure that you are isolating your code to purely examine the test at hand. When I was first performing the benchmark above, I explicitly referenced sysdate for each of the 100,000 rows being processed, namely:

```
for i in 1 .. 100000 loop
  insert into DEMO values (i, sysdate, to_char(i));
end loop;

for i in 1 .. 100000 loop
  l_rows(i).x := i;
  l_rows(i).y := sysdate;
  l_rows(i).z := to_char(i);
```

■ **Note**   Both tests ran very slowly, and the bulk binding results did not outperform the single row test by the order magnitude I had expected. Some more careful experimenting showed that it was in fact the 100,000 calls to sysdate that was the dominant factor in the test. In fact, had I performed the test on earlier versions of Oracle, where references to the 'sysdate' would silently issue a 'select sysdate from dual', then the tests would suggest bulk binding was of no benefit at all. Always examine your tests carefully before concluding what the results might mean.

Monitoring Memory Usage

Just like bulk collect, if you have a large number of rows that you need to bulk bind, this does not necessarily mean that you should be pre-storing all of them in array before passing them to the database. There are diminishing returns on performance as the number of rows you bind goes up, at the ever increasing cost of PGA memory. You can bulk bind in batches to ensure that you do not exhaust session memory. Here is an example (`bulk_bind_pga.sql`) similar to that of the bulk collect memory demo demonstrating the PGA consumption with increasing bulk bind sizes:

```
SQL> set serverout on
SQL> declare
  2     type t_row_list is table of hardware.descr%type;
  3     l_rows t_row_list;
  4
  5     l_start_of_run timestamp;
  6
  7     l_pga_ceiling  number(10);
  8
  9     type t_bulk_sizes is table of pls_integer;
```

```
10    l_bulk_sizes t_bulk_sizes := t_bulk_sizes(10,100,1000,10000,100000,1000000);
11
12    tot_rows pls_integer := 10000000;
13
14  begin
15    select value
16    into   l_pga_ceiling
17    from   v$mystat m, v$statname s
18    where  s.statistic# = m.statistic#
19    and    s.name = 'session pga memory max';
20
21    dbms_output.put_line('Initial PGA: '||l_pga_ceiling);
22
23    for i in 1 .. l_bulk_sizes.count
24    loop
25
26      execute immediate 'truncate table hardware';
27
28      l_start_of_run := systimestamp;
29
30      l_rows := t_row_list();
31      l_rows.extend(l_bulk_sizes(i));
32      for j in 1 .. l_bulk_sizes(i)
33      loop
34        l_rows(j) := rpad('x',50);
35      end loop;
36
37      for iter in 1 .. tot_rows / l_bulk_sizes(i) loop
38        forall j in 1 .. l_bulk_sizes(i)
39          insert into hardware ( descr )  values (l_rows(j));
40      end loop;
41
42      select value
43      into   l_pga_ceiling
44      from   v$mystat m, v$statname s
45      where  s.statistic# = m.statistic#
46      and    s.name = 'session pga memory max';
47
48      dbms_output.put_line('Bulk size: '||l_bulk_sizes(i));
49      dbms_output.put_line('- Elapsed: '||( systimestamp - l_start_of_run));
50      dbms_output.put_line('- PGA Max: '||l_pga_ceiling);
51
52    end loop;
53
54  end;
55  /
Initial PGA: 3470120
Bulk size: 10
- Elapsed: +000000000 00:00:53.478000000
- PGA Max: 4042888
Bulk size: 100
- Elapsed: +000000000 00:00:14.760000000
```

149

```
- PGA Max: 4042888
Bulk size: 1000
- Elapsed: +000000000 00:00:10.588000000
- PGA Max: 4042888
Bulk size: 10000
- Elapsed: +000000000 00:00:11.872000000
- PGA Max: 4108424
Bulk size: 100000
- Elapsed: +000000000 00:00:16.431000000
- PGA Max: 12890248
Bulk size: 1000000
- Elapsed: +000000000 00:00:17.507000000
- PGA Max: 99266696

PL/SQL procedure successfully completed.
```

Similar to bulk collect, once you are binding above 1,000 rows per array, the benefits are negligible and the increase in memory consumption will certainly become a scalability threat if your application consists of hundreds or thousands of sessions all consuming large amounts of memory on the server. In this example, performance actually got worse as the bulk bind sizes got larger than 1,000.

Improvements in 11g

The sample code in this chapter has been written assuming version 11 of the database. If you are running the bulk bind samples on an earlier version, then you may see an error like this:

```
SQL> create table DEMO ( x int, y int);

Table created.

SQL> declare
  2     type t_rows is
  3        table of demo%rowtype
  4        index by pls_integer;
  5     l_rows t_rows;
  6  begin
  7     l_rows(1).x := 1;
  8     l_rows(1).y := 1;
  9
 10     l_rows(2).x := 2;
 11     l_rows(2).y := 2;
 12
 13     forall i in 1 .. l_rows.count
 14        insert into DEMO
 15        values ( l_rows(i).x, l_rows(i).y );
 16  end;
 17  /
```

PL/SQL procedure successfully completed.

```
 values ( l_rows(i).x, l_rows(i).y );
                *
ERROR at line 15:
PLS-00436: implementation restriction: cannot reference
               fields of BULK In-BIND table of records
```

In versions of Oracle prior to 11g, bulk bind operations were not able to access the individual elements of a record or object type within an associative array. However, all is not lost—it just takes a little more coding. You can still bulk bind arrays of simple datatypes, thus you can use an associative array for *each* attribute that you need to bulk bind. The previous example can be recast into a version that will work on earlier versions of Oracle.

```
SQL>  declare
  2      type t_x_list is table of demo.x%type
  3         index by pls_integer;
  4
  5      type t_y_list is table of demo.y%type
  6         index by pls_integer;
  7
  8      l_x_rows t_x_list;
  9      l_y_rows t_y_list;
 10   begin
 11      l_x_rows(1) := 1;
 12      l_x_rows(2) := 2;
 13
 14      l_y_rows(1) := 1;
 15      l_y_rows(2) := 2;
 16
 17      forall i in 1 .. l_x_rows.count
 18         insert into DEMO
 19         values ( l_x_rows(i), l_y_rows(i) );
 20   end;
 21   /
```

PL/SQL procedure successfully completed.

■ **Tip**   For other techniques to avoid this restriction on earlier versions of Oracle, see www.oracle-developer.net/display.php?id=410

Error Handling with Bulk Bind

There are large benefits to had from bulk binding. But one area where extra care is required is in error handling. In a development model where rows are modified on a row-at-a-time basis, when a SQL statement fails with an error, the erroneous row in question is implicit—it's the row you are working with. For example, in the following simple PL/SQL block (bulk_error_1.sql) with two insert statements, it is obvious which insert statement is the problem one:

```
SQL> alter table hardware
  2    add constraint
  3    hardware_chk check ( item > 0 );

Table altered.

SQL> begin
  2    insert into hardware ( item ) values (1);
  3    insert into hardware ( item ) values (-1);
  4    insert into hardware ( item ) values (2);
  5    insert into hardware ( item ) values (3);
  6    insert into hardware ( item ) values (4);
  7    insert into hardware ( item ) values (-2);
  8  end;
  9  /
begin
*
ERROR at line 1:
ORA-02290: check constraint (MCDONAC.HARDWARE_CHK) violated
ORA-06512: at line 3
```

When you make the transition to modifying rows in bulk, things get a little more complicated, so more care is needed. A single FORALL statement might be canvassing hundreds rows. When the previous example is repeated in bulk mode (bulk_error_2.sql), it's not immediately obvious where row caused the error.

```
SQL> declare
  2    type t_list is table of hardware.item%type;
  3    l_rows t_list := t_list(1,-1,2,3,4,-2);
  4  begin
  5    forall i in 1 .. l_rows.count
  6      insert into hardware ( item ) values (l_rows(i));
  7  end;
  8  /
declare
*
ERROR at line 1:
ORA-02290: check constraint (MCDONAC.HARDWARE_CHK) violated
ORA-06512: at line 5
```

As per normal statement level operations, the default is for the entire bulk bind operation, so even though one of the rows in the array was valid, there will be no rows present in the target table.

```
SQL> select count(*) from HARDWARE;

no rows selected.
```

Note that rollback of changes is not a property of the bulk bind per se; it's a standard part of the PL/SQL transactional management. A common misconception with PL/SQL is that it is just a wrapper around a series of independent SQL statements. Thus, in the first example where the second insert statement failed

```
begin
  insert into DEMO values (1);
  insert into DEMO values (-1);
end;
```

developers then feel the need to take reparative action to undo the first insert. It is common to see exception handling code like the following in PL/SQL modules:

```
begin
  insert into DEMO values (1);
  insert into DEMO values (-1);
exception
  when others then
    rollback;
    raise;
end;
```

There is no requirement to perform such a rollback. Moreover, such a rollback will typically result in data corruption within your application. PL/SQL blocks implicitly create a savepoint into the code. Thus, independent of where an error occurs in a PL/SQL block, all changes in the block are automatically rolled back to a point as if the PL/SQL routine was never called. This behavior is one of the truly great features in PL/SQL. Very few other languages make transaction management so easy.

Now returning to the bulk bind example, simple code inspection shows that the second array entry with a value of -1 is the problem row. However, this is because the example is so trivial. There is no information from the actual error message that reveals which array entry was the cause—just that one or more of the entries have violated the constraint. In Oracle 9, this was addressed by extending the bulk bind syntax to add the SAVE EXCEPTIONS clause. The error still occurs, but additional information to allow diagnosis of which array entries are in error. Let's amend the example as follows (bulk_error_3.sql) to demonstrate how to use SAVE EXCEPTIONS:

```
SQL> declare
  2    type t_list is table of hardware.item%type;
  3    l_rows t_list := t_list(1,-1,2,3,4,-2);
  4  begin
  5    forall i in 1 .. l_rows.count save exceptions
  6      insert into hardware ( item ) values (l_rows(i));
  7  end;
  8  /
ERROR:
ORA-24381: error(s) in array DML
ORA-06512: at line 5
```

At first glance, it appears not much has been achieved, but this example demonstrates that a new exception is raised (ORA-24381) rather than the previous constraint violation (ORA-02290). By handling this particular bulk bind exception, I gain access to a number of special attributes that allow drilling down into the errors. For example, the following code (bulk_error_4.sql) introduces more code into the exception handler to reveal the true cause of the error:

```
SQL> set serverout on
SQL> declare
  2    type t_list is table of hardware.item%type;
  3    l_rows t_list := t_list(1,-1,2,3,4,-2);
  4
```

```
 5    bulk_bind_error exception;
 6    pragma exception_init(bulk_bind_error,-24381);
 7
 8  begin
 9    forall i in 1 .. l_rows.count save exceptions
10      insert into hardware ( item ) values (l_rows(i));
11
12  exception
13    when bulk_bind_error then
14      dbms_output.put_line(
15        'There were '||sql%bulk_exceptions.count||' errors in total');
16      for i in 1 .. sql%bulk_exceptions.count loop
17        dbms_output.put_line(
18          'Error '||i||' occurred at array index:'||
19          sql%bulk_exceptions(i).error_index);
20        dbms_output.put_line('- error code:'||
21          sql%bulk_exceptions(i).error_code);
22        dbms_output.put_line('- error text:'||
23          sqlerrm(-sql%bulk_exceptions(i).error_code));
24      end loop;
25
26  end;
27  /
There were 2 errors in total
Error 1 occurred at array index:2
- error code:2290
- error text:ORA-02290: check constraint (.) violated
Error 2 occurred at array index:6
- error code:2290
- error text:ORA-02290: check constraint (.) violated

PL/SQL procedure successfully completed.
```

When the SAVE EXCEPTIONS syntax is used within a FORALL, any errors become available within a new collection named SQL%BULK_EXCEPTIONS that contains a row for each error. Each row in that new collection contains the following:

- error_index: The index from the collection used in the FORALL

- error_code: The oracle error code; note that the error code is positive (unlike the SQLCODE built-in function in PL/SQL).

■ **Tip** Take care with older versions of the Oracle documentation. Some code examples position the SQL%BULK_EXCEPTIONS inline within the code, directly under the FORALL statement, thus suggesting that an exception will not be raised. As seen from the previous demo, you must code the references to SQL%BULK_EXCEPTIONS collection within your exception handler code section.

Also, since the SQL%BULK_EXCEPTIONS attribute is a collection, multiple errors can be caught and handled. In the previous example, because the exception handler did not re-raise the error back to the calling environment, the successfully inserted rows are still retained within the table.

```
SQL> select item from HARDWARE;

         X
----------
         1
         2
         3
         4
```

SAVE EXCEPTIONS with Batches

As described earlier, when bulk binding a large number of rows, you will be processing the rows in smaller size chunks to avoid consuming excessive session PGA memory. But if you are bulk binding in batches, then each FORALL call will re-initialize the SQL%BULK_EXCEPTIONS structure. So, in this circumstance, the structure can't be used to house the entire set of rejected rows during a series of bulk bind calls. One possible workaround is to catch any errors out of each bulk bind call, save them to a table, then process the next batch of 1,000 rows. An example (bulk_error_5.sql) of this approach is presented below:

```
SQL> create table ERRS
  2    ( error_index   number(6),
  3      error_code    number(6),
  4      item          number );

Table created.

SQL> set serverout on
SQL> declare
  2      type t_list is table of hardware.item%type;
  3      l_rows t_list := t_list(1,-1,2,3,4,-2);
  4
  5      bulk_bind_error exception;
  6      pragma exception_init(bulk_bind_error,-24381);
  7
  8      type t_err_list is table of ERRS%rowtype index by pls_integer;
  9      l_err_list t_err_list;
 10
 11  begin
 12      forall i in 1 .. l_rows.count save exceptions
 13          insert into hardware ( item ) values (l_rows(i));
 14
 15  exception
 16      when bulk_bind_error then
```

If there are rows in error, then a new structure (l_err_list) is populated with all of the information from the sql%bulk_exceptions collection.

```
17        for i in 1 .. sql%bulk_exceptions.count loop
18            l_err_list(i).error_index := sql%bulk_exceptions(i).error_index;
19            l_err_list(i).error_code := sql%bulk_exceptions(i).error_code;
20            l_err_list(i).item := l_rows(sql%bulk_exceptions(i).error_index);
21        end loop;
```

Then these will saved into the ERRS table, using bulk bind, of course!

```
22        forall i in 1 .. l_err_list.count
23            insert into ERRS values l_err_list(i);
24
25    end;
26    /
```

```
PL/SQL procedure successfully completed.

SQL> select * from errs;

ERROR_INDEX ERROR_CODE       ITEM
----------- ---------- ----------
          2       2290         -1
          6       2290         -2
```

LOG ERRORS Clause

Alternatively, you can achieve something similar by converting your code to a pure SQL approach and take advantage of the LOG ERRORS clause. From 10g onwards, if the DML operation you were planning to use bulk bind for can be expressed natively in SQL, you can catch errors in a similar fashion to the SAVE EXCEPTIONS clause. The DDL and code below are contained in bulk_log_errors.sql.

First, create a table to catch any errors using the supplied DBMS_ERRLOG package.

```
SQL> exec DBMS_ERRLOG.CREATE_ERROR_LOG('HARDWARE');

PL/SQL procedure successfully completed.
```

This execution creates a table with the columns from the HARDWARE table, plus additional columns to indicate what kind of error has occurred. Here's what the resulting table will look like:

```
SQL> desc err$_HARDWARE
 Name                         Null?    Type
 -------------------------- -------- ----------------
 ORA_ERR_NUMBER$                      NUMBER
 ORA_ERR_MESG$                        VARCHAR2(2000)
 ORA_ERR_ROWID$                       ROWID
 ORA_ERR_OPTYP$                       VARCHAR2(2)
 ORA_ERR_TAG$                         VARCHAR2(2000)
 AISLE                                VARCHAR2(4000)
 ITEM                                 VARCHAR2(4000)
 DESCR                                VARCHAR2(4000)
 STOCKED                              VARCHAR2(4000)
```

Then execute the SQL statement with the additional log error clause to capture errors, like so:

```
SQL> insert
  2  into HARDWARE ( item )
  3  with SRC_ROWS as
  4    ( select -3 + rownum      x from dual
  5        connect by level <= 6 )
  6  select x
  7  from SRC_ROWS
  8  log errors reject limit unlimited;

3 rows created.
```

You'll find that, similar to the bulk bind example (`bulk_bind_error_5.sql`), the erroneous rows have been captured along with the reason for the error.

```
SQL> select
  2     item
  3    ,ora_err_number$
  4    ,ora_err_mesg$
  5  from err$_HARDWARE;

ITEM  ORA_ERR_NUMBER$ ORA_ERR_MESG$
----- --------------- ----------------------------------------------------------------
-2               2290 ORA-02290: check constraint (MCDONAC.HARDWARE_CHK) violated
-1               2290 ORA-02290: check constraint (MCDONAC.HARDWARE_CHK) violated
0                2290 ORA-02290: check constraint (MCDONAC.HARDWARE_CHK) violated
```

A complete coverage of the `LOG ERRORS` extension is beyond the scope of this book, but the previous example demonstrates how it can be used in a very similar fashion to the `SAVE EXCEPTIONS` feature in PL/SQL, with the added benefit of having the erroneous data readily available within a table for further processing.

Robust Bulk Bind

When you bulk collect into a collection, the array is populated from index 1. Almost all of the examples in the standard documentation make this assumption, the code typically being along the lines of:

```
begin
  select ...
  bulk collect into <array>
  from ...

  for i in 1 .. <array>.count loop
    <processing>
  end loop;
end;
```

It is very unlikely that Oracle will ever change this behavior, so its reasonably safe to assume that any collection initialized with bulk collect will always start at an array index of 1. However, collections don't fall solely under the domain of the bulk collect/bulk bind feature in PL/SQL. In fact, collections pre-date bulk operations, going all the way back to Oracle 7. Once data has been fetched into a collection, the developer is free to do whatever they like to the contents of a collection. So what happens to a bulk bind operation if the collection no longer contains a set of elements starting from index=1. Let's explore some scenarios.

Scenario 1: Elements Do Not Start at 1

As long as an array's indices are contiguous, you can use the attributes of the array itself to continue to use bulk bind. Consider the following example (**bulk_bind_scenario1.sql**) where the array starts from 10. The array attributes FIRST and LAST can be used to define the extrema of the array for bulk binding.

```
SQL> declare
  2     type t_num_list is table of hardware.item%type index by pls_integer;
  3
  4     val t_num_list;
  5  begin
  6
  7     val(10) := 10;
  8     val(11) := 20;
  9     val(12) := 20;
 10
 11     FORALL i IN val.first .. val.last
 12        insert into hardware ( item ) values (val(i));
 13
 14  end;
 15  /

PL/SQL procedure successfully completed.
```

In fact, it's probably reasonable to adopt a standard that .FIRST and .LAST attributes should be used in preference to 1 and .COUNT. However, the next scenario demonstrates that doing so does not provide a total safeguard.

Scenario 2: Elements Are Not Contiguous

Let's repeat the preceding example with one slight alteration: a missing entry in the array. The following is the example and the resulting error caused by the missing entry (**bulk_bind_scenario2a.sql**):

```
SQL> declare
  2     type t_num_list is table of hardware.item%type index by pls_integer;
  3
  4     val t_num_list;
  5  begin
  6
  7     val(10) := 10;
  8  --   val(11) := 20;
  9     val(12) := 20;
 10
 11     FORALL i IN val.first .. val.last
 12        insert into hardware ( item ) values (val(i));
 13
 14  end;
```

```
 15  /
declare
*
ERROR at line 1:
ORA-22160: element at index [11] does not exist
ORA-06512: at line 11
```

Once collections become sparse, bulk bind will not automatically work using low and high boundary index values. However, from version 10.2 onwards, the FORALL syntax has been extended to include the INDICES OF and VALUES OF specification. The use of INDICES OF fixes the ORA-22160 issue encountered above as demonstrated here (bulk_bind_scenario2b.sql):

```
SQL> declare
  2    type t_num_list is table of hardware.item%type index by pls_integer;
  3
  4    val t_num_list;
  5  begin
  6
  7    val(10) := 10;
  8  --  val(11) := 20;
  9    val(12) := 20;
 10
 11    FORALL i IN INDICES OF val
 12        insert into hardware ( item ) values (val(i));
 13
 14  end;
 15  /
```

```
PL/SQL procedure successfully completed.
```

I really like this syntax. There is no dependency on the array attributes, and the code is independent of how the data is spread throughout the array. I recommend adopting a standard of using the INDICES OF clause whenever you want to process an entire collection, and that use of .FIRST, .LAST, and .COUNT should be deprecated in your PL/SQL code. Sadly, the INDICES OF extension can only be used in a FORALL statement, not in a standard FOR loop.

If, however, the bulk binding you need to perform is more along the lines of cutting and slicing an existing collection, then this is where the VALUES OF syntax can be useful. The VALUES OF clause allows a level of indirection, somewhat similar to pointers, to allow you to bulk bind selected subsets of a larger collection.

In this next example (bulk_bind_values_of.sql), a collection will be populated that contains a STATUS attribute in that rows flagged with a status of NEW will be inserted into the HARDWARE table and rows flagged with status of UPD will update their matching rows in the HARDWARE table. The example thus emulates a MERGE statement. The collection will be examined to determine which indices should be used for update and which should be used for insert. The VALUES OF clause will then be used to process the rows.

First, I'll create some structures representing the input data. The variable src will be the input data, containing 100 rows each with a status of NEW or UPD.

```
SQL> set serverout on
SQL> declare
  2    type t_input_row is record (
  3        item    hardware.item%type,
  4        descr   hardware.descr%type,
```

```
 5        status varchar2(3)
 6        );
 7
 8    type t_input_list is
 9        table of t_input_row
10        index by pls_integer;
11
12    src t_input_list;
```

Now two variables (**IND_N** and **IND_Y**) are defined and will hold the index values of the appropriate rows in SRC. In this way, rather than copying the source data into separate collections (one for status = NEW and one for status = UPD), a record of just the index entries is retained. Avoiding the need to copy is of particular importance if the source data is large.

```
13
14    type t_target_indices is
15        table of pls_integer
16        index by pls_integer;
17
18    ind_new  t_target_indices;
19    ind_upd  t_target_indices;
20
21  begin
```

Now the source data is seeded with some fictitious values (80 rows of status = UPD, and 20 rows of status = NEW). In a real world example, the data would probably be initialized elsewhere and passed into the application for processing.

```
22    for i in 1 .. 100 loop
23        src(i).item   := i;
24        src(i).descr  := 'Item '||i;
25        src(i).status :=  case when mod(i,5) = 0 then 'NEW' else 'UPD' end;
26    end loop;
27
```

Now the data is scanned and the indices arrays are populated with the indices that correspond to the two different status values.

```
28
29    for i in 1 .. 100 loop
30        if src(i).status = 'NEW' then
31            ind_new(ind_new.count) := i;
32        else
33            ind_upd(ind_upd.count) := i;
34        end if;
35    end loop;
```

And finally, the VALUES OF syntax is used to transfer the changes into the HARDWARE table. Even though the rows relevant to each table are sparsely distributed throughout the 'src' collection, the **VALUES OF** syntax gives direct access to them for bulk binding.

```
36
37    forall i in values of ind_new
38        insert into hardware ( aisle, item)
```

```
39        values (1, src(i).item);
40     dbms_output.put_line(sql%rowcount||' rows inserted');
41
42     forall i in values of ind_upd
43        update hardware
44        set descr = src(i).descr
45        where aisle = 1
46        and item = src(i).item;
47     dbms_output.put_line(sql%rowcount||' rows updated');
48
49  end;
50  /
20 rows inserted
80 rows updated
```

The VALUES OF and INDICES OF syntax completes the bulk bind implementation. Any permutation of entries within an array can be manipulated and bound into a database table.

Earlier Versions of Oracle

If you own Oracle 10.1 or below, then your version of Oracle does not yet support the VALUES OF or INDICES OF extensions, but all is not lost. If a collection is possibly sparse, then transferring that collection to one that is dense will solve the problem. This is not something to done lightly, because if the collection is large in size, then you will be holding two copies of the collection in memory while you densify the data. I'll return to the first example in this section where the input array did not contain contiguous entries and solve the problem without using VALUES OF (bulk_bind_scenario_oldver.sql).

First, here is the code to declare the first collection val, which will be the sparse collection:

```
SQL> declare
 2     type t_num_list is table of hardware.item%type
 3        index by pls_integer;
 4
 5     val t_num_list;
```

Now a second array is defined, which will contain the entries from the sparse collection val:

```
 6
 7     dense_val t_num_list;
 8     idx        pls_integer;
 9
10  begin
11
12     val(10) := 10;
13     val(12) := 20;
14
```

Population of the dense_val array is performed by walking along the entries of the val collection, using the collection attributes .FIRST and .NEXT. The collection dense_val will start at 0 (because dense_val.count is initially zero) and grows up to the number of elements in val.

```
15     idx := val.first;
16     while idx is not null loop
17        dense_val(dense_val.count) := val(idx);
```

```
18        idx := val.next(idx);
19    end loop;
```

The dense_val collection is then used rather than sparse val to perform the bulk bind:

```
20
21    FORALL i IN dense_val.first .. dense_val.last
22        insert into hardware ( item )
23        values (dense_val(i));
24
25  end;
26  /
```

PL/SQL procedure successfully completed.

A Justification for Massive Collections

As seen throughout this chapter, once you start working with collections, you need to be aware of the implications with regard to memory consumption. However, sometimes your performance requirements have their motivation in other parts of the database infrastructure.

Many of the examples you have seen involve inserting large amounts of rows into a table. While bulk binding is dramatically faster than single row inserts, it will still consume large amounts of redo because the inserts are still DML issued via the conventional path, so performance may still compromised to a slight degree. For example, performance may be compromised due to freelist or segment space bitmap management, or due to advancing the high watermark of the table.

Oracle Database 11.2 introduces the APPEND_VALUES hint, which will convert a conventional path insert statement into a direct path load. Here's an example of the hint in use (bulk_bind_append_values_1.sql):

```
SQL> insert /*+ APPEND_VALUES */
  2  into HARDWARE ( item ) values (1);

1 row created.

SQL> select item from HARDWARE;
select item from HARDWARE
                  *
ERROR at line 1:
ORA-12838: cannot read/modify an object after modifying it in parallel

SQL> commit;

Commit complete.

SQL> select item from HARDWARE;

      ITEM
----------
        1
```

When the APPEND_VALUES hint was announced, its usefulness was questioned. After all, who would want to lock a table, advance its high watermark, and be bound to end the transaction immediately all to insert just a *single* row? However, when combined with bulk bind, the usefulness of the feature becomes more apparent. In the next example (bulk_bind_append_values_2.sql), the session level statistics are measured to compare the difference in redo consumption between a conventional insert and a direct load insert via a bulk bind:

```
SQL> declare
  2     type t_list is table of hardware.descr%type;
  3     l_rows t_list := t_list();
  4     l_now timestamp;
  5     l_redo1 int;
  6     l_redo2 int;
  7     l_redo3 int;
  8  begin
  9
 10     select value
 11     into   l_redo1
 12     from   v$mystat m, v$statname s
 13     where  s.statistic# = m.statistic#
 14     and    s.name = 'redo size';
 15
```

An array of 1,000,000 rows to be inserted via a standard bulk bind is prepared, and the before and after redo consumption by this session is captured.

```
 16     for i in 1 .. 1000000 loop
 17        l_rows.extend;
 18        l_rows(i) := i;
 19     end loop;
 20
 21     l_now := systimestamp;
 22     forall i in 1 .. l_rows.count
 23       insert into hardware ( descr ) values (l_rows(i));
 24     dbms_output.put_line('Elapsed = '||(systimestamp-l_now));
 25
 26     select value
 27     into   l_redo2
 28     from   v$mystat m, v$statname s
 29     where  s.statistic# = m.statistic#
 30     and    s.name = 'redo size';
 31
```

Then the table is truncated, and the load is re-performed using APPEND_VALUES for direct path load.

```
 32     execute immediate 'truncate table hardware';
 33
 34     dbms_output.put_line('Redo conventional = '||(l_redo2-l_redo1));
 35
 36     l_now := systimestamp;
 37     forall i in 1 .. l_rows.count
 38       insert /*+ APPEND_VALUES */ into hardware ( descr ) values (l_rows(i));
```

```
39     dbms_output.put_line('Elapsed = '||(systimestamp-l_now));
40
41     select value
42     into   l_redo3
43     from   v$mystat m, v$statname s
44     where  s.statistic# = m.statistic#
45     and    s.name = 'redo size';
46
47     dbms_output.put_line('Redo direct load = '||(l_redo3-l_redo2));
48
49  end;
50  /
Elapsed = +000000000 00:00:03.057000000
Redo conventional = 67599300
Elapsed = +000000000 00:00:02.668000000
Redo direct load = 146912

PL/SQL procedure successfully completed.
```

As expected, the direct path load operation was faster and used much less redo. So while it's always important to be aware of the memory consumption with collections, when it comes to using bulk bind for direct load inserts, you may find yourself using larger-than-normal collection sizes if the memory on your database server permits.

The Real Benefit: Client Bulk Processing

As I mentioned at the start of the chapter, my repeated meanderings within the hardware store are hurting my efficiency. However, sometimes things are much, much worse: I pay for an item, drive home, and *then* realize I need to get back in the car, drive back to the hardware store, and purchase something else. (For the sake of sensitive readers, I won't include the term of "endearment" my wife uses when this happens!)

This chapter has described the efficiency of using bulk operations in PL/SQL to access data, but that is equivalent to *already being* at the hardware store. The cost of coming from an external client application to the database (network trip) and processing data in a row-at-a-time basis is equivalent to driving back and forth to the store in a car. The cost of this can be quantified with some simple demos. First, I'll build (using PL/SQL, of course!) a replica of what many client applications implement in 3GL code, namely a routine to open a cursor on the table and a routine a fetch a single row. Here is the code, which you'll find in bulk_network_1.sql:

```
SQL> create or replace
  2  package PKG1 is
  3
  4    procedure open_cur(rc in out sys_refcursor);
  5
  6    procedure fetch_cur(rc in out sys_refcursor, p_row out hardware.item%type);
  7
  8  end;
  9  /

Package created.
```

```
SQL> create or replace
  2  package body PKG1 is
  3
  4    procedure open_cur(rc in out sys_refcursor) is
  5    begin
  6      open rc for select item from hardware;
  7    end;
  8
  9    procedure fetch_cur(rc in out sys_refcursor, p_row out hardware.item%type) is
 10    begin
 11      fetch rc into p_row;
 12    end;
 13
 14  end;
 15  /
```

Package body created.

SQL Plus will suffice as the client application calling this package. SQL Plus is, of course, a genuine SQL client in its own right, and the number of rows it will fetch per fetch call is a preference you have explicit control over, so the demo above could be written just as

```
set arraysize n   (n=1 for single row fetch, n=1000 for multirow fetch)
select item from HARDWARE;
```

but I want to mimic what a 3GL application will do, namely, contain explicit calls to open the cursor, fetch from it repeatedly, and then close it. To open the cursor, and then repeatedly fetch rows until the resultset is exhausted, I can use the script bulk_single_fetch_100000.sql, which performs the following:

```
variable rc refcursor
exec pkg1.open_cur(:rc)
variable n number
exec    pkg1.fetch_cur(:rc,:n);
exec    pkg1.fetch_cur(:rc,:n);
[repeat 100000 times]
```

In order to view the elapsed time for the demo, without scrolling through 100,000 lines of output, I switch off terminal output and record before and after timestamps.

```
SQL> variable rc refcursor
SQL> exec pkg1.open_cur(:rc)
SQL> select to_char(systimestamp,'HH24:MI:SS.FF') started from dual;

STARTED
------------------
12:11:18.779000

SQL> set termout off
SQL> @bulk_single_fetch_1000.sql    -- contains 1000 fetch calls
[repeated 100 times]

SQL> set termout on
SQL> select to_char(systimestamp,'HH24:MI:SS.FF') ended from dual;
```

```
ENDED
------------------
12:12:47.270000
```

You can see that 100,000 trips to the database took approximately 90 seconds. I repeated that demo with a session trace enabled and examined the resultant tkprof-formatted file. Here are the results:

```
SELECT ITEM
FROM   HARDWARE

call     count      cpu    elapsed      disk      query    current       rows
-------  ------  --------  ----------  --------  --------  ----------  ----------
Parse         1     0.00        0.05         0         1          0           0
Execute       1     0.00        0.00         0         0          0           0
Fetch    100000     1.17        0.94         0    100003          0      100000
-------  ------  --------  ----------  --------  --------  ----------  ----------
total    100002     1.17        1.00         0    100004          0      100000
```

You can see that out of this 90 seconds, only one second was spent actually doing work in the database. The other 89 seconds are spent jumping back and forth across the network. The database is doing nothing, but from the perspective of the client application, it is waiting on the database. In motoring parlance, I'm spinning my wheels but going nowhere. At my current workplace, whenever we encounter 3GL programs on the middle tier server exhibiting this behavior, we call it "middleware fail." It is amazing how labeling poor quality code in this way sharpens the focus of the development team!

Now, let's apply this newfound knowledge of bulk processing to fetch the data from the database in bulk and pass that data back to the client in bulk. The following code (bulk_network_2.sql) is the new implementation and the performance will be much better:

```
SQL> create or replace
  2  package PKG2 is
  3
  4    type t_num_list is table of hardware.item%type index by pls_integer;
  5
  6    procedure open_cur(rc in out sys_refcursor);
  7
  8    procedure fetch_cur(rc in out sys_refcursor, p_rows out t_num_list);
  9
 10  end;
 11  /

Package created.

SQL> create or replace
  2  package body PKG2 is
  3
  4    procedure open_cur(rc in out sys_refcursor) is
  5    begin
  6      open rc for select item from hardware;
  7    end;
  8
  9    procedure fetch_cur(rc in out sys_refcursor, p_rows out t_num_list) is
 10    begin
 11      fetch rc bulk collect into p_rows limit 1000;
```

```
12   end;
13
14   end;
15   /
```

Package body created.

Rerun the demo. Each time, 1,000 rows will be bulk collected from the database and passed back to the client. Because SQL Plus does not natively understand the array that comes back, the data will simply be appended to a large VARCHAR2 variable (the_data) to simulate the client receiving the array data. Here is an example (bulk_multi_fetch_in_bulk.sql):

```
SQL> variable rc refcursor
SQL> exec pkg2.open_cur(:rc)

PL/SQL procedure successfully completed.

SQL> select to_char(systimestamp,'HH24:MI:SS.FF') started from dual;

STARTED
-------------------
12:39:09.704000

SQL> variable the_data varchar2(4000);
SQL> set termout off

SQL> declare
  2    n pkg2.t_num_list;
  3  begin
  4    :the_data := null;
  5    pkg2.fetch_cur(:rc,n);
  6    for i in 1 .. n.count loop
  7      :the_data := :the_data||n(i);
  8    end loop;
  9  end;
[repeated 100 times]

SQL> select to_char(systimestamp,'HH24:MI:SS.FF') ended from dual;

ENDED
-------------------
12:39:09.837000
```

The difference is astounding. Immediate turnaround time is down from 90 seconds to 0.13 seconds. Re-running the demo with trace enabled reveals the reduction in database trips.

```
SELECT ITEM
FROM HARDWARE
```

call	count	cpu	elapsed	disk	query	current	rows
Parse	1	0.00	0.00	0	0	0	0
Execute	1	0.00	0.00	0	0	0	0

Fetch	100	0.04	0.04	0	256	0	100000
total	102	0.04	0.04	0	256	0	100000

100,000 rows were still fetched (far right column), but 100 fetch calls were made. I cannot overstate the benefit that has been realized here, even with just this simple demo. It's not uncommon for customers of Oracle to spend large sums of money performing optimization exercises in order to glean perhaps an extra 10-15 *percent* performance out of their system through such methods as caching, index creation, SQL tuning, etc. Sometimes, customers even purchase more hardware along with associated license cost increases. But consider the performance benefits gained here in this demo:

From 90 seconds down to 0.13 seconds, an almost 700-fold improvement.

As an application developer, if you're making modifications to code that makes it hundreds of times faster, that's going to make your applications that much more successful and you very popular! Reducing network trips in a client application's interaction with the database comes down largely the tools at the disposal of the developer in the language of their client application, the design of the application to take advantage of passing data to the database in an intelligent fashion, and the diligence of the developer. But as a *database* developer, if you can ensure that your PL/SQL interfaces to the database are equipped to allow client applications to pass and receive data in bulk, then you are that much closer to successful application performance.

Summary

One of the reasons I enjoy writing, presenting, or talking about the bulk operations in PL/SQL is that using them is virtually a guaranteed success story. Many Oracle features, new or old, apply only to a particular niche of customers or address a specific technical issue, and moreover, require a large amount of careful testing to ensure that using the features does not result in negative impacts elsewhere within the database or its applications. On the other hand, adopting bulk collection and bulk binding in PL/SQL benefits applications in the overwhelming majority of occasions. The effort required to move from row-centric fetching of data to the set-centric bulk fetching of data is small or perhaps even zero. Your choices are pretty simple.

- If you are already using FOR cursor_variable in (QUERY or CURSOR) syntax, then getting bulk collection is simply a matter of being on a recent version of Oracle and ensuring the PL/SQL compilation settings are at their default.

- If you are not that fortunate, then it's still just a matter of some simple re-coding to change FETCH CURSOR INTO style to the FETCH CURSOR BULK COLLECT INTO. Just a couple of keywords and some PL/SQL type definitions and you're done!

The effort required to move from row-centric modification of data to set-centric bulk bind modification of data is equally small.

- If you are already issuing DML (insert, update, delete) in a loop, simply adding some appropriate type definitions and recasting the FOR loop into FORALL and the job is done.

It is that easy, and whereas performance improvement in applications is often described in terms of a few-percentage-point gain here and there, you've seen in this chapter that moving to bulk operations can give *orders of magnitude* improvements in performance. In past releases of Oracle, some elements of PL/SQL did not support bulk operations (for example, native dynamic SQL and dynamic ref cursors). However, all of these restrictions have been lifted in the recent releases of the database, thus there's never a reason why bulk operations can't be considered.

So the effort is small, the risks are low, and the payback is huge. The moment your approach within PL/SQL becomes set-centric, you'll be amazed at how quickly your newfound, set-centric thinking will spread to other areas of your Oracle skillset. You will find yourself achieving more in SQL rather than by procedural logic and you will also be taking of advantage of facilities that process data en-masse such as pipeline functions. The same skills you learn with bulk operations will become the motivations for a set-centric mindset throughout all of your database development.

I hope you share my excitement about bulk operations, and that you will see the rewards at your own workplace. As for me, I'm off to the hardware store—this time with a trolley.

CHAPTER 7

Know Your Code

by Lewis Cunningham

The name of this chapter is "Know Your Code." You might think that if you wrote a piece of code, you know it well. You probably do. You know it at least as well as anyone else. Even if you've written the code, however, you will still make assumptions based from your memory. These assumptions will likely move further and further from reality as time goes on. You have a best guess—an educated assumption—but that is subjective and dependent on human frailty. And if you didn't write the code, all bets are off.

Why guess when you can know? I first heard that question in a performance context. I think it was Cary Milsap (author and performance guru) who said it (at least the first time I heard it). I'll talk more about knowing your code from a performance perspective later but the concept holds true for so much more than just performance.

If you are making a big purchase and need to write a check, are you just going to hope (and assume) you have enough money in your account? What if it is within a few hundred dollars of what you think is in your account? Would you use an ATM or a web page to verify first? My bank even allows me to send an SMS message and get my balance. Why would I guess when I can know?

Oracle gives you ATM access to your code. Everything you could possibly need to know about your PL/SQL code can be found within the Oracle data dictionary and/or by using tools provided by Oracle. You don't even need a PIN code (although you'll need to log into the database and perhaps get a few permissions).

This chapter will show you where to find the best place for an account update. Instead of SMS, you'll send some SQL. The chapter starts with a static analysis of your code using the Oracle data dictionary (as it relates to your PL/SQL code) and PL/Scope. It will then move on to time-based and event-based profiling (pre-11g) and finally context-sensitive, time-based profiling (11g+).

By the end of this chapter, you will be able to take a piece of code you have never seen before and know what the code looks like, the data types used, what variables are using them, and where they are using them. You will know where runtime is spent (efficiently or not) within the application. By the end of this chapter, you will have the tools to know your code. No guesses; you will know the code.

What This Chapter Will (and Will Not) Cover

From an architect's perspective (by that I mean from the viewpoint of correctness of design, correctness of code, and compliance to standards), by the time an application or program unit hits production, there should be absolutely no surprises. All designs should have been peer reviewed—early—for compliance to business requirements and design standards. All code should have been reviewed for compliance to coding standards, performance standards, logic errors, and basic documentation. The better code complies with standards and the better tested an application is, the less likely you are to find "oopsy" type errors. You may find logic errors regardless of how well an application complies with standards. Testing should catch most of these but a few usually still get through. But what does get through should not be a common error. Those common errors are exactly what standards and regression testing are designed to catch.

This chapter will provide you with the tools to help make the best decisions possible by using the valuable data provided by Oracle in the form of the data dictionary, profiling, and the PL/SQL compiler. Much of the validation can be automated and this chapter will show where this is possible. Anything that can be offloaded to a computer should be. Let the humans concentrate on the things that require humans. Even if the full analysis/discovery can't be automated, at least the gathering of the data can be automated or simplified.

Some things are not so automation friendly. Even today, it still requires a human to validate much of a review. If I could develop an automated tool to catch every possible logic error in any possible application, I would have something very valuable to sell and would be raking in large amounts of money. Logic reviews are still in the domain of a human performing a manual check, either through reviewing code or through testing.

Documentation is also difficult. It's easy to see that there are comments in the code, but it's difficult to verify that a given comment is useful (or even relevant). Logic and commenting are highly specific to the task at hand. This chapter will not try to cover logic or documentation issues as there is very little that Oracle can provide to help in that area.

Understanding your application's performance profile is critical to the success of the application. The downside to this, though, is that performance checks require human intelligence to validate. While you can automate a system to raise an alert if a function takes longer than x seconds to complete, a human will need to validate if this is or is not acceptable.

Oracle provides tools to help gather the information required to analyze a system in a way that allows a developer to make intelligent performance decisions. Tuning an application is far beyond the scope of this chapter. However, Chapter 13 provide the means to interpret performance profiling results.

Instead of tuning recommendations, what this chapter will provide, from the perspective of knowing your code as it relates to performance, is what tools are available to gather these performance metrics (primarily a profiler), where the data is stored, and how to use that data for regression. A regression test is the easiest way to validate that what worked before a change is still working after a change. By saving the data provided by Oracle, you can keep an eye on performance over time and compare one release to the next. You can program thresholds into your tests so that automated runs of the profiler will alert someone only on exception. A human must make sure the performance results are correct on the first run, but once a good metric has been gathered, a human only needs to intervene should a metric fall outside a threshold.

Another testing benefit, beyond regression, is code coverage. While not infallible, code coverage testing does provide some assurance that at least the code will execute for some data set. Using a combination of Oracle-provided tools and a little sweat, it is possible to validate that every executable line in a program has been executed. As valuable as that is, even more valuable is the ability to see what lines have not been executed. This is where you want to automate as much as possible. If every line is executed, test passed. If every line is not executed, test failed. A human intervenes and creates a test, or tests, that do cover every line.

The bulk of this chapter will use data provided by the data dictionary and the PL/SQL compiler to ensure compliance to corporate standards. Standards are anything but standard, so a one-size-fits-all solution is impossible. Instead, this chapter will provide the tools and guidance for you to create your own solution in whatever detail you require. Using plain SQL and the data dictionary, you can validate naming standards, find unused variables, find variables defined at multiple scopes, perform impact analysis, find unacceptable data type usage, and more.

I will not explain every option, column, or report provided by, or for, these tools. If the documentation from Oracle is good, and it usually is, I will not regurgitate it. This chapter is not a general tutorial on using these tools. It is an explanation of how you can incorporate these tools into your development workflow to implement better applications.

Automated Code Analysis

Code analysis, also known as program analysis, is the analysis of source code. Manual code analysis is code review by a human. Such analysis may also include reviewing log data and system output from running programs. Automated analysis allows an analyst (usually a developer, in my experience) to skip the boring parts of analysis and jump to the more interesting things. Instead of eyeballing everything, you get to run some kind of a program to do the tedious work for you.

Let's take an example. You're a developer and you're at work. You're handed some new requirements that mean you must change an existing procedure. Maybe a calculation has changed and the procedure will need to add a variable. The business wants an estimate of the time it will take to make the change. To make it really interesting, the person who wrote this procedure and has maintained it for years recently won the lottery and quit. You've never even seen the code (you were out sick on the day of the code review).

How do you provide the estimate? Reach up high (or in deep) and pull a number out of the air (or somewhere else)? I have seen that method used quite a bit and it's never really been all that successful in my experience.

The next method I've seen is to scramble, pull out the source code, and make an emergency review of it. After a quick perusal, you decide that it's a simple change and you only need two hours to code and unit test it.

Nice. A quick analysis and you're ready to start coding. One of the business people is amazed that you can change the call in all 673 places where this calculation is called (it is a *very* popular calculation). Now you get a bit worried. You do a quick grep in the file system to see all the places from where the procedure is called.

Realizing your procedure is called from so many places, you multiply your original estimate by two. That's usually a bit more accurate than not multiplying, but there is a better way. Would you believe me if I said you can find everywhere it is called by running a few simple queries? Not only can you find where the function is being called but these queries can also cover impact analysis and naming standards compliance as well as show code and variable usage, scope collisions, and code coverage for testing.

You can get all of this information by manually reviewing source code, program log data, etc., but by automating the process, you get a repeatable, predictable process that is less error-prone and vastly less time consuming. You can't replace a good developer when it comes to interpreting the data provided by automated or manual analysis, but automation saves you a lot of time.

Static Analysis

Static analysis is analyzing the source code of a program without actually running it. You are looking at things the compiler knows at compile time. Static analysis provides information about the program based on the functionality actually utilized within the program.

Static analysis can give information about the data types being used, about naming standards, about security, about objects accessed, etc. Static analysis may utilize the source code directly or may use tools. If you manually review code for compliance to naming standards, you are performing a manual static analysis of that source code. Peer reviews are a kind of static analysis. If you have ever found a SQL injection flaw in a co-worker's program while reviewing it, you understand the importance of static analysis.

In Oracle PL/SQL, there are a variety of places where you can get information for your analysis. You will generally start with the data dictionary. With each release, Oracle enhances the data dictionary with valuable data. Later, in the "Performing Static Analysis" section, I will walk you through some important data dictionary views (as well as some analysis queries) before introducing you to a new data dictionary view that brings code analysis into the 21st century. The new view is provided by PL/Scope, an 11g compiler addition.

Dynamic Analysis

Dynamic analysis tells you what you will find out when you run the program. Dynamic analysis is also called program profiling. With profiling, you run a program and either intrusively or non-intrusively gather statistics of where the program has been and what it has done.

DBMS_PROFILER and DBMS_TRACE were the pre-11g profiling tools. DBMS_PROFILER is a flat profiler. A flat profiler provides simple timing information such as how long different procedure and function calls take without any contextual information such as which function was called and in what order. Oracle added call context to the mix with DBMS_TRACE, but ended up creating a tool that was intrusive (required DEBUG) and noisy (optionally producing a lot of data). It's much better to use DBMS_PROFILER.

DBMS_HPROF is an 11g+, hierarchical profiling tool that is non-intrusive and simple to use. DBMS_HPROF provides timing information, like the flat profiler DBMS_PROFILER, but it also includes contextual information like DBMS_TRACE. It can deliver some reports that are very valuable for performance tuning but it also populates some tables that you can then write queries against. This is very beneficial for comparing metrics over time and as an additional tool for understanding your code.

When to Analyze?

The whole purpose of analyzing your code is to understand your code. The vast majority of people who use these analysis tools (at least those who have asked me how to use these tools) are doing so at crunch time: an upgrade gone bad, users screaming about a slow database, a nasty logic bug that seems to be hiding.

Like performance tuning, code analysis can be called upon when things go bad. But wouldn't you agree that a system designed for performance is less likely to wake you up in the middle of the night? The same is true for a well analyzed, standards compliant system: both static (human or automated) and dynamic. Both types of analysis should be baselined.

Analysis should be performed when an application is written (or when you take ownership of it). I have no doubt that everyone is familiar with a code review. As mentioned, a code review (or peer review) is a human-powered type of static analysis. The automated analysis provided by Oracle (especially PL/Scope) should be considered an extension to the code review.

This pre-production analysis/review should be documented, version controlled, and retained. The automated analysis, being data in a dictionary view, is very easily archived and can be recalled whenever needed (although you need to build that functionality yourself). With each and every change, a new version of your analysis will need to be gathered and saved. In addition to saving the analysis, you have to look at it. You really should study it.

With static analysis (as discussed with the data dictionary and PL/SCOPE) you will understand the dependencies of your code, the identifiers used by your code, and where/how those identifiers are used.

With dynamic analysis, you can see the bottlenecks in your code (fixable or not); you can see how varying input data changes the execution profile of your code; you can validate code coverage; etc.

Using reports provided by the various tools (or written in SQL yourself), you will have an excellent start for debugging any issues that should pop up in the middle of the night. You will also have documentation to share with new developers (or to convince management you are actually doing some work).

Once your code is in production, you will be able to use the old information you've collected and verify that everything is still performing to expectations. While you're developing, you will use the profiler to continually verify that your code is working correctly, both from a code path perspective as well as a performance perspective. There's no need to save every profiler run to a version control system, but you should save a version that was run before every implementation or upgrade.

CODE ANALYSIS VS. INSTRUMENTATION

Sometimes there is confusion between analysis and instrumentation. The term *instrumentation* refers to code added to a system in support of analysis, especially dynamic analysis. Instrumentation enables analysis, but it is not the same thing.

To decide what kind of instrumentation an application needs (and if it does need instrumentation) or to do any performance tuning, you will have to analyze the code (to a degree). Profilers are a kind of instrumentation and are valuable for tuning. Likewise, understanding the performance profile of an application or code base is important to really understanding your code. How will the application handle various loads, data inputs, and so forth? The answers to these questions are some of the things you want to capture during analysis.

I say all this to make the point that none of this analysis is done in a vacuum. Code analysis is performed to ensure compliance to the standards you want, or are forced, to follow. A program that can't perform is worthless. A program that can't be maintained is just as worthless. Over the life of a program, the vast majority of time (and money) will be in maintenance. Maintainability is determined at design time.

Instrumentation is a tool, used over the life of an application, to log interesting information. Code analysis is a tool to provide interesting information about your program before it's running in production. Both are critical to a successful, performant, maintainable application.

Performing Static Analysis

You can perform static analysis using two resources. First, you have the data dictionary at your disposal. Every database, no matter the version, implements a data dictionary, and the information you can derive from this dictionary can be incredibly helpful in analyzing your code. The dictionary is your first line of offense, and it is always available.

If you're running Oracle Database 11g or higher, you also have available a feature called PL/Scope. It gives you visibility into compile-time data that otherwise is not available from the data dictionary. I'll discuss both resources—the dictionary and PL/Scope—in the following two subsections.

The Data Dictionary

Since you're reading this book, I will assume that you are at least somewhat familiar with Oracle's data dictionary. If not, you are probably reading this chapter a bit early in your career. I'm not going to explain what the data dictionary is; there are plenty of other books that cover that topic.

I am, however, going to discuss the views that are pertinent to understanding your code. I'm not getting into a discussion about DBA_*, ALL_* and USER_*. I am going to use USER_* for this discussion but you can assume, that the ALL and DBA counterparts exist. In the same vein, I am not going to do a bunch of describes on these views. I'll stick to covering the columns pertinent to this particular discussion.

■ **Note** I am providing examples that use partial strings and string formats. In a real life, implementation of the concepts shown in these examples, the select criteria and things in the where clause, the format strings and such, would exist in a table rather than being hardcoded. For brevity, I am hardcoding such values into the examples. Also, in a real implementation you may use regular expressions to narrow down query results. However, I stick with regular PL/SQL functions as most readers will be familiar with them.

If you've compiled the example code provided for this chapter (available from the book's catalog page at apress.com), you will have the basic set of programs that I will show as the results of the examples. It will make it much easier to follow along with the text if you have that code. It might make it more interesting, though, if you run it against your own schemas and see what kind of results you get.

USER_SOURCE

Around since PL/SQL was just a carving in stone, the USER_SOURCE view is very simply a line-by-line listing of your code. If you want to browse or export your code (kind of like that manual eyeballing), USER_SOURCE is the view for you. I have used this data for reversing engineering a piece of code (DBMS_METADATA is a better way now) and I frequently use it for a quick analysis of where an object is used. It is, very simply, a line-by-line copy of the course code.

The following is an example of using USER_SOURCE to extract lines of code that contain specific content, in this case "jobs_api.validate_job":

```
SELECT name, line
  FROM user_source
  WHERE lower(text) like '%jobs_api.validate_job%';
```

NAME	LINE
EMPLOYEE_API	40
TEST_CALLS_FNC	5
TEST_CALLS_PRC	4
TEST_CALLS_PRC	8

This query was once the basic method of code analysis in the database. It still works for a fast lookup against the database but if you look at the use case of a query like this, you'll see that you can get even better information by using other views.

The query in the example is an attempt to find all programs that invoke the JOBS_API.VAIDATE_JOB program unit. Unfortunately, the query will also return all calls that include "jobs_api.validate_job" in a comment. The primary problem with USER_SOURCE is that it is just a listing. I would need to parse the code to throw away comments (which can be hidden within /* */ when you look at the code line by line), and I would need to parse and separate the various type of variables, executable statements, and more to get any real intelligence from the results. I personally don't want to maintain my own PL/SQL parser.

USER_DEPENDENCIES

USER_DEPENDENCIES is a better approach when you want to see who is calling whom. Unfortunately, the view is not at a very granular level and does not allow for dynamic dependencies such as DBMS_SQL or native dynamic SQL. An analyst would have to have specific knowledge of the code or review the code manually. The following query and results show where the JOBS_API package is being reference by the code in the current schema:

```
SELECT name, type
FROM user_dependencies
WHERE referenced_name = 'JOBS_API';
```

```
NAME                          TYPE
----------------------------  ------------------
TEST_CALLS_PRC                PROCEDURE
TEST_CALLS_FNC                FUNCTION
JOBS_API                      PACKAGE BODY
EMPLOYEE_API                  PACKAGE BODY
```

With these results, you see exactly which program units are really calling the JOBS_API, but the view only provides it at the package level. You have no idea which procedure within the package is making the call nor do you know how many times the program unit is being called.

░ **Note** Oracle is adding fine-grained dependencies and may, in the future, make a view available to give us the missing granular level details that we would like.

The rest of the views that I discuss have been created using the source that is stored in the USER_SOURCE view (by the compiler at compile time). To see the actual code, which is required frequently when analyzing the code, you can join back to this view.

USER_PROCEDURES

For many purposes, a view that is better than USER_SOURCE for getting to know a piece of code is the USER_PROCEDURES view. This view will give you compilation details about your code, such as what type of program it is (function, procedure, package, etc.), and if it is an aggregate, deterministic, etc.

Arguably the most important feature related to code analysis is that you can combine USER_PROCEDURES with the dictionary view USER_ARGUMENTS discussed in the next section to get detailed information about the parameters used by a program.

The USER_PROCEDURES view is hierarchical so that not only can you identify all of your programs, you can identify which procedures and functions exist within a package. You can also see object types that implement methods in this view (more on objects and methods later).

USER_PROCEDURES, like USER_ARGUMENTS, contains information related to any code objects in the database. That means you can find information related to packages, procedures, functions, triggers, and types. I refer to these code objects generically as programs and program units. The same is true of the additional data dictionary views that I cover later.

USER_PROCEDURES can be a little confusing at first. The OBJECT_NAME column identifies the object. PROCEDURE_NAME is null unless you are looking at an object that exists within the namespace of another object (PACKAGE or TYPE). For example, when you select data from USER_PROCEDURES, PROCEDURE_NAME will be null for a standalone procedure or function while OBJECT_NAME will be the name of the procedure or function. For a package or a type, PROCEDURE NAME will be null (for the package or type object) and OBJECT_NAME will be the name of the package or type. However, each package or type will have another entry in the view for each function, procedure, or method. In this case, the OBJECT_NAME will be the name of the package and the PROCEDURE_NAME will be the name of the procedure or function (method for an object type).

The following query shows that the PROCEDURE_NAME column is null even though the object is a procedure. This is due to the fact that procedure name is only populated for objects containing multiple program units (such as packages and types).

```
select object_name, procedure_name, object_type
  from user_procedures
  where object_name = 'SECURE_DML';
```

```
OBJECT_NAME      PROCEDURE_NAME      OBJECT_TYPE
---------------  ------------------  -------------------
SECURE_DML                           PROCEDURE
```

On the other hand, the next query shows that if an object is a package or type, OBJECT_NAME is the name of the package and PROCEDURE_NAME will have the name of the packaged procedure or function:

```
select object_name, procedure_name, object_type
  from user_procedures
  where object_name = 'DEPARTMENTS_API';
```

```
OBJECT_NAME      PROCEDURE_NAME          OBJECT_TYPE
---------------  ----------------------  -------------------
DEPARTMENTS_API  DEPARTMENT_EXISTS       PACKAGE
DEPARTMENTS_API  DEPARTMENT_MANAGER_ID   PACKAGE
DEPARTMENTS_API  DEPARTMENT_MANAGER_ID   PACKAGE
DEPARTMENTS_API                          PACKAGE
```

If an object is an implementation of a user defined aggregate or a pipelined function, the IMPLTYPEOWNER and IMPLTYPENAME will be of the base type below the aggregate. The next query shows that the built-in aggregate function SYS_NT_COLLECT is an example of a function that is an implementation of a type while the built-in DM_CL_BUILD is a pipelined function that implements a type.

```
select object_type, aggregate, pipelined, impltypeowner, impltypename
  from all_procedures
  where owner = 'SYS'
    and (object_name = 'SYS_NT_COLLECT'
         or
         object_name = 'DM_CL_BUILD');
```

```
OBJECT_TYPE   AGGREGATE PIPELINED IMPLTYPEOWNER    IMPLTYPENAME
-----------   --------- --------- ---------------  ----------------------------
FUNCTION      YES       NO        SYS              SYS_NT_COLLECT_IMP
FUNCTION      NO        YES       SYS              DMCLBIMP
```

Each object in this view has an OBJECT_ID and a SUBPROGRAM_ID. OBJECT_ID can be considered the primary key of this view (of the object in the dictionary, actually). When joining to other dictionary objects (as I will do later with USER_ARGUMENTS, OBJECT_ID is the unique ID I will use to join). If the code is standalone, such as a procedure or function, SUBPROGRAM_ID is always a 1. If the code is a package, the subprogram_id will be 0, and each procedure and function in the package will increment the subprogram_id by 1.

One feature that can be incredibly useful in understanding a piece of code is the OVERLOAD column. If a procedure or function is overloaded within a package, OVERLOAD will start with 1 and will increment by 1 for each iteration of the overloaded subprogram. The SUBPROGRAM_ID always increments so an overloaded procedure will have a different SUBPROGRAM_ID from an overloaded version of the procedure.

When combined with the USER_ARGUMENTS view, you can query exactly how overloaded procedures differ. I will provide an example of this in the next section. By itself, the USER_PROCEDURES view can be used for naming standards and to check compilation information that might interest you, such as PIPELINED, AUTHID, or DETERMINISTIC.

USER_ARGUMENTS

When you add USER_ARGUMENTS into the mix, you can start finding some fine-grained details about the code and the arguments to that code. Querying this data can be confusing when you first start using it. The object naming is distinctly different from the USER_PROCEDURES view.

In this view, the OBJECT_NAME is the name of the program that owns the arguments. Whether the program is standalone or inside of a package or type, the procedure or function name will be in the OBJECT_NAME field. If the PROCEDURE or FUNCTION is in a package, PACKAGE_NAME will have a value—it will be NULL otherwise. The ARGUMENT_NAME is the actual name of the argument.

Note that in USER_PROCEDURES, the object_name is the top-level object. In the case of a package, it will be the package or type name. For standalone code, it will be the procedure name, trigger name, or function name. In USER_ARGUMENTS, object_name is the sub-program name. It is always the name of a procedure, function, or trigger. In the case of a package, object name will be the sub-programs, and package name will be the name of the package. This is very important for joining the two tables (see the next query example).

If an argument is an anchored type (EMPLOYEES.EMPLOYEE_ID%TYPE) you will not see the anchor type. You will see the underlying data type (NUMBER, for example) as the argument type. However, if the code is created with anchored types, you will see, along with the data type, the scale and precision of that anchored value. Normally you can't include scale or precision in an argument but since Oracle is aware of the base objects scale and precision, it can keep track of that information. That doesn't really help if you want to know *which* anchored type. Still, the information is useful when available.

One of the big objects that I am concerned with as a database architect is standards compliance. Are things being named correctly? Are the correct data types being used? The following example is a query I used until PL/Scope became available. It was an easy way to ensure naming standard compliance for program unit parameters.

```
select package_name, object_name, argument_name,
        position, in_out, data_type
  from user_arguments
  where argument_name not like 'P_%';
```

PACKAGE_NAME	OBJECT_NAME	ARGUMENT_NAME	POSITION	IN_OUT	DATA_TYPE
JOBS_API	JOB_EXISTS	JOB_TITLE	1	IN	VARCHAR2

The next example is a query that shows the differences in arguments for an overloaded procedure. I could have written it against only the USER_ARGUMENTS view but I wanted to show an example of joining the two views.

```
select ua.package_name, up.procedure_name, ua.argument_name, up.overload, position, IN_OUT
  from user_procedures up
  join user_arguments ua
  on (ua.object_name = up.procedure_name
  and ua.subprogram_id = up.subprogram_id)
  where up.overload is not null
  order by overload, position;
```

PACKAGE_NAME	PROCEDURE_NAME	ARGUMENT_NAME	OVERLOAD	POSITION	IN_OUT
DEPARTMENTS_API	DEPARTMENT_MANAGER_ID		1	0	OUT
DEPARTMENTS_API	DEPARTMENT_MANAGER_ID	P_DEPARTMENT_NAME	1	1	IN
DEPARTMENTS_API	DEPARTMENT_MANAGER_ID		2	0	OUT
DEPARTMENTS_API	DEPARTMENT_MANAGER_ID	P_DEPARTMENT_ID	2	1	IN

Notice the POSITION and IN_OUT columns. The procedure, DEPARTMENT_MANAGER_ID, is actually a function. The IN_OUT column is "OUT" and the position is 0. For a function, position 0 is the return value (a function must always have a return value). You can infer that a program unit is a function by looking at position. Function return values also do not have an argument name. If you have a record in the USER_ARGUMENTS table that does not have a name, it is the RETURN. If a program unit has no parameters, it will not have a record in the USER_ARGUMENTS view.

The following query shows that the procedure SECURE_DML exists in the USER_PROCEDURES view:

```
SELECT count(*) FROM user_procedures
WHERE object_name = 'SECURE_DML';
```

```
COUNT(*)
----------------------
1
```

The next query, however, shows that even though the procedure SECURE_DML exists as a procedure, it has no parameters so it will not have any records in the USER_ARGUMENTS view:

```
SELECT count(*) FROM user_arguments
WHERE object_name = 'SECURE_DML';


COUNT(*)
----------------------
0
```

Another standard that is worth checking, especially since it can be so easily automated, is validating the data types that your standards prohibit (CHAR, LONG, VARCHAR, etc) can be easily queried and questioned. Even though LONG in PL/SQL is just a sub-type of VARCHAR2 now (as opposed to a LONG in a table), I have seen many standards require that PL/SQL code use VARCHAR2(32767) instead.

You can validate data type information for parameters fairly easily by using the following query:

```
SELECT object_name, argument_name, data_type
  FROM user_arguments
  WHERE data_type IN ('CHAR', 'LONG', 'VARCHAR');


OBJECT_NAME                    ARGUMENT_NAME                    DATA_TYPE
------------------------------ ------------------------------   ------------------------------
BAD_DATA_TYPES_PRC             P_DATA_IN                        CHAR
BAD_DATA_TYPES_PRC             P_DATA_OUT                       LONG
```

Unfortunately, you can *only* get this for parameters from this view. When you validate this kind of information, you really want to validate variables as well as parameters. The section on PL/Scope shows you how to do this.

USER_TYPES

The USER_TYPES view provides information about your types. While you may not think of types as PL/SQL objects, many types, but not all, have type bodies. A type body is PL/SQL like any other program unit. From a purely PL/SQL point of view, the important columns in this view are the number of methods, local_methods, and the supertype columns, name and owner. I am going to assume an understanding of Oracle's object type system for the next couple of paragraphs.

A quick query of this view can determine if the type contains any PL/SQL. If the number of methods is greater than 0, there will be code behind the spec (i.e., a body). Also, if the supertype columns are not null, this means that this is a sub-type. It contains an inherited spec (and potentially an inherited body) from its supertype. Also important is the LOCAL_METHODS column; this is the number of methods defined in the sub-type (0 if not a sub-type or maybe 0 if nothing is over-ridden or extended).

The following query is running against the three object types provided in the demo code for this chapter. The three types include a type with no body (no PL/SQL), a collection type, and a type with a body.

```
SELECT type_name, typecode, attributes, methods, supertype_name, local_methods
FROM user_types;
```

```
TYPE_NAME            TYPECODE     ATTRIBUTES    METHODS    SUPERTYPE_NAME        LOCAL_METHODS
------------------   ------------ -------------- ---------- --------------------  -------------
CODE_INFO            OBJECT       7             0
CODE_INFOS           COLLECTION   0             0
DEMO_TYPE            OBJECT       1             3
```

You can see from the output that CODE_INFO has seven attributes, no code (no methods), does not inherit from a supertype, and that means no local methods. CODE_INFOS is a collection. Notice that it has no attributes of its own. DEMO_TYPE has a single attribute and three methods. That one has PL/SQL for you to look at.

USER_TYPE_METHODS

When debugging PL/SQL in a type body, there is important information you need to know—not just in how the code is written but in how the methods are defined. While all of the columns have value, the important ones for knowing your code are METHOD_NO, METHOD_TYPE, PARAMETER, RESULTS, OVERIDING and INHERITED.

When you join USER_TYPE_METHODS to USER_PROCEDURES, you join the type name in USER_TYPE_METHODS to the OBJECT_NAME in USER_PROCEDURES and the METHOD_NO to the SUBPROGRAM_ID . The SUBPROGRAM_ID also flows into the USER_ARGUMENTS view.

If you have overloaded methods, the OVERLOAD column will have an incremental sequence. If OVERLOAD is null, the method is not overloaded. Overloading methods are very common when using Oracle's type system, especially with constructors.

The following query shows that the DEMO_TYPE type provides three methods. The OVERLOAD_PROC member procedure is overloaded and the FUNC member function is not.

```
SELECT utm.type_name, utm.method_type, utm.method_name, up.overload,
       utm.parameters, utm.results
  FROM user_type_methods utm
  JOIN user_procedures up
   ON (utm.type_name = up.object_name
       AND
       utm.method_no = up.subprogram_id)
  WHERE utm.type_name = 'DEMO_TYPE';
```

```
TYPE_NAME       METHOD_TYPE METHOD_NAME     OVERLOAD   PARAMETERS    RESULTS
--------------  ----------- --------------  ---------- ------------- ----------------------
DEMO_TYPE       PUBLIC      FUNC                       2             1
DEMO_TYPE       PUBLIC      OVERLOAD_PROC   1          2             0
DEMO_TYPE       PUBLIC      OVERLOAD_PROC   2          2             0
```

METHOD_TYPE tells you the basics of the method. Is it a PUBLIC method (regular usage) or is it an ORDER or MAP type (for equivalency)?

PARAMETERS and RESULTS provide the input and output to a method. These two columns actually provide the number of values in and out, respectively. In an upcoming example, I will show how using this view and your knowledge of the PARAMETERS to lookup the parameters via USER_ARGUMENTS. You might be wondering why all of the methods say they have two parameters when they are defined with only a single parameter. Type methods always include the SELF parameter, even when it is not included in the spec or referenced in the body of the method. It is *always* passed in.

INHERITED and OVERRIDING tell you if the method was inherited from a supertype or if it is overriding a method from a supertype, respectively. Knowing if the code comes from the supertype is important when debugging and analyzing. It's important to ensure you are looking at the right code.

Not only can USER_TYPE_METHODS be joined to USER_PROCEDURES but it can also be joined to USER_ARGUMENTS for additional detailed information about your object types. The following query shows a few lines of results from the join. It is a great query for validating your naming standards and/or catching invalid data type usages.

```
SELECT utm.type_name, utm.method_name, ua.argument_name,
    position, sequence, data_type
FROM user_type_methods utm
JOIN user_procedures up
 ON (utm.type_name = up.object_name
     AND
     utm.method_name = up.procedure_name)
 JOIN user_arguments ua
 ON (up.procedure_name = ua.object_name
     AND
     up.object_name = ua.package_name)
WHERE utm.type_name = 'DEMO_TYPE'
  AND rownum < 5;  -- usign rownum just to keep the example short
```

TYPE_NAME	METHOD_NAME	ARGUMENT_NAME	POSITION	SEQUENCE	DATA_TYPE
DEMO_TYPE	FUNC		0	1	NUMBER
DEMO_TYPE	FUNC	SELF	1	2	OBJECT
DEMO_TYPE	FUNC	P_VALUE	2	3	VARCHAR2
DEMO_TYPE	OVERLOAD_PROC	SELF	1	1	OBJECT

USER_TRIGGERS

USER_TRIGGERS contains information about triggers that are defined in your database. While it is a useful place to find code, and it does contain useful information about the trigger and how the trigger is defined, it does not contain much information about the code. Use this view as a loop through USER_SOURCE to quickly view the code line by line.

PL/SCOPE

PL/SCOPE is a feature of the PL/SQL compiler that provides data for an extension to the data dictionary. This feature takes information gathered at compile time (information the compiler needs anyway) and drops it into a view (the usual three: USER_*, ALL_* and DBA_*) called USER_IDENTIFIERS. The data dictionary provides information about variables and other identifiers that are used in your PL/SQL code. In addition to showing the name of all identifiers, it also identifies what the variables are (data types as well as variables vs. parameter vs. etc.), how they are used (declared, referenced, assigned, etc.) and where they are used (the context of the declaration, assignment, etc.).

■ **Note**   PL/Scope is a version 11+ feature. If you are still using a version less than 11.0, you will need to upgrade to take advantage of both PL/Scope and DBMS_HPROF (dynamic profiling is discussed later). If you are using an earlier version, you can get some of this information from the dictionary views discussed earlier. I recommend an upgrade because you will benefit by many more things in 11g than just code analysis.

Every identifier used in your code (and this is true for any language, not just PL/SQL) has a context. This context is the most important part of usage analysis. A variable may be defined in a procedure (DEFINITION) within a package (the DECLARATION). The assignment of a value may be with the definition or it may come later as an assignment step in the body of the code. For a variable or iterator, you will be able to see any variables not REFERENCEd anywhere in the code. For a procedure or function, you can find if it has ever been CALLed. I will show examples of this in more detail next.

What is an identifier?

An identifier is anything that you can use within you code. You can use a procedure (you CALL it). You can use a variable (you can give it values or read values from it). You can use data types (seems odd but you use them when you declare a variable, constant, iterator, etc.). You can use triggers, synonyms, formal parameters, and even exceptions. An identifier is pretty much anything you can use or reference (with the exception of embedded SQL) within your code.

The following are the different types of identifiers that you will encounter when working with PL/SQL:

- Data types and subtypes used (including collections)

- Cursors and ref cursors

- Procedures

- Functions

- Packages and package bodies

- Triggers

- Object types and type bodies

- Parameters

- Function return values

- Variables, iterators, constants

- Exceptions

- Synonyms (are not resolved to any actual objects, there is no validation)

Every identifier has a unique signature that is a column in the USER_IDENTIFIERS view. This signature is a HEX string provided by Oracle—it is a unique string across a database. If you have an identifier named v_my_id declared in two different packages or standalone procedures, the signature will be unique across those program units. If you have the same variable identified at multiple scopes within the same program unit, each will have its own signature. An overloaded procedure within a package will also have two different signatures.

Scope of Identifiers

PL/Scope, by understanding the context, can provide the scope of a variable, hence the name PL/Scope. This ability is not super important for the most part, but it can help in some situations. One example is that when you have a variable defined in two scopes and don't realize it. You may think you are assigning a value to the variable at the higher scope when in fact you are assigning to the local scope. The assignment that PL/Scope shows can't tell you what you meant to do, but at least you will see the same variable declared at multiple scopes in the same call stack (bad practice alert). You can minimize this danger by always referencing the named scope of a variable but I find this makes the code less maintainable rather than more. I just try not to reuse names.

PL/Scope, also by understanding the context, can provide a call stack of procedural code. One of the uses of dynamic code analysis (which will be covered later) is to verify code coverage. Code coverage is the actual execution of all code in a regression test. PL/Scope can give you a static view that at least each program unit is referenced. If you have a procedure that is defined but never called, that's not necessarily a bad thing (it may be called from an external context), but it does give additional information that can be reviewed.

Speaking of external contexts, PL/Scope does show identifiers CALLed or REFERENCEd with an external context. You can then join to the external reference as long as that external context is compiled with PL/Scope turned on. An example of this is when you declare a variable of NUMBER, it makes an external reference to DATATYPENUMBER, which is a subtype declared in DBMS_STANDARD (an Oracle standard package). This would be an external context (external from the view point of the current program unit).

If a procedure in one program unit makes a call to a procedure in another program unit, you can see the complete call stack if both procedures are utilizing PL/Scope. You would not be able to follow the stack into an external C procedure or a Java unit as they are not covered by PL/Scope. Instead, you would see the CALL and the stack would end there (well, not end; you would pick the stack back up when the external reference returned).

Data Gathered

The data gathered by PL/Scope includes the name of an identifier, the usage, and the context of the identifier's usage. It also includes the object where the identifier is defined, the type of object, and the line and column of the usage.

Usage is the way the identifier is used. A data type is used by a variable definition; a procedure can be declared, defined and called. The following are the usages tracked by PL/Scope:

- **Declaration:** First identification of an identifier, such as a package.

- **Definition:** Implementation of an identifier, such as a procedure in a package body.

- **Assignment:** Change the value of an identifier, such as a variable or iterator.

- **Reference:** Inspect the value of an identifier (including raising an exception).

- **Call:** Execute an identifier, such as a procedure, function, cursor.

> ■ **Note** Data Type is a context of an identifier, as opposed to a property of an identifier, because not all identifiers have a data type. A procedure is an identifier but it has no data type.

All of the columns in the USER_IDENTIFIERS view are important. Table 7-1 contains the columns in the view and a brief description of the columns.

Table 7-1. Columns in the USER_IDENTIFIERS View

Column	Description
NAME	The name of an identifier (this can also be an object)
SIGNATURE	The unique signature of the identifier
TYPE	The type of the identifier
OBJECT_NAME	The name of the program unit being referenced
OBJECT_TYPE	The type of object (program unit) being referenced
USAGE	How the identifier is being used in the current context
USAGE_ID	The unique key for the identifier's usage in the current context
LINE	The line number for the usage
COL	The column number for the usage
USAGE_CONTEXT_ID	Hierarchical connection to the parent usage of the identifier's current context

To understand the usage columns a bit better, you need to look at the raw data in the view. The following is an example query against the view. The output is representative of what you will see in your own queries. Note that the view will be empty until you have compiled your code with PL/Scope turned on (which is explained in the next section "Configuring PL/Scope").

```
SELECT * FROM (
  SELECT object_name, name, type, usage, usage_id, usage_context_id
    FROM user_identifiers
    WHERE object_name = 'JOBS_API'
      AND object_type = 'PACKAGE BODY'
    ODER BY line, col, usage_id)
WHERE rownum < 6; -- keeping it small
```

OBJECT_NAME	NAME	TYPE	USAGE	USAGE_ID	USAGE_CONTEXT_ID
JOBS_API	JOBS_API	PACKAGE	DEFINITION	1	0
JOBS_API	JOB_EXISTS	FUNCTION	DEFINITION	2	1
JOBS_API	JOB_TITLE	FORMAL IN	DECLARATION	3	2
JOBS_API	V_JOB_ID	VARIABLE	DECLARATION	4	2
JOBS_API	V_JOB_ID	VARIABLE	ASSIGNMENT	5	2

The first usage (USAGE_ID = 1), is the package definition. The context for this program unit is 0. It is the first usage in the program unit so the USAGE_CONTEXT_ID is 0. You can't mix and match usages or contexts between program units, not even between a spec and a body.

The second row is a function definition. The USAGE_ID is 2 and the context is 1. This means that USAGE_ID 2 is a child of USAGE_ID 1. The function falls under the package.

The third row is a parameter, the fourth line is a variable declaration, and the fifth row is an assignment into the variable defined on row four. All of these usages are children of the function so the USAGE_CONTEXT_ID is 2 (they all fall within the function body).

If you have an overloaded program unit, the SIGNATURE column will uniquely identify which version is being called. The signature is always the signature of the identifier being referenced, not necessarily the current identifier in the object.

The following query shows that overloaded procedures will have different signatures even though they have the same name:

```
SELECT name, usage, signature
FROM user_identifiers
WHERE object_name = 'PLSCOPE_SUPPORT_PKG'
  AND object_type = 'PACKAGE'
  AND name = 'SOURCE_LOOKUP'
ORDER BY line, col, usage_id;
```

NAME	USAGE	SIGNATURE
SOURCE_LOOKUP	DECLARATION	A633B1818ABD9AE3739E5A0B6D86EBB8
SOURCE_LOOKUP	DECLARATION	3ED2FA822BD27B5B10F44226DCB93E0E

Configuring PL/Scope

The Oracle documentation states that PL/Scope is intended for application developers and is usually used in development. I would extend that. It should be used by anyone compiling PL/SQL and it should be used in any database you work in (development, test, and production). PL/Scope stores its data in the SYSAUX tablespace and uses very little space at all (so that should not be a concern). Running PL/Scope is also a compile time activity and not a runtime activity so there is no performance penalty (as there is with compiling with debug turned on). It may slightly increase compile time but not enough that I have been aware of it.

PL/Scope is very easily configured. As mentioned, it is a compile time activity so it is enabled prior to compilation of a program unit. The compiler setting used is called PLSCOPE_SETTINGS. The user, or most likely the user's IDE, will use an ALTER SESSION command to turn on PL/Scope. You can also set it globally by ALTER SYSTEM or per program unit with the ALTER COMPILE statement. I'll show an example of each below.

At this point, there is only an on (ALL) or off (NONE) switch, but in the future there may be some granularity allowed. The default in 11.2 and below is NONE. I would expect that in time ALL would be the default but that's just my personal preference.

To turn on PL/Scope collection at the session level, use this command:

```
ALTER SESSION SET PLSCOPE_SETTINGS = 'IDENTIFIERS:ALL';
```

To turn off identifier collection, use this command:

```
ALTER SESSION SET PLSCOPE_SETTINGS = 'IDENTIFIERS:NONE';
```

Turning it on and off at the system level is similar. I'm not going to go into the details of the ALTER SYSTEM command and how it stores the values, but an example might be the following:

```
ALTER SYSTEM SET PLSCOPE_SETTINGS = 'IDENTIFIERS:ALL';
```

To compile an object with identifier collection, use the appropriate alter (PROCEDURE, PACKAGE, TRIIGER, FUNCTION, TYPE, etc.), like so:

```
ALTER PACKAGE batch_overlord COMPILE PLSCOPE_SETTINGS = 'IDENTIFIERS:ALL';
```

Once you have compiled the program unit, you can use the view USER_PLSQL_OBJECT_SETTINGS to see the settings, like so:

```
SQL> SELECT type, plscope_settings
        FROM user_plsql_object_settings
        WHERE name = 'EMPLOYEE_API';

TYPE          PLSCOPE_SETTINGS
------------  ----------------------------------------------------------------------
PACKAGE       IDENTIFIERS:ALL
PACKAGE BODY  IDENTIFIERS:ALL
```

That's all there is to it. Once it's set up, you can start using it. Don't forget to recompile your code with PL/Scope turned on.

Change Impact Analysis

Change impact analysis allows a developer or analyst to assess the impact of intended changes in code to other areas of the code. In my experience, impact analysis is very rare. The norm seems to be to make changes and discover the repercussions after the fact. This can be very expensive in terms of time, money, and reputation. It is far better to know ahead of time, so that impacts can be analyzed and planned for instead of running into issues after moving code to test (or worse, production) environments.

When impact analysis is completed, you, or the person doing the analysis, should have a fairly deep understanding of the objects that will require changes. Not only will you know which objects require changes but test cases can be created for each object to be changed, and regression tests can be planned and estimated for all changed objects. By knowing ahead of time which objects to test, you will also be able to schedule time for appropriate performance testing to ensure the changes do not negatively affect application performance.

The problem with impact analysis is that there are really no one-size-fits-all approaches to the analysis. In a database application, multiple types of changes are possible: data change (changes to types or volumes of data, such as adding new sources), schema changes (changes to database structures), and code changes. There's not much a PL/SQL book can give you to handle data changes; that's very application specific. For schema changes, the USER_DEPENDENCIES view is still your best bet to see which objects have references to other objects in the schema. The rest of this section will deal with code changes (which may be related to, or a result of, data or schema changes).

The way impact analysis has been done in most organizations where I have worked is to either assume you have omniscient knowledge of the application and everything that uses it or to change an object and see where it invalidates downstream objects. Both approaches are just ugly. For one thing, if you are already changing objects, then you are past the estimation phase, which is where you really want to start this process. For another, there's no indication of exactly what caused the invalidation. This is a highly tedious and error-prone approach.

Isn't it a better approach to use the data available in the data dictionary to run a report and get a listing of exactly the data related to a change? A human being can then use this (mostly, hopefully) automated data gathering.

The way to begin an impact change analysis is to break down the requirements into component parts. Each part contains a change and that change has some impact (normally) to the application. The next step is to identify all of the units that will be impacted.

This breaking down can be done at an object level (such as at the package level). At that high of a level, though, you are hit with all of the issues as described earlier in the sections on USER_SOURCE and USER_DEPENDENCIES. Ideally, you would have a very granular view of the source code without resorting to a line-by-line scan of the code. PL/Scope can provide a very fine-grained view of the program units called by other program units. Note that PL/Scope does not help with external code or code called from views. You would use the dependency views for view support and tools external to the database for external code and Java.

I don't include it in this book but I also frequently pull out related information and store it in my own tables. I will collapse parent/child records into a single record (for example, collapse rows to combine a package.function call). In this way, I have a multi-pass system that allows for a greater range of programs that use easier-to-maintain queries. Explaining the full system I use is way out of scope here but when you start writing your own queries, remember that you can write parts of the query, save those results, and then write queries against the saved data.

In the demo code provided for this chapter is a package called PLSCOPE_SUPPORT_PKG. This package contains some useful code for dealing with various aspects of PL/Scope. I'll start with the procedure PRINT_IMPACTS, which is an overloaded procedure. The version I will use first takes as parameters a program unit owner (P_OWNER), name (P_OBJECT), and sub unit name (P_UNIT).

Let's take an example. Suppose you planned to change the HR.JOBS_API.VALIDATE_JOB procedure so that it took an extra parameter or changed the return data type. You would want to know where all calls to that function are. The example call to the support package would look like this:

```
SQL> exec plscope_support_pkg.print_impacts('HR', 'JOBS_API', 'VALIDATE_JOB');

Impact to PACKAGE BODY HR.EMPLOYEE_API.CREATE_EMPLOYEE at line 40 and column 12
Impact to PROCEDURE HR.TEST_CALLS_PRC at line 8 and column 8
Impact to PROCEDURE HR.TEST_CALLS_PRC at line 4 and column 6
Impact to FUNCTION HR.TEST_CALLS_FNC at line 5 and column 10

PL/SQL procedure successfully completed.
```

From this view, you can see that three objects are impacted and one of those objects (HR.TEST_CALLS_PRC) is impacted twice. In an application this small, it is probably just as easy to query USER_SOURCE or grep your code repository and eyeball the results. However, in a very large system, this kind of conciseness makes analysis much easier.

If you wanted to see the source text with your output, you could pass in an optional BOOLEAN with the call to PRINT_IMPACTS, like so:

```
SQL> set serveroutput on format wrapped
SQL> exec plscope_support_pkg.print_impacts('HR', 'JOBS_API', 'VALIDATE_JOB', TRUE);

Impact to PACKAGE BODY HR.EMPLOYEE_API.CREATE_EMPLOYEE at line 40 and column 12
    TEXT:
              IF NOT jobs_api.validate_job(p_job_t
          tle, p_department_name)

Impact to PROCEDURE HR.TEST_CALLS_PRC at line 8 and column 8
    TEXT:
              IF JOBS_API.VALIDATE_JOB('a', 'b')

Impact to PROCEDURE HR.TEST_CALLS_PRC at line 4 and column 6
    TEXT:
              IF JOBS_API.VALIDATE_JOB('a', 'b')

Impact to FUNCTION HR.TEST_CALLS_FNC at line 5 and column 10
    TEXT:
              RETURN JOBS_API.VALIDATE_JOB('a', 'b')

PL/SQL procedure successfully completed.
```

This code is just a demo but it shows how you can use PL/Scope to walk through the hierarchy of identifiers to find so much valuable information about your code. The meat of these impact analysis procedures is this query from PLSCOPE_SUPPORT_PKG.GET_IMPACT_INFO. (Note that I simplified both the procedures and the main query so that they would better serve as an example. An example that can handle nested blocks is a bit more complex, needlessly so for the purpose of this section. Just know that this code is a demo and a starting point, not a complete impact analysis program.) The following code is from PLSCOPE_SUPPORT_PKG.GET_IMPACT_INFO and is the FOR LOOP query starting at line 54:

```
SELECT code_info( ai.owner,
                  prior_object_name,
                  CASE
                  WHEN ai.object_type IN ('PROCEDURE', 'FUNCTION')
                  THEN NULL
                  ELSE
                    ai.name
                  END,
                  ai.object_type,
                  'CALL',
                  cnctby_vw.line,
                  cnctby_vw.p_col ) code_value
        FROM all_identifiers ai, (
    SELECT usage, level, usage_id, usage_context_id, PRIOR usage_id p_usage_id,
          PRIOR usage_context_id prior_usagectx_id,
          object_name, name, object_type, type, line, PRIOR col p_col,
          PRIOR object_name prior_object_name, PRIOR name p_name,
          PRIOR object_type prior_object_type
       FROM all_identifiers
```

```
        WHERE OWNER = p_owner
          AND OBJECT_TYPE IN ('PACKAGE BODY', 'PROCEDURE', 'FUNCTION', 'TRIGGER', 'TYPE BODY')
          AND USAGE NOT IN ('DECLARATION', 'ASSIGNMENT', 'DEFINITION')
          AND type IN ('PACKAGE BODY', 'FUNCTION', 'PROCEDURE', 'TYPE', 'TYPE BODY')
        CONNECT BY PRIOR usage_id = usage_context_id
          AND PRIOR name = p_object
          AND name = p_unit
          AND prior usage_context_id != 0 )  cnctby_vw
  WHERE ai.usage_id = cnctby_vw.prior_usagectx_id
    AND ai.object_name = cnctby_vw.prior_object_name
    AND ai.object_type = cnctby_vw.prior_object_type  )
```

The inner query (cnctby_vw) is a hierarchical query that gets the changed program unit information. This query is specifically looking for packaged calls. It's easily modified to find any kind of calls; I leave that exercise to you. Modifying it to find procedure or function calls is easier than finding packaged calls or object methods.

The outer query ties the changed unit (the CALLED program unit) to the sub-unit (procedure or function in a package) or, if standalone, to the standalone unit.

Before creating your own impact analysis queries using this query as a basis, I suggest that you start with the inner query and play with that for a while. That basic query can be modified to return almost any two related items that PL/Scope provides.

Validating Naming Standards Compliance

Like USER_PROCEDURES, USER_ARGUMENTS and the USER_TYPE family of views, PL/Scope can provide intelligence on naming standards compliance. PL/Scope is even better, though, because you can verify the naming of variables internal to packages as well as in the body of procedures and functions, as opposed to just parameters and program unit naming.

The following query will find all variables that don't begin with 'V_' and parameters that don't begin with 'P_'. It could be extended using a hierarchical query like the one in the code analysis section to validate globals and sub-types.

```
SELECT  ui_var.name, type, usage, line, col
  FROM user_identifiers ui_var
  WHERE ui_var.object_name = 'JOBS_API'
    AND ui_var.object_type = 'PACKAGE BODY'
    AND (
          (ui_var.type = 'VARIABLE' AND name NOT LIKE 'V_%')
      OR
          (ui_var.type IN ('FORMAL IN', 'FORMAL OUT', 'FORMAL IN OUT')
             AND name NOT LIKE 'P_%')
        )
    AND ui_var.usage = 'DECLARATION'
  ORDER BY line, col;
```

NAME	TYPE	USAGE	LINE	COL
JOB_TITLE	FORMAL IN	DECLARATION	4	5

If you look at the code in JOBS_API starting at line 4, you will find the following code:

```
FUNCTION job_exists(
  job_title  IN jobs.job_title%TYPE )
RETURN jobs.job_id%TYPE AS
  v_job_id jobs.job_id%TYPE;
BEGIN
  SELECT job_id
    INTO v_job_id
    FROM jobs
    WHERE UPPER(job_title) = upper(job_title);
```

From this code, you can see that it does indeed have a parameter named JOB_TITLE. Looking at the query in the code, you will find that the query has a problem. The problem lies in the WHERE clause where the same column name is referenced twice. The person writing the function intended to compare the table column to the parameter, but that's not the comparison that will happen. Here is the offending comparison:

```
WHERE UPPER(job_title) = UPPER(job_title);
```

If someone were to run that select, every record in the table would match (the SQL parser will use job_title from the table instead of the job_title parameter). The fix is to rewrite the function specification as follows, adding a p_ to the parameter name:

```
FUNCTION job_exists(
  p_job_title  IN jobs.job_title%TYPE )
 RETURN jobs.job_id%TYPE;
```

Modify the filter criteria in the WHERE clause to add the p_ that was added to the parameter, like so:

```
WHERE UPPER(job_title) = upper(p_job_title);
```

The reason the query would not run successfully is that, as far as Oracle is concerned, the filter was comparing the value in the column job_title to the value in the column job_title. That would be the same as the criteria WHERE 1=1. The result is that every row in the table would be returned—obviously not what was intended. By adding the p_ prefix to both the parameter and its usage, the filter will only return the row where the job title in the table matches the job_title passed into the function.

Finding Unused Identifiers

Many organizations have standards about variable usage, such as "no global variables and/or all variables must be used." I don't particularly agree with the no globals rule (although the usage of globals should be carefully considered). However, I do agree that having unused variables in a program makes maintaining it more complex (cluttery mostly).

With PL/Scope, it is easy to see which variables, at any scope, are not used. You will have a declaration and no reference. The next several queries will build up to a query that will find a procedure that defines an unused global protected variable, an unused parameter, and an unused local variable.

First, list all of the declared variables in a package body (note that this will not pick up globals defined in the spec, only protected globals defined in the body), like so:

```
SELECT  ui_var.name, type, usage, line, col
  FROM user_identifiers ui_var
  WHERE ui_var.object_name = 'VARIABLES_PKG'
    AND ui_var.object_type = 'PACKAGE BODY'
```

```
      AND ui_var.type IN ('VARIABLE', 'FORMAL IN', 'FORMAL OUT', 'FORMAL IN OUT')
      AND ui_var.usage = 'DECLARATION'
    ORDER BY line, col;
```

NAME	TYPE	USAGE	LINE	COL
G_PROTECTED_VARIABLE_USED	VARIABLE	DECLARATION	3	3
G_PROTECTED_VARIABLE_UNUSED	VARIABLE	DECLARATION	4	3
P_KEYNUM	FORMAL IN	DECLARATION	7	5
P_DATE	FORMAL IN OUT	DECLARATION	8	5
P_LOB	FORMAL OUT	DECLARATION	9	5
V_USED_VARIABLE	VARIABLE	DECLARATION	11	5
V_UNUSED_VARIABLE	VARIABLE	DECLARATION	12	5

The easiest way to validate that all of these parameters/variables are used is to check that they are referenced. However, you could do an assignment and never reference a variable (what would be the use of that?) and you can also assign a variable in the same step that it is declared. For me, I want to be sure all variables are being used (which means a reference regardless of assignment).

To see the variables that are being referenced, it's as easy as changing the usage from DECLARATION to REFERENCE, which the following query does:

```
SELECT  ui_var.name, type, usage, line, col
  FROM user_identifiers ui_var
  WHERE ui_var.object_name = 'VARIABLES_PKG'
    AND ui_var.object_type = 'PACKAGE BODY'
    AND ui_var.type IN ('VARIABLE', 'FORMAL IN', 'FORMAL OUT', 'FORMAL IN OUT')
    AND ui_var.usage = 'REFERENCE'
  ORDER BY line, col;
```

NAME	TYPE	USAGE	LINE	COL
P_KEYNUM	FORMAL IN	REFERENCE	14	24
V_USED_VARIABLE	VARIABLE	REFERENCE	16	22
G_PROTECTED_VARIABLE_USED	VARIABLE	REFERENCE	16	40
P_LOB	FORMAL OUT	REFERENCE	17	39

This shows that there are three missing variables. Using a simple bit of SQL, they are easily findable. This final query returns the declared variables that are not being used:

```
SELECT  name, type, usage, line, col
  FROM user_identifiers
  WHERE object_type = 'PACKAGE BODY'
    AND usage = 'DECLARATION'
    AND (name, type) IN (
SELECT  ui_var.name, type
  FROM user_identifiers ui_var
  WHERE ui_var.object_name = 'VARIABLES_PKG'
    AND ui_var.object_type = 'PACKAGE BODY'
    AND ui_var.type IN ('VARIABLE', 'FORMAL IN', 'FORMAL OUT', 'FORMAL IN OUT')
    AND ui_var.usage = 'DECLARATION'
MINUS
  SELECT  ui_var.name, type
  FROM user_identifiers ui_var
```

```
  WHERE ui_var.object_name = 'VARIABLES_PKG'
    AND ui_var.object_type = 'PACKAGE BODY'
    AND ui_var.type IN ('VARIABLE', 'FORMAL IN', 'FORMAL OUT', 'FORMAL IN OUT')
    AND ui_var.usage = 'REFERENCE')
  ORDER BY line, col;
```

NAME	TYPE	USAGE	LINE	COL
G_PROTECTED_VARIABLE_UNUSED	VARIABLE	DECLARATION	4	3
P_DATE	FORMAL IN OUT	DECLARATION	8	5
V_UNUSED_VARIABLE	VARIABLE	DECLARATION	12	5

If you remove the outer query where criteria (the fourth line in the previous query),

```
AND usage = 'DECLARATION'
```

you can add additional records indicating those variables that are declared and assigned a value but are never referenced (the results from that change follow).

NAME	TYPE	USAGE	LINE	COL
G_PROTECTED_VARIABLE_UNUSED	VARIABLE	ASSIGNMENT	4	3
G_PROTECTED_VARIABLE_UNUSED	VARIABLE	DECLARATION	4	3
P_DATE	FORMAL IN OUT	DECLARATION	8	5
V_UNUSED_VARIABLE	VARIABLE	DECLARATION	12	5

Finding Scope Issues

Another bad coding practice is creating variables of the same name at different scopes in a program. If you always include the scope in a reference, then you ensure you are accessing the correct item. However, it makes for painful maintenance and is generally a bad idea.

To provide an example, I am using the SCOPE_PKG demo package provided. The package specification and body are listed here for easy reference:

```
create or replace PACKAGE SCOPE_PKG AS
  i CONSTANT NUMBER := 0;

  g_global_variable NUMBER := 10;

  PROCEDURE proc1 ;
END SCOPE_PKG;
/

create or replace PACKAGE BODY SCOPE_PKG AS

  PROCEDURE proc1
  AS
    i PLS_INTEGER := 30;
  BEGIN
```

```
    FOR i IN 1..10
    LOOP
      DBMS_OUTPUT.PUT_LINE(i);
    END LOOP;

    DBMS_OUTPUT.PUT_LINE(i);
  END;

END SCOPE_PKG;
/
```

The next query shows all variables identifiers (VARIABLES, CONSTANTS, and ITERATORS) that are declared at different scopes in the same program (in this case, a package). A package can declare variables in both a spec and a body. It's up to you to decide if the scoping is an error.

```
WITH source_ids AS (
  SELECT    *
    FROM user_identifiers
      WHERE object_name = 'SCOPE_PKG'
        AND object_type IN ('PACKAGE BODY', 'PACKAGE')
)
SELECT name, type, usage, prior name, object_type, line, col
  FROM source_ids si
  WHERE type IN ('VARIABLE', 'ITERATOR', 'CONSTANT')
    AND usage = 'DECLARATION'
    AND EXISTS (
      SELECT count(*), name
        FROM user_identifiers
        WHERE object_Name = si.object_name
          AND name = si.name
          AND usage = si.usage
        GROUP BY name
        HAVING count(*) > 1 )
  START WITH usage_context_id = 0
  CONNECT BY PRIOR usage_id = usage_context_id
    AND PRIOR object_type = object_type;
```

NAME	TYPE	USAGE	PRIORNAME	OBJECT_TYPE	LINE	COL
I	CONSTANT	DECLARATION	SCOPE_PKG	PACKAGE	3	3
I	VARIABLE	DECLARATION	PROC1	PACKAGE BODY	5	5
I	ITERATOR	DECLARATION	PROC1	PACKAGE BODY	8	9

The variable I is declared in the package spec, in a procedure in the body, and as a loop iterator in the same procedure.

You can include additional criteria to the query and only return values that are definite collisions. You would do that by including the hierarchy—if one declaration is included in a USAGE_ID that is also covered by a higher USAGE_CONTEXT_ID, such as if the usage is a child of a previous usage.

Data Types Checks

In the section on USER_ARGUMENTS, I showed how you can validate data types but also how it is limited to just parameters. With PL/Scope, I can extend that to include variables defined anywhere in a program. Using the same demo procedure, BAD_DATA_TYPES_PRC, the following query shows how you can find those variables (and parameters):

```
SELECT * FROM (
WITH source_ids AS (
  SELECT    line,
            col,
            name,
            type,
            usage,
            usage_id,
            usage_context_id,
            object_name
    FROM user_identifiers
      WHERE object_name = 'BAD_DATA_TYPES_PRC'
        AND object_type = 'PROCEDURE')
SELECT  prior name "Identifier",
        CASE
        WHEN prior type IN ('FORMAL IN', 'FORMAL OUT', 'FORMAL IN OUT')
        THEN 'PARAMETER'
        WHEN prior type IN ('VARIABLE', 'CONSTANT', 'ITERATOR')
        THEN 'VARIABLE'
        ELSE prior name
        END "Identififer Type",
        Name "Data Type",
        Usage
  FROM source_ids
  START WITH usage_context_id = 0
  CONNECT BY PRIOR usage_id = usage_context_id
  ORDER SIBLINGS BY line, col
)
WHERE usage =   'REFERENCE';
```

Identifier	Identififer Type	Data Type	USAGE
P_DATA_IN	PARAMETER	CHAR	REFERENCE
P_DATA_OUT	PARAMETER	LONG	REFERENCE
V_CHAR	VARIABLE	CHAR	REFERENCE
V_VARCHAR	VARIABLE	VARCHAR	REFERENCE
V_LONG	VARIABLE	LONG	REFERENCE

One thing that is still not available is being able to verify if a data type is anchored or not. Having that as part of PL/Scope as just another child of the identifier declaration would be excellent. You can infer that (using user_arguments) a data length or data precision means that an argument is anchored but null does not mean not anchored. Date data types, for example, do not have a scale.

Performing Dynamic Analysis

Moving on from static analysis to dynamic analysis, let's look at the tools available in a pre-11g Oracle database (DBMS_PROFILER and DBMS_TRACE) and what is available in post 11g (those plus DBMS_HPROF). Even though DBMS_HPROF is a better tool for performance metrics (much better, in my opinion), DBMS_PROFILER and DBMS_TRACE still provide some usability for code coverage testing.

This section is not intended to be a tutorial on how to use the built-in packages mentioned, but it will cover some basics to get you up and running. This section will point out which parts of the built-ins are useful for knowing your code.

There are two primary benefits to be gained by running dynamic analysis using these Oracle-provided tools. The first is insight into the performance profile of your application. By profiling, you can identify bottlenecks in your code before putting it into production. The second, which is sort of an unintentional side benefit, is the ability to test for code coverage (more on this later).

Note that Chapter 13 specifically covers profiling and instrumentation from a performance perspective but does not cover the Oracle-supplied packages discussed here. For a complete introduction to the packages discussed in the chapter, the Oracle documentation outlines all of the parameters and such.

DBMS_PROFILER and DBMS_TRACE

DBMS_PROFILER is a flat profiler. It provides timing information between two procedure calls in a PL/SQL program. You "turn on" the profiler to start a timer and then "turn it off" when you want to stop the timer. The time between the "on" and "off" is the amount of time that it took to run (with some minimal overhead from the DBMS_PROFILER code).

Form a performance perspective, DBMS_PROFILER is most powerful when used with DBMS_TRACE. The DBMS_TRACE package provides context for the timings that are gathered by DBMS_PROFILER. It provides a dynamic version of the static hierarchy provided by PL/Scope. PL/Scope shows you identifiers, and by inference the code, in the order that it can happen. PL/Scope shows you every possibility; DBMS_TRACE shows you the hierarchy that was *actually* executed.

DBMS_TRACE requires all code that will be traced to be compiled with DEBUG=TRUE. Running procedures compiled for debug is not recommended in production, so that makes the DBMS_TRACE package useless as instrumentation. However, as a way to know your code, there is still value to the package.

The output of a DBMS_TRACE session shows which procedure called which procedure, in order. The output of DBMS_TRACE combined with the line-by-line profiling from DBMS_PROFILER is the easiest way to do semi-automated code coverage that I have found. Even in a post 11g world, there is still some value to DBMS_TRACE and DBMS_PROFILER that can't be captured any other way. DBMS_TRACE will create a record for every line executed. When used in conjunction with PL/Scope (11g+ only), you get a great tool for line-oriented code coverage.

Configuring DBMS_PROFILER and DBMS_TRACE

Setting up both tools is a fairly simple process. You need EXECUTE on both DBMS_PROFILER and DBMS_TRACE. The packages should already exist in the database.

Before using the tools, you (or a DBA) will need to run a couple of scripts to create the underlying tables. The scripts are available in the $ORACLE_HOM/RDBMS/ADMIN directory. `PROFTAB.sql` will create the tables needed for DBMS_PROFILER and `TRACETAB.sql` for DBMS_TRACE. Note that `TRACETAB.sql` must be run as SYS. The tables that get created in these scripts will be described later.

If you are running multiple applications on a single server, you may want to create a common PROFILER user and run PROFTAB.sql as that user. This way, you can grant access to the tables and create synonyms for them and all applications can share the same tables. When you run reports about relationships between program calls, you can span schemas. If you want to keep runs separate or you only have a single application schema, you can run it as the script schema.

When running DBMS_PROFILER and DBMS_TRACE, you are required to have specific permissions and compiler options set. For any code to trace or profiled, you will need execute granted to the profiling schema. Also, for DBMS_PROFILER, it needs CREATE access on any program units to be profiled. Finally, DBMS_TRACE requires that the program unit be compiled with DEBUG=TRUE.

You will need SELECT access granted to your user account to query from the DBMS_TRACE tables. If the database user you are connecting as owns the DBMS_PROFILER tables, you will not need any additional grants. If a common profiler user owns the tables, that schema needs to grant SELECT to your schema.

That's it for configuration. After performing these setup steps, you are ready to gather some information.

DBMS_PROFILER and DBMS_TRACE Example Session

This section provides an example profiling and tracing session using both DBMS_PROFILER and DBMS_TRACE. All of the resultant trace and profiling information displayed in this section was generated using the code presented here:

```
DECLARE
  v_employee_id employees.employee_id%TYPE;
BEGIN
  -- Start the profiling session
  dbms_profiler.start_profiler;
  dbms_trace.set_plsql_trace(
                DBMS_TRACE.trace_enabled_calls
                +
                DBMS_TRACE.trace_enabled_exceptions
                +
                DBMS_TRACE.trace_all_sql
                +
                DBMS_TRACE.trace_all_lines);

  -- call the top level procedure to be profiled
  v_employee_id := employee_api.create_employee(
        p_first_name => 'Lewis',
        p_last_name => 'Cunningham',
        p_email => 'lewisc@yahoo.com',
        p_phone_number => '888-555-1212',
        p_job_title => 'Programmer',
        p_department_name => 'IT',
        p_salary => 99999.99,
        p_commission_pct => 0 );
```

```
   -- Stop the profiling session
   dbms_trace.clear_plsql_trace;
   dbms_profiler.stop_profiler;

END;
```

DBMS_PROFILER.start_profiler begins the profiling session and DBMS_TRACE.set_plsql_trace starts the event tracing. Both procedures take optional parameters as input. The DBMS_TRACE parameter TRACE_LEVEL identifies how much information to gather. In this case, I wanted a record created for all enabled calls (calls to program units compiled with DEBUG), all enabled exceptions, all SQL calls, and for all lines. This is really overkill for the most part. The output is shown next.

DBMS_PROFILER and DBMS_TRACE Output

When run, DBMS_TRACE compiles data into two tables. These tables are as follows:

- PLSQL_TRACE_RUNS – DBMS_TRACE: The top-level table that identifies each individual run.

- PLSQL_TRACE_EVENTS – DBMS_TRACE: A very useful table that can log every line executed in a trace session, can quickly get very large very, and requires monitoring.

When run, DBMS_TRACE compiles data into the following tables:

- PLSQL_PROFILER_RUNS – DBMS_PROFILER: The top-level table that identifies each individual profiler session.

- PLSQL_PROFILER_UNITS – DBMS_PROFILER: Describes the program units executed during a profiling session.

- PLSQL_PROFILER_DATA – DBMS_PROFILER: Timing and execution statistics for each unit run during a session.

You can identify a DBMS_PROFILER run by the RUN_DATE and RUN_COMMENT (optional; defaults to the SYSDATE of the run initiation). The following query shows the data stored in the PLSQL_PROFILER_RUNS table after two profiler sessions:

```
select runid, run_date, run_comment, run_total_time
from plsql_profiler_runs;
```

```
RUNID      RUN_DATE                RUN_COMMENT       RUN_TOTAL_TIME
---------- --------------------    ----------------  ----------------------
2          13-MAR-2011 11:56:54    13-MAR-11         133000000
3          13-MAR-2011 12:30:18    13-MAR-11         80000000
```

From this output, you can identify the run you are looking for. When analyzing for performance, you will often average over many runs of the same program code. For the needs of this example, I will use a distinct program run.

Identifying a trace sessions is much the same as identifying a profiler session. The session is identified by a RUNID and a RUN_DATE. The following query shows the data stored in the PLSQL_TRACE_RUNS table after a tracing session:

```
SELECT runid, run_date
FROM plsql_trace_runs;

RUNID                   RUN_DATE
---------------------   -------------------------
10                      26-MAR-2011 11:04:35
```

DBMS_PROFILER provides timing information about the executable lines in a run. You gather the information and then analyze that information to determine if there is a bottleneck in the code. Code that runs for a long time may be okay; then again, it may not. That determination comes from your analysis. The profiler can't tell you where you have a performance problem. The profiler can only give you a performance profile for your analysis. Once you have analyzed the output and made any changes, you would then run another profiling session to validate your changes.

The following query lists the timing gathered by the profiler line by line. I have removed many lines of output to keep the size down. I'm ignoring the ANONYMOUS BLOCK entries as they are noise from the run itself.

```
SELECT unit_name, unit_type, line#, total_occur, ppd.total_time, max_time
   FROM plsql_profiler_units ppu
   JOIN plsql_profiler_data ppd
     ON (ppu.runid = ppd.runid
         AND
         ppu.unit_number = ppd.unit_number)
WHERE ppu.runid = :RUNID
   AND unit_type != 'ANONYMOUS BLOCK'  ;
```

UNIT_NAME	UNIT_TYPE	LINE#	TOTAL_OCCUR	TOTAL_TIME	MAX_TIME
EMPLOYEE_API	PACKAGE BODY	3	1	11982	9985
EMPLOYEE_API	PACKAGE BODY	20	1	1997	1997
EMPLOYEE_API	PACKAGE BODY	21	1	2995	2995
DEPARTMENTS_API	PACKAGE BODY	3	1	7988	6989
DEPARTMENTS_API	PACKAGE BODY	8	1	0	0
JOBS_API	PACKAGE BODY	3	1	7988	6989
JOBS_API	PACKAGE BODY	7	1	0	0
.					
.					
.					

```
 80 rows selected
```

This listing shows the line executed for each program unit profiled. It gives you the number of occurrences and the total time spent on that line (including calls to called program units). The max time is the longest time spent on any particular call. Using this information, you should be able to get a good feel of where you would begin your investigation into any performance issues.

While the performance metrics are great, it would be better if you knew the context, or call hierarchy, of the times. DBMS_TRACE does not quite give you that, but it does give you the call structure. To view the executed code hierarchy (remember that this is the actual execution, not the expected or possible execution), you can run the following very simple query:

```
SELECT event_unit, event_proc_name,
       CASE
         WHEN proc_unit IS NOT NULL and proc_name IS NOT NULL
           THEN proc_unit || '.' || proc_name || '(' || proc_line || ')'
         WHEN proc_unit IS NULL and proc_name IS NOT NULL
           THEN proc_name || '(' || proc_line || ')'
         ELSE
           substr(event_comment,1,30)
       END executed_code
FROM plsql_trace_events pse
WHERE runid = :RUNID
 AND event_unit NOT IN ('<anonymous>', 'DBMS_TRACE')
 AND event_kind NOT IN (50, 51)
ORDER BY event_seq;
```

```
EVENT_UNIT         EVENT_PROC_NAME          EXECUTED_CODE
----------------   --------------------     --------------------------------------------
EMPLOYEE_API       CREATE_EMPLOYEE          DEPARTMENTS_API.DEPARTMENT_EXISTS(3)
DEPARTMENTS_API    DEPARTMENT_EXISTS        SELECT DEPARTMENT_ID FROM DEPA
EMPLOYEE_API       CREATE_EMPLOYEE          JOBS_API.JOB_EXISTS(3)
JOBS_API           JOB_EXISTS               SELECT JOB_ID FROM JOBS WHERE
EMPLOYEE_API       CREATE_EMPLOYEE          JOBS_API.VALIDATE_JOB(21)
EMPLOYEE_API       CREATE_EMPLOYEE          DEPARTMENTS_API.DEPARTMENT_MANAGER_ID(29)
DEPARTMENTS_API    DEPARTMENT_MANAGER_ID    SELECT MANAGER_ID FROM DEPARTM
EMPLOYEE_API       CREATE_EMPLOYEE          Select EMPLOYEES_SEQ.NEXTVAL f
EMPLOYEE_API       CREATE_EMPLOYEE          INSERT INTO EMPLOYEES (EMPLOYE
EMPLOYEE_API       CREATE_EMPLOYEE          EMPLOYEE_API.ASSIGN_SALARY(74)
EMPLOYEE_API       ASSIGN_SALARY            UPDATE EMPLOYEES SET SALARY =
```

```
11 rows selected
```

This listing (and query) provides the order of execution from the run. EMLOYEE_API.CREATE_EMPLOYEE called DEPARTMENTS_API.DEPARTMENT_EXISTS (which is defined on line 3 in the DEPARTMENTS_API package body). The called program unit then ran a query before returning.

DBMS_TRACE can be very verbose. The examples I am using in this section are fairly simple and back office-ish. When you have very large applications or applications that run for a while and call the same program units over and over, the value of DBMS_TRACE starts to drop off as the complexity increases. For example, there is a demo procedure provided for this chapter called TEST_CALLS_PRC. It is a simple for loop (100 iterations) that calls two procedures for each iteration. Using DBMS_TRACE and DBMS_PROFILER with the same options that I used earlier, compare the differences in number of rows (the lower RUNID is the trace seen earlier for both counts). The following query compares the number of output lines produced between the two runs by DBMS_PROFILER:

```
SELECT ppd.runid, count(*)
  FROM plsql_profiler_units ppu
  JOIN plsql_profiler_data ppd
    ON(ppu.runid = ppd.runid
    AND ppu.unit_number = ppd.unit_number)
```

```
WHERE ppu.runid IN (9,10)
  AND ppd.total_time != 0
  AND unit_type != 'ANONYMOUS BLOCK'
GROUP BY ppd.runid;
```

```
RUNID                    COUNT(*)
---------------------- ----------------------
9                        29
10                       15
```

The next query produces the same line counts but for two DBMS_TRACE sessions:

```
SELECT runid, count(*)
  FROM plsql_trace_events
  WHERE runid IN (12,13)
  GROUP BY runid;
```

```
RUNID                    COUNT(*)
---------------------- ----------------------
12                       100
13                       5545
```

DBMS_PROFILER has fewer rows for the less complex code but DBMS_TRACE has many, many more rows. When writing queries against the DBMS_TRACE tables, you need to account for that. Use the options to gather only the data you really want and then plan to be creative on filtering out those things you don't want but can't option out of.

Code Coverage Testing and Performance Metrics

Code coverage testing is a method of testing in which you verify that each line of a program that *can be* executed is actually executed. This kind of testing is regression testing as opposed to functional testing. Just because a piece of code was executed does not mean it was executed correctly. However, if it was executed at least once, then you know it will in fact, under certain circumstances, execute without error.

Code coverage testing is fairly meaningless by itself. However, as part of an automated build process or as one component of an overall test plan, it does have its uses. I like using code coverage for the same reason I like compiler errors. It catches plenty of oopsy. Without the proper tools though, this is very difficult testing to accomplish. Fortunately, Oracle has given us most of what we need.

I'm not particularly concerned with performance metrics here (although there is no reason not to include them). What I want to see is that all of the code that can be executed is executed.

It is possible to combine the output from DBMS_TRACE and DBMS_PROFILER to get a nice trace of each line that executed along with some context. To do so requires creating a funky query and some knowledge of individual runs that are related by being run together or very close together. If you combine a run of the profiler with a run of the trace from different versions of the code, you will get a very ugly mess. However, if you know that you have matching runs, the information is highly useful.

The following query joins the DBMS_PROFILER output and the DBMS_TRACE output. To simplify the query, I am leaving out the PLSQL_TRACE_RUNS and the PLSQL_PROFILER_RUNS tables, which is really where you would start. I'm just manually picking a run from each. I'm dropping certain event types, specifically SQL calls (54) and returns from procedure calls (50). You can get a list of all of the event kinds from the documentation or from the `tracetab.sql` install code. When looking at the total_time, I like to see who is being called, from where, and exactly what the code is doing. The who and where comes from the DBMS_TRACE data and the what comes from USER_SOURCE. Here is the query:

```
BREAK ON event_unit ON event_proc_name
SELECT event_unit, event_proc_name, line# line,
       total_time time, pse.proc_unit, pse.proc_name,
       substr(ltrim(rtrim(text)),1,30) source_text
FROM (
  (SELECT ppu.runid, ppu.unit_type, ppu.unit_name,
          ppd.line#, ppd.total_time
     FROM plsql_profiler_units ppu
     JOIN plsql_profiler_data ppd
       ON(ppu.runid = ppd.runid
       AND ppu.unit_number = ppd.unit_number)
      WHERE ppu.runid = :PROF_RUNID
        AND ppd.total_time != 0)) prof_data
JOIN (
    SELECT event_unit, event_proc_name, event_line,
           proc_unit, proc_name, event_unit_kind,
           event_kind, min(event_seq) event_seq
      FROM plsql_trace_events trace_data
     WHERE runid = :TRACE_RUNID
       AND event_kind NOT IN (50, 54)
     GROUP BY event_unit, event_proc_name, event_line,
           proc_unit, proc_name, event_unit_kind,
           event_kind) pse
  ON (pse.event_unit = prof_data.unit_name
  AND pse.event_line = prof_data.line#)
JOIN user_source us
  ON (us.name = pse.event_unit
  AND us.type = pse.event_unit_kind
  AND us.line = pse.event_line)
ORDER BY event_seq;


EVENT_UNIT          EVENT_PROC_NAME          LINE    TIME PROC_UNIT
----------------    ----------------------   -----  ------- -----------------
PROC_NAME           SOURCE_TEXT
----------------    ------------------------------
EMPLOYEE_API        CREATE_EMPLOYEE              3   12933
                    FUNCTION create_employee(

                                               20    2984
                    v_exception BOOLEAN := FALSE;

                                               21    3979
                    v_exception_message CHAR(2048)

                                               24  247720
                    v_department_id := departments

                                               24  247720 DEPARTMENTS_API
```

```
DEPARTMENT_EXISTS        v_department_id := departments

DEPARTMENTS_API    DEPARTMENT_EXISTS         3     7958
                        FUNCTION department_exists(

                                        9    185044
                        SELECT department_id

                                       14     1989
                        RETURN v_department_id;

EMPLOYEE_API       CREATE_EMPLOYEE          24    247720
                        v_department_id := departments
.
.
.
38 rows selected.
```

It was fairly difficult to format this output to fit the page, but hopefully you can see what is going on. The output starts at EMPLOYEE_API.CREATE_EMPLOYEE on line 3 of the package body. The time for that line is 12,933 and the actual code that is being executed (at least the first 30 bytes of it) is FUNCTION create_employee.

The second row of output corresponds to line 20 of the package body and is an assignment that had an elapsed time of 2,984. You can compare the code in this output to the actual source and see that line 20 is the first executable line. Everything before it was parameters and declarations. The assignment (while being declared) makes it an executable line. Line 20 is followed by 21, which is another assignment.

Finally, at line 24, an assignment is made by making a call to DEPARTMENTS_API.DEPARTMENT_EXISTS. That moves the EVENT_UNIT from EMPLOYEE_API to DEPARTMENTS_API. The next few lines are the executable lines in that program unit until it hits the return at line 14 (of the DEPARTMENTS_API package body). The last line displayed returns control to EMPLOYEE_API. The rest of the lines were suppressed to save space.

In a single report/query, you have a code coverage report, a code analysis report (by including executable code, line number, timing, and the actual source code), and performance metrics. If this report is saved to a table (your own user-created table), you can rerun this query after any changes to the code and compare output. You just need to be careful how you compare individual lines as they will change over time.

Unexecuted Code

It would be nice if there were an easy way to select all of the executable code that was not executed. PL/Scope does some of the information that you need but the way DBMS_TRACE executes a query (it captures the line with the select but not any of the other lines) presents some issues. Also, PL/Scope doesn't capture all potential executable lines, only lines with identifiers. If you look at the demo procedure TEST_PLSCOPE that follows, you'll see that the PROCEDURE has two executable lines (ignoring the declaration and definition of the procedure): the IF 1=1 and the "execute immediate."

```
CREATE OR REPLACE PROCEDURE TEST_PLSCOPE AS
BEGIN
  IF 1=1
  THEN
    execute immediate 'declare v1 number; begin select 1 into v1 from dual; end;';
  END IF;
END TEST_PLSCOPE;
```

As the next query shows, if you query USER_IDENTIFIERS, you only see the declaration and definition:

```
  SELECT object_name, line, usage
  FROM user_identifiers
  WHERE object_name = 'TEST_PLSCOPE'
    AND object_type = 'PROCEDURE'
ORDER BY usage_id;
```

OBJECT_NAME	LINE	USAGE
TEST_PLSCOPE	1	DECLARATION
TEST_PLSCOPE	1	DEFINITION

Right now, you can automate the code coverage gathering what was executed but you can't automate the gathering of what was not executed. About the closest you can get is an automated report that can then be picked over by human eyes. Such a report is better than nothing but not quite as sophisticated as I would like it to be.

The following query attempts to make the code coverage from the preceding query more robust by using USER_IDENITIFERS to retrieve all executable rows that are not included in the DBMS_TRACE run:

```
SELECT id_data.object_name, id_data.line, us.text
  FROM (
    SELECT DISTINCT object_type, object_name, line
      FROM user_identifiers ui
      WHERE (object_type, object_name) IN
            (SELECT distinct event_unit_kind, event_unit
                FROM plsql_trace_events pse
               WHERE pse.event_unit = ui.object_name
                 AND pse.event_unit_kind = ui.object_type
                 AND pse.runid = :TRACE_RUNID
                 AND pse.event_kind NOT IN (50, 54))
                 AND usage NOT IN ('DEFINITION', 'DECLARATION')
    MINUS
    SELECT event_unit_kind, event_unit, event_line
      FROM plsql_trace_events pse
      WHERE pse.runid = :TRACE_RUNID
        AND pse.event_kind NOT IN (50, 54)
        AND event_line IS NOT NULL) id_data
  JOIN user_source us
    ON (us.name = id_data.object_name
    AND us.type = id_data.object_type
    AND us.line = id_data.line)
  ORDER BY id_data.object_name, id_data.line;
```

In this part of the results (the following output is from the middle of the output), you can see what I would like to be the output from the PL/Scope data:

```
OBJECT_NAME                    LINE TEXT
-----------------------------  ----- ------------------------------
DEPARTMENTS_API                 42       WHEN NO_DATA_FOUND
DEPARTMENTS_API                 44        RETURN v_manager_id;
EMPLOYEE_API                    27      v_exception := TRUE;
EMPLOYEE_API                    28      v_exception_message := v
                                     _exception_message || chr(10)
                                        ||

EMPLOYEE_API                    29                  'Department '
                                     || p_department_name || ' not
                                     found.';

EMPLOYEE_API                    35      v_exception := TRUE;
EMPLOYEE_API                    36      v_exception_message := v
                                     _exception_message || chr(10)
                                        ||
```

Unfortunately, the result set starts with an example that I would like to filter out.

```
OBJECT_NAME                    LINE TEXT
-----------------------------  ----- ------------------------------
DEPARTMENTS_API                 10       INTO v_department_id
DEPARTMENTS_API                 12       WHERE upper(department_n
                                     ame) = upper(p_department_name
                                     );
```

These lines were executed as part of the select that started on line 9. PL/Scope includes lines 10 and 12 because they contain identifiers: v_department_id and p_department_name. Line 11 is the FROM clause that does not contain any identifiers.

All the other lines shown in the preceding example really were not executed. They are embedded in exception code, which is exactly the type of thing you want code coverage to show. Ideally, you would see that those lines were not executed and create tests that would exercise that code.

DBMS_HPROF

DBMS_HPROF is the Oracle 11g and up answer to PL/SQL code profiling. This is definitely the preferred tool for gathering performance metrics. It provides everything DBMS_PROFILER and DBMS_TRACE together provide, minus the line information for code coverage; it's easier to use, easier to read, and doesn't require changes to the environment to work. DBMS_HPROF can easily be run in a production environment, which is something lacking in DBMS_PROFILER and DBMS_TRACE.

DBMS_HPROF is a hierarchical profiler. DBMS_HPROF gives you not only what ran and how long it ran, it gives you the hierarchical context of who called what and in what order. You can also compare time spent in SQL vs. PL/SQL (critical for performance tuning). When combined with proper code instrumentation, you will be able to verify complete code coverage.

When a profiling session is run, the PL/SQL virtual machine keeps track of runtime information. DBMS_HPROF makes that information available to interested parties by writing the information to an operating system file. The output from a profiling session is called the raw output.

The raw output is human readable but not very friendly. With the raw output, you can take two directions. There is a command line tool called plshprof that takes in raw DBMS_HPROF output files and generates HTML reports that contain all kinds of goodness related to performance. With that tool, you can even compare the output of two profiling sessions (for example, before and after a code change) to see how the change has impacted the performance profile of the code. (Chapter 13 specifically covers instrumentation and profiling for performance so I will leave the details to that chapter.) I would rather discuss using the analyzed data for you to write your own reports.

The second path to take with the raw output is a function in the DBMS_HPROF package: DBMS_HPROF.ANALYZE. The ANALYZE function takes several input parameters, most importantly the directory and file name of the raw output, and returns a RUN_ID. When ANALYZE is run, three tables are populated and RUN_ID is the primary key of the parent table.

The three tables that get populated contain information about the profiling session, the information about the run, and the relationship between program calls within the run session. With this information (ignoring the performance information for now), you can find exactly what was called and by whom. What you do not get is what was not called. When combined with PL/Scope, you can find what was not called—this is the value that profiling adds to code coverage.

Configuring DBMS_HPROF

Configuring DBMS_HPROF requires only a couple of very simple steps. The first is that you need execute on the DBMS_HPROF package. The second is that you need read/write access to an OS directory. If you have permissions to create directories, you can create your own. If not, ask you DBA to create one and give you READ and WRITE.

For the purpose of this discussion, I will be logged in as SYSTEM. The following DDL has to be executed before the examples will work:

```
CREATE DIRECTORY plshprof_dir AS 'c:\temp';
GRANT READ, WRITE ON DIRECTORY PLSHPROF_DIR TO HR;
```

For performance tuning, this access to the directory is all that you need. Run the plshprof, available in $ORACLE_HOME/bin) utility to generate your HTML reports and start your analysis. I generally copy the HTML output locally and review it in my browser.

However, for the purpose of understanding the code and automating analysis, I want that raw output in the database so that I can query it. Oracle provides that with three tables (described in more detail later). To create these tables, you need to run a script supplied by Oracle and available in $ORACLE_HOME/RDBMS/ADMIN, dbmshptab.sql.

Like the script for DBMS_PROFILER, you can run this script as an application user or you can create a common PROFILER schema. I generally lean towards having a dedicated user that will contain all of the profiling data for a database; this way you will have cross schema profiling sessions stored together for easy querying and you can create the same schema on all of your databases. This allows you to keep consistency across instances, which enhances the maintainability of your code.

That's all that's required to configure the DBMS_HPROF profiler.

DBMS_HPROF Example Session

When running the profiler, it's much like using DBMS_TRACE or DBMS_PROFILER. A profiling session is started with START_PROFILING and the session is ended with STOP_PROFILING. The following session will use the exact same call to create_employee:

```
DECLARE
```

```
    v_employee_id employees.employee_id%TYPE;
    v_runid dbmshp_runs.runid%TYPE;
    v_plshprof_dir all_directories.directory_name%TYPE := 'PLSHPROF_DIR';
    v_plshprof_file VARCHAR2(30) := 'create_employee.raw';
BEGIN
    -- Start the profiling session
    dbms_hprof.start_profiling(v_plshprof_dir, v_plshprof_file);

    -- call the top level procedure to be profiled
    v_employee_id := employee_api.create_employee(
        p_first_name => 'Lewis',
        p_last_name => 'Cunningham2',
        p_email => 'lewisc2@yahoo.com',
        p_phone_number => '888-555-1212',
        p_job_title => 'Programmer',
        p_department_name => 'IT',
        p_salary => 99999.99,
        p_commission_pct => 0 );

    -- Stop the profiling session
    dbms_hprof.stop_profiling;

    -- Analyze the raw output and create the table data
    v_runid := dbms_hprof.analyze(v_plshprof_dir, v_plshprof_file);

    DBMS_OUTPUT.PUT_LINE('This Run: ' || to_char(v_runid) );

END;
```

The DBMS_HPROF.ANALYZE returns a RUNID to identify a particular run. If, however, you need to come back at some later point in time, the DBMS_HPROF.START_PROFILING procedure takes an optional COMMENT parameter, which is the easiest way to identify a particular ANALYZED run.

DBMS_HPROF Output

DBMS_HPROF tracks all kinds of PL/SQL calls including triggers and anonymous blocks, as well as DML and native dynamic SQL. It is truly a powerful profiling tool. DBMS_HPROF.analyze writes to three tables.

- DBMSRP_RUNS: Run header info.

- DBMSHP_FUNCTION_INFO: Stored program details and timings.

- DBMSHP_PARENT_CHILD_INFO: The hierarchy of calls with timing.

These tables store all of the information you need to generate complete trace reports with timing at whatever level of detail you want to see them. As a side note, SQL Developer (the free GUI IDE from Oracle) supports DBMS_HPROF out of the box.

The HTML reports generated by the plshprof command line utility are very powerful tools in your performance arsenal. It would be silly for me to duplicate them with a bunch of screen shots; however, I do want to make you aware of the information available in these reports.

When you run plshprof, it produces a set of related HTML files. You navigate between the various reports and can drill down from the top level to more detailed level reports. Figure 7-1 shows the index page produced by plshprof.

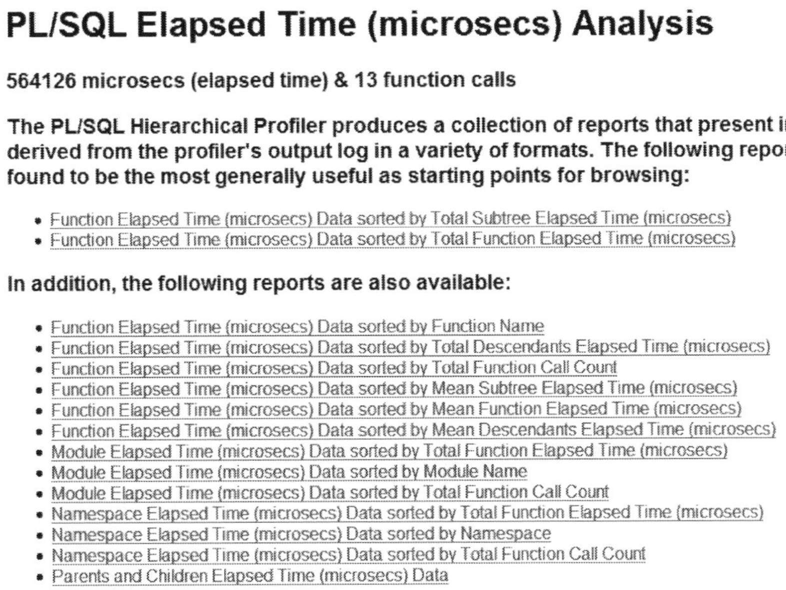

PL/SQL Elapsed Time (microsecs) Analysis

564126 microsecs (elapsed time) & 13 function calls

The PL/SQL Hierarchical Profiler produces a collection of reports that present information derived from the profiler's output log in a variety of formats. The following reports have been found to be the most generally useful as starting points for browsing:

- Function Elapsed Time (microsecs) Data sorted by Total Subtree Elapsed Time (microsecs)
- Function Elapsed Time (microsecs) Data sorted by Total Function Elapsed Time (microsecs)

In addition, the following reports are also available:

- Function Elapsed Time (microsecs) Data sorted by Function Name
- Function Elapsed Time (microsecs) Data sorted by Total Descendants Elapsed Time (microsecs)
- Function Elapsed Time (microsecs) Data sorted by Total Function Call Count
- Function Elapsed Time (microsecs) Data sorted by Mean Subtree Elapsed Time (microsecs)
- Function Elapsed Time (microsecs) Data sorted by Mean Function Elapsed Time (microsecs)
- Function Elapsed Time (microsecs) Data sorted by Mean Descendants Elapsed Time (microsecs)
- Module Elapsed Time (microsecs) Data sorted by Total Function Elapsed Time (microsecs)
- Module Elapsed Time (microsecs) Data sorted by Module Name
- Module Elapsed Time (microsecs) Data sorted by Total Function Call Count
- Namespace Elapsed Time (microsecs) Data sorted by Total Function Elapsed Time (microsecs)
- Namespace Elapsed Time (microsecs) Data sorted by Namespace
- Namespace Elapsed Time (microsecs) Data sorted by Total Function Call Count
- Parents and Children Elapsed Time (microsecs) Data

Figure 7-1. PLSHPROF Output—Report Index

From here, a click on the first link, Function Elapsed Time, brings up the page in Figure 7-2.

Function Elapsed Time (microsecs) Data sorted by Total Subtree Elapsed Time (microsecs)

564126 microsecs (elapsed time) & 13 function calls

Subtree	Ind%	Function	Ind%	Descendants	Ind%	Calls	Ind%	Function Name
564126	100%	4871	0.9%	559255	99.1%	1	7.7%	HR.EMPLOYEE API.CREATE EMPLOYEE (Line 3)
262267	46.5%	78	0.0%	262189	46.5%	1	7.7%	HR.EMPLOYEE API.ASSIGN SALARY (Line 74)
262189	46.5%	262189	46.5%	0	0.0%	1	7.7%	HR.EMPLOYEE API. static sql exec line80 (Line 80)
158664	28.1%	140	0.0%	158524	28.1%	1	7.7%	HR.DEPARTMENTS API.DEPARTMENT EXISTS (Line 3)
158524	28.1%	158524	28.1%	0	0.0%	1	7.7%	HR.DEPARTMENTS API. static sql exec line9 (Line 9)
98035	17.4%	98035	17.4%	0	0.0%	1	7.7%	HR.EMPLOYEE API. static sql exec line64 (Line 64)
35494	6.3%	137	0.0%	35357	6.3%	1	7.7%	HR.JOBS API.JOB EXISTS (Line 3)
35357	6.3%	35357	6.3%	0	0.0%	1	7.7%	HR.JOBS API. static sql exec line8 (Line 8)
2629	0.5%	118	0.0%	2511	0.4%	1	7.7%	HR.DEPARTMENTS API.DEPARTMENT MANAGER ID (Line 29)
2511	0.4%	2511	0.4%	0	0.0%	1	7.7%	HR.DEPARTMENTS API. static sql exec line35 (Line 35)
2161	0.4%	2161	0.4%	0	0.0%	1	7.7%	HR.EMPLOYEE API. static sql exec line62 (Line 62)
5	0.0%	5	0.0%	0	0.0%	1	7.7%	HR.JOBS API.VALIDATE JOB (Line 21)
0	0.0%	0	0.0%	0	0.0%	1	7.7%	SYS.DBMS HPROF.STOP PROFILING (Line 59)

Figure 7-2. PLSHPROF Elapsed Time Report

The report in Figure 7-2 shows the overall time of the process sorted by the amount of time taken in each call. This report is a quick sanity check for where the time in a process is spent. The call with the most time, not coincidentally, is the top level CREATE_EMPLOYEE. From this report, I can click on one of the function calls and drill down to a detail report of that specific call, as shown in Figure 7-3.

HR.EMPLOYEE_API.__static_sql_exec_line64 (Line 64)

Subtree	Ind%	Function	Ind%	Descendants	Ind%	Calls	Ind%	Function Name
98035	17.4%	98035	17.4%	0	0.0%	1	7.7%	HR.EMPLOYEE API. static sql exec line64 (Line 64)
Parents:								
98035	100%	98035	100%	0	N/A	1	100%	HR.EMPLOYEE API.CREATE EMPLOYEE (Line 3)

HR.EMPLOYEE_API.__static_sql_exec_line80 (Line 80)

Subtree	Ind%	Function	Ind%	Descendants	Ind%	Calls	Ind%	Function Name
262189	46.5%	262189	46.5%	0	0.0%	1	7.7%	HR.EMPLOYEE API. static sql exec line80 (Line 80)
Parents:								
262189	100%	262189	100%	0	N/A	1	100%	HR.EMPLOYEE API.ASSIGN SALARY (Line 74)

HR.JOBS_API.__static_sql_exec_line8 (Line 8)

Subtree	Ind%	Function	Ind%	Descendants	Ind%	Calls	Ind%	Function Name
35357	6.3%	35357	6.3%	0	0.0%	1	7.7%	HR.JOBS API. static sql exec line8 (Line 8)
Parents:								
35357	100%	35357	100%	0	N/A	1	100%	HR.JOBS API.JOB EXISTS (Line 3)

Figure 7-3. PLSHPROF Function Drilldown

You can see in Figure 7-3 that the procedures shown all made static SQL calls and how much time was spent in SQL versus PL/SQL. Generally, I would rather run my own queries to get concise information on my runs to give me a snapshot of my performance. If something in my homegrown queries stands out, then I can run the HTML reports and dig in a little deeper.

The following query is a fairly simple report of who called who and how long it is taking. I will usually compare this data with the data from a previous run; in that way I can get a very quick look at how the changes have impacted performance.

```
SELECT parent_info.owner || '.' || parent_info.module || '.' ||
                parent_info.function || '(' || parent_info.line# || ')' caller,
       child_info.owner || '.' || child_info.module || '.' ||
                child_info.function || '(' || child_info.line# || ')' callee,
       child_info.function_elapsed_time elapsed
  FROM dbmshp_parent_child_info dpci
  JOIN dbmshp_function_info parent_info
    ON parent_info.runid = dpci.runid
  JOIN dbmshp_function_info child_info
    ON child_info.runid = dpci.runid
  WHERE dpci.runid = :HPROF_RUNID
  START WITH dpci.runid = :HPROF_RUNID
    AND dpci.childsymid = child_info.symbolid
    AND dpci.parentsymid = parent_info.symbolid
    AND parent_info.symbolid =1
  CONNECT BY dpci.runid = PRIOR dpci.runid
    AND dpci.childsymid = child_info.symbolid
    AND dpci.parentsymid = parent_info.symbolid
    AND prior dpci.childsymid = dpci.parentsymid;
```

```
CALLER                                   CALLEE                                      ELAPSED
---------------------------------------- ------------------------------------------- ----------
.._anonymous_block(0)                    HR.EMPLOYEE_API.CREATE_EMPLOYEE(3)              189
HR.EMPLOYEE_API.CREATE_EMPLOYEE(3)       HR.DEPARTMENTS_API.DEPARTMENT_EXISTS(3)          57
HR.DEPARTMENTS_API.DEPARTMENT_EXISTS(3)  HR.DEPARTMENTS_API.__static_sql_exec_lin        473
                                         e9(9)

HR.EMPLOYEE_API.CREATE_EMPLOYEE(3)       HR.DEPARTMENTS_API.DEPARTMENT_MANAGER_ID         24
                                         (29)

HR.DEPARTMENTS_API.DEPARTMENT_MANAGER_ID HR.DEPARTMENTS_API.__static_sql_exec_lin         99
(29)                                     e35(35)

HR.EMPLOYEE_API.CREATE_EMPLOYEE(3)       HR.EMPLOYEE_API.ASSIGN_SALARY(74)                51
HR.EMPLOYEE_API.ASSIGN_SALARY(74)        HR.EMPLOYEE_API.__static_sql_exec_line80       2634
                                         (80)
.
.
.
```

The anonymous block called CREATE_EMPLOYEE, CREATE_EMPLOYEE called DEPARTMENT_EXISTS, etc. The elapsed time is the rightmost column; it is the function elapsed time. In your own reports you can include any of the other columns that are important to you. There is a subtree elapsed time that is also useful. The function time elapsed is just the time spent in the function; subtree elapsed includes the time spent in descendants. The CALLS column contains the number of calls to a subprogram (useful in repeated calls and loops).

You can write your own queries against these tables and return the performance information you require. I would also highly recommend running the HTML reports and browsing through them. They contain some incredibly useful information, as shown in the previous screenshots.

Summary

This chapter explained how to best understand the code that you are responsible for. It explained the different types of code analysis available natively from Oracle and showed how to use those tools in your daily development. You should now understand the benefits of both static code analysis and dynamic code analysis. You should also be able to sit down to configure these tools, use them, and understand the output.

I reviewed the data dictionary views that are most important for static analysis and showed how they compare to the PL/Scope utility provided by Oracle in 11g. The chapter then moved onto dynamic analysis and the type of data available to you from those tools.

One of the beauties of implementing the suggestions in this chapter is that there is nothing here that you should not already be doing—this chapter just shows you how to it all more efficiently and how to avoid human errors. You should already have standards; you should already be doing code reviews; you should be intelligently instrumenting your code and profiling that code, before production, so that you know that when you get to production it will run reliably and be maintainable.

The effort to make the best use of these tools in your environment is a onetime expense that you put out up front and then benefit from on every project going forward. Before creating your own reports and tools based on the information in this chapter, I suggest you either create or firm up your coding and testing standards. You will get much more value from these tools, as well as the ability to automate more of your reviews and tests, if everyone is using the same standards when developing their PL/SQL.

You don't have to use the tools provided by Oracle. There are third party tools that will provide much of this functionality, most probably using the items discussed in the chapter. The important thing is that you decide to incorporate impact analysis and other code analysis into your workflow for better quality applications.

Also, don't feel like you are "stuck" with the out-of-the-box functionality. Create your own tables for querying and use things like PL/Scope as a starting point. Massage the data until you get what you feel is valuable. Don't take what is presented in this chapter as the end point. It is meant as the starting point.

After having read this chapter, I hope you "get" why source code analysis is useful. I also sincerely hope that you are not thinking that code reviews and profiling are not worth the work. If you do think this, I only ask you to please read the rest of this book (especially Chapter 13) and think about it.

Anything new can seem complex and intrusive to your normal routine. If you have never participated in a code review, it is frightening the first time. Once you start getting the benefits of fewer bugs and better code, you will get on board with the idea. The same is true of code analysis: once you've done the work of analysis the first time, it's really not very hard thereafter, and the benefits pays dividends for the life time of the program.

Don't make knowing your code an add-on to your development. Build it in. Know; don't guess.

Contract-Oriented Programming

by John Beresniewicz

This chapter will introduce you to a powerful software engineering paradigm called Design by Contract and a method for applying it to PL/SQL programming.

Design by Contract

The following quote struck me as a revelation of software-truth when I first read it sometime in the year 2000:

> *Design by Contract is a powerful metaphor that...makes it possible to design software systems of much higher reliability than ever before; the key is understanding that reliability problems (more commonly known as bugs) largely occur at module boundaries, and most often result from inconsistencies in both sides' expectations. Design by Contract promotes a much more systematic approach to this issue by encouraging module designers to base communication with other modules on precisely defined statements of mutual obligations and benefits, not on vague hopes that everything will go right.*

> —Bertrand Meyer, *Object Success*

I had written quite a lot of PL/SQL code as part of developing an Oracle performance diagnostic tool for DBAs and had come to loathe chasing down runtime bugs, many of which were of precisely the kind noted by Meyer, which is to say misuse or confusion regarding APIs between modules. The promise of engineering such bugs out of my code motivated me to learn more about Design by Contract and apply it somehow to PL/SQL programming.

Software Contracts

Design by Contract makes the observation that software modules have client-supplier relationships that can be modeled after legal contracts where two parties enter into an agreement of mutual self-interest and obligation. Each party expects to benefit somehow from the contract, and each party is usually also under some obligation from the contract. In the world of software, contracts can be thought of as the rules under which the APIs between calling and called modules must function. The calling module provides some input values or other system state when the API is invoked, and the called module is expected to reliably compute some output or resultant system state upon completion. If the rules governing these inputs and outputs are broken, there is a contract violation and the software has a defect, or bug.

The concept of software contracts governing APIs is powerful for many reasons, but most especially because a high percentage of bugs are due to confusion or misuse at API boundaries, as suggested in the quote from Meyer. If we can enforce API contracts in some way such that contract violations are exposed immediately, we can discover an entire class of bugs quickly and improve the reliability of software greatly.

Basic Contract Elements

Three basic formal elements are used to define the terms of software contracts: preconditions, postconditions, and invariants. These abstract contract elements are documented and enforced in the code by using software mechanisms typically called assertions.

Preconditions

Preconditions are conditions or states that must be true in order for a module to compute correct results. They represent obligations on the callers of a module under the contract and accrue benefits to the module itself. Preconditions benefit the module because they represent hard facts that the module's algorithms can rely on. Preconditions oblige callers because it is the responsibility of callers to make sure the preconditions are met prior to calling the module.

It is a contract violation to call the module while failing to satisfy the preconditions; therefore precondition violations indicate bugs in the calling code. The module is not even under any obligation to compute a result in this case, as the "terms of the deal" have not been met.

At the code level, preconditions are ideally checked prior to module entry by the execution environment itself. Since PL/SQL does not offer native support for contract elements, it is recommended that all modules enforce their preconditions immediately upon module entry, especially those that govern the validity of input variable values.

Postconditions

Postconditions specify conditions on the output or computed results that the module guarantees will be true when it completes its computation, provided the preconditions have been met. They represent a fundamental obligation on the module to compute correct results. Postconditions are a benefit to the callers of the module precisely in that they allow callers to trust the module's output.

Failure to satisfy postconditions is a contract violation by the module itself, and indicates defects are present in the module. As a practical matter at the code level, it can be very difficult to assert the full correctness of a module's outputs at runtime either from within or without the module, as doing so can imply having independent implementations of the module's computational requirements to compare against each other for equality.

However, it may often be the case that limited or partial postconditions can be imposed on the module's outputs that are sufficient to indicate a contract violation. For instance, if a function is intended to compute some result that should always be a positive number, then it will be a contract violation for it to return a negative number, and this can be imposed as a postcondition on the module.

Unit and regression testing can be thought of as validating postconditions under known preconditions and input values.

Invariants

Invariants specify states or conditions that should always hold true. For instance, a PL/SQL package may make use of private shared data structures accessed and perhaps modified by the package's modules. There may be various consistency or integrity requirements over these data structures that can be defined and considered shared contract elements imposed on the entire package itself.

A module that completes execution and causes the invariants to become invalid has a bug. Invariants can be difficult to identify and express programmatically and are often expensive to enforce.

Assertions

Assertions are the basic mechanism for expressing and enforcing software contract elements in the code itself. Assertions basically encapsulate statements about system state that must be true or there is an error. That is, when an assertion tests false, the system is known to be in error; this should be communicated out, usually in the form of an exception.

Technically, preconditions, postconditions, and invariants are all different kinds of assertions as they capture different contract elements. In applying Design by Contract to PL/SQL programming, I recommend building a simple and consistent assertion mechanism and using that mechanism to express and enforce preconditions, postconditions, and invariants (where possible.)

Assertions are essentially correctness tests built directly into the software that find and signal bugs at runtime and as such are a powerful means of ensuring software reliability.

References

You can find much more information about the principles and practice of Design by Contract in the following books:

- *Object-Oriented Software Construction, Second Edition* by Bertrand Meyer (Prentice Hall PTR, 1997)

- *The Pragmatic Programmer* by Andrew Hunt and Dave Thomas (Addison Wesley Longman, Inc., 2000)

- *Design by Contract by Example* by Richard Mitchell and Jim McKim (Addison-Wesley, 2002)

- *Design Patterns and Contracts* by Jean-Marc Jezequel, Michel Train, Christine Mingins (Addison Wesley Longman, 2000)

Implementing PL/SQL Contracts

With the conceptual framework for Design by Contract in place, the next step is to design and implement a PL/SQL assertion mechanism (or mechanisms) with which to enforce software contracts between PL/SQL programs.

Basic ASSERT Procedure

A very simple assertion mechanism can be implemented in PL/SQL as a procedure that accepts a Boolean input argument and either exits silently when it tests TRUE or complains loudly by raising an exception when it tests FALSE. The simple procedure in Listing 8-1 implements exactly this logic.

Listing 8-1. Basic Assert Procedure

```
PROCEDURE assert (condition_in IN BOOLEAN)
IS
BEGIN
   IF NOT NVL(condition_in,FALSE)
   THEN
      RAISE_APPLICATION_ERROR(-20999,'ASSERT FAILURE');
   END IF;
END assert;
```

As simple as it is, there are a couple of points to note about this procedure. First and very importantly, the procedure takes the position that a NULL input value will test as FALSE and raise the exception. This means that the procedure expects an actual value to be passed in or the assertion itself is invalid—in other words, the procedure has been improperly called. In contract terms, the procedure has a precondition that the input parameter (condition_in) is NOT NULL.

Another thing to note is that while the procedure provides a message indicating the exception signals an assertion failure, this message does not communicate anything about the failing condition itself. Since assertion failures always indicate bugs, it would be useful to have additional information specific to the condition that failed for debugging purposes.

The assertion procedure can be improved by adding parameters to supply contextual information along with the Boolean condition for use in creating a more informative error message to return with the ASSERTFAIL exception. Listing 8-2 provides an example.

Listing 8-2. Improved Basic Assert Implemented as a Public Procedure

```
CREATE OR REPLACE
PROCEDURE assert (condition_IN IN BOOLEAN
               ,msg_IN   IN VARCHAR2 := null
               ,module_IN IN VARCHAR2 := null)
IS
  ASSERTFAIL_C CONSTANT INTEGER := -20999;
  BEGIN
    IF NOT NVL(condition_IN,FALSE) -- assertfail on null
    THEN
      RAISE_APPLICATION_ERROR        -- per doc accepts 2048
            ( ASSERTFAIL_C, 'ASSERTFAIL:'||SUBSTR(module_IN,1,30)||':'||
              SUBSTR (msg_IN,1,2046) ); -- fill 2048 with msg
```

```
    END IF;
END assert;
/
CREATE OR REPLACE PUBLIC SYNONYM assert FOR assert;
GRANT EXECUTE ON assert TO PUBLIC;
```

Here the assert procedure is made globally available via public synonym and execute privileges. In this example, the ASSERTFAIL error number is provided to RAISE_APPLICATION_ERROR via reference to a local constant (ASSERTFAIL_C) in the example but that could also reference a package-level constant. Using the constant avoids hardcoding a literal number in the call to RAISE_APPLICATION_ERROR and affords better maintainability should there be a need to change its value.

The signature of this assert includes two new parameters: module_IN and msg_IN. The module_IN parameter allows the assertion-calling code to identify its source module. The second parameter, msg_IN, permits the calling code to provide some diagnostic detail about the contract element.

When the condition_IN parameter tests FALSE, there is a contract violation and ASSERTFAIL exception is raised. The actual message returned with an ASSERTFAIL exception is constructed as a colon-delimited composite of the string "ASSERTFAIL", the program name (module_IN), and finally a message passed in the call to assert (msg_IN.) In this way, the ASSERTFAIL exception can provide very specific information about location and cause of the contract violation, greatly assisting bug isolation and diagnosis.

I can execute a simple test of the procedure in SQL*Plus as follows:

```
SQL> l
  1  declare
  2  procedure my_proc(i number)
  3  is
  4  begin
  5    assert(i>3,'i>3','my_proc');
  6  end;
  7  begin
  8  my_proc(1);
  9* end;
SQL> /
declare
*
ERROR at line 1:
ORA-20999: ASSERTFAIL:my_proc:i>3
ORA-06512: at "APPLO1.ASSERT", line 9
ORA-06512: at line 5
ORA-06512: at line 8
```

Note how the exception message tells us where and why the ASSERTFAIL was raised: the condition that the parameter i must be greater than 3 failed in module my_proc. This is incredibly useful; the ASSERTFAIL indicates a bug in the code and the exception message helps isolate and triage the bug. The call stack indicates the initiating line of code is number 8 of the anonymous PL/SQL block, which calls my_proc, which calls APPLO1.ASSERT at its line number 5 to assert the contract condition on the input parameter (namely i>3). The specific module and failing condition are exposed in the ASSERTFAIL error message by making good use of the module_IN and msg_IN parameters of assert. If the assertion is enforcing a precondition, it will be important to diagnose the caller of the module failing the assertion, as precondition bugs implicate the calling code.

Standard Package-Local ASSERT

Most substantive programming in PL/SQL takes place inside packages, so deciding how to enforce contracts within the context of a package is an important consideration. I developed simple, standardized package-local assertion implementation to use in all my PL/SQL packages. Using only this relatively simple construct and associated coding discipline, significant progress can be made in defining and enforcing PL/SQL software contracts rigidly.

The first thing to standardize relative to contract enforcement is the mechanism and meaning for signaling contract violations. The mechanism adopted is to raise a specific exception (called ASSERTFAIL) using the RAISE_APPLICATION_ERROR built-in procedure. The specification for package DBC_example in Listing 8-3 illustrates declaring the ASSERTFAIL exception and associating it to a specific exception number using the PRAGMA compiler directive.

Listing 8-3. Standardized Package Specification Template

```
CREATE OR REPLACE PACKAGE DBC_example
AS
   ------------------------------------------------------------
   -- SLPA declarations (standard local packaged assertion)
   ------------------------------------------------------------
   ASSERTFAIL      EXCEPTION;
   ASSERTFAIL_C    CONSTANT INTEGER := -20999;
   PRAGMA EXCEPTION_INIT(ASSERTFAIL, -20999);
   ------------------------------------------------------------
END DBC_example;
/
```

All packages within an application scope should standardize on a single error number to use for the ASSERTFAIL exception to avoid confusion. In this way, ASSERTFAIL obtains a common meaning across the entire application. This is important, as clear contract enforcement requires unambiguous and common interpretation of contract violations, the whole purpose of ASSERTFAIL. Finally, the exception number for ASSERTFAIL (-20999) is also assigned to a package constant for referencing inside the assert procedure itself. Similarly, begin all packages with a standardized implementation as shown in Listing 8-4, taken from the body for the DBC_example package.

Listing 8-4. Standardized Package Body Example

```
CREATE OR REPLACE PACKAGE BODY DBC_example
AS
   -- package name for assertfail msg
   PKGNAME_C       CONSTANT VARCHAR2(20) := $$PLSQL_UNIT;  -- NOTE 10g construct
   -- foreward declare assert so all module implementations can reference it
   PROCEDURE assert (condition_IN IN BOOLEAN
                    ,msg_IN       IN VARCHAR2 := NULL
                    ,module_IN    IN VARCHAR2 := NULL);
   ------------------------------------------------------------
   -- standard local packaged assertion procedure
   ------------------------------------------------------------
   PROCEDURE assert (condition_IN IN BOOLEAN
                    ,msg_IN       IN VARCHAR2 := NULL
                    ,module_IN    IN VARCHAR2 := NULL)
```

```
IS
  l_assertmsg VARCHAR2(2048) := 'ASSERTFAIL:'||SUBSTR(PKGNAME_C,1,30)||'.'; -- assertmsg
BEGIN
  -- test the asserted condition
  IF NOT NVL(condition_IN,FALSE)    -- fail on null input
  THEN
    -- finish initializing assertmsg
    l_assertmsg := l_assertmsg || SUBSTR(NVL(module_IN,'?MODULE?')||':'||msg_IN,1,2046);
    -- raise the standardized exception
    RAISE_APPLICATION_ERROR (ASSERTFAIL_C, l_assertmsg, FALSE); -- FALSE
  END IF;
END assert;

BEGIN
  assert(TRUE); -- pkg initilization token
END DBC_example;
/
```

The assert in Listing 8-4 closely resembles the one presented earlier as a public procedure in Listing 8-2 with the slight change that it uses the Oracle 10g inquiry directive $$PLSQL_UNIT to identify the package rather than rely on a separately declared (and potentially erroneously initialized) constant. The call to RAISE_APPLICATION_ERROR will trim a long message to just fit into 2048 characters, allowing up to 30 characters for the package name. In practice, messages that challenge this limit would not necessarily be so helpful but the use of substrings helps correctness and robustness of the code.

Listing 8-4 does not represent much code penalty to pay for having a local assert available in all packages independent of other procedures. I prefer the idea of packages that can compile completely independently, at least at inception (and even somewhat resent RAISE_APPLICATION_ERROR for this reason.)

So my personal preference is to begin all PL/SQL packages using standard specification and body templates like these, such that standardized usages for contract enforcement can be adopted within and across packages.

Alternatively, you could adopt a simple, standardized PUBLIC assert procedure as in Listing 8-2 and have all contract enforcement depend on it.

Finally, I could suggest you create a really slick shared package implementation of assert with fancy call stack processing to assist bug diagnosis, but will not recommend it. The purpose of this chapter is to educate and convince you to enforce contracts with simplicity in your code, not to impress with fancy assertion mechanisms.

LOCAL OR GLOBAL ASSERT?

Astute readers steeped in conventional PL/SQL wisdom will likely question my recommendation to embed a standardized assertion construct into all packages rather than to create a single shared mechanism using either standalone procedure or a dedicated assertion package.

To be honest, the reasons I prefer a package-local assertion are less technical than they are emotional and political, but I will try to make the case anyway.

For one thing, taking a contract-oriented approach has been for me much more than adopting a new technique. It is rather more like a religious conversion and as such can meet with heavy resistance among the unconverted. So the political headwinds to getting agreement over deploying and using a common mechanism may be considerable, and religious battles are never won anyway. It is far easier to worship privately within the safe confines of your local package, at least until the masses are converted.

Secondly, I like to pretend and use assert as if it were a PL/SQL language primitive, and so always using a package-qualified reference would be a constant reminder that this is not the case. Having local asserts with identical implementations everywhere helps preserve my illusion.

Third, another personal preference is to always begin new packages without any external dependencies (even though almost no packages I have developed remained truly standalone).

Finally, there is a slight technical advantage to having every package locally declare the ASSERTFAIL exception, which is that exceptions are distinguishable between packages. So, for instance, if some code block makes calls to modules from two different packages, it can distinguish which ASSERTFAIL was raised. This is rarely of consequence, however, since ASSERTFAIL should really never be handled but rather allowed to propagate all the way out.

So there you have it: four truly uncompelling reasons for preferring and recommending a package-local assertion mechanism over shared global constructs. But as mentioned already, although the reasoning is weak, the preference is strong.

Lucky for me, Oracle 11g introduced the optimizing PL/SQL compiler that actually provides a new and reasonably strong performance argument in favor of my recommendation, namely code inlining. The topic and its implications for favoring a package-local assert are discussed briefly near the end of the chapter.

Enforcing Contracts Using ASSERT

Having decided to standardize on an assertion mechanism and embed it in every package, the question now becomes how to put it into use enforcing contracts? For this a little discipline is required; however, in my experience, the extra investment in coding up front is far more than paid back by the assurance that an entire class of important bugs is either not present or will be immediately detected by the code itself.

The procedure in Listing 8-5 illustrates using the standardized assert to enforce a good singular: precondition and silly postcondition directly in code. The precondition is that the single input parameter be not null, which is not declaratively enforceable and is often a very important requirement to demand, as discussed later. The postcondition illustrates by contrast the value of adopting calling discipline when using assert in code. The assertion fails to make use of module_IN or msg_IN parameters and thus provides little to go on relative to debugging the issue.

Listing 8-5. An Example Procedure Making Good and Bad Use of Assert

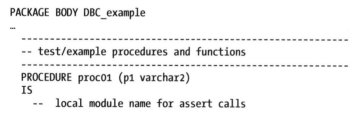

```
PACKAGE BODY DBC_example
...
    ------------------------------------------------------------
    -- test/example procedures and functions
    ------------------------------------------------------------
    PROCEDURE proc01 (p1 varchar2)
    IS
      --   local module name for assert calls
```

```
  l_module VARCHAR2(30) := 'PROC01';
BEGIN
  -- enforce NOT NULL inputs precondition
  assert(p1 IS NOT NULL,'p1 NOT NULL', l_module);

  -- procedure logic
  null;

  -- a very bad postcondition!
  assert(FALSE,'Boo hoo on you');  -- assertfail w/out passing module
END proc01;
```

Proc01 takes a single input parameter p1 and asserts the contract precondition that it be NOT NULL using this line of code:

```
assert(p1 IS NOT NULL,'p1 NOT NULL',l_module);
```

Note that this precondition is tested in the very first line of the module's main code block. Remember that under software contracts modules are not obliged to compute outputs if preconditions are not met, so testing them immediately allows modules to fail early and not waste compute cycles unnecessarily.

Also note the conventions adopted for passing extra information to assert through the parameters msg_IN and module_IN. In the first case, the message is simply a string literal of the Boolean expression constituting the contract condition to be asserted. In the second, the module declares a local variable l_module and initializes it with its own name, which is also passed to assert.

In addition to asserting the contract precondition against NULL inputs, proc01 implements some illustrative buggy logic: it asserts a final postcondition that will always throw the ASSERTFAIL exception but without passing any useful diagnostic information to include in the error message.

Testing proc01 by calling it using a NULL input value spools the following results from SQL*Plus:

```
BEGIN DBC_example.proc01(null); END;

*
ERROR at line 1:
ORA-20999: ASSERTFAIL:DBC_EXAMPLE.PROC01:p1 NOT NULL
ORA-06512: at "APPL01.DBC_EXAMPLE", line 104
ORA-06512: at "APPL01.DBC_EXAMPLE", line 25
ORA-06512: at line 1
```

At first glance, these results may not seem all that impressive, but to me they are pure gold. For example, the first ORA-20999 error indicates the following:

- There is a contract violation bug in the code, indicated by the ASSERTFAIL.

- The bug was caught in module PROC01 of the DBC_EXAMPLE package.

- The contract violation was that input variable p1 failed the NOT NULL check.

- Call stack indicates the assertion check in line 25 of the DBC_EXAMPLE package failed.

A bug has been identified for certain, the code location where bug was caught is known, and the nature of the bug is also revealed. Think for a minute about the last time you tried to chase down a bug involving unexpected run-time data values, and then tell me this is not totally cool.

Reading the call stack is not intuitive and requires some knowledge of the implementation. Beginning with the ORA-20999 error, which is the call to RAISE_APPLICATION_ERROR inside the local assert, the next in the stack must be the assert procedure itself, so the third entry on stack is the code location that called assert. This is important in that the next entry on the stack is the caller of the module making the call to assert. When the assertion is a precondition then this caller violated the contract condition, so the calling code has a bug exposed at the line indicated (line 1 in the trivial example here.) Executing a second test of proc01 that passes the non-NULL input precondition but trips on the bad assertion gives the following output:

```
BEGIN DBC_example.proc01('VALUE'); END;

*
ERROR at line 1:
ORA-20999: ASSERTFAIL:DBC_EXAMPLE.?MODULE?:Boo hoo on you
ORA-06512: at "APPL01.DBC_EXAMPLE", line 104
ORA-06512: at "APPL01.DBC_EXAMPLE", line 29
ORA-06512: at line 1
```

This second ASSERTFAIL helps illustrate the value of adopting the extra discipline required to pass in informative values for the module name and message parameters to assert. In this case, it is still known there is a contract violation bug and in which package the bug was caught, but the lack of additional diagnostic information is clearly disadvantageous.

My strong recommendation is that you take the time to always include both the module name and an informative description of the failing condition in your calls to assert. Many modules may have multiple input parameters, and each of them may be subject to one or even more than one contract preconditions. It will seem like a lot of extra typing to do without furthering the computational goals of the module. Believe me, the first time an ASSERTFAIL exception jumps out at runtime and informs you exactly the where and what of a previously undiscovered bug, you will be extremely glad you invested the effort.

An Additional Improvement

As noted already, precondition violations indicate bugs in calling modules while postcondition violations are bugs in the called module. Therefore, it is vitally important for assigning responsibility for contract violation bugs to know whether an ASSERTFAIL issued from a precondition or postcondition assertion.

The improvement in Listing 8-6 was suggested by my friend Steven Feuerstein as a means of distinguishing between pre- and postcondition violations.

Listing 8-6. Distinguishing between Pre- and Postconditions

```
-- assert for preconditions
PROCEDURE assertpre (condition_IN IN BOOLEAN
                    ,msg_IN      IN VARCHAR2 := NULL
                    ,module_IN   IN VARCHAR2 := NULL)
IS
BEGIN
   assert (condition_IN,'Pre:'||msg_IN,module_IN);
END assertpre;
```

```
-- assert for postconditions
PROCEDURE assertpost(condition_IN IN BOOLEAN
                    ,msg_IN       IN VARCHAR2 := NULL
                    ,module_IN    IN VARCHAR2 := NULL)
IS
BEGIN
   assert (condition_IN,'Post:'||msg_IN,module_IN);
END assertpost;
```

The idea is simply to have separately named procedures to assert preconditions and postconditions that call the original assert but add either "Pre:" or "Post:" to the message. These extra routines do not add much code baggage and significantly improve bug diagnostics, so I have added them to the standardized package template. Of course, they must be called in the right context to avoid confusion: never call assertpost to check preconditions nor assertpre for postconditions.

Contract-Oriented Function Prototype

PL/SQL functions offer additional opportunity to impose more contract discipline into code. Consider the function in Listing 8-7 as a prototype for all PL/SQL functions.

Listing 8-7. Prototype PL/SQL Function

```
FUNCTION  func01 (p1 varchar2) RETURN NUMBER
IS
  l_return NUMBER;
  l_module VARCHAR2(30) := 'FUNC01';
BEGIN
  -- preconditions
  assertpre(p1 IS NOT NULL,'p1 NOT NULL',l_module);

  -- function logic
  null;

  -- postcondition check and return
  assertpost(l_return IS NOT NULL, 'RETURN NOT NULL',l_module);

  RETURN l_return;
END func01;
```

Note the following key points about this function:

- It returns results through a local variable declared with a standardized name (and proper type of course).

- It asserts preconditions using module identifier and message conventions at the beginning.

- It exits using RETURN in exactly one place: the last line of code.

- It asserts postconditions using standard conventions immediately preceding the RETURN statement.

Since functions will always have a single return value, they can and should be coded such that there is a single exit point at which this value is returned to the calling module. Following this convention allows postcondition checks to be specified in exactly one place, immediately preceding the RETURN statement.

The use of a local variable with a standard name to always use for the RETURN statement allows me to know whenever the return value is being manipulated by the function logic. Clever functions with complex expressions computing outputs directly in the RETURN statement may seem elegant but they compromise the level of control over postcondition assertions that following my simple convention provides.

Adhering to the function prototype's coding conventions greatly benefits code reliability, as functions can enforce contract terms at well-defined entry and exit points. Functions (or procedures) with multiple possible exit points may introduce the need for postcondition assertions to be duplicated, which can itself be a source of bugs should contract terms need to be altered.

Example: Testing Odd and Even Integers

The examples so far have been trivial showcases for calling precondition and postcondition assertions without any real computational requirements. This section will present a pair of functions with actual computational requirements, albeit very modest and perhaps not very practical ones.

Imagine an application with logic that depends critically on whether specific data values are odd or even integers. In such an application, it may be useful to have modules that conform to the following contractual agreements:

- A function that accepts a non-NULL integer as input and returns the Boolean TRUE if the integer is an odd integer and FALSE otherwise.

- A function that similarly accepts a non-NULL integer and returns TRUE when the input integer is even and FALSE otherwise.

These two functions are clearly related in that for any given integer they should return exactly opposite results since the integer can only be either even or odd and must be one of these two. The code in Listing 8-8 uses the function prototype and coding conventions presented earlier to meet the first requirement.

Listing 8-8. A Function to Test a Number for Oddity

```
FUNCTION  odd (p1 number) RETURN BOOLEAN
IS
  l_return BOOLEAN;
  l_module VARCHAR2(30) := 'ODD';
BEGIN
  -- preconditions
  assertpre(p1 IS NOT NULL,'p1 NOT NULL',l_module);
  assertpre(p1 = TRUNC(p1), 'p1 INTEGER',l_module);

  -- function logic: returns TRUE if p1 ODD
  l_return := MOD(p1,2)=1;
```

```
-- postcondition check and return
assertpost(l_return IS NOT NULL, 'RETURN NOT NULL',l_module);

RETURN l_return;
END odd;
```

Listing 8-8's function is almost identical to the function prototype in Listing 8-7. The function in Listing 8-8 asserts preconditions and postconditions at the beginning and end of the function respectively, returning the computational result in the final line of code.

The function asserts two preconditions: that the input is non-NULL and additionally that it is an integer. Clever readers may observe that the second assertion implies the first, in the sense that if the input value for **p1** is NULL then this second assertion will fail as well and the first can be considered redundant in some sense. It may be tempting in such instances to only assert the second condition; however, this represents a shortcut that obfuscates the fact that there really are two separate preconditions: that the input be non-NULL and that it be an integer-valued number. Part of the motivation for adopting a contract-oriented approach to coding is the desire to be very explicit about contract requirements in the code itself, so compound assertions should be preceded by any simpler assertions on their components, even if these are implied by the compound expression. This illustrates an important added benefit of assertions in code: they document as well as enforce software contracts.

The computational requirements of the odd function are met in a single line of code, yet the function itself contains five lines of executable code. A minimal implementation of our functional requirements could be met by the function in Listing 8-9.

Listing 8-9. Minimal Implementation of the Test for Oddity

```
FUNCTION  odd2 (p1 number) RETURN BOOLEAN
IS
BEGIN
  RETURN MOD(p1,2)=1;
END odd2;
```

While the implementation in Listing 8-9 meets the basic computational requirement to return TRUE when **p1** is an odd integer, it does not enforce the contractual requirements to accept only non-NULL integers and return only TRUE or FALSE. If a NULL value for **p1** is passed, the function will return NULL as output even though it purports to be a Boolean. This obliges calling modules to either assert non-NULL on input values themselves or to accommodate NULL outputs using NVL or other special-case constructs. So, the extra code required to ensure correctness has not disappeared, rather it is moved into the calling applications, all of which must get it right.

Similarly, the minimal implementation does not check that **p1** is an integer, and the MOD function will happily return results for non-integer values of its arguments so the function will not fail in this case; however, it is very unlikely that a system that depends on oddness or evenness of integers will be satisfied with routines that accept non-integer inputs and makes statements about whether they are odd or not.

Now consider the implementation in Listing 8-10 of the complementary function **even** that computes whether an input integer is an even number.

Listing 8-10. A Function to Test for Evenness

```
FUNCTION  even (p1 number) RETURN BOOLEAN
IS
  l_return BOOLEAN;
```

```
    l_module VARCHAR2(30) := 'EVEN';
BEGIN
  -- preconditions
  assertpre(p1 IS NOT NULL,'p1 NOT NULL',l_module);
  assertpre(p1 = TRUNC(p1), 'p1 INTEGER',l_module);

  -- function logic: returns TRUE if p1 EVEN
  l_return := p1/2 = TRUNC(p1/2);

  -- postcondition check and return
  assertpost(l_return IS NOT NULL, 'RETURN NOT NULL',l_module);
  assertpost(NOT(l_return AND odd(p1)),'NOT(EVEN AND ODD)',l_module);
  assertpost(l_return OR odd(p1),'EVEN OR ODD',l_module);

  RETURN l_return;
END even;
```

Listing 8-10's function looks very similar to the **odd** function (Listing 8-8) in that it closely follows the contract-oriented function prototype, yet there are some important differences to note. For one thing, the function logic could easily have used modulo logic just as the **odd** function did by using l_return := MOD(p1,2)=0 but instead uses simple division by 2 and the TRUNC function:

```
  l_return := p1/2 = TRUNC(p1/2);
```

This introduces the most interesting feature to note about **even**, which is the extensive assertion of postconditions. First the simple expectation that l_return is non-NULL is asserted, followed by these logic puzzles:

```
  assertpost(NOT(l_return AND odd(p1)),'NOT(EVEN AND ODD)',l_module);
  assertpost(l_return OR odd(p1),'EVEN OR ODD',l_module);
```

These two complex assertions actually test the correctness of the value about to be returned by **even** using the complementary **odd** function. The first asserts that the two functions **even** and **odd** cannot both agree about **p1**, if one is FALSE the other is TRUE and vice versa. The second asserts that at least one of them must be FALSE for any given **p1**.

The assertions test the correctness of the function results by checking them against results of a computationally independent function with a different algorithmic strategy. This is one of those rare cases when the correctness of computational results can actually be asserted as a postcondition.

Of course, nothing comes entirely for free and in this case asserting the complex postcondition really amounts to performing the computational logic three times - once in the **even** function itself and twice again in calling the **odd** function in postcondition assertions. Tight coupling with the **odd** function also means that if there is a bug in that function it will extend as a bug into the **even** function as well.

Useful Contract Patterns

There are several useful contract patterns that I have come to recognize and appreciate in my own code, described in the following subsections. Adopting well-understood and agreed patterns like these for modules promotes code correctness and clarity in that certain contracts are understood to apply based on the pattern and do not require module-by-module specification or analysis.

Not-NULL IN / Not-NULL OUT

Perhaps the most basic and useful software contracts in a PL/SQL context are those that eliminate the problematic and often ambiguous circumstances that surround the handling of NULL values. Most algorithms expect to compute over actual data and may need to special case or provide alternate computational results in the presence of missing or NULL data values. This can introduce unnecessary ambiguity or complexity into APIs, much better to simply outlaw NULL values wherever possible.

Figuring out bugs due to NULL values can be very difficult, especially when computations do not explicitly fail as a result. Computer program logic is by its very nature binary, and NULL is an unwelcome third wheel.

So one of my favorite contracts can be simply described (from the called module's point of view) as follows: if you agree NOT to pass me NULL input values, you will certainly receive non-NULL output values back. This contract agreement is almost universally valuable whenever it can be imposed. In practice, a large majority of contract enforcement is validating input preconditions and this often means accepting only non-NULL values. Of course, the module must then also adhere to and enforce wherever possible its obligation under the postcondition that only non-NULL outputs will be generated. There is also an inherent fairness in this contract pattern: both parties are held to the same obligation and accrue similar benefits of certainty.

FUNCTION RETURN Not-NULL

This pattern is a specialization of the previous one that recognizes the significant advantages of using functions instead of procedures when a module must return output to callers. The function-based programming model lends itself to disciplined contract enforcement as illustrated in the function prototype discussed previously. In addition, functions that reliably return non-NULL values can be referenced in calling code in place of constants or variables. For instance, imagine a function called my_function that takes a single input parameter p1 and guarantees to return a non-NULL number as output. This allows me to safely write code like the following:

```
IF my_function(p1=>'X') > my_function(p1=>'Y')
THEN do_something;
END IF;
```

The intent here is clear, unambiguous, and reads directly from the code: compare my_function results over the parameter values 'X' and 'Y' and take action if the former is greater than the latter.

Now suppose that my_function does not guarantee non-NULL output values. Now any code that calls it must itself make decisions about what to do in that case, for example:

```
IF NVL(my_function(p1=>'X'), 0) > NVL(my_function(p1=>'Y'), 1)
THEN do_something;
END IF;h
```

This code is much more difficult to read due to the distracting syntax clutter introduced by the pair of NVL function calls. In addition, the intent is far less obvious, especially given that NULL output from my_function is cast to 0 when the input value is 'X' and to 1 when the input value is 'Y'. Why is this the case? Is it a bug in this code or some mysterious consequence of the inner purpose of my_function? This is what happens when function contracts are weak and callers must adapt to ambiguous outputs.

FUNCTION RETURN BOOLEAN Not-NULL

A specific case of the non-NULL function pattern occurs when the function's RETURN datatype is BOOLEAN. Such functions can safely be referenced in conditional statements to implement powerful and expressive logic.

For instance, suppose there is a procedure to perform some complex processing on records of some type my_rectype, but these must pass some sophisticated criteria in order to be successfully processed. These criteria may actually be preconditions to the processing procedure, or perhaps they are additional criteria that are not required by that procedure but which the program logic wishes to impose. These criteria can be encapsulated in a function whose contract is to test these criteria and unambiguously return TRUE or FALSE.

```
FUNCTION ready_to_process (rec1 my_rectype) RETURN BOOLEAN;
```

The code that performs processing of records might look like this:

```
IF ready_to_process(rec1=>local_rec)
THEN
  process_record(rec1=>local_rec);
ELSE
  log_error;
END IF;
```

Again, not having to deal with NULL function output combined with expressive function names makes the intent of such code clear.

Check Functions: RETURN TRUE OR ASSERTFAIL

The previous example leads to an interesting consideration regarding asserting the truth-value of functions that return BOOLEAN. For instance, should the process_record procedure assert the ready_to_process function as a precondition?

```
PROCEDURE process_record (rec1 my_rectype)
IS
    l_module VARCHAR2(30) := 'PROCESS_RECORD';
BEGIN
  -- precondition: test that record ready to process
  assertpre(ready_to_process(rec1), 'REC1 ready to process', l_module);
```

The answer as to whether this is OK or not is, it depends. Bertrand Meyer has this to say about it:

> *If you exert the proper care by sticking to functions that are simple and self-evidently correct, the use of function routines in assertions can provide you with a powerful means of abstraction.*

> Bertrand Meyer, *Object-Oriented Software Construction*, Second Edition

I love the phrase "simple and self-evidently correct" as it succinctly captures the essence of bug-free code. In my own programming, I have sometimes found that multiple modules within the same package may all reference and manipulate some private global data structures and all need to assert a common set of preconditions over these structures to guarantee correctness. In this case, implementing a function that combines these assertions together can eliminate significant code duplication.

```
FUNCTION check_all_ok(module_IN VARCHAR2) RETURN BOOLEAN
IS
BEGIN
  assert(condition1, 'condition1', module_IN);
  assert(condition2, 'condition2', module_IN);

  …
  assert(conditionN, 'conditionN', module_IN);

  RETURN TRUE;
END check_all_ok;
```

As long as the conditions tested are themselves simple expressions limited to package variables or data structures and PL/SQL language primitives, such "check functions," can be considered "simple and self-evidently correct" in that they can clearly only return TRUE or throw an ASSERTFAIL exception, the check_all_ok function can safely be asserted in the various modules that depend on it.

```
assertpre(check_all_ok(l_module), 'check_all_ok', l_module);
```

Note that the local module name of the caller is passed into the check_all_ok function so that any ASSERTFAIL exceptions generated will be correctly tagged with the module name in which the check failed.

Principles For Bug-Free Code

This chapter has actually covered a considerable amount of material rapidly and with brevity. The references cited earlier near the beginning of the chapter can give you a much fuller treatment of the depth and richness of Design by Contract. I mentioned my attraction to contract-oriented programming is rooted in an abhorrence of bugs, especially those in my own code. Software contracts are purposed to eliminating ambiguity at software interfaces by being explicit about assumptions and expectations, and enforcing these directly in the code itself. Through these means an entire class of bugs can be pre-engineered out of programs—or at least exposed and dispatched quickly.

The mechanism and techniques presented here do not by any means represent full support for Design by Contract in PL/SQL. In fact, Bertrand Meyer created an entire programming language called Eiffel and a development environment to support it, precisely because existing languages and tools were not entirely capable of fully supporting this paradigm. However, we must live with PL/SQL and do the best we can, and I have tried to present a practical approach to adopting the Design by Contract philosophy within a PL/SQL context.

In wrapping up, I will briefly discuss a few contract-oriented principles for developing bug-free code.

Assert Preconditions Rigorously

PL/SQL programs typically execute their algorithms on simple or complex data structures passed to them via input parameter values or available to them as package global variables. They are no different than programs written in any other language in this respect. Program algorithms typically have very specific requirements about the data on which they execute and may very well fail or give unreliable results when those requirements are not met. These requirements are precisely what Design by Contract refers to as preconditions and enforcing precondition requirements rigorously is the first and best step that you can take to insuring that your algorithms will execute successfully every time. This probably sounds obvious, yet how many programs are written with detailed attention to identifying each and every assumption about the inputs that its algorithms make and documents them explicitly? And of these, how many actually enforce those requirements in the code itself, such that invalid inputs cannot get past the front door, so to speak?

As mentioned several times already, many algorithms are not designed to operate on NULL inputs, or they employ special case code producing special case outputs where they are. Why not simply excise NULL values altogether and limit such programs to the straightforward cases they are designed for? This is not to say that NULL inputs can always be outlawed, but perhaps that is where contract negotiations should begin. If clients absolutely cannot comply then perhaps the precondition will need to be relaxed and the program adapted appropriately, but at least then you will know why it is the case.

It is also good practice to tease out and explicitly enforce each separate precondition rather than overload multiple preconditions into one assertion. For instance, if two input parameters x and y are required to have non-NULL values and x must be greater than y, all three preconditions can be enforced with

```
assertpre(x > y,'x > y', l_module)
```

This assertion will fail if either x or y (or both) is NULL; however, these requirements are not explicit in the assertion and must be inferred. Contract-orientation is about being explicit and precise, with no tolerance for inference and innuendo. So there should be three precondition assertions in this example.

The previous example also illustrates a major benefit of assertions I have not emphasized so much, which is that they not only enforce but also document software contracts. If programmers writing code to use your modules can read the source, requirements for proper usage can be read directly from the preconditions.

Require good inputs explicitly, and good outputs are much easier to guarantee.

Modularize Ruthlessly

Having required of callers that they provide good inputs and enforced these requirements in your code, your modules are obliged to produce correct outputs. Programs with hundreds or thousands of lines of code making many transformations to data structures are difficult or impossible to verify for correctness. However, compact computational units with very specific algorithms over well understood and verified data structures may actually have the property of being "self-evidently correct." This can only be achieved through modularization, which is to say breaking large and complex computations down into smaller and smaller self-contained computational sub-components, and then stringing these together to achieve the larger goals. Each sub-component should be algorithmically as simple as possible, such that confidence in its correctness can be gained through inspection and a minimum of mental gymnastics.

Note that modularizing code may not always mean breaking it into independent executable modules; it could be organizing a single large program into a set of sub-transformations that progressively develop intended outputs from supplied inputs. In these cases, you will want to make assertions on intermediate computational states as one sub-transformation ends and another begins.

By modularizing your code into more and smaller components, you create more interfaces and more opportunities to express contracts. If you adhere to the first principle of rigorous precondition testing, this means there will be more and more assertions built into your code, protecting the contractual requirements of all these interfaces. Each of these assertions is a correctness test executed at runtime: your code becomes hardened like tempered steel in the fire of assertions. How can bugs possibly survive?

Simple and self-evidently correct algorithms operating on trusted data is the virtuous path to bug-free code.

Adopt Function-Based Interfaces

Having adopted the first two principles, what should your simple and self-evidently correct modules look like? Functions offer distinct advantages to enforcing contracts whenever modules must pass computational results back to callers. These advantages were alluded to earlier but are worth reiterating.

- Functions provide a single output and are thus consistent with singularity of purpose.

- Functions can be written such that postcondition assertions can be located precisely, immediately preceding the RETURN statement.

- Functions can be used interchangeably with variables or conditional tests such that highly compact and expressive code is possible, especially when they assert NON NULL postconditions.

This is not to say procedures do not have their place and that you should avoid them. However, much of the PL/SQL code I have seen is procedure-heavy and function-light. When requirements are such that specific input data is computationally transformed and some output data returned, function-based interfaces offer better opportunities to adopt a rigorous contract orientation.

Crash on ASSERTFAIL

In Design by Contract, assertion failures signal bugs, period. Programs that catch ASSERTFAIL exceptions and handle them in some way that masks or hides their occurrence are effectively lying about what is going on: a correctness bug has been identified yet it is not being reported. Better to allow the program to crash and use the diagnostic information provided in the exception message to find and fix the bug.

In the words of Andy Hunt and Dave Thomas (see References above):

Dead Programs Tell No Lies

If you do find yourself compelled to catch and handle ASSERTFAIL because correct computation can proceed in spite of it, then perhaps there are contract issues to iron out. Contract-orientation does not mean exercising dictatorial control over client modules through non-negotiable preconditions. Contracts are an agreement between two parties, and the terms need to be acceptable on both sides. So, rather than catching and handling ASSERTFAIL, it is much better to renegotiate contracts wherever possible.

Regression Test Your Postconditions

Much emphasis has been placed on rigorous assertion of preconditions and far less on postconditions. The requirement to absolutely guarantee output correctness given the preconditions can be difficult at best in most cases, and in some almost impossible. The example provided by the function even is unusual, where having an alternative algorithm for the complementary function odd provides a means of asserting output correctness. And even when possible, the computational cost of asserting complete postcondition correctness is likely to effectively double the cost of computing the output itself.

However, there is a common case in which correct outputs for given inputs is well known, and that is unit testing. Typical unit testing consists of matching program outputs to well-known expected results under specific sets of inputs. This effectively amounts to asserting that the program has met postconditions given these inputs. So hopefully if you are doing production-level PL/SQL programming, you have a testing framework in place and are validating correctness of your modules through regular regression testing.

One caveat here is that only externally declared modules can be regression tested. A possible workaround is to have two versions of the package specification: one that exposes only the modules intended for external use and another that exposes internal modules as well for regression tests. Both versions should, of course, use the same package body, and great care must be taken not to diverge the specifications except in the modules declared. It's not ideal, but it is possible.

Avoid Correctness-Performance Tradeoffs

Finally, a cautionary principle: avoid what I call the false correctness-performance tradeoff. If you adopt the contract-oriented approaches recommended here, you may find that not only does rigorous assertion of contract elements cause you lots of extra typing, each call to assert is actual code executed and, while extremely inexpensive, is not entirely free. Modules that assert long lists of complex preconditions many thousands of times (perhaps over many rows of a cursor loop) could see these assertions show up as "expensive" when code is profiled.

In such cases, you may be tempted to remove these assertions on the basis of their computational cost; my recommendation is to avoid this temptation as much as possible. Assertions are about insuring correctness of code; performance is about executing code quickly. There is no such thing as a correctness-performance tradeoff: incorrect results obtained quickly are still incorrect and therefore useless.

However, if the performance impact of contract assertions seems too high to tolerate and the modules involved are highly trusted, it may become necessary to relax this dictum and stop testing some assertions. Rather than removing them altogether from the source code, it's much better to simply comment them out. Remember that assertions in source code are also important documentation artifacts of the contracts to which a module adheres.

Alternatively, in Oracle 10g and higher releases, you can somewhat have your cake and eat it too using the PL/SQL conditional compilation feature. Consider the following procedure that conditionally includes a precondition assertion whenever compiled with the conditional compilation flag DBC is set to TRUE:

```
PROCEDURE proc02
IS
  l_module VARCHAR2(30) := 'PROC02';
BEGIN
  -- conditional precondition assertion
  $IF $$DBC $THEN
  assertpre(FALSE,'Assert FALSE precondition',l_module);
  $END

  -- procedure logic
  null;
END proc02;
```

The procedure can be compiled with the flag set as TRUE for testing purposes and recompiled with it set as FALSE for releasing to production. In production, if program issues are suspected, the flag can be set back to TRUE and code recompiled to re-enable the assertion testing for bug discovery and diagnosis. Again, this is not recommended as correctness testing in production is where it matters most, but it is possible in situations where the impact on performance is unacceptably high.

Oracle 11g Optimized Compilation

Oracle 11g introduced optimized compilation of PL/SQL including subprogram inlining that can gain significant performance advantages where small local programs are frequently called. An in-depth discussion of the topic is beyond the scope of this chapter, but basically inlining can replace calls to modules local to the compilation unit with a copy of the called module's code "inline" with the calling code and thereby eliminating call stack overhead.

Inlining is preferentially performed for smaller and simpler local modules, which exactly describes the package-local assertion mechanism I have been using and recommending for years now. Finally, some real vindication for my unorthodox preference to localize the assertion inside each package! So adopting the package-local assertion and enabling full optimization can minimize the cost of enforcing software contracts in your PL/SQL code. Sounds like a win to me.

PL/SQL inlining is enabled by setting the PLSQL_OPTIMIZE_LEVEL parameter to value 3 prior to compilation, as below:

```
ALTER SESSION SET PLSQL_OPTIMIZE_LEVEL=3;
```

You can be informed about inlining optimizations and other compiler warnings using the PLSQL_WARNINGS parameter, like so:

```
ALTER SESSION SET PLSQL_WARNINGS='ENABLE:ALL';
```

It will be interesting to experiment and measure the performance benefits of PL/SQL inlining on packages heavily laden with contract enforcing assertions.

Summary

Design by Contract is a powerful software engineering paradigm for engineering bugs related to module interfaces (APIs) out of your code. Software contracts are specified by preconditions representing requirements imposed on calling modules, and postconditions representing obligations imposed on the called module. These contract elements are enforced by a software mechanism called assert. Assertion failures always signal bugs in the code in either the calling or called module, depending on whether a precondition or postcondition has been violated, respectively.

Adopting a contract-oriented approach to PL/SQL can be achieved using a simple, standardized assertion mechanism and adopting disciplined, standardized usage across the body of your code. This chapter showed you specific techniques I developed for doing just that, and I sincerely hope you find these techniques valuable should you choose to adopt them.

CHAPTER 9

PL/SQL from SQL

by Adrian Billington

Functions are an integral part of any well-designed PL/SQL application. They are an embodiment of programming best practices, such as code modularization, reuse, and the encapsulation of business or application logic. When used as simple building-blocks for larger programs, they can be an elegant and simple way to extend functionality while reducing code-complexity at minimal cost.

Conversely, when PL/SQL functions are heavily used, particularly in SQL statements, there can be a range of associated costs, most notably for performance. Depending on the nature of the function, simply calling PL/SQL from SQL and/or excessive I/O can degrade performance of even the most trivial of queries.

Given this, I will describe a variety of costs associated with calling PL/SQL functions from SQL and, more importantly, demonstrate a range of techniques that you can use to reduce their impact. By the end of this chapter, you will have a greater awareness of the costs of using PL/SQL functions in your applications. You will therefore be better placed to make good design decisions for your new or re-factored applications and improve your performance tuning efforts on critical parts of your system.

Note   The examples in this chapter have all been run on an 11.2.0.2 Oracle Enterprise Linux database. The code listings are available for download in their entirety from the Apress web site. In many cases I have reduced the output to the minimum required to convey my message and maintain the flow of the chapter. All examples can be executed in SQL*Plus and the download pack includes any utilities that I've used in addition to those provided in the Oracle Database software.

The Cost of Using PL/SQL Functions in SQL

The SQL and PL/SQL languages are seamlessly integrated. Since Oracle Database 9*i*, the two languages have even shared the same parser. We use this inter-operability to our advantage in most of the code that we write, such as SQL cursors in PL/SQL programs or PL/SQL functions that are called from SQL. We often do this with little concern for what Oracle Database has to do under the covers to run our programs.

Despite this integration, there is a runtime cost to combining them, in particular when calling PL/SQL from SQL (the focus of this chapter, of course). I'm going to spend the next few pages exploring some of these costs. What is interesting is that Oracle has been working hard to reduce the impact of combining SQL and PL/SQL code over several versions, so the issues I describe are not necessarily in their final state.

My investigation of the costs of using PL/SQL functions in SQL can be broken down into three main areas:

- Performance

- Predictability (which is related to performance)

- Side effects

■ **Note**   I do not cover syntactic or operational restrictions (such as DML being prohibited in PL/SQL functions called from SQL). These are not runtime costs as such and are well-documented elsewhere.

Context-Switching

Context-switching is an almost-irreducible cost of computing that occurs in CPUs, operating systems, and software. The mechanics differ depending on where it is occurring, but it is often a CPU-intensive operation that designers attempt to tune as much as is possible.

When we consider "context switching" in relation to Oracle Database, we specifically refer to the exchange of processing control between the SQL and PL/SQL engines (without necessarily understanding what occurs in such a process). These two engines are separate and distinct but we use them interchangeably. This means that when we call SQL from PL/SQL or vice versa, the calling context needs to store its process state and hand over control and data to its counterpart engine (which may or may not be picking up from an earlier switch). This switching cycle is computationally intensive and can typically be repeated so many times that its effects on response times can become quite noticeable.

For many, the first encounter with context-switching in Oracle Database would have been the introduction of the BULK COLLECT and FORALL PL/SQL features in Oracle 8*i*, designed *specifically* to reduce context-switching. These performance features made it possible to bind arrays of data between the SQL and PL/SQL engines in a single context-switch, dramatically reducing the number of context-switches that were generated by the row-by-row PL/SQL techniques that were prevalent at the time. For several major releases, almost all of the performance benefits of these language features could be attributed to the reduction in context-switching they facilitated. (In more recent releases, some further benefits such as redo optimization for bulk INSERT operations can also be realized when using PL/SQL array processing.)

■ **Note**   The reduction of context-switching is such an effective performance technique that the Oracle designers added an implicit BULK COLLECT for cursor-for-loops to the PL/SQL optimizing compiler introduced in Oracle Database 10*g*.

All of which is good news for PL/SQL programmers, of course, but the effects of excessive context-switching are still encountered elsewhere. In particular, context-switching is a performance penalty to pay for calling PL/SQL functions from SQL.

Measuring Context-Switching

As good as Oracle Database's instrumentation is (and it is truly excellent), context-switching is not something that can be directly measured; it's performed way down in the depths of the kernel and there is no simple statistic or counter available to quantify it. But given that context-switching is a fact of calling PL/SQL from SQL (and vice versa, though I shall cease to remind readers of this), its impact can be inferred with a simple set of measurements and supplied utilities.

Listing 9-1 shows a simple comparison between two SQL statements, one of which calls a PL/SQL function for every row. The function does nothing but return the input parameter and the timings are compared using the SQL*Plus timer. I've used an array size of 500 and Autotrace to suppress the output.

Listing 9-1. The Cost of Calling a PL/SQL Function from SQL (Baseline)

```
SQL> SELECT ROWNUM AS r
  2  FROM   dual
  3  CONNECT BY ROWNUM <= 1e6;

1000000 rows selected.

Elapsed: 00:00:01.74

Statistics
----------------------------------------------------------
          0  recursive calls
          0  db block gets
          0  consistent gets
          0  physical reads
          0  redo size
    6290159  bytes sent via SQL*Net to client
      40417  bytes received via SQL*Net from client
       2001  SQL*Net roundtrips to/from client
          1  sorts (memory)
          0  sorts (disk)
    1000000  rows processed
```

The baseline SQL statement generated 1 million rows in less than 2 seconds. As you can see from the Autotrace output, a SQL statement of this form is light on resources other than CPU (and network transfer and memory at larger rowcounts). Adding a PL/SQL function call to the SQL makes quite a difference to the elapsed time, as the Listing 9-2 demonstrates.

Listing 9-2. The Cost of Calling a PL/SQL Function from SQL (Using the Function)

```
SQL> CREATE FUNCTION plsql_function(
  2                  p_number IN NUMBER
  3                  ) RETURN NUMBER AS
  4  BEGIN
```

```
5      RETURN p_number;
6  END plsql_function;
7  /
```

Function created.

```
SQL> SELECT plsql_function(ROWNUM) AS r
  2  FROM   dual
  3  CONNECT BY ROWNUM <= 1e6;
```

1000000 rows selected.

Elapsed: 00:00:05.61

I've omitted the Autotrace output as it is almost identical to that of the baseline SQL, but you can see that adding a call to the function has added almost 4 seconds to the runtime of this simplest of queries.

As stated earlier, it is not possible to directly measure context-switching as such, but you can use tools such as SQL trace, the PL/SQL Hierarchical Profiler (an Oracle Database 11*g* feature), or the V$SESS_TIME_MODEL view to measure the time spent in the PL/SQL engine overall. Listing 9-3 shows the summary results of a Hierarchical Profiler session for the previous SQL.

Listing 9-3. The Cost of Calling a PL/SQL Function from SQL (Hierarchical Profiler Results)

FUNCTION	LINE#	CALLS	SUB_ELA_US	FUNC_ELA_US
__plsql_vm	0	1000003	3122985	2006576
PLSQL_FUNCTION	1	1000000	1116012	1116012
__anonymous_block	0	3	397	311
DBMS_OUTPUT.GET_LINES	180	2	86	82
DBMS_OUTPUT.GET_LINE	129	2	4	4
DBMS_HPROF.STOP_PROFILING	59	1	0	0

This profile clearly shows that the PL/SQL function was called 1 million times and this accounted for a little over 1 second of elapsed time. What is also interesting is the fact that the PL/SQL VM (the PL/SQL engine) spent 2 seconds of processing time outside of the function. Some of this time can be attributed to context-switching. Overall, the PL/SQL engine accounted for over 3 seconds of elapsed time. (Note that the DBMS_OUTPUT calls are a consequence of the serveroutput setting in SQL*Plus and are no more than background noise in this instance.)

■ **Note** For a detailed discussion on the PL/SQL Hierarchical Profiler, see Chapter 13.

These figures are validated by an extended SQL trace of the query, as the TKProf output in Listing 9-4 demonstrates.

Listing 9-4. The Cost of Calling a PL/SQL Function from SQL (tkprof Output)

call	count	cpu	elapsed	disk	query	current	rows
Parse	1	0.00	0.00	0	0	0	0
Execute	1	0.00	0.00	0	0	0	0
Fetch	2001	4.92	5.08	0	0	0	1000000
total	2003	4.92	5.08	0	0	0	1000000

<snip>

Rows (1st)	Row Source Operation
1000000	COUNT (cr=0 pr=0 pw=0 time=3595520 us)
1000000	CONNECT BY WITHOUT FILTERING (cr=0 pr=0 pw=0 time=1693263 us)
1	FAST DUAL (cr=0 pr=0 pw=0 time=28 us cost=2 size=0 card=1)

I've removed the Rows (max) and Rows (avg) statistics to shrink the output, but you can see from the rowsource statistics that it took approximately 3.6 seconds to project the 1 million rows for the resultset (this includes a small amount of network transfer time that was shown in the associated waits summary), yet it took just 1.7 seconds to generate the rows in the first place.

These examples are as simple as possible to demonstrate the cost of calling of PL/SQL functions from SQL. Despite their trivial timings, you can clearly see that the PL/SQL function adds a significant overhead to the response time (over 300%). Of course, PL/SQL functions that have much longer elapsed times (especially those functions that include SQL) will cause you far greater performance issues than context-switching problem. For PL/SQL-only functions (i.e. no SQL in the function body), however, context-switching can be a major part of the PL/SQL VM's elapsed time.

Context-switching can also have a performance impact on queries that have plenty of other work to do, such as accessing and joining sets of data. In Listing 9-5, I have a lightweight PL/SQL function and I've used this to format part of a sales report. As before, I've used Autotrace and SQL*Plus timing to record the runtime statistics.

Listing 9-5. Context-Switching in More Intensive Queries

```
SQL> CREATE FUNCTION format_customer_name (
  2                    p_first_name IN VARCHAR2,
  3                    p_last_name  IN VARCHAR2
  4                    ) RETURN VARCHAR2 AS
  5  BEGIN
  6     RETURN p_first_name || ' ' || p_last_name;
  7  END format_customer_name;
  8  /

Function created.

SQL> SELECT t.calendar_year
  2  ,        format_customer_name(
  3              c.cust_first_name, c.cust_last_name
  4              )                  AS cust_name
  5  ,        SUM(s.quantity_sold) AS qty_sold
```

```
 6  ,          SUM(s.amount_sold)    AS amt_sold
 7  FROM    sales      s
 8  ,          customers c
 9  ,          times      t
10  WHERE   s.cust_id = c.cust_id
11  AND     s.time_id = t.time_id
12  GROUP   BY
13              t.calendar_year
14  ,          format_customer_name(
15                 c.cust_first_name, c.cust_last_name
16                 )
17  ;
```

11604 rows selected.

Elapsed: 00:00:06.94

```
Statistics
----------------------------------------------------------
       3216   consistent gets
          0   physical reads
```

Note that I've trimmed the Autotrace output to include just the I/O statistics. The report completed in approximately 7 seconds. I've compared this to a SQL-only implementation in Listing 9-6.

Listing 9-6. Context-Switching in More Intensive Queries (SQL Implementation)

```
SQL> SELECT t.calendar_year
 2  ,          c.cust_first_name || ' ' || c.cust_last_name AS cust_name
 3  ,          SUM(s.quantity_sold)                          AS qty_sold
 4  ,          SUM(s.amount_sold)                            AS amt_sold
 5  FROM    sales      s
 6  ,          customers c
 7  ,          times      t
 8  WHERE   s.cust_id = c.cust_id
 9  AND     s.time_id = t.time_id
10  GROUP   BY
11              t.calendar_year
12  ,          c.cust_first_name || ' ' || c.cust_last_name
13  ;
```

11604 rows selected.

Elapsed: 00:00:01.40

```
Statistics
----------------------------------------------------------
       3189   consistent gets
          0   physical reads
```

By removing the function in favor of a SQL expression, the runtime of the report reduced to less than 1.5 seconds. You can see, therefore, that even when accessing and joining multiple rowsources, the presence of a PL/SQL function can still impact the overall response time of the query.

Other PL/SQL Function Types

The context-switching penalty applies to any PL/SQL source that is invoked from SQL (including user-defined aggregate functions, type methods, or table functions). A good example is the STRAGG function that Tom Kyte wrote many years back to demonstrate user-defined aggregate functions (then a new feature of Oracle 9*i*). Until Oracle Database 11*g*, there was no built-in equivalent to STRAGG, so this utility function became extremely popular as a solution to string-aggregation problems on Oracle forums.

The release of the LISTAGG built-in function provides a significant performance boost over STRAGG by simply removing the need for the SQL engine to perform context-switching. I've demonstrated this in Listing 9-7 with a simple example of aggregating the range of IDs for each customer in the supplied SH.CUSTOMERS table.

Listing 9-7. Built-in vs. User-Defined Aggregate Function

```
SQL> SELECT cust_first_name
  2  ,      cust_last_name
  3  ,      LISTAGG(cust_id) WITHIN GROUP (ORDER BY NULL)
  4  FROM   customers
  5  GROUP  BY
  6         cust_first_name
  7  ,      cust_last_name;

5601 rows selected.

Elapsed: 00:00:00.23

SQL> SELECT cust_first_name
  2  ,      cust_last_name
  3  ,      STRAGG(cust_id)
  4  FROM   customers
  5  GROUP  BY
  6         cust_first_name
  7  ,      cust_last_name;

5601 rows selected.

Elapsed: 00:00:01.40
```

I've suppressed the Autotrace output, but neither method incurs any physical I/O and the logical I/O is identical. Yet the user-defined aggregate function takes over six times longer than the built-in equivalent.

In summary, I've demonstrated that simply calling PL/SQL functions from SQL can be expensive, regardless of the nature of the function itself. Later, I'll demonstrate various methods you can apply to reduce or remove this cost altogether from your SQL queries.

Executions

It is often said that the fastest way to do something is not to do it at all. It's also commonly said that even when something is nanoseconds-fast, if you execute it enough times, its elapsed time will start to mount up. This is what commonly happens with PL/SQL functions that are executed from SQL. It follows that the more times a PL/SQL function is executed from a SQL statement, the greater the time and resources that are spent in both the function itself and the associated context-switching.

When a PL/SQL function is included in a SQL statement, how many times should that function be executed? There are a number of factors to be considered when attempting to answer this question; even assuming that you have some knowledge of the function's usage in the query, you can't be certain.

SQL is a non-procedural language, yet trying to predict the number of times that a PL/SQL function is executed by a SQL query is a decidedly procedural way of thinking. You have no way of controlling the innermost workings of the SQL engine and therefore no absolute control over how many times a PL/SQL function is called. (I say absolute because there are techniques you can use to reduce a function's executions, but you can't reliably predict the number of calls that you ultimately reduce it to.) If you don't attempt to control the number of executions, then it follows that you won't have any influence over the contribution that your function makes to the response time of your SQL statement.

Query Rewrite and the CBO

There are also the effects of the Cost Based Optimizer (CBO) to consider. With every release of Oracle Database, the CBO becomes more sophisticated (read complex); in particular, it finds more ways to optimize queries through transformation techniques. This means that the query block you call your PL/SQL function from might not exist in the final version of the query that the CBO generates.

This can easily be demonstrated with a small example of the CBO's view-merging transformation. Listing 9-8 contains a mock report that aggregates product sales by customer and calendar year. The PL/SQL function in this example maintains a counter to trace the number of executions. It is called from an in-line view of the CUSTOMERS table in an attempt to pre-compute and also limit the number of function calls.

Listing 9-8. CBO Query Transformation and Function Executions

```
SQL> SELECT t.calendar_year
  2  ,        c.cust_name
  3  ,        SUM(s.quantity_sold) AS qty_sold
  4  ,        SUM(s.amount_sold)   AS amt_sold
  5  FROM     sales     s
  6  ,        (
  7             SELECT cust_id
  8             ,       format_customer_name (
  9                       cust_first_name, cust_last_name
 10                       ) AS cust_name
 11             FROM    customers
 12           )         c
 13  ,        times     t
 14  WHERE    s.cust_id = c.cust_id
 15  AND      s.time_id = t.time_id
```

```
16  GROUP  BY
17         t.calendar_year
18  ,      c.cust_name
19  ;
```

11604 rows selected.

Having executed the report, I can retrieve the latest counter to see how many times the function was executed, as demonstrated in Listing 9-9. Note that you can refer to the source code on the Apress web site for implementation details of the COUNTER package and its use in the FORMAT_CUSTOMER_NAME function.

Listing 9-9. CBO Query Transformation and Function Executions (Displaying Function Calls)

```
SQL> exec counter.show('Function calls');
```

Function calls: **918843**

```
PL/SQL procedure successfully completed.
```

The PL/SQL function has been executed over 918,000 times, although my intention was that the in-line view would limit the function executions to just 55,500 (i.e. once per row in the CUSTOMERS table). This hasn't worked, however, because the CBO has simply merged the inline view with the outer query block, and as a result, my PL/SQL function has been applied to a much larger rowsource than I intended. The execution plan in Listing 9-10 shows that the inline view has been factored out (i.e. merged) and the projection information clearly shows that the function calls have been applied at the very last step in the plan.

Listing 9-10. CBO Query Transformation and Function Executions (Projection of the PL/SQL Function)

```
-----------------------------------------------------
| Id | Operation                   | Name      |
-----------------------------------------------------
|  0 | SELECT STATEMENT            |           |
|  1 |  HASH GROUP BY              |           |
|  2 |   HASH JOIN                 |           |
|  3 |    PART JOIN FILTER CREATE  | :BF0000   |
|  4 |     TABLE ACCESS FULL       | TIMES     |
|  5 |    HASH JOIN                |           |
|  6 |     TABLE ACCESS FULL       | CUSTOMERS |
|  7 |     PARTITION RANGE JOIN-FILTER|        |
|  8 |      TABLE ACCESS FULL      | SALES     |
-----------------------------------------------------

Column Projection Information (identified by operation id):
-----------------------------------------------------------

   1 - "T"."CALENDAR_YEAR"[NUMBER,22],
       "FORMAT_CUSTOMER_NAME"("CUST_FIRST_NAME","CUST_LAST_NAME")[4000],
       SUM("S"."AMOUNT_SOLD")[22], SUM("S"."QUANTITY_SOLD")[22]
```

```
2 - (#keys=1) "T"."CALENDAR_YEAR"[NUMBER,22],
    "CUST_LAST_NAME"[VARCHAR2,40], "CUST_FIRST_NAME"[VARCHAR2,20],
    "S"."AMOUNT_SOLD"[NUMBER,22], "S"."QUANTITY_SOLD"[NUMBER,22]
3 - "T"."TIME_ID"[DATE,7], "T"."TIME_ID"[DATE,7],
    "T"."CALENDAR_YEAR"[NUMBER,22]
4 - "T"."TIME_ID"[DATE,7], "T"."CALENDAR_YEAR"[NUMBER,22]
5 - (#keys=1) "CUST_LAST_NAME"[VARCHAR2,40],
    "CUST_FIRST_NAME"[VARCHAR2,20], "S"."AMOUNT_SOLD"[NUMBER,22],
    "S"."TIME_ID"[DATE,7], "S"."QUANTITY_SOLD"[NUMBER,22]
6 - "CUST_ID"[NUMBER,22], "CUST_FIRST_NAME"[VARCHAR2,20],
    "CUST_LAST_NAME"[VARCHAR2,40]
7 - "S"."CUST_ID"[NUMBER,22], "S"."TIME_ID"[DATE,7],
    "S"."QUANTITY_SOLD"[NUMBER,22], "S"."AMOUNT_SOLD"[NUMBER,22]
8 - "S"."CUST_ID"[NUMBER,22], "S"."TIME_ID"[DATE,7],
    "S"."QUANTITY_SOLD"[NUMBER,22], "S"."AMOUNT_SOLD"[NUMBER,22]
```

View-merging, subquery unnesting, and other complex query transformations are not the only CBO-related issues that can affect the number of executions of your PL/SQL function. The CBO is also free to ignore the order that your tables or predicates are listed (although with the latter there is a notable exception, specific to PL/SQL functions, and I'll be describing it later). The ordering of joins and predicates can have a dramatic effect on the cardinality of each step of an execution plan; this, in turn, will probably cause your PL/SQL function to be executed more, or less perhaps, than you expect.

Internal Optimizations

In addition to the numerous CBO optimizations, Oracle Database also has a range of internal optimizations that are applied at runtime, and trying to second-guess the behavior of these can often be an exercise in futility. Not only will they probably change with database version, they can also be dependent on a wide range of factors, some of which you can derive and others that are hidden from you.

Oracle Database's optimization for DETERMINISTIC functions is one such example. Because a deterministic function will, by definition, always return the same result for a particular input value, Oracle Database can avoid re-executing the PL/SQL function if it encounters the same inputs. The efficiency of this optimization is, however, dependant on other factors, such as data type, data length, cardinality (i.e. the number of distinct values), the database version, and even environmental settings such as array fetch size. For a good discussion of how these factors can result in a wildly varying reduction in function executions, see Dom Brooks' "*Determining Deterministic*" series of articles on http://orastory.wordpress.com.

Similar behavior is seen when PL/SQL function calls are encapsulated in scalar-subqueries (a commonly-used technique to reduce the impact of functions in SQL and one that I demonstrate later in this chapter). While the scalar subquery cache appears to be a more effective optimization than that for deterministic functions, it is still dependant on some of the same factors (such as data type, length, and order) in addition to the size of the internal cache (which varies by database version). See *Cost-Based Oracle Fundamentals* by Jonathan Lewis *(Apress, 2005)* for a more in-depth description of the internal hash table that supports the scalar subquery cache. The fact that this hash table is quite small means that collisions (i.e. cache "misses") are almost inevitable on all but the more trivial set of input values. Because you can't predict when these collisions will occur, you should accept that you can usually derive *some* benefit by using the scalar subquery cache, but not of a precisely quantifiable amount.

Suboptimal Data Access

What happens when a PL/SQL function contains a SQL statement? An extremely common design pattern that can be found in most large database applications is that of SQL lookups wrapped in PL/SQL functions. In general, the principles behind such "getter" functions are sound (i.e. the encapsulation of common lookups, reusable data access methods, etc.), but the performance implications of such design decisions can be devastating, especially when the PL/SQL functions are called from SQL statements.

When a SQL statement is wrapped in a PL/SQL function and called from SQL queries, the cost of context-switching is automatically doubled—it now occurs both inside and outside the function. Far more critical, however, is the fact that by wrapping SQL lookups in functions, the optimization choices that the CBO would otherwise have had if the lookup were in the main body of the calling SQL statement are effectively disabled. The impact that this can have on your queries' elapsed times can be severe (it's fair to say that the cost of context-switching pales into insignificance in these scenarios).

Consider the example in Listing 9-11. I have a PL/SQL function that returns an exchange rate between two currencies for a given date. Note that I've kept this deliberately simple for the purposes of the example.

Listing 9-11. Encapsulating SQL Lookups in PL/SQL Functions (Create PL/SQL Function)

```
SQL> CREATE FUNCTION get_rate(
  2                     p_rate_date IN rates.rate_date%TYPE,
  3                     p_from_ccy  IN rates.base_ccy%TYPE,
  4                     p_to_ccy    IN rates.target_ccy%TYPE
  5                     ) RETURN rates.exchange_rate%TYPE AS
  6     v_rate rates.exchange_rate%TYPE;
  7  BEGIN
  8     SELECT exchange_rate INTO v_rate
  9     FROM   rates
 10     WHERE  base_ccy   = p_from_ccy
 11     AND    target_ccy = p_to_ccy
 12     AND    rate_date  = p_rate_date;
 13     RETURN v_rate;
 14  END get_rate;
 15  /

Function created.
```

In the report of sales by product and calendar year shown in Listing 9-12, I've used this function to calculate revenue in GBP as well as USD. Note that I've used Autotrace to suppress the resultset and enabled the SQL*Plus timer.

Listing 9-12. Encapsulating SQL Lookups in PL/SQL Functions (SQL with PL/SQL)

```
SQL> SELECT t.calendar_year
  2  ,        p.prod_name
  3  ,        SUM(s.amount_sold)                                    AS amt_sold_usd
  4  ,        SUM(s.amount_sold * get_rate(s.time_id, 'USD', 'GBP')) AS amt_sold_gbp
  5  FROM     sales    s
  6  ,        products p
  7  ,        times    t
  8  WHERE    s.prod_id = p.prod_id
```

```
 9   AND     s.time_id = t.time_id
10   GROUP   BY
11           t.calendar_year
12   ,       p.prod_name
13   ;
```

272 rows selected.

Elapsed: 00:01:05.71

The elapsed time of this query is roughly 66 seconds—a poor response time for an aggregate query over less than 1 million rows. The Autotrace output for this statement is provided in Listing 9-13.

Listing 9-13. Encapsulating SQL Lookups in PL/SQL Functions (Autotrace Output for SQL with PL/SQL)

```
Statistics
-----------------------------------------------------------
    918848  recursive calls
        12  db block gets
   1839430  consistent gets
         0  physical reads
      3196  redo size
     16584  bytes sent via SQL*Net to client
       449  bytes received via SQL*Net from client
         2  SQL*Net roundtrips to/from client
         0  sorts (memory)
         0  sorts (disk)
       272  rows processed
```

As highlighted, that's over 1.8 million consistent gets for the report (and over 918,000 recursive calls relating to the execution of the SQL statement embedded in the GET_RATE function). In Listing 9-14, I've converted this query into a "straight SQL" alternative by joining directly to the RATES table and calculating the currency conversion in an expression.

Listing 9-14. Encapsulating SQL Lookups in PL/SQL Functions (SQL-only Solution)

```
SQL> SELECT t.calendar_year
  2  ,       p.prod_name
  3  ,       SUM(s.amount_sold)                 AS amt_sold_usd
  4  ,       SUM(s.amount_sold*r.exchange_rate) AS amt_sold_gbp
  5  FROM    sales     s
  6  ,       times     t
  7  ,       products  p
  8  ,       rates     r
  9  WHERE   s.time_id          = t.time_id
 10  AND     s.prod_id          = p.prod_id
 11  AND     r.rate_date   (+)  = s.time_id
 12  AND     r.base_ccy    (+)  = 'USD'
 13  AND     r.target_ccy  (+)  = 'GBP'
```

```
14   GROUP   BY
15           t.calendar_year
16   ,       p.prod_name
17   ;
```

272 rows selected.

Elapsed: 00:00:00.97

The performance difference is staggering! By removing the PL/SQL function and joining directly to the RATES table, the response time has dropped from 66 seconds to just 1 second.

■ **Note** An unusual "feature" of PL/SQL functions called from SQL is that unhandled NO_DATA_FOUND exceptions silently return NULL rather than propagate the error. I haven't explicitly handled the NO_DATA_FOUND exception in the GET_RATE function in Listing 9-11, so my query in Listing 9-12 won't fail, even if the exchange rate I'm looking up doesn't exist. Rather, the function will return NULL and my query will be lossless (in terms of rows). To emulate this in the SQL-only version of the query in Listing 9-14, I've simply used an outer join to the RATES table.

The Autotrace statistics for the SQL-only report are shown in Listing 9-15.

Listing 9-15. Encapsulating SQL Lookups in PL/SQL Functions (Autotrace Output for SQL-only Report)

```
Statistics
----------------------------------------------------------
        0   recursive calls
        0   db block gets
     1758   consistent gets
        0   physical reads
        0   redo size
    16584   bytes sent via SQL*Net to client
      425   bytes received via SQL*Net from client
        2   SQL*Net roundtrips to/from client
        0   sorts (memory)
        0   sorts (disk)
      272   rows processed
```

The Autotrace output highlights a striking difference in the logical I/O required to satisfy the two SQL statements. The PL/SQL function incurs a penalty of over 1.8 million consistent gets. The TKProf report in Listing 9-16 clearly shows the cost of encapsulating the rates lookup in a function.

Listing 9-16. Encapsulating SQL Lookups in PL/SQL Functions (tkprof Output)

```
SELECT t.calendar_year
,      p.prod_name
,      SUM(s.amount_sold)                               AS amt_sold_usd
,      SUM(s.amount_sold * get_rate(s.time_id, 'USD', 'GBP')) AS amt_sold_gbp
```

```
FROM    sales     s
,       products  p
,       times     t
WHERE   s.prod_id = p.prod_id
AND     s.time_id = t.time_id
GROUP   BY
        t.calendar_year
,       p.prod_name
```

call	count	cpu	elapsed	disk	query	current	rows
Parse	1	0.00	0.00	0	0	0	0
Execute	1	0.00	0.00	0	0	0	0
Fetch	2	105.53	106.38	0	1734	0	272

<snipped output>

```
********************************************************************************
SQL ID: ajp04ks60kqx9 Plan Hash: 139684570

SELECT EXCHANGE_RATE
FROM
 RATES WHERE BASE_CCY = :B3 AND TARGET_CCY = :B2 AND RATE_DATE = :B1
```

call	count	cpu	elapsed	disk	query	current	rows
Parse	0	0.00	0.00	0	0	0	0
Execute	918843	12.50	13.85	0	0	0	0
Fetch	918843	9.74	10.86	0	1837686	0	918843

The TKProf report shows that the SQL inside the PL/SQL function is treated as a separate query; in this case it has accounted for all of the additional logical I/O that the sales query generated and almost half of the additional runtime (if you're wondering where the remaining runtime was spent for this example, a Hierarchical Profiler report showed that almost 59 seconds were spent in the PL/SQL engine overall. Some 47 seconds of this PL/SQL time was accounted for by the rates-lookup SQL itself—double that reported by the SQL trace above—meaning that approximately 23 seconds was PL/SQL overhead). The base query itself has incurred very little logical I/O and is in fact comparable to the SQL-only implementation.

This separation highlights an important point. If the embedded SQL is treated as a query in its own right, the CBO cannot optimize it in the context of the outer query. The CBO is completely ignorant of what the function actually does, so the RATES table does not even feature in the CBO's decision-making. The results, as you can see, can be catastrophic.

You can see, therefore, that it makes good sense (from a performance perspective) to convert PL/SQL lookup functions to SQL. If performance is critical and such lookup functions are heavily used in your application, you are encouraged to remove them wherever possible. There are alternative encapsulation methods that I'll demonstrate later in this chapter that can help you with this.

However, I recognize that it's not always possible to "sweep" a legacy application to convert its SQL (it might be embedded in many different application tiers and technologies, or the regression testing overhead might be too prohibitive). In such cases, there are methods you can use to reduce the costs of the PL/SQL functions and again I'll show some of these later.

Optimizer Difficulties

Many of the examples so far have shown PL/SQL functions called from the SELECT block (projection) of SQL statements but it is equally common to see user-written functions being used in predicates. This can give rise to a range of issues. Firstly, as I demonstrated earlier, a PL/SQL function used in a predicate will be executed an unpredictable number of times. Secondly, a PL/SQL function (or indeed any function) applied to an indexed column will prevent the use of the index. Thirdly, the CBO knows very little about PL/SQL functions as it usually has no statistics with which to work. This can lead to suboptimal execution plans. I will concentrate on the third issue here, as I described the first issue earlier and the second is well understood by the Oracle DBA/developer community.

PL/SQL Functions and Statistics

Why does the CBO have difficulties with PL/SQL functions? The answer is statistics. You know that the CBO relies on good-quality statistics to enable it to make sensible optimization decisions. When it comes to PL/SQL functions, however, the CBO almost always has no statistics to work with and has to resort to default heuristics instead. For example, when encountering a predicate of the form `WHERE plsql_function(expression-involving-some-column) = value`, the CBO defaults the predicate's selectivity to just 1% (in the absence of statistics for the function, it has no alternative).

In Listing 9-17, I demonstrate this heuristic using a small table of 1,000 rows, a PL/SQL function, and a simple query with CBO tracing enabled (10053 event).

Listing 9-17. Default Selectivity for PL/SQL Function Predicate

```
SQL> CREATE TABLE thousand_rows
  2  AS
  3     SELECT ROWNUM            AS n1
  4     ,       RPAD('x',50,'x') AS v1
  5     FROM   dual
  6     CONNECT BY ROWNUM <= 1000;

Table created.

SQL> BEGIN
  2     DBMS_STATS.GATHER_TABLE_STATS(user, 'THOUSAND_ROWS');
  3  END;
  4  /

PL/SQL procedure successfully completed.

SQL> CREATE FUNCTION plsql_function (
  2                  p_id IN INTEGER
  3                  ) RETURN INTEGER AS
  4  BEGIN
  5     RETURN 0;
  6  END plsql_function;
  7  /

Function created.
```

```
SQL> ALTER SESSION SET EVENTS '10053 trace name context forever, level 1';

Session altered.

SQL> set autotrace traceonly explain

SQL> SELECT *
  2  FROM    thousand_rows
  3  WHERE   plsql_function(n1) = 0;

Execution Plan
-----------------------------------------------------------
Plan hash value: 4012467810


-----------------------------------------------------------------------------------
| Id  | Operation          | Name          | Rows  | Bytes | Cost (%CPU)| Time     |
-----------------------------------------------------------------------------------
|   0 | SELECT STATEMENT   |               |    10 |   550 |     5   (0)| 00:00:01 |
|*  1 |  TABLE ACCESS FULL | THOUSAND_ROWS |    10 |   550 |     5   (0)| 00:00:01 |
-----------------------------------------------------------------------------------

Predicate Information (identified by operation id):
---------------------------------------------------

   1 - filter("PLSQL_FUNCTION"("N1")=0)

SQL> ALTER SESSION SET EVENTS '10053 trace name context off';

Session altered.
```

In the absence of statistics for the PL/SQL function, the CBO has defaulted to a 1% selectivity to determine the cardinality of the predicate. You can see this reflected in the cardinalities (Rows) displayed in the execution plan above. An excerpt from the 10053 trace file in Listing 9-18 also demonstrates the CBO's calculations.

Listing 9-18. Default Selectivity for PL/SQL Function Predicate (10053 Trace File)

```
***************************************
BASE STATISTICAL INFORMATION
***********************
Table Stats::
  Table: THOUSAND_ROWS  Alias: THOUSAND_ROWS
    #Rows: 1000  #Blks:  12  AvgRowLen:  55.00  ChainCnt:  0.00
Access path analysis for THOUSAND_ROWS
***************************************
SINGLE TABLE ACCESS PATH
  Single Table Cardinality Estimation for THOUSAND_ROWS[THOUSAND_ROWS]
  No statistics type defined for function PLSQL_FUNCTION
  No default cost defined for function PLSQL_FUNCTION
  No statistics type defined for function PLSQL_FUNCTION
  No default selectivity defined for function PLSQL_FUNCTION
  Table: THOUSAND_ROWS  Alias: THOUSAND_ROWS
```

```
      Card: Original: 1000.000000  Rounded: 10  Computed: 10.00  Non Adjusted: 10.00
    Access Path: TableScan
      Cost:  5.10  Resp: 5.10  Degree: 0
        Cost_io: 5.00  Cost_cpu: 3285657
        Resp_io: 5.00  Resp_cpu: 3285657
    Best:: AccessPath: TableScan
```

I've highlighted some important information in this trace file. It states that there are no default statistics or statistics types defined for either cost or selectivity of the PL/SQL function. This shows you, therefore, that it is possible to provide statistics on PL/SQL functions; I'll demonstrate how to do this later.

Predicate Ordering

When statistics for PL/SQL functions are missing, other potential issues can arise as a result of the order in which the predicates are coded. For example, if you write a WHERE clause that contains two PL/SQL function predicates, in the absence of statistics the functions will be executed simply in the order in which they appear in the SQL.

I've demonstrated this in Listing 9-19, where I have a SQL statement that filters on two PL/SQL functions, SLOW_FUNCTION and QUICK_FUNCTION. As their names suggest, one function is more costly than the other, so I've executed the SQL statement twice with the predicates in different orders, using Autotrace and a SQL*Plus timer to compare the results.

Listing 9-19. PL/SQL Functions and Predicate Ordering

```
SQL> CREATE FUNCTION quick_function (
  2                   p_id IN INTEGER
  3                   ) RETURN INTEGER AS
  4  BEGIN
  5     RETURN MOD(p_id, 1000);
  6  END quick_function;
  7  /

Function created.

SQL> CREATE FUNCTION slow_function (
  2                   p_id IN INTEGER
  3                   ) RETURN INTEGER AS
  4  BEGIN
  5     DBMS_LOCK.SLEEP(0.005);
  6     RETURN MOD(p_id, 2);
  7  END slow_function;
  8  /

Function created.

SQL> set autotrace traceonly

SQL> SELECT *
```

```
  2  FROM    thousand_rows
  3  WHERE   quick_function(n1) = 0
  4  AND     slow_function(n1) = 0;
```

1 row selected.

Elapsed: 00:00:00.02

Execution Plan

Plan hash value: 4012467810

```
-------------------------------------------------------------------------------
| Id  | Operation            | Name          | Rows  | Bytes | Cost (%CPU)| Time     |
-------------------------------------------------------------------------------
|   0 | SELECT STATEMENT     |               |    1  |   55  |    5   (0)| 00:00:01 |
|*  1 |  TABLE ACCESS FULL|   THOUSAND_ROWS  |    1  |   55  |    5   (0)| 00:00:01 |
-------------------------------------------------------------------------------
```

Predicate Information (identified by operation id):
----

    1 - filter("QUICK_FUNCTION"("N1")=0 AND "SLOW_FUNCTION"("N1")=0)


```
SQL> SELECT *
  2  FROM    thousand_rows
  3  WHERE   slow_function(n1) = 0
  4  AND     quick_function(n1) = 0;
```

1 row selected.

Elapsed: 00:00:11.09

Execution Plan

Plan hash value: 4012467810

```
-------------------------------------------------------------------------------
| Id  | Operation            | Name          | Rows  | Bytes | Cost (%CPU)| Time     |
-------------------------------------------------------------------------------
|   0 | SELECT STATEMENT     |               |    1  |   55  |    5   (0)| 00:00:01 |
|*  1 |  TABLE ACCESS FULL|   THOUSAND_ROWS  |    1  |   55  |    5   (0)| 00:00:01 |
-------------------------------------------------------------------------------
```

Predicate Information (identified by operation id):
----

    1 - filter("SLOW_FUNCTION"("N1")=0 AND "QUICK_FUNCTION"("N1")=0)

I've removed the Autotrace statistics but kept the Explain Plan sections to show the order in which the PL/SQL functions were executed for each SQL statement. You can see that this matches the order in which they were coded and that this made quite a difference to the relative performance of the two statements. This is the point. The CBO has no idea that SLOW_FUNCTION has a lower selectivity or that it takes longer to execute than QUICK_FUNCTION. In the absence of supplied statistics, how can it? It makes no sense for the CBO to re-order the predicates, because it has no basis for doing so.

The good news is that there are several methods for generating or setting statistics for PL/SQL functions to mitigate this issue. These are described in the section entitled *"Assisting the CBO."*

The Read-Consistency Trap

Listing 9-13 clearly demonstrates the resource-cost of putting SQL lookups into PL/SQL functions (and these costs are easy to quantify). However, there is another important pitfall of using such a design, although it is much harder to quantify the potential impact that this might have on your application(s). That is, the SQL inside the PL/SQL function is not read-consistent with the main SQL statement that is calling the function.

The TKProf report from Listing 9-12 (shown in Listing 9-16) demonstrated that the SQL inside the PL/SQL function was treated as a separate statement. This means that under the READ COMMITTED isolation level, it has its own read-consistency and not that of the SQL statement that calls the function.

In Listings 9-20 through 9-23, I've demonstrated this read-consistency trap. I have two sessions; the first of which (*Session One*) executes a long-running query that includes a call to a PL/SQL lookup function. The second session (*Session Two*) updates one of the lookup records at a random point in time, but importantly, this is while the first session's query is still running.

I'll begin with the PL/SQL lookup function in Listing 9-20.

Listing 9-20. The Read-Consistency Trap (Create PL/SQL Function)

```
SQL> CREATE FUNCTION get_customer_name (
  2                     p_cust_id IN customers.cust_id%TYPE
  3                     ) RETURN VARCHAR2 AS
  4     v_customer_name VARCHAR2(200);
  5  BEGIN
  6     SELECT cust_first_name || ' ' || cust_last_name
  7     INTO   v_customer_name
  8     FROM   customers
  9     WHERE  cust_id = p_cust_id;
 10     RETURN v_customer_name;
 11  END get_customer_name;
 12  /

Function created.
```

You can see that the lookup function fetches a customer name by primary key. In addition, I have created a small SLEEPER function to enable me to slow down *Session One's* query and simulate a long-running SQL statement (this function simply calls DBMS_LOCK.SLEEP and returns a constant 0).

Continuing with the example, *Session One* issues the following query shown in Listing 9-21.

Listing 9-21. The Read-Consistency Trap (Session One's Long-Running Query)

Session One
```
-----------
22:47:23 SQL> SELECT s.cust_id
22:47:23    2 ,      get_customer_name(s.cust_id) AS cust_name
22:47:23    3 ,      sleeper(1)                   AS sleep_time
22:47:23    4 FROM   sales s
22:47:23    5 WHERE  ROWNUM <= 10;
```

Note the time at which *Session One* issues this SQL. The 10-row resultset and the 1 second sleep for each row means that this query should complete in just over 10 seconds. While this is executing, *Session Two* updates one of the customer names that *Session One* is repeatedly querying, as shown in Listing 9-22.

Listing 9-22. The Read-Consistency Trap (Session Two's Customer Update)

Session Two
```
-----------
22:47:26 SQL> UPDATE customers
22:47:26    2 SET    cust_last_name = 'Smith'
22:47:26    3 WHERE  cust_id = 2;
```

1 row updated.

22:47:26 SQL> COMMIT;

Commit complete.

Again, note the time that this update is committed (approximately 3 seconds into *Session One's* long-running query). Listing 9-23 shows the effect of this on *Session One's* report.

Listing 9-23. The Read-Consistency Trap (Session One's Resultset)

Session One
```
-----------
   CUST_ID CUST_NAME                      SLEEP_TIME
---------- ------------------------------ ----------
         2 Anne Koch                               1
         2 Anne Koch                               1
         2 Anne Koch                               1
         2 Anne Koch                               1
         2 Anne Smith                              1
         2 Anne Smith                              1
         2 Anne Smith                              1
         2 Anne Smith                              1
         2 Anne Smith                              1
         2 Anne Smith                              1
```

10 rows selected.

Elapsed: 00:00:10.02

Approximately halfway through *Session One's* resultset, the customer name for ID=2 changed, because the lookup function operates outside of the main query's read-consistent image of data. The report itself is therefore inconsistent.

What does this mean if you use such PL/SQL functions? Clearly you are at risk of inconsistent resultsets every time you include the function in a query, particularly if your users can update the lookup table at any time. You would need to assess this risk in the context of your own application patterns, of course. Users who received an inconsistent report would naturally question what they were seeing, and even worse, question your application.

Unfortunately, the options for protecting yourself against this are less than satisfactory. Short of removing all PL/SQL lookup functions, you have a range of options, such as

- Using the SERIALIZABLE isolation level.

- Using SET TRANSACTION READ ONLY.

- Making your PL/SQL function use flashback query with a given SCN to match the start of the main query.

- Making your readers block writers with FOR UPDATE queries (which even then would only work if the lookup table was accessed directly elsewhere in your main query. At which point you'd need to question the need for your PL/SQL lookup function in the first place!)

Any of these options would solve the issue but would more likely cause you greater headaches by seriously limiting your application's concurrency and performance.

Other Issues

I've described in some detail the major issues you need to be aware of when using PL/SQL functions in SQL. Needless to say, there are others and perhaps you've encountered a particular corner-case that I haven't thought of. I'll complete this section with a very brief mention of other issues that you might encounter at some stage.

Parallel Query

PL/SQL functions can be enabled to work with Oracle Database's parallel query option (PQ). While many PL/SQL functions can be executed by PQ slaves without issue, it is sometimes possible to disable PQ by referencing a PL/SQL function that is not explicitly parallel-enabled. If you are having trouble parallelizing a SQL statement and it contains a PL/SQL function, check to see if the function is parallel-enabled. Assuming your PQ hints, session PQ settings, and PQ system parameters are valid for parallel query yet it's simply not "taking," re-create your PL/SQL function to include the PARALLEL_ENABLE clause and try again. Note that for a PL/SQL function to be parallel-enabled, it should not reference session state variables that a PQ-slave might not be able to access (such as package state).

NO_DATA_FOUND

I described this earlier in the commentary for Listing 9-12 but it's worth reiterating for completeness. A NO_DATA_FOUND exception raised in a PL/SQL function called from a SQL statement will not propagate the exception! Instead, the function will return NULL.

Reducing the Cost of PL/SQL Functions

I've just spent several pages describing many of the difficulties, costs, and pitfalls that you might encounter when using PL/SQL functions. Yet this is a book for PL/SQL professionals, so I'm going to spend the remainder of this chapter describing a range of techniques to reduce the impact of using PL/SQL functions.

A Sense of Perspective

Before I continue, I think it is important to give a sense of perspective. Nothing in the world of Oracle development and performance is absolute and, fortunately, there are times when a basic implementation of a PL/SQL function will be more than adequate. Listings 9-24 and 9-25 demonstrate such an example. I'm going to create an isNumber checker to validate in-bound raw data and compare a PL/SQL function implementation with a SQL-only version. To do this, I've created an external table of seven fields (all as VARCHAR2(30)), dumped the data in the SALES table to a flat-file and modified 1 in every 10,000 AMOUNT_SOLD values to include non-numeric characters (AMOUNT_SOLD maps to FIELD_07 in the external table). Finally, I've created the IS_NUMBER function shown in Listing 9-24 to validate that strings are in fact of numeric format.

Listing 9-24. Validating Numeric Data (IS_NUMBER Function)

```
SQL> CREATE FUNCTION is_number (
  2                      p_str IN VARCHAR2
  3                      ) RETURN NUMBER IS
  4      n NUMBER;
  5  BEGIN
  6      n := TO_NUMBER(p_str);
  7      RETURN 1;
  8  EXCEPTION
  9      WHEN VALUE_ERROR THEN
 10          RETURN 0;
 11  END;
 12  /

Function created.
```

In Listing 9-25, I've used two alternative approaches to validate that the data in FIELD_07 is of numeric format. First, I've used the IS_NUMBER PL/SQL function (which returns 1 if the input value is a number). Second, I've used a SQL built-in regular expression, taken from an example in an OTN forum thread. I've used Autotrace to suppress the output and the SQL*Plus timer to record the timings.

Listing 9-25. Validating Numeric Data (PL/SQL Function vs. SQL Built-in)

```
SQL> SELECT *
  2  FROM   external_table
  3  WHERE  is_number(field_07) = 1;

918752 rows selected.
```

Elapsed: 00:00:10.19

```
SQL> SELECT *
  2  FROM    external_table
  3  WHERE   REGEXP_LIKE(
  4              field_07,
  5              '^( *)(\+|-)?((\d*[.]?\d+)|(d+[.]?\d*)){1}(e(\+|-)?\d+)?(f|d)?$',
  6              'i');
```

918752 rows selected.

Elapsed: 00:00:28.25

You can see that the PL/SQL function implementation is much quicker (almost three times) than the regular expression. It is better still when reversing the two methods to find the small number of non-numeric records. Regular expressions are very CPU-intensive; compare the CPU times for the two SQL statements in V$SQL or trace the two queries with DBMS_UTILITY.GET_CPU_TIME to see the difference for yourself.

This example shows that the validity of using PL/SQL functions in SQL statements cannot be dismissed outright. Your requirements, your knowledge of the systems you are developing, and your testing will help you to determine whether a PL/SQL function is viable or not. And if it is viable, the techniques I will describe in the remainder of this chapter should help you to get a lot more from your implementations.

Using SQL Alternatives

It is, however, quite rare that a PL/SQL function will be quicker than a SQL-only expression or built-in function. You should consider whether it is possible or desirable to change some of your application's critical queries (that use PL/SQL functions) to use SQL-only alternatives. If you are developing new applications, you have a good opportunity to build-in performance from the outset.

Some considerations will be required here, of course, and if any of the following are true, you might decide to favour some PL/SQL functions over a SQL implementation:

- A PL/SQL function is not heavily used.

- A PL/SQL function is too complicated to be easily expressed in SQL.

- A SQL statement is not displaying any of the issues I've described.

- You have simply too much SQL to change or regression-testing would be too prohibitive.

I'll demonstrate the performance benefits of using SQL and offer some alternative techniques that you can use to refactor those critical SQL statements (or even consider as a standard for new applications).

Use SQL

In Listing 9-12, I ran a sales report that generated over 918,000 executions of a GET_RATE PL/SQL function. I demonstrated that a SQL-only implementation of the same report (i.e. a simple join to the RATES table) reduced the runtime of that query from 66 seconds to just 1 second (there was also a massive reduction in logical I/O). The SQL-only technique can also make a difference to the elapsed time of queries that use quicker PL/SQL functions, such as those that don't contain any SQL.

SQL is an extremely flexible and rich language for processing sets of data quickly. Assuming that performance is your goal, you can use SQL such as analytic functions, subquery factoring, and a wide range of applications of the built-in functions to refactor your PL/SQL functions to SQL (visit the OTN SQL and PL/SQL forum or http://oraqa.com/ for examples of innovative uses for SQL).

Use a View

An argument in favour of retaining PL/SQL functions is that they encapsulate and centralize application logic, preventing a proliferation of the same rules throughout the code base. There are alternative encapsulation methods, such as using views, which have the added benefits of also providing the performance of SQL. In Listing 9-26, I've converted the sales report by calendar year and product from using the GET_RATE PL/SQL function to using a view, where the logic is encapsulated in a SQL expression.

Listing 9-26. Encapsulating Function Logic in a View

```
SQL> CREATE VIEW sales_rates_view
  2  AS
  3     SELECT s.*
  4     ,       s.amount_sold * (SELECT r.exchange_rate
  5                              FROM   rates r
  6                              WHERE  r.base_ccy   = 'USD'
  7                              AND    r.target_ccy = 'GBP'
  8                              AND    r.rate_date  = s.time_id) AS amount_sold_gbp
  9     FROM    sales    s;

View created.
```

With this view, I've converted the GET_RATE PL/SQL function to a scalar subquery lookup. The entire rates conversion is now projected as a single column. I've used a scalar subquery instead of a simple join to RATES to take advantage of an optimization with views known as column-elimination. With this optimization, the scalar subquery will only be executed when the AMOUNT_SOLD_GBP column is referenced in a query. This means that queries that don't need the converted rate can also take advantage of this view without penalty, widening the scope for re-use. The timing and statistics for the sales report when using this view are shown in Listing 9-27.

Listing 9-27. Exploiting Column-Elimination in Views (No Column-Elimination)

```
SQL> SELECT t.calendar_year
  2  ,       p.prod_name
  3  ,       SUM(s.quantity_sold)    AS qty_sold
  4  ,       SUM(s.amount_sold)      AS amt_sold_usd
  5  ,       SUM(s.amount_sold_gbp)  AS amt_sold_gbp
  6  FROM    sales_rates_view s
  7  ,       times            t
  8  ,       products         p
  9  WHERE   s.time_id     = t.time_id
```

```
10  AND     s.prod_id    = p.prod_id
11  GROUP   BY
12          t.calendar_year
13  ,       p.prod_name;
```

272 rows selected.

Elapsed: 00:00:01.29

```
Execution Plan
-----------------------------------------------------------
Plan hash value: 625253124

-----------------------------------------------------------
| Id  | Operation                    | Name     | Rows  |
-----------------------------------------------------------
|   0 | SELECT STATEMENT             |          |   252 |
|*  1 |  INDEX UNIQUE SCAN           | RATES_PK |     1 |
|   2 |   HASH GROUP BY              |          |   252 |
|*  3 |    HASH JOIN                 |          |  918K |
|   4 |     PART JOIN FILTER CREATE  | :BF0000  |  1826 |
|   5 |      TABLE ACCESS FULL       | TIMES    |  1826 |
|*  6 |     HASH JOIN                |          |  918K |
|   7 |      TABLE ACCESS FULL       | PRODUCTS |    72 |
|   8 |      PARTITION RANGE JOIN-FILTER|       |  918K |
|   9 |       TABLE ACCESS FULL      | SALES    |  918K |
-----------------------------------------------------------

Statistics
-----------------------------------------------------------
          8  recursive calls
          0  db block gets
      10639  consistent gets
          0  physical reads
          0  redo size
      17832  bytes sent via SQL*Net to client
        437  bytes received via SQL*Net from client
          2  SQL*Net roundtrips to/from client
          0  sorts (memory)
          0  sorts (disk)
        272  rows processed
```

I've highlighted the critical parts of the output. There is slightly more logical I/O than with a simple join to RATES, but this is minor compared with the I/O generated by the PL/SQL function. The sales report is still much quicker than the version with the PL/SQL function and the business logic is encapsulated.

Listing 9-28 demonstrates column-elimination. I've excluded the AMOUNT_SOLD_GBP column from the report and captured the statistics again.

Listing 9-28. Exploiting Column-Elimination in Views (Column-Elimination)

```
SQL> SELECT t.calendar_year
  2  ,       p.prod_name
  3  ,       SUM(s.quantity_sold)   AS qty_sold
  4  ,       SUM(s.amount_sold)     AS amt_sold_usd
  5  FROM    sales_rates_view s
  6  ,       times            t
  7  ,       products         p
  8  WHERE   s.time_id   = t.time_id
  9  AND     s.prod_id   = p.prod_id
 10  GROUP   BY
 11          t.calendar_year
 12  ,       p.prod_name;
```

272 rows selected.

Elapsed: 00:00:00.61

```
Statistics
-----------------------------------------------------------
          8  recursive calls
          0  db block gets
       1736  consistent gets
          0  physical reads
          0  redo size
      11785  bytes sent via SQL*Net to client
        437  bytes received via SQL*Net from client
          2  SQL*Net roundtrips to/from client
          0  sorts (memory)
          0  sorts (disk)
        272  rows processed
```

This time, the query completes in half the time and the logical I/O decreases again. This is because the RATES table lookup has been eliminated from the view projection at runtime. The execution plan and projection in Listing 9-29 clearly demonstrate this.

Listing 9-29. Exploiting Column-Elimination in Views (Execution Plan)

```
PLAN_TABLE_OUTPUT
--------------------------------------------------------------------------
Plan hash value: 171093611
```

```
-------------------------------------------------------
| Id  | Operation                | Name      |
-------------------------------------------------------
|   0 | SELECT STATEMENT         |           |
|   1 |  HASH GROUP BY           |           |
|   2 |   HASH JOIN              |           |
|   3 |    TABLE ACCESS FULL     | PRODUCTS  |
|   4 |    VIEW                  | VW_GBC_9  |
|   5 |     HASH GROUP BY        |           |
```

```
|   6 |      HASH JOIN                     |         |
|   7 |        PART JOIN FILTER CREATE     | :BF0000 |
|   8 |          TABLE ACCESS FULL         | TIMES   |
|   9 |        PARTITION RANGE JOIN-FILTER|          |
|  10 |          TABLE ACCESS FULL         | SALES   |
--------------------------------------------------------
```

```
Column Projection Information (identified by operation id):
-----------------------------------------------------------

    1 - "ITEM_4"[NUMBER,22], "P"."PROD_NAME"[VARCHAR2,50],
        SUM("ITEM_2")[22], SUM("ITEM_3")[22]
    2 - (#keys=1) "P"."PROD_NAME"[VARCHAR2,50], "ITEM_4"[NUMBER,22],
        "ITEM_2"[NUMBER,22], "ITEM_3"[NUMBER,22]
    3 - "P"."PROD_ID"[NUMBER,22], "P"."PROD_NAME"[VARCHAR2,50]
    4 - "ITEM_1"[NUMBER,22], "ITEM_2"[NUMBER,22], "ITEM_3"[NUMBER,22],
        "ITEM_4"[NUMBER,22]
    5 - "T"."CALENDAR_YEAR"[NUMBER,22], "S"."PROD_ID"[NUMBER,22],
        SUM("S"."AMOUNT_SOLD")[22], SUM("S"."QUANTITY_SOLD")[22]
    6 - (#keys=1) "T"."CALENDAR_YEAR"[NUMBER,22],
        "S"."PROD_ID"[NUMBER,22], "S"."AMOUNT_SOLD"[NUMBER,22],
        "S"."QUANTITY_SOLD"[NUMBER,22]
    7 - "T"."TIME_ID"[DATE,7], "T"."TIME_ID"[DATE,7],
        "T"."CALENDAR_YEAR"[NUMBER,22]
    8 - "T"."TIME_ID"[DATE,7], "T"."CALENDAR_YEAR"[NUMBER,22]
    9 - "S"."PROD_ID"[NUMBER,22], "S"."TIME_ID"[DATE,7],
        "S"."QUANTITY_SOLD"[NUMBER,22], "S"."AMOUNT_SOLD"[NUMBER,22]
   10 - "S"."PROD_ID"[NUMBER,22], "S"."TIME_ID"[DATE,7],
        "S"."QUANTITY_SOLD"[NUMBER,22], "S"."AMOUNT_SOLD"[NUMBER,22]
```

This highlights the fact that views can be a higher-performing alternative to PL/SQL functions, without compromising the need for encapsulation and centralization. As a final consideration, you could rename the base table and allow the view to take on its name. With these actions, you will have "slotted in" the business logic columns into the SALES "table" and your DML statements will not be compromised, as Listing 9-30 shows.

Listing 9-30. DML on a Table through a View with a Scalar Subquery

```
SQL> RENAME sales TO sales_t;

Table renamed.

SQL> CREATE VIEW sales
  2  AS
  3     SELECT s. prod_id, s.cust_id, s.time_id, s.channel_id,
  4            s.promo_id, s.quantity_sold, s.amount_sold,
  5            s.amount_sold * (SELECT r.exchange_rate
  6                             FROM   rates r
  7                             WHERE  r.base_ccy   = 'USD'
  8                             AND    r.target_ccy = 'GBP'
  9                             AND    r.rate_date  = s.time_id) AS amount_sold_gbp
 10     FROM   sales_t  s;
```

```
View created.

SQL> INSERT INTO sales
  2      ( prod_id, cust_id, time_id, channel_id, promo_id,
  3        quantity_sold, amount_sold )
  4  VALUES
  5      ( 13, 987, DATE '1998-01-10', 3, 999, 1, 1232.16 );

1 row created.

SQL> UPDATE sales
  2  SET     amount_sold = 10000
  3  WHERE   ROWNUM = 1;

1 row updated.

SQL> DELETE
  2  FROM    sales
  3  WHERE   amount_sold = 10000;

1 row deleted.
```

To use this approach, consideration needs to be given to any existing code base, such as %ROWTYPE declarations, PL/SQL record-based DML, unqualified INSERT or SELECT lists (i.e. those without explicit column references), and so on. Fortunately, derived columns in views cannot be modified, as the final example for this section demonstrates in Listing 9-31.

Listing 9-31. DML on a Table through a View with a Scalar Subquery

```
SQL> INSERT INTO sales
  2      ( prod_id, cust_id, time_id, channel_id, promo_id,
  3        quantity_sold, amount_sold, amount_sold_gbp )
  4  VALUES
  5      ( 13, 987, DATE '1998-01-10', 3, 999, 1, 1232.16, 1000 );
     quantity_sold, amount_sold, amount_sold_gbp )
                                  *
ERROR at line 3:
ORA-01733: virtual column not allowed here
```

Use a Virtual Column

To wrap up this section on using SQL expressions in place of PL/SQL functions, I'm going to demonstrate how to replace a PL/SQL function with a virtual column.

A feature of Oracle Database 11g, virtual columns are expressions stored as column metadata in tables (they don't use any storage as such). They are logically similar to columns in views but are far more flexible as they can have statistics gathered for them or be indexed. Virtual columns are an excellent tool for encapsulating simple business rules and, because they are stored as metadata against tables, they are also self-documenting declarations of your data logic.

To demonstrate virtual columns as an alternative to PL/SQL functions, I've converted the sales report from Listing 9-6. To recap, this used the FORMAT_CUSTOMER_NAME function to format a customer name and took almost 7 seconds to execute (compared with just 1 second as a SQL-only query). To begin the conversion, I've added a virtual column to the CUSTOMERS table, as shown in Listing 9-32.

Listing 9-32. Converting a PL/SQL Function to a Virtual Column (Syntax)

```
SQL> ALTER TABLE customers ADD
  2  ( cust_name VARCHAR2(100) GENERATED ALWAYS AS (cust_first_name||' '||cust_last_name) )
  3  ;

Table altered.
```

The GENERATED ALWAYS AS (expression) syntax is specific to virtual columns (I've omitted an optional VIRTUAL keyword to keep the display on a single line). The CUSTOMERS table now looks as follows in Listing 9-33.

Listing 9-33. Converting a PL/SQL Function to a Virtual Column (Table Description)

```
SQL> SELECT column_name
  2  ,      data_type
  3  ,      data_default
  4  FROM   user_tab_columns
  5  WHERE  table_name = 'CUSTOMERS'
  6  ORDER  BY
  7         column_id;
```

COLUMN_NAME	DATA_TYPE	DATA_DEFAULT
CUST_ID	NUMBER	
CUST_FIRST_NAME	VARCHAR2	
CUST_LAST_NAME	VARCHAR2	
CUST_GENDER	CHAR	
<...output removed...>		
CUST_VALID	VARCHAR2	
CUST_NAME	**VARCHAR2**	**"CUST_FIRST_NAME"||' '||"CUST_LAST_NAME"**

Using the virtual column in a SQL statement is no different from any other table, view, or other column. The converted sales report is shown in Listing 9-34.

Listing 9-34. Converting a PL/SQL Function to a Virtual Column (Usage)

```
SQL> SELECT t.calendar_year
  2  ,      c.cust_name
  3  ,      SUM(s.quantity_sold) AS qty_sold
  4  ,      SUM(s.amount_sold)   AS amt_sold
  5  FROM   sales     s
  6  ,      customers c
  7  ,      times     t
  8  WHERE  s.cust_id = c.cust_id
  9  AND    s.time_id = t.time_id
 10  GROUP  BY
```

```
 11        t.calendar_year
 12  ,     c.cust_name;
```

11604 rows selected.

Elapsed: 00:00:01.20

As you can see from the elapsed time of this query, by moving the customer name formatting to a virtual column, I've eliminated the overhead of the PL/SQL function while retaining the encapsulation of the business logic with the very data to which it applies.

Reducing Executions

Earlier in this chapter, I described the fact that you can't reliably predict the number calls to a PL/SQL function that a SQL statement will make. Further, each execution carries a context-switching penalty in addition to the work the PL/SQL function has to do. There are, however, techniques you can use to reliably *reduce* the function calls and I will demonstrate some of these next.

Pre/Post-Computing with SQL Hints

I gave an example of the CBO's cost-based query transformation in Listings 9-8 to 9-10, where my attempt to pre-compute formatted customer names in an inline view was negated by view merging. The result was 918,000 PL/SQL function executions (i.e. once per row in the larger SALES table) instead of an intended 55,500 calls (i.e. once per row in the CUSTOMERS table). For some queries, such an order of magnitude or more function executions can be disastrous.

I've repeated the customer sales report in Listing 9-35. This time, however, I've used a couple of hints to ensure that the pre-computation of the customer names in an inline view "sticks" and the CBO doesn't merge the query blocks.

Listing 9-35. Reducing Function Calls through SQL

```
SQL> SELECT /*+ NO_MERGE(@customers) */
  2        t.calendar_year
  3  ,     c.cust_name
  4  ,     SUM(s.quantity_sold) AS qty_sold
  5  ,     SUM(s.amount_sold)   AS amt_sold
  6  FROM  sales     s
  7  ,     (
  8        SELECT /*+ QB_NAME(customers) */
  9               cust_id
 10        ,      format_customer_name (
 11                   cust_first_name, cust_last_name
 12                   ) AS cust_name
 13        FROM   customers
 14        )      c
 15  ,     times     t
 16  WHERE s.cust_id = c.cust_id
 17  AND   s.time_id = t.time_id
 18  GROUP BY
```

```
 19         t.calendar_year
 20   ,     c.cust_name
 21   ;
```

11604 rows selected.

Elapsed: 00:00:01.49

SQL> exec counter.show('Function calls');

Function calls: 55500

You can see that this time, I've used hints to instruct the CBO to leave my inline view unmerged. The aim is to ensure that my PL/SQL function only executes against the CUSTOMERS dataset and not the larger SALES set. I've done this by using the NO_MERGE hint, adopting the query block naming syntax introduced in Oracle Database 10g. The QB_NAME hint is used to label the inline view query block; I'm therefore able to reference the inline view from the main query block, as you can see in the NO_MERGE hint.

I can go one step further with this query, however. In this particular example, the FORMAT_CUSTOMER_NAME function only needs to be applied to the final resultset of just11,604 rows (far fewer than the 55,500 customer records). I can therefore pre-group the entire resultset using the same hints as previously, but only call the PL/SQL function at the very last stage. Listing 9-36 shows the impact of this.

Listing 9-36. Reducing Function Calls through SQL (Restructured Query)

```
SQL> SELECT /*+ NO_MERGE(@pregroup) */
  2         calendar_year
  3   ,     format_customer_name(
  4              cust_first_name, cust_last_name
  5              ) AS cust_name
  6   ,     qty_sold
  7   ,     amt_sold
  8   FROM  (
  9            SELECT /*+ QB_NAME(pregroup) */
 10                   t.calendar_year
 11            ,      c.cust_first_name
 12            ,      c.cust_last_name
 13            ,      SUM(s.quantity_sold) AS qty_sold
 14            ,      SUM(s.amount_sold)   AS amt_sold
 15            FROM   sales     s
 16            ,      customers c
 17            ,      times     t
 18            WHERE  s.cust_id = c.cust_id
 19            AND    s.time_id = t.time_id
 20            GROUP  BY
 21                   t.calendar_year
 22            ,      c.cust_first_name
 23            ,      c.cust_last_name
 24         );
```

11604 rows selected.

Elapsed: 00:00:01.14

SQL> exec counter.show('Function calls');

Function calls: 11604

This is better still, because I have managed to pre-aggregate all the data prior to calling the PL/SQL function, reducing its number of calls to 11,604 and saving more time on the report.

This technique can be applied in targeted cases where PL/SQL function calls absolutely must be kept to a minimum. For example, by adopting this technique for the earlier sales report with the GET_RATE function, I managed to reduce 918,000 function executions to just 36,000, which decreased the overall response time from 66 seconds to just 4 seconds.

A more strategic method for reducing function calls, however, is to exploit a caching solution, which I'll now describe.

Caching to Reduce Function Calls

There are several options for caching data in Oracle Database, depending on your version. I'm going to briefly describe two caching techniques for reducing function calls that you might wish to investigate and/or apply to your application. These are:

- Scalar-subquery caching

- Cross-session PL/SQL function result cache

Scalar-Subquery Caching

This caching feature is an internal optimization designed to reduce the number of executions of SQL statements or PL/SQL functions embedded in scalar subqueries. Although the efficiency of this internal cache can't be reliably predicted, it can be used to reduce PL/SQL function calls to some extent. In Listing 9-37, I've converted the sales report with the GET_RATES lookup function to exploit the scalar subquery cache.

Listing 9-37. Using Scalar-Subquery Caching to Reduce PL/SQL Function Calls

```
SQL> SELECT t.calendar_year
  2  ,       p.prod_name
  3  ,       SUM(s.amount_sold)                                          AS amt_sold_usd
  4  ,       SUM(s.amount_sold * (SELECT get_rate(s.time_id, 'USD', 'GBP')
  5                                 FROM   dual))                        AS amt_sold_gbp
  6  FROM    sales     s
  7  ,       products  p
  8  ,       times     t
  9  WHERE   s.prod_id = p.prod_id
 10  AND     s.time_id = t.time_id
 11  GROUP   BY
```

```
 12          t.calendar_year
 13   ,      p.prod_name
 14   ;
```

272 rows selected.

Elapsed: 00:00:02.54

Statistics

```
      19451  recursive calls
          0  db block gets
      40634  consistent gets
          0  physical reads
          0  redo size
      16688  bytes sent via SQL*Net to client
        437  bytes received via SQL*Net from client
          2  SQL*Net roundtrips to/from client
          0  sorts (memory)
          0  sorts (disk)
        272  rows processed
```

```
SQL> exec counter.show('Function calls');
```

Function calls: 19450

By encapsulating the call to GET_RATE in a scalar subquery, I've managed to reduce the query's elapsed time from 66 seconds to just under 3 seconds. The counter shows that the PL/SQL function calls have dropped to just 19,450 (from over 918,000), resulting in an enormous saving in time and logical I/O (over 1.8 million consistent gets were prevented by the caching).

As noted earlier, the cache's efficiency is dependent on a range of factors, including the order of the input data. With this in mind, I know that the range of input-values to the GET_RATE function in my SALES data is quite small, so in Listing 9-38, I have attempted to reduce the function calls further still by ordering the inputs into the scalar subquery.

Listing 9-38. Using Scalar Subquery Caching to Reduce PL/SQL Function Calls (Effect of Sorted Data)

```
SQL> SELECT /*+ NO_MERGE(@inner) */
  2         calendar_year
  3   ,     prod_name
  4   ,     SUM(amount_sold)                                    AS amt_sold_usd
  5   ,     SUM(amount_sold * (SELECT get_rate(time_id, 'USD', 'GBP')
  6                            FROM   dual))                    AS amt_sold_gbp
  7   FROM  (
  8         SELECT /*+ QB_NAME(inner) NO_ELIMINATE_OBY */
  9                t.calendar_year
 10         ,      s.time_id
 11         ,      p.prod_name
 12         ,      s.amount_sold
 13         FROM   sales      s
 14         ,      products   p
 15         ,      times      t
```

```
16           WHERE   s.prod_id = p.prod_id
17           AND     s.time_id = t.time_id
18           ORDER   BY
19                   s.time_id
20         )
21   GROUP   BY
22           calendar_year
23   ,       prod_name
24   ;
```

272 rows selected.

Elapsed: 00:00:02.14

Statistics

```
     1461   recursive calls
        0   db block gets
     4662   consistent gets
        8   physical reads
        0   redo size
    16688   bytes sent via SQL*Net to client
      437   bytes received via SQL*Net from client
        2   SQL*Net roundtrips to/from client
        2   sorts (memory)
        0   sorts (disk)
      272   rows processed
```

```
SQL> exec counter.show('Function calls: ordered inputs');
```

Function calls: ordered inputs: 1460

By ordering the inputs to the scalar subquery cache, I've reduced the PL/SQL function calls further to just 1,460 (and therefore reduced the logical I/O by an order of magnitude and trimmed the overall elapsed time by a small margin). This demonstrates that ordering (or clustering) of calls into the subquery cache can make a difference to its efficiency. In my case, the savings I made through the further reduction in PL/SQL function calls "paid for" the cost of pre-sorting the SALES data.

Cross-Session PL/SQL Function Result Cache

The cross-session PL/SQL function Result Cache was introduced in Oracle Database 11g. The principle behind result caching is simple. First, a PL/SQL function is flagged for caching (using the RESULT_CACHE directive). Thereafter, each time the function is invoked with new parameters, Oracle Database executes the function, adds the return value(s) to the Result Cache, and returns the result(s) to the calling context. If a call is repeated, Oracle Database retrieves the results from the cache rather than re-execute the function. Under certain circumstances, this caching behavior can result in significant performance gains. It also has the benefit of requiring very little re-factoring (just a small function change, in fact).

I'll demonstrate the effect of the Result Cache on the GET_RATE function. First, I need to re-compile the function with the cache directive, as shown in Listing 9-39.

Listing 9-39. Preparing a Function for the PL/SQL Function Result Cache

```
SQL> CREATE OR REPLACE FUNCTION get_rate(
  2                               p_rate_date IN rates.rate_date%TYPE,
  3                               p_from_ccy  IN rates.base_ccy%TYPE,
  4                               p_to_ccy    IN rates.target_ccy%TYPE
  5                               ) RETURN rates.exchange_rate%TYPE
  6                               RESULT_CACHE RELIES_ON (rates) AS
  7      v_rate rates.exchange_rate%TYPE;
  8  BEGIN
     <...snip...>
 15  END get_rate;
 16  /

Function created.
```

I've added two pieces of syntax specific to the Result Cache, as highlighted above. The RESULT_CACHE keyword is self-explanatory and tells Oracle Database to enable this function for the Result Cache. The RELIES_ON (rates) syntax is required only in Oracle Database 11*g* Release 1 and declares the fact that the function is dependent on the data in the RATES table (Oracle Database 11*g* Release 2 automatically recognizes such dependencies). Therefore, any transaction against RATES will cause Oracle Database to invalidate the cached results and suspend caching this function until the transaction is complete (at which point the cache will commence a new refresh cycle).

Now that I have cache-enabled this function, I can re-execute my original sales query, as demonstrated in Listing 9-40.

Listing 9-40. Query Performance with a Result-Cached PL/SQL Function

```
SQL> SELECT t.calendar_year
  2  ,      p.prod_name
  3  ,      SUM(s.amount_sold)                      AS amt_sold_usd
  4  ,      SUM(s.amount_sold *
  5             get_rate(s.time_id, 'USD', 'GBP')) AS amt_sold_gbp
  6  FROM   sales     s
  7  ,      products  p
  8  ,      times     t
  9  WHERE  s.prod_id = p.prod_id
 10  AND    s.time_id = t.time_id
 11  GROUP  BY
 12         t.calendar_year
 13  ,      p.prod_name
 14  ;

272 rows selected.

Elapsed: 00:00:08.74

Statistics
----------------------------------------------------------
       1481  recursive calls
          0  db block gets
```

```
 4683  consistent gets
    0  physical reads
    0  redo size
16688  bytes sent via SQL*Net to client
  437  bytes received via SQL*Net from client
    2  SQL*Net roundtrips to/from client
    0  sorts (memory)
    0  sorts (disk)
  272  rows processed
```

By caching the function results, the elapsed time of this query has dropped by 57 seconds. This isn't quite as quick as the SQL-only implementation (that completed in 1 second) or the scalar subquery version (that completed in 2 seconds), but you might consider this to be an acceptable performance gain, given that no SQL needed to be re-written to achieve it and its behavior is predictable.

Another issue with the original query was the I/O generated by the encapsulated RATES lookup. With the Result Cache, the logical I/O has reduced to a more acceptable level.

To quantify the reduction in function executions, I traced the query with the PL/SQL Hierarchical Profiler. The profile report is provided in Listing 9-41.

Listing 9-41. PL/SQL Hierarchical Profiler Session Report for a Query with a Result-Cached PL/SQL Function

FUNCTION	LINE#	CALLS	SUB_ELA_US	FUNC_ELA_US
__plsql_vm	0	918846	3777356	3651587
GET_RATE	1	1460	125433	25731
GET_RATE.__static_sql_exec_line9	9	1460	99702	99702
__anonymous_block	0	3	336	276
DBMS_OUTPUT.GET_LINES	180	2	60	57
DBMS_OUTPUT.GET_LINE	129	2	3	3
DBMS_HPROF.STOP_PROFILING	59	1	0	0

You can see that the cache-enabled GET_RATES function was executed just 1,460 times (the same result as the best scalar subquery cache example). Interestingly, context-switching into the PL/SQL VM is *not* reduced by using the Result Cache, so Oracle Database therefore passed control to the PL/SQL engine once for each of the 918,000 rows the query needed to process. For this reason, it rarely pays to convert a PL/SQL-only function (i.e. one without any embedded SQL) to use the Result Cache. First, there is no reduction in context-switching and second, you'll possibly find that diverting a function call to the Result Cache and acquiring the RC latch that protects it will take longer than an execution of the function itself.

To wrap up, Oracle Database also provides several performance views for the Result Cache. For example, the V$RESULT_CACHE_STATISTICS view can provide a useful overview of the cache's efficiency. Listing 9-40 ran with an empty cache, so the statistics in Listing 9-42 are entirely attributed to this query.

Listing 9-42. Investigating Result Cache Hits with V$RESULT_CACHE_STATISTICS

```
SQL> SELECT name, value
  2  FROM   v$result_cache_statistics
  3  WHERE  name IN ('Find Count','Create Count Success');
```

NAME	VALUE
Create Count Success	1460
Find Count	917383

These statistics demonstrate a very efficient cache. The GET_RATE function was executed just 1,460 times to load the cache (as demonstrated by the Create Count Success statistic , which also corresponds to the GET_RATE statistics in the Hierarchical Profiler report in Listing 9-41). Once cached, the results were heavily reused (the Find Count statistic shows that the cached results were used over 917,000 times). If I were to repeat the sales query at this point, the PL/SQL function would not be executed at all (assuming the cached results were not invalidated) and the response time would be further reduced, albeit by a small margin.

■ **Note** If you're not running Oracle Database 11*g*, you can simulate the Result Cache (to a degree) by creating your own session-based PL/SQL cache with associative arrays. While this will not reduce function executions in the same way, it will dramatically reduce the impact of the SQL lookups embedded inside the function. See the *"Tuning PL/SQL"* section at the end of this chapter for an example that converts the GET_RATE function from the result-cached version to a user-defined array-cached implementation. However, make sure that you consider the potential shortcomings of such an approach, as described in that section.

Deterministic Functions

As stated earlier, Oracle Database has an internal optimization for deterministic functions which can sometimes make them a useful feature for reducing PL/SQL function calls. In Listing 9-43, I've demonstrated the effect of declaring the GET_CUSTOMER_NAME function to be deterministic (i.e. by using the DETERMINISTIC keyword in the function specification) and running a variation on the sales-by-customer report from Listing 9-5.

Listing 9-43. Effect of Declaring a DETERMINISTIC Function

```
SQL> CREATE OR REPLACE FUNCTION format_customer_name (
  2                          p_first_name IN VARCHAR2,
  3                          p_last_name  IN VARCHAR2
  4                        ) RETURN VARCHAR2 DETERMINISTIC AS
<snip>
  9 /

Function created.

SQL> SELECT /*+ NO_MERGE(@inner) */
  2           calendar_year
  3  ,        format_customer_name(
  4              cust_first_name, cust_last_name
  5              )                            AS cust_name
```

```
 6  ,         SUM(quantity_sold)                    AS qty_sold
 7  ,         SUM(amount_sold)                      AS amt_sold
 8  FROM   (
 9         SELECT /*+
10                     QB_NAME(inner)
11                     NO_ELIMINATE_OBY
12                 */
13                 t.calendar_year
14             ,   c.cust_first_name
15             ,   c.cust_last_name
16             ,   s.quantity_sold
17             ,   s.amount_sold
18         FROM    sales     s
19             ,   customers c
20             ,   times     t
21         WHERE   s.cust_id = c.cust_id
22         AND     s.time_id = t.time_id
23         ORDER   BY
24                 c.cust_first_name
25             ,   c.cust_last_name
26         )
27  GROUP   BY
28          calendar_year
29      ,   format_customer_name(
30              cust_first_name, cust_last_name
31              )
32  ;
```

11604 rows selected.

Elapsed: 00:00:07.83

```
Statistics
-----------------------------------------------------------
      3189  consistent gets
         0  physical reads
```

SQL> exec counter.show('Deterministic function calls');

Deterministic function calls: 912708

You can see from the results that the number of PL/SQL function calls has reduced by a very small margin (approximately 6,000 fewer than the original query in Listing 9-5) so it hasn't been particularly effective (this report is actually slower than the original). In fact, to benefit from the deterministic function optimization *at all* with this example, I needed to pre-order the input data to ensure that customer names passing into the function were clustered together. In this case, the cost of sorting the data outweighed the marginal gains from 6,000 fewer calls to FORMAT_CUSTOMER_NAME and my report ran slower as a result.

That is not to say that the optimization for deterministic functions doesn't work. As noted earlier, there are a range of factors that affect its efficiency. It can be quite effective in some cases, particularly when your resultset contains very few distinct function inputs. For example, there are approximately 3,700 distinct customers in the SALES table, so I simplified my sales query to join SALES to CUSTOMERS, order the data in an in-line view and call the `FORMAT_CUSTOMER_NAME` function with no aggregation. With this simplified query, the PL/SQL function was executed just 36,000 times for 918,000 rows. This is better than the standard sales report, of course, albeit quite a restricted optimization when compared with the alternative techniques I've demonstrated.

■ **Caution**   By their very nature, PL/SQL functions that return randomized data or perform SQL lookups are not deterministic. Don't be tempted to declare a function as deterministic unless it really is or you will risk returning wrong results from your queries.

Assisting the CBO

As described earlier, there are several ways in which PL/SQL functions can trip up the Cost-Based Optimizer, largely due to the lack of statistics and the reliance on defaults. There are a range of methods you can use to improve the CBO's handling SQL with PL/SQL functions and I'll demonstrate the following techniques:

- Function-based indexes

- Extended statistics

- Default statistics

- The Extensible Optimizer

Function-Based Indexes

Functions applied to an indexed column completely disable the index for use in an execution plan. To counter this, function-based indexes have been available since Oracle 8*i* and allow such expressions to be indexed. In the following listings, I've demonstrated the use of a function-based index on a query that uses a PL/SQL function predicate. Listing 9-44 begins with a simple PL/SQL function applied to a highly–selective indexed column.

Listing 9-44. PL/SQL Function Applied to Indexed Column

```
SQL> CREATE FUNCTION promo_function(
  2                    p_promo_category IN VARCHAR2
  3                    ) RETURN VARCHAR2 DETERMINISTIC IS
  4  BEGIN
  5     RETURN UPPER(p_promo_category);
  6  END promo_function;
  7  /

Function created.
```

```
SQL> SELECT *
  2  FROM    sales       s
  3  ,       promotions  p
  4  ,       times       t
  5  WHERE   s.promo_id = p.promo_id
  6  AND     s.time_id  = t.time_id
  7  AND     t.time_id BETWEEN DATE '2000-01-01' AND DATE '2000-03-31'
  8  AND     promo_function(p.promo_category) = 'AD NEWS';

Execution Plan
----------------------------------------------------------

-------------------------------------------------------------
| Id | Operation                    | Name       | Rows  |
-------------------------------------------------------------
|  0 | SELECT STATEMENT             |            | 51609 |
|* 1 |  HASH JOIN                   |            | 51609 |
|  2 |   PART JOIN FILTER CREATE    | :BF0000    |    92 |
|  3 |    TABLE ACCESS BY INDEX ROWID| TIMES     |    92 |
|* 4 |     INDEX RANGE SCAN         | TIMES_PK   |    92 |
|* 5 |   HASH JOIN                  |            | 52142 |
|* 6 |    TABLE ACCESS FULL         | PROMOTIONS |     5 |
|  7 |    PARTITION RANGE SINGLE    |            | 62197 |
|* 8 |     TABLE ACCESS FULL        | SALES      | 62197 |
-------------------------------------------------------------
```

You can see that despite having an index on the PROMO_CATEGORY column, applying the PL/SQL function to the column forces the CBO to choose a full table scan of PROMOTIONS (it has no other choice). Fortunately, I can use a function-based index to work around this (only because PROMO_FUNCTION is deterministic). In Listing 9-45, I've created the function-based index and included the new execution plan.

Listing 9-45. Using a Function-Based Index

```
SQL> CREATE INDEX promotions_fbi
  2      ON promotions (promo_function(promo_category))
  3      COMPUTE STATISTICS;

Index created.

Execution Plan
----------------------------------------------------------
Plan hash value: 3568243509

-------------------------------------------------------------
| Id | Operation                    | Name       | Rows  |
-------------------------------------------------------------
|  0 | SELECT STATEMENT             |            | 51609 |
|* 1 |  HASH JOIN                   |            | 51609 |
|  2 |   PART JOIN FILTER CREATE    | :BF0000    |    92 |
|  3 |    TABLE ACCESS BY INDEX ROWID| TIMES     |    92 |
|* 4 |     INDEX RANGE SCAN         | TIMES_PK   |    92 |
```

```
|*  5 |    HASH JOIN                        |                | 52142 |
|   6 |      TABLE ACCESS BY INDEX ROWID| PROMOTIONS     |     5 |
|*  7 |        INDEX RANGE SCAN             | PROMOTIONS_FBI |     2 |
|   8 |      PARTITION RANGE SINGLE         |                | 62197 |
|*  9 |        TABLE ACCESS FULL            | SALES          | 62197 |
---------------------------------------------------------------------
```

```
Predicate Information (identified by operation id):
---------------------------------------------------

  1 - access("S"."TIME_ID"="T"."TIME_ID")
  4 - access("T"."TIME_ID">=TO_DATE(' 2000-01-01 00:00:00', 'syyyy-mm-dd hh24:mi:ss') AND
            "T"."TIME_ID"<=TO_DATE(' 2000-03-31 00:00:00', 'syyyy-mm-dd hh24:mi:ss'))
  5 - access("S"."PROMO_ID"="P"."PROMO_ID")
  7 - access("SH"."PROMO_FUNCTION"("PROMO_CATEGORY")='AD NEWS')
  9 - filter("S"."TIME_ID"<=TO_DATE(' 2000-03-31 00:00:00', 'syyyy-mm-dd hh24:mi:ss'))
```

This time the CBO has chosen to use the function-based index. Not only does the index exist, but the CBO also has some statistics to work with in choosing an optimal plan.

If you wish to investigate function-based indexes, you will find metadata regarding their implementation in views such as USER_INDEXES, USER_IND_EXPRESSIONS, and USER_TAB_COLS/USER_IND_COLUMNS (the indexed expression is stored as a hidden virtual column in the table being indexed).

Extended Statistics

Statistics are one of the benefits of function-based indexes. These can be invaluable to the CBO (even if it chooses not to use the index, it can make use of the statistics in deciding join or predicate orders). However, indexing a PL/SQL function predicate might not always be possible. In such cases, Oracle Database 11*g* provides an alternative known as extended statistics.

Extended statistics can be created on expressions without requiring a supporting index. Such statistics are known as *extensions* and they have an added benefit over function-based indexes of being applicable to *all* PL/SQL function expressions in a query (i.e. not just those in predicates).

To demonstrate this, I have re-executed the sales report by customer with extended statistics in place. Listing 9-46 is a reminder of the query without extended statistics, together with its execution plan and function call output from Listing 9-5.

Listing 9-46. Using Extended Statistics on a Projected PL/SQL Function (Plan without Statistics from Listing 9-5)

```
SQL> SELECT t.calendar_year
  2  ,         format_customer_name(
  3                 c.cust_first_name, c.cust_last_name
  4                 )                     AS cust_name
  5  ,         SUM(s.quantity_sold) AS qty_sold
  6  ,         SUM(s.amount_sold)   AS amt_sold
  7  FROM    sales      s
  8  ,         customers c
  9  ,         times      t
 10  WHERE    s.cust_id = c.cust_id
```

```
11   AND    s.time_id = t.time_id
12   GROUP  BY
13          t.calendar_year
14   ,      format_customer_name(
15              c.cust_first_name, c.cust_last_name
16              )
17   ;
```

11604 rows selected.

Elapsed: 00:00:06.94

```
Execution Plan
-----------------------------------------------------------
Plan hash value: 3113689673
```

```
---------------------------------------------------------------
| Id  | Operation                     | Name      | Rows  |
---------------------------------------------------------------
|   0 | SELECT STATEMENT              |           |  918K |
|   1 |  HASH GROUP BY                |           |  918K |
|*  2 |   HASH JOIN                   |           |  918K |
|   3 |    PART JOIN FILTER CREATE    | :BF0000   |  1826 |
|   4 |     TABLE ACCESS FULL         | TIMES     |  1826 |
|*  5 |    HASH JOIN                  |           |  918K |
|   6 |     TABLE ACCESS FULL         | CUSTOMERS | 55500 |
|   7 |     PARTITION RANGE JOIN-FILTER|          |  918K |
|   8 |      TABLE ACCESS FULL        | SALES     |  918K |
---------------------------------------------------------------
```

```
Statistics
-----------------------------------------------------------
       3189   consistent gets
          0   physical reads
```

```
SQL> exec counter.show('Function calls');
```

Function calls: 918843

```
PL/SQL procedure successfully completed.
```

As you can see, this performs over 918,000 function calls and completes in roughly 7 seconds. In Listing 9-47, I've used DBMS_STATS to generate extended statistics on the PL/SQL function call and show the execution plan from the re-executed query.

Listing 9-47. Generating and Using Extended Statistics

```
SQL> BEGIN
  2     DBMS_STATS.GATHER_TABLE_STATS(
  3        ownname    => USER,
  4        tabname    => 'CUSTOMERS',
```

```
   5          method_opt => 'FOR COLUMNS (format_customer_name(cust_first_name,cust_last_name))
SIZE AUTO'
   6          );
   7  END;
   8  /
```

PL/SQL procedure successfully completed.

SQL> SELECT t.calendar_year...

11604 rows selected.

Elapsed: 00:00:00.90

Execution Plan

Plan hash value: 833790846

```
---------------------------------------------------------------
| Id  | Operation                    | Name      | Rows  |
---------------------------------------------------------------
|   0 | SELECT STATEMENT             |           | 19803 |
|   1 |  HASH GROUP BY               |           | 19803 |
|*  2 |   HASH JOIN                  |           | 24958 |
|   3 |    VIEW                      | VW_GBC_9  | 24958 |
|   4 |     HASH GROUP BY            |           | 24958 |
|*  5 |      HASH JOIN               |           | 918K  |
|   6 |       PART JOIN FILTER CREATE| :BF0000   | 1826  |
|   7 |        TABLE ACCESS FULL     | TIMES     | 1826  |
|   8 |       PARTITION RANGE JOIN-FILTER|       | 918K  |
|   9 |        TABLE ACCESS FULL     | SALES     | 918K  |
|  10 |    TABLE ACCESS FULL         | CUSTOMERS | 55500 |
---------------------------------------------------------------
```

SQL> exec counter.show('Extended stats');

Extended stats: 237917

PL/SQL procedure successfully completed.

With the benefit of the extended statistics for the PL/SQL function, the CBO has made an informed decision to rewrite the query and pre-group the SALES and TIMES data. This is represented by Step 3 of the execution plan. Because this pre-groups and therefore reduces the resultset, the PL/SQL function calls are reduced to below 238,000. Overall, the effect on the response time is dramatic.

Extended statistics are a good alternative to the NO_MERGE hint demonstrated earlier. Without extended statistics, the query shown in Listing 9-48 was merged into the main query block by the CBO, resulting in 918,000 function executions. Fortunately, generating the extended statistics works nicely to prevent this transformation, again with good results.

Listing 9-48. Extended Statistics and Impact on Cost-Based Query Transformation

```
SQL> SELECT t.calendar_year
  2  ,       c.cust_name
  3  ,       SUM(s.quantity_sold) AS qty_sold
  4  ,       SUM(s.amount_sold)   AS amt_sold
  5  FROM    sales      s
  6  ,       (
  7            SELECT cust_id
  8            ,      format_customer_name (
  9                     cust_first_name, cust_last_name
 10                     ) AS cust_name
 11            FROM   customers
 12          )          c
 13  ,       times      t
 14  WHERE   s.cust_id = c.cust_id
 15  AND     s.time_id = t.time_id
 16  GROUP   BY
 17          t.calendar_year
 18  ,       c.cust_name
 19  ;

11604 rows selected.
```

Elapsed: 00:00:00.94

```
Execution Plan
----------------------------------------------------------
Plan hash value: 833790846
```

```
---------------------------------------------------------------------
| Id  | Operation                      | Name      | Rows  |
---------------------------------------------------------------------
|   0 | SELECT STATEMENT               |           | 19803 |
|   1 |  HASH GROUP BY                 |           | 19803 |
|*  2 |   HASH JOIN                    |           | 24958 |
|   3 |    VIEW                        | VW_GBC_9  | 24958 |
|   4 |     HASH GROUP BY              |           | 24958 |
|*  5 |      HASH JOIN                 |           | 918K  |
|   6 |       PART JOIN FILTER CREATE  | :BF0000   | 1826  |
|   7 |        TABLE ACCESS FULL       | TIMES     | 1826  |
|   8 |       PARTITION RANGE JOIN-FILTER|         | 918K  |
|   9 |        TABLE ACCESS FULL       | SALES     | 918K  |
|  10 |    TABLE ACCESS FULL           | CUSTOMERS | 55500 |
---------------------------------------------------------------------
```

```
SQL> exec counter.show('Extended stats + inline view');
```

Extended stats + inline view: 17897

Interestingly, the CBO has generated the same execution plan for this re-arranged query, although the function executions have dropped dramatically from 234,000 to just 18,000. This is another excellent example of the function executions being unpredictable—I have the same execution plan yet more than an order of magnitude difference in function calls. Nevertheless, these listings clearly highlight how important statistics on PL/SQL functions are for the CBO and that extended statistics are an excellent mechanism for supplying them.

▓ **Note** Extended statistics, or extensions, are implemented using system-generated virtual columns (similar to function-based indexes). To investigate more about this feature, query dictionary views such as USER_TAB_COLS and USER_STAT_EXTENSIONS.

Default Statistics

Unlike extended statistics, default statistics are user-generated and only apply to PL/SQL functions in predicates. Furthermore, the CBO will not use default statistics to inform cost-based query transformations, but it will use them to determine predicate ordering in the event that you have more than one function call in your WHERE clause.

Default statistics are supplied using the ASSOCIATE STATISTICS SQL command and with these you can define statistics on selectivity, CPU, and I/O costs for your PL/SQL functions (thereby improving on the defaults that the CBO otherwise adopts).

In Listing 9-19, I highlighted the impact of default predicate ordering when I referenced two functions in a query (these were appropriately named QUICK_FUNCTION and SLOW_FUNCTION). Listing 9-49 demonstrates how applying default statistics can ensure that the CBO applies the function predicates in the most efficient order.

Listing 9-49. Setting Default Statistics for PL/SQL Function Predicates

```
SQL> ASSOCIATE STATISTICS WITH FUNCTIONS quick_function DEFAULT SELECTIVITY 0.1;

Statistics associated.

SQL> ASSOCIATE STATISTICS WITH FUNCTIONS slow_function DEFAULT SELECTIVITY 50;

Statistics associated.

SQL> SELECT *
  2  FROM    thousand_rows
  3  WHERE   slow_function(n1) = 0
  4  AND     quick_function(n1) = 0;

1 row selected.
```

Elapsed: 00:00:00.02

```
Execution Plan
-----------------------------------------------------------
Plan hash value: 4012467810

--------------------------------------------------------------------------------
| Id  | Operation         | Name          | Rows  | Bytes | Cost (%CPU)| Time     |
--------------------------------------------------------------------------------
|   0 | SELECT STATEMENT  |               |     1 |    55 |     5   (0)| 00:00:01 |
|*  1 |  TABLE ACCESS FULL| THOUSAND_ROWS |     1 |    55 |     5   (0)| 00:00:01 |
--------------------------------------------------------------------------------

Predicate Information (identified by operation id):
---------------------------------------------------
```

1 - filter("QUICK_FUNCTION"("N1")=0 AND "SLOW_FUNCTION"("N1")=0)

Because of the selectivity statistics associated with SLOW_FUNCTION and QUICK_FUNCTION, you can see that the CBO has chosen to re-order the predicates to good effect. I have told Oracle Database that an equality predicate against QUICK_FUNCTION will only be true 1 in 1,000 times, whereas the SLOW_FUNCTION predicate will be true 1 in 2 times. It clearly made sense to apply QUICK_FUNCTION first to reduce the rowsource as soon as possible. An excerpt from the 10053 trace file in Listing 9-50 shows the workings of the CBO for this query.

Listing 9-50. 10053 Trace File Excerpt for Default Selectivity Statistics

```
****************************************
BASE STATISTICAL INFORMATION
***********************
Table Stats::
  Table: THOUSAND_ROWS  Alias: THOUSAND_ROWS
    #Rows: 1000  #Blks:  12  AvgRowLen:  55.00  ChainCnt:  0.00
Access path analysis for THOUSAND_ROWS
****************************************
SINGLE TABLE ACCESS PATH
  Single Table Cardinality Estimation for THOUSAND_ROWS[THOUSAND_ROWS]
  No statistics type defined for function SLOW_FUNCTION
  No default cost defined for function SLOW_FUNCTION
  No statistics type defined for function SLOW_FUNCTION
  Default selectivity for function SLOW_FUNCTION: 50.00000000%
  No statistics type defined for function QUICK_FUNCTION
  No default cost defined for function QUICK_FUNCTION
  No statistics type defined for function QUICK_FUNCTION
  Default selectivity for function QUICK_FUNCTION: 0.10000000%
  Table: THOUSAND_ROWS  Alias: THOUSAND_ROWS
    Card: Original: 1000.000000  Rounded: 1  Computed: 0.50  Non Adjusted: 0.50
  Access Path: TableScan
    Cost:  5.10  Resp: 5.10  Degree: 0
      Cost_io: 5.00  Cost_cpu: 3288527
      Resp_io: 5.00  Resp_cpu: 3288527
  Best:: AccessPath: TableScan
        Cost: 5.10  Degree: 1  Resp: 5.10  Card: 0.50  Bytes: 0
```

The ASSOCIATE STATISTICS command can also be used to supply *cost* information for PL/SQL functions and this has a similar impact to the selectivity statistics above. Listing 9-51 shows how to set default cost statistics for the GET_RATE PL/SQL function:

Listing 9-51. Setting Default Cost Statistics for a PL/SQL Function

```
SQL> ASSOCIATE STATISTICS WITH FUNCTIONS get_rate DEFAULT COST (403416, 2, 0);

Statistics associated.
```

I calculated these cost statistics as follows (in parameter order):

- *CPU cost* (403416): Calculated by the DBMS_ODCI.ESTIMATE_CPU_UNITS(<ms>) function, where <ms> is the number of milliseconds it takes to execute the GET_RATE function once (as reported by the Hierarchical Profiler).

- *I/O cost* (2): The sum of logical and physical I/Os of one execution of GET_RATE (reported by Autotrace).

- *Network cost* (0): This is not yet implemented so it can be left at 0.

It is possible to set both selectivity and costs in a single ASSOCIATE STATISTICS command and it makes sense to supply both when using this strategy.

Extensible Optimizer

I'll finish this walkthrough of supplying statistics to the CBO with a brief overview of the Extensible Optimizer. This feature (part of the Oracle Data Cartridge toolset), takes default statistics one stage further by associating selectivity and cost by means of an object type, rather than by hardcoded defaults such as those previously mentioned.

It is possible to spend many pages describing the Extensible Optimizer so I'll just provide a flavor of the technology to show you how to build a method for estimating statistics for your PL/SQL functions that can adapt to your data patterns.

Consider Listing 9-52. I have a simple function that returns a product code in uppercase. Without statistics, the CBO will assume that any predicate using this function will have a 1% selectivity as follows.

Listing 9-52. Default Selectivity for a PL/SQL Function Predicate

```
SQL> CREATE FUNCTION format_prod_category(
  2                    p_prod_category IN VARCHAR2
  3                    ) RETURN VARCHAR2 DETERMINISTIC IS
  4  BEGIN
  5     RETURN UPPER(p_prod_category);
  6  END format_prod_category;
  7  /

Function created.
```

```
SQL> SELECT *
  2  FROM    products
  3  WHERE   format_prod_category(prod_category) = 'SOFTWARE/OTHER';

Execution Plan
-----------------------------------------------------------
Plan hash value: 1954719464


---------------------------------------------
| Id | Operation           | Name     | Rows |
---------------------------------------------
|  0 | SELECT STATEMENT    |          |    1 |
|* 1 |   TABLE ACCESS FULL| PRODUCTS |    1 |
---------------------------------------------
```

The CBO has estimated a cardinality of just 1 row for this predicate, but I know for a fact that there are more rows for the Software/Other category as the data profile in Listing 9-53 shows.

Listing 9-53. Data Profile for PRODUCTS Table

```
SQL> SELECT prod_category
  2  ,        c                                           AS num_rows
  3  ,        ROUND(RATIO_TO_REPORT(c) OVER () * 100, 1) AS selectivity
  4  FROM    (
  5           SELECT prod_category
  6           ,       COUNT(*) AS c
  7           FROM    products
  8           GROUP   BY
  9                   prod_category
 10          )
 11  ORDER   BY
 12          num_rows;
```

PROD_CATEGORY	NUM_ROWS	SELECTIVITY
Hardware	2	2.8
Photo	10	13.9
Electronics	13	18.1
Peripherals and Accessories	21	29.2
Software/Other	26	36.1

You can see a range of selectivity in this data, so a default statistics solution wouldn't be flexible enough to cover all categories. Therefore, you can use the Extensible Optimizer to build a dynamic statistics parser for this function predicate. As stated earlier, this is implemented using an object type, the specification for which is provided in Listing 9-54.

Listing 9-54. Creating a Statistics Type for the Extensible Optimiser

```
SQL> CREATE TYPE prod_stats_ot AS OBJECT (
  2
  3      dummy_attribute NUMBER,
  4
```

```
 5      STATIC FUNCTION ODCIGetInterfaces (
 6                      p_interfaces OUT SYS.ODCIObjectList
 7                      ) RETURN NUMBER,
 8
 9      STATIC FUNCTION ODCIStatsSelectivity (
10                      p_pred_info      IN  SYS.ODCIPredInfo,
11                      p_selectivity    OUT NUMBER,
12                      p_args           IN  SYS.ODCIArgDescList,
13                      p_start          IN  VARCHAR2,
14                      p_stop           IN  VARCHAR2,
15                      p_prod_category  IN  VARCHAR2,
16                      p_env            IN  SYS.ODCIEnv
17                      ) RETURN NUMBER,
18
19      STATIC FUNCTION ODCIStatsFunctionCost (
20                      p_func_info      IN  SYS.ODCIFuncInfo,
21                      p_cost           OUT SYS.ODCICost,
22                      p_args           IN  SYS.ODCIArgDescList,
23                      p_prod_category  IN  VARCHAR2,
24                      p_env            IN  SYS.ODCIEnv
25                      ) RETURN NUMBER
26 );
27 /
```

Type created.

The Extensible Optimizer uses well-defined interface methods and Listing 9-54 uses the three that are needed to generate selectivity and cost statistics. You must use the exact method names that Oracle prescribes, as I have done.

The parameter data types and order are also prescribed by the Extensible Optimizer, although you can use parameter names of your own choosing, with one notable exception. You must include the same parameter names in your type methods that you have in the PL/SQL function(s) that will eventually be associated with the statistics type. In my case, the FORMAT_PROD_CATEGORY function that I am building this statistics type for has a single parameter named p_prod_category (so I've included this in the relevant methods).

The type body implements the statistics type and can include any logic you like that enables the CBO to determine the selectivity and cost of your associated PL/SQL function(s). The type body for the PROD_STATS_OT.ODCIStatsSelectivity method is provided in Listing 9-55 (the remaining methods are available from the Apress web site).

Listing 9-55. Creating a Statistics Type for the Extensible Optimiser (Excerpt of the Type Body)

```
SQL> CREATE TYPE BODY prod_stats_ot AS
  2
  3      STATIC FUNCTION ODCIGetInterfaces ...
<snip>
 13      STATIC FUNCTION ODCIStatsSelectivity (
 14                      p_pred_info      IN  SYS.ODCIPredInfo,
 15                      p_selectivity    OUT NUMBER,
 16                      p_args           IN  SYS.ODCIArgDescList,
 17                      p_start          IN  VARCHAR2,
```

```
18                    p_stop            IN  VARCHAR2,
19                    p_prod_category   IN  VARCHAR2,
20                    p_env             IN  SYS.ODCIEnv
21                    ) RETURN NUMBER IS
22      BEGIN
23
24          /* Calculate selectivity of predicate... */
25          SELECT (COUNT(CASE
26                          WHEN UPPER(prod_category) = p_start
27                          THEN 0
28                       END) / COUNT(*)) * 100 AS selectivity
29          INTO    p_selectivity
30          FROM    sh.products;
31
32          RETURN ODCIConst.success;
33      END ODCIStatsSelectivity;
34
35      STATIC FUNCTION ODCIStatsFunctionCost ...
<snip>
76
77  END;
78  /
```

As its name suggests, the ODCIStatsSelectivity method is used to calculate the selectivity for the associated PL/SQL function predicate for a given set of values. How it does this is the interesting part. Imagine that I have a predicate of the form WHERE format_prod_category(p.prod_category) = 'SOFTWARE/OTHER'. When the CBO optimizes this predicate, it invokes the ODCIStatsSelectivity method and passes the value 'SOFTWARE/OTHER' on to the statistics method in the p_start and p_stop parameters. (If you have a range predicate, p_start and p_stop will contain the lower and upper bounds, respectively.) This means, therefore, that I can specifically count the number of occurrences of 'SOFTWARE/OTHER' in the PRODUCTS table to determine the selectivity, as above.

Once the statistics type is created, it can be associated with the PL/SQL function. Listing 9-56 demonstrates the syntax for associating the statistics type and a couple of small queries to show its dynamic nature.

Listing 9-56. Associating and Using the Statistics Type for Dynamic PL/SQL Function Statistics

```
SQL> ASSOCIATE STATISTICS WITH FUNCTIONS format_prod_category USING prod_stats_ot;

Statistics associated.

SQL> SELECT *
  2  FROM    products
  3  WHERE   format_prod_category(prod_category) = 'SOFTWARE/OTHER';

Execution Plan
-----------------------------------------------------------
Plan hash value: 1954719464
```

```
-----------------------------------------------------
| Id  | Operation            | Name     | Rows  |
-----------------------------------------------------
|   0 | SELECT STATEMENT    |          |    26 |
|*  1 |   TABLE ACCESS FULL | PRODUCTS |    26 |
-----------------------------------------------------
```

```
SQL> SELECT *
  2  FROM    products
  3  WHERE   format_prod_category(prod_category) = 'HARDWARE';
```

Execution Plan

Plan hash value: 1954719464

```
-----------------------------------------------------
| Id  | Operation            | Name     | Rows  |
-----------------------------------------------------
|   0 | SELECT STATEMENT    |          |     2 |
|*  1 |   TABLE ACCESS FULL | PRODUCTS |     2 |
-----------------------------------------------------
```

You can see that by using the Extensible Optimizer, I've provided accurate and dynamic statistics on my PL/SQL function to the CBO (in this example, these match the data profile of the PRODUCTS table perfectly). Note that the ODCI* methods are called *once* during the SQL optimization phase (i.e. the "hard parse") and bind variables are also supported (as long as bind-variable peeking is enabled). However, you should give some consideration to the time it takes to execute your statistics methods and ensure that this is more than offset by the performance improvements they provide or by the fact that you reuse the shared cursor many times over.

▓ **Note** If you want to see how the CBO invokes the statistics type methods to extract the selectivity and costs, you can run a 10053 trace and view the resulting trace file.

Tuning PL/SQL

I've described many techniques for improving the performance of queries that use PL/SQL functions. Unless you are going to eliminate or dramatically reduce your PL/SQL function calls, however, you should also consider tuning the functions themselves.

You have a range of tuning options at your disposal (especially with later versions of Oracle Database), such as native compilation, subprogram-inlining, new integer data types, array fetching, associative array caching, and so on. For your critical queries and/or heavily-executed PL/SQL functions, you should find that you can reduce their elapsed time by using some of the wide range of PL/SQL tuning techniques available to you.

That said, I'm only going to demonstrate a tuning technique involving array-caching here, because it's closely related to the Result Cache option I demonstrated earlier and can have dramatic results.

User-Defined PL/SQL Session Cache

I mentioned earlier that caching lookup data in associative arrays is an alternative to the Cross-Session PL/SQL Function Result Cache when the built-in feature is not available. There are several ways to do this and in Listing 9-57, I have provided one such method. I've created a PL/SQL array cache for the rates data (using a private global associative array) and provided a single GET_RATES function to load and access the cached data.

Listing 9-57. A User-Defined PL/SQL Cache for Rates

```
SQL> CREATE OR REPLACE PACKAGE BODY rates_pkg AS
  2
  3      /* Index subtype for cache... */
  4      SUBTYPE key_st IS VARCHAR2(128);
  5
  6      /* Rates cache... */
  7      TYPE rates_aat IS TABLE OF rates.exchange_rate%TYPE
  8          INDEX BY key_st;
  9      rates_cache rates_aat;
 10
 11      /* Cache-enabled function... */
 12      FUNCTION get_rate (
 13              p_rate_date IN rates.rate_date%TYPE,
 14              p_from_ccy  IN rates.base_ccy%TYPE,
 15              p_to_ccy    IN rates.target_ccy%TYPE
 16              ) RETURN rates.exchange_rate%TYPE IS
 17
 18      v_rate rates.exchange_rate%TYPE;
 19      v_key  key_st := TO_CHAR(p_rate_date, 'YYYYMMDD')
 20                          || '~' || p_from_ccy || '~' || p_to_ccy;
 21
 22   BEGIN
 23
 24      IF rates_cache.EXISTS(v_key) THEN
 25
 26          /* Cache hit... */
 27          v_rate := rates_cache(v_key);
 28
 29      ELSE
 30
 31          /* Cache miss. Fetch and cache... */
 32          SELECT exchange_rate INTO v_rate
 33          FROM    rates
 34          WHERE   rate_date  = p_rate_date
 35          AND     base_ccy   = p_from_ccy
 36          AND     target_ccy = p_to_ccy;
 37          rates_cache(v_key) := v_rate;
 38
 39      END IF;
 40
 41      RETURN v_rate;
```

```
42
43     END get_rate;
44
45  END rates_pkg;
46  /
```

I've omitted the package specification (it only has the GET_RATES function signature) and listed just the package body. To keep the example short, I've excluded the exception-handling that would be needed to cater for NO_DATA_FOUND, among others. Some other points to note about the implementation are as follows:

> *Lines 7-9:* I've created a private global associative array type and variable to store the cached data.

> *Lines 19-20:* The index of the array is a string representation of the primary key for the RATES table. I've assigned this key directly in the function's declaration to save space, but for best practice, any assignments should be performed in the executable block of the PL/SQL program.

> *Lines 24-27:* I test to see if the rate is already cached. If it is, I simply return it directly from the cache.

> *Lines 32-37:* If the rate is not already in the cache, I fetch it from the RATES table and add it to the cache. I've decided to cache only what is needed to reduce the potential PGA memory footprint (as an alternative, you might prefer to pre-load small lookup tables into associative arrays on instantiation).

In Listing 9-58, I've repeated the sales report that I used in Listing 9-40 (when demonstrating the Result Cache) but replaced the call to the result-cached GET_RATES function with my new user-defined cache equivalent.

Listing 9-58. Query Performance with a User-Defined PL/SQL Session Cache Function

```
SQL> SELECT t.calendar_year
  2  ,        p.prod_name
  3  ,        SUM(s.amount_sold)                              AS amt_sold_usd
  4  ,        SUM(s.amount_sold *
  5             rates_pkg.get_rate(s.time_id, 'USD', 'GBP')) AS amt_sold_gbp
  6  FROM     sales     s
  7  ,        products  p
  8  ,        times     t
  9  WHERE    s.prod_id = p.prod_id
 10  AND      s.time_id = t.time_id
 11  GROUP    BY
 12           t.calendar_year
 13  ,        p.prod_name
 14  ;

272 rows selected.
```

Elapsed: 00:00:11.93

Statistics

```
    1591  recursive calls
       0  db block gets
    4729  consistent gets
       0  physical reads
       0  redo size
   16688  bytes sent via SQL*Net to client
     437  bytes received via SQL*Net from client
       2  SQL*Net roundtrips to/from client
       9  sorts (memory)
       0  sorts (disk)
     272  rows processed
```

Like the Result Cache example, the user-defined cache has dramatically reduced the logical I/O and runtime of the query to acceptable levels. In fact, the statistics for the user-defined session cache are similar to those of the Result Cache (the cache misses are identical), although the user-cache is slightly slower overall. Listing 9-59 shows the Hierarchical Profiler report for the query and demonstrates where the additional time (over the Result Cache example) was spent.

Listing 9-59. Query Performance with a User-Defined PL/SQL Session-Cache Function (Hierarchical Profiler Report)

FUNCTION	LINE#	CALLS	SUB_ELA_US	FUNC_ELA_US
__plsql_vm	0	918848	7734487	2202214
RATES_PKG.GET_RATE	12	918843	5531933	5434184
RATES_PKG.__static_sql_exec_line32	32	1460	97749	97749
__anonymous_block	0	3	328	270
DBMS_OUTPUT.GET_LINES	180	2	58	58
RATES_PKG.__pkg_init	0	1	12	12
DBMS_HPROF.STOP_PROFILING	59	1	0	0

You can see from the calls to the SQL inside the rates function that there were 1,460 cache misses, which is identical to the earlier scalar subquery cache and Result Cache examples. This accounts for a dramatic reduction in the number of lookups against the RATES table. However, remember that the Result Cache also eliminated the calls to the GET_RATES PL/SQL function itself. In this respect, the user-defined cache is less optimal as calls to the RATES_PKG.GET_RATES function are not reduced at all; in fact, the function calls account for all of the additional runtime.

By using your own PL/SQL array cache, as I have done, you are essentially tuning the function rather than reducing or eliminating its use. Nonetheless, the user-defined PL/SQL session cache is a useful tuning technique for reducing the cost of SQL embedded in PL/SQL functions.

▓ **Caution**   If you choose your own PL/SQL array cache over the Result Cache, you should be aware of three potential shortcomings. Firstly, each array cache will be visible to a single session and will not be shared. Secondly, each session will need to cache its own copy of the data at the expense of private PGA memory (conversely, the Result Cache stores a single shared copy of its results in the SGA). Thirdly, and most critically, is that if you cache data from tables that are regularly updated, you'll need some form of cache-management, which will be difficult to implement. The Result Cache comes with this facility "out of the box", but in your PL/SQL programs, you'll not have this luxury.

Summary

To wrap up this chapter, I have demonstrated a range of costs that you should consider when designing PL/SQL functions into your applications and queries. In addition, I've demonstrated a wide range of techniques that are at your disposal to eliminate, reduce, or optimize the use of PL/SQL functions in your SQL statements.

CHAPTER 10

Choosing the Right Cursor

by Melanie Caffrey

Anyone who has ever written a PL/SQL function or procedure that performs any looping logic knows the pain of choosing just the right type of cursor—or the pain of choosing the *wrong* type of cursor. Choosing the right type of cursor for the right programmatic situation is what this chapter strives to teach you. Choosing the wrong type of cursor may result in your users, your peers, or your managers (or all of them) losing faith in your ability to serve the technical needs of the business requirements. Choosing the wrong type of cursor may also lead to a great amount of time debugging system slowdowns in production and, as what you may deem a worst-case scenario, a diminished paycheck. Given the potential pitfalls and consequences, every PL/SQL programmer should strive to choose a type of cursor that works best for each individual technical problem she must solve.

This chapter highlights four types of cursors—not because they are the only four types of cursors available to you, but because they are the most *common* types of cursors most PL/SQL programmers typically implement. Implementing them correctly, given a particular set of business requirements, is key to having PL/SQL code that is performant and scalable. The four types of cursors discussed in this chapter are

- Explicit

- Implicit

- Static REF Cursors

- Dynamic REF Cursors

Your goal in writing any PL/SQL program that obtains sets of records for processing programmatically (either individually or in bulk) is to choose a type of cursor that allows you and the Oracle database to obtain the correct answer with the least amount of work. It is really just that simple. Of course, there are many types of cursors you *can* use in many situations. But *should* you? This is the question you need to ask yourself each time you write a PL/SQL program. Choose knowledgeably. Know first what business question you are trying to answer, and then choose the best programmatic tool to answer it quickly and correctly given each individual situation.

Explicit Cursors

The most common type of cursor used in any PL/SQL program, hands down, is the explicit cursor. Everyone learns the explicit cursor upon first learning the PL/SQL language, and most PL/SQL programmers feel instantly drawn to it because they are under the impression that it gives them more programmatic control over their processing. Programmers (at least the newly minted ones) are all about control; their impression is often that if they do not have control over every aspect of their program, then it will not execute correctly.

Explicit cursors are often referred to as *open, fetch, close* cursors due to their required keywords: OPEN, FETCH, and CLOSE. If you write an explicit cursor, you are required to explicitly open the cursor, fetch from the cursor, and close the cursor. So far, that doesn't sound too bad and may even give an all-about-control programmer peace of mind. However, it is important to find out not only in which cases such types of cursors may reasonably be used, but also in which cases they may actually be doing more harm than good. Consider the following explicit cursor example in Listing 10-1:

Listing 10-1. An Explicit Cursor Used to Fetch Just One Value

```
CREATE FUNCTION f_get_name (ip_emp_id in number ) RETURN VARCHAR2
AS
CURSOR c IS SELECT ename FROM emp WHERE emp_id = f_get_name.ip_emp_id;
lv_ename emp.ename%TYPE;
BEGIN
OPEN c;
FETCH c INTO lv_ename;
CLOSE c;
RETURN lv_ename;
END;
```

■ **Note**   The naming conventions for parameter names and variable names in this chapter are as follows: `ip_` for *input parameters*, `op_` for *output parameters*, `lv_` for *local variables*, and `gv_` for *global variables*. When input and output parameters are referenced in a function or procedure, they are prepended with the function or procedure name in order to avoid confusion and to illustrate scope. In the previous example, in Listing 10-1, `ip_emp_id` is referenced as `f_get_name.ip_emp_id`.

At first glance, this function probably looks like any typical example of a get function (a function whose sole purpose is to obtain, or *get*, one row or even one value). The business requirement is obviously to grab at least one (and at most one) employee name, ename, from the emp table given an entered employee ID, emp_id. The cursor is opened; the single value is fetched from the open cursor and placed into the variable, lv_ename; the cursor is closed; and finally the function returns the value stored in the lv_ename variable to the calling program. So, why might this type of cursor be an inappropriate choice for this type of business requirement? Because the function, f_get_name, is a bug waiting to happen.

What might end up in `lv_ename` after a fetch that fetches nothing? You wouldn't know whether you received a value or not. Furthermore, what if the data is bad? What if there ends up being more than one row returned for your entered `ip_emp_id` value? Listing 10-2 illustrates a more correct version of this explicit cursor:

Listing 10-2. A More Correct Explicit Cursor Used to Fetch Just One Value (11.2.0.1)

```
CREATE FUNCTION f_get_name (ip_emp_id IN NUMBER) RETURN VARCHAR2
AS
CURSOR c IS SELECT ename FROM emp WHERE emp_id = f_get_name.ip_emp_id;
lv_ename emp.ename%TYPE;
BEGIN
    OPEN c;
    FETCH c INTO lv_ename;
        IF (SQL%NOTFOUND) THEN
            RAISE NO_DATA_FOUND;
        ENDIF;
    FETCH c INTO lv_ename;
        IF (SQL%FOUND) THEN
            RAISE TOO_MANY_ROWS;
        ENDIF;
    CLOSE c;
    RETURN lv_ename;
END;
```

As you can see, however, this is becoming really complex. This is why an explicit cursor is a bad choice when coding a simple get function. It becomes quickly apparent that your simple function is suddenly not so simple. The problem is two-fold:

- Many people do the open/fetch/close and that's it. That is a bug waiting to happen.

- If, on the other hand, you code correctly, you are writing *much* more code than you need to. MORE CODE = MORE BUGS. Just because you *can* get the right answer to the previous business question using an explicit cursor doesn't mean you should. In the section "Implicit Cursors," you will see an example of this same business problem answered with the use of an implicit cursor.

The Anatomy of an Explicit Cursor

Knowing how an explicit cursor goes about its work can help you to decide whether it is appropriate for your business function. It was noted earlier that explicit cursors have the syntax: open, fetch, close. So, what does this mean? What is actually happening during each step? The following outlines the process or programmatic function each step performs:

1. OPEN: This step initializes the cursor and identifies the result set. Note that it does not actually have to *assemble* the result set. It just sets the point in time the result set will be "as of."

2. FETCH: This step executes repeatedly until all rows have been retrieved (unless you are using BULK COLLECT (described later), which fetches all of the records at once).

3.   CLOSE: This step releases the cursor once the last row has been processed.

Additionally, as Listing 10-1 illustrates, an explicit cursor must be *declared* before it is fetched from. An explicit cursor must always be declared in the declaration section of any procedure or function (or package, as it can be declared globally in a package specification or body) before it is actually invoked. However, what makes it *explicit* is that you have to explicitly open/fetch/close from it. Note that you can declare a cursor and then use it implicitly. Declaring a cursor is not what makes it explicit; it's how you code your subsequent interaction with it. In the "Implicit Cursors" section, you'll see that when using implicit cursors, this declaration step is not necessary. Implicit cursors *may be* declared, but, unlike their explicit counterparts, they don't *have to be.*

■ **Note**   REF cursors (discussed shortly) are not explicitly declared with the actual SELECT statement. The SELECT statement does not come into play until they are explicitly opened.

The details involved in working with a cursor are a lot to keep track of, especially if you happen to have multiple cursors open and in the process of fetching records. Given the amount of work an explicit cursor goes through (as outlined previously in the three-step list), it is important to only use an explicit cursor when absolutely necessary. So in which cases might an explicit cursor be needed? The most obvious reason to use an explicit cursor is when you have a requirement to process records in bulk.

Explicit Cursors and Bulk Processing

In instances where it is necessary to process thousands (or millions) of records at a time, you cannot process all records at once. Sure, you may *try.* But the performance slowdown would be so tremendous that you wouldn't want to. In instances where you must process a very large dataset in smaller chunks, bulk processing is one of the best ways to handle the requirement. Consider the following bulk processing example in Listing 10-3.

Listing 10-3. An Explicit Cursor Used to Perform Bulk Processing

```
CREATE OR REPLACE PROCEDURE refresh_store_feed AS
   TYPE prod_array     IS TABLE OF store_products%ROWTYPE INDEX BY BINARY_INTEGER;
   l_prod              prod_array;
   CURSOR c IS
     SELECT  product
       FROM  listed_products@some_remote_site;
   BEGIN
   OPEN C;
   LOOP
   FETCH C BULK COLLECT INTO l_prod LIMIT 100;
   FOR i IN 1 .. l_csi.COUNT
   LOOP
      /*   ... do some procedural code here that cannot be done in SQL to l_csi(i) ... */
   END LOOP;
      FORALL i IN 1 .. l_csi.COUNT
         INSERT INTO store_products (product) VALUES (l_prod(i));
```

```
    EXIT WHEN c%NOTFOUND;
    END LOOP;
    CLOSE C;
    END;
    /
```

Since bulk processing that involves piece-wise processing like that illustrated in Listing 10-3 cannot be accomplished using an implicit cursor, you must use an explicit cursor to complete the task. In the previous example, you may ask "If the goal is simply to select from one table and insert into another, why not simply use *INSERT AS SELECT* methodology?" It's a reasonable question, since using SQL before resorting to PL/SQL is usually the fastest way to accomplish a task. But not in the case outlined in Listing 10-3. If you must perform some type of intermediate processing on the data just after you've selected it—but before you insert it—and you'd like to perform the task in bulk, then you'll need an explicit cursor. Furthermore, though you can use an implicit cursor to array fetch (as of Oracle10g, an implicit cursor will automatically perform an array fetch of 100 rows), and you can process them (read them, then perform DML), you cannot perform DML in bulk. Only when using FORALL functionality can you perform DML in bulk. And only when using an explicit cursor can you use FORALL functionality.

Another example of when you would need to use an explicit cursor is somewhat dynamic in nature. It may sound counterintuitive, but when you do not know until runtime what the query will be, then you need a special type of explicit cursor to help you determine what result set will actually be processed. In this case, the type of explicit cursor you would use is called a REF (for *reference*) cursor. If you need to return a resultset to a client, this is one of the easiest ways to do it. A REF cursor offers you flexibility that regular PL/SQL cursors cannot.

REF Cursors in Brief

Though there are two other sections in this chapter that cover REF cursors more fully ("Static REF Cursors" and "Dynamic REF Cursors"), a brief overview regarding these types of cursors warrants mention in this section due to their structure: they must be explicitly opened, fetched from, and closed. If you are returning a result set to a client, a great way to avoid lots of repetitive code is to use a REF cursor. Essentially, the cursor you open usually depends on what input you receive from the requesting client. Listing 10-4 provides a brief example of a REF cursor scenario in PL/SQL:

Listing 10-4. REF Cursors Work Dynamically, But Are Declared

```
DECLARE
    prod_cursor sys_refcursor;
BEGIN
IF ( input_param = 'C' )
THEN
    OPEN prod_cursor FOR
        SELECT * FROM prod_concepts
         WHERE concept_type = 'COLLATERAL'
            AND concept_dt  < TO_DATE( '01-JAN-2003', 'DD-MON-YYYY');
ELSE
    OPEN prod_cursor FOR
        SELECT * FROM prod_concepts
         WHERE concept_category = 'ADVERTISING';
END IF;
LOOP
```

```
        FETCH prod_cursor BULK COLLECT INTO .... LIMIT 500;
        ...procedural code to process results here...
        EXIT WHEN prod_cursor%NOTFOUND;
END LOOP;
    CLOSE prod_cursor;
END;
```

Listing 10-4 illustrates how REF cursors are opened dynamically dependent on the input received from the client. In the example displayed in Listing 10-4, if the input received is 'C,' then one cursor is opened. However, if the input is not 'C,' an entirely different cursor is opened. Only after the correct cursor is opened is it then fetched from and closed. This works because the name of the cursor variable does not change—only its contents do.

It is important to note that this REF cursor is an example of a *static* REF cursor. It is called a static REF cursor because it is associated with a query known at compile time, as opposed to a *dynamic* REF cursor whose query is not known until runtime. The query associated with a static REF cursor is *static* (never changing). When using REF cursors, if it is possible to use a static REF cursor, you should do so. Dynamic code of any kind breaks dependencies since you are waiting until runtime to discover either

- the number or types of columns you will be working with, or

- the number or types of bind variables you will be working with.

If you *do* know both of these things before creating your REF cursor, then you should defer to creating a static REF cursor. Static code is almost always better than dynamic code since it is known to the RDBMS at compile time and, therefore, the compiler can catch many errors for you. Dynamic code is not known to the RDBMS until runtime and can therefore be unpredictable and prone to error.

REF cursors will be elaborated upon in subsequent sections. For now, it is enough to know that a REF cursor is yet another reason to use explicit cursors. There are only a handful of situations in which explicit cursors would actually be a more useful programmatic choice than implicit cursors. When performing bulk processing that cannot be performed using SQL or when returning a dataset to a client, you need to use explicit cursors. In almost all other cases, you should try to use SQL or implicit PL/SQL cursors before resorting to explicit cursors.

Implicit Cursors

Implicit cursors, unlike their explicit counterparts, do not need to be declared before they are invoked, though they can be, if you prefer (you'll see an example of declaring an implicit cursor shortly). Additionally, implicit cursors do not need to be opened from, fetched from, and closed from explicitly. Instead of the open, fetch, close syntax, they use either the for … in syntax or a simple select ... into syntax. An example of a typical implicit cursor is shown in Listing 10-5.

Listing 10-5. An Implicit Cursor Used to Fetch Just One Value

```
CREATE FUNCTION f_get_name (ip_emp_id IN NUMBER) RETURN VARCHAR2
AS
lv_ename emp.ename%TYPE;
BEGIN
    SELECT ename INTO lv_ename FROM emp WHERE emp_id = f_get_name.ip_emp_id;
    RETURN lv_ename;
END;
```

You may recognize the business question being asked here. It's the same business question asked in Listing 10-2. The main difference between the two is that, obviously, the solution in Listing 10-5 employs the use of an implicit cursor. When your goal is merely to fetch just one value, you should always defer to using an implicit cursor first. Compare the simplicity of this code with the verbosity and error-proneness of the explicit cursor example in Listing 10-2. In this implicit cursor example, there are no checks for `SQL%FOUND` or `SQL%NOTFOUND`. The code is very clear. There is one simple `select ... into` cursor. If just one name is selected, then just one name is returned. An exception-handling section could be written to handle the two cases where either no name exists for an entered employee ID or more than one name exists due to bad data.

■ **Note** Notice that the examples thus far omit an exception-handling section. This is intentional. If there is a bug in your code and you don't have an exception-handling section, Oracle will display the exact line item within your PL/SQL code where the error occurred. With an exception-handling section, the error line displayed is where your exception-handling section begins. This may be useful if you are providing instructions delivered up the stack to the user for the user to do something differently when interacting with your program. However, if the error message is for you and other programmers, then noting the exact line item on which your error occurred is essential for you to be able to debug quickly and effectively.

When there is at most one answer to the question you are asking, a `for ... in` cursor is not necessary at all. In that case, use a simple SQL `SELECT` statement to retrieve an answer that could potentially have either zero records or one record to process. Listing 10-5 assumes that the business question asked will never return more than one record. If that is the case, the simple SQL `select ... into` statement is the best programmatic choice for implementing the solution. If more than one record exists, your program would return an error. That is a good thing. You want to know if the data is bad. Similarly, your program would return an error if no record exists. Your program is expecting one and only one answer—any other result is an error and your program would fail immediately. Using the explicit cursor would typically not have the second fetch (described in Listing 10-2) to test whether there are more rows and that would be a bug. The `select ... into` version is "bug free."

The Anatomy of an Implicit Cursor

As mentioned previously, an implicit cursor can take one of two forms. It can be implemented using either a FOR LOOP or, more specifically, using the form `for ... in`, or it can be implemented using simple SQL `select ... into` syntax. An implicit cursor does not require that you open it explicitly. When using the `for ... in` form to implement an implicit cursor, keep the following in mind:

- Once your implicit cursor enters its for loop structure, the cursor is initialized and the result set is identified.

- The `IN` step is very similar to the `FETCH` step outlined in the "The Anatomy of an Explicit Cursor" section, with one key difference. When using an explicit cursor, if you want to ensure that there are no more rows to process, you need to add syntax similar to the following (an example of this is illustrated in Listings 10-3 and 10-4):

```
EXIT WHEN cursor%NOTFOUND;
```

Such extra syntax is not a requirement of implicit cursors. They do not need to check whether the cursor has more data to process to know when to exit.

- Similarly, the CLOSE syntax is not required of an implicit cursor as it will exit automatically once the FOR loop has terminated.

The select … into cursor behaves differently from the way the for … in cursor behaves. Listing 10-6 illustrates the difference between the two implementations.

Compare each of the BEGIN … END anonymous blocks with the DECLARE … BEGIN … END anonymous blocks that immediately follow.

Listing 10-6. A Select … Into Cursor vs. a For … In Cursor

```
BEGIN
    FOR x IN (SELECT * FROM dual) LOOP ... END LOOP;
END;



DECLARE
    CURSOR c IS SELECT * FROM dual;
BEGIN
    OPEN c;
    LOOP
        FETCH c INTO …
        EXIT WHEN c%NOTFOUND;
            …
    END LOOP;
    CLOSE c;
END;



BEGIN
    SELECT *INTO ...FROM dual;
END;



DECLARE
    CURSOR c IS SELECT * FROM dual;
    l_rec dual%ROWTYPE;
BEGIN
    OPEN c;
    FETCH c INTO l_rec;
        IF (SQL%NOTFOUND)
        THEN
            RAISE NO_DATA_FOUND;
        END IF;
    FETCH c INTO l_rec;
        IF (SQL%FOUND)
```

```
      THEN
          RAISE TOO_MANY_ROWS;
      END IF;
    CLOSE c;
END;
```

Conceptually, `select … into` is like the two procedural blocks shown in the listing. However, an implicit cursor's `for … in` processing performs an array fetch (as of Oracle10g), and is really, therefore, more like a bulk fetch and collect, making it much more efficient than its explicit cursor counterpart.

The `select … into` cursor uses different keywords and should be implemented when you expect zero records to, at most, one record. The `for … in` cursor should be implemented when you expect to be processing more than one record. Once you `SELECT … INTO` some PL/SQL variable, the cursor is initialized with the `SELECT` keyword, it *fetches* `INTO` the PL/SQL variable implicitly, then *closes* automatically because it has no more data to retrieve.

The Implicit Cursor and the Extra Fetch Theory

An oft batted-around theory regarding why implicit cursors should be avoided (and one that has been debunked for many years, though I still see it outlined in the odd company policy database programming guideline) is that implicit cursors engage in wasted work by performing an extra row fetch to test for row existence. This theory has been proposed in several (to remain anonymous) independent educational texts regarding the Oracle RDBMS. The problem with this theory is that it is rarely supported with actual evidence. It is easy enough to test this theory on any version of Oracle from version 7.1 onwards. In fact, it should be your moral imperative to challenge any edict that makes its way into a company database programming policy. If it is stated, then it should be provable. If it is not provable, then you should question whether it is an edict that should remain in force.

It is simple enough to test this theory using any implicit cursor of your choosing. For illustrative purposes, you may want to try a more universally-available case like a simple `SELECT` from an Oracle data dictionary table to test this theory. Listing 10-7 outlines a simple test case:

Listing 10-7. A Simple Implicit Cursor Fetch Test Case

```
SQL> DECLARE
  2      v_test NUMBER := 0;
  3  BEGIN
  4      SELECT user_id INTO v_test FROM all_users WHERE username = 'SYS';
  5  END;
  6  /
PL/SQL procedure successfully completed.
```

This is an easy test to conduct because it includes no looping constructs. At least and at most one value is expected. If the `SELECT` statement needs to perform an extra fetch, then the extra fetch should be visible in the TKPROF output of a simple SQL traced session. Listing 10-8 displays the TKPROF output for the test case illustrated in Listing 10-7.

Listing 10-8. TKPROF Output for Implicit Cursor Extra Fetch Test (11.2.0.1)

```
********************************************************************************

SQL ID: bs5v1gp6hakdp
Plan Hash: 3123615307
SELECT USER_ID
FROM
 ALL_USERS WHERE USERNAME = 'SYS'

call     count       cpu     elapsed       disk      query    current       rows
-------  ------  --------  ----------  ---------  ---------  ---------  ----------
Parse        1      0.00        0.00          0          0          0           0
Execute      1      0.00        0.00          0          0          0           0
Fetch        1      0.00        0.00          0          6          0           1
-------  ------  --------  ----------  ---------  ---------  ---------  ----------
total        3      0.00        0.00          0          6          0           1

Misses in library cache during parse: 1
Optimizer mode: ALL_ROWS
Parsing user id: 84     (recursive depth: 1)

Rows     Row Source Operation
-------  ---------------------------------------------------
      1  NESTED LOOPS  (cr=6 pr=0 pw=0 time=0 us cost=3 size=32 card=1)
      1   NESTED LOOPS  (cr=4 pr=0 pw=0 time=0 us cost=2 size=29 card=1)
      1    TABLE ACCESS BY INDEX ROWID USER$ (cr=2 pr=0 pw=0 time=0 us cost=1 size=26 card=1)
      1     INDEX UNIQUE SCAN I_USER1 (cr=1 pr=0 pw=0 time=0 us cost=0 size=0 card=1)(object↵
id 46)
      1    TABLE ACCESS CLUSTER TS$ (cr=2 pr=0 pw=0 time=0 us cost=1 size=3 card=1)
      1     INDEX UNIQUE SCAN I_TS# (cr=1 pr=0 pw=0 time=0 us cost=0 size=0 card=1)(object↵
id 7)
      1   TABLE ACCESS CLUSTER TS$ (cr=2 pr=0 pw=0 time=0 us cost=1 size=3 card=1)
      1    INDEX UNIQUE SCAN I_TS# (cr=1 pr=0 pw=0 time=0 us cost=0 size=0 card=1)(object↵
id 7)

********************************************************************************
```

As you can see from the TKPROF output, no extra fetch is performed. Therefore, I can think of only a handful of reasons why you would not want to do everything you can to ensure that you are using implicit cursors over explicit cursors. As mentioned in the "Explicit Cursors and Bulk Processing" subsection, when needing to perform FORALL bulk processing on data fetched from the database, you will need to use explicit cursors. In other words, if you are merely selecting data and using htp.p to output the data in APEX, or you are using utl_file.put_line to send the selected data to a file, for example, there is no need to bulk process using an explicit cursor. Behind the scenes, the Oracle RDBMS already *is* bulk processing in those types of instances.

It is only when you fetch data out, process it procedurally, and then put it back into the database using FORALL updates, inserts, and/or deletes that you would have a need for explicit cursor processing. In the same section, REF cursors were briefly illustrated as yet another reason to use explicit cursors if your requirement is to pass data to a client (residing outside of, but connecting to, the database) application. The next two sections introduce the two types of REF cursors available to you.

Static REF Cursors

As mentioned in the section "REF Cursors in Brief," if you are returning a result set to a client, REF cursors (also referred to as *reference* cursors or *cursor variables*) are the best way to do so. A REF cursor often depends on the input of the client to decide exactly which cursor to open, and therefore, which result set to return. Given the quantity of unknowns that can be present when returning data to a client, the ability to select (no pun intended) the query to be run at runtime provides your program with a great amount of flexibility. This ability also helps you to avoid writing repetitive code. You see an example of a static REF cursor in section "REF Cursors in Brief." Listing 10-9 illustrates an expansion on this example of a static REF cursor with package parameter specifications:

Listing 10-9. A Static REF Cursor Declared in a PL/SQL Package (11.2.0.1)

```
CREATE OR REPLACE PACKAGE product_pkg
AS
-- In Package Specification, declare the cursor variable type
TYPE my_cv IS REF CURSOR;

PROCEDURE get_concepts ( ip_input    IN   NUMBER,
                         op_rc       OUT  my_cv);

END product_pkg;

CREATE OR REPLACE PACKAGE BODY product_pkg
AS
-- In Package Body procedure, declare the cursor variable using the type declared in↩
 the package specification

PROCEDURE get_concepts (ip_input    IN   NUMBER,
                        op_rc       OUT  my_cv)
IS
    BEGIN
       IF ( ip_input = 1 )
       THEN
          OPEN op_rc FOR
             SELECT * FROM prod_concepts
              WHERE concept_type  = 'COLLATERAL'
                AND concept_dt    < TO_DATE( '01-JAN-2003', 'DD-MON-YYYY');
       ELSE
          OPEN op_rc FOR
             SELECT * FROM prod_concepts
              WHERE concept_category = 'ADVERTISING';
       END IF;
    END get_concepts;

END product_pkg;
```

The package and package body in Listing 10-9 illustrate code that makes use of a cursor variable. The package specification declares a REF cursor type, as shown by this line of code:

```
TYPE my_cv IS REF CURSOR;
```

Note that this type of cursor variable is *weak-typed*. The weak-typed cursor variable provides you with more flexibility as to the result set returned. However, because it is not created as a specific type of record like the following

```
TYPE my_cv IS REF CURSOR RETURN prod_concepts%ROWTYPE;
```

or

```
TYPE ProdConTyp IS RECORD (
    prod_id              NUMBER,
    con_id               NUMBER,
    req_id               NUMBER,
    concept_type      VARCHAR2(30),
    concept_category  VARCHAR2(30),
    concept_dt                DATE);
    TYPE my_cv IS REF CURSOR RETURN ProdConTyp;
```

it is more prone to error. If you find yourself having to use cursor variables, it is better to create them *strong-typed* (as just shown), than weak-typed whenever possible. The type declared in the package specification is then referenced in the package body to declare the actual cursor variable, as illustrated with the following line of code:

```
op_rc       OUT  my_cv)
```

From this point forward, this cursor variable may be used and re-used for any result set you would like, as evidenced by the following code that opens the REF cursor and returns it as an out parameter in the procedure get_concepts:

```
IF ( ip_input = 1 )
THEN
   OPEN op_rc FOR
            SELECT * FROM prod_concepts
              WHERE concept_type = 'COLLATERAL'
                AND concept_dt   < TO_DATE( '01-JAN-2003', 'DD-MON-YYYY');
  ELSE
          OPEN op_rc FOR
            SELECT * FROM prod_concepts
              WHERE concept_category = 'ADVERTISING';
END IF;
```

Note that in this code, all columns from the PROD_CONCEPTS table are returned dependent upon the WHERE clause that ultimately is executed. In this case, it would be better to strong-type the cursor variable used to return either of these result sets since they both contain the same column list. However, for purposes of illustration, if a third outcome were possible, expanding the IF statement as follows

```
ELSIF ( ip_input = 2 )
THEN
   OPEN op_rc FOR
            SELECT prod_name FROM products p, prod_concepts pc
             WHERE p.prod_id    = pc.prod_id
               AND concept_type = 'COLLATERAL'
               AND concept_dt   < TO_DATE( '01-JAN-2003', 'DD-MON-YYYY');
```

this result set would be completely different from either of the others. In this particular instance, all things being equal, a weak-typed cursor variable such as the example shows would be the only type of cursor variable that would work for this scenario. In other words, because the example's chosen type of cursor variable can accept virtually any type of result set, it will likely succeed.

However, because its structure is not known to the compiler at compile time, if a failure were to occur regarding this REF cursor, it would occur at runtime. You always take a risk when you sidestep possible compiler errors and allow them to occur (if they are going to occur) at runtime because such errors affect your users. Remember, just because you *can* use a particular type of cursor, doesn't mean it is your best choice. Your goal is to write PL/SQL as efficiently as possible. If you are using a REF cursor, it is assumed that either

- You are passing a result set to a client, and/or

- You don't know until runtime what the query will be, and/or

- There is no method available to you in achieving your goal using implicit cursors.

There are several items to keep in mind when using REF cursors. REF cursors are owned by whomever (whether a client program or a PL/SQL program) is processing/fetching their records at a current point in time. Because a REF cursor is a pointer to a cursor and can, in fact, be pointed to many different cursors, it is not cached in PL/SQL. Statement caching is extremely important in reducing overall parse calls and, therefore, increasing application scalability. Repeated parsing of the same SQL lowers your scalability and increases the amount of work you do. By using non-REF cursors in PL/SQL, you decrease your parsing greatly. More regarding the PL/SQL cursor cache is discussed in the section "A Few Words About Parsing."

There is a caveat to this in that you can limit the amount of soft parsing work (or rather, the amount of work soft parsing performs, since you cannot limit soft parsing) that will inevitably take place by setting your initialization file's value for the `session_cached_cursors` parameter appropriately. With REF cursors, PL/SQL doesn't know what the cursor will be until a request is made for it and the associated code is run. Therefore, since the overhead is slightly higher in using REF cursors, it's a good idea to see if you can accomplish what you'd like to do by using regular cursors first.

Why are all of these points important? Because there are a slew of restrictions on using cursor variables. If you think you've chosen the easy way to accomplish your goal by using REF cursors instead of using non-REF cursors, you've actually chosen a method that will be much harder to manage long-term.

Cursor Variable Restrictions Laundry List

Consider these very important points regarding cursor variables:

- You can't declare cursor variables in a package (specification or body, that is). They may only be declared in a procedure or function.

- You can't pass cursor variables back and forth over a database link. If you pass a host cursor variable to PL/SQL, you can't fetch from it on the server side unless you also open it within the same server call.

- Cursors and cursor variables are not interoperable. You can't use one where the other is expected.

- You can't use comparison operators to test cursor variables for equality, inequality, or nullity.

- You can't use a REF CURSOR type to specify the element type of a collection. Therefore, collection elements can't store the values of cursor variables. This may be something to consider, especially if you are planning on using REF cursors to aid in bulk processing, for example.

- By the same token, you can't use REF CURSOR types to specify column types in a CREATE TABLE or CREATE VIEW statement. In other words, database columns can't store the values of cursor variables.

- You can't assign null values to a cursor variable.

This is a lot to think about. Given all of these restrictions on using cursor variables, your choice to use them, therefore, must be well considered. However, using cursor variables is definitely preferable to putting all of your database access logic directly into the application. So, if you choose to use cursor variables, it's important to not only have an idea about how you'd structure your PL/SQL code portion, but additionally, how you'd structure your Java code portion.

Your Client and REF Cursors

Remember that the client *owns* the REF cursor once it is returned to them. Your PL/SQL program opens the REF cursor, sometimes based on input it receives from the client, and then returns the result set it opens to the client. Listing 10-10 provides a brief example of a Java program used to accept the result set received from the PL/SQL program outlined in Listing 10-9.

Listing 10-10. A Java Program Used for REF Cursor Processing (11.2.0.1)

```
import java.sql.*;
import java.io.*;
import oracle.jdbc.driver.*;
class ProdConRefCursor
{
public static void main (String args [ ])
throws SQLException, ClassNotFoundException
{
   String query  = "BEGIN " + "product_pkg.get_concepts( ?, ?); " + "end;";
   DriverManager.registerDriver
       (new oracle.jdbc.driver.OracleDriver());
   Connection conn =
       DriverManager.getConnection
       ("jdbc:oracle:thin:@proximo-dev:1521:mozartora112dev", "mktg", "mktg");
   Statement trace = conn.createStatement();
   CallableStatement  cstmt = conn.prepareCall(query);
   cstmt.setInt(1, 37);
   cstmt.registerOutParameter(2 ,OracleTypes.CURSOR);
   cstmt.execute();
   ResultSet rset = (ResultSet)cstmt.getObject(2);
   for(int i = 0;  rset.next(); i++ )
       System.out.println( "rset " + rset.getString(1) );
   rset.close();
}
}
```

This is a rather simplistic, yet straightforward example of a client accepting the result set returned by a REF cursor. The salient parts of this are the following code snippets:

```
cstmt.registerOutParameter(2 ,OracleTypes.CURSOR);
cstmt.execute();
ResultSet rset = (ResultSet)cstmt.getObject(2);
```

Your return type is a cursor of OracleTypes. Once you receive the cursor, you iterate over each record until there are no more records to process on the client side, like so:

```
for(int i = 0;  rset.next(); i++ )
      System.out.println( "rset " + rset.getString(1) );
```

Finally, it is the job of the client to close the REF cursor. It cannot pass the REF cursor back to your PL/SQL program. Therefore, once it is done processing the records returned by your REF cursor, it simply closes the cursor with the following statement:

```
rset.close();
```

A Few Words about Parsing

Though this may sound like a bit of an aside, parsing is something to be kept high on your list of priorities when choosing which cursor will suit you best for each type of programmatic situation. As mentioned earlier, REF cursors, even the static type, generally perform a soft parse each time they are opened (see the caveat regarding setting a value in `session_cached_cursors` mentioned earlier). Though a soft parse is infinitely better than a hard parse, it is *much* worse than no parse at all. Your goal when writing any kind of SQL or PL/SQL is to reduce parsing whenever and wherever possible. So what can you do to reduce parsing?

If you are using PL/SQL implicit cursors or explicit (non-REF) cursors and you are not using literal values for your predicates, you are using bind variables. This means that, by default, you have opened up the opportunity to reduce parsing since you have reduced the number of unique SQL statements. Your cursor queries will parse the first time they are accessed and remain in the shared pool to be reused by multiple accesses until they are aged out. This is a huge savings for the runtime and scalability of your application. Your cursor queries will not be seen as individual, new cursors to be parsed, executed, closed, and reopened (wash, rinse, repeat) over and over again.

In addition to being cached in the shared pool, PL/SQL itself can "cache" these queries. It will cache them in an *open* state. This means they can be executed later again without having to even open (parse) them. So, not only will you have excellent shared SQL in the shared pool, but you'll also eliminate all but one parse call per SQL statement in your session. That is one of the best reasons to use non-REF cursors. PL/SQL does not close them, it keeps them open and avoids the parse altogether.

REF cursors, on the other hand, always perform a soft parse. On the one hand, they provide you with great coding flexibility, particularly if you are required to pass a result set back to a client, which many database applications are required to do. On the other hand, that flexibility comes with the tradeoff of possible reduced scalability and excessive soft parses. And with excessive soft parsing comes possible latch contention. So if you can't write static implicit cursors and you must write REF cursors, what can you do to work towards reducing the effects of inevitable soft parsing?

Consider setting an appropriate value for your `session_cached_cursors` initialization file parameter. Your goal is to reduce the effects (latching) of excessive soft parses. Caching cursors system-wide is generally a very good thing because it will reduce the effects of too much latching and help your application to avoid latch contention. Using `session_cached_cursors` helps you to make a soft parse softer. It makes soft parsing *easier*, so it is, therefore, a good setting to have in place when your applications use REF cursors. When you close a cursor in PL/SQL, implicitly or explicitly, PL/SQL does not close the cursor. It caches it open. And the size of the PL/SQL cache is controlled by the value supplied for the session_cached_cursors parameter.

Static SQL using non-REF cursors in PL/SQL is what helps to reduce parsing, due to the PL/SQL cursor cache. More than one parse will take place when the application parses the query more than once. The parses might be hard or soft. For example, say you have a script similar to the following:

```
ALTER SESSION SET SQL_TRACE = true;

BEGIN
    FOR i IN 1 .. 2000 LOOP
        FOR x IN ( SELECT /*+ implicit cursor query goes here */ * FROM dual )
        LOOP
            NULL;
        END LOOP;
    END LOOP;
END;
/

DECLARE
    TYPE rc_type IS REF CURSOR;
    rc rc_type;
BEGIN
    FOR i IN 1 .. 2000 LOOP
        OPEN rc FOR SELECT /*+ REF cursor query goes here */ * FROM dual;
        CLOSE rc;
    END LOOP;
END;
/
```

The resultant TKPROF output reveals the following:

```
****************************************************

SQL ID: dybuvv2j10gxt
Plan Hash: 272002086
SELECT /*+ implicit cursor query goes here */ *
FROM
 DUAL


call     count      cpu    elapsed       disk      query    current       rows
-------  ------  -------- ---------- ---------- ---------- ----------  ----------
Parse        1     0.00       0.00          0          0          0           0
Execute   2000     0.01       0.02          0          0          0           0
Fetch     2000     0.03       0.04          2       6000          0        2000
-------  ------  -------- ---------- ---------- ---------- ----------  ----------
total     4001     0.05       0.07          2       6000          0        2000

Misses in library cache during parse: 1
Optimizer mode: ALL_ROWS
Parsing user id: 84      (recursive depth: 1)
```

```
Rows     Row Source Operation
-------  ---------------------------------------------------
      1  TABLE ACCESS FULL DUAL (cr=3 pr=2 pw=0 time=0 us cost=2 size=2 card=1)
```

****

The TKPROF output illustrates how the query was parsed once and executed 2,000 times. PL/SQL cached the cursor. The "misses in library cache during parse" line in the output also demonstrates this was a hard parse. It wasn't found in the shared pool. Here's another example:

****

```
SQL ID: gc72r5wh91y0k
Plan Hash: 272002086
SELECT /*+ REF cursor query goes here */ *
FROM
 DUAL
```

call	count	cpu	elapsed	disk	query	current	rows
Parse	2000	0.02	0.02	0	0	0	0
Execute	2000	0.02	0.02	0	0	0	0
Fetch	0	0.00	0.00	0	0	0	0
total	4000	0.04	0.05	0	0	0	0

```
Misses in library cache during parse: 1
Optimizer mode: ALL_ROWS
Parsing user id: 84     (recursive depth: 1)

Rows     Row Source Operation
-------  ---------------------------------------------------
      0  TABLE ACCESS FULL DUAL (cr=0 pr=0 pw=0 time=0 us cost=2 size=2 card=1)
```

****

This time the TKPROF output demonstrates the query was parsed 2000 times. It was opened with a REF cursor, and PL/SQL can't cache such cursors. The output also demonstrates one hard parse and (therefore) 1,999 soft parses. The second parse was done by finding the already existing plan in the shared pool's library cache. Optimally, you should see parse =1 but it is not unusual to see parse = execute = N.

Dynamic REF Cursors

Dynamic REF cursors are, for all practical purposes, very similar to static REF cursors, except for a few notable differences. The query for a dynamic REF cursor is not known until runtime *and* is also built dynamically. You may ask how this is different from static REF cursors, since a static REF cursor's query is also not known until runtime. Strongly-typed REF cursors cannot be dynamically opened. Weakly-typed REF cursors can be dynamically opened.

Example and Best Use

Consider the example in Listing 10-11 that outlines a procedure that uses a dynamic REF cursor:

Listing 10-11. A Procedure That Uses a Dynamic REF Cursor (11.2.0.1)

```
PROCEDURE get_concepts (ip_input       IN  NUMBER,
                        ip_con_type    IN  VARCHAR2,
                        ip_con_dt      IN  DATE,
                        ip_con_cat     IN  VARCHAR2,
                        op_rc          OUT my_cv)
IS
    lv_query VARCHAR2 (512) DEFAULT 'SELECT * FROM prod_concepts';
    BEGIN
        IF ( ip_con_type IS NOT NULL )
           lv_query := lv_query ||
        '  WHERE concept_type LIKE ''%''||:ip_con_type||''%'' ';
        ELSE
           lv_query := lv_query ||
        ' WHERE (1 = 1 OR :ip_con_type IS NULL) ';
        END IF;
        IF ( ip_con_dt IS NOT NULL )
           lv_query := lv_query ||
        '  AND concept_dt < :ip_con_dt ';
        ELSE
           lv_query := lv_query ||
        ' AND (1 = 1 OR :ip_con_dt IS NULL) ';
        END IF;
        IF ( ip_con_cat IS NOT NULL )
           lv_query := lv_query ||
        '  AND concept_category LIKE ''%''||:ip_con_cat||''%'' ';
        ELSE
           lv_query := lv_query ||
        ' AND (1 = 1 OR :ip_con_cat IS NULL) ';
        END IF;
            OPEN op_rc FOR
                lv_query USING ip_con_type, ip_con_dt, ip_con_cat;

    END get_concepts;
```

So, how is this version of the get_concepts procedure different from the one illustrated in Listing 10-9? To begin with, unlike the static OPEN-FOR version, the dynamic version has an *optional* USING clause—*optional* because it would also be possible to code this procedure using literals, as opposed to bind variables, similar to the following:

```
'SELECT * FROM prod_concepts
  WHERE concept_type  = ''||COLLATERAL||''
    AND concept_dt    < ''||TO_CHAR('''01-JAN-2003''', '''DD-MON-YYYY''')||''';
```

Obviously, this appears to be a non-ideal and cumbersome way to build your query. It would also lead to the dreaded hard parse since all queries would be unique, which would *kill* performance. If it is necessary to build a dynamic query of any kind, ask the reasons for doing so. You need dynamic SQL in the following situations:

- You want to execute a SQL data definition statement (such as CREATE), a data control statement (such as GRANT), or a session control statement (such as ALTER SESSION). In PL/SQL, such statements cannot be executed via static SQL.

- You want more flexibility. For example, you might want to wait until runtime to choose which schema objects you use. Or, you might want your program to build different search conditions for the WHERE clause of a SELECT statement as is being done in Listing 10-11. Dynamically building a WHERE clause is a very common reason to use dynamic SQL. A more complex program might choose from various SQL operations, clauses, etc.

If you don't need to perform any of the above, but you do need a REF cursor, then you should definitely use a static REF cursor. If you *do* need to use any of the above, ensure that you are using bind variables, as with the first example in Listing 10-11.

Now, because the structure you are using is a REF cursor, it will still be performing soft parses, but at least, if you are using bind variables, it won't be performing hard parses. Because the cursor *could* be different, the Oracle RDBMS assumes that it might be, since it is dynamic, and therefore some type of parse always takes place. Of all the cursor types you have to choose from, this one should definitely be your last resort. Dynamic SQL is extremely fragile, hard to code, hard to tune, and simply hard to maintain. The chain of code dependencies no longer exists and you are therefore *hoping* that data structure changes do not adversely affect your code.

But you learned in the previous section that REF cursors perform, at a minimum, soft parsing. Other than the cumbersome coding that dynamic REF cursors present, what might be other reasons to avoid them? The biggest reason I can think of to avoid dynamic REF cursors is the possibility of SQL injection. SQL injection is a very real threat to your applications and, more importantly, your data. If your application code allows malicious users to attach their own SQL statements to your dynamically built queries, such attacks can pose a dangerous threat to the security of your data.

The Threat of SQL Injection

Dynamic SQL that allows a user to concatenate strings into statements without bind variables is not only a parsing, scalability, and maintainability nightmare; it also presents a very tangible security threat. Each time you allow someone to provide inputs from outside your control, your data is no longer safe. And to top it all off, the malicious user, because they are using *your* code, is executing their statements as *you*. You've opened the door and left your data vulnerable. Consider the example in Listing 10-12 that outlines an innocent-looking procedure subject to SQL injection:.

Listing 10-12. A Procedure Subject to SQL Injection (11.2.0.1)

```
PROCEDURE get_concepts (ip_input      IN  NUMBER,
                        ip_con_type   IN  VARCHAR2,
                        ip_con_dt     IN  DATE,
                        ip_con_cat    IN  VARCHAR2,
                        op_rc         OUT my_cv)
IS
   BEGIN
```

```
            IF ( ip_input = 1 )
            THEN
            OPEN op_rc FOR
                  'SELECT * FROM prod_concepts
                    WHERE concept_type  = ''||ip_con_type||''
                      AND concept_dt    < ''||ip_con_dt||''' ;
            ELSE
               OPEN op_rc FOR
                 'SELECT * FROM prod_concepts
                    WHERE  concept_category = ''||ip_con_cat||''' ;
            END IF;
        END get_concepts;
```

If someone wishes to do something they shouldn't, such as gain access or something destructive, then these harmless looking parameters (obviously intended for input regarding product concept data) can easily be manipulated to where the resultant dynamic SQL queries end up looking similar to the following:

```
CREATE OR REPLACE
    PROCEDURE get_concepts (ip_input       IN   NUMBER,
                            ip_con_type    IN   VARCHAR2,
                            ip_con_dt      IN   DATE,
                            ip_con_cat     IN   VARCHAR2,
                            op_rc          OUT  sys_refcursor )
    IS
        BEGIN
          IF ( ip_input = 1 )
          THEN
                   DBMS_OUTPUT.PUT_LINE(
                 'SELECT * FROM prod_concepts
                   WHERE concept_type  = ''' ||ip_con_type|| '''
                     AND concept_dt    < ''' || to_char(ip_con_dt, 'dd-mon-yyyy' )↵
||'''' );
          ELSE
                   DBMS_OUTPUT.PUT_LINE(
                 'SELECT * FROM prod_concepts
                   WHERE  concept_category = ''' || ip_con_cat||'''' );
          END IF;
      END get_concepts;
  /
scott%ORA11GR2> variable x refcursor
scott%ORA11GR2> exec get_concepts( ip_input => 2, ip_con_type => null, ip_con_dt => null,↵
 ip_con_cat => '''||admin_pkg.change_app_passwd( ''INJECTED'' ) --', op_rc => :x );
SELECT * FROM prod_concepts
 WHERE concept_category =
''||admin_pkg.change_app_passwd( 'INJECTED' ) --'

PL/SQL procedure successfully completed.
```

What has taken place here? In the call to this procedure, the input the user provides does not care about matching either the concept_type or the concept_dt and thus provides the actual SQL they intend to execute: admin_pkg.change_app_passwd('INJECTED'); . The addition of the notation, --, just at the end of that input marks the start of an SQL comment. This is a clever way to *consume* the final quote provided by the application and not worry about having to match it.

As you can see, dynamic SQL leaves the door wide open to malicious intruders. Any time you are not using bind variables, you are not only impeding application performance, you are putting your data at severe risk. Therefore, since dynamic REF cursors (and dynamic SQL of any kind) are fragile and prone to both error and risk, you need to ask yourself whether the added flexibility of coding applications that use REF cursors is worth the security risks and maintainability headaches. And if you have no other choice but to use REF cursors, keep the following in mind:

- If you must use REF cursors, use strongly-typed static REF cursors.

- If you cannot use a static REF cursor, then ensure that your dynamic REF cursor uses bind variables.

Describing REF Cursor Columns

In Oracle versions gone by, it was never the case that you could describe the columns of a REF cursor. You had to use a client external to the database if you wanted this functionality. This situation has changed as of Oracle version 11.1 and later. As of Oracle 11.1, DBMS_SQL, a supplied package that lets you procedurally process a result set much like JDBC, works in tandem with REF cursor functionality to allow you to be able to describe your columns programmatically after opening your REF cursor. This functionality is possible because Oracle 11g allows a REF cursor to be converted to DBMS_SQL and vice versa. Consider the example in Listing 10-13.

Listing 10-13. A REF Cursor That Uses DBMS_SQL to Describe Columns (11.2.0.1)

```
DECLARE
            lv_ref_cursor    SYS_REFCURSOR;
            lv_col_cnt       NUMBER;
            lv_desc_tab      DBMS_SQL.DESC_TAB;
BEGIN
            OPEN lv_rcursor FOR SELECT * FROM prod_concepts;

            DBMS_SQL.DESCRIBE_COLUMNS
            ( cur_id        => DBMS_SQL.TO_CURSOR_NUMBER(lv_ref_cursor),
              col_cnt       => lv_col_cnt,
              desc_tab      => lv_desc_tab );

            FOR i IN 1 .. lv_col_cnt
            LOOP
                    DBMS_OUTPUT.PUT_LINE( lv_desc_tab(i).col_name );
            END LOOP;
END;
/
```

The salient part of this example is the following code snippet:

```
cur_id        => DBMS_SQL.TO_CURSOR_NUMBER(lv_ref_cursor)
```

The function TO_CURSOR_NUMBER can convert any REF cursor (either strongly or weakly typed) to a SQL cursor number, which can then be passed to any DBMS_SQL subprograms. You can harness the capability of DBMS_SQL within REF cursor processing and provide your programs with further flexibility. Be aware, however, that once you convert a REF cursor to a DBMS_SQL cursor number, you can no longer use native dynamic SQL operations to access it. You can use the DBMS_SQL.TO_REFCURSOR function to switch the cursor number back to a REF cursor, but be aware that this latest version of the REF cursor will be weakly typed, even if it was strongly typed originally. So, as with any other PL/SQL cursor functionality, use this functionality with full knowledge of its side effects, as well as its benefits.

Summary

Choosing the right types of cursors for your application needs can make or break your application. If you have the opportunity to use static SQL, do so and don't look back. When choosing between implicit and explicit cursors, defer to implicit cursors whenever possible. Your performance will be increased, your scalability will be measurable, and your users will thank you. However, if you are performing bulk processing where you need to also process the data procedurally, or you are passing a result set to a client application, you will have little choice but to use an explicit cursor.

When choosing a REF cursor (that your application needs have deemed inevitable), see if you can meet your goal by use of a strongly-typed REF cursor. Creating compiler-aware code should be one of your paramount goals. Remember that dynamic code is fragile and error-prone by its very nature. But if you must use dynamic REF cursors, ensure that you are using bind variables—not just for the runtime gains, but for the security peace of mind as well. SQL injection is just waiting for any application caught unaware.

Your job, as a developer, is to use the right tools for the right job. All of these cursor types are right for a particular purpose. Ensure you have a good understanding of the risks and pitfalls, in addition to the benefits. Your cursor choice should be made in a way that maximizes your performance, decreases your concerns, and increases your popularity amongst your application user community. So, try out things different ways. Weigh one method versus another. Keep the order of precedence in mind, and when you must use something other than an implicit cursor, do so judiciously and wisely.

CHAPTER 11

PL/SQL Programming in the Large

by Martin Büchi

Most business applications are data-centric and therefore require a database at their core. These applications are commonly used for years or even decades. During this time, the user interface is sometimes completely replaced or extended to keep it state of the art. The data model and the business logic, on the other hand, usually evolve more steadily along with the supported business processes. Many of these applications end up large, whether they start small (such as an APEX replacement of a spreadsheet) or are complex from the onset. Thus, we need an architecture and a programming language suitable for developing and maintaining data-centric business logic for years. PL/SQL in the Oracle database ideally fits these requirements.

Business logic in PL/SQL can lead to lots of PL/SQL code; my company's flagship application, for example, has 11 million lines and is maintained by 170 developers. This is true programming in the large. Effective and efficient programming in the large in any language requires good modularization and high uniformity based on strict adherence to programming conventions. PL/SQL provides solid foundations to implement and enforce these aspects. Furthermore, it allows for object-oriented programming, which significantly increases reuse and thereby leads to a cost reduction and quality increase.

This chapter first describes when and why business logic in PL/SQL is a good option, then explains ways to master the key success factors for PL/SQL programming in the large.

The Database as PL/SQL-Based Application Server

Software architectures and programming languages must be chosen to best satisfy business requirements. Therefore, the most convincing argument for coding business logic in PL/SQL is a long-term successful application based on this architecture. The Avaloq Banking System is such an application and serves as case study. From this case study, I deduce the strengths of this architecture. Because no architecture is universally applicable, it is also important to know its limits.

Case Study: The Avaloq Banking System

The Avaloq Banking System (ABS) is a complete core banking system with payment, investment, and financing functionality. It provides an end-user GUI and batch processing of messages and files. Over 65 banks with 20 to 5,000 concurrent end users each use it in seven countries. Real-time OLTP and reporting are implemented in the same database.

The ABS has a physical three-tier architecture, as depicted in Figure 11-1. The thin rich client implemented in .NET provides for efficient user interaction with optimal Windows integration. The middle tier is responsible for telephony integration, external authentication, and protocol conversion between Oracle Net and Windows Communication Foundation, so that no Oracle client is required on desktops, firewalls can prohibit direct SQL access from end-user PCs, and network encryption in the client network is available for free. Neither the client nor the middle tier contains any business logic; in fact, they could be used as-is for an arbitrary ERP application.

The business logic resides in the backend—that is, the Oracle database. The database serves as a PL/SQL-based application server and is based on a logical three-tier architecture with data access, business logic, and presentation layers. The same PL/SQL business logic code is executed in batch processing and GUI sessions. For example, a payment transaction is handled the same way whether it is read into the system from a file or entered by a clerk on the GUI.

In the Avaloq Banking System, the state of GUI sessions is stored in PL/SQL package body global variables. Every field value is sent to the server for validation and calculation of derived fields. Business transactions are built up in PL/SQL memory and are persisted upon finalization by the user. The best location of the session state (database tables, database server memory, middle tier, or client) is an often emotional topic of debate. Because large parts of the business logic can be implemented in PL/SQL even if the session state is not kept in the database, this chapter is relevant no matter where your application stores the session state.

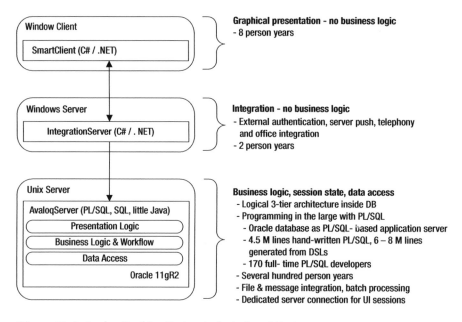

Figure 11-1. Avaloq Banking System technical architecture

Development of the Avaloq Banking System started in 1993 with Oracle 7. The basic architecture with the business logic in the Oracle database has been the same since the beginning. The original GUI was written in HyperCard; it has since been replaced three times by Java AWT, Java Swing, and .NET based implementations and may well become a Web GUI in the future.

Avaloq is a commercial company that wants to maximize profit. We have chosen the described architecture to maximize customer satisfaction and developer productivity and periodically reevaluate it. Admittedly, no commercial application servers existed in 1993 when development of the Avaloq Banking System started. However, we keep the current architecture because it works very well and not because a migration to an application server would be very expensive. In fact, we chose a similar architecture for our database provisioning and continuous integration system, which was designed in 2006 by an engineer with JEE background and Java certification. We sometimes have to explain the reasons for our architecture choice, but we haven't lost a single sales case in the past 17 years because of our architecture.

Many other ERP and banking applications, including IFS Applications, Oracle E-Business Suite, and Oracle Fusion Applications contain several million lines of PL/SQL. Oracle's strong commitment to PL/SQL is manifested by its implementation of Application Express (APEX) in PL/SQL and by the continuous enhancements of PL/SQL, such as edition-based redefinition in 11gR2.

Strengths of Business Logic in the Database with PL/SQL

Avaloq profits from the following strengths of coding the business logic in the database:

- *Simplicity*. Most developers need to code in only one language for a single tier. They can code complete business functions without losing time coordinating with and waiting for developers of other tiers to do their jobs. Furthermore, the concurrency model makes it easy to develop programs that run parallel to others.

- *Performance*. Data access including bulk operations is fastest directly in the database. It's the same basic idea as in Exadata: bring the processing closer to the data and send only the minimum over the network. For batch processing, which is the majority of the OLTP banking activity, all processing can be done in the database.

- *Security*. Definer rights procedures make it easier to ensure that no critical information can be accessed by unauthorized persons from outside the database. All data can reside in locked schemas and external access can be restricted to a few packages. No direct table or view access needs to be granted. If the business logic is outside the database, there are (at least after some time) multiple applications that directly access the database. This makes it hard to enforce consistent security. Passwords stored in application servers can be easily misused to directly access data. Furthermore, the session state in the server prevents spoofing attacks.

- *Consistency*. I trust Oracle's read consistency. I wouldn't sleep well if I had to display real-time customer portfolios based on middle-tier caches simultaneous with heavy OLTP activity.

- *Availability from any environment*. Many applications need to interface with others. Stored procedures can be invoked from any language through JDBC, OCI, ODBC, etc. Of course, this is true for web services as well.

- *Participation in distributed transactions:* Distributed transactions are crucial for interfaces in business systems to ensure once and only once execution. Distributed transactions with Oracle as transaction participant are simple to set up and are supported by most transaction coordinators. Setting up distributed transactions for arbitrary interfaces over a Web service or CORBA middle tier connected to a database in a multi-vendor environment, on the other hand, is a nightmare.

- *Centralized, single-tier deployment:* Most enhancements and bug fixes require a change on only a single tier, even if tables and business logic need to be modified.

- *Scalability:* The Oracle database scales nicely in the box thanks to ever more powerful servers and horizontally outside the box with Real Application Cluster.

- *Stability and reliability:* The Oracle database is an exceptionally stable and reliable execution environment.

Most benefits of three-tier architectures stem from the logical rather than the physical separation of data access, business logic, and presentation. The logical separation, and therefore the benefits, can also be achieved with modularization inside the database, as described later.

Stored procedures can be coded in PL/SQL, in Java, in .NET, or in almost any language as external procedures. PL/SQL is my default.

PL/SQL Stored Procedures

PL/SQL, an imperative 3GL designed specifically for seamless processing of SQL, provides additional benefits for coding business logic. Selected key benefits are illustrated in Figure 11-2.

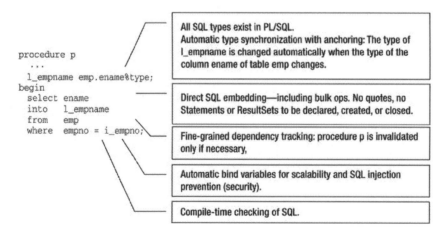

Figure 11-2. Selected key benefits of PL/SQL

Furthermore, edition-based redefinition provides for online application upgrades of PL/SQL code together with other object types. PL/SQL also runs in the TimesTen in-memory database, thereby bringing the same advantages to data cached in memory for even high performance.

Java Stored Procedures

Java stored procedures don't provide the same seamless SQL integration as PL/SQL. In fact, Java doesn't have any of the benefits listed in Figure 11-2. Furthermore, as of Oracle 11gR2, the performance of SQL calls from within a Java stored procedure is significantly worse than those from PL/SQL or Java running outside the database. This may well improve given that with the JDBC performance from outside the database is excellent. The algorithmic performance with the 11g just-in-time compiler, on the other hand, is better than that of PL/SQL and almost on par with Java outside the database.

Avaloq uses Java if something is not possible in PL/SQL, such as OS calls prior to Oracle 10g, or where an existing Java library greatly simplifies the work. For example, the Avaloq installer checks the signature of ZIP files using Java and the database provisioning system transfers LOBs between databases using Java over JDBC—rather than PL/SQL over database links, which only support LOBs in DDL and not DML. The availability of many libraries is definitely a strength of the Java ecosystem. This fact is, however, often overrated. For business applications, often only infrastructure libraries are useful, and even those might be insufficient. For example, none of the Java logging frameworks support per-entry security, grouping of log calls of the same problem into a single entry, or a workflow on entries. Furthermore, the constant appearance of new libraries can lead to Compulsive Latest Framework Adoption Disorder, which commonly manifests itself in many similar libraries being used in a single product because the effort for a complete refactoring of large products is prohibitive. Last but not least, PL/SQL also comes with a formidable number of libraries: the *PL/SQL Packages and Types Reference* has grown to 5,900 pages in 11gR2.

A benefit of Java is that the same code, such as data validation, can run in the database and in another tier. An alternative for the latter case is the generation of code in PL/SQL and another language from a domain-specific language. In the Avaloq Banking System, over half of the PL/SQL code is generated from higher-level domain-specific languages.

Whereas Oracle lets the developer decide between PL/SQL and Java as implementation language on a subprogram (procedure or function) by subprogram basis, I try to avoid a difficult-to-maintain wild mix.

Java stored procedure is actually a misnomer. The Oracle database includes a complete Java Virtual Machine (JVM). It is, therefore, possible to write stored procedures in any of the dozens of language with a compiler that generates Java byte code. From aspect-oriented programming with AspectJ to functional programming with Scala, however, none of the languages sport a seamless SQL embedding.

SQLJ, a preprocessor-based extension of Java, adds syntactic sugar for simpler SQL integration and automatic bind variables. However, it lacks compile-time checking of embedded SQL and dependency tracking for automatic invalidation after modifications of referenced objects. Automatic invalidation would require an enhancement of the JVM and cannot be added by means of a language extension.

SQLJ support is spotty. Few IDEs support SQLJ. Oracle itself ceased supporting SQLJ in the original 10g release. Following customer complaints, SQLJ reappeared in the 10.1.0.4 patch set.

.NET and C-Based External Procedures

External procedures, or subprograms as they are interchangeably called in the Oracle documentation, are subprograms with a PL/SQL call specification and an implementation in another language. By coding stored procedures in .NET, you restrict yourself to running the Oracle database on Windows. External procedures, written in C or another language callable from C, hamper portability. Furthermore, they run in their own processes. Thus, C-based external procedures have no significant advantage over business logic in a middle tier except that they can be called through the database.

Limits of the Database as PL/SQL-Based Application Server

If you are a hammer, everything looks like a nail. As a software engineer, on the other hand, you should be aware of the applicability limits of an architecture blueprint. The described business logic in PL/SQL in the database solution is an excellent fit for data centric ERP applications. On the other hand, it is not a good fit for computationally intensive applications requiring little data interaction.

Furthermore, PL/SQL is not my first choice for the following tasks:

- *CPU intensive tasks*: PL/SQL's algorithmic performance is below that of C and Java. Furthermore, Oracle license costs apply to PL/SQL. Java in commercial application servers incurs similar license costs, whereas no runtime license is required to run C or standalone Java programs. In the Avaloq Banking System, less than 50 percent of the CPU usage is PL/SQL; the rest is SQL.

- *Programs using very large collections in memory*: PL/SQL collections may require significantly more memory than their C counterparts. I take an in-depth look at memory usage later in this chapter.

- *Very complex data structures*: PL/SQL collections and records are sufficient for most tasks. However, others can be more easily expressed in a language with generic types, in-memory references, and automated garbage collection.

■ **Note** Vendor independence is sometimes cited as a reason against proprietary stored procedure languages. This argument is invalid because most applications are never ported to another database and because achieving good performance and correct concurrency handling on different databases requires multiple specific implementations rather than a single generic implementation. Tom Kyte argues this point in detail in *Expert Oracle Database Architectures* (Apress, 2005). I support every word he says on this topic in his book (and my paycheck doesn't come from Oracle). It's a different point if you don't like a particular database vendor. But you should make the best use of the database you choose.

Soft Factors

Even though Java may have more sex appeal than PL/SQL, I've found that it is not harder (and, unfortunately, not easier) to hire PL/SQL programmers than to hire their Java counterparts. The learning curve is not much different. PL/SQL is easy to learn. The big challenges, especially for new graduates, are to understand the business requirements, learn programming in the large, grasp the application-specific frameworks and patterns, and write efficient SQL.

SQL is also a problem if the business logic is written in Java. Of course, the trivial SQL statements can be generated by an object relation mapper. But the SQL statements that follow a few simple patterns are not the problem in PL/SQL either—it's the complex statements that must be hand coded for optimal performance.

Making the start easy for a new hire in a company with a multimillion line application is one of the main requirements of successful programming in the large.

Requirements of Programming in the Large

Having established the case for business logic in the database, let's see how best to master all the PL/SQL you will write. Programming in the large can involve programming by larger groups of people or by smaller groups over longer time periods. Often the people maintaining a software solution change. As a case in point, none of the creators of PL/SQL in Oracle 6 work in the PL/SQL group anymore. Because it is common for over two thirds of the lifetime cost of a piece of software to go to maintenance, efficiency in maintenance is a key requirement.

Programming in the large requires an approach that delivers in time, budget, and external product quality to the users during the initial creation and future maintenance of software. Ignoring the process aspects, which are largely independent of the architecture and programming language, you need a high internal product quality to achieve the external goals. The main factors of internal product quality are simplicity, ease of understanding, extendibility, and reusability. The business-logic-in-the-database architecture is the cornerstone for simplicity. The other goals are achieved with naming and coding conventions, modularization, and object-oriented programming. The implementation of these aspects differs among programming languages. In this chapter, I explain how to implement these aspects in PL/SQL. Due to space constraints, I omit other relevant aspects of programming in the large, such as tooling, and of handling the usually associated large data volumes, such as information lifecycle management and design for performance and scalability.

Successful programming in the large requires successful programming in the small. If code that somebody else wrote five years ago crashes, you will be thankful if she or he followed proper exception handling and error logging practices (which I omit in this chapter for brevity). Likewise, you'll be glad if the code you modify contains unit tests or contracts in the form assertions, so you know you aren't likely to break any of the 200 callers of the subprogram you change to fix the bug. Any type of programming requires logical thinking and pedantic exactness.

Uniformity through Conventions

Uniformity is a necessity for programming in the large because it allows developers to understand each other's code quickly and thoroughly. For example, if the primary key column of every table is called id and every reference to it is <table>_id, anybody who comes across a foo_id knows immediately that it references foo.id. Uniformity also ensures that developers don't constantly reformat someone else's code and thereby waste time, introduce regressions, and create diffs in which it is hard to distinguish the semantic changes from the cosmetic changes.

Uniformity can be achieved through conventions. In most cases, no conventions are better or worse than others; their sole value lies in providing the foundation for uniformity. For example, driving on the right-hand side of the road is as good as driving on the left-hand side. The choice is arbitrary. But every country must adopt one of the two conventions to avoid chaos. Likewise, there is no advantage in using trailing commas rather than leading commas to separate parameters. However, mixing the two in a single program impedes readability.

Unfortunately, there are no standard naming and formatting conventions for PL/SQL as there are for Java. Chapter 14 provides a set of coding conventions and Steven Feuerstein has three sets of PL/SQL coding conventions at `http://bit.ly/8WPRiy`. Whether you adopt one of the aforementioned conventions or make up your own is unimportant as long as you have a convention to which everybody in your organization adheres.

There are three ways to guarantee adherence to a convention. The best is to use an IDE that automatically establishes the convention either as you type or upon selecting auto format. Whatever cannot be handled in this manner must be enforced—ideally, through automatic tools rather than reliance on manual reviews. The last option to guarantee adherence is hope, which might work with a small project but not when programming in the large.

Sometimes large applications contain sources that, for historical reasons, adhere to different conventions. In this case, you must decide whether it is worth the effort to make all sources comply with one standard; if you want to keep multiple standards for different, clearly separated parts of the application; or if all new sources should adhere to a single standard. In any case, every source must consistently follow a single convention. If the chosen approach is to move to a single convention, complete sources must be adapted at once. Syntactic adaptations to adhere to a different convention must not be mixed with semantic changes, such as bug fixes, in a single repository check in. Otherwise, code auditing becomes very difficult.

The rationale behind a convention can be rendered obsolete by a new Oracle release or other changes. For example, before Oracle 10g, the PL/SQL compiler accepted different default values for input parameters in the package specification and body and just used the values provided in the package specification. To avoid wrong assumptions, the Avaloq convention was not to specify any default values for exported subprograms in the package body. Starting in 10g, the compiler checks that the default values are the same if listed in both the specification and the body. Thus, you can duplicate the default values without risk so that the developer doesn't have to open the specification when working in the body. The moral of the story is that you should periodically check the rationale behind every convention, especially if the convention also has disadvantages.

For most aspects regulated by conventions, it doesn't matter what the convention says because the sole benefit of the convention is the resulting uniformity. There are, however, aspects for which good reasons exist to go one way rather than another. For example, if your IDE supports only auto-formatting with leading commas, it doesn't make sense if your convention prescribes trailing commas. I present here selected aspects specific to PL/SQL for which there is a strong rationale to follow a particular practice.

Abbreviations

Identifiers in SQL and PL/SQL can be only 30 bytes long. To make a descriptive name fit these requirements, you need to omit unnecessary words (such as "get") and abbreviate long words. You can achieve consistency in abbreviations by maintaining a list of abbreviations and checking all names against that list. You must also add to that list those words which you specifically choose never to abbreviate. You can even add a synonym list against which you check new entries to avoid multiple entries for the same concept.

To check consistent abbreviation usage, all identifiers must be split into their parts and checked against the abbreviation registry. The identifiers to be checked can be found in the Oracle data dictionary, in views such as user_objects and user_tab_columns. From Oracle 11g onward, all identifiers used in PL/SQL programs are stored in user_identifiers if the unit is compiled with `plscope_settings="identifiers:all"`. You may want to enable this new feature called PL/Scope at the system level by issuing

```
SQL> alter system set plscope_settings="identifiers:all";
```

and recompiling all user PL/SQL units. The view user_plsql_object_settings shows for which objects this setting is in effect.

Because lower-case and mixed-case identifiers require double quotes in SQL and PL/SQL, they are not used. Instead, identifier parts are usually separated by an underscore.

The following code listing shows a simplified version of an abbreviation checker. The table abbr_reg holds the registered abbreviations. The package abbr_reg# provides a procedure ins_abbr to insert a new abbreviation and chk_abbr to check whether only registered abbreviations are used as identifier parts.

You can populate the registry with calls such as abbr_reg#.ins_abbr('abbr', 'abbreviation') and check consistent usage with abbr_reg#.chk_abbr.

```
create table abbr_reg(
  abbr                      varchar2(30)  primary key  -- Abbreviation, e.g., ABBR
  ,text                     varchar2(100) not null     -- Abbreviated text, e.g., ABBREVIATION
  ,descn                    varchar2(400)              -- Description, explain concept
) organization index;
create unique index abbr_reg#u#1 on abbr_reg(text);

create or replace package abbr_reg#
is
  ----------------------------------------------------------------------------
  -- Registry of abbreviations for SQL and PL/SQL identifier parts, such as
  -- ABBR for ABBREVIATION and REG for REGISTRY. All identifiers must be made up
  -- of registered abbreviations separated by underscores, e.g. abbr_reg.
  -- Contains also terms not to be abbreviated.
  ----------------------------------------------------------------------------


  ----------------------------------------------------------------------------
  -- Insert an abbreviation into the registry.
  ----------------------------------------------------------------------------
  procedure ins_abbr(
    i_abbr                  varchar2
    ,i_text                 varchar2
    ,i_descn                varchar2 := null
  );

  ----------------------------------------------------------------------------
  -- Check whether only registered abbreviations are used as identifier parts.
  ----------------------------------------------------------------------------
  procedure chk_abbr;
end abbr_reg#;

create or replace package body abbr_reg#
is
  procedure ins_abbr(
    i_abbr                  varchar2
    ,i_text                 varchar2
    ,i_descn                varchar2
  )
  is
  begin
    insert into abbr_reg(abbr, text, descn)
    values(upper(trim(i_abbr)), upper(trim(i_text)), i_descn);
  end ins_abbr;

  ----------------------------------------------------------------------------
  procedure chk_ident(
    i_ident                 varchar2
    ,i_loc                  varchar2
  )
```

```
is
  l_start_pos              pls_integer := 1;
  l_end_pos                pls_integer := 1;
  l_abbr_cnt               pls_integer;
  l_part                   varchar2(30);
  c_ident_len      constant pls_integer := length(i_ident);
begin
  while l_start_pos < c_ident_len loop
    -- DETERMINE NEXT PART --
    while    l_end_pos <= c_ident_len
          and substr(i_ident, l_end_pos, 1) not in ('_', '#', '$')
    loop
      l_end_pos := l_end_pos + 1;
    end loop;
    l_part := upper(substr(i_ident, l_start_pos, l_end_pos - l_start_pos));

    -- CHECK WHETHER THE PART IS A REGISTERED ABBREVIATION --
    select count(*)
    into   l_abbr_cnt
    from   abbr_reg
    where  abbr = l_part;

    if l_abbr_cnt = 0 then
      dbms_output.put_line('Unregistered part ' || l_part || ' in ident ' || i_ident
                       || ' at ' || i_loc || '.');
    end if;

    -- INIT VARIABLES FOR NEXT LOOP --
    l_end_pos := l_end_pos + 1;
    l_start_pos := l_end_pos;
  end loop;
end chk_ident;

----------------------------------------------------------------------------
procedure chk_abbr
is
begin
  -- PL/SQL USING PL/SCOPE --
  for c in (
    select name
          ,object_type
          ,object_name
          ,line
    from   user_identifiers
    where  usage = 'DECLARATION'
    order by object_name, object_type, line
  ) loop
    chk_ident(
      i_ident => c.name
     ,i_loc   => c.object_type || ' ' || c.object_name || ' at line ' || c.line
    );
  end loop;
```

```
    -- OTHER ITEMS: USER_OBJECTS, USER_TAB_COLUMNS, ... --
    -- ...
  end chk_abbr;

end abbr_reg#;
```

Since only one hundred lines of PL/SQL code are needed to build the checker, there is no excuse not to build one. PL/Scope makes this process much easier than trying to parse your source from user_source or your source code repository.

▓ **Note** Oracle does not use abbreviations consistently in the data dictionary. For example, the term "index" is spelled out once and abbreviated differently twice in the views user_indexes and user_ind_columns and the column idx of user_policies. Presumably, Oracle doesn't fix this because backward compatibility in public APIs is more important than consistent abbreviations.

Pre- and Suffixes for PL/SQL Identifiers

Many PL/SQL developers add prefixes to identifiers to indicate their scope or type. For example, local variables are prefixed with l_, constants with c_, input parameters with i_, and types with t_. There are two good reasons to add a prefix or a suffix to every PL/SQL identifier. Both have to do with avoiding scope capture.

PL/SQL automatically turns PL/SQL variables in static SQL statements into bind variables. Consider the following function, which should return the employee name for the specified employee number from the emp table of the SCOTT schema created by demobld.sql script from Oracle. In this example, I don't use any prefixes for the parameter empno and the local variable ename.

```
create or replace function emp#ename(empno emp.empno%type)
return emp.ename%type
is
  ename                        emp.ename%type;
begin
  select  ename
  into    ename
  from    emp
  where   empno = empno;

  return ename;
end emp#ename;
```

The function doesn't do what I would like it to do. Both occurrences of empno in the where clause refer to the table column empno rather than to the input parameter because every identifier is resolved to the most local declaration. In this case, the most local scope is the SQL statement with the table emp. Hence, the where condition is equivalent to emp.empno = emp.empno, which is the same as emp.empno is not null. Unless I have exactly one entry in the table emp, the function will throw an exception.

```
SQL> truncate table emp;
```

```
Table truncated.

SQL> insert into emp(empno, ename) values (7369, 'SMITH');

1 row created.
```

With exactly one row in the table, the function returns the name of this row independent of the actual parameter. I ask for the name of the employee with empno 21 and get the name of the employee with empno 7369.

```
SQL> select emp#ename(21) from dual;

EMP#ENAME(21)
----------------------------------------------------------------
SMITH

1 row selected.
```

With two or more rows in the table, the function always returns an ORA-01422.

```
SQL> insert into emp(empno, ename) values (7499, 'ALLEN');

1 row created.

SQL> select emp#ename(7369) from dual;
select emp#ename(7369) from dual
       *
ERROR at line 1:
ORA-01422: exact fetch returns more than requested number of rows
ORA-06512: at "K.EMP#ENAME", line 5
```

You can avoid scope capture by adding a prefix or a suffix to the input parameter empno, such as i_empno. Let's generalize this rule to say that every PL/SQL identifier should have a prefix or a suffix that is not used in column names. The minimum length for the prefix or suffix is two bytes—that is, a letter and an underscore as separator. You can use this prefix to convey additional semantics, such as the scope of a variable or the mode of a parameter without wasting another precious one of the thirty bytes.

An alternative to the prefix is to qualify all PL/SQL variables inside SQL statements with the name of the declaring block, e.g., empno = emp#ename.empno. The advantage of this approach is that it prevents unnecessary invalidation when a column is added to the table because the compiler knows that no scope capture can occur. Bryn Llewellyn describes this aspect of Oracle 11g fine-grained dependency tracking in http://bit.ly/dSMfto. I don't use this approach because edition-based redefinition is the better solution to prevent invalidation during online upgrades and because I find the syntax clumsy.

Of course, adding an l_ prefix to every local variable does not avoid scope capture in nested PL/SQL blocks. Fully qualified notation for all PL/SQL identifiers in all nested blocks would solve this at the cost of wordiness.

The second reason for including prefixes or suffixes in PL/SQL identifiers is to avoid confusion with the large number of keywords in SQL and PL/SQL and the built-in functions declared in standard and dbms_standard. As of Oracle 11gR2, there are 1,844 SQL keywords such as *table* and names of built-in functions such as *upper*, which are listed in v$reserved_words.

```
SQL> select count(distinct keyword)
  2  from    v$reserved_words;

COUNT(DISTINCTKEYWORD)
----------------------
                  1844
```

1 row selected.

The PL/SQL keywords are listed in appendix D of the *PL/SQL Language Reference*, but not available in a view. If you're not careful in the selection of your own identifiers, you shadow the Oracle implementation. In the following example, the implementation of upper, which returns the argument in lowercase rather than the Oracle-provided standard function with the same name, is executed:

```
create or replace procedure test
  authid definer
is
  function upper(i_text varchar2) return varchar2
  is
  begin
    return lower(i_text);
  end upper;
begin
  dbms_output.put_line(upper('Hello, world!'));
end test;

SQL> exec test
hello, world!

PL/SQL procedure successfully completed.
```

What appears artificial in this small example may well occur in practice in a large package maintained by someone other than the original author. For example, the original author may have implemented a function regexp_count when the application still ran under 10g. After the upgrade to 11gR2, the new maintainer may have added a call to regexp_count somewhere else in the package, expecting the newly added SQL built-in function with the same name (but possibly different semantics) to be invoked.

Oracle provides warnings to prevent the abuse of keywords. Unfortunately, warnings are usually disabled. If you enable all and recompile the test procedure, you get the desired error or warning, depending upon whether you set plsql_warnings to error:all or enable:all.

```
SQL> alter session set plsql_warnings='error:all';

Session altered.

SQL> alter procedure test compile;

Warning: Procedure altered with compilation errors.

SQL> show error
Errors for PROCEDURE TEST:
```

```
LINE/COL ERROR
-------- --------------------------------------------------------------------
4/12    PLS-05004: identifier UPPER is also declared in STANDARD or is a SQL built-in
```

In summary, adding a prefix or a suffix to every PL/SQL identifier can solve problems with scope capture. I use prefixes for variables and parameters to avoid scope capture in static SQL, but I don't bother to add prefixes or suffixes to functions or procedures because clashes with keywords are rare and because scope capture cannot occur in SQL with functions with parameters.

To differentiate between lists and elements thereof, it is common to add a plural suffix to lists such as associative arrays. Alternatively, suffixes to indicate the type, such as _rec for record and _tab for associative array types, are used to distinguish between elements and lists and at the same time convey additional semantic information at the cost of several characters. I use the type suffix notation in this chapter for clarity because I will be comparing implementations using different types. I use the hash sign as suffix for packages to avoid name clashes with tables of the same name.

■ **Note** The proper usage of prefixes and suffixes can also easily be checked with PL/Scope. Lucas Jellema has an example of this at http://technology.amis.nl/blog/?p=2584.

Modularization of Code and Data

Proper modularization is the foundation for scalability of the development team and maintainability of an application. Modularization brings the benefits of "divide and conquer" to software engineering. The key aspects of modularization are the following:

- *Decomposability*: It must be possible to decompose every complex problem into a small number of less complex subproblems that can be worked on separately.

- *Modular understandability*: In a large application, it must be possible to understand any part in isolation without knowing much or anything at all about the rest of the application. This property is called modular understandability. Programming in the large often means that a person works on an application with several million lines of code that already existed before she or he joined the company. Clearly, this can be done in an efficient manner only if the application satisfies modular understandability.

- *Modular continuity*: Continuity has two aspects. First, a small change to the specification must lead to a change in only one or a few modules. Second, a change in a module must easily be shown not to cause a regression in other modules. Modular continuity is especially important for interim patches that, due to their frequency and urgency, may not be as well tested as major releases.

- *Reusability*: A solution to a problem in one part of an application must be reusable in another part. The more general goal of composability (that is, the construction of new, possibly very different systems out of existing components) is commonly required only for basis frameworks.

> ■ **Note** Decomposability and composability are often conflicting goals. Decomposability is achieved by top-down design. It leads to specific modules, which may be unsuitable for composition in general. Composability, on the other hand, is based on bottom-up design, which leads to general designs that are often inefficient and too costly for special cases (unless a module can be reused many times, justifying a large investment).

These aspects of modularization can be achieved with modules by adhering to the following rules:

- *Information hiding (abstraction)*: Every module explicitly separates the public interface for its clients from its private implementation. This can be compared to a TV: its interface is a remote control with a few buttons and its implementation consists of complex circuits and software. TV viewers don't need to understand the implementation of the TV.

- *Small interfaces*: The interfaces are as small as possible in order not to restrict future improvements of the implementation.

- *Few interfaces and layering*: Every module uses as few interfaces from other modules as possible to reduce collateral damage if an interface needs to be changed in an incompatible way and to generally improve modular continuity. Most architectures are layered, where modules from higher layers, such as the business logic, may call modules from lower layers, such as data access, but not vice versa.

- *Direct mapping*: Each module represents a dedicated business concept and encompasses the data and operations necessary to do a single task and to do it well.

How do these general requirements and design principles translate to PL/SQL? A module maps on different levels of granularity to a subprogram, a package, a schema, or sets of any of the previous items. Subprograms as units of abstraction are the same in PL/SQL and most other procedural language and therefore not discussed here in more detail.

I restrict the discussion to technical modularization and ignore modularization in source code versioning, deployment, customization, marketing, and licensing, for which the technical modularization is often a precondition. I start with packages and then describe how to implement larger modules with and without schemas.

Packages and Associated Tables as Modules

PL/SQL explicitly provides packages to be used as modules that meet the previously mentioned requirements. Information hiding is supported by separating the package specification from its implementation. To ensure that the clients need to consult only the specification and don't rely on implementation details that may change, the package specification must be properly documented. A brief description of the semantics and intended usage of the overall package and each interface element (such as subprograms and types) suffices. The fact that there is no standard HTML API generation tool similar to JavaDoc available for PL/SQL is no excuse not to document package specifications. Users won't mind reading the documentation in the package specification. In fact, in an ad-hoc survey, most Java developers told me that they look at JavaDoc in the Java sources rather than the generated HTML.

Information hiding can even be implemented literally by wrapping the body but not the specification. Oracle does this for most public APIs, such as dbms_sql. Be aware, though, that wrapped code can be unwrapped, losing only comments in the process.

Every element exposed in a package specification can be used by any other program in the same schema and in another schema that has been granted execute privilege on the package. PL/SQL does not support protected export like Java or read-only export of variables like Oberon-2. This is not needed: APIs for different types of clients can be implemented by different packages.

Packages also provide for efficient development with separate, type-safe compilation. Clients can be compiled against the package specification and are never invalidated if only the body is modified. With the introduction of fine-grained dependency tracking in 11g, clients are invalidated only if the package specification changes in a relevant way. The drawback of this approach is that without a just-in-time compiler (which PL/SQL doesn't have) no cross-unit inlining is possible (except for standalone procedures, which PL/SQL doesn't currently support either).

▓ **Note** To keep the interface small, most procedures should be declared only in the package body and not exported through the specification in production code. To test them, they can be exported in test builds using conditional compilation, as described by Bryn Llewellyn at `http://bit.ly/eXxJ9Q`.

To extend modularization from PL/SQL code to table data, every table should be modified by only a single package. Likewise, all select statements referencing only a single table should be contained in this single package. On the other hand, select statements referencing multiple tables associated with different packages are allowed to break the one-to-one mapping. Views may be used to introduce an additional layer of abstraction. However, it is usually not practical to introduce a view for every join between two tables associated with different packages.

There are multiple approaches to detect violations of the previously mentioned rules for table accesses. All approaches described here must be viewed as software engineering tools to find bugs during testing and not as means to enforce security. Except for the trigger and the fine-grained auditing approaches, a transitive closure (e.g., with a hierarchical query) is required to drill down through views to the underlying tables.

I describe two compile-time approaches in summary form in a single section and three runtime approaches in detail under separate headings. The runtime approaches are more complex and contain techniques of interest beyond the specific cases. The main problem with the runtime approaches is that they require test cases that trigger the execution of all relevant SQL statements.

Detecting Table Accesses by Static Analysis

There are two compile-time approaches based on static analysis:

- *Searching in the source text*: This approach is usually surprisingly quick with a good tool, unless there are lots of views whose occurrences also need to be searched. However, this approach requires a PL/SQL parser to be automated.

- *Dependencies*: The view user_dependencies lists only static dependencies and does not distinguish between DML and read-only access. PL/Scope does not contain information on SQL statements.

Detecting Table Accesses by Probing the Shared Pool

The view v$sql contains recently executed SQL that is still in the shared pool. The column program_id references the PL/SQL unit that caused the hard parse. For example, the following statement shows all PL/SQL sources that issued DML against the above table abbr_reg. To also see select statements, simply remove the condition on command_type.

```
SQL> select ob.object_name
  2         ,sq.program_line#
  3         ,sq.sql_text
  4  from   v$sql         sq
  5         ,all_objects ob
  6  where  sq.command_type in (2 /*insert*/, 6 /*update*/, 7 /*delete*/, 189 /*merge*/)
  7    and sq.program_id = ob.object_id (+)
  8    and upper(sq.sql_fulltext) like '%ABBR_REG%';

OBJECT_NAME          PROGRAM_LINE# SQL_TEXT
-------------------- ------------- --------------------------------------------------------
ABBR_REG#                       10 INSERT INTO ABBR_REG(ABBR, TEXT, DESCN) VALUES(UPPER(:

1 row selected.
```

The shared pool probing approach has several shortcomings.

- Only the PL/SQL unit that caused the hard parse is returned. If the same SQL occurs in multiple units (even though it shouldn't in hand-written code), you won't find the others. If the hard parse is triggered by an anonymous block, you don't get any relevant information.

- You have to catch the SQL before it is flushed out of the shared pool. The Statspack, ASH, and AWR views on SQL don't contain the column program_id.

- You need to use an approximate string match, which may return too much data, because the target table of a DML is visible only in the SQL text. Tables from a select clause can be matched exactly by joining v$sql_plan. Alternatively, you can create on-the-fly wrapper procedures containing the SQL texts, get the references from all_dependencies, and drop the wrapper procedures again.

- Truncates are listed as generic lock table in the SQL text.

Detecting Table Accesses with Triggers

Triggers are another option to log or block access. The following trigger checks that all DML to the table abbr_reg is made from the package abbr_reg# or a subprogram called from it:

```
create or replace trigger abbr_reg#b
before update or insert or delete or merge
on abbr_reg
begin
```

```
  if dbms_utility.format_call_stack not like
      '%package body% K.ABBR_REG#' || chr(10) /*UNIX EOL*/|| '%' then
    raise_application_error(-20999,'Table abbr_reg may only be modified by abbr_reg#.');
  end if;
end;
```

As expected, DML from abbr_reg# is tolerated, but direct DML or DML from another package is not.

```
SQL> exec abbr_reg#.ins_abbr('descn', 'description')

PL/SQL procedure successfully completed.

SQL> insert into abbr_reg(abbr, text) values('reg', 'registry');
insert into abbr_reg(abbr, text) values('reg', 'registry')
            *
ERROR at line 1:
ORA-20999: Table abbr_reg may only be modified by abbr_reg#.
ORA-06512: at "K.ABBR_REG#B", line 3
ORA-04088: error during execution of trigger 'K.ABBR_REG#B'
```

Instead of calling the expensive dbms_utility.format_call stack, you can use a package body global variable in abbr_reg#, set the variable to true before accesses to the table abbr_reg and false after, and call from the trigger a procedure in abbr_reg# that checks whether the variable is true or not.

Detecting Table Accesses with Fine-Grained Auditing

Since Oracle doesn't provide on-select triggers, you have to use a workaround to detect read access. The three options are fine-grained auditing, RLS predicates, and Database Vault. All require the Enterprise Edition. Database Vault is an additionally priced option. Here is the approach with fine-grained auditing. I log all distinct callers into the table call_log.

```
create table call_log(
   object_schema            varchar2(30)
  ,object_name              varchar2(30)
  ,policy_name              varchar2(30)
  ,caller                   varchar2(200)
  ,sql_text                 varchar2(2000 byte)
  ,constraint call_log#p primary key(object_schema, object_name, policy_name
                                     ,caller, sql_text)
) organization index;
```

■ **Note** Oracle puts a limit onto the maximum size of an index entry based on the block size as described in My Oracle Support (MOS) Note 136158.1. I ran this example on a database with 8K block size and AL32UTF8 character set, in which each character can occupy up to 4 bytes. To get the most information into the index, which is used to avoid duplicate entries upon creation, I specify the length semantics of the column sql_text to be byte.

The table gets filled by the procedure call_log_ins, which is called by the fine-grained auditing framework for every SQL statement execution, corresponding roughly to a statement-level trigger.

```
create or replace procedure call_log_ins(
  i_object_schema             varchar2
,i_object_name               varchar2
,i_policy_name               varchar2
)
is
  pragma autonomous_transaction;
  l_caller                    call_log.caller%type;
  l_current_sql               call_log.sql_text%type;

  -------------------------------------------------------------------------------
  -- Returns the call stack below the trigger down to the first non-anonymous block.
  -------------------------------------------------------------------------------
  function caller(
    i_call_stack              varchar2
  ) return varchar2
  as
    c_lf            constant varchar2(1) := chr(10);
    c_pfx_len       constant pls_integer := 8;
    c_head_line_cnt constant pls_integer := 5;
    l_sol                    pls_integer;
    l_eol                    pls_integer;
    l_res                    varchar2(32767);
    l_line                   varchar2(256);
  begin
    l_sol := instr(i_call_stack, c_lf, 1, c_head_line_cnt) + 1 + c_pfx_len;
    l_eol := instr(i_call_stack, c_lf, l_sol);
    l_line := substr(i_call_stack, l_sol, l_eol - l_sol);
    l_res := l_line;
    while instr(l_line, 'anonymous block') != 0 loop
      l_sol := l_eol + 1 + c_pfx_len;
      l_eol := instr(i_call_stack, c_lf, l_sol);
      l_line := substr(i_call_stack, l_sol, l_eol - l_sol);
      l_res := l_res || c_lf || l_line;
    end loop;
    return l_res;
  end caller;

begin
  l_caller := nvl(substr(caller(dbms_utility.format_call_stack), 1, 200), 'external');
  l_current_sql := substrb(sys_context('userenv','current_sql'), 1, 2000);
  insert into call_log(
    object_schema
   ,object_name
   ,policy_name
   ,caller
   ,sql_text
  ) values (
    i_object_schema
```

```
      ,i_object_name
      ,i_policy_name
      ,l_caller
      ,l_current_sql
    );
    commit;
exception
    when dup_val_on_index then
      rollback;
end call_log_ins;
```

Finally, I need to add the policy. I want the procedure call_log_ins to be called for every access to the table abbr_reg in a select statement. To audit DML as well, I must add the parameter statement_types => 'select,insert,update,delete' to the call or create separate policies for select and for DML.

```
begin
    dbms_fga.add_policy(
      object_name     => 'ABBR_REG'
      ,policy_name    => 'ABBR_REG#SELECT'
      ,handler_module => 'CALL_LOG_INS'
    );
end;
/
```

I test the implementation by calling abbr_reg#.chk_abbr from my running example, like so:

```
SQL> exec abbr_reg#.chk_abbr

PL/SQL procedure successfully completed.

SQL> select object_name, policy_name, caller, sql_text from call_log;
```

OBJECT_NAME	POLICY_NAME	CALLER	SQL_TEXT
ABBR_REG	ABBR_REG#SELECT	35 package body K.ABBR_REG#	SELECT COUNT(*) FROM ABBR_REG WHE

```
1 row selected.
```

Neither the DML trigger nor the fine-grained auditing fires on truncate of a table or partition. To log or block these, a DDL trigger is required.

Modules Containing Multiple Packages or Submodules

Subprograms and packages are necessary building blocks. Yet higher level modules are required to group the thousands of packages in large programs. For example, the Avaloq Banking System is divided functionally into core banking, execution & operation, and front modules. Each module is further subdivided, such as execution & operation into finance and payment. On each modularization level, accepted dependencies are declared.

Orthogonally, the system is divided technically into data access, business logic, and presentation layers. The two modularizations can be treated separately or be combined as shown on the left side of Figure 11-3. Atomic modules, such as Finance UI, are defined as intersections of the two modularizations. Technical modules are shown as enclosing boxes, first-level functional modules by identical shading and name prefixes of the atomic modules belonging together.

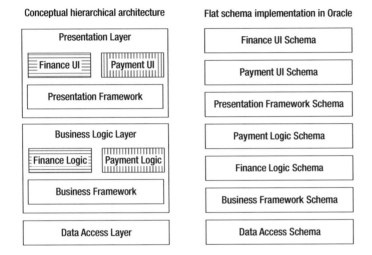

Figure 11-3. Nested layer and module architecture and a flat implementation with schemas

Modules as sets of packages and other object types can be represented in Oracle with schemas and grants. Both schemas and grants are very flexible, yet low level. For example, schemas cannot be nested. Thus the conceptual hierarchical architecture on the left side of Figure 11-3 must be mapped to a flat set of schemas, as shown on the right side. Furthermore, interfaces have to be implemented as individual grants to each client schema.

Therefore, the introduction of a modularization model with a higher abstraction level than Oracle schemas and grants improves the understandability by reducing the number of items. Oracle schemas and grants can be generated from this model if desired or the model can be used to check the modularization within a schema.

The precise requirements for the metamodel depend upon the chosen modularization. Typically, the model must meet the following requirements:

1. Represent the modules of the system, such as Payment Logic and Business Framework in Figure 11-3.

2. Map every database object to exactly one module, such as the PL/SQL package pay_trx# to the module Payment Logic.

3. Declare the dependencies between modules, such as Payment Logic using Business Framework but not vice versa. Only acyclic dependencies should be permitted.

4. Declare the interfaces (APIs) of each module—that is, which objects may be referenced from depending modules.

5. Provide an extension/upcall mechanism that allows a module to be extended by another module that depends on it. For example, the Presentation Framework may declare an extension point for menu items and the Payment UI may create a menu item. When this menu item is selected, the Presentation Framework must make an upcall to the Payment UI. This call is termed *upcall* because it goes against the dependency chain: the Payment UI depends on the Presentation Framework and not the other way around.

In PL/SQL, upcalls are usually implemented with generated dispatchers or dynamic SQL as described in the section on object-oriented programming. If modules are implemented with schemas, the appropriate execute object privilege must be granted.

Grants derived from dependencies and grants required for upcalls can be separated by placing generated code, such as upcall dispatchers, into a separate schema.

No additional privileges are required at all if upcalls are implemented with dynamic dispatch as provided by user defined types.

Optionally, the metamodel can provide the following:

6. Support hierarchical nesting of modules along one or more dimensions, such as functionality and technical layering. Alternatively, dedicated entities, such as layers and functional components, can be introduced. Dedicated entities can be defined with specific semantics, such as layers allowing only downward dependencies.

7. Allow for friend modules, which may use additional APIs not available to normal client modules. For example, the Payment Logic module may provide additional APIs only for the Payment UI module. Likewise, it may be justified to widen the interface between selected modules for performance reasons. Friendship can be declared individually or be derived from other entities, such as functional domain modules.

8. Manage exceptions. Upon the introduction of a (new) target modularization, it may not be feasible to immediately remove all illegal dependencies, yet no additional illegal dependencies must be created going forward. Therefore, the temporarily tolerated illegal dependencies must be managed.

The target architecture model of an application can be defined centrally in a single file and/or on a per-module basis. The central definition is suited for global high-level entities, such as layers. The per-module configuration is more scalable and is required for multiple independent module providers. The manifest files of OSGi modules (called bundles in OSGi terminology) are examples of a per-module declaration.

Figure 11-4 shows a possible metamodel in form of an entity-relationship diagram. I list the previously mentioned requirements in parentheses behind the element that satisfies it. At the top of Figure 11-4 are the modules (requirement 1) and the module types. Hierarchies of modules (requirement 6) and dependencies between modules (requirement 3) are shown below. With these entities you can model the architecture depicted on the left in Figure 11-3.

The objects (such as PL/SQL units, tables, and views) come next. Each object belongs to exactly one module (requirement 2). Each object is either private to its containing module or is an interface of some type (requirement 4). In the example are several types of interfaces: interfaces for other atomic modules with the same functional module parent, interfaces for other modules in the same application, and public interfaces that can be used by external applications. The additional code table code_object_intf_mode is used to differentiate between read-only access and read-write access to tables.

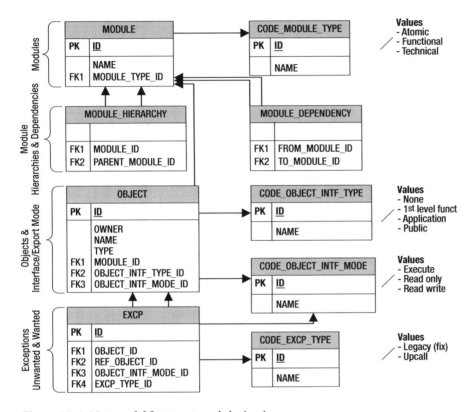

Figure 11-4. Metamodel for target modularization

At the bottom of Figure 11-4 are the structures to represent the two types of exceptions as described by the two values at the bottom right.

- Legacy bugs to be fixed (requirement 8). These should occur only temporarily if an application is newly modularized or if the target modularization is changed.

- Accepted exceptions for upcalls (requirement 5).

Friend modules (requirement 7) are only supported implicitly by functional modules. Explicit friend modules could be supported by introducing different module dependency types or by modeling friends as additional exception type.

Modules as groups of PL/SQL packages and other object types can be implemented with database schemas or within schemas. The two approaches can be combined, such as schemas for the top level modules and grouping within schemas for the submodules.

Schemas as Modules

Schemas provide a common modularization for all types of objects from PL/SQL units to tables at a higher granularity than packages. Every object belongs to a schema. Schemas can be used to divide an application into parts. For example, an application could be divided into three schemas containing the data access, business logic, and presentation layer, respectively.

Schemas are synonymous with users in Oracle. I create the schemas for the three-layer architecture as follows:

```
SQL> create user data_access identified by pwd account lock;

User created.

SQL> create user business_logic identified by pwd account lock;

User created.

SQL> create user presentation identified by pwd account lock;

User created.
```

Grants for Object Privileges

To access objects in another schema, the respective object privilege needs to be granted. I first create a table and a procedure in the data_access schema to have a concrete example.

```
SQL> create table data_access.t(x number);

Table created.

SQL> create or replace procedure data_access.d(
  2    i_x                       number
  3  )
  4  is
  5  begin
  6    insert into t(x) values (abs(i_x));
  7  end d;
  8  /
```

■ **Note**   To create these objects, you must log on with a user that has the "Create any table" and "Create any procedure" privileges or grant create session, table, and procedure to data_access.

Without an explicit grant, the procedure data_access.d cannot be accessed from a subprogram in the schema business_logic:

```
SQL> create or replace procedure business_logic.b(
  2     i_x                          number
  3  )
  4  is
  5  begin
  6    data_access.d(trunc(i_x));
  7  end b;
  8  /

Warning: Procedure created with compilation errors.

SQL> show error
Errors for PROCEDURE BUSINESS_LOGIC.B:

LINE/COL ERROR
-------- --------------------------------------------------------
6/3      PL/SQL: Statement ignored
6/3      PLS-00201: identifier 'DATA_ACCESS.D' must be declared
```

After granting the execute privilege, I can successfully compile the procedure.

```
SQL> grant execute on data_access.d to business_logic;

Grant succeeded.

SQL> alter procedure data_access.d compile;

Procedure altered.
```

Grants are a flexible, yet low-level construct:

- Grants are always on individual items. A separate grant is required for each of the interface packages.

- Grants are always to a specific schema. Just because business_logic can access data_access.d doesn't mean that presentation can access data_access.d. By granting presentation privileges only on business_logic and not on data_access, you could enforce a strict layering in which all calls from presentation to data_access must go through business_logic. Grants provide selective information hiding whereas a package exports an item either for all clients or for none.

- If two schemas should be granted the same privileges on a set of objects (such as Finance Logic and Payment Logic on Business Framework in Figure 11-3), the grants must be made individually because roles are not considered in definer rights procedures.

- It is not possible to grant a schema (for example, one containing generated code) access to all objects of another schema. Separate grants for each object are required.

- For tables, the select, insert, update, and delete privileges can be granted separately. Thus, schemas make it possible to enforce data consistency by restricting DML to a single schema and allowing other modules direct read access for optimal performance. There is no performance overhead for accessing object in other schemas with definer rights procedures.

Because grants are so low level and because a large application may require thousands of grants, it is best to generate the grants from a metamodel, as in Figure 11-4.

■ **Note** All privileges on individual objects are visible in the view all_tab_privs. System, role, and column privileges can be found in all_sys_privs, all_role_privs, and all_column_privs, respectively.

Accessing Objects in Other Schemas

Like packages, schemas introduce namespaces. There are two options to reference an object in another schema. The fully-qualified notation requires the schema name in each reference (such as data_access.d in the previous example). Alternatively, you can create a synonym for the procedure d in the schema business_logic and then access the procedure directly as d.

```
SQL> create or replace synonym business_logic.d for data_access.d;

Synonym created.
```

Some developers prefer the synonym approach to reduce the amount of typing and to avoid strong coupling. Because interfaces should be few and explicit, I prefer the fully-qualified notation, which prevents name clashes.

■ **Note** If a schema contains an object of the same name as another schema, it becomes impossible to reference objects in this other schema using the fully-qualified notation because the scoping rules of PL/SQL resolve the reference to the object. For example, if you add a table data_access to the schema business_logic, you can no longer reference any objects in PL/SQL from data_access in business_logic except through synonyms.

Optimal Usage of Schemas

The ideal number of schemas for an application depends upon the architecture. For hand-written code, 20–100 packages might be a desirable average size for a schema. With fewer packages, the number of modules as well as the sizes and number of interfaces may become too high, which violates the aforementioned rules for modularization and causes administration overhead for grants and structural changes. With more packages, the units of modular understandability are too big.

Schemas have several additional features that should be considered during design. They are useful for deploying third-party components because their namespaces prevent name clashes. Schemas can be used to enforce security because the security is checked in all cases (including dynamic SQL) by the database. Beyond the object privileges described previously, schemas can be used to centralize critical operations into a small, "micro-kernel"-like schema with many system privileges. Furthermore, schemas have various properties (such as quotas on tablespaces) and are units of enabling editioning.

The Road to Modularization with Schemas

In spite of all these benefits, most large applications that I know use only one or a handful of schemas. The reasons seem to be nontechnical or historic and unrelated to any problems with schemas in current versions of Oracle. The aforementioned synonym approach for referencing objects in other schemas provides a relatively simple migration path to using schemas for modularization. Only DDL statements and queries against the data dictionary might have to be adapted, and dynamic SQL needs to be checked to find missing grants. Of course, such a migration provides only a starting point for future cleanup and yields no magic modularization improvement.

After the migration to schemas, no additional modularization violations referencing previously unreferenced schema private objects are possible. For example, if there is no reference from the new schema business_logic to the table data_access.t before the migration, no object privilege needs to be granted for the migration. If a developer later tries to reference data_access.t in a package in business_logic, the PL/SQL compiler will catch the error. On the other hand, additional references to already-used schema private objects are possible because grants are to schemas rather than to individual objects therein. If, in this example, an existing package body of business_logic accessed data_access.t before the migration, the grant would have been required for the one-to-one migration, and additional violations would not be flagged by the compiler. It is therefore necessary keep a list of pre-existing violations and check for new violations. The check can be fine granular using all_identifiers for references between PL/SQL units and using all_dependencies for references involving other object types.

Modularizing an existing application is very expensive because if the modularization was not enforced in the past, the application is full of illegal references to non-referenceable modules and to non-interface objects. The high cost of changing these reference is attributed to past sins and not to any shortcomings of schemas. The lessons to be learned are that new applications must be modular from the beginning and that modularity must be enforced.

Modularization within Schemas

If an application is confined to a single schema for backward compatibility or organizational reasons or if schemas are only to be used for top-level modules, the application can still be subdivided into logical modules inside a schema.

Modules within schemas are often implicitly represented by name prefixes, such as da_ for objects in the data access layer. The correct usage of module prefixes can be checked as previously described for scope prefixes.

Since modularization without enforcement is worthless and because the database doesn't help with enforcement of modularization within schemas, you need to create your own checks. For the checks you need the target and the actual modularization. The target modularization is given by an instance of the metamodel of Figure 11-4 (shown earlier). The actual modularization is in the code. Static dependencies are listed in all_dependencies and all_identifiers. I have already discussed the detection of references to tables in dynamic SQL. For references to PL/SQL in dynamic SQL and PL/SQL, you can use the SQL area or Database Vault.

Database Vault is a security option that restricts access to specific areas in an Oracle database from any user, including users who have administrative access. You use access restrictions to catch modularization violations—that is, direct accesses of non-interface units of other modules. In the example, I assume that every PL/SQL unit has a module prefix in its name and that interface units have a _intf# suffix. Database Vault provides the option to execute a custom PL/SQL function to check the validity of each PL/SQL call (or other object usage) in a rule. The function gets the call stack and verifies that the topmost caller/callee pair of units in the schema to be checked (in the example k) satisfies the modular reference requirements. To avoid checks for the checking function, I create the latter in a separate schema x.

```
create or replace function x.valid_call
return pls_integer
is
  c_lf                constant varchar2(1)     := chr(10);       -- UNIX
  c_intf_like         constant varchar2(8)     := '%\_INTF#';    -- Interface unit suffix
  c_owner_like        constant varchar2(5)     := '% K.%';       -- Schema to be checked
  c_module_sep        constant varchar2(1)     := '_';           -- Separator of module prefix
  c_head_line_cnt     constant pls_integer     := 4;             -- Ignored lines in call stack
  l_call_stack                 varchar2(4000);                   -- Call stack
  l_sol                        pls_integer;                      -- Start pos of current line
  l_eol                        pls_integer;                      -- End pos of current line
  l_callee                     varchar2(200);                    -- Called unit
  l_caller                     varchar2(200);                    -- Calling unit
  l_res                        boolean;                          -- Valid call?
begin
  l_call_stack := dbms_utility.format_call_stack;
  l_sol := instr(l_call_stack, c_lf, 1, c_head_line_cnt);
  l_eol := instr(l_call_stack, c_lf, l_sol + 1);
  l_callee := substr(l_call_stack, l_sol, l_eol - l_sol);
  -- ONLY CALLS TO NON INTERFACE UNITS OF K MAY BE INVALID --
  if l_callee like c_owner_like and l_callee not like c_intf_like escape '\' then
    l_callee := substr(l_callee, instr(l_callee, '.') + 1);
    -- FIND TOPMOST CALLER OF SCHEMA K, IF ANY, AND CHECK FOR SAME MODULE PREFIX --
    loop
      l_sol := l_eol + 1;
      l_eol := instr(l_call_stack, c_lf, l_sol + 1);
      l_caller := substr(l_call_stack, l_sol, l_eol - l_sol);
      if l_caller like c_owner_like then
        l_caller := substr(l_caller, instr(l_caller, '.') + 1);
        l_res := substr(l_callee, 1, instr(l_callee, c_module_sep))
                   = substr(l_caller, 1, instr(l_caller, c_module_sep));
      end if;
      exit when l_eol = 0 or l_res is not null;
    end loop;
  end if;
  return case when not l_res then 0 else 1 end;
end valid_call;
```

The Database Vault schema needs to be granted the execute privilege on this function so it can be used in rules.

```
SQL> grant execute on x.valid_call to dvsys;

Grant succeeded.
```

Then I create the rule set, rule, and command rule to execute the function valid call on the execution of each PL/SQL unit logged in as Database Vault Owner.

```
declare
  c_rule_set_name  varchar2(90)  := 'Modularization within schema check';
  c_rule_name      varchar2(90)  := 'CHKUSER';
begin
  -- RULE SET: CHECK RULES AND FLAG VIOLATIONS
  dvsys.dbms_macadm.create_rule_set(
    rule_set_name    => c_rule_set_name
   ,description      => null
   ,enabled          => dvsys.dbms_macutl.g_yes
   ,eval_options     => dvsys.dbms_macutl.g_ruleset_eval_all
   ,audit_options    => dvsys.dbms_macutl.g_ruleset_audit_off
   ,fail_options     => dvsys.dbms_macutl.g_ruleset_fail_show
   ,fail_message     => 'Modularization check failed'
   ,fail_code        => -20002
   ,handler_options  => dvsys.dbms_macutl.g_ruleset_handler_off
   ,handler          => null
  );
  -- RULE: CHECK WHETHER CALL IS VALID
  dvsys.dbms_macadm.create_rule(
    rule_name => c_rule_name
   ,rule_expr => 'X.VALID_CALL = 1'
  );
  -- ADD RULE TO RULE SET
  dvsys.dbms_macadm.add_rule_to_rule_set(
    rule_set_name => c_rule_set_name
   ,rule_name     => c_rule_name
  );
  -- MATCH CRITERIA: EXECUTE RULE SET ON PL/SQL EXECUTE OF OBJECTS OWNED BY USER K
  dvsys.dbms_macadm.create_command_rule(
    command        => 'EXECUTE'
   ,rule_set_name  => c_rule_set_name
   ,object_owner   => 'K'
   ,object_name    => '%'
   ,enabled        => dvsys.dbms_macutl.g_yes
  );
  commit;
end;
/
```

With this in place, a call from k.m1_2 to k.m1_1 is legal because both units have the same module prefix of m1. On the other hand, a call from k.m2_3 to k.m1_1 is blocked because the caller belongs to module m2 and the callee to module m1.

```
SQL> create or replace procedure k.m1_1 is begin null; end;
  2  /

Procedure created.
```

```
SQL> create or replace procedure k.m1_2 is begin execute immediate 'begin m1_1; end;'; end;
  2  /

Procedure created.

SQL> exec k.m1_2

PL/SQL procedure successfully completed.

SQL> create or replace procedure k.m2_3 is begin execute immediate 'begin m1_1; end;'; end;
  2  /

Procedure created.

SQL> exec k.m2_3
BEGIN k.m2_3; END;

*
ERROR at line 1:
ORA-01031: insufficient privileges
ORA-06512: at "K.M1_1", line 1
ORA-06512: at "K.M2_3", line 1
ORA-06512: at line 1
```

This approach works for both static and dynamic SQL (native and dbms_sql). Instead of blocking violations, they could also be permitted and logged.

■ **Note**   To install Database Vault you must relink the binaries, as explained in appendix B of the *Database Vault Administrator's Guide*, and add the Oracle Label Security (precondition) and Oracle Database Vault options with the Database Creation Assistant dbca. As of 11.2.0.2, there are few gotchas with the installation. The option must be installed with dbca as the SQL*Plus scripts don't install NLS properly. The required special character in the password for the DV Owner must not be the last character. If you use deferred constraints, patch 10330971 is required. With AL32UTF8 as database character set, a tablespace with 16K or bigger block size is required because of the aforementioned maximum size of an index entry based on the block size. If your default block size is smaller, set db_16k_cache_size and create a tablespace with 16 K block size for database vault. Furthermore, Database Vault purposely introduces some restrictions, which you may need to lift again for your application to work properly.

Modularization with Schemas vs. within Schemas

Table 11-1 summarizes the pros and cons of modularization with and within schemas. An abstract model of the target modularization is required in both cases.

Table 11-1. Comparison of Modularization with Schemas and within Schemas

Property	With Schemas	Within Schemas
Access rights without low-level object privileges	(generated)	✓
Modularization enforced by database	✓	
Risk-free dynamic SQL and PL/SQL (no runtime errors due to missing privileges)		✓
Full 30 bytes for identifier (no loss of real estate for module prefix)	✓ (using fully qualified notation)	

Object-Oriented Programming with PL/SQL

With modularization you are still missing two important pieces to efficiently create large programs. First, all your memory structures have been restricted to the representation of singletons. However, most applications must support multiple instances of a kind, such as multiple banking transactions. Second, reuse has been restricted to reuse exactly as is. In practice, though, reuse commonly requires adaptations—without having to duplicate the source code and maintain multiple copies going forward. For example, payment and stock-exchange transactions in a banking system share many commonalities but differ in other aspects, such as their booking logic. The goal is to have only a single implementation of the shared functionality rather than just reuse of ideas and developers. Object-oriented programming addresses these issues.

Reuse brings many benefits: it reduces the time to market, the implementation cost, and the maintenance effort because there is only one implementation to maintain. Because there is only one implementation, more expert resources can be spent on making it correct and efficient.

Object-oriented programming increases reuse in two ways.

- *Reuse with adaptations:* Inheritance and subtype polymorphism allow you to extend a data type and treat instances of its subtypes as if they were instances of the supertype. In the example, you can define a generic banking transaction type as supertype and subtypes for payment and stock exchange transactions. Dynamic binding (also called late binding, dynamic dispatch, and virtual methods) adds the final piece to the puzzle. You can declare, possibly abstract without an implementation, a procedure book on the supertype banking transaction and adapt it for the two subtypes. The generic framework calls the procedure book, and each banking transaction executes the logic corresponding to its actual subtype.

- *Reuse of data and associated functionality:* Object-oriented analysis promotes decomposition based on data rather than functionality. Because data is longer lived than the particular functionality provided on it, this typically provides for better reuse.

Bertrand Meyer summarizes both aspects in his book *Object-Oriented Software Construction:* "Object-oriented software construction is the building of software systems as structured collections of possibly partial abstract data type implementations."

■ **Note**   Generic types (F-bounded polymorphism) are sometimes mistakenly considered to be a requirement for object-oriented programming, especially since their addition to Java 5. However, generic types are an orthogonal concept that is, for example, also present in the original version of Ada, which is not object-oriented. Generic types are most commonly used for collections. PL/SQL supports strongly typed collections, such as associative arrays, as built-in language construct. This suffices in most cases.

Whereas PL/SQL is not an object-oriented programming language per se, it is possible to program in an object-oriented way using user-defined types (UDT) or PL/SQL records. Multiple instances and reuse with adaptations are implemented as follows:

- PL/SQL does not support in-memory references (pointers) directly. The only way to create an arbitrary number of instances of an object at runtime is to store the instances in collections, such as associative arrays. References are represented as collection indexes.

- UDTs support dynamic binding out of the box. With records, you can implement dynamic dispatch yourself using dynamic SQL or a static dispatcher.

I start with UDTs because their alternate name object types suggests that they are the natural choice for object-oriented programming and then explain why records are the better option in most cases.

Object-Oriented Programming with User-Defined Types

Oracle added user-defined types (UDT) in Oracle 8 amid the object hype, addressing mostly storage aspects and leaving out some useful programming features. UDTs are schema-level objects. I can create a base type for banking transactions as follows:

■ **Note**   Oracle uses two synonymous terms for user-defined types (UDT). In the *Database Object-Relational Developer's Guide*, they are called *object types* because Oracle wanted to support object orientation in the database. The same term *object type* has been used for much longer as the type of an entry in all_objects, such as packages and tables. The second synonym *abstract data type* (ADT) is used in the *PL/SQL Language Reference*, because UDTs can be used to implement the mathematical concept of an ADT—that is, a data structure defined by a list of operations and properties of these operations. I use the unambiguous term *UDT* in this chapter. UDTs include varrays and nested tables, which I don't discuss here. UDTs are useful as types of parameters for subprograms called externally.

```
create or replace type t_bank_trx_obj is object (
  s_id                     integer
 ,s_amount                 number

  ---------------------------------------------------------------------------
  -- Returns the amount of the transaction.
  ---------------------------------------------------------------------------
 ,final member function p_amount return number

  ---------------------------------------------------------------------------
  -- Books the transaction.
  ---------------------------------------------------------------------------
 ,not instantiable member procedure book(
   i_text                  varchar2
   )
) not instantiable not final;
```

The type t_bank_trx_obj has two attributes s_id and s_amount to hold the state. In addition, it has two methods. The function p_amount is declared as final, meaning that it cannot be overridden in subtypes. The procedure book is declared as non-instantiable (abstract), meaning that it just declared and specified, but not implemented. The syntax for the type body is PL/SQL extended by the modifiers for subprograms, like so:

```
create or replace type body t_bank_trx_obj is
  final member function p_amount return number
  is
  begin
    return s_amount;
  end p_amount;
end;
```

Inheritance and Dynamic Dispatch with UDTs

UDTs provide for inheritance. I can define a payment transaction type as a specialization of the general banking transaction type.

```
create or replace type t_pay_trx_obj under t_bank_trx_obj (
  ---------------------------------------------------------------------------
  -- Creates a payment transaction. Amount must be positive.
  ---------------------------------------------------------------------------
  constructor function t_pay_trx_obj(
   i_amount                number
  ) return self as result

 ,overriding member procedure book(
   i_text                  varchar2
   )
);
```

I can also add an explicit constructor to prohibit payment transactions with negative amounts. The constructor only takes the amount as input parameter, assuming that the ID gets initialized from a sequence. The keyword "self" denotes the current instance, like "this" in other languages.

■ **Note** Oracle creates a default constructor with all attributes in the order of declaration and the names of the attributes as input parameters. To prevent that, the default constructor creates a loophole (e.g., allowing the caller to create a payment with a negative amount), an explicit constructor with the same signature as the default constructor must be declared.

```
create or replace type body t_pay_trx_obj is
  constructor function t_pay_trx_obj(
   i_amount                 number
  ) return self as result
  is
  begin
    if nvl(i_amount, -1) < 0 then
      raise_application_error(-20000, 'Negative or null amount');
    end if;
    self.s_amount := i_amount;
    return;
  end t_pay_trx_obj;


  -------------------------------------------------------------------------
  overriding member procedure book(
   i_text                  varchar2
  )
  is
  begin
    dbms_output.put_line('Booking t_pay_trx_obj "' || i_text || '" with amount '
      || self.p_amount);
  end book;
end;
```

I can now use the two types to illustrate the dynamic dispatch. I assign a payment transaction to a variable of type t_bank_trx_obj and call the procedure book. Even though the static type of the variable is t_bank_trx_obj, the implementation of the actual type t_pay_trx_obj is executed.

```
SQL> declare
  2    l_bank_trx_obj              t_bank_trx_obj;
  3  begin
  4    l_bank_trx_obj := new t_pay_trx_obj(100);
  5    l_bank_trx_obj.book('payroll January');
  6  end;
  7  /
Booking t_pay_trx_obj "payroll January" with amount 100

PL/SQL procedure successfully completed.
```

Limitations of UDTs

So far, you have seen the good aspects of UDTs for object-oriented programming. Unfortunately, UDTs also have two major shortcomings.

- UDTs can use only SQL types, but not PL/SQL types (such as record and Boolean) in their specification because UDTs can be persisted in SQL.

- Unlike PL/SQL packages, UDTs don't support information hiding. It is not possible to declare any attributes or methods as private, or to add more attributes and methods in the body. Any client can access all members, as shown in the following example, in which I directly modify the amount:

```
create or replace procedure access_internal
is
  l_bank_trx_obj              t_bank_trx_obj;
begin
  l_bank_trx_obj := new t_pay_trx_obj(100);
  l_bank_trx_obj.s_amount := 200;
  l_bank_trx_obj.book('cheating');
end;
```

At least PL/Scope gives you a way to detect such accesses. The following select lists all static accesses to attributes and private methods, indicated by the prefix p_, from outside the declaring type and its subtypes:

```
SQL> select us.name, us.type, us.object_name, us.object_type, us.usage, us.line
  2  from   all_identifiers pm
  3         ,all_identifiers us
  4  where  pm.object_type = 'TYPE'
  5    and (
  6              pm.type = 'VARIABLE'
  7          or (pm.type in ('PROCEDURE', 'FUNCTION') and pm.name like 'P\_%' escape '\')
  8        )
  9    and pm.usage       = 'DECLARATION'
 10    and us.signature   = pm.signature
 11    and (us.owner, us.object_name) not in (
 12         select ty.owner, ty.type_name
 13         from   all_types ty
 14         start with ty.owner       = pm.owner
 15                and ty.type_name = pm.object_name
 16         connect by ty.supertype_owner = prior ty.owner
 17                and ty.supertype_name  = prior ty.type_name
 18       );

NAME      TYPE      OBJECT_NAME     OBJECT_TYPE  USAGE       LINE
--------  --------  --------------- ------------ ----------  ----
S_AMOUNT  VARIABLE  ACCESS_INTERNAL PROCEDURE    ASSIGNMENT   6

1 row selected.
```

PL/Scope distinguishes between assignment and reference. Unfortunately, hidden assignments in the form of passing an attribute as actual parameter for an out or in out parameters are visible only as references.

Persistence of UDTs

Object types can be persisted as table columns or as object tables. For example, all transactions can be stored in the following table:

```
create table bank_trx_obj of t_bank_trx_obj(s_id primary key)
object identifier is primary key;
```

This table can store objects of any subtype, such as payment transaction.

```
SQL> insert into bank_trx_obj values(t_pay_trx_obj(1, 100));
```

```
1 row created.
```

What looks easy at the beginning becomes very complex and cumbersome when type specifications change. The details are beyond the scope of this chapter. Furthermore, edition-based redefinition of types (and as of 11gR2, type bodies) is impossible for types with table dependents and subtypes thereof. Storing UDTs in tables is bad practice that may be justified only in Advanced Queuing tables and for some varrays. Of course, it is also possible to store the content of UDTs into relational tables with a table column per UDT attribute as described for records below.

Object-Oriented Programming with PL/SQL Records

PL/SQL record types provide an alternative implementation basis to UDTs for object-oriented programming in PL/SQL. Most people I know who do object-oriented programming in PL/SQL use records for object-oriented programming. Using records instead of UDTs solves several problems.

- PL/SQL types are allowed as types of fields and as parameters of subprograms.

- Multiple inheritance and subtyping are possible.

The disadvantage of using records is that you have to implement the dynamic dispatch yourself. Before I get to the dynamic dispatch, I will describe how to create an arbitrary number of object instances at runtime in memory and how to reference them.

Multiple Instances and In-Memory References with Collections

The object instances are stored in a collection. The collection and the record type are declared in the package body to implement information hiding. References are indexes into the collection. The index type is declared as subtype of pls_integer in the package specification because the references are used as arguments to exported subprograms. The following example shows the implementation of a heap using an associative array of bank transactions. I intersperse the code with explanatory text.

```
create or replace package bank_trx#
is
   ----------------------------------------------------------------------
   -- Type for references to t_bank_trx and subtypes thereof.
   ----------------------------------------------------------------------
   subtype t_bank_trx        is pls_integer;
```

I need to keep track of the actual type of each banking transaction instance.

```
   ----------------------------------------------------------------------
   -- Type for subtypes of t_bank_trx.
   ----------------------------------------------------------------------
   subtype t_bank_trx_type is pls_integer;
```

The constructor takes the type of the transaction as well as the individual elements. I prefix the subprograms with the name of the type. This allows me to wrap multiple types with a single package and give the types direct access to each other's internal representation.

```
   ----------------------------------------------------------------------
   -- Creates a banking transaction.
   ----------------------------------------------------------------------
   function bank_trx#new(
     i_bank_trx_type_id      t_bank_trx_type
    ,i_amount                number
   ) return t_bank_trx;
```

All other subprograms take the self reference i_bank_trx as the first argument. The procedure bank_trx#remv is required because there is no automatic garbage collection.

```
   ----------------------------------------------------------------------
   -- Removes (deletes) the banking transaction.
   ----------------------------------------------------------------------
   procedure bank_trx#remv(
     i_bank_trx             t_bank_trx
   );

   ----------------------------------------------------------------------
   -- Returns the amount of the transaction.
   ----------------------------------------------------------------------
   function bank_trx#amount(
     i_bank_trx             t_bank_trx
   ) return number;

   ----------------------------------------------------------------------
   -- Books the transaction.
   ----------------------------------------------------------------------
   procedure bank_trx#book(
     i_bank_trx             t_bank_trx
    ,i_text                 varchar2
   );
end bank_trx#;
```

■ **Note** The index of the associative array must not be confused with the ID stored inside the banking transaction. The index is the current in-memory "address" which can change if the transaction is persisted and read again. The ID is the unique and immutable identifier of the transaction. Using the ID as the index wouldn't work because the index is of type pls_integer, which has a smaller range than ID. Changing the associative array to be indexed by varchar2(38) instead of pls_integer to store any positive integer would result in higher memory usage and lower performance. For added type safety, a record with a single pls_integer element could be used as type of t_bank_trx instead.

The implementation of the package body bank_trx# is straightforward.

```
create or replace package body bank_trx#
is
```

The state of an object is represented in a record. The set of records is stored in an associative array.

```
type t_bank_trx_rec is record (
  bank_trx_type_id          t_bank_trx_type
 ,id                        integer
 ,amount                    number
);
type t_bank_trx_tab is table of t_bank_trx_rec index by t_bank_trx;
b_bank_trx_list             t_bank_trx_tab;
```

The function bank_trx#new assigns the record to the next free index.

```
function bank_trx#new(
  i_bank_trx_type_id        t_bank_trx_type
 ,i_amount                  number
) return t_bank_trx
is
  l_bank_trx                t_bank_trx;
begin
  l_bank_trx := nvl(b_bank_trx_list.last, 0) + 1;
  b_bank_trx_list(l_bank_trx).bank_trx_type_id := i_bank_trx_type_id;
  b_bank_trx_list(l_bank_trx).amount := i_amount;
  return l_bank_trx;
end bank_trx#new;
```

The procedure bank_trx#remv deletes the element.

```
procedure bank_trx#remv(
  i_bank_trx                t_bank_trx
)
is
begin
  b_bank_trx_list.delete(i_bank_trx);
end bank_trx#remv;
```

The function **bank_trx#amount** has the same implementation for all types of banking transactions, which can be given in the base type.

```
function bank_trx#amount(
   i_bank_trx                  t_bank_trx
) return number
is
begin
   return b_bank_trx_list(i_bank_trx).amount;
end bank_trx#amount;
```

The overridable procedure bank_trx#book has a different implementation for each type of banking transaction. The implementation in bank_trx# needs to call the code of the subtypes.

```
procedure bank_trx#book(
   i_bank_trx                  t_bank_trx
   ,i_text                     varchar2
)
is
begin
   <Dynamic dispath according to b_bank_trx_list(i_bank_trx).bank_trx_type_id>
end bank_trx#book;
end bank_trx#;
```

Subtypes

Before I illustrate the implementation of the dynamic dispatch, I will introduce the payment transaction subtype. As with the UDT implementation, the subtype in form of a package contains a constructor and its specialized implementation of the procedure book. Here is the code for the subtype:

```
create or replace package body pay_trx#
is
  function pay_trx#new(
     i_amount                   number
  ) return bank_trx#.t_bank_trx
  is
  begin
    if nvl(i_amount, -1) < 0 then
      raise_application_error(-20000, 'Negative amount');
    end if;
    return bank_trx#.bank_trx#new(
      i_bank_trx_type_id => bank_trx_type#.c_pay_trx
      ,i_amount          => i_amount
    );
  end pay_trx#new;

  ---------------------------------------------------------------------------
  procedure bank_trx#book(
     i_bank_trx                 bank_trx#.t_bank_trx
     ,i_text                    varchar2
  )
  is
```

```
  begin
    dbms_output.put_line('Booking t_pay_trx "' || i_text || '" with amount '
                         || bank_trx#.bank_trx#amount(i_bank_trx));
  end bank_trx#book;
end pay_trx#;
```

The package body pay_trx# references the list of banking transaction subtypes. The constant declaration package bank_trx_type# can be hand coded or generated.

```
create or replace package bank_trx_type#
is
  -- LIST OF SUBTYPES OF BANKING TRX. HAS NO BODY. --
  c_pay_trx          constant bank_trx#.t_bank_trx_type := 1;
end bank_trx_type#;
```

Dynamic Dispatch

UDTs natively support dynamic dispatch. With objects as records, you need to implement dynamic dispatch yourself. This can be done with dynamic SQL or a static dispatcher.

Dynamic Dispatch with Dynamic SQL

The statement to be invoked for bank_trx#book for each type of bank transaction is stored in a table.

```
SQL> create table bank_trx_dsp(
  2      method_name                varchar2(30)
  3     ,bank_trx_type_id           number(9)
  4     ,stmt                       varchar2(200)
  5     ,primary key(method_name, bank_trx_type_id)
  6   ) organization index;

Table created.

SQL> begin
  2      insert into bank_trx_dsp(
  3       method_name
  4      ,bank_trx_type_id
  5      ,stmt
  6      ) values (
  7       'bank_trx#book'
  8      ,bank_trx_type#.c_pay_trx
  9      ,'begin pay_trx#.bank_trx#book(i_bank_trx => :1, i_text => :2); end;'
 10      );
 11      commit;
 12  end;
 13  /

PL/SQL procedure successfully completed.
```

The implementation of the procedure bank_trx#.bank_trx#book executes the correct dynamic SQL based on the bank_trx_type_id:

```
procedure bank_trx#book(
  i_bank_trx               t_bank_trx
  ,i_text                  varchar2
)
is
  l_stmt                   bank_trx_dsp.stmt%type;
begin
  select stmt
  into   l_stmt
  from   bank_trx_dsp
  where  method_name       = 'bank_trx#book'
    and bank_trx_type_id = b_bank_trx_list(i_bank_trx).bank_trx_type_id;
  execute immediate l_stmt
  using i_bank_trx, i_text;
end bank_trx#book;
```

With all pieces in place, I can create and book a payment transaction.

```
SQL> declare
  2     l_my_payment              bank_trx#.t_bank_trx;
  3  begin
  4     l_my_payment := pay_trx#.pay_trx#new(100);
  5     bank_trx#.bank_trx#book(l_my_payment, 'payroll');
  6  end;
  7  /
Booking t_pay_trx "payroll" with amount 100

PL/SQL procedure successfully completed.
```

The call with dynamic SQL is slower and less scalable than a static PL/SQL call. Thanks to single statement caching in 10g and newer, the differences are small if every session uses mostly one type of banking transactions. Another difference to the static call is that if a dynamic call returns an exception, a rollback is performed to the savepoint set implicitly before the call.

Dynamic Dispatch with a Static Dispatcher

A static dispatcher in form of an if statement is the alternative to dynamic SQL. Such a dispatcher can be generated from metadata or coded by hand. The procedure bank_trx#.bank_trx#book calls the dispatcher with the type of the transaction.

```
procedure bank_trx#book(
  i_bank_trx               t_bank_trx
  ,i_text                  varchar2
)
is
```

353

```
begin
  bank_trx_dsp#.bank_trx#book(
    i_bank_trx          => i_bank_trx
   ,i_bank_trx_type_id => b_bank_trx_list(i_bank_trx).bank_trx_type_id
   ,i_text             => i_text
  );
end bank_trx#book;
```

The dispatcher, of which I only show the body, simply calls the correct implementation based on the type.

```
create or replace package body bank_trx_dsp#
is
  procedure bank_trx#book(
    i_bank_trx              bank_trx#.t_bank_trx
   ,i_bank_trx_type_id      bank_trx#.t_bank_trx_type
   ,i_text                  varchar2
  )
  is
  begin
    if i_bank_trx_type_id = bank_trx_type#.c_pay_trx then
      pay_trx#.bank_trx#book(
        i_bank_trx => i_bank_trx
       ,i_text            => i_text
      );
    else
      raise_application_error(-20000, 'Unknown bank_trx_type_id: ' || i_bank_trx_type_id);
    end if;
  end bank_trx#book;
end bank_trx_dsp#;
```

If there are very many subtypes, the if statement in the dispatcher has many branches. A binary search with nested if statements provides the best runtime performance in this case. If the dispatcher is coded by hand, it can be implemented in bank_trx# instead of a separate package.

Additional Attributes and Methods in Subtypes

If payment transactions require additional methods not present in general banking transactions, I just add them to the package pay_trx#. If payment transactions require an additional attribute (say, a settlement type), I create a corresponding record type and associative array in the body of pay_trx#, show in bold here:

```
create or replace package body pay_trx#
is
  type t_pay_trx_rec is record (
    settle_type_id          t_settle_type
  );
  type t_pay_trx_tab is table of t_pay_trx_rec index by bank_trx#.t_bank_trx;
  b_pay_trx_list          t_pay_trx_tab;
```

```
function pay_trx#new(
  i_amount                     number
 ,i_settle_type_id            t_settle_type
) return bank_trx#.t_bank_trx
is
  l_idx                        bank_trx#.t_bank_trx;
begin
  if nvl(i_amount, -1) < 0 then
    raise_application_error(-20000, 'Negative amount');
  end if;
  l_idx := bank_trx#.bank_trx#new(
    i_bank_trx_type_id => bank_trx_type#.c_pay_trx
   ,i_amount           => i_amount
  );
  b_pay_trx_list(l_idx).settle_type_id := i_settle_type_id;
  return l_idx;
end pay_trx#new;
```

To free the additional state I also need bank_trx#.bank_trx#remv to call a remove method in pay_trx# through the dispatcher.

Persistence of Objects as Records

To persist banking transactions implemented in memory with the record approach, I create a plain vanilla table with the respective columns.

```
create table bank_trx(
  id                           integer
 ,bank_trx_type_id            integer
 ,amount                       number
 ,constraint bank_trx#p primary key(id)
);
```

The additional attributes of subtypes, such as the settlement type of payment transactions, can be stored in supplementary tables.

```
create table pay_trx(
  bank_trx_id                  integer
 ,settle_type_id              integer
 ,constraint pay_trx#p primary key(bank_trx_id)
 ,constraint pay_trx#f#1 foreign key(bank_trx_id) references bank_trx(id)
);
```

The disadvantage of this approach is that multiple tables must be accessed. Alternatively, you can store the additional fields in the base table, a fine solution if there are few fields and you don't mind the conceptual ugliness. A third approach is to get rid of the base table bank_trx and store all attributes in pay_trx. The disadvantages of this form of object-relational mapping are two-fold: you have to create a union-all view over all subtypes to find a transaction if you know only its ID, and Oracle cannot enforce unique IDs over all types of transactions stored in multiple tables using a simple primary key constraint.

Assessment

The good news is that it is possible to do object-oriented programming in PL/SQL as well as in C and most other procedural programming languages. The bad news is that getting all the features requires some additional glue code. Fortunately, the glue code may largely be generated.

If an application requires only a handful of type hierarchies and if they are just a few levels deep, PL/SQL is suitable. If, on the other hand, hundreds of different types with subtypes are required, I'd look for a different solution. The Avaloq Banking System described at the beginning of this chapter has two type hierarchies: banking transactions and static data objects. Each hierarchy has only two levels: a base type and hundreds of subtypes. In addition, there are dozens of standalone types without any subtypes. For these standalone types, no dispatchers are required, resulting in an implementation as simple as in an object-oriented language.

Memory Management

Large programs commonly require lots of memory, whether objects are stored in collections as described earlier or whether other patterns are used. Therefore, you need to know how to measure memory usage to detect problems, such as memory leaks. Collections consume most of the PL/SQL memory; therefore you need to understand how they allocate memory.

Most large PL/SQL applications use dedicated rather than shared server processes. Therefore, I focus on dedicated server processes and ignore shared server processes, in which the UGA (and, therefore, most PL/SQL memory) resides in the SGA.

■ **Note** With PL/SQL variables you can allocate more memory than defined by pga_aggregate_target, which specifies the target aggregate PGA memory available to all server processes attached to the instance. PL/SQL memory is considered untunable. Oracle simply allocates memory as requested as long as the OS provides it.

Measuring Memory Usage

There are multiple ways to measure the memory usage of processes, corresponding one-to-one to connections and in most cases also sessions. The view v$process is often used as a starting point.

```
SQL> select se.sid
  2         ,se.username
  3         ,round(pr.pga_used_mem / power(1024, 2))      pga_used_mb
  4         ,round(pr.pga_alloc_mem / power(1024, 2))     pga_alloc_mb
  5         ,round(pr.pga_freeable_mem / power(1024, 2)) pga_freeable_mb
  6         ,round(pr.pga_max_mem / power(1024, 2))       pga_max_mb
  7  from   v$session se
  8         ,v$process pr
  9  where  se.paddr = pr.addr
 10    and se.type != 'BACKGROUND'
 11  order by pr.pga_alloc_mem desc;
```

SID	USERNAME	PGA_USED_MB	PGA_ALLOC_MB	PGA_FREEABLE_MB	PGA_MAX_MB
173	K	35	39	3	39
91	K	16	28	10	28
50	K	19	23	3	24
376	K	13	13	0	13

The first three memory figures denote the currently used, allocated, and freeable memory, where used plus freeable roughly equals allocated. The column pga_max_mem returns the maximum size the process ever had. Note that your system may show slightly different values for all experiments in this section as memory usage depends upon the exact Oracle release and operating system.

The view v$process_memory, introduced in 10g but buggy prior to 11g, provides a drill-down. I illustrate this with a procedure that prints the current memory usage of the session.

```
create or replace procedure print_session_mem
is
begin
  dbms_output.put_line('Category  Allocated KB    Used KB  Max all KB');
  dbms_output.put_line('--------------------------------------------');
  for c in (
    select pm.*
    from   v$session         se
          ,v$process         pr
          ,v$process_memory pm
    where  se.sid   = sys_context('userenv', 'sid')
      and  se.paddr = pr.addr
      and  pr.pid   = pm.pid
  ) loop
    dbms_output.put_line(rpad(c.category, 10)
                      || to_char(round(c.allocated     / 1024), '999G999G999')
                      || to_char(round(c.used          / 1024), '999G999G999')
                      || to_char(round(c.max_allocated / 1024), '999G999G999'));
  end loop;
end print_session_mem;
```

I then print the initial memory usage.

```
SQL> set serveroutput on
SQL> exec print_session_mem
Category  Allocated KB    Used KB  Max all KB
--------------------------------------------
SQL               44         38          44
PL/SQL            38         33          38
Other            982        982

PL/SQL procedure successfully completed.
```

To allocate memory, I create a package with a global associative array.

```
create or replace package mem#
is
  type t_char1000_tab is table of varchar2(1000) index by pls_integer;
  g_list                        t_char1000_tab;
end mem#;
```

Next, I fill the global variable with data and print the memory usage again.

```
SQL> begin
  2     select lpad('x', 1000, 'x')
  3     bulk collect into mem#.g_list
  4     from   dual
  5     connect by level <= 100000;
  6  end;
  7  /

PL/SQL procedure successfully completed.

SQL> exec print_session_mem
Category  Allocated KB    Used KB  Max all KB
---------------------------------------------
SQL                 58         46       4,782
PL/SQL         114,052    113,766     114,056
Other            7,594      7,594

PL/SQL procedure successfully completed.
```

The PL/SQL memory usage jumped from 33 KB to 113,766 KB. The category Other, which contains miscellaneous structures, also increased. Next, I delete the associative array and measure the memory usage once more.

```
SQL> exec mem#.g_list.delete

PL/SQL procedure successfully completed.

SQL> exec print_session_mem
Category  Allocated KB    Used KB  Max all KB
---------------------------------------------
SQL                 58         45       4,782
PL/SQL         114,060         45     114,060
Other            7,586      7,586

PL/SQL procedure successfully completed.
```

The used PL/SQL memory decreased almost back to the initial value. The allocated memory stayed the same. Freeable memory can be returned to the operating system by calling the procedure dbms_session.free_unused_user_memory in the session. Because of the cost of deallocation and allocation, it should not be called too frequently.

```
SQL> exec dbms_session.free_unused_user_memory

PL/SQL procedure successfully completed.
```

```
SQL> exec print_session_mem
Category  Allocated KB   Used KB  Max all KB
---------------------------------------------
SQL               50         37       4,782
PL/SQL            58         49     114,068
Freeable       1,024          0
Other          1,084      1,830

PL/SQL procedure successfully completed.
```

The view v$process_memory_detail provides even more detail for a single process at a time. A snapshot is created by executing `alter session set events 'immediate trace name pga_detail_get level <pid>'`, where pid is obtained from v$process. The usefulness of v$process_memory_detail for PL/SQL developers is limited, because the returned heap names are not fully documented and because the breakdown is not by PL/SQL type or compilation unit. A detailed description is given in MOS Notes 822527.1 and 1278457.1.

The procedure dbms_session.get_package_memory_utilization, introduced in 10.2.0.5 and 11gR1, allows you to drill down to the PL/SQL units using the memory. This is perfect for finding memory leaks. This example shows the memory utilization after filling mem#.g_list:

```
SQL> declare
  2     l_owner_names              dbms_session.lname_array;
  3     l_unit_names               dbms_session.lname_array;
  4     l_unit_types               dbms_session.integer_array;
  5     l_used_amounts             dbms_session.integer_array;
  6     l_free_amounts             dbms_session.integer_array;
  7  begin
  8     dbms_session.get_package_memory_utilization(
  9       owner_names   => l_owner_names
 10      ,unit_names    => l_unit_names
 11      ,unit_types    => l_unit_types
 12      ,used_amounts  => l_used_amounts
 13      ,free_amounts  => l_free_amounts
 14     );
 15     for i in 1..l_owner_names.count loop
 16       dbms_output.put_line(
 17         case l_unit_types(i)
 18           when  7 then 'PROCEDURE    '
 19           when  8 then 'FUNCTION     '
 20           when  9 then 'PACKAGE      '
 21           when 11 then 'PACKAGE BODY'
 22           else        'TYPE     ' || lpad(l_unit_types(i), 3)
 23         end || ' '
 24      || rpad(l_owner_names(i) || '.' || l_unit_names(i), 26)
 25      || ' uses ' || to_char(round(l_used_amounts(i) / 1024), '999G999G999')
 26      || ' KB and has ' || to_char(round(l_free_amounts(i) / 1024), '999G999G999')
 27      || ' KB free.');
 28     end loop;
 29  end;
 30  /
PACKAGE BODY SYS.DBMS_SESSION            uses          2 KB and has          1 KB free.
PACKAGE      SYS.DBMS_SESSION            uses          0 KB and has          1 KB free.
```

```
PACKAGE BODY SYS.DBMS_OUTPUT            uses           2 KB and has        1 KB free.
PACKAGE      SYS.DBMS_OUTPUT            uses           0 KB and has        1 KB free.
PACKAGE      K.MEM#                     uses     108,035 KB and has    5,414 KB free.
PACKAGE BODY SYS.DBMS_APPLICATION_INFO  uses          1 KB and has        0 KB free.
PACKAGE      SYS.DBMS_APPLICATION_INFO  uses          0 KB and has        1 KB free.

PL/SQL procedure successfully completed.
```

The downside is that the procedure can analyze the memory usage of only the session it runs in.

The hierarchical profiler dbms_hprof provides an undocumented method for profiling memory allocation and deallocation in 11g. The procedure start_profiling has two new parameters, profile_pga and profile_uga. The following example shows how the latter can be used:

```
SQL> create or replace directory hprof_dir as '/tmp';

Directory created.

SQL> begin
  2    dbms_hprof.start_profiling(
  3      location    => 'HPROF_DIR'
  4     ,filename    => 'hprofuga'
  5     ,profile_uga => true
  6    );
  7  end;
  8  /

PL/SQL procedure successfully completed.

SQL> declare
  2      procedure alloc
  3      is
  4      begin
  5        select lpad('x', 1000, 'x')
  6        bulk collect into mem#.g_list
  7        from   dual
  8        connect by level < 100000;
  9      end alloc;
 10      procedure dealloc
 11      is
 12      begin
 13       mem#.g_list.delete;
 14       dbms_session.free_unused_user_memory;
 15      end dealloc;
 16  begin
 17      alloc;
 18      dealloc;
 19  end;
 20  /
```

```
PL/SQL procedure successfully completed.

SQL> exec dbms_hprof.stop_profiling

PL/SQL procedure successfully completed.
```

To analyze the generated profile, you can either use the same undocumented parameters in DBMS_HPROF.ANALYZE (which stores the byte output in the _TIME columns of DBMSHP_PARENT_CHILD_INFO) or pass the parameter -pga or -uga to plshprof.

```
oracle@af230d:af230d > $ORACLE_HOME/bin/plshprof -uga -output hprofuga hprofuga
PLSHPROF: Oracle Database 11g Enterprise Edition Release 11.2.0.2.0 - 64bit Production
[10 symbols processed]
[Report written to 'hprofuga.html']
```

This produces a HTML report, as shown in Figure 11-5.

Function UGA mem (bytes) Data sorted by Total Subtree UGA mem (bytes)

`23536 bytes (uga mem) & 17 function calls`

Subtree	Ind%	Function	Ind%	Descendants	Ind%	Calls	Ind%	Function Name
116922816	N/A	5800	24.6%	116917016	N/A	1	5.9%	anonymous_block.ALLOC (Line 2)
-116918984	-496766.6%	-116918984	-496766.6%	0	0.0%	1	5.9%	SYS.DBMS_SESSION.FREE_UNUSED_USER_MEMORY (Line 250)
116917016	N/A	116917016	N/A	0	0.0%	1	5.9%	static_sql_exec_line5 (Line 5)
-116910424	-496730.2%	8560	36.4%	-116918984	-496766.6%	1	5.9%	anonymous_block.DEALLOC (Line 10)
23536	100%	0	0.0%	23536	100%	4	23.5%	plsql_vm
23536	100%	6984	29.7%	16552	70.3%	4	23.5%	anonymous_block
4160	17.7%	4160	17.7%	0	0.0%	2	11.8%	SYS.DBMS_OUTPUT.GET_LINES (Line 180)
0	0.0%	0	0.0%	0	0.0%	1	5.9%	SYS.DBMS_SESSION._pkg_init
0	0.0%	0	0.0%	0	0.0%	1	5.9%	K_MEM#_pkg_init
0	0.0%	0	0.0%	0	0.0%	1	5.9%	SYS.DBMS_HPROF.STOP_PROFILING (Line 59)

Figure 11-5. UGA allocation and deallocation memory profile

The profile shows allocation and deallocation of memory for the UGA rather than allocation and deallocation within the UGA. Comparable information can be gathered by tracing OS calls with truss or similar utilities. Remember that this usage of the hierarchical profiler is undocumented and not supported by Oracle.

I have seen several cases where the memory reported by Oracle's dynamic performance views did not correspond to the figures reported by the OS. If you experience memory issues, it's always worthwhile to check on the OS as well. Help for analyzing out of process memory error can be found in MOS Notes 1088267.1 and 396940.1.

Historic PGA and UGA snapshot values of V$SYSSTAT and V$SESSTAT can be found in the workload repository and in Statspack views DBA_HIST_SYSSTAT, PERFSTAT.STATS$SESSTAT, and PERFSTAT.STATS$SYSSTAT. In my experience, this information is insufficient to analyze problems. Therefore, it is worthwhile to check the memory usage of long-running processes in an outer loop and log detailed information if a specified threshold is exceeded. If possible, processes should periodically restart themselves to recover from memory leaks and unreleased locks.

Collections

Because collections usually consume the majority of the PL/SQL memory, it is important to understand how memory is allocated for them and how to reduce their footprint. Oracle does not document the implementation of collections to allow for modifications in future releases. Therefore, you must measure the memory allocation yourself and be aware that information gathered this way may be rendered obsolete by a future Oracle release.

Many data types use up to double the space on 64bit versions of Oracle as compared to the 32bit versions. My measurements were made on Solaris 10 x86-64.

I illustrate the following points that may be relevant for your coding with associative arrays indexed by pls_integer:

- Associative arrays have an overhead of roughly 27 bytes for the key. This overhead is significant for an array of pls_integer or Boolean, but not for a larger payload (such as a complex record or a large string). In most cases it is better in terms of memory usage, performance, and conceptual clarity to use an associative array of a record instead of several associative arrays of basic types as in dbms_session.get_package_memory_utilization. With out-of-line allocation of the payload, the total overhead per element may be significantly larger than the 30 bytes for the key.

- Space for roughly 20 consecutive indices is allocated at once. Thus, in terms of memory usage and performance, it is better to use consecutive indices.

- As of 11.2.0.2, memory is freed for other usage or returned to the OS only upon deletion of the last element of an array. This holds true for the keys and small payloads stored inline. Memory for large payloads that are stored out of line is usually freed immediately.

- There may be a benefit in defining elements, such as varchar2, only as large as needed to avoid overallocation.

Associative arrays indexed by varchar2 differ in all but the last point. The overhead of the key is larger and depends on the actual length of the string. Space is allocated for only one element at a time and, in some cases, freed immediately upon deletion. Furthermore, arrays indexed by varchar2 are significantly slower than their counterparts indexed by pls_integer.

In terms of memory usage and performance, there is no benefit in using other collection types (namely varrays and nested tables).

So let me prove the above claims with the following procedure. I use conditional compilation to vary the length of the strings in the collection and to use the procedure with different collection types.

```
create or replace procedure coll_mem_usage(
  i_step                    pls_integer := 1
 ,i_elem_cnt                pls_integer := 1000000
)
is
  $IF $$COLL_TYPE = 0 $THEN
  type t_char_tab is table of varchar2($$string_len) index by pls_integer;
  $ELSIF $$COLL_TYPE = 1 $THEN
  type t_char_tab is table of varchar2($$string_len) index by varchar2(10);
  $ELSIF $$COLL_TYPE = 2 $THEN
  type t_char_tab is table of varchar2($$string_len);
  $ELSIF $$COLL_TYPE = 3 $THEN
```

```
    type t_char_tab is varray(2147483647) of varchar2($$string_len);
    $END
    c_string_len        constant pls_integer := $$string_len;
    l_str               constant varchar2($$string_len) := lpad('x', c_string_len, 'x');
    l_list                          t_char_tab;


    ---------------------------------------------------------------------------
    procedure print_plsql_used_session_mem(
      i_label                     varchar2
    )
    is
      l_used                      number;
    begin
      $IF DBMS_DB_VERSION.VERSION < 11 $THEN
      select pr.pga_used_mem
      $ELSE
      select pm.used
      $END
      into    l_used
      from    v$session         se
             ,v$process         pr
             ,v$process_memory pm
      where   se.sid        = sys_context('userenv', 'sid')
          and se.paddr      = pr.addr
          and pr.pid        = pm.pid
          and pm.category = 'PL/SQL';
      dbms_output.put_line(rpad(i_label, 18) || ' PL/SQL used '
                            || to_char(round(l_used / 1024), '999G999G999') || ' KB');
    end print_plsql_used_session_mem;
begin
    -- INIT --
    dbms_output.put_line(i_elem_cnt || ' elements of length ' || c_string_len || ' step '
                          || i_step || ' type ' || $$coll_type);
    print_plsql_used_session_mem('Init');

    -- ALLOCATE ELEMENTS --
    $IF $$COLL_TYPE = 2 OR $$COLL_TYPE = 3 $THEN /* NESTED TABLE, VARRAY */
    l_list := t_char_tab();
    l_list.extend(i_elem_cnt * i_step);
    $END
    for i in 1..i_elem_cnt loop
      l_list(i * i_step) := l_str;
    end loop;
    print_plsql_used_session_mem('Allocated');

    -- REMOVE ALL BUT 1 ELEMENT --
    for i in 2..i_elem_cnt loop
      $IF $$COLL_TYPE != 3 $THEN /* ASSOCIATIVE ARRAYS, NESTED TABLE */
      l_list.delete(i * i_step);
      $ELSE /* NO SINGLE ELEMENT DELETE IN VARRAY */
      l_list(i * i_step) := null;
      $END
```

363

```
  end loop;
  print_plsql_used_session_mem('1 element left');

  -- ADD ANOTHER c_element_cnt ELEMENTS --
  $IF $$COLL_TYPE = 2 OR $$COLL_TYPE = 3 $THEN /* NESTED TABLE, VARRAY */
  l_list.extend(i_elem_cnt * i_step);
  $END
  for i in (i_elem_cnt + 1)..(2 * i_elem_cnt) loop
    l_list(i * i_step) := l_str;
  end loop;
  print_plsql_used_session_mem('Allocated on top');

  -- DELETE ALL --
  l_list.delete;
  print_plsql_used_session_mem('All deleted');
end coll_mem_usage;
```

The procedure is invalid upon creation. It needs to be compiled with valid conditional compilation flags, such as collection type "associative array index by pls_integer", denoted by coll_type equal to 0, and string_len 10.

```
SQL> alter procedure coll_mem_usage compile plsql_ccflags='coll_type:0,string_len:10';

Procedure altered.
```

The valid procedure can be executed.

```
SQL> exec coll_mem_usage
1000000 elements of length 10 step 1 type 0
Init              PL/SQL used         0 KB
Allocated         PL/SQL used    36,144 KB
1 element left    PL/SQL used    36,144 KB
Allocated on top  PL/SQL used    72,272 KB
All deleted       PL/SQL used        16 KB

PL/SQL procedure successfully completed.
```

This output shows that the overhead for the key is 27 bytes. 36,144 KB divided by 1,000,000 entries gives 37 bytes per entry, of which 10 bytes are used by the string array element. Deleting all but one element doesn't free up any space, as shown by the column "1 element left" being unchanged from the column "Allocated." New elements cannot reuse the space of deleted elements, as show by "Allocated on top" doubling the used memory.

Table 11-2 summarizes the results of running the procedure with different parameters. The second row shows that by using only every tenth index, ten times as much memory is used. Increasing the step further would show that space for about twenty consecutive elements is allocated at once.

With a string length of 100, the strings are allocated out of line and the freed memory of the strings, but not the indices, can be reused as shown on the third row. In this case, there is an overhead and alignment loss of 37 bytes per entry for the out-of-line storage.

For consecutive indices, associative arrays indexed by varchar2 are six times slower and use more than double the memory than their pls_integer counterparts. On the other hand, their memory usage is independent of the step.

The memory usage and performance of nested table and varrays is roughly the same as for associative arrays index by pls_integer.

Table 11-2. Memory Usage and Execution Duration of Collection Tests

Collection type	String length	Step	Allocated	1 element left	Allocated on top	Duration
Associative array index by pls_integer	10	1	36,144 KB	36,144 KB	72,272 KB	1.7 s
		10	361,237 KB	361,237 KB	722,458 KB	8.3 s
	100	1	160,315 KB	160,313 KB	178,378 KB	6.6 s
Associative array index by varchar2	10	1	94,853 KB	94,853 KB	189,667 KB	10.4 s
		10	94,853 KB	94,853 KB	189,667 KB	11.2 s
	100	1	201,519 KB	201,503 KB	261,287 KB	14.5 s
Nested table	10	1	36,128 KB	36,144 KB	72,272 KB	1.7 s
Varray	10	1	35,567 KB	35,583 KB	71,138 KB	1.7 s

Summary

Business logic of data-centric applications belongs in the database. This claim is supported by both technical reasons and successful practical examples. There are plenty of technical benefits for this practice, such as simplicity of the design, high performance, and increased security. Furthermore, many concrete examples of ERP systems that use this design have been successful for many years, and new systems are built based on this design.

Business logic in PL/SQL in the database leads to a large PL/SQL code base. Naturally, the question arises of how to deliver to users an initial version that meets time, budget, and external product quality parameters and that can be maintained in the future. On an abstract level, the answers are the same for any architecture. The concrete implementation in PL/SQL is unique in four areas that I covered in this chapter.

- Uniformity allows developers to understand each other's code more quickly and thoroughly. Uniformity is more important than the concrete convention. Still, there are good reasons to incorporate certain aspects into your PL/SQL coding conventions.

- Modularization is the foundation for scalability of the development team and maintainability of an application. Modularization brings the benefits of divide and conquer to software engineering. PL/SQL provides strong modularization constructs in the form of subprograms, packages, and schemas as well as excellent analysis capabilities based on dependency views and PL/Scope.

- Object-oriented programming allows for increased reuse, which is key to reducing cost and time to market and improving quality in programming in the large. Whereas reuse as-is has a limited applicability, reuse with adaptations as provided by object-oriented programming enables reuse in more cases. PL/SQL is not an object-oriented language but can be used to program in an object-oriented way via the set of described patterns.

- The memory requirements of large applications must be measured and optimized using the described techniques. There are many good resources on design for scalability and performance, including several chapters of this book.

CHAPTER 12

Evolutionary Data Modeling

by Robyn Sands

I worked for Lockheed right after college. In my first year, I was part of a team assigned to evaluate Manufacturing Resources Planning (MRP) methods and tools. I was familiar with MRP; it had been part of the required curriculum for my bachelor's degree, plus I had some prior experience with MRP systems. However, MRP was a very new idea at Lockheed, and it was the antithesis of the philosophy behind the existing systems. My boss and mentor, Skip Christopherson, had been at Lockheed more years than I'd been on the planet and he knew every aspect of Lockheed's scheduling system, down to the very smallest detail. You attended classes in MRP together after work and it was like a classic comedy scene with the smart-mouthed rookie breezing through the material while the grizzled older employee who actually knows how things work struggles to grasp the point of this new fangled technology with all its bells and whistles. At the end of the class each night, you'd walk back to our windowless office while Skip talked about all that was wrong with this inane idea that a system could process changes and regenerate the schedule every night without throwing the assembly line into utter chaos. I'd been learning about how Lockheed approached scheduling at the same time you were taking the MRP class and I'd begun to understand and appreciate how it worked. Skip was right: MRP was exactly opposite our process flow model, which was based on math, statistics, and learning curves. Using the knowledge gained from decades of successful aircraft programs, you calculated the boundaries for the specific phases of the assembly process and tied them to positions on the shop floor. These positions and dates created a window in time for each crew to contain their contribution to the assembly. Within those boundaries, parts and schedules might shuffle madly while the crew worked insane hours, but the men on line knew that meeting the scheduled move date for the next position was critical and they'd learned to make it happen no matter what. The plane always moved forward, even if an assembly crew three positions further down the line had to rip out four positions worth of work to add a fabricated part that hadn't been available when it was needed.

As our class got more intense, Skip's concerns about MRP heightened and his after-class rants got more animated. He knew everything the assembly line went through to make their schedules now. If the schedules changed nightly, how could workers possibly keep up with the influx of information, much less the actual parts and planes? One night, I considered my words carefully before I expressed what I was thinking to my mentor. Once I had worked up my courage, I said, "Skip, the schedule is already changing every day. The only difference is that you'll be able to see it if it's it the system." He suddenly got very quiet and that was the last time I ever heard him complain about MRP. Later he went on to champion the MRP system implementation and became an expert in both the technology and the implementation process.

Change happens, whether you're building airplanes or software. You have a choice: you either manage it or you get blindsided.

Lessons from Two Decades of System Development

I met Skip in 1989 when he interviewed me on recruitment trip to my college and he taught me many things in the time I worked for him. Since that first post-college job, I've been a contributor on many different kinds of software system projects. Some of them were small enough that I could design and build the entire application myself, while others involved global teams with hundreds of people. Most of the projects I've been involved with were complex, and every one of them was expected to meet an expedited design and implementation schedule. In spite of the differences, there have been some basic realities of system development that were always the same.

- Customers don't know what they want until they see it. Only once they see what can be done with their data will they begin to understand the real possibilities of a new application. This is also the point in time when they will begin to shower the project with change requests. If you want to build an exceptional product, the last thing you want to do is shut down their ideas by refusing to change.

- To paraphrase Gregory House, MD, customers lie. Ask a customer to describe their process, and most of the time, they will answer with the documented version of the process. Customers don't intend to mislead us, but the ISO certification process has taught them to answer questions about process by describing the currently documented steps. However, many processes are flawed and there are likely to be additional steps that may not be included in the written documentation. *Watch what a customer does* and you will see the real process. When you see the steps that are not in the documentation, that's where you will find the best opportunities to build an innovative product.

- If you build a system that makes a user's job easier, they will use it and demand more: more options, more functionality, and more performance. Build an application that creates work without providing sufficient benefit, and users will work around the application, using it in ways that were never intended or avoiding it all together. This is a perfectly reasonable way for them to react: users have a job to do and the application and code that is so important to us as the creators of the application may only be a small part of the users' workday. When users have to work around an application to get their job done, more bugs will be reported and data will become inaccurate over time. You need to remember as database and software developers that your customers are not as fascinated with the details of the technology as you are. Users need tools that work consistently and predictably.

- If you cannot provide a tool or a product quickly, someone else will. This applies to both the end product and the development environment it is built in. If a product is late to market, potential customers will find another solution and another vendor. If the database is not available to support the application developers, they will find another solution to get their job done. Even if that solution does not work as well as it might have using the database, it can be very difficult to remove or optimize it later. Usually, such solutions have long ranging repercussions in application functionality, performance, or both.

Database management systems excel at storing, searching, and transforming data. When combined with a well-designed data model, they will perform each of these tasks faster than any application method. Here is the challenge: a database system must be well designed to perform and to continue to perform even as it is placed under increasing demands of more users or more data. It takes time to design a database system that will scale to support these demands. When shortcuts are taken in the design process, the database system will fail to meet performance requirements; this usually leads to a major redesign or hardware expenditure. Both of these options represent waste and inefficiency: the redesign requires extra time and effort, and even if the hardware is able to bring the system up to acceptable performance levels, think of how much more capable the system could have been with a good design AND powerful hardware.

This all sounds quite discouraging: if customers don't know what they want, don't accurately describe their processes, and will misuse a tool to minimize their workload, software developers and the applications they build seem doomed to fail. You can't create a good design up front because you don't have a complete picture of what the application and data will eventually become, and even if you did have complete and accurate information about the final requirements at the beginning of the project, you don't have time for data modeling and system design when the competition is aiming for the same customer base. Yet if the database design is flawed, your users will be unhappy with system response time and your project will be plagued with slow response time and system crashes.

There is another option. You can do something revolutionary: you can recognize that change is inevitable, prepare for it and manage it. If you expect change, or better yet, encourage it and learn from it, you open up the possibility that you will create exactly what the customer needs. If you watch the end user perform their work rather than ask them to describe it, you will find the pain points in the current process and you may be able to remove those pain points easily. This gives you an opportunity to truly innovate and build tools your users need but no one has thought of. If you build your applications with customer involvement, getting new functionality in their hands early in the process, requesting feedback and then using that feedback to improve the application early in the development process, the result is a collaborative process and a better product. If you watch the customer use the tools you build, you will find even more ways to improve your products. This is called *iterative design* and I believe it leads to better products, happier customers, and a more satisfying work environment for software developers.

The Database and Agile Development

Iterative development is not a new concept: there are a multitude of books and experts covering software development and iterative design. However, when it comes to the database, there is little useful information about how to manage iterative database design. At the same time, more and more application databases are created without an adequate database design. Whether it is the conceptual, logical, or physical design, the one common thread is that intentional design is absent in far too many cases. This leads to a far-too-common end result: the database and application do not perform to expectations. The application might pass functional test requirements, but once it is placed under the expected user load, performance may be far from acceptable. While it is possible to make a poorly designed application perform better, to build a database that will continue to perform to expectations under an increasing number of concurrent users with an ever-growing amount of data, you MUST have a well designed schema. You may be able to add more hardware resources and improve performance, but think about it. What portion of those hardware resources are simply compensating for a bad design? And how much more could you get out of your hardware investment if the design flaws didn't exist? When the schema is flawed, the amount of rework required in the application code increases. This creates a very big problem as the database schema remains frozen in time while the application functionality continues to expand. As change requests continue to flow in and additional fields are tacked on to the already problematic schema design, performance problems become increasingly difficult to repair.

The net result of these kinds of problems is that architects and developers have come to the conclusion that the solution is to put as little functionality in the database as possible. Perhaps this is understandable: because they've learned to see database changes as painful, they attempt to avoid the pain by avoiding the database. They even avoid using the database for the tasks the database does best because they are afraid they may have to change it someday. The desire to be *database agnostic* adds to the problem as some of the best features and functions in the DBMS go unused. The unfortunate and somewhat ironic result is that a very expensive DBMS sits idle while teams of workers struggle to recreate functionality that is available and paid for under their existing license. Choosing to license a powerful product and then design the application as if you'd purchased the lowest common denominator is one of the most expensive mistakes a development team can make. This is true whether the DBMS is Oracle, MySQL, Postgres, or SQL Server. Good developers are hard to find. Why spend their time recreating what has already been built by another company and purchased by yours? If the goal is to build a competitive product, one that will give the customer what they need while maximizing the return on our investment, you should be fully exploiting every last useful feature available in the DBMS platform you've purchased.

Thus far, I've listed the contradictory goals for software development projects: you need to build it fast, you need to proceed before you have sufficient knowledge, you need to design to support the long term performance goals and those performance goals are probably unknown as well. If you don't have a product yet, how do you know how many users you will attract someday? If you create something amazing and innovative, you will have more users than you ever thought possible in a much shorter time frame than you expected. Then your enthusiastic users will promptly overload the system, resulting in one of those front-page stories about the latest software product experiencing a very public failure. You need to aim for stability and yet encourage change through an iterative design process. You want your systems to be transparent and simple to use so users are able to do their work without having to relearn the steps every time they connect, but you must recognize that your understanding of the user's work may be inaccurate. Considering all the potential ways a project can fail to meet these challenges, how do software projects ever succeed? The one thing you can't do is turn back the clock to times when development didn't move so fast. Instead, you must expect that designs will change, and equip database administrators, database developers, and application developers to manage today's change while remaining focused on the longer term impacts these changes will have on the system as a whole.

■ **Note** In this chapter, there will be references to *database development* and *application development*. Both of these labels can refer to development of the same application, and one developer may be responsible for both layers of development. My intention for this chapter is to differentiate between the code that accesses and processes the data, and the code that builds the tool to present the data to the end user, not to suggest that an additional organizational layer or group of people is required.

Evolutionary Data Modeling

In spite of the challenging picture I've painted, I believe it is possible to achieve your goals—but it's not by doing less in the DBMS. The best way to create both an agile development environment and a truly agile application database is by coding more functionality inside the database and exploiting the DBMS for the kind of work it does best. Your database designs need to evolve and adapt to the changing needs of the development team, the customer, and the end users. You need to walk a fine line of building what is needed now, while keeping your eyes on the future and preparing for it. This is why I prefer the term *evolutionary data modeling* to *iterative data modeling*. The term *iterative* implies that the design cycle is repeated throughout the development process: this is a good start but it's not enough. *Evolutionary* also implies ongoing change, but with evolution, each change builds on the foundation created thus far. When the design evolves, you recognize that it should be capable of extending to meet needs and requirements that are not fully defined. You still don't want to build functionality before it is required, but neither should you make choices that limit options in the name of YGANI (You Ain't Gonna Need It). Some design decisions you make create more options for future design phases, while others remove options and limit the potential solutions in the next round of development. Until you are certain about what is coming next, make the choice that keeps as many options open as possible.

░ **Note** To the best of my knowledge, the term "Evolutionary Data Modeling" originated with Scott W. Ambler on his website at `agiledata.org`. He also coauthored a book, *Refactoring Databases: Evolutionary Database Design*, which includes some excellent methodologies for Agile development. The approach described in this chapter for achieving an easily refactorable database differs from any recommendation I've seen by Mr. Ambler to date.

For example, the database for one development project had been loaded from a .csv file provided by the customer. About half of the columns in the file did not have a defined use in the first round of functional specifications. The development team was divided into two schools of thought as to what should be done with the extraneous fields. One side stated that all the columns that were not required should be removed as they were not being actively used. The other side recognized that although these fields were not in use, the values had a clear relationship to the data values that were central to the application. They thought the fields might have value in helping the team better understand the required data and how it was processed by the end users.

The unnecessary fields were retained and although they appeared to be parent values of the data in a central table, the solution was to leave the fields as attributes so the relationships could be further evaluated without creating work, and eventually rework, for the database developers. This decision broke several rules of traditional data modeling: the table contained unnecessary data and some of the data in the schema was not normalized. Since the central table was still small and reasonably narrow, the impact of the rule breaking was negligible. A few releases later, the customer began to make references to these unused fields, which confirmed the previously suspected relationships. Gradually, those data values were incorporated into the application as new functionality was requested, with some data values moving to parent tables while others were left as attributes. Removing the data too soon would have limited the team's options. Retaining the data could have created rework if the data had been formally incorporated into the schema too early. Keeping the data in form that minimized the impact on the application while leaving the door open for later use was the better decision in this case.

In the next section, you'll see code that illustrates a simple schema change and how such changes can ripple through an average development environment. Next, you'll examine why using PL/SQL as the API supports evolutionary design by making it easier to refactor the database design without impacting other application components. Later, you'll review some agile development concepts and discuss how evolutionary data modeling and a PL/SQL API supports the values and principles of agile development.

Refactoring the Database

You will use the Human Resources (HR) schema from Oracle's sample schemas to illustrate a simple change to a database schema and demonstrate how those changes can have an unexpected impact on other functionality within the application. The default HR schema as delivered by Oracle contains one phone number field in the employee table. The customer has requested that the application be modified to store and display both an office and a mobile phone number for each employee. Screens and reports will need to be changed, as some will continue to require one specific phone number while others will need to utilize both phone numbers. For example, the company directory may show both the employees' desk and mobile numbers, while a facilities report only needs the desk numbers.

The original structure of the HR schema is shown in Figure 12-1. You need to determine where to store the new data and how to present the information to the user. You should consider multiple plausible solutions and decide which one (or ones) should be tested.

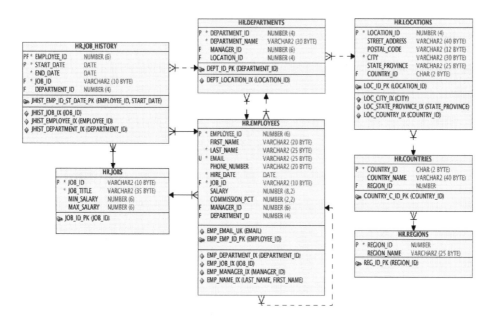

Figure 12-1. Human Resourse schema, unchanged

A common solution to this kind of request would be to add an additional column to the EMPLOYEES table (EMPLOYEES.MOBILE_NUMBER). While this may resolve the initial requirement, there are better ways to solve the problem as this approach only addresses the immediate need. What happens when HR decides they need the employee's home number as well? You could continue to add columns but if you solve every request for new data by adding a column to the end of the EMPLOYEES table, your table will soon be very wide with sparsely distributed data. This first option is also a relatively limited solution. What if an employee works from two different offices and has two different office numbers? What if one employee prefers to be reached on their mobile while another is easier to contact at the office, and the department administrator needs a report of all the employees and the best way to reach them? You could add another column to store an indicator of the kind of phone the employee prefers and then have the application loop through the data pulling the office number for some employees and the mobile number for others. This type of design process is a good example of how performance problems get started. Columns continue to get tacked on to tables and more application code is needed to process the data in those columns. Eventually, the tables grow very wide, code to access the data becomes increasingly complex as code outside the database does more of the sorting and grouping that should be in the DBMS, and performance starts its downward spiral.

A better solution is to create another table that will store multiple phones number and use the EMPLOYEE_ID to link back to the EMPLOYEES table. This approach offers a few advantages over the first proposal: the database will not artificially limit the number of phone numbers that can be stored for each employee, plus you can store additional attributes about the phone numbers such as phone type and preferred phone.

Listing 12-1 shows how to add a table to store the employee ID, phone numbers, phone types, and an indicator of which phone number is the employee's preferred method of contact. This code will create the new table and populate it from the existing table. All phone numbers will be set to a default type "Office" and the preferred indicator is set to "Y".

Then you'll populate the new table using the data from the EMPLOYEES table. Since all employees have had only one phone in the system, you can set the default phone type and the preferred indicator to the same values for all employees.

Listing 12-1. Create Table and Populate EMP_PHONE_NUMBER

```
SQL>   CREATE TABLE emp_phone_numbers
          (employee_id    NUMBER(6)                  NOT NULL,
           phone_number   VARCHAR2(20)               NOT NULL,
           preferred      VARCHAR2(1)   DEFAULT 'N'  NOT NULL,
           phone_type     VARCHAR2(10)               NOT NULL,
             CONSTRAINT   emp_phone_numbers_pk
             PRIMARY KEY (employee_id, phone_number)
          ) ;

Table created.

SQL>   alter table EMP_PHONE_NUMBERS add constraint emp_phone_numbers_fk1
          foreign key (employee_id)
          references EMPLOYEES (employee_id) ;

Table altered.

SQL>   insert into emp_phone_numbers (
          select employee_id, phone_number, 'Y', 'Office' from employees) ;

107 rows created.

SQL>   commit;

Commit complete.
```

Some approaches to database refactoring suggest that you should keep the old column in the database, populating both data points until you are certain all references to the old column have been resolved. Anytime you store the same data in multiple places in a database, you run the risk that the data will get out of sync. Then you need to reconcile it, determine which values are correct, and repair the data. In a real HR database, data reconciliation and repair can be a huge effort. There are options to minimize the risk of such issues, but they usually involve duplicating the data from one source to the other, which may not prevent the target column from being updated independently. If all of the changes to the database require maintaining multiple data sources, even temporarily, the net result is a development environment that is very difficult to manage. This approach becomes even more complex when you realize that the typical development team is responding to multiple change requests at any given time. As the developers are making other change requests, will they have to build their new code to support both the old and the new field? And how long might these leftover data values remain in the system? The key to good performance is to eliminate unnecessary work: this is as true for processes as it is for systems. If the development team is going to be agile, you must minimize the amount of work they need to do. Maintaining multiple code paths for weeks, months, or years is not the best use of your development resources.

The changes required to update a query to use the new table are simple: you add another table to the from clause and connect the EMPLOYEES table and the EMP_PHONE_NUMBERS table via the EMPLOYEE_ID in the where clause. If the application has been written with SQL calls directly in the application code layer (Java, PHP, etc) then queries like the first one shown in Listing 12-2 could be found throughout the application code in every module that references basic employee information. Listing 12-2 shows a query to get employee information including the employee's phone number before the change to the table design, and how that query would be changed to request the same data after the table changes were complete.

Listing 12-2. Employee Data Request

```
SQL>  select dept.department_name,
             loc.street_address,
             loc.city,
             loc.state_province,
             loc.postal_code,
             cty.country_name ,
             emp.employee_id ,
             emp.last_name,
             emp.first_name,
             emp.email,
             emp.phone_number
        from departments dept,
             locations loc,
             countries cty,
             employees emp
       where dept.department_id = &DepartmentID
         and dept.location_id = loc.location_id
         and loc.country_id = cty.country_id
         and dept.department_id = emp.department_id
       order by dept.department_name, emp.last_name, emp.first_name ;

SQL>  select dept.department_name,
             loc.street_address,
             loc.city,
             loc.state_province,
             loc.postal_code,
             cty.country_name ,
             emp.employee_id EMP_ID,
```

```
       emp.last_name,
       emp.first_name,
       emp.email,
       epn.phone_number
  from departments dept,
       locations loc,
       countries cty,
       employees emp,
       emp_phone_numbers epn
 where dept.department_id = &DepartmentID
   and dept.location_id = loc.location_id
   and loc.country_id = cty.country_id
   and dept.department_id = emp.department_id
   and emp.employee_id = epn.employee_id
 order by dept.department_name, emp.last_name, emp.first_name ;
```

Since only one phone number is currently populated for each employee, the result sets for the Purchasing Department are exactly the same for both queries. At this point, either query will return the data shown in Listing 12-3.

Listing 12-3. Abbreviated Employee Data for Department 30 (Purchasing)

DEPT_NAME	EMP_ID	LAST_NAME	FIRST_NAME	EMAIL	PHONE_NO
Purchasing	114	Raphaely	Den	DRAPHEAL	515.127.4561
Purchasing	115	Khoo	Alexander	AKHOO	515.127.4562
Purchasing	116	Baida	Shelli	SBAIDA	515.127.4563
Purchasing	117	Tobias	Sigal	STOBIAS	515.127.4564
Purchasing	118	Himuro	Guy	GHIMURO	515.127.4565
Purchasing	119	Colmenares	Karen	KCOLMENA	515.127.4566

■ **Note**   To keep the examples readable, results sets may be edited to shorten column names and/or to remove data that is not significant to the example. Results that are not critical to the example may not be shown.

The changes in the table structure create several potential problems for your application, problems that are likely to impact the user interface and generate new bug reports. Resolving these issues will require feedback from the functional side of the business, as you need to know how the customer wants the application to behave. The following are a few questions you need answered:

- How does the customer expect to input employee phone number data? The answer to this question will help you determine your options for keeping the two data sources synchronized until you are sure it is safe to remove the original column.

- Should you add the phone type and preferred flag to the queries in question? Having this information in the query will give you more options for your screens and reports.

- Which queries need to return one phone number per employee, and which queries should return multiple phone numbers? Once the employee's mobile numbers are in the system, the results sets from the queries in Listing 12-2 will NOT be identical, as the original query would only return one row, while the new query could return multiple rows for one employee.

- If there are views built on queries like these, will adding additional fields to the views break the application? If someone has used a Select * from EMPLOYEES_BY_DEPT_VW to request the data, it will.

Once you've answered these questions, you need to confirm the same information for all queries or updates that reference the EMPLOYEES table and use the phone number data. Otherwise, your small change may impact the application front end in places not intended by the customer's initial request.

There may be many similar but slightly different queries within your application: a different column order, different result sets due to different where clauses, different selections of included columns. Every piece of code that uses the original phone number field needs to be found, updated, and tested. Keeping the old column and synchronizing the data will give you more time to find all the code that needs correction, but all that work still needs to be done.

The single, biggest challenge in refactoring a database schema is finding and changing all of the components that reference the tables you alter. If the developers have been diligent, perhaps they've built reusable modules to handle requesting EMPLOYEE data and you will have less code to find. But can you really be sure that someone hasn't written a small but unknown query or update that will fail when the table structure changes? In this example, you've only considered one select statement. In a real HR system, there will be extensive application code to add employees, change employee data, and produce reports that use the phone number data. Looking at the schema diagram in Figure 12-1, you'll notice there is a circular reference, as the employee's manager is identified in the employee record by the manager's employee ID. Queries, updates, and reports that include employee and manager phone numbers may require more complex changes. And just to make things really interesting, the Order Entry schema also makes use of the EMPLOYEES table, using the EMPLOYEE_ID to indicate the sales representative that made the sale so your very small changes now impact multiple schemas and multiple application modules. When you think of how simple this schema is, and imagine how complex most data stores can be, the fear created by the mention of a schema change becomes a little more understandable.

Creating an Access Layer via PL/SQL

What if you created your modular, reusable code in the database itself, so that all access to your application data was encapsulated within PL/SQL packages, procedures, and functions? The query referenced in Listing 12-2 would instead be incorporated into a procedure as shown in Listing 12-4. Listing 12-5 shows the code to execute that procedure, and Listing 12-6 shows the results from an example execution. This exercise creates a procedure that can be called by components outside the database to return the same data that is returned by the first query in Listing 12-2.

Listing 12-4. Procedure to Return Employee Data by Department

```
CREATE OR REPLACE PROCEDURE GetEmployeeData(
        p_dept_id        IN  NUMBER,
        p_emp_cursor        OUT SYS_REFCURSOR,
        p_status_code       OUT NUMBER,
        p_status_message OUT VARCHAR2) IS
```

```
/****************************************************************************
    NAME: GetEmployeeData
 PURPOSE: This procedure returns contact information for employees by department

  NOTES:

      p_status_code  status_message
      =============  =======================================================
                 0   Success
            -20102   Input parameter p_dept_id must not be null.

*******************************************************************************/
BEGIN -- GetEmployeeData

--validate parameters
IF ((p_department_id) IS NULL ) THEN
    RAISE_APPLICATION_ERROR(-20102, Input parameter p_dept_id must not be null.',TRUE);
END IF;

OPEN p_emp_cursor FOR
    SELECT
          dept.department_id,
          dept.department_name,
          loc.street_address,
          loc.city,
          loc.state_province,
          loc.postal_code,
          cty.country_name,
   CURSOR (select emp.employee_id,
                  emp.last_name,
                  emp.first_name,
                  emp.email,
                  emp.phone_number
             from employees emp
            where emp.department_id = dept.department_id) emp_cursor
      FROM
            departments dept, locations loc, countries cty
      WHERE
            dept.department_id = p_dept_id
        AND dept.location_id = loc.location_id
        AND loc.country_id = cty.country_id
      ORDER BY 2,3;

   p_status_code:= 0;
   p_status_message:= NULL;
```

```
EXCEPTION
  WHEN OTHERS THEN
    p_status_code:= SQLCODE;
    p_status_message:= SQLERRM;

END GetEmployeeData;
/
```

Listing 12-5. Procedure Execution Script

```
set serveroutput on

          var p_main_cursor REFCURSOR

DECLARE
          v_dept_id          departments.department_id%TYPE;
          v_status_code      NUMBER;
          v_status_message   VARCHAR2(200);

          t0 timestamp;
          t1 timestamp;

BEGIN
          t0:= systimestamp;

          v_dept_id := &Department_ID;

  GetEmployeeData
          (v_dept_id, :p_main_cursor, v_status_code, v_status_message);

  t1:= systimestamp;

 DBMS_OUTPUT.PUT_LINE('Code=' || v_status_code || 'Message=' || v_status_message);
 DBMS_OUTPUT.PUT_LINE('ela=' || (t0 - t1) );

END;
/

    print :p_main_cursor
```

Listing 12-6. Procedure Execution and Results Set

```
SQL> @exec_GetEmployeeData.prc

Enter value for department_id: 30
  old  13:    v_dept_id := &Department_ID;
  new  13:    v_dept_id := 30;
  status_code=0  status_message
  ela=-000000000 00:00:00.000091000
```

```
PL/SQL procedure successfully completed.


DEPT_ID DEPT_NAME     STREET_ADDRESS    CITY      STATE        EMP_CURSOR
30      Purchasing    2004 Charade Rd   Seattle   Washington   CURSOR STATEMENT : 8

CURSOR STATEMENT : 8

EMPLOYEE_ID     LAST_NAME     FIRST_NAME    EMAIL       PHONE_NUMBER
        114     Raphaely      Den           DRAPHEAL    515.127.4561
        115     Khoo          Alexander     AKHOO       515.127.4562
        116     Baida         Shelli        SBAIDA      515.127.4563
        117     Tobias        Sigal         STOBIAS     515.127.4564
        118     Himuro        Guy           GHIMURO     515.127.4565
        119     Colmenares    Karen         COLMENA     515.127.4566
```

6 rows selected.

With a procedure in place, your refactoring exercise changes and becomes more complete. This time you can create and populate the new table, and once you are sure the data has been correctly populated, drop the old column, removing the duplicate data and the potential for inconsistent entries. You can also use your execution script to complete the first round of testing, verifying that the procedure executes and returns the expected results set. While you can always test a query in the database, that test is of limited value if the application can contain its own version of the code. Later in this chapter you learn how to use schema permissions to ensure that the procedures have been used consistently throughout the application so you can remain confident that refactoring the database will not impact the application layer. For now, execute the code in Listing 12-7.

Listing 12-7. Refactoring Exercise Using a PL/SQL API

```
SQL>  CREATE TABLE emp_phone_numbers
          (employee_id     NUMBER(6)                      NOT NULL,
           phone_number    VARCHAR2(20)                   NOT NULL,
           preferred       VARCHAR2(1)    DEFAULT 'N'     NOT NULL,
           phone_type      VARCHAR2(10)                   NOT NULL,
             CONSTRAINT   emp_phone_numbers_pk
             PRIMARY KEY (employee_id, phone_number)
          ) ;

Table created.

SQL>  alter table EMP_PHONE_NUMBERS add constraint emp_phone_numbers_fk1
          foreign key (employee_id)
          references EMPLOYEES (employee_id) ;

Table altered.

SQL> insert into emp_phone_numbers (
     select employee_id, phone_number, 'Y', 'Office'
      from employees) ;
```

```
107 rows created.

SQL> commit;

Commit complete.

SQL> alter table employees drop column phone_number;

Table altered.
```

With the changes shown in Listing 12-7 complete, you achieved your target design immediately. The new table has been created and populated and the old data column as been removed. There is no need to code to keep duplicate values synchronized or to revisit this change later to remove the old column and the code built to support it. You've reduced the work that must be done by both the application and by the development team. Figure 12-2 shows your new schema design.

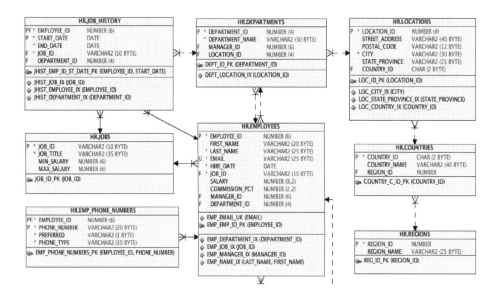

Figure 12-2. Human Resourse schema, target design

Once you've populated the new table and dropped the old column, be sure to check for any objects in the application schema that have been invalidated by your changes. Listing 12-8 will show that not only is your GetEmployeeData procedure invalid, as expected, but two triggers have been invalidated. The first thing you need to do is see what these triggers do and how they are associated to the EMPLOYEES table.

As part of verifying your changes, select the source text for each invalid trigger and evaluate how they are using the EMPLOYEES table. In Listing 12-8, you'll use the data dictionary to see how the changes made in Listing 12-7 impacted other objects in the schema. You will recompile the invalid objects and ensure all objects are valid. The UPDATE_JOB_HISTORY trigger references the EMPLOYEES table, but not the column you've moved to another table. The SECURE_EMPLOYEES trigger references another procedure. You'll check the SECURE_DML procedure and verify that it is not using the phone number data either. This means both triggers can be recompiled as is to restore them to a valid state.

Listing 12-8. Verifying and Recompiling Related Objects

```
SQL> select object_type, object_name, status
       from user_objects
      where status = 'INVALID'
      order by object_type, object_name ;

OBJECT_TYPE    OBJECT_NAME            STATUS
-------------  --------------------   -------
PROCEDURE      GETEMPLOYEEDATA        INVALID
TRIGGER        SECURE_EMPLOYEES       INVALID
TRIGGER        UPDATE_JOB_HISTORY     INVALID

3 rows selected.

SQL> select text
       from user_source
      where name = 'UPDATE_JOB_HISTORY'
        and type = 'TRIGGER'
      order by line ;

TEXT
----------------------------------------------------------------------
TRIGGER update_job_history
        AFTER UPDATE OF job_id, department_id ON employees
           FOR EACH ROW
BEGIN
  add_job_history(:old.employee_id,
                  :old.hire_date,
                   sysdate,
                  :old.job_id,
                  :old.department_id);
END;

7 rows selected.

SQL> alter trigger update_job_history compile ;

Trigger altered.

SQL> select text
       from user_source
      where name = 'SECURE_EMPLOYEES'
        and type = 'TRIGGER'
      order by line ;

TEXT
----------------------------------------------------------------------
```

```
TRIGGER secure_employees
     BEFORE INSERT OR UPDATE OR DELETE ON employees
BEGIN
     secure_dml;
END secure_employees;

5 rows selected.

SQL> select object_type, object_name, status
            from user_objects
         where object_name = 'SECURE_DML' ;

OBJECT_TYPE   OBJECT_NAME           STATUS
------------------ ---------------------- -------
PROCEDURE     SECURE_DML            VALID

1 row selected.

SQL> select text
       from user_source
      where name = 'SECURE_DML'
      order by line ;

TEXT
----------------------------------------------------------------------
PROCEDURE secure_dml
  IS
BEGIN
  IF TO_CHAR (SYSDATE, 'HH24:MI') NOT BETWEEN '08:00' AND '18:00'
  OR TO_CHAR (SYSDATE, 'DY') IN ('SAT', 'SUN') THEN
    RAISE_APPLICATION_ERROR (-20205,
      'You may only make changes during normal office hours');
  END IF;
END secure_dml;

9 rows selected.

SQL> alter trigger secure_employees compile;

Trigger altered.

SQL> select object_type, object_name, status
       from user_objects
      where status = 'INVALID'
      order by object_type, object_name ;

OBJECT_TYPE   OBJECT_NAME        STATUS
------------- ----------------- ------------
PROCEDURE     GETEMPLOYEEDATA    INVALID

1 row selected.
```

Now you are ready to update the GetEmployeeData procedure to use the EMP_PHONE_NUMBERS table; here again, using procedures gives you options that you don't have when you code SQL directly into your application layer. Instead of altering this procedure to provide the new functionality requested by your customer, you will change the select statement so the procedure returns the same results set as in the past but from the new data source. This is accomplished by adding an additional limiting factor to the where clause, which will now specify that you wish to receive the preferred phone number for each employee. An alternative would be to specify that the procedure always return the office number for the employee. The best way to make this determination is to offer the customer a choice in behavior.

Pause here for a moment and consider what you have accomplished. You refactored the database, changing the table definitions and the location of the data without impacting the front-end application in any way. Every time the application code calls the GetEmployeeData procedure, it will behave exactly as it always has. If the application uses only procedures, then you know there are no unfound bits of select statements missed during your analysis and testing. Even better, since you are able to test the execution and the results in the database before you deliver the changes to development, you can be certain that development can be immediately productive with the real work they need to complete, which is incorporating the new functionality.

Now it's time to make an application change, or at least to change the procedure that the application invokes. Listing 12-9 shows how to modify the GetEmployeeData procedure to use the new table. You'll change the GetEmployeeData procedure to use the new EMP_PHONE_NUMBERS table to return the employees preferred phone number. You'll then execute the test script from Listing 12-5 to confirm the procedure works as expected.

Listing 12-9. Alter the GetEmployeeData Procedure

```
SQL>  CREATE OR REPLACE PROCEDURE GetEmployeeData(
                p_dept_id        IN NUMBER,
                p_emp_cursor     OUT SYS_REFCURSOR,
                p_status_code    OUT NUMBER,
                p_status_message OUT VARCHAR2) IS


/*********************************************************************************
   NAME:    GetEmployeeData
  PURPOSE:  This procedure returns contact information for employees by department

   NOTES:

  p_status_code   status_message
  =============   ===========================================================
            0   Success
       -20102   'Input parameter p_dept_id must not be null.'


*********************************************************************************/
BEGIN -- GetEmployeeData

     --validate parameters
```

```
IF ((p_dept_id) IS NULL ) THEN
  RAISE_APPLICATION_ERROR(-20102, 'Input parameter p_dept_id must not be null.', TRUE);
    END IF;

OPEN p_emp_cursor FOR
    SELECT
            dept.department_id, dept.department_name,
            loc.street_address,
            loc.city, loc.state_province, loc.postal_code,
            cty.country_name,
      CURSOR (select emp.employee_id,
                     emp.last_name,
                     emp.first_name,
                     emp.email,
                     eph.phone_number
               from employees emp , emp_phone_numbers eph
              where emp.department_id = dept.department_id
                and emp.employee_id = eph.employee_id
                and eph.preferred = 'Y'
              order by emp.employee_id) emp_cursor
       FROM
            departments dept, locations loc, countries cty
      WHERE dept.department_id = p_dept_id
        AND dept.location_id = loc.location_id
        AND loc.country_id = cty.country_id ;

  p_status_code:= 0;
  p_status_message:= NULL;

EXCEPTION
  WHEN OTHERS THEN
      p_status_code:= SQLCODE;
      p_status_message:= SQLERRM;

END GetEmployeeData;
/

----  Confirm that all schema objects are valid:

SQL>  select object_type, object_name, status
        from user_objects
        where status = 'INVALID'
        order by object_type, object_name ;

no rows selected

---- Execute test script and confirm the procedure works as expected:

SQL> @exec_GetEmployeeData.prc
```

```
Enter value for department_id: 30
  old  13:    v_dept_id := &Department_ID;
  new  13:    v_dept_id := 30;
  status_code=0  status_message=
  ela=-000000000 00:00:00.000128000


PL/SQL procedure successfully completed.

DEPT_ID DEPT_NAME   STREET_ADDRESS  CITY      STATE      EMP_CURSOR
30      Purchasing  2004 Charade Rd Seattle   Washington CURSOR STATEMENT : 8

CURSOR STATEMENT : 8

EMPLOYEE_ID    LAST_NAME   FIRST_NAME   EMAIL      PHONE_NUMBER
        114    Raphaely    Den          DRAPHEAL   515.127.4561
        115    Khoo        Alexander    AKHOO      515.127.4562
        116    Baida       Shelli       SBAIDA     515.127.4563
        117    Tobias      Sigal        STOBIAS    515.127.4564
        118    Himuro      Guy          GHIMURO    515.127.4565
        119    Colmenares  Karen        KCOLMENA   515.127.4566

6 rows selected.
```

At this point, you made the schema design changes and you completed several steps to test and confirm your changes. You know that all schema objects that were impacted by the table changes have been found, recompiled, and are now valid. The only change you made to the GetEmployeeData procedure ensures that it will continue to behave as it always has. The next step is to incorporate the requested functionality change and provide the employee data by department with multiple phone numbers. To accomplish this, you will create a new procedure, GetEmployeeData_MultiPhoneNo, as shown in Listing 12-10. Listing 12-11 then shows how to test the new procedure.

▓ **Note** There is another, more elegant approach to solving this problem: you add a new parameter to the original procedure to indicate which phone number or combination of phone numbers should be returned to the application. The new parameter should default to returning a single phone number, either the preferred phone number or the office number, whichever option was chosen by your customer. This alternative approach ensures that the procedure will continue to produce the same results set with no changes to the application, and when development is ready to include the new functionality, they will use the same procedure but specify the phone number behavior via one additional value in the procedure call.

Listing 12-10. Create the GetEmployeeData_MultiPhoneNo Procedure

```
SQL>  CREATE OR REPLACE PROCEDURE GetEmployeeData_MultiPhoneNo(
            p_dept_id        IN NUMBER,
            p_emp_cursor     OUT SYS_REFCURSOR,
            p_status_code    OUT NUMBER,
            p_status_message OUT VARCHAR2) IS


/*********************************************************************************
    NAME: GetEmployeeData_MultiPhoneNo
  PURPOSE: This procedure returns contact information for employees by department

    NOTES:

    p_status_code  status_message
    ============   =========================================================
              0    Success
         -20102    Input parameter p_dept_id must not be null.


*********************************************************************************/
BEGIN -- GetEmployeeData_MultiPhoneNo

      --validate parameters
 IF ((p_dept_id) IS NULL ) THEN
   RAISE_APPLICATION_ERROR(-20102, 'Input parameter p_dept_id must not be null.', TRUE);

END IF;

   OPEN p_emp_cursor FOR
     SELECT
            dept.department_id,
            dept.department_name,
            loc.street_address,
            loc.city,
            loc.state_province,
            loc.postal_code,
            cty.country_name,
     CURSOR (select emp.employee_id,
                    emp.last_name,
                    emp.first_name,
                    emp.email,
                    eph.preferred,
                    eph.phone_type,
                    eph.phone_number
               from employees emp , emp_phone_numbers eph
              where emp.department_id = dept.department_id
                and emp.employee_id = eph.employee_id
              order by emp.employee_id) emp_cursor
       FROM
            departments dept, locations loc, countries cty
```

```
        WHERE dept.department_id = p_dept_id
          AND dept.location_id = loc.location_id
          AND loc.country_id = cty.country_id ;

  p_status_code:= 0;
  p_status_message:= NULL;

  EXCEPTION
    WHEN OTHERS THEN
      p_status_code:= SQLCODE;
      p_status_message:= SQLERRM;

END GetEmployeeData_MultiPhoneNo;
/

---- Create new test script to execute this procedure
---- only the procedure name is changed

set serveroutput on

  var p_main_cursor        REFCURSOR

DECLARE
  v_dept_id             departments.department_id%TYPE;

  v_status_code      NUMBER;
  v_status_message VARCHAR2(200);

  t0 timestamp;
  t1 timestamp;

BEGIN
  t0:= systimestamp;

  v_dept_id := &Department_ID;

  GetEmployeeData_MultiPhoneNo
     (v_dept_id, :p_main_cursor, v_status_code, v_status_message);

  t1:= systimestamp;
  DBMS_OUTPUT.PUT_LINE('code=' || v_status_code || 'message=' || v_status_message);
  DBMS_OUTPUT.PUT_LINE('ela=' || (t0 - t1) );

END;
/
    print :p_main_cursor
```

At this point, the results set from the new procedure looks exactly like the old procedure as none of the employees actually have more than one phone number in the system. In Listing 12-11, you will add multiple phone numbers for one employee and confirm the correct results are returned from the original test script. You'll add two phone numbers for one of your executives, Mr. Steven King. He'll now have three phone numbers: office, mobile, and home. You will also switch his mobile number to become his preferred number and confirm that his mobile number will be returned from the original GetEmployeeData procedure.

Listing 12-11. Extended Phone Number Functionality Testing

```
SQL>  select * from emp_phone_numbers
        where employee_id = 100;

EMPLOYEE_ID PHONE_NUMBER       P PHONE_TYPE
----------- ----------------- - ----------
        100 515.123.4567       Y Office

SQL> 1 row selected.

SQL> insert into emp_phone_numbers
      values (100,'555.312.9876','N','Mobile');

1 row created.

SQL> insert into emp_phone_numbers
      values (100,'555.321.7345','N','Home');

1 row created.

Commit complete.

SQL> select * from emp_phone_numbers
        where employee_id = 100;

EMPLOYEE_ID PHONE_NUMBER       P PHONE_TYPE
----------- ----------------- - ----------
        100   515.123.4567     Y Office
        100   555.312.9876     N Mobile
        100   555.321.7345     N Home

SQL> 3 rows selected.

SQL> @exec_GetEmployeeData_MultiPhoneNo.sql

Enter value for department_id: 90
  old  13:    v_dept_id := &Department_ID;
  new  13:    v_dept_id := 90;
  status_code=0   status_message=
  ela=-000000000 00:00:00.000110000

PL/SQL procedure successfully completed.

DEPT_ID DEPT_NAME       STREET_ADDRESS    CITY      STATE         EMP_CURSOR
     90 Executive       2004 Charade Rd   Seattle   Washington    CURSOR STATEMENT : 8

CURSOR STATEMENT : 8
```

```
EMPLOYEE_ID    LAST_NAME    FIRST_NAME    EMAIL       P    PHONE_TYPE    PHONE_NUMBER
       100     King         Steven        SKING       Y    Office        515.123.4567
       100     King         Steven        SKING       N    Mobile        555.312.9876
       100     King         Steven        SKING       N    Home          555.321.7345
       101     Kochhar      Neena         NKOCHHAR    Y    Office        515.123.4568
       102     De Haan      Lex           LDEHAAN     Y    Office        515.123.4569
```

```
---- Set Mr. Kings' mobile number to be his preferred number
---- Execute the GetEmployeeData procedure
---- Confirm default behavior returns preferred number

SQL>  update emp_phone_numbers set preferred = 'N'
        where employee_id = 100
          and phone_type = 'Office';

1 row updated.

SQL>  update emp_phone_numbers set preferred = 'Y'
        where employee_id = 100
          and phone_type = 'Mobile';

1 row updated.

SQL> commit ;

Commit complete.

SQL> select * from emp_phone_numbers
       where employee_id = 100;

EMPLOYEE_ID PHONE_NUMBER       P PHONE_TYPE
----------- ----------------- - -----------------
        100 515.123.4567       N Office
        100 555.312.9876       Y Mobile
        100 555.321.7345       N Home

3 rows selected.

SQL> @exec_GetEmployeeData

Enter value for department_id: 90
  old  13:    v_dept_id := &Department_ID;
  new  13:    v_dept_id := 90;
  status_code=0  status_message=
  ela=-000000000 00:00:00.002270000

PL/SQL procedure successfully completed.

DEPT_ID DEPT_NAME    STREET_ADDRESS    CITY      STATE       EMP_CURSOR
     90 Executive    2004 Charade Rd   Seattle   Washington  CURSOR STATEMENT : 8
```

```
CURSOR STATEMENT : 8

EMPLOYEE_ID    LAST_NAME   FIRST_NAME   EMAIL       PHONE_NUMBER
        100    King        Steven       SKING       555.312.9876
        101    Kochhar     Neena        NKOCHHAR    515.123.4568
        102    De Haan     Lex          LDEHAAN     515.123.4569
```

If you compare this results set to the one just above it, you'll notice that phone number listed for Mr. King is his mobile number. Your goal in any refactoring exercise should be to identify the desired behavior in the majority of existing application screens and reports, and code the original procedure to return those results. The unique cases can be dealt with by adding new procedures or by adding additional parameters set to default to the commonly requested value. This will minimize the number of application code changes needed to incorporate the changes.

By approaching the database design and refactor steps to minimize the impact on front-end application development, you have truly decoupled the database from the application. There is a clean line between database development and application development; for the database, this line can be verified and tested in the schema or schemas containing application objects. This allows the application developers to incorporate new functionality at their own pace, prioritizing their tasks independent of the database changes. The database changes will have no impact on the application until the developer chooses to call the procedure that returns the new version of the data. `

Does this mean that application developers, database developers, and DBAs no longer need to work together and communicate? Far from it. In the next section, you'll take a look at the values behind agile and consider some guidelines for making the most of PL/SQL in an agile database development environment.

The Agile Manifesto

A few years ago, I found myself very puzzled by the phrase *agile development*. I heard many new terms like *scrum* and *sprint*, bumped into groups of people standing in hallways (usually blocking access to wherever I was trying to go), and noticed a steady deluge of e-mail about build candidates. At the same time, copies of a Dilbert comic strips explaining that specifications, documentation, and training were no longer needed because everyone had been trained to be *agile* appeared throughout cubicle land. All of this was vaguely entertaining to me until I noticed that the Entity Relationship Diagram (ERD) and well-designed database schemas had also gone missing in this new world. At that point, I decided it was time to learn something about agile.

Unfortunately, most of my reading turned up very little information about databases. The few sources I did find seemed very limited in their understanding of all the options available in modern database products and how the use of those options impacted database performance. I wondered if the lack of attention to database design had been intended by the creators of the agile movement because they did not consider it necessary, or if database design had been overlooked because the typical use cases in most books dealt with building an application on pre-existing databases.

So I started at the beginning by looking at The Agile Manifesto, shown in Figure 12-3. I found that I agreed wholeheartedly with both the Manifesto and every one of The Twelve Principles supporting it. I also found no reference to scrum, sprints, standup meetings, or any desire to obliterate database design. I've copied The Agile Manifesto below, you can find The Twelve Principles at agilemanifesto.org.

Manifesto for Agile Software Development

We are uncovering better ways of developing
software by doing it and helping others do it.
Through this work we have come to value:

Individuals and interactions over processes and tools

Working software over comprehensive documentation

Customer collaboration over contract negotiation

Responding to change over following a plan

That is, while there is value in the items on
the right, we value the items on the left more.

Kent Beck	James Grenning	Robert C. Martin
Mike Beedle	Jim Highsmith	Steve Mellor
Arie van Bennekum	Andrew Hunt	Ken Schwaber
Alistair Cockburn	Ron Jeffries	Jeff Sutherland
Ward Cunningham	Jon Kern	Dave Thomas
Martin Fowler	Brian Marick	

© 2001, the above authors
This declaration may be freely copied in any form,
but only in its entirety through this notice.

Figure 12-3. The Agile Manifesto

The Agile Manifesto lists four values: *Individuals and Interaction, Working Software, Customer Collaboration,* and *Response to Change.* These first four values are comparable to four traditional values: *Processes and Tools, Comprehensive Documentation, Contract Negotiation,* and *Following a Plan.* Notice the phrasing of each line. The Manifesto doesn't state that the second set of values is no longer necessary; it simply says that the first set of values are more important. Nor does the Manifesto tell you exactly how to achieve agile and there is a reason for that. Teams are different, and what works well for one may be detrimental to another. Since individuals and interactions are more important than tools and processes and are the first value pair listed, you need to recognize that tools and processes should support the individuals on the team and encourage interaction among the team members. When existing tools and processes do not meet this goal, the tools and processes should be changed.

People who hear me say this are usually surprised. After all, I wrote a paper back in 2008 called "An Industrial Engineer's Guide to Database Management." In my paper, I noted ways that good database management practices were similar to Industrial Engineering, and processes and standardization were very heavily emphasized. I still believe that process and standardization are very important to building a reliable product with a repeatable build but if the existing process is not making it easier for the team to get their job done, the process is flawed, not the team. Just like a user will readily use an application that makes it easier to do their job, a team will follow a process that makes it easier to do theirs. The first sign of a flawed process is that people don't like to follow it. The best fix is to ensure that the process is adding value and that the benefits are visible. If the process is adding value but using the process is painful, then you need tools to make it easier to comply. Processes are most beneficial when they are consistently followed by everyone on the team, and teams are generally very willing to comply with processes that make it easy to comply with a known requirement.

This is, of course, a circular argument but that's not a bad thing. In this case, you have a healthy feedback loop in that people will follow a process that adds value; as more people follow the process, the more valuable it becomes. Early Industrial Engineering techniques, i.e. Taylorism, recognized the importance of finding and eliminating bottlenecks in process (system) optimization but they did so at the expense of the humans involved in the process. Later techniques, such as those proposed by Dr. W. Edwards Deming and used in Lean Manufacturing, recognized the value of the individuals within the process. By changing processes to optimize the team's ability to get their job done in the simplest and most expedient way possible, Toyota was able to build better quality cars faster at a lower cost than the companies who followed the recognized processes of that time period. This is what agile is all about: focus on the values and the goals of the team, define the principals that support those goals, and then create the process (practices) that ensure members are able to achieve their goals as effectively and as efficiently as possible.

Using PL/SQL with Evolutionary Data Modeling

In this section, I'll list some of the techniques that have I have either experienced or seen to be effective. This isn't an exhaustive list, nor is it intended to be a list of commandments that must be followed. As you read through these techniques, consider the values in The Agile Manifesto. Each of the techniques below aligns with at least one of the core values and supports the team's ability adapt to changes, keep change visible, and continuously improve their software products.

Define the Interface

Rather than beginning by designing a database schema, start by defining the interface between the database and the front-end application. What is the functionality the application must perform? Define the data needed by the users and the values they will enter to request the result set. Define the data they need to update and how they will confirm their updates. If data needs to be manipulated or transformed, determine what needs to happen to it and how the transformation can be verified. This process should include database architects, database developers, and application developers, and when it's complete, the end result is an agreement of the functionality the database will provide for the application. The agreement must include names of any object the application team will call. If views are needed, column names and data types should be included. Procedure definitions should include all required input and output parameters. Once an agreement is reached, everyone should have what they need to focus on optimizing the design within their area of responsibility. Any changes must be negotiated. If bugs are identified later that indicate a mismatch between the database and application, a review of the interface agreement will help identify how the bug should be resolved. The process of defining the interface increases the direct interaction between team members and engages them on the most important topic: the functionality needed by the end user.

Think Extensible

One of the principles behind The Agile Manifesto is simplicity and minimizing the work to be done. Some interpretations of agile use the idea of minimizing work to insist that nothing but the minimal code to provide for the immediate needs should be written. The problem with this kind of thinking is that performance and scalability can't be added to the build when the customer notices response time is slowing. I've heard people say "The customer isn't paying for a Cadillac. Just build the Yugo for now." However, has anyone ever successfully turned a Yugo into a Cadillac? Anyone who knows cars—or software—knows that it just doesn't work that way.

Instead, you need to start by building a solid and extensible frame. Structural changes are major changes for cars, houses, or software systems. If you have a solid foundation, you can add functionality so that your Yugo/Cadillac begins to take shape and gives the customer an initial feel for what is possible. Maybe the customer will be happy with a Yugo; maybe the application will be so successful it will eventually become a Cadillac. Using an evolutionary approach to database design and using PL/SQL as an API allows you to adapt the database to changing needs while controlling how and when changes are implemented in the next layer of the application.

Many proponents of agile mention how easy it is to make the changes later when new customer needs are identified. This depends on which system components are considered part of the design. If the team has an architect and that architect is responsible for the design of the application only, this may be true. However, *architect* is a widely used term these days, and if the architect in question is responsible for the hardware or software platform, making changes later can become a very complicated and expensive option. The goal should be to focus on the essential: the features and functionality that will provide the results the customer requested while planning for the likely direction of the final product. Short release cycles and iterative development provide you with feedback to ensure you are interpreting our customer's requests accurately. The feedback you receive provides the first clues when your product's direction needs to shift.

Test Driven Development

One of the most beneficial tools to come from agile and Extreme Programming is test driven development (TDD). The concept is simple: before any code is written, design the test that will prove that the planned code changes have achieved their goal. Some people wonder how a test can be written for software functionality that doesn't exist yet, but turn that question around. How can code be written if the measures of success or failure have not been defined?

When using PL/SQL as the API, the first step to determining the necessary tests is to consider the agreed upon interface. The interface provides the information about the procedure name, the parameters, and the desired results. Testing changes made to a procedure should include verifying the accuracy of the results, of course, but what other kinds of errors might influence the procedure's behavior? As you consider this question, you will see options to improve the code. Some error conditions can be captured, and then the procedure can return a message to the front end application. What will happen if the application passes a completely unexpected value? What happens when the results are not what are expected? What happens when the application session calling a procedure goes away without completing its task? Each of these conditions represents a real possibility for any application but when the code is able to capture errors and handle them in a way that helps the developer identify why the input was invalid or how the results were influenced, the resulting application becomes more robust and stable for the end user, which increases the software's value significantly.

Each procedural test should be scripted and repeatable. These repeatable scripts form the foundation for regression testing, providing a tool to confirm that changes to one procedure did not impact other areas of the application. As a side benefit, these scripts can be made available to others, providing a tool for troubleshooting or verifying system integration. Once tests are repeatable, then they can be incorporated into a test harness, allowing an entire series of tests to be executed as a package. If the test scripts can be executed using shell script or PL/SQL code, then the database developer can confirm that all the functionality required by the interface agreement is working as expected before the application development side begins working with it. This will minimized the issues the front end development team experiences as they incorporate their changes with the database changes. Better yet, if an application developer does hit an error, the results from the database only level testing can be compared to the parameters and results at the next level of development. This expedites troubleshooting and error correction, making both sides of this development process more agile.

Use Schemas and Users Wisely

One of the advantages of using PL/SQL as the interface layer is that structural objects can be changed, database code can be recompiled, and the data dictionary can be checked to confirm that the entire schema is valid. If the new changes had any impact on other packages, procedures, or views, it will be visible immediately and "bugs" can be repaired before they've propagated into other application layers. In order to be able to do this, there should be one application schema containing the all the application objects. In a complex application, the functionality can be divided into modules that will allow subsets of the code to be tested independently of each other. This does not mean that complete system integration testing should not be performed, or that it should be delayed until late in the project. But problems can often be solve more easily and quickly if the scope of the problem can be narrowed.

Create a distinct application user and grant that user permission to execute the procedures defined in the interface agreement and central schema(s). If you grant more access to the application user than this, you run the risk that someone will build a direct SQL statement into another part of the application and this will defeat the compile test. It will also make it more difficult to identify how much application code is impacted by a proposed change, adding complexity and uncertainty to the planning process.

While limiting the access and permissions of the application user IDs provides benefits, it's important to note that the developers need access to schema objects and this is not just true for database developers. The more the front-end application developers know and understand about the DBMS and the data within it, the better use they will be able to make of this toolset. Developers should be encouraged to safely explore the database schema, and there are a couple of options for achieving this goal. Provide as much access as possible to the database early in the development cycle and reduce access as changes are migrated from the development databases, through functionality testing, systems integration testing, and quality testing. How this access is provided depends on the skill of the team. If the team is knowledgeable about the database, allow direct access to the schema. If they are inexperienced with the DBMS and database techniques, create additional users with different kinds of permissions. This also provides benefits in monitoring: if you see a runaway query but the process was initiated by the read only user rather than the user expected to execute the procedures in the application, the process can be safely terminated without impacting the application. If developers cannot be trusted to NOT change code or data without authorization or at the wrong stage of the migration process, they should not be given direct access. Auditing provides an accurate and easy way to make all changes made within the database transparent.

Summary

Agility is being able to adapt quickly to changing conditions. More than that, being able to adapt and evolve to meet changing conditions and requirements is critical to your ability to remain competitive. The DBMS software doesn't limit your ability to implement change, but how you choose to use the software and how you design our applications can. First, you need to acknowledge and prepare for the inevitable change that will come your way. Then you need to evaluate the goals of your projects and the tools you have to meet these goals. It is possible to support an agile development process AND have a well designed data model. Using PL/SQL as an API can buffer some of the changes that will need to be made by providing a means to allow the database and the application to evolve and support changing customer needs.

Profiling for Performance

by Ron Crisco

Performance and *profiling* are critical words in our everyday conversations in the office where I work, in our engagements with clients, and in our teaching. Both words apply equally well to all aspects of life, including software engineering and the topic at hand, PL/SQL.

I first encountered PL/SQL at its inception in the beta release of SQL*Forms 3, Oracle's character-based interactive application development tool. Over the years, I have learned much about writing high performance PL/SQL code, and I am excited to share what I have learned with you.

What exactly does performance mean in the context of PL/SQL? By the end of this chapter, my goal is to arm you with the knowledge and understanding needed to win the battle against poorly performing code.

> *Amateurs practice until they get it right. Professionals practice until they can't get it wrong.*
>
> —Anonymous

In addition to my career in software development and education, I perform professionally as a classical musician on the most heroic instrument, the Horn. Experts in any field share many things in common. Music and software engineering are no exception—the more I think about it, the more I find. For example, these two fields share a common word: performance. Although at first glance it appears to have very different meanings in the two contexts, the word implies some really important things about how we go about the business of music and software development.

In music, performance is defined as an interpretation of a musical composition presented before an audience. In software development, performance is defined as the manner in which or the efficiency with which software fulfills its intended purpose. Both of these definitions explain performance as an end result. In music, as the end result of preparation includes learning the fundamental techniques of the musician's chosen instrument, learning musical notation in general, learning the specific notations of the chosen composition, practicing the specific techniques needed for that composition, and then preparing mentally and physically for the actual performance. But as a professional musician, I know that performance is not simply a single event at the end of this process.

Never practice, always perform!

—Bud Herseth, Chicago Symphony Orchestra

In other words, I realize that my performance will always sound just like my practice, and that's a scary thought unless I practice performing. In order to discover ahead of time what my performance will sound like, I need to perform the music as if my audience were right there listening as I practice. Only by practicing in this way will I be able to assess the parts of the composition on which I need to focus improvement efforts.

How does all of this relate to software performance, specifically for software performance of PL/SQL code? The real key is to be able to look at your software before you put it into production using the same perspective as people will use to see it in production. An expert's perspective requires understanding of these important concepts: performance, profiling, instrumentation, and problem diagnosis.

A MUSICAL NOTE

Many English speakers use the word *Horn* to refer to a general category of instruments including trumpets, saxophones, and trombones. What is commonly called a *French Horn* is neither French in origin or design, and is correctly called the Horn. See `http://en.wikipedia.org/wiki/Corno` for more information. This may seem insignificant, but to many Horn players, including me, it's a big deal.

I described the Horn as the most heroic instrument. When great composers write music for the Horn, they take advantage of the wide variety of musical expression possible with the instrument. One pattern repeats throughout musical history—when the hero enters, the Horn is most often chosen to provide the musical theme. In the classical repertoire, composers like Richard Wagner, Richard Strauss, Pyotr Ilyich Tchaikovsky, and Gustav Mahler produced exciting and vivid heroic themes. In the movie music of the twentieth century, John Williams, Erich Korngold, and Howard Shore continued and expanded the tradition.

What Is Performance?

The word *performance* in the software context does have a few different meanings, so I'll begin by clarifying my use of the word. In the context of PL/SQL code specifically—and really any code in general—performance can be thought of in four ways.

Functional Requirements

Performance can sometimes be used to describe the extent to which software execution meets the so-called functional specifications and requirements defined. If the software program runs to completion without any errors, processes input accurately, and produces correct output, then one might say that the software performed well. How many times have you wished for software that you purchased for your own use to live up to that standard? It seems to be a normal expectation, of course, but it's important to see this basic part of the definition.

Response Time

Writers of requirements have learned that there's more to it than that. Performance is also about time. Software that completes the work that you expect—but completes in 34 hours when you expect completion in minutes—fails the qualitative description of "performs well." When we describe software that performs well, we must introduce the element of time in the description. Software requirements are usually expressed in terms of a single unit of work, a business task. So the requirement must state the expected function of that task and also the expected time it should take for the software to complete that task. This is usually referred to as *response time*: the duration of an execution of a business task measured in units of time.

Throughput

But sometimes it makes more sense to measure performance in a different way. *Throughput* is the number of executions of the business task that complete within a specified duration. The software requirement for an order entry application might state a minimum throughput of 1,000 orders entered per hour. That requirement certainly implies some limits on the response time of any one specific order, but the metric makes more sense to the business manager responsible for the order entry application.

To the manager, the individual response times of each order entered are irrelevant as long as the throughput goal is met. To the order entry clerks and the customers on the phone, throughput is of no consideration. They only care about the response time of one specific order entry task, their own.

Optimizing response time is a necessary prerequisite to optimizing throughput, but not sufficient. Getting a response time of 1/1,000 second per order doesn't guarantee a throughput of 1,000 orders per second. Optimizing throughput also requires attention to queuing delay and coherency delay, but a satisfactory treatment of these is beyond the scope of this chapter. For a clear explanation, I recommend Cary Millsap's paper called "Thinking Clearly About Performance," which can be downloaded from http://method-r.com/downloads/doc_download/44-thinking-clearly-about-performance.

Resource Utilization

Another way to consider performance is with the measurement of resources used during the execution of the software to complete the business task. Common metrics include CPU utilization, memory usage, and I/O latency. Typical diagnoses discuss these metrics only in the aggregate form—in other words, separated from the execution of a single business task. While these metrics are useful in describing system health overall, I have not found them to be useful as the starting point for performance problem diagnosis. Instead, I see these as far more useful when tightly coupled with the measurement of response time. Consider the following examples.

Nathan complains that the month-end sales report is far too slow. Last month it took only 5 minutes to complete. For this month, he started the report 15 minutes ago and it's still not finished. System monitoring shows that the CPU utilization is running at 95%. Average disk I/O latency looks great at 4 ms, and the network administrator tells us the throughput is well under capacity at 9,000 tx/s. Table 13-1 shows a summary of this information.

Table 13-1. Nathan's Sales Report

Resource	Measurement
CPU 95%	
Disk I/O	4 ms
Network 9,00	0 tx/s

Matt complains that the month-end payroll report is far too slow. Last month it took only 5 minutes to complete. Of the 5 minutes, 20% was spent on the CPU, 70% was spent on disk I/O operations, and 10% was spent on network calls. For this month, he started the report 15 minutes ago and it's still not finished. Response time metrics show that of the 15 minutes, 5% was spent on CPU, 25% on I/O operations, and 70% on network calls. Table 13-2 shows a summary of this information.

Table 13-2. Matt's Payroll Report

Resource	Response Time (seconds)
CPU 1	3
Disk I/O	65
Network 182	
Total 260	

I would much rather respond to Matt's situation, given the information provided. The tables are visually similar but convey completely different information. When trying to diagnose Nathan's problem with Table 13-1, I can only *guess* whether or not CPU utilization is a problem for the sales report, because aggregation of data hides the detail that I need. I certainly know that CPU is high for the entire system, but in order to solve the problem for the sales report, I need to know if that task is actually waiting on CPU resources in order to finish.

In Matt's example, I have valuable information about resource utilization applied to his task alone. With Table 13-2, I can *know* where to look, and with great confidence start investigating how and why the payroll report is spending time in the network layer.

Performance Is a Feature

You should think of performance as a feature. It's not a serendipitous result of your work; rather it's something you approach with intent as you design and deliver a product. Karen Morton really captures the importance of this concept when she says:

*So, first and foremost, I think managing performance is about integrating one simple principle into your mindset: **I am responsible for the performance of the code I write or maintain.***

—Karen Morton, *Expert Oracle Practices* (Apress 2010)

Regardless of your adherence to Agile or Waterfall, XP or RAD, Prototyping or Spiral, performance should be a prominent feature at the beginning of the process, during the process, and after the process has "completed."

Functional requirements should be accompanied by performance expectations, and in some business cases those expectations are formal requirements expressed as a Service Level Agreement (SLA). These expectations can't be forced onto the software after delivery. That seems like such an obvious statement, but in practice that's exactly what happens in the real world. Karen Morton's quote describes the essential mindset for every person in every role in the software development team. From the very start, performance must include the concepts of function and time.

When Matt calls and complains about the performance of the payroll report, who will he call? Probably the DBA responsible for the application. That DBA was probably never involved in the software development process. Will the software application documentation lead the DBA by the hand through the problem diagnosis? Probably not. Should it? Absolutely! Will the software itself provide adequate information to point the DBA to the probable cause? Probably not. Should it? Of course! Why is it that performance problems are considered a defect in production implementations but not during development and testing?

Whatever the reasons, the DBAs or performance analysts end up with the problem to solve. Their ability to resolve the problem will depend on the quality of information they can gather about the problem. If Matt complains, that "the whole system is slow" without identifying a specific problem, solving Matt's problem can be agonizing. System-wide aggregated, usually sampled, data may or may not surface the problems that are affecting Matt's report. Analysts can spend endless time and money chasing the wrong problems if they depend solely on aggregated data. They may improve some parts of the system, but they aren't really finished until they fix the root problem that is causing Matt's slow report.

That's not meant to imply that good DBAs and performance analysts don't solve problems like Matt's all the time—of course they do. They ask good questions that lead to resolutions of the problems, such as the following:

- What exactly were you doing while the system was slow?

- Which business task will you execute immediately after I tell you that the system is no longer slow, in order to test my assertion?

Performance analysts use various tools for measuring the critical details—where the time was spent and on what resources during the execution of that business task. So how should you write code that actually helps performance analysts—code that provides performance information beyond the functional requirements?

What Is Profiling?

Profiling is emitting a log of code steps as they execute. In some cases, profiling is done without emphasis on time, but focused more on the sequence of events and the number of iterations. In other cases, each code step is logged with an elapsed time measurement.

Profiling is a common activity, even a daily practice, for many software developers. Profiling is a great way to know your code during development. Chapter 7 describes how to profile PL/SQL code with Oracle provided packages. You might recognize these profilers from other software languages:

```
gcc -pg …; gprof …
```

```
java -prof …; java ProfilerViewer …
```

```
perl -d:Dprof …; dprofpp …
```

Each of these tools displays the results of profiling in different ways. In able to more clearly describe profiling results that work best, specifically for performance, I'll start with a quick explanation of a tool that can help developers understand the passage of time more clearly: the sequence diagram.

Sequence Diagrams

As part of the Unified Modeling Language (UML), sequence diagrams are used primarily to show the interactions between objects in the sequential order that those interactions occur. In software architecture, the objects are usually defined as application tiers like the database, web server, or browser.

In software development, the objects are sometimes defined as layers in the application code, high level procedures calling successively lower level procedures. In the lowest layers, these procedures typically represent calls to basic system resources.

A sequence diagram is most valuable for performance optimization when the element of time is introduced. Seeing a visual representation of each tier or layer where your response time is consumed, with each interaction scaled in proportion to the duration of time elapsed, allows you to focus your attention on the areas of code where the most performance gains can be achieved.

Diagrams work wonderfully for high level understanding of processes, but as more and more objects and interactions are added to the diagram, the details crowd the picture so much that the overall value is lost. When I get lost in details, I find it most helpful to summarize or aggregate the data to find the information I need.

The Magic of Profiles

A *profile* is a tabular representation of a sequence diagram. It is a decomposition of response time, typically listed in descending order of component response time contribution. A receipt from the grocery store is a similar decomposition (although usually not ordered by cost), providing the total amount paid at the bottom and a list of the cost for each of the individual items purchased. Table 13-3 shows a profile of a task that consumed 60 seconds of time, decomposed into the component functions of the task.

Table 13-3. Profile Showing Decomposition of a 60 Second Response Time

Function Call	Response Time (sec)	% Response Time
r	42 70%	
q	15 25%	
s	3 5%	
Total 60		100%

A profile can be aggregated so that all calls to the same function are reported in one row. Adding a column in the table showing the number of times each function was called is sometimes helpful, especially of you would like to know the average response time for each call.

The magic happens when you see exactly where your slow task spent the 60 seconds. You now *know* that 70% of your task's response time is consumed by function r calls. Just as helpful, you know where your task is *not* spending time.

Benefits of Profiling

There are many benefits to profiling your code in this way. The real key is the visibility provided by the unique format of the profile. The benefits include the following:

- You *know* where your code is spending its time. Without accurate measurement of response time, you can only *guess*.

- You optimize only relevant code path. The profile focuses your attention on the top contributors to response time. Without that information, you succumb to Compulsive Tuning Disorder (CTD), tuning everything you can and never knowing when enough is enough. Gaja Krishna Vaidyanatha defines and describes CTD in Chapter 7 of *Oracle Insights: Tales of the Oak Table* (Apress 2004).

- You focus your learning on the topics that matter to you right now. If your response time is completely dominated by `latch: cache buffers chains` calls, then today's your lucky day: you'll need to study only one of the more than 1,000 types of calls that are instrumented within the Oracle Database.

- You can stop optimizing when your objective is achieved. With the profile, you know the possible improvement for each component of the business task. You make economic decisions about improvement with real data to prove your assertions.

- You can *predict* what impact your remedies will have, quantitatively. Then you can verify the results directly in the same units of measure as you predicted. Profiles act then as both the tool for optimization and the proof of benefits gained.

Using profiles in these ways simply make you a better software developer. In order to take full responsibility for the performance of your code, you must make a habit of profiling.

Instrumentation

As a musician and a software developer, of course, the term instrumentation also has multiple meanings to me. When I'm thinking about music, instrumentation is defined as the number and types of different instruments to be used in a particular musical composition or arrangement. The composer specifies the number of different instruments required and a minimum number of players required for each instrument, notated as separate parts. The conductor and performers of the composition make the final decision on how many players will perform each part, guided by both desired musical effect and availability of the correct number of musicians.

When I'm thinking about software, instrumentation takes on a different meaning. If a profile is built by aggregating sequential measurements, where do the measurements come from? Instrumentation is the part of your code that provides those measurements. Like musical instrumentation, the type and amount of measurements provided by your code contribute to the overall performance of your software.

Consider the circumstance that typically leads to the topic of instrumentation. When something goes wrong and the performance of a program is not acceptable, the magic question arises: "Why is this program slow?"

Why is This Program Slow?

Moving from theory to practice, let's examine program p. Why is program p slow?

```
SQL> exec p
PL/SQL procedure successfully completed.
SQL>
```

Obviously, I'm missing a crucial element. Without more information, I can only guess about why program p is slow. Around the office, I have heard countless times what could be described as our corporate mantra.

> *Why guess when you can know?*
>
> —Cary Millsap

Of course I can know—I just need to measure. "Slow" is measured in units of time, so I need to measure the elapsed time of program p.

```
SQL> set timing on
SQL> exec p
PL/SQL procedure successfully completed.
Elapsed 00:03:07.42
SQL>
```

Now I know that program p executed in 3 minutes, 7.42 seconds. That's a good start, but in order to have any idea about what parts of the code in program p I need to improve, I need to measure all of the parts of the code in detail. (That's Step 2 in Method R, which I'll describe in detail later). The detailed measurements are best presented in a profile. How then do I get the right measurements to create a profile? I need *instrumentation*. Instrumentation is what you add to the code to make generation of a profile possible.

First, here's what the code looks like now:

```
CREATE OR REPLACE PROCEDURE p AS
BEGIN
  q;
  r;
  s;
END;
```

Now I add the instrumentation.

```
CREATE OR REPLACE PROCEDURE p AS
  t0 NUMBER;
  t1 NUMBER;
  t2 NUMBER;
  t3 NUMBER;
BEGIN
  t0 := DBMS_UTILITY.GET_TIME;
  q;
  t1 := DBMS_UTILITY.GET_TIME;
  DBMS_OUTPUT.PUT_LINE ('Procedure q: ' || (t1 - t0)/100 || ' seconds');
  r;
  t2 := DBMS_UTILITY.GET_TIME;
  DBMS_OUTPUT.PUT_LINE ('Procedure r: ' || (t2 - t1)/100 || ' seconds');
  s;
  t3 := DBMS_UTILITY.GET_TIME;
  DBMS_OUTPUT.PUT_LINE ('Procedure s: ' || (t3 - t2)/100 || ' seconds');
  DBMS_OUTPUT.PUT_LINE ('Total Elapsed: ' || (t3 - t0)/100 || ' seconds');
END;
```

Here are the results after execution of this instrumented code:

```
SQL> set timing on serveroutput on
SQL> exec p
Procedure q: 1.05 seconds
Procedure r: 172.59 seconds
Procedure s: 14.11 seconds
Total Elapsed: 187.75 seconds
Elapsed 00:03:07.75
SQL>
```

I now know something very important that I could never have known without instrumentation of some kind. The results provide a *profile*, an invoice of where my time was spent in the code. I admit that the instrumentation shown here is clunky, and I wouldn't recommend calling such code "finished," but even instrumentation as clunky as this is powerful. I'll discuss improvements to the instrumentation method in the next section.

Now I know that spending my time optimizing procedure q will gain very little benefit—no more than 1.05 seconds (0.56%) of 187.75 seconds total. Likewise, optimizing procedure s will gain no more than 14.11 seconds (7.52%). The majority of my time was spent in procedure r, so that's where I should spend my optimization time and effort. What if I had decided to start working on procedure q or s? I may have been able to improve the individual response times of those procedures drastically, but if my objective had been to reduce the overall response time by 1 minute, my efforts would have been unsuccessful. Why *guess*? You can *know* where to focus your attention.

Instrumentation makes your code faster, easier to maintain, and cheaper to write. Instrumentation makes your code faster because it shows you all of your opportunities for making your code more efficient, both while you're writing it and after you're done. Instrumentation makes your code easier to maintain because it shows you exactly what your analysts are talking about when they say that your code is too slow. Instrumentation makes your code cheaper to write because it focuses your tuning efforts only upon the parts of your code where performance really matters. Good instrumentation is your proof that the performance requirements for your code have been met.

Measurement Intrusion

Notice in my short example that the elapsed time after adding instrumentation was 3:07.75 seconds, 0.33 seconds longer than the original 3:07.42 seconds. Imagine that those measurements had been computed as an average over the course of a thousand executions. Instrumentation is code, and all code contributes to the overall response time of a unit of work. Smart developers know that removing extraneous and unnecessary code is critical to performance optimization.

So should you consider this instrumentation code extraneous and unnecessary? Absolutely not! Code must not only fulfill the requirements of the task but also perform well throughout the life of the software.

Tom Kyte, the "Tom" behind http://asktom.oracle.com/, was once asked at a conference how much the measurement intrusion effect was for all of the instrumentation built into the Oracle database (the data published through the various V$ and X$ fixed views, the extended SQL trace data, and so on). He paused thoughtfully and then responded confidently that the measurement intrusion amounted to *negative* ten percent or possibly less. He went on to explain that without the instrumentation coded in the Oracle Database kernel, the developers in Oracle Server Technologies would have been unable to optimize their code effectively. As a direct result of having the level of detail their instrumentation provides, the developers are able to improve the performance of the code in every release.

Identification

In addition to code that provides response time values for individual program units, instrumentation can also be used to identify application code in the database. The ability to associate resources consumed in the database directly with specific business tasks is a critical component of performance optimization. Oracle provides many different ways to accomplish this goal.

DBMS_SESSION.SET_IDENTIFIER

DBMS_SESSION.SET_IDENTIFIER should be used to make performance analysis easier at runtime. Using this command lets the instance know which end user is associated with each session. Oracle introduced this "End to End Application Tracing" feature in version 10. For example, if your application authenticates users at the database level with unique accounts, you could set the identifier to the user name and IP address in a logon trigger.

```
CREATE OR REPLACE TRIGGER LOGON_TRIGGER
AFTER LOGON ON DATABASE
DECLARE
  l_identifier VARCHAR2(64);
```

```
BEGIN
  L_identifier := SYS_CONTEXT('USERENV', 'OS_USER') || ':' ||
                  SYS_CONTEXT('USERENV', 'IP_ADDRESS');
  DBMS_SESSION.SET_IDENTIFIER(l_identifier);
END;
```

The end user identifying information is now visible in the column V$SESSION.CLIENT_IDENTIFIER, in dozens of other views, and in any extended SQL trace files generated for that session. To enable tracing for a known end user identifier, call the Oracle built-in procedure, like so:

```
DBMS_MONITOR.CLIENT_ID_TRACE_ENABLE(client_id=>'HR:Claire:425542',
                                    waits=>TRUE,
                                    binds => TRUE,
                                    plan_stat => 'ALL_EXECUTIONS'     -- 11g and later
                                    );
```

The trace file will contain a line formatted like

```
*** CLIENT ID:(HR:Claire:425542) 2011-03-16 01:59:13.317
```

If your application shares sessions among end users, then this information needs to be set from the application layer instead of the database. Instead of IP address, use an application level session ID or user name. The key is to use the information necessary to identify the end user responsible for the work being done in the database session.

Enabling tracing for the end user identifier will now output data to multiple trace files, since your application is sharing sessions. The Oracle utility trcsess can be used to consolidate information from multiple trace files containing the same CLIENT ID. For example:

```
trcsess output=425542.trc clientid=HR:Claire:425542 *.trc
```

▓ **Caution**   Don't confuse V$SESSION.CLIENT_IDENTIFIER with V$SESSION.CLIENT_INFO, which is set using the DBMS_APPLICATION_INFO.SET_CLIENT_INFO procedure. Although DBMS_MONITOR has procedures for enabling and disabling extended SQL tracing based on MODULE and ACTION set from DBMS_APPLICATION_INFO, the CLIENT_INFO column has no counterpart in DBMS_MONITOR.

DBMS_APPLICATION_INFO.SET_SESSION_LONGOPS

If you have a task that you know in advance will be long-running, identify the task with DBMS_APPLICATION_INFO.SET_SESSION_LONGOPS. This procedure populates a row in the V$SESSION_LONGOPS view that can be used to monitor the progress of your long-running task. The procedure parameters loosely correspond to columns in the view, so visibility of application-specific details is easily achieved, and in an extremely lightweight way.

Note that Oracle automatically populates this view during tasks like statistics gathering, parallel query execution, and Server Managed Recovery, so your data will be interspersed with that data. The following code shows an example of using this procedure:

```
DECLARE
    l_rindex       BINARY_INTEGER;
    l_slno         BINARY_INTEGER; -- Oracle internal use
    l_op_name      VARCHAR2(64)    := 'Month end posting';
    l_target       BINARY_INTEGER; -- Object ID being worked on
    l_target_desc  VARCHAR2(32);   -- Description of target
    l_context      BINARY_INTEGER; -- A number relevant to task, amount processed, etc.
    l_sofar        NUMBER(6,2);    -- The amount of work done so far
    l_totalwork    NUMBER := 100;  -- An estimate of the amount of work to be done
    l_units        VARCHAR2(32)    := 'records';
BEGIN
    -- rindex is used to identify the row in V$SESSION_LONGOPS
    -- the _nohint call will create a new row and rindex for us to use
    l_rindex := DBMS_APPLICATION_INFO.SET_SESSION_LONGOPS_NOHINT;

    FOR i IN 1 .. l_totalwork LOOP

        -- In practice, this would be a more complex calculation.
        -- This simple example assumes uniform processing time for each sub task
        l_sofar := i;

        DBMS_APPLICATION_INFO.SET_SESSION_LONGOPS(rindex      => l_rindex,
                                                  slno        => l_slno,
                                                  op_name     => l_op_name,
                                                  target      => l_target,
                                                  target_desc => l_target_desc,
                                                  context     => l_context,
                                                  sofar       => l_sofar,
                                                  totalwork   => l_totalwork,
                                                  units       => l_units);

        -- processing occurs here

        COMMIT;
    END LOOP;
END;
/
```

■ **Tip**   Oracle doesn't currently provide a procedure for removing the row in V$SESSION_LONGOPS. This view represents data from one of Oracle's fixed-size underlying tables, so rows aren't really deleted anyway. New rows replace older rows after the maximum number of rows is reached. For rows inserted by Oracle features like statistics gathering, the TIME_REMAINING column will be set to 0 when the operation completes. For your own data, ensure that you set SOFAR and TOTALWORK to the same value when your task is complete, since the TIME_REMAINING column is not accessible through the procedure.

DBMS_APPLICATION_INFO.SET_MODULE

While the DBMS_APPLICATION_INFO.SET_SESSION_LONG_OPS procedure is intended specifically for the identification of long running tasks, Oracle does provide a lightweight method for identifying all of your application tasks currently executing in the database. The values of module and action are visible in V$SESSION and in many of the dynamic performance views. DBMS_MONITOR.SERV_MOD_ACT_STAT_ENABLE can be used to see real-time statistics for any module and action in the view V$SERV_MOD_ACT_STATS.

Setting the values of module and action correctly is absolutely the best way to correlate performance statistics in the database with your business tasks. For example:

```
CREATE OR REPLACE PROCEDURE p AS
BEGIN
  DBMS_APPLICATION_INFO.SET_MODULE(module_name => 'Month End Posting',
                                   action_name => 'p');
  q;
  r;
  s;
  DBMS_APPLICATION_INFO.SET_MODULE(module_name => NULL,
                                   action_name => NULL);
END;
```

Note that like DBMS_SESSION.SET_IDENTIFIER, Oracle provides (in 10g and later) the ability to turn on extended SQL tracing based on module and action values with the DBMS_MONITOR package. To enable tracing for a known module and action, call the Oracle procedure, like so:

```
DBMS_MONITOR.SERV_MOD_ACT_TRACE_ENABLE(service_name => 'V11202',
                                       module_name => 'Month End Posting',
                                       action_name => 'p',
                                       waits => TRUE,
                                       binds => TRUE,
                                       plan_stat => 'ALL_EXECUTIONS'     -- 11g and later
                                       );
```

The trace file will contain lines formatted like this:

```
*** SERVICE NAME:(V11202) 2011-05-13 20:26:22.919
*** MODULE NAME:(Month End Posting) 2011-05-13 20:26:22.919
*** ACTION NAME:(p) 2011-05-13 20:26:22.919
```

What values should be used for module and action? The module name should uniquely identify a part of your application. The action name should represent a logical unit of work that is being executed within the module. Both module and action should mimic business terminology as closely as possible.

■ **Note**   Oracle provides hooks into the module and action identifiers for other languages in addition to PL/SQL. In OCI, use the procedure OCIAttrSet to set the OCI_ATTR_MODULE and OCI_ATTR_ACTION values. See `http://download.oracle.com/docs/cd/E11882_01/appdev.112/e10646/ociaahan.htm` for details.

In Java, use the JDBC method `OracleConnection.setEndToEndMetrics()`, provided first in Oracle 10g. See `http://download.oracle.com/docs/cd/E11882_01/java.112/e16548/dmsmtrc.htm` for details.

In Perl, use the `DBI->connect` function (in `DBD::Oracle`) to set attributes `ora_module_name` and `ora_action`. See `http://kobesearch.cpan.org/htdocs/DBD-Oracle/DBD/Oracle.html` for details.

These languages, as well as any other language with access to the database layer, can also use PL/SQL calls to set the values directly with DBMS_APPLICATION_INFO. Unlike the OCI, Java, and Perl examples, this method does incur an additional network round trip, so consider carefully before making these PL/SQL calls inside code loops.

The DBMS_APPLICATION_INFO package doesn't keep track of nested actions. When you use the SET_MODULE procedure, the former values of module and action are lost, so you're responsible for handling this problem correctly in your code. Unsetting them at the end of the procedure makes sense at the highest level of the code, but how should SET_MODULE be used in the inner procedures q, r, and s? One option is to avoid setting module and action in called procedures and only setting them in the highest level procedure. For example:

```
CREATE OR REPLACE PROCEDURE p AS
BEGIN
  DBMS_APPLICATION_INFO.SET_MODULE(module_name => 'Month End Posting',
                                   action_name => 'q');
  q;
  DBMS_APPLICATION_INFO.SET_MODULE(module_name => 'Month End Posting',
                                   action_name => 'r');
  r;
  DBMS_APPLICATION_INFO.SET_MODULE(module_name => 'Month End Posting',
                                   action_name => 's');
  s;
  DBMS_APPLICATION_INFO.SET_MODULE(module_name => NULL,
                                   action_name => NULL);
END;
```

A better option is to handle the nesting by storing the prior values before calling set_module and then restoring them at completion. Instead of instrumenting only the highest level code, each called procedure should have similar code. Each exit point of the procedure will need to reset the module and action, including the exception handling section. For example:

```
CREATE OR REPLACE PROCEDURE p AS
  l_module VARCHAR2(48);
  l_action VARCHAR2(32);
  l_sqlcode NUMBER;
  l_sqlerrm VARCHAR2(512);
BEGIN
```

```
DBMS_APPLICATION_INFO.READ_MODULE(module_name => l_module,
                                  action_name => l_action);
DBMS_APPLICATION_INFO.SET_MODULE(module_name => 'Month End Posting',
                                 action_name => 'p');
q;
r;
s;
DBMS_APPLICATION_INFO.SET_MODULE(module_name => l_module,
                                 action_name => l_action);
EXCEPTION WHEN OTHERS THEN
  l_sqlcode := SQLCODE;
  l_sqlerrm := SQLERRM;
  DBMS_APPLICATION_INFO.SET_MODULE(module_name => l_module,
                                   action_name => l_action);
  -- handle exceptions here
END;
```

I can't overstate the value of incorporating the use of DBMS_APPLICATION_INFO in your application. Keeping track of the module/action stack is troublesome, but I'll soon discuss a way to simplify that.

Conditional Compilation

Chapter 4 describes instrumenting PL/SQL code with timing information using the Conditional Compilation feature of PL/SQL. This method can be used in cases where performance analysts have control over the runtime application and the performance problems are easily reproducible.

If the problem is reproducible in a test environment, then the PL/SQL code can be recompiled with the Timing instrumentation turned on. If the production environment must be used (and let's face it, this happens all too frequently), there are ways to minimize the intrusion. Instead of recompiling the PL/SQL in the active schema, duplicate the PL/SQL in a separate schema. Then the code can be recompiled in the new schema without affecting production users.

To redirect a specific user to the newly created schema, either modify the application or create a login trigger. Then reproduce the problem. Finally, based on the data provided by the timing code, construct a profile of the response time for the problem task and amaze your friends by solving the performance problem.

Built-in Profilers

Chapter 7 encourages you to know your code with the assistance of several packages included with the Oracle database: DBMS_HPROF, DBMS_TRACE, and DBMS_PROFILER. These packages provide functionality for profiling your PL/SQL code, each with slightly different area of focus. I will only mention them quickly here, since I am really more interested in solutions that will span the entire software life cycle.

Knowing your code during development is crucial, so tools that easily profile code at the line or subprogram level are invaluable. But how easily can these tools be integrated into your application? How heavy is the measurement intrusion? Can a performance analyst easily get response time data for a specific business task without incurring the penalty of intrusion on all other business tasks?

Using these built-in packages may be just what you're looking for, but I have not found them to answer these questions well enough. Fortunately, I have found a better answer: a PL/SQL library that provides a standard for instrumenting with DBMS_APPLICATION_INFO and enabling Oracle's internal instrumentation. Before I cover the library in detail, I need to introduce this instrumentation.

Extended SQL Trace Data (Event 10046)

Oracle's kernel instrumentation, extended SQL trace data, was originally known as "pseudo error debugging event number 10046." This instrumentation was added to Oracle's code for the optimization of database applications as well as optimization of the kernel itself. The trace files generated by this instrumentation provide exactly what developers want: a linear sequential record of how their code spends time.

The level of detail included in the trace files allows analysts an intimate view of the inner workings of a database session. Much like the built-in profilers, sometimes this level of detail can be overwhelming. Instrumentation *at the right level* is the real key. Oracle's tkprof aggregates the data to make some sense of the details, but in doing so, it hides important relationships. What's really needed is aggregation of the data in the format of a profile, summarizing the details in a way that focuses your attention on where the largest amounts of response time for a specific business task were spent.

Constructing profiles of slow performing business tasks is critical to successful optimization. I use the Method R Profiler software to generate a profile, identify the top contributors to response time, and resolve performance problems. Sometimes the problems are in poor SQL, sometimes in poor PL/SQL, sometimes in configuration issues, and sometimes in more complex situations. But in every case, the profile is the best place to start. Sometimes DBA staff are resistant to enabling tracing or to providing access to their development teams.

> *I will run trace, even if it does take an act of Congress and a letter from my doctor to get the DBAs to give me the necessary privileges.*

> —Frustrated Client

But getting those trace files is well worth the effort. Applications that are instrumented really well may report enough detailed timing information to resolve most issues. But in some cases, the real performance problem is hidden from the application at the database layer. In those cases, performance analysts need the correlation of instrumentation: extended SQL trace files that include details of the business tasks being executed. And better yet, smart applications should generate trace files when needed with this correlated information included.

Instrumentation Library for Oracle (ILO)

ILO, the Instrumentation Library for Oracle, is an open source project. I'm the current caretaker, but the credit for its creation belongs to Eric Evans. ILO consists of PL/SQL packages with procedures for identifying and measuring tasks using Oracle extended SQL trace and procedures for collecting and storing response time data for specific business tasks. The packages are installed and compiled in the target Oracle instance and can be called by code written in any language that has access to the Oracle database tier. ILO is fully integrated with the Method R SLA Manager, which allows you to organize and analyze response time data for your entire application system.

▒ **Note** ILO is open source software available at SourceForge, `http://sourceforge.net/projects/ilo/`. It requires Oracle Database version 9.2.0.1 or newer. It is released free of charge under the GNU Lesser General Public License (LGPL), `http://gnu.org/copyleft/lgpl.html`. SLA Manager is commercial software from Method R Corporation, `http://method-r.com/software/slam`.

Why Should You Use ILO?

The benefits of instrumenting code with ILO include the following:

- It's very easy for operators and analysts running ILO-instrumented applications to profile the exact duration of a specified business task. Imagine that a user complains that "adding an employee" in an HR system is too slow. With ILO instrumentation, it's trivially easy for a performance analyst to obtain exactly the Oracle-extended SQL trace data he needs to diagnose and repair the user's specific problem.

- Developers no longer need to worry about understanding when or why to use DBMS_APPLICATION_INFO or DBMS_SESSION to register parts of their applications with the Oracle database. Business tasks are now visible in **V$** views identified by Module and Action.

- Developers no longer need to worry about inserting lines of code into their applications to manage Oracle's "extended SQL tracing" feature (also known as 10046 tracing, `DBMS_SUPPORT` tracing, or `DBMS_MONITOR` tracing).

- With ILO, your Oracle trace files will be properly time-scoped and will contain *only* descriptions of elapsed time that are part of your response time.

- ILO contains hooks that allow you to store response time histories for specific tasks. You'll then be able to report on performance trends or violations of service level agreements.

- ILO is real-world tested. It's lightweight and trustworthy.

How It Works

ILO is very easy to use. You mark the beginning and end of each task with a single line of code, giving each task a module and action name. Think of the action as the name of the task itself and the module as the part of the application that the task represents.

Marking the beginning of any task is as simple as making a procedure call and including the values for module, action, and comment. When marking the end of a task, you again make a simple procedure call. Be sure to include all possible exit points of the marked task including any EXCEPTION sections in your code. For example:

```
DECLARE
  l_sqlcode NUMBER;
  l_sqlerrm VARCHAR2(512);
BEGIN
  ilo_task.begin_task(module  => 'Load Transaction Tables',
                      action  => 'Begin overall load',
                      comment => 'Execution of procedure all_trx_table_loads');

  ... code for your task goes here

  ilo_task.end_task;
EXCEPTION
  WHEN ex_insert_problem THEN
      l_sqlcode := SQLCODE;
      l_sqlerrm := SQLERRM;
      ilo_task.end_task(error_num => l_sqlcode);
      ... handle the exception
  WHEN others THEN
      l_sqlcode := SQLCODE;
      l_sqlerrm := SQLERRM;
      ilo_task.end_task(error_num => l_sqlcode);
      ... handle the exception
END;
```

■ **Tip**   SQLCODE and SQLERRM are active at all times in the EXCEPTION section of your code. If your exception handling raises another exception, the original SQLCODE will be replaced by the new error. Note that almost any line of code can cause an exception to be raised. Before referencing these built-ins, save the contents in local variables. Your logging and instrumentation procedures should then use the local variables to document the correct error. Also note that ILO exception handling is configurable. By default, ILO procedures will suppress their own exceptions to avoid affecting production code negatively.

The enabling and disabling of extended SQL tracing should be performed at application runtime, long after the developer's involvement in the project has completed. The ilo_task.begin_task call checks to see whether someone has expressed the intent to trace a specific module/action pair by calling ilo_timer.get_config. This procedure determines which tasks should be traced, and is usually customized at each ILO installation.

A developer who wishes to unit test his code can call the special procedure ilo_timer.set_mark_all_tasks_interesting(TRUE,TRUE); to override the normal ilo_timer.get_config processing, but calls to this procedure are typically not going to be present in production code unless they are implemented as menu options (for example, Help ➤ Debug ➤ Trace All). The greatest benefit of using ILO is that the choice of tracing is a precisely controlled runtime decision. Instead of manual intervention by a DBA to turn on trace for a session, ILO provides the mechanism for expressing the intent to turn on trace from the application and task specific tracing to occur without intervention.

Example

A common use for PL/SQL code is in DML triggers that handle multiple code paths. In the following example, the trigger performs different actions depending on whether the originating DML was an insert or an update. Good instrumentation should not only inform you of code coverage but also help you to measure the right thing.

```
CREATE OR REPLACE TRIGGER insert_or_update_example
    INSTEAD OF INSERT OR UPDATE ON table_abc
DECLARE
  v_storage_value VARCHAR2(32000);
  l_sqlcode       NUMBER;
BEGIN
  IF INSERTING THEN
    ilo_task.begin_task(module => 'Table_ABC',
                        action => 'Instead of insert',
                        comment => 'Insert or Update Trigger on Table_ABC');
    example_package.create_value
    (p_value_name     => :NEW.value_name
    ,p_value          => :NEW.value
    ,p_description     => :NEW.description
    ,p_storage_value => v_storage_value
    );
    example_package.setup_something_else
    (p_storage_value => v_storage_value
    );
  ELSIF UPDATING THEN
    example_package.update_value
    (p_value_name     => :NEW.value_name
    ,p_value          => :NEW.value
    ,p_description     => :NEW.description
    ,p_storage_value => v_storage_value
    );
  ENDIF;
  ilo_task.end_task;
EXCEPTION WHEN OTHERS THEN
  l_sqlcode := SQLCODE;
  ilo_task.end_task(error_num => l_sqlcode);
  ... handle the exception
END;
```

Assuming that you have already instrumented the individual program units in the example_package, you might think further instrumentation is overkill in this trigger. But if your goal for instrumentation is to provide the right performance metric for testing and for diagnosing performance problems, then this instrumentation is critical.

One of the many benefits of using ILO is that the library correctly handles nesting of module/action pairs. Imagine what would happen to the module and action if that weren't the case. The last procedure or function that sets the values gets the blame for all the time spent until the values are set again, and you lose visibility to the actual response time of that task.

Problem Diagnosis

How should you solve performance problems? When something takes too long, ask one question: "Where did my time go?" That's Method R.

Method R

"Method R" is the name that Cary Millsap and Jeff Holt unassumingly called their four-step method for diagnosing and repairing performance problems, documented in the book *Optimizing Oracle Performance* (O'Reilly, 2003). The "R" stands for response time, in contrast to the conventional approach, which they called "Method C."

Method R prescribes four simple steps.

- Identify the task that's most important to you.

- Measure its response time in detail.

- Optimize that response time in the most economically efficient way.

- Repeat until your system is economically optimal.

It's the act of optimizing software like you optimize anything else in life.

Step 1: Identify

Identify the task that's the most important to you. Ask the business stakeholder of your software the following questions:

- What slowly performing business task is most negatively impacting the business?

- Which task would be nicest to fix first?

Inevitably, you will get an answer of many tasks that are all of utmost priority. Don't panic, though, this is not unexpected. Simply ask this follow-up question: "If all of these tasks are of equal priority, then can we start with task X?"

You will either get agreement or clarification. Maybe task Y really does need to be addressed first. In either case, the key is to pick *one* task and move on to the next step of Method R. If the entire system really is slow, and a single underlying cause exists, then addressing any slow task will quickly lead to that underlying cause. Fixing the performance problems for that task will then benefit the rest of the system as well.

If, instead, that task has a unique underlying cause, then you'll waste no time in solving the problem, since you started with a task known to be important to the business. The key to any process or method is getting started correctly. As Mary Poppins said, quoting Aristotle:

> *Well begun is half done.*

> —Aristotle

Step 2: Measure

Measure the task's response time in detail. Measurement should be the primary focus of your attention during any performance analysis activity. Accurate measurement can point clearly to the root problem. Inaccurate measurement can send you on fruitless hunts down ratholes.

When I say "response time," I mean the response time of that top priority task from the moment the end user makes the request for the work to be done until the moment the end user receives the information requested or notification of completed processing. Getting those measurements is sometimes difficult but always worth the trouble.

When I say "in detail," I mean in the form of a profile. Know where every moment of the response time was spent and focus on the largest consumers of time. The profile can detail program code units or resource utilization, but the total at the bottom *must* be 100% of the response time you measured. If not, you need to measure again, more accurately, or you need to reconsider how you are building the profile.

Software performance analysis is often portrayed as art rather than science, but I disagree with that portrayal. Good performance analysis is all about measurement.

> *There are two possible outcomes: if the result confirms the hypothesis, then you've made a measurement. If the result is contrary to the hypothesis, then you've made a discovery.*
>
> —Enrico Fermi

Step 3: Optimize

Optimize that response time in the most economically efficient way. First, find and eliminate unnecessary work. I repeatedly find this to be the best starting point when assessing a new performance issue. Is that 600-page report that runs every morning at 8 a.m. absolutely necessary? Does someone actually read it? Has the job that runs every night to rebuild indexes been evaluated recently? Asking the right question at the business task level is the best place to start.

If it's really needed, then maybe the report could it be run at 2 a.m. instead? Perhaps it could be executed in SQL*Plus in the data center rather than in Excel 2,000 miles away. If you can't eliminate all the work, the next best thing is to reduce the amount of work being done. Moving business rules from mid-tier applications to the database tier is a great way of accomplishing this. Chapter 11 provides an extensive case study showing the benefits of code in the database.

If you have a critical task that depends heavily on a resource, consider rescheduling other work competing for that resource at the same time. Load management is a very effective tool that is often overlooked. Including the business stakeholders in performance optimization is crucial. If you take your pickup truck to the shop and ask the technician to tune your vehicle, how will they tune? Each technician will have his own interpretation of what "tuned" means. Do you want to use your pickup truck to haul a bed full of steel rods up a steep incline for 2 hours? Do you want to win a 200-mile race at the local dirt track on Friday night? The technician that knows the answer to these questions will get the job done right. The performance analyst that knows the business expectations for workload will also get the job done right.

Reduction of work is also the goal when optimizing code path in your application or optimizing individual SQL statements. The key is to focus on efficiency, accomplishing the right amount of work with the last amount of resource utilization. With the right measurements at hand, you *know* where the improvements are needed.

The fastest way to do anything is to not do it at all.

—Cary Millsap

▨ **Tip**   Moving business rules to the database tier is a hotly debated subject, but Toon Koppelaars argues for the case better than anyone else I have heard. If you desire the performance benefits of moving code to the lowest tier possible, check out Toon's vision and his explanation of "The Helsinki Declaration (IT Version)" at `http://thehelsinkideclaration.blogspot.com/`.

Step 4: Repeat

Repeat until your system is economically optimal. A system's performance can always be improved, but at ever increasing cost. By measuring response time of a business task accurately, you can predict the improvement associated with a given change to the software or hardware resources. That quantified improvement can then be weighed against the cost needed to achieve the improvement. The tuning process finishes when the cost of the improvement exceeds the business value gained. When the ball is in the hole—stop.

> *Go play golf. Go to the golf course. Hit the ball. Find the ball. Repeat until the ball is in the hole. Have fun. The end.*

—Chuck Hogan

ILO Example

What does the process of a diagnosing a performance problem look like when your code is properly instrumented? Here I present a case study from our own application development at Method R Corporation. The example comes from work we're doing for a client that contracted us specifically because of our commitment to delivering code that is fast now and fast later.

In many cases, ILO is implemented through calls from an application written in Java or another language external to the database. In this example, the application is written in Java, but all database access is done through a PL/SQL API. Each of the API procedures is instrumented with appropriate module and action names using ILO.

Following the Method R approach, the first step is *identification* of the task most in need of performance improvement. Based on end user feedback, the task in question was identified by module name: `assignment`.

Because the code was already instrumented with ILO, the second step of *measurement* was trivial. When we encountered the performance problem, there was no need to add any sort of debugging or logging code. We used ILO to emit performance data and turn on extended SQL tracing for the `assignment` task. After execution of the production code in a load test, we analyzed the response time data provided by ILO, using the following query:

```
SELECT
  ilo_module,
  ilo_action,
  SUM(elapsed_seconds)                              total_duration,
  AVG(elapsed_seconds)                              avg_duration,
  COUNT(*)                                          cnt
FROM ilo_run_vw
GROUP by ilo_module,
        ilo_action
ORDER BY SUM(elapsed_seconds) DESC;
```

		TOTAL DURATION	AVG DURATION	
ILO_MODULE	ILO_ACTION	(SECONDS)	(SECONDS)	COUNT
--------------	-----------------	--------------	------------	-----
assignment	SetLocationData	9.064287	0.09064287	100
SetLocationData	get_device	8.315280	0.08315280	100
SetLocationData	get_location	0.502014	0.00502014	100
SetLocationData	update_location	0.036686	0.00036686	100
SetLocationData	insert_reservation	0.035895	0.00035895	100
SetLocationData	update_device	0.034592	0.00034592	100
SetLocationData	merge_device	0.031978	0.00031978	100

The information provided is exactly what we need to pinpoint the performance issue. In the results of the query, you can see that the get_device procedure was the largest contributor to the response time, over 8 seconds of a 9 second task, SetLocationData. With the extended SQL trace data for this task, a profile was generated that led to *optimization* of the procedure. The details of the optimization are omitted here to emphasize the importance of the method.

In many cases, examining the variance in executions can be a powerful performance analysis technique. The response time of the get_device procedure was our primary concern in this case, but what if this had not been a current performance issue? We can use Oracle's statistical analysis functions to find tasks with the most variance, like so:

```
SELECT
  ilo_module,
  ilo_action,
  VARIANCE(elapsed_seconds)                              variance,
  STDDEV(elapsed_seconds)                                standard_deviation,
  ROUND(VARIANCE(elapsed_seconds)/AVG(elapsed_seconds),3) variance_to_mean_ratio,
  ROUND(STDDEV(elapsed_seconds)/AVG(elapsed_seconds),3)   coefficient_of_variation
FROM ilo_run_vw
GROUP by ilo_module,
        ilo_action
ORDER BY 5 DESC, 3 DESC;
```

			STANDARD	VARIANCE TO	COEFFICIENT
ILO_MODULE	ILO_ACTION	VARIANCE	DEVIATION	MEAN RATIO	OF VARIATION
---------------	---------------	----------	-----------	-----------	------------
SetLocationData	get_location	0.00004253	0.00652182	0.008	1.299
SetLocationData	get_device	0.00033352	0.01826257	0.004	0.243
assignment	SetLocationData	0.00013663	0.01168871	0.002	0.129
SetLocationData	update_location	5.8995E-09	0.00007680	0.000	0.209

SetLocationData insert_reservation	5.3832E-09 0.00007337	0.000	0.204
SetLocationData update_device	3.7374E-09 0.00006113	0.000	0.177
SetLocationData merge_device	7.8088E-09 0.00008837	0.000	0.276

The query results show that both get_location and get_device have a high variance to mean ratio (VMR) and coefficient of variation. If these procedures do the same amount of processing each time they are called, then the variation in response times is an issue worth pursuing. For further explanation of statistical analysis techniques in performance problem diagnosis, I highly recommend Robyn Sands's work in Chapter 13 of *Expert Oracle Practices* (Apress, 2010). There she explains the significance of the coefficient of variation and variance to mean ratio calculations shown in the output above.

The following code excerpt is just a small sample from the application that generated the ILO data above. I have included the code here to more clearly show the simplicity of the instrumentation.

```
PROCEDURE SetLocationData(…) IS

-- code omitted

PROCEDURE get_location(…) IS
BEGIN
   ilo_wrapper.begin_task(module => 'assignment',
                          action => 'get_location',
                          comment => 'P_ID=' || p_id || ' p_key=' || p_key);

   -- code omitted

   ilo_wrapper.end_task(widget_count => p_data_count);
EXCEPTION WHEN OTHERS THEN
   ilo_wrapper.end_task(error_num => SQLCODE);
END get_location;

PROCEDURE get_device() IS
BEGIN --get_device
   ilo_wrapper.begin_task(module => 'assignment', action => 'get_device');

   -- code omitted

   ilo_wrapper.end_task;
EXCEPTION WHEN OTHERS THEN
   ilo_wrapper.end_task(error_num => SQLCODE);
END get_device;

ilo_wrapper.end_task(error_num => status_code, widget_count => v_cnt);

EXCEPTION WHEN OTHERS THEN
   ilo_wrapper.end_task(error_num => SQLCODE);
END SetLocationData;
```

The real take-away here is that performance optimization in general and instrumentation specifically need to become foremost in your mindset during development. By instrumenting the code, we were able to eliminate all the portions of the code that were irrelevant to the problem. Knowing the true problem is the first and most important step in the solution.

■ **Tip**   Notice that the calls to ILO are wrapped in an application-specific package called ilo_wrapper. This is a good idea. If you use ILO or any other external library, it makes sense to abstract that code. If changes to the API of ILO happen, then only your wrapper package needs to change to match.

Profiling Example

What does the process of profiling look like in practice? Here's an example that I executed in SQL*Plus to answer the same question I asked earlier: Why is program p slow? This time I'll use ILO for instrumentation instead of DBMS_OUTPUT.PUT_LINE.

```
CREATE OR REPLACE PROCEDURE q AS
  l_sqlcode NUMBER;
  l_sqlerrm VARCHAR2(512);
BEGIN
  ilo_task.begin_task(module => 'Procedure P',
                        action => 'q');
  FOR rec IN (SELECT * FROM V$SESSION) LOOP
    NULL;
  END LOOP;
  ilo_task.end_task;
EXCEPTION WHEN OTHERS THEN
  l_sqlcode := SQLCODE;
  l_sqlerrm := SQLERRM;
  ilo_task.end_task(error_num => l_sqlcode);
  -- handle exceptions here
END;
/


CREATE OR REPLACE PROCEDURE r AS
  l_sqlcode NUMBER;
  l_sqlerrm VARCHAR2(512);
BEGIN
  ilo_task.begin_task(module => 'Procedure P',
                        action => 'r');
  FOR rec IN (SELECT * FROM ALL_OBJECTS) LOOP
    NULL;
  END LOOP;
  ilo_task.end_task;
EXCEPTION WHEN OTHERS THEN
  l_sqlcode := SQLCODE;
  l_sqlerrm := SQLERRM;
  ilo_task.end_task(error_num => l_sqlcode);
  -- handle exceptions here
END;
/
```

```
CREATE OR REPLACE PROCEDURE s AS
  l_sqlcode NUMBER;
  l_sqlerrm VARCHAR2(512);
BEGIN
  ilo_task.begin_task(module => 'Procedure P',
                      action => 's');
  FOR rec IN (SELECT * FROM USER_TABLES) LOOP
    NULL;
  END LOOP;
  ilo_task.end_task;
EXCEPTION WHEN OTHERS THEN
  l_sqlcode := SQLCODE;
  l_sqlerrm := SQLERRM;
  ilo_task.end_task(error_num => l_sqlcode);
  -- handle exceptions here
END;
/

CREATE OR REPLACE PROCEDURE p AS
  l_sqlcode NUMBER;
  l_sqlerrm VARCHAR2(512);
BEGIN
  ilo_task.begin_task(module => 'Month End Posting',
                      action => 'p');
  q;
  r;
  s;
  ilo_task.end_task;
EXCEPTION WHEN OTHERS THEN
  l_sqlcode := SQLCODE;
  l_sqlerrm := SQLERRM;
  ilo_task.end_task(error_num => l_sqlcode);
  -- handle exceptions here
  raise;
END;
/

DELETE FROM ilo_run WHERE ilo_module IN ('Month End Posting', 'Procedure P');

EXEC ilo_timer.set_mark_all_tasks_interesting(true,true);

EXEC p;

EXEC ilo_timer.flush_ilo_runs;

set pages 1000
COLUMN ILO_MODULE FORMAT A20
COLUMN ILO_ACTION FORMAT A10
SELECT ILO_MODULE, ILO_ACTION, ELAPSED_SECONDS
FROM ilo_run_vw WHERE ilo_module IN ('Month End Posting', 'Procedure P') ORDER BY 3 DESC;
```

ILO_MODULE	ILO_ACTION	ELAPSED_SECONDS
Month End Posting	p	8.566376
Procedure P	r	8.418068
Procedure P	s	.135682
Procedure P	q	.005708

The results of the query in the SQL*Plus script show me exactly where my time was spent, associated with each business task, identified by module and action name. The query results are a profile (assuming that I know the hierarchical relationship of the procedures and the first row returned represents the total line that usually displays at the bottom instead), so I can easily see that if my goal is optimizing response time, procedure r needs my attention.

In addition to storing the elapsed time information in the database, ILO turned on extended SQL tracing so a trace file was generated. Oracle's trace data stream allows me to drill down into procedure p to see all of the database and system calls made that comprised the response time. Since the module and action names are emitted in the trace file as well, I'm also able to drill down specifically into calls corresponding just to procedure r.

First, I would like to see where my response time went for each module/action pair. Summarizing the response time data in the trace file looks like this:

Module:Action	DURATION	%	CALLS	MEAN	MIN	MAX
Procedure P:r	8.332521	98.4%	545	0.015289	0.000000	1.968123
Procedure P:s	0.132008	1.6%	4	0.033002	0.000000	0.132008
Procedure P:q	0.000000	0.0%	16	0.000000	0.000000	0.000000
Month End Posting:p	0.000000	0.0%	66	0.000000	0.000000	0.000000
SQL*Plus:	0.000000	0.0%	2	0.000000	0.000000	0.000000
TOTAL (5)	8.464529	100.0%	633	0.013372	0.000000	1.968123

In this profile, the data shown for parent procedure p does not include any of the response time contributions of the children. The total elapsed time represented in the trace file is about 8.46 seconds. That doesn't exactly match the values shown in my ILO query, but that's not a problem because the numbers are close enough for my analysis. For more information about the reasons for the difference, see *Optimizing Oracle Performance* (O'Reilly, 2003).

▓ **Note** In this example I am using mrskew from the MR Tools suite sold by Method R Corporation to generate the summary information. Oracle's tkprof and Trace Analyzer tools do provide some aggregation, but they don't provide the *profile* that you need.

Next, I would like to see where the time was spent while executing just procedure r. To do this, I'll drill down into the trace file data, summarizing only the calls executed while module and action were set to Month End Posting and r respectively:

Call	DURATION	%	CALLS	MEAN	MIN	MAX
FETCH	8.332521	100.0%	542	0.015374	0.000000	1.968123
PARSE	0.000000	0.0%	1	0.000000	0.000000	0.000000
CLOSE	0.000000	0.0%	1	0.000000	0.000000	0.000000
EXEC	0.000000	0.0%	1	0.000000	0.000000	0.000000
TOTAL (4)	8.332521	100.0%	545	0.015289	0.000000	1.968123

Now I see clearly what the database is doing during the 8.33 seconds of time spent. All of the time was spent in the FETCH database call. That's not really surprising, since all r does is execute a single query of ALL_OBJECTS. But the value is still here—I *know* where the time is spent. But the trace file contains a lot more detail than this, so drilling down further can provide valuable insight. I would like to know which lines in the trace file represent the largest time contributions to my r procedure. Are all the FETCH calls the same duration? Here's the answer to that question (again provided by mrskew):

Line Number	DURATION	%	CALLS	MEAN	MIN	MAX
4231	1.968123	23.6%	1	1.968123	1.968123	1.968123
2689	0.380023	4.6%	1	0.380023	0.380023	0.380023
4212	0.316020	3.8%	1	0.316020	0.316020	0.316020
4233	0.304019	3.6%	1	0.304019	0.304019	0.304019
2695	0.156010	1.9%	1	0.156010	0.156010	0.156010
281	0.144009	1.7%	1	0.144009	0.144009	0.144009
362	0.100007	1.2%	1	0.100007	0.100007	0.100007
879	0.064004	0.8%	1	0.064004	0.064004	0.064004
1348	0.056003	0.7%	1	0.056003	0.056003	0.056003
2473	0.052003	0.6%	1	0.052003	0.052003	0.052003
532 others	4.792300	57.5%	532	0.009008	0.000000	0.044003
TOTAL (542)	8.332521	100.0%	542	0.015374	0.000000	1.968123

In fact, all of the FETCH calls are not the same duration. The single FETCH call on line 4231 of the trace file comprised almost 24% of the total response time of 8.33 seconds. Instrumentation and profiling allow me to drill down exactly where I need to be to make improvements to my software. In this contrived example, optimizing procedure r means optimizing the query, SELECT * FROM ALL_OBJECTS. The long FETCH call in this case was an anomaly due to the recursive SQL but does serve well to show the method.

Summary

In the software development lifecycle, you should treat PL/SQL with the same disciplines as any other software language—especially the discipline of instrumentation. In order to write fast code that continues to be fast throughout the life of the application, you must properly instrument the code during development. Tools for low level debugging and profiling exist and are useful during development, but these are not well suited for use in production environments.

When performance problems arise in a production environment, an analyst needs to quickly find the area of code that is the largest contributor to response time. Proper instrumentation will provide data for a profile that clearly shows this information, leading to a successful analysis and resolution of the problem. You can *know* that you're measuring the right things and that you've instrumented the right way, when you are able to generate profiles of your code in action that clearly point to the portions of the code where the largest amount of time is being spent. Adding good instrumentation to your code isn't difficult, and ILO, the Instrumentation Library for Oracle, makes it painless.

Coding Conventions and Error Handling

by Stephan Petit

Can you wear a Tuxedo and Birkenstocks at the same time? Yes, you can! Anyone who spent some time at a particle physics laboratory knows it is technically possible. However, some may say that such an outfit clashes with the conventions of elegance. You may also like to wear a combination of green and blue clothes. (Personally I prefer mixing red and black). We can argue endlessly about our respective taste: everyone is right; everyone is wrong. At the same time, conventions, written or not, help with living and working together. They have their own history and reasons.

It is often fun to write code and we all want to make it as good as possible: efficient in terms of execution, compact, and if possible, with style. But we do not usually write code just for ourselves. If you ever had to read a piece of code written by somebody else in order to understand in details what it does or to debug it or to modify it, you probably thought "hmm, I wouldn't have done it that way." It works but it can be hard to understand—a bit like listening to a cousin who speaks with a strong accent. The goal of this chapter is to propose one way of writing PL/SQL. I will first discuss the advantages of coding conventions, then propose specific formatting conventions. I will then discuss error handling and provide examples of error handling conventions. At the end, you will find a template summarizing the conventions outlined in this chapter

---

▨ **Note** I definitely do not pretend that the conventions I have outlined are the only possible ones, but they have proved their efficiency in my day-to-day work. I think it's important to understand the reason of each convention and see the benefits of one method compared to another.

Why coding conventions?

Why even bother? Do we really need coding conventions? Wouldn't it be better for each person to let their own artistic talents flourish, giving free reign to everyone on naming of variables, indenting of loops, and more? Such freedom may sound enticing, but it's the road to ruin—or at least the road to not getting home for dinner on time because you're stuck in the office debugging some inscrutable code. The following are some benefits that accrue from creating structure and adhering to a good set of rules:

Quick understanding: It is easier, hence quicker, to read code that was written following conventions. With just a little bit of practice, the eyes of the reader immediately identify patterns in the code. The structure appears clearly, the various types of elements and the logical blocks become obvious. It also has the advantage of minimizing the possibility of misunderstanding. It is better to say "I like chocolate" than "I do not deny that I don't dislike chocolate," even if both sentences mean the same thing.

Reliability: Once your code is complete, it is nice to have it reviewed by a colleague in order to find possible bugs, inconsistencies, and make sure that its logic is clear. Code that is easy to read and easy to understand benefits from a better review and then is potentially more reliable. From my experience, I know it is also easier to find a reviewer for my work when he or she knows that reading my code won't be a pain because it is an expression of my twisted style.

Maintainability: Maintaining code over time is a challenge. You may find even your own code to be difficult to understand when you revisit it a few months later. It gets worse when a whole package has been written by several individuals. Making sure a common style is being used during the life of a system is of great help when it comes to maintain it.

Security: Coding conventions can enhance the level of security of a system. For instance, a systematic use of bind variables can insulate against code injection threats. This aspect is described in more detail in a following paragraph.

Trainability: When half of the team in charge of a system changes almost every year, it is crucial to train every single newcomer as quickly as possible. When everyone speaks the same way, training is faster. It may happen that a newcomer is reluctant to learn a new way of using a language he or she is already mastering. Dare to impose the standards used by the whole team and if possible, ask the newcomer to work on existing modules. Finding the same coding style everywhere will quickly appear as an advantage.

Speed in coding: Why reinvent the wheel every time you start coding a new module? Using coding conventions removes several questions you may ask yourself about the style of your code. For instance, when modifying an existing procedure, should you follow the style used by the original author or should you use your own? When everyone uses the same style, such a dilemma simply vanishes.

Error handling: Making sure that all errors are gracefully trapped and correctly treated is another tricky part of delivering good software. Therefore, it is important to have a systematic approach to errors and a standardized way of reporting them. Coding conventions can bring a powerful solution to this aspect of software programming.

Formatting

Let's begin by looking at detailed conventions concerning how code is physically formatted. Formatting is one aspect of convention that picky people prefer. Dare to be picky. Following some simple rules makes code easier to read, reuse, and maintain.

The following sections describe some formatting rules that have worked well for me over the years. I follow them. My team follows them. Please though, do not take them as gospel. Feel free to adopt or adapt them, even invent your own! What is important is that everyone walks the same way.

Case

Use upper case for all SQL and PL/SQL keywords, names of procedures, functions, exceptions, and constants.

Use lower case for variables, comments, table names, and column names.

Comments

There are two ways of writing comments in the middle of some code: every single line beginning with -- or a whole block of text between /* and */. I decided to use the syntax --. I think it nicely highlights the text itself, so you don't need to look for where it starts and where it ends. Moreover, it has some technical advantage: you still can use /*... */ to comment a block of code for debugging reasons, even when this block contains some comments (prefixed with --) which you can't do if your code uses the /*... */ syntax. It is slightly heavier to use but can be very handy. You choose. Any comment?

The following is an example of how I comment code within a block:

```
l_book_author := NULL; -- I make sure there is no old value in this variable

IF l_book_id < 0 THEN
  -- This case should not happen unless the book was lost.
  -- Carry on by checking the list of lost books.
  ...
END IF;
```

■ **Note** Use comments as often as you can! What is obvious to you today may be obscure to somebody else (or even to you) tomorrow.

Comparisons

Use <> instead of !=. The <> syntax avoids confusion with = when quickly reading,

Indentation

If ever there was a programming topic to cause controversy, it is probably the topic of how to indent your code. Programmers in all languages have been doing battle with this issue for decades. COBOL programmers perhaps have it easiest. At least in their language, much of the critical indentation is proscribed by the language specification.

The following sections address specific aspects of indenting PL/SQL code. The overall goal is to ease the reading of the code and visually identify logical blocks. I chose to use two blanks. One thing: avoid tabulations as they can be interpreted in different ways by various software development environments and printers.

General Indentation

Use two blanks to indicate that a block is a child of another one, like so:

```
BEGIN
  l_author := 'Pierre Boulle';
  IF p_book_id = 123456 THEN
    FOR l_counter IN 1..100 LOOP
      ...
    END LOOP;
  END IF;
EXCEPTION
  WHEN NO_DATA_FOUND THEN
    -- Deal with this error
    ...
END;
```

Select Statements

Use one line per fetched column, one line per variable, and one line per element of the statement. This approach takes some space but eases the reading and the understanding of the whole statement. See in the following example a useful way of aligning various items:

```
SELECT editor
      ,publication_date
  FROM books
 WHERE book_id = 12345
    OR (book_title   = 'Planet of the Apes'
        AND book_author = 'Pierre Boulle'
       );
```

■ **Note** This example also shows how parenthesis can be aligned in order to clearly show where they start and where they end. Please also note the subtle alignment of the equal signs (or when coding becomes painting!)

This example shows how table aliases can be used:

```
SELECT b1.book_title
      ,b1.book_id
      ,b2.book_id
  FROM books b1
      ,books b2
 WHERE b1.book_title = b2.book_title
   AND b1.book_id <> b2.book_id;
```

Insert Statements

Use one line per column and one line per value. Always indicate the names of the columns in order to avoid ambiguity. This example shows how things can be aligned:

```
INSERT INTO books (
            book_id
           ,title
           ,author
           )
     VALUES (
            12345
           ,'Planet of the Apes'
           ,'Pierre Boulle'
           );
```

Update and Delete Statements

They look pretty much the same. Use one line per column and value, and one line per element of the statement.

```
UPDATE books
   SET publication_year = 1963
 WHERE book_id = 12345;

DELETE FROM books
 WHERE book_id = 12345;
```

If Statements

Use one line per element. For better reading, it's useful to add a comment after the END IF keyword, especially when many lines separate it from the matching IF. Here is an example of a series of IF blocks:

```
IF l_var IS NULL THEN
  ...
ELSE
  IF l_var > 0 AND l_var < 100 THEN
    ...
```

```
  ELSE
    ...
  END IF; -- l_var is between 0 and 100
END IF; -- l_var is null
```

■ **Note** In IF blocks, make sure you always have an ELSE part in order to avoid non-handled cases, unless you are sure that there is nothing to do at all. Then, a little comment is a nice thing to write, just to keep in mind that the ELSE was not purely forgotten. Non-explicitly handled cases can make your application behave oddly and difficult to debug.

Case Statements

Use one line per element, like so:

```
CASE l_var
  WHEN value_1 THEN
    -- Explanation
    ...
  WHEN value_2 THEN
    -- Explanation
    ...
  ELSE
    -- Explanation
    ...
END CASE;
```

Cursors

Use lower case for naming cursors and the suffix _cursor. Note the alignment of keywords on the left, as in the previous examples, improving the readability of the statement.

```
CURSOR books_cursor IS
  SELECT book_id
        ,title
    FROM books
   WHERE registration_date >= TO_DATE('1971-01-01', 'YYYY-MM-DD')
   ORDER BY title;
```

For...loop Statements

Use the l_ prefix for naming the variable used in the loop. When looping on a cursor, use the name of the cursor and the suffix _rec. Understanding where values come from is then easier when reading the code, as in this example:

```
FOR l_book_rec IN books_cursor LOOP
  FOR l_counter IN 1..100 LOOP
    ...
  END LOOP; -- Counter
  ...
END LOOP; -- List of books
```

String Concatenation

Use one line per concatenated element. Reading and modifying are easier this way. Building a string from several parts looks like this:

```
l_text := 'Today, we are '||TO_DATE(SYSDATE, 'YYYY-MM-DD')
                          ||' and the time is '
                          ||TO_DATE(SYSDATE, 'HH24:MI')
                          ;
```

Dynamic Code

Dynamic SQL can be an open door to SQL or statement injection. Using coding templates can help in forcing the use of bind variables, which is one solution against such a threat. The following example shows how it can be dangerous to execute a statement built by concatenating strings , one of them given by an end user (as a parameter, for instance).

Imagine a module that registers books reservations at a library. It may contain some dynamic code, for instance because the table into which the data are inserted depends on the type of book. It may look like this:

```
l_statement := 'BEGIN'
               ||'  INSERT INTO book_reservations (
               ||'            res_date
               ||'           ,res_book_id
               ||'           )
               ||'     VALUES ('
               ||          SYSDATE
               ||'         ,'
               ||          p_book_id
               ||'         );'
               ||'END;'
               ;
EXECUTE IMMEDIATE l_statement;
```

The user is simply asked to input the requested book ID. In case of a gentle and standard user, the generated statement would look like the following, with "123456" the given input:

```
BEGIN
  INSERT INTO book_reservations (
            res_date
           ,res_book_id
           )
```

```
        VALUES (
                SYSDATE
                ,123456
                );
END;
```

But if the end user has bad intentions, he or she can use the same input to inject malicious code. Giving the following input "123456); delete from books where (1=1", the generated statement is this one:

```
BEGIN
  INSERT INTO book_reservations (
              res_date
              ,res_book_id
              )
      VALUES (
              SYSDATE
              ,123456
              );
  DELETE FROM books where (1=1);
END;
```

The operation to be executed would then be made of two statements: a harmless one followed by a very nasty instruction emptying a table.

The following is a rewrite of the code using a bind variable. The use of the bind variable prevents any user-entered string from being interpreted as part of the statement itself. The risk of SQL or statement injection is eliminated.

```
l_statement := 'BEGIN'
               ||'   INSERT INTO book_reservations (
               ||'                res_date
               ||'                ,res_book_id
               ||'                )
               ||'        VALUES (:p_date'
               ||'                ,:p_book_id'
               ||'                );'
               ||'END;'
               ;
EXECUTE IMMEDIATE l_statement
  USING IN SYSDATE
        ,IN p_requested_book_id
        ;
```

Packages

Although it is possible to compile standalone stored procedures and functions in a database, it can quickly become a nightmare to search for one module in a large, flat list. Instead, use packages to group procedures and functions by semantic field or by usage. It is quicker to scan a correctly named package that is most probably containing what you are looking for than it is to scan a list of all functions and procedures in your whole schema.

Separate the *kernel* packages (the ones directly dealing with the data) from the ones that are responsible for *user interface*. More than helping their management and usage, this will allow you to fine tune execution grants, such as having wide access on interface package, more restricted access on kernel packages used as APIs, and no access at all to the very core of your application.

Name your packages using upper case (avoid double quotes around object names, making them case sensitive) and meaningful names. Use prefixes to indicate the type of modules that a package contains. For example, you might use the following prefixes:

> `KNL_` for a package containing kernel modules.

> `GUI_` for a package containing modules dealing with user interface.

Your package names might look as follows:

> `PACKAGE KNL_BOOKS;` for a package containing modules dealing with books.

> `PACKAGE GUI_LIBRARY;` for a package containing modules dealing with a library's user interface.

Stored Procedures

Stored procedures (standalone or in a package) should be considered black boxes that perform a given task. The term "black box" means that they are expected to cope with any kind of input (valid or not), and then do their job or leave the database in the same state as when they were called (for example, in case of error). Usually you want procedures to report any problem encountered in doing the work.

It is better to dedicate one procedure to one single task. This is the basis for good modularity in your application. It is better to have several small modules that you can use and reuse as elementary bricks than to have a few large and heavy modules that are difficult to reuse.

The various kinds of tasks can be separated as follows: retrieving records, checking information, inserting or modifying data, handled by kernel or API packages, producing display for a user interface, handled by interface packages.

Next I'll show you a way of naming stored procedures according to the kind of task they perform. This procedure naming policy, in combination with the package separation naming policy, will ensure an easier understanding of the source code. Moreover, it can also act as a guide for good modularity.

Naming

Use upper case and meaningful names. Use a prefix that indicates the type of the procedure (the $ sign is here as a cosmetic element to visually make a difference with package names and to separate the type prefix from the name). For example, the following are some prefix examples:

> `CHK$` for a procedure checking data.

> `GET$` for a procedure retrieving information from the database or calculating something.

> `EXE$` for a procedure inserting, modifying, or deleting data.

> `DSP$` for a procedure displaying information in a user interface.

And the following are some actual procedure names developed using the preceding list of prefixes:

PROCEDURE CHK$BOOK_AVAILABITLIY; for a procedure checking the availability of a book.

PROCEDURE GET$BOOK_AUTHOR; for a procedure retrieving the author of a book.

PROCEDURE EXE$STORE_BOOK; for a procedure storing data about a book.

PROCEDURE DSP$BOOK_INFO; for a procedure displaying information about a book in a user interface.

Also consider developing the habit of adding a comment repeating the name of the procedure after the final END closing the declaration. Doing so eases the task of reading packages containing a long list of modules, as you can see here:

```
PROCEDURE CHK$TITLE_LENGTH (
                    p_title                      IN          VARCHAR2
                ) IS
BEGIN
  ...
END; -- CHK$TITLE_LENGTH
```

Parameters

Use lower case and the prefix *p_* to name parameters. It is then easier to distinguish them from local variables within the body of the procedure. Use one line per parameter and a fixed distance between the names, the in/out attribute, type, and the default assignment value, like so:

```
PROCEDURE GET$BOOK_AUTHOR (
                p_book_id             IN      NUMBER    := NULL
                ,p_book_title         IN      VARCHAR2 := NULL
                ,p_author                 OUT  VARCHAR2
                );
```

Notice how using one line per parameter makes the code easy to read. It is also easy add or remove one parameter if necessary, specially when the comma is at the beginning of each line.

■ **Note** I also recommend that you specify NULLs as your default parameter values. Otherwise, it can be difficult to know whether a given parameter value was actually passed or whether it was left at its default. If a parameter defaults to X, and the value in a given procedure call is indeed X, your code has no way to know whether that value X was passed to the procedure or whether the parameter defaulted. Should you need a non null default value, there's always time to use a good old NVL later on when using the parameter.

Calls

Always prefix the procedure name with its package name, even when calling a procedure within the same package. It eases reading and debugging and makes the relocation of a piece of code into another package a piece of cake.

Always use the => syntax to pass parameter values. List parameters one value to the line. The => syntax makes the call unambiguous regarding the ordering of parameters; each parameter receives the value it is intended to receive. Moreover, the syntax also avoids any ambiguity when calling overloaded modules (some call them *polymorphic* modules). Here's an example:

```
KNL_BOOKS.GET$BOOK_AUTHOR (
            p_book_id     => 123456
            ,p_author     => l_author
            );
```

Local Variables

Use lower case and the prefix *l_* to name local variables. It is then easier to distinguish them from parameters within the body of the procedure. Use one line per declaration and a fixed distance between the names and the types, like so:

```
l_author                           VARCHAR2(50);
```

Constants

Use upper case and the prefix *C_* to name your constants, like so:

```
C_TITLE_HEADER                     CONSTANT VARCHAR2(50) := 'Title';
```

Create a constant as soon as a value (a string or a number) is used at more than one place in the code. In other words, avoid hardcoded values. Using constants instead of hardcoded values multiple times will avoid typos and hours spent trying to understand why a module is not behaving as expected. For instance, imagine that you want to check that a button is pressed in a user interface. Using a constant for the name of the button and for checking what was clicked ensures consistency between the interface and the behavior of the application. Here's an example:

```
IF p_button = 'Ok' THEN -- Bad if the button is named 'OK' (in upper case)

C_OK_BUTTON                        CONSTANT VARCHAR2(50) := 'OK';
IF p_button = C_OK_BUTTON THEN -- Far better !
```

▨ **Note** It is possible to dimension a constant string with a length that is too short (such as VARCHAR2(1) := 'Hello') without triggering a compilation error. The code fails only when the given constant is called. Debugging this is very difficult, as the origin of the problem is not in the body of any module. Therefore, I always declare constant strings with a good length, like 50, even for very short values (VARHCAR2(50) := 'Y').

Types

Use upper case and the prefix *T_* to name your types, like so:

```
TYPE T_SEARCH_RESULT IS TABLE OF NUMBER
    INDEX BY BINARY_INTEGER;
```

Global Variables

Use lower case and the prefix *g_* to name global variables, as in the following example:

```
g_book_record                           BOOKS%ROWTYPE;
```

Local Procedures and Functions

It is possible to declare procedures or functions that are local to a given procedure. Use upper case and the prefix *LOCAL$* in their names. A local procedure would look like this:

```
PROCEDURE KNL$REGISTER_AUTHOR (
                    p_name                  IN      VARCHAR2
                    ) IS

  PROCEDURE LOCAL$COMPUTE_CODE_NAME(
                    p_local_name            IN      VARCHAR2
                    ) IS
  BEGIN
    ...
  END; -- LOCAL$COMPUTE_CODE_NAME

  l_code_name                                 VARHCAR2(80);

BEGIN
      l_code_name := LOCAL$COMPUTE_CODE_NAME(
                      p_local_name => p_name
                      );
  ...
    END; -- KNL$REGISTER_AUTHOR
```

Procedure Metadata

Even if you use software version management tools (such as Subversion), it can be useful to keep some dates and names in your source code. Other in-code documentation is also helpful. I suggest adding a block of comments such as the following before the declaration of each module. Having the name of who did what change and for what reason can help when it comes to modifying a module. It also acts as part of the technical documentation of the system.

```
/*------------------------------------------------------------------*/
/*                                                                  */
/* Module   : MODULE_NAME                                           */
/* Goal     : Short description of the module.                      */
/* Keywords : Few keywords describing what the module does.         */
/*                                                                  */
/*------------------------------------------------------------------*/
/* Description:                                                     */
/*                                                                  */
/* Long description of the module: its goal.                        */
/* Explanation about parameters (Input and Output).                 */
/* How the procedure works, the "tricks", etc.                      */
/*                                                                  */
/*------------------------------------------------------------------*/
/* History:                                                         */
/*                                                                  */
/* YYYY-MM-DD : First name and Name - Creation.                     */
/*                                                                  */
/* YYYY-MM-DD : First name and Name - Review.                       */
/*                                                                  */
/* YYYY-MM-DD : First name and Name                                 */
/*              Description of the modification.                    */
/*                                                                  */
/*------------------------------------------------------------------*/
```

Functions

My coding conventions for functions are the same as for procedures. Only the naming is different. I name my functions using the prefix *STF$* (standing for Stored Function), like the following:

```
FUNCTION STF$IS_BOOK_AVAILABLE (
              p_book_id            IN      NUMBER
       ) RETURN BOOLEAN;
```

Functions are usually designed to return a single value. It may be useful to define one constant meaning that something went wrong. Note that functions can also have OUT parameters but I think it is mixing with the role of procedures. Therefore, I usually limit my use of functions to very safe processes or to cases that absolutely require them.

Error Handling

One of the key elements of robust, maintainable, and scalable software is modularity and avoidance of logic duplication. A strong system relies on a series of elementary bricks, each one having a unique function. Put together, these bricks implement more complex functionalities. Should a module fail, it must not crash the module that calls it. The first step of error handling, then, is to create a confinement hull that is designed to prevent any damage outside the procedure that fails. The second step is to report this error to the caller, so it can be nicely taken into account and propagated to the highest level without harm. The third step is to make sure that the state of the system remains consistent after an error; in other words, that no action was partially done.

Error Trapping

PL/SQL has a powerful error trapping mechanism in the form of *exceptions*. The one with the widest spectrum is called OTHERS. As its name says, it is designed to catch everything that was not otherwise trapped. I strongly recommend protecting all stored procedures by an exception handler for OTHERS. Doing so is the chance to log or output any valuable information for later debugging, such as which module failed with which parameter values. It won't prevent the application from crashing but you will know where and how. See the "Error Reporting" section for more details.

Should you need to add a user defined exception, use upper case, a meaningful name, and the prefix *L_*. You can use a different prefix if you prefer. My own convention here is to use *L_*.

The following is a skeleton procedure showing how I typically structure the error handling logic:

```
PROCEDURE GET$BOOK_AUTHOR (
                p_book_id             IN      NUMBER   := NULL
               ,p_book_title          IN      VARCHAR2 := NULL
               ,p_author                  OUT  VARCHAR2
               ) IS

   L_MY_EXCEPTION                           EXCEPTION;

BEGIN
   ...
EXCEPTION
   WHEN L_MY_EXCEPTION THEN
      -- Handling of the specific error
      ...
   WHEN OTHERS THEN
      -- Handling of the generic error
      ...
END; -- GET$BOOK_AUTHOR
```

Also, while not a coding convention per se, do give thought to checking all input parameters. At least be sure not to fully trust them. Just because a module has a parameter called p_book_id does not mean the value passed into that parameter will always be a genuine book ID.

Error Reporting

Once you have built a system of modules, you want to know when one of them fails in order to correctly treat the problem. Transmitting error messages becomes vital towards having a stable architecture.

Error messaging can have two aspects: one for machines and one for humans. Error messaging for machines is based upon codes that can be easily interpreted, like (ORA-)01403 standing for "No data found." Error messaging for humans is based on clear text explaining the given error. I recommend creating your own set of errors (codes and explanations) in a specific table. Make your errors specific to your application. For example, create a message such as "No book with such a title" and associate that message with a code of your choosing. Such a list of errors is useful to programmers *and* to end users. Make sure your messages are clear and friendly.

In order to propagate errors from one module to another, I use two output parameters called p_exitcode and p_exittext. The first is for machines; the second one is for humans. I ensure those parameters are present in every single stored procedure that I write. By convention, an exit code equal to 0 means that the execution of the procedure went fine. A code different from 0 indicates that an error occurred, with the code number indicating just which error that was.

Stop the execution as soon as a problem is detected; it's not worth going further. You may want to use a generic exception called L_PB_FATAL (standing for *Local Problem Fatal*, but you may choose any dramatic name you wish) that is raised as soon as there is no reason to carry on.

The following is an enhanced version of the procedure skeleton from the previous section. This version of the skeleton implements the additional parameters, and also the exception, that I've just described.

```
PROCEDURE GET$BOOK_AUTHOR (
                p_book_id              IN      NUMBER   := NULL
               ,p_book_title           IN      VARCHAR2 := NULL
               ,p_author                   OUT  VARCHAR2
               ,p_exitcode                 OUT  NUMBER
               ,p_exittext                 OUT  VARCHAR2
               ) IS

   L_PB_FATAL                                  EXCEPTION;

BEGIN
   -- Init
   p_exitcode := 0;
   p_exittext := NULL;
   ...
EXCEPTION
   WHEN L_PB_FATAL THEN
      IF p_exitcode = 0 THEN -- To avoid forgotten values
         p_exitcode := -1;     -- Return something <> 0 indicating an error
      END IF;
   WHEN OTHERS THEN
      p_exitcode := SQLCODE;
      p_exittext := SUBSTR('Error in GET$BOOK_AUTHOR: '||SQLERRM, 1, 500);
END; -- GET$BOOK_AUTHOR
```

Any call to a procedure following the convention illustrated in this skeleton should be followed by a check on the exit code and an appropriate action in case of problem. Then you can decide whether to take the appropriate emergency action or to stop the execution and propagate the error using the same mechanism, like so:

```
PROCEDURE GET$BOOK_DATA (
                p_book_id              IN      NUMBER
               ,p_book_author              OUT  VARCHAR2
               ,p_book_editor              OUT  VARCHAR2
               ,p_exitcode                 OUT  NUMBER
               ,p_exittext                 OUT  VARCHAR2
               ) IS

   L_PB_FATAL                                  EXCEPTION;

BEGIN
   -- Init
   p_exitcode := 0;
   p_exittext := NULL;
```

```
   -- Get the author of the book
   KNL_BOOKS.GET$BOOK_AUTHOR (
                   p_book_id  => p_book_id
                   ,p_author   => p_book_author
                   ,p_exitcode => p_exitcode  -- The values of error code and text
                   ,p_exittext => p_exittext  -- are propagated to the caller
                   );
   IF p_exitcode <> 0 THEN
     RAISE L_PB_FATAL;
   END IF;

   -- Get the editor of the book
   KNL_BOOKS.GET$BOOK_EDITOR (
   ...
EXCEPTION
   WHEN L_PB_FATAL THEN
     IF p_exitcode = 0 THEN -- To avoid forgotten values
       p_exitcode := -1;    -- Return something <> 0 indicating an error
     END IF;
   WHEN OTHERS THEN
     p_exitcode := SQLCODE;
     p_exittext := SUBSTR('Error in GET$BOOK_DATA: '||SQLERRM, 1, 500);
END; -- GET$BOOK_DATA
```

Error Recovery

Following the black box paradigm, a procedure that inserts, updates, or deletes information should leave the database in a consistent state. Should the procedure fail, it has to rollback to the state the system was in when entering the procedure. Use upper case to name savepoints and make sure to include rollback calls in the global exceptions of the procedure, like so:

```
PROCEDURE EXE$REGISTER_NEW_BOOK (
                   p_title                  IN      VARCHAR2
                   ,p_author                IN      VARCHAR2
                   ,p_book_id                   OUT  NUMBER
                   ,p_exitcode                  OUT  NUMBER
                   ,p_exittext                  OUT  VARCHAR2
                   ) IS

   L_PB_FATAL                               EXCEPTION;

BEGIN
   -- Init
   p_exitcode := 0;
   p_exittext := NULL;

   SAVEPOINT BEFORE_REGISTER_NEW_BOOK;
```

```
  IF p_title IS NULL OR p_author IS NULL THEN
    p_exitcode := 12345;  -- Error code for invalid new book data
    p_exittext := 'Missing title or author information';
    RAISE L_PB_FATAL;
  END IF;

  ...

EXCEPTION
  WHEN L_PB_FATAL THEN
    ROLLBACK TO BEFORE_REGISTER_NEW_BOOK;
    IF p_exitcode = 0 THEN -- To avoid a forgotten value
      p_exitcode := -1;
    END IF;
  WHEN OTHERS THEN
    ROLLBACK TO BEFORE_REGISTER_NEW_BOOK;
    p_exitcode := SQLCODE;
    p_exittext := SUBSTR('Error in KNL_BOOKS.EXE$REGISTER_NEW_BOOK: '||SQLERRM, 1, 500);
END; -- EXE$REGISTER_NEW_BOOK
```

Test First. Display Second.

If you are writing a module to drive a user interface, it is better to first check and get all the required data first, then to display the interface. That way, all the possible errors are trapped before anything is displayed. You can then easily avoid having a message like "An error occurred" appear in a middle of a page or a screen for the user to see. Also, if you do need to display an error message, you can do so without confusing the user. If you begin display data only to interrupt with an error, users can become flustered and frustrated.

Summary

Coding conventions are not intended to solve all the problems you may encounter while implementing a system or maintaining software. However, they are very handy in order to standardize large source code bases and to ease the maintenance and sharing of modules. Following coding standards is a sign of respect for your fellow programmers and project leaders. As a programmer, you may find them difficult to use in the beginning, because they may not match your own style. Believe me; it takes only a short time before a given set of standards become your natural way of coding. Moreover, once you start managing a large set of modules, what a pleasure it is to "plug and play" them in a consistent way in order to build complex mechanisms! As a project leader, you may find difficult to impose standards upon a whole team, but the gain in quality is worth it.

The following is one final template. It summarizes in one place many of the conventions described in this chapter.

```
/*-------------------------------------------------------------------*/
/*                                                                   */
/* Module   : MODULE_NAME                                            */
/* Goal     : Short description of the module.                       */
/* Keywords : Few keywords describing what the module does.          */
/*                                                                   */
```

```
/*----------------------------------------------------------------------*/
/* Description:                                                         */
/*                                                                      */
/* Long description of the module: its goal.                           */
/* Explanation about parameters (Input and Output).                    */
/* How the procedure works, the "tricks", etc.                         */
/*                                                                      */
/*----------------------------------------------------------------------*/
/* History:                                                             */
/*                                                                      */
/* YYYY-MM-DD : First name and Name - Creation.                        */
/*                                                                      */
/* YYYY-MM-DD : First name and Name - Review.                          */
/*                                                                      */
/* YYYY-MM-DD : First name and Name                                    */
/*              Description of the modification.                       */
/*                                                                      */
/*----------------------------------------------------------------------*/
PROCEDURE TYPE$MODULE_NAME(
                p_param1              IN      VARCHAR2 -- Here comment on p_param1
                ,p_param2             IN      NUMBER    := NULL
                ,p_exitcode             OUT   NUMBER
                ,p_exittext             OUT   VARCHAR2
                ) IS

-- DECLARE Section

CURSOR one_cursor IS
  SELECT *
    FROM table
   WHERE condition;

  L_PB_FATAL                              EXCEPTION;
  l_variable                              VARCHAR2(1);

BEGIN
  -- Init
  p_exitcode := 0;
  p_exittext := NULL;

  SAVEPOINT BEFORE_TYPE$MODULE_NAME;

  -- Check the input
  PACKAGE.CHK$PARAM1 (
                p_value      => p_param1
                ,p_exitcode => p_exitcode
                ,p_exittext => p_exittext
                );
  IF p_exittext <> 0 THEN
     RAISE L_PB_FATAL;
  END IF;
```

```
  -- Gather the required data
  BEGIN
    SELECT col
      INTO l_variable
      FROM table
     WHERE condition1
       AND condition2;
  EXCEPTION
     WHEN OTHERS THEN
        p_exitcode := 123456;
        p_exittext := 'Error in getting information in TYPE$MODULE_NAME
        RAISE L_PB_FATAL;
  END;

  -- Get data from cursor
  FOR l_one_rec FROM one_cursor LOOP
     IF l_one_rec.col <> PACKAGE.C_CONSTANT THEN
       -- Explanation about the test above
       ...
     ELSE
       ...
     END IF;
  END LOOP; -- One cursor

  -- Display
  ...

EXCEPTION
  WHEN L_PB_FATAL THEN
     ROLLBACK TO BEFORE_TYPE$MODULE_NAME;
     IF p_exitcode = 0 THEN          -- To avoid a forgotten exitcode
       p_exitcode := -1;             -- Return something <> 0 indicating an error
     END IF;
  WHEN OTHERS THEN
     ROLLBACK TO BEFORE_TYPE$MODULE_NAME;
     p_exitcode := SQLCODE;
     p_exittext := SUBSTR('Error in PACKAGE.TYPE$MODULE_NAME: '||SQLERRM, 1, 500);
END TYPE$MODULE_NAME;
```

Dependencies and Invalidations

by Arup Nanda

Dependencies between PL/SQL packages can a perplexing source of application errors. Database administrators and developers unacquainted with how dependencies work can find themselves scratching their heads over sporadic and unrepeatable errors that are seemingly without cause. For example, while executing a procedure in a package you are responsible for, an application throws the following error:

```
ORA-04068: existing state of package has been discarded
```

This particular procedure has been executed a million times before. You can swear on your great grandmother's grave that you haven't changed the package in a long time, definitely not in the last few seconds and yet the application gets this error, the customer orders fail, and the organization loses money.

Not finding an obvious explanation, you blame a coworker for messing with this package, resulting in a heated argument which you regret instantly. Your manager intervenes and calmly asks you to show her the error. You manually re-execute the procedure in the package and (surprise, surprise) it executes without any error! Amidst that glaring from your accused coworker and the oh-you-need-help look from your manager, you are now thoroughly perplexed as to what happened. Sabotage, Oracle bug, bad karma, or none of the above?

What is this error? And why did it get resolved immediately afterwards without your intervention? The problem is not voodoo, but how PL/SQL code dependencies work. Some object referenced in the package was altered, which caused the package to be invalidated. Then the package revalidated (or, recompiled) later and had to be reinitialized.

Understanding the dependency chain and causes of invalidation is very important when you develop an application. The preceding scenario is an example of how poorly designed application code can cause an outage. This chapter explains dependencies and how you can code to reduce invalidations, thus reducing and possibly eliminating interruptions to the application during runtime.

Dependency Chains

First, you must understand dependency chains and their impact upon PL/SQL code. Suppose you have a table ORDERS and a procedure UPD_QTY that updates the column QUANTITY. Their definitions are as follows (note the dependency of the procedure upon the table; the two objects form a dependency chain):

```
SQL> desc orders
Name                                     Null?    Type
---------------------------------------- -------- ---------------------------
ORDER_ID                                 NOT NULL NUMBER(5)
CUST_ID                                  NOT NULL NUMBER(10)
QUANTITY                                          NUMBER(10,2)

create or replace procedure upd_qty (
        p_order_id in orders.order_id%type,
        p_quantity in orders.quantity%type
) as
begin
    update orders
    set quantity = p_quantity
    where order_id = p_order_id;
end;
```

What happens if you drop the column QUANTITY? The procedure will become meaningless, of course, so Oracle rightfully makes it invalid. Later you make another modification, either by adding the column back to the table or by removing that column from the procedure and replacing it with another in such a way that the procedure is now syntactically valid. If you added the column back into the table, you can recompile the procedure by executing:

```
SQL> alter procedure upd_qty compile reuse settings;
```

■ **Tip**   The RESUSE SETTINGS clause in the recompilation is a handy and powerful tool. Any special compile time parameter such as plsql_optimize_level or warning_level set earlier for the procedure will remain the same after the recompilation. If you didn't use that clause, the settings for the current sessions would have taken effect. So, unless you want to change those settings, it's a good idea to use that clause every time.

The compilation will check the existence of all the components referenced in the procedure. This establishment of validity occurs only when the procedure is compiled—not at runtime. Why? Imagine the contents of a typical stored code base: thousands of lines long with hundreds of tables, columns, and synonyms, views, sequences, and other stored code trying to validate every object at every execution. The performance will be terrible, making the process infeasible. Therefore, the validation is done at compilation time, which is likely a one-time act. When an object (such as this table) changes, Oracle can't immediately determine whether the changes will affect the dependent objects (such as this procedure), so it reacts by marking it as invalid. The dependency among objects is clearly shown in the data dictionary view DBA_DEPENDENCIES (or, its counterpart – USER_DEPENDENCIES).

```
SQL> desc dba_dependencies
Name                                     Null?    Type
---------------------------------------- -------- ---------------------------
OWNER                                    NOT NULL VARCHAR2(30)
NAME                                     NOT NULL VARCHAR2(30)
TYPE                                              VARCHAR2(18)
REFERENCED_OWNER                                  VARCHAR2(30)
```

```
REFERENCED_NAME                                      VARCHAR2(64)
REFERENCED_TYPE                                      VARCHAR2(18)
REFERENCED_LINK_NAME                                 VARCHAR2(128)
DEPENDENCY_TYPE                                      VARCHAR2(4)
```

The REFERENCED_NAME shows the object being referenced—the other object that the current object is dependent on. The following query against the table lists dependencies for UPD_QTY. Each such dependency represents an object upon which UPD_QTY is dependent.

```
select referenced_owner, referenced_name, referenced_type
from dba_dependencies
where owner = 'ARUP'
and name = 'UPD_QTY'
/
```

REFERENCED_OWNER	REFERENCED_NAME	REFERENCED_TYPE
SYS	SYS_STUB_FOR_PURITY_ANALYSIS	PACKAGE
ARUP	ORDERS	TABLE

This output shows that the procedure UPD_QTY depends on the table ORDERS, as we expected. Had there been another object in the procedure's code, it would have been listed here as well.

■ **Note** See the upcoming sidebar "What About SYS_STUB_FOR_PARITY_ANALYSIS?" for an explanation of this particular dependency.

Whenever the structure of the table ORDERS is changed, the procedure's validity becomes questionable and Oracle makes it invalid. However, being questionable does not necessarily mean invalid. For instance, when you add a column to the table, it is technically a change to the table. Will it make the procedure invalid?

```
SQL> alter table orders add (store_id number(10));
```

```
Table altered.
```

If you examine the status of the UPD_QTY procedure, yes.

```
SQL> select status from user_objects where object_name = 'UPD_QTY';
```

```
STATUS
-------
INVALID
```

But the procedure does not actually reference the new column, so it shouldn't have been affected. However, Oracle does not necessarily know that. It preemptively marks the procedure invalid just to be safe. You can, at this point, recompile the procedure; it will compile fine. Otherwise, Oracle will recompile the procedure automatically when it is invoked next time.

Let's see the new procedure, including the automatic recompilation, in action.

```
SQL> exec upd_qty (1,1)

PL/SQL procedure successfully completed.
```

The procedure executed just fine, even though it was marked invalid. How was that possible? It was executed successfully because the execution forced a recompile (and re-validation) of the procedure. The recompile succeeded because the procedure does not actually have any referenced to the component in the underlying table that changed—the new column STORE_ID. The procedure compiled fine and was marked valid. You can confirm that by checking the status once again.

```
SQL> select status from user_objects
  2  where object_name = 'UPD_QTY';

STATUS
-------
VALID
```

So far the events seem pretty benign; these forced recompilations take care of any changes that do not affect the validity of the program and the world just goes on as usual. Why should you care? You should care a lot.

EXECUTED IMMEDIATE IS A SPECIAL CASE

If a table is referenced inside of an *execute immediate* string, then dependency checking does not capture that table as a referenced object. For instance, consider the following code:

```
create or replace procedure upd_qty as
begin
    execute immediate 'update orders set quantity = ...';
end;
```

In this case, ORDERS table will not be shown as referenced object for UP_QTY, which is yet another reason for not using dynamic SQL (or, using it, based on your perspective).

The compilation of stored code (and for that matter other dependent objects such as views on a table) forces another process in the database called parsing. Parsing is akin to compilation of source code. When you execute an SQL statement such as `select order_id from orders`, Oracle can't just execute the statement as is. It must ask a lot of questions, some which are:

- *What* is `orders`? Is it a table, a view, a synonym?

- Is there indeed a *column* in the table called `order_id`?

- Is there a *function* called `order_id`?

- Do you have *privileges* to select from this table (or the function, as is the case)?

After making sure you have all the necessary pre-conditions, Oracle makes an executable version of that SQL statement and puts it in the library cache. This process is known as *parsing*. Subsequent execution of the SQL will use the parsed version only and not go through the process of parsing. During the execution phase, Oracle must ensure that the components (the table ORDERS, the procedure

UPD_QTY, etc.) are not changed. It does that by placing a *parse lock* on those objects and other structures such as cursors.

Parsing is very CPU intensive. Frequent parsing and recompilation rob the server of CPU cycles, starving other useful processes from getting their share of CPU power. You can examine the effect by checking the statistics related to parsing in a view called v$mystat which shows statistics for your current session. The view shows the stats as statistic# only; their names are available in another view called v$statname. The following is a query that joins both views and shows stats on parsing. Save the query as ps.sql to examine the effect of reparsing and recompilation.

```
select name, value
from v$mystat s, v$statname n
where s.statistic# = n.statistic#
and n.name like '%parse%';
```

The view v$mystat is a cumulative view, so the values in there do not show the current data; they are incremented. To know the stats for a period of time, you have to select from the view twice and get the difference. To find out the parse-related stats, collect the stats first by running ps.sql, execute the procedure upd_qty(), and collect the stats once again by running ps.sql, like so:

```
SQL> @ps

NAME                               VALUE
------------------------------ ----------
parse time cpu                        20
parse time elapsed                    54
parse count (total)                  206
parse count (hard)                    16
parse count (failures)                 1

SQL> exec upd_qty(1,1)

PL/SQL procedure successfully completed.

SQL> @ps

NAME                               VALUE
------------------------------ ----------
parse time cpu                        20
parse time elapsed                    54
parse count (total)                  208
parse count (hard)                    16
parse count (failures)                 1
```

Note the values. Nothing has increased; in other words, there was no parsing as a result of executing the procedure upd_qty. On a *different* session, alter the table by adding a column, like so:

```
SQL> alter table orders add (amount number(10,2));

Table altered.
```

Now, in the first session execute the procedure and collect the statistics.

```
SQL> exec upd_qty(1,1)

PL/SQL procedure successfully completed.

SQL> @ps

NAME                              VALUE
-----------------------------  ----------
parse time cpu                       26
parse time elapsed                   60
parse count (total)                 279
parse count (hard)                   19
parse count (failures)                1
```

Notice how the parse-related statistics have increased. Hard parsing, which means the SQL statement was either not found in the library cache or whatever version was found was not usable and therefore had to be parsed fresh, jumped from 16 to 19—indicating 3 hard parses. Total parse count jumped from 208 to 279, a jump of 71. Since there are 3 hard parses, the other 68 are soft parses, which means the structures were found in the library cache and were revalidated rather than being parsed from scratch. The CPU time for parsing jumped from 20 to 26, indicating that the parsing consumed 6 centi-seconds of CPU. These CPU cycles could have been used for doing some otherwise useful work had there been not a need for parsing. It may not sound like much, but consider situations where thousands of such cases occur in a normal database system causing significant CPU consumption.

■ **Note** In a RAC database, this parsing effect is even more pronounced. Since there are multiple instances, each with a library cache of its own, the parsing and invalidation must be carefully coordinated. For instance, when a table ORDERS is modified in instance INST1, the UPD_QTY procedure must be invalidated not only in the instance INST1; but in INST2 as well (assuming a two-node RAC database). The instance INST1 sends a message to INST2 to immediately mark the loaded versions of UPD_QTY invalid. Since there is a possibility someone may access the UPD_QTY procedure incorrectly, this message is sent with the high priority as a type of message known as a Direct Message. Since direct messages supersede the other types of messages, such as request for a block (which is called an Indirect Message), the other messages may not get their chance to be transmitted. That results in a lag in getting the blocks; the session that requested the blocks must wait, adding to the performance problems.

The problem does not stop there. As you saw, the procedure is recompiled automatically when executed. It's validated, and that message is transmitted to INST2 immediately. The RAC interconnect is flooded with the messages like this, affecting the flow of other messages and blocks, and thus causing performance problems. The problem is exacerbated when the number of instances goes up since the amount of coordination goes up exponentially. Unlike blocks, there is no "master instance" of an object (cursor, table, package, etc.) in a library cache, so RAC must notify all the instances in the cluster to invalidate (and validate) the object.

In a typical application, you probably have a lot of procedures, which call a lot of other procedures. Suppose procedure P1 calls procedure P2, which in turn calls P3, which accesses the table T1. Diagrammatically, we can represent this situation as follows, with → signifying "depends on," like so:

P1 → P2 → P3 → T1

This is known as a *dependency chain*. If T1 is modified, all the dependent objects in the chain left of it (the ones that depend on it) could be invalidated and must be recompiled before being used. The recompilation must be in the order of dependency, e.g. first P3, then P2 followed by P1.This recompilation could be automatic, but it consumes CPU cycles in parsing and needs parse locks in any case. The longer the dependency chain, the more the demand for parsing, and the more the CPU consumption and need for parse locks. In a RAC database, it becomes extremely important that this cost be controlled; otherwise, the effects will spiral out of control. Therefore, your objective should be to reduce the cycle of revalidations and shorten the dependency chains.

WHAT ABOUT SYS_STUB_FOR_PURITY_ANALYSIS?

Did you notice the strangely named package in the output, SYS_STUB_FOR_PURITY_ANALYSIS? I'm pretty sure you didn't create it and you surely didn't use it in the procedure. If you check the data dictionary, you will see specification but not the body of the package. In any case, you haven't even referenced the package, so why is that listed as a parent of the procedure UPD_QTY?

This is yet another hidden working of the parsing mechanism. Remember the purity model of the PL/SQL code segments? In summary, it specifies the possibility of stored code to change database and package state, such as Write No Database State (WNDS) or Read No Package State (RNPS). These are known as the purity level of the stored code. While compiling a stored code, Oracle assumes one of these purity states. However, consider this complex case: there was a public synonym called ORDERS. When you create this procedure, the parsing must assume you are referring to *your* object ORDERS; not the public synonym ORDERS. But suppose another user is creating a procedure with the same name (with the same code) but does not have a table called ORDERS? In that case, parsing will point to the public synonym. This creates an interesting problem for the parser—the object's scope and purity must be considered. Oracle addresses this problem by accessing a special package that has procedures defined for the purity states. Here is how the package is defined:

```
Create or replace package sys_stub_for_purity_analysis as
  procedure prds;
  pragma restrict_references(prds, wnds, rnps, wnps);

  procedure pwds;
  pragma restrict_references(pwds, rnds, rnps, wnps);

  procedure prps;
  pragma restrict_references(prps, rnds, wnds, wnps);

  procedure pwps;
  pragma restrict_references(pwps, rnds, wnds, rnps);
end sys_stub_for_purity_analysis;
```

Since the procedures are merely there to provide a pointer to the purity levels, there is no other purpose, thus the body does not exist. How can the dependency tree exist for a package only and not the body? This interesting topic is discussed later in this chapter. For the time being, we hope you are satisfied with this explanation of the strangely referenced package sys_stub_for_purity_analysis.

Shortening Dependency Chains

How can you reduce this vicious cycle of parsing-invalidation-parsing events? One bit of good news is that Oracle development has taken notice and the normal dependency model has been changed in Oracle Database11g. Instead of relying on modification of a table or view to invalidate dependent objects, Oracle Database 11g adopts a fine-grained dependency mechanism that looks at the column changes as well. The dependent objects are invalidated only if the columns referenced in them are modified; otherwise, they are left valid.

What about the cases where you do have to modify a column? In Oracle Database 11g, that could trigger invalidations. It may not be possible to avoid it completely, but you can reduce the impact if you shorten the dependency chain. For instance, if the above dependency chain had been just two levels instead of four, there would be fewer recompilations, resulting in lesser CPU consumption and parse locks. How can you accomplish this objective?

The answer lies in another type of stored code: packages. Packages handle invalidation differently and are much less susceptible than procedures and functions to this ripple effect of invalidations in case of a change in an upstream object. Let's see this with an example. First, you create a series of tables, packages, and procedures.

```
-- Create two tables
create table test1 (
    col1   number;
    col2   number
)
/
create table test2 (
    col1   number;
    col2   number
)
/
-- Create a package to manipulate these tables
create or replace package pack1
is
    g_var1   number;
    l_var1   number;
    procedure p1 (p1_in test1.col1%TYPE);
    procedure p2 (p1_in number);
end;
/
create or replace package body pack1
```

```
as
    procedure p1 (p1_in test1.col1%type) is
    begin
        update test1
        set col2 = col2 + 1
        where col1 = p1_in;
    end;
    procedure p2 (p1_in number) is
    begin
        update test2
        set col2 = col2 + 1
        where col1 = p1_in;
    end;
end;
/
create or replace package pack2
is
    procedure p1 (p1_in number);
    procedure p2 (p1_in number);
end;
/
create or replace package body pack2
as
    procedure p1 (p1_in number) is
    begin
        pack1.p1(p1_in);
    end;
    procedure p2 (p1_in number) is
    begin
        pack1.p2(p1_in);
    end;
end;
/
-- Create two procedures calling these packages.
create or replace procedure p1
(
    p1_in    in number
)
is
begin
    pack2.p1 (p1_in);
end;
/
create or replace procedure p2
(
    p1_in    in number
)
is
begin
    p1(p1_in);
end;
```

You've created two tables, then two packages that reference those tables (which then become dependents of the tables), a procedure that calls one of the packages, and finally another procedure that calls this procedure. From the definition the dependency chain *appears* to be like this:

P2 → P1 → PACK1,PACK2 → TEST1,TEST2

Now to modify a column of the table TEST2:

```
SQL> alter table test2 modify (col2 number(9));
```

Table altered.

As per the dependency rules, all objects (PACK1, PACK2, P1, and P2) should have been invalidated and remain so until they are recompiled either manually or automatically. Confirm it by checking the status of all the objects in question.

```
select object_type, object_name, status
from user_objects;
```

OBJECT_TYPE	OBJECT_NAME	STATUS
PROCEDURE	P1	VALID
PROCEDURE	P2	VALID
PACKAGE	PACK1	VALID
PACKAGE BODY	**PACK1**	**INVALID**
PACKAGE	PACK2	VALID
PACKAGE BODY	PACK2	VALID
TABLE	TEST1	VALID
TABLE	TEST2	VALID

Interestingly, the only invalid object is package body PACK1; all others are still valid. How did that happen? Why were all the objects dependent on table TEST2 not invalidated?

The answer lies in the way the dependencies work for packages. Let's check these dependencies by running a SQL statement. Since you have to run it multiple times, save the following as dep.sql:

```
select referenced_type, referenced_owner, referenced_name
from dba_dependencies
where owner = '&1'
and name = '&2'
and type = '&3'
```

Now you can call this script several times with appropriate arguments to get the dependency information.

```
SQL> @dep ARUP P2 PROCEDURE
```

REFERENCED_TYPE	REFERENCED_OWNER	REFERENCED_NAME
PACKAGE	SYS	SYS_STUB_FOR_PURITY_ANALYSIS
PACKAGE	SYS	STANDARD
PROCEDURE	ARUP	P1

```
SQL> @dep ARUP P1 PROCEDURE
```

```
REFERENCED_TYPE    REFERENCED_OWNER              REFERENCED_NAME
----------------   ----------------------------  ------------------------------
PACKAGE            SYS                           SYS_STUB_FOR_PURITY_ANALYSIS
PACKAGE            SYS                           STANDARD
PACKAGE            ARUP                          PACK2

SQL> @dep ARUP PACK2 PACKAGE

REFERENCED_TYPE    REFERENCED_OWNER              REFERENCED_NAME
----------------   ----------------------------  ------------------------------
PACKAGE            SYS                           STANDARD

SQL> @dep ARUP PACK2 'PACKAGE BODY'

REFERENCED_TYPE    REFERENCED_OWNER              REFERENCED_NAME
----------------   ----------------------------  ------------------------------
PACKAGE            SYS                           STANDARD
PACKAGE            ARUP                          PACK1
PACKAGE            ARUP                          PACK2

SQL> @dep ARUP PACK1 PACKAGE

REFERENCED_TYPE    REFERENCED_OWNER              REFERENCED_NAME
----------------   ----------------------------  ------------------------------
PACKAGE            SYS                           STANDARD

SQL> @dep ARUP PACK1 'PACKAGE BODY'

REFERENCED_TYPE    REFERENCED_OWNER              REFERENCED_NAME
----------------   ----------------------------  ------------------------------
PACKAGE            SYS                           STANDARD
TABLE              ARUP                          TEST1
PACKAGE            ARUP                          PACK1
TABLE              ARUP                          TEST2
```

If you put this dependency information, which is really a dependency chain, into a diagram, it would look like Figure 15-1. The arrows point from *dependent* to *referenced*. I prefer those terms instead of *child* and *parent* simply because parent/child connotes a foreign key relationship. Not all dependencies are about referential integrity constraints (which are on data). Dependencies are about the references to actual objects, even if the objects may contain no data at all.

Studying Figure 15-1 carefully, you may notice an interesting fact: the package bodies depend on the *packages*, not on other package *bodies*. This is a very important property of packages and plays a beneficial role in invalidation of the objects in the dependency chain. Since the package bodies are dependent, and not the packages, they get invalidated, not the packages themselves. Objects that depend on the packages are also left valid since their referenced object is valid. In this example, no other object depends on PACK1 package body, so nothing else was invalidated.

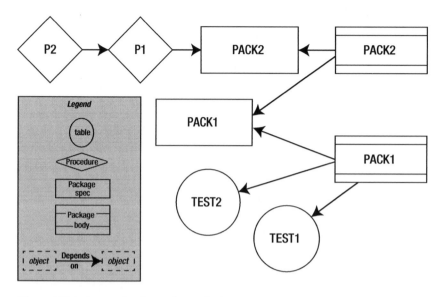

Figure 15-1. A complex dependency chain

When does the PACK1 body get revalidated (or recompiled)? Since the modification of the table column does not fundamentally change anything, the objects can be recompiled automatically when they are called. Let's execute procedure P2, which is at the top of the dependency chain (i.e. it's the last, so nothing else depends on it).

```
SQL> exec p2 (1)

PL/SQL procedure successfully completed.
```

After execution, check the status of the objects.

OBJECT_TYPE	OBJECT_NAME	STATUS
PROCEDURE	P1	VALID
PROCEDURE	P2	VALID
PACKAGE	PACK1	VALID
PACKAGE BODY	PACK1	VALID
PACKAGE	PACK2	VALID
PACKAGE BODY	PACK2	VALID
TABLE	TEST1	VALID
TABLE	TEST2	VALID

Note how the package body was automatically recompiled. Execution of P2 executed procedure P1, which executed PACK2.P1, which in turn executed PACK1.P1. Since PACK1 was invalid, this execution forced the compilation and revalidated it. Only one package body was compiled here, not an entire chain of objects, which reduced the CPU consumption and parse locks. Consider the same case if the packages were procedures. It would have invalidated all the dependent procedures. The forced recompilation would have resulted in significantly more CPU consumption and need for parse locks.

Datatype Reference

Sometimes two best practices are desirable on their own but fail when they are used together. Such is the case with dependency tracking and some datatypes used in PL/SQL code. To illustrate the issue, I want to demonstrate a slightly different scenario. Instead of modifying table TEST2, let's modify TEST1 to add a column, like so:

```
SQL> alter table test1 modify (col2 number(8,3));

Table altered.
```

If you check for the status of the objects, you will see the following:

```
OBJECT_TYPE          OBJECT_NAME                     STATUS
-------------------  ------------------------------  -------
PROCEDURE            P1                              VALID
PROCEDURE            P2                              VALID
PACKAGE              PACK1                           INVALID
PACKAGE BODY         PACK1                           INVALID
PACKAGE              PACK2                           VALID
PACKAGE BODY         PACK2                           INVALID
TABLE                TEST1                           VALID
TABLE                TEST2                           VALID
```

Note the objects invalidated as a result of this modification—many more this time. Both the package and package body PACK1 are invalidated in this case, while only the package body was invalidated in the previous case. Why?

To answer, look at the declaration of P1 in the package specification.

```
procedure p1 (p1_in test1.col1%type) is
```

The datatype is a not a primitive such as NUMBER; it is referenced with the datatype of COL1 in the table TEST1. Defining parameters this way instead of a primitive is a good idea for performant code since the compilation ties it to the object components and makes the code faster. However, it also makes it dependent on table TEST1 more intimately than TEST2. Modifying TEST2 does not impact the datatype inside the package PACK1, but modifying datatype of COL1 in TEST1 changes the datatype of one of the parameters. Therefore, when TEST1 was modified, Oracle sensed that the package specification also changed and hence marked the package invalid. In case of the alteration of the table TEST2, the parameters passed to the procedures were not altered, the package specifications were not affected, and the package specification remained valid.

This invalidation should be automatically recompiled next time the topmost object is executed, right? No; this time the automatic recompilation will actually fail.

```
SQL> exec p2 (1)
BEGIN p1(1); END;

*
ERROR at line 1:
ORA-04068: existing state of packages has been discarded
ORA-04061: existing state of package "ARUP.PACK1" has been invalidated
ORA-04065: not executed, altered or dropped package "ARUP.PACK1"
```

```
ORA-06508: PL/SQL: could not find program unit being called: "ARUP.PACK1"
ORA-06512: at "ARUP.PACK2", line 5
ORA-06512: at "ARUP.P1", line 7
ORA-06512: at line 1
```

At this point, if you check for the validity of objects, you get the following:

OBJECT_TYPE	OBJECT_NAME	STATUS
PROCEDURE	P1	VALID
PROCEDURE	P2	VALID
PACKAGE	PACK1	VALID
PACKAGE BODY	**PACK1**	**INVALID**
PACKAGE	PACK2	VALID
PACKAGE BODY	PACK2	VALID
TABLE	TEST1	VALID
TABLE	TEST2	VALID

The two invalid objects were re-validated as a result of this attempted execution. Only one object remained invalid: the body of the package PACK1. How do you explain this and the error earlier?

The problem lies in a concept called *package state*. When a package is called for the very first time, it initializes its state in the memory. For instance, the global variables are one of the components in the package that are initialized. When the package specification becomes invalidated, the state is invalidated as well. The state is reinitialized, but right *after* the error, so the error occurs anyway. If you re-execute this procedure, you will not get the same error because the state has already been initialized this time. When the package was not recompiled the first time, its body was not recompiled either. Later, when the package state was initialized and the package recompiled fine, Oracle didn't go back and attempt *another* recompilation of the body and the body was left with invalid status.

At this point, if you re-execute procedure P2, package body PACK2 will be recompile and become valid, too. The application getting this error should do nothing other than simply re-executing the procedure it executed earlier. However, the application may not be able to handle it properly, throwing an exception and eventually causing an application outage—not a very desirable outcome. Therefore you should try to avoid this type of invalidation. You can easily avoid it by using primitives (such as NUMBER, DATE, etc.) for datatypes of parameters in the declaration section rather than the **%type** declaration. Unfortunately, doing so will result in less performing code. This brings up an interesting conundrum: would you code for performance or for more uptime?

Is there a way to accomplish both goals: writing performant code that does not invalidate easily? Fortunately, there is and it's described in the next section.

View for Table Alterations

One of the tricks to avoid or lessen the chances of cascading invalidations as a result of table modifications as you saw earlier is to use a view inside your stored code in place of a table. The view adds another layer of abstraction and will insulate the changes on the table from the dependent code. Let's see this benefit in action with an example. Let's assume there is a table called TRANS, which you can create as follows:

```
create table trans
(
    trans_id        number(10),
    trans_amt       number(12,2),
    store_id        number(2),
    trans_type      varchar2(1)
);
```

Now build the following package to manipulate the data in this table:

```
create or replace package pkg_trans
is
        procedure upd_trans_amt
        (
                p_trans_id      trans.trans_id%type,
                p_trans_amt     trans.trans_amt%type
        );
end;
/
create or replace package body pkg_trans
is
        procedure upd_trans_amt
        (
                p_trans_id      trans.trans_id%type,
                p_trans_amt     trans.trans_amt%type
        ) is
        begin
                update trans
                set trans_amt = p_trans_amt
                where trans_id = p_trans_id;
        end;
end;
/
```

You now want to write several other business code units using this package. One such unit is a function called ADJUST that updates the transaction amounts by a certain amount. Here is the code to create this function:

```
create or replace function adjust
(
        p_trans_id      trans.trans_id%type,
        p_percentage    number
)
return boolean
is
        l_new_trans_amt number(12);
begin
        select trans_amt * (1 + p_percentage/100)
        into l_new_trans_amt
        from trans
```

```
        where trans_id = p_trans_id;
        pkg_trans.upd_trans_amt (
                p_trans_id,
                l_new_trans_amt
        );
        return TRUE;
exception
        when OTHERS then
                return FALSE;
end;
/
```

■ **Note** Proponents of a school of a certain coding practices will argue to place all the code to manipulate a specific table in a single package instead of spreading that code among many stored code segments, while others will argue that such a practice would have made the package long and unmanageable. I think the right answer is situation specific and therefore best left as a decision made at design time. In this example, I am not endorsing either approach but resorting to a separate procedure merely for illustration purposes.

With the new objects in place, let's add a column in the view.

```
SQL> alter table trans add (vendor_id number);
```

Table altered.

Now check the status of the objects.

OBJECT_NAME	OBJECT_TYPE	STATUS
PKG_TRANS	PACKAGE BODY	INVALID
PKG_TRANS	PACKAGE	INVALID
ADJUST	FUNCTION	INVALID

It shouldn't be a surprise that the function got invalidated. It was invalidated because the components it depends on (the package specification and body of PKG_TRANS) were invalidated. Those invalidations were caused by the modification of the table TRANS. The next time these invalid components are executed, they will be automatically recompiled, but that will result in parsing, leading to increased CPU consumption and the placing of parse locks.

To avoid this scenario, you can build a view on the table.

```
create or replace view vw_trans
as
select trans_id, trans_amt, store_id, trans_type
from trans
/
```

Use this view in the package and function instead:

```
create or replace package pkg_trans
is
        procedure upd_trans_amt
        (
                p_trans_id        vw_trans.trans_id%type,
                p_trans_amt       vw_trans.trans_amt%type
        );
end;
/
create or replace package body pkg_trans
is
        procedure upd_trans_amt
        (
                p_trans_id        vw_trans.trans_id%type,
                p_trans_amt       vw_trans.trans_amt%type
        ) is
        begin
                update vw_trans
                set trans_amt = p_trans_amt
                where trans_id = p_trans_id;
        end;
end;
/
create or replace function adjust
(
        p_trans_id        vw_trans.trans_id%type,
        p_percentage      number
)
return boolean
is
        l_new_trans_amt number(12);
begin
        select trans_amt * (1 + p_percentage/100)
        into l_new_trans_amt
        from vw_trans
        where trans_id = p_trans_id;
        pkg_trans.upd_trans_amt (
                p_trans_id,
                l_new_trans_amt
        );
        return TRUE;
exception
        when OTHERS then
                return FALSE;
end;
/
```

Now add a column and then check the status of the objects.

```
SQL> alter table trans add (vendor_id number);
```

Table altered.

OBJECT_NAME	OBJECT_TYPE	STATUS
PKG_TRANS	PACKAGE BODY	VALID
PKG_TRANS	PACKAGE	VALID
ADJUST	FUNCTION	VALID
VW_TRANS	VIEW	VALID

All the objects are valid. This is because the package body depends on the view, not the table. The new column was not referenced in the view, so the view itself was not affected by the change in the table and was not invalidated, thanks to the fine grained dependency implemented in Oracle 11g.

■ **Note** The view will be invalidated in Oracle 10g because in that version the fine-grained dependency control was not implemented. In 10g, the dependency is of the view on the table and any change in the table, even if it is a column addition that is not even referenced in the view, will invalidate the view.

The power of fine-grained dependency is such that it not only looks at named columns, it applies to implicit columns as well. For instance, had you defined the view as `create or replace view vw_trans as select * from trans` (note the *; it means *all columns* instead of *named columns earlier*), the dependency wouldn't have mattered and view would not have been invalidated. However, if you recreate the view, the new column will be added to the view and makes the dependent object (the function) invalid. However, had you used a packaged function instead of a standalone function, it would not have been invalidated, as you observed earlier.

Adding Components into Packages

Now that you understand how packages are extremely valuable in shortening the dependency chain and reducing the cascading invalidations, you should always use packages, not standalone code segments in your applications. You should create packages as logical groups around functionalities. When you enhance the functionality of the applications, you may need to add new functions and procedures to the existing packages instead of creating new ones. That leads to a question. Since you altered existing packages, will doing so affect the dependent objects?

Let's examine the issue using the earlier example involving the table TRANS, the view VW_TRANS, the package PKG_TRANS, and the function ADJUST. Suppose with the revised requirements you need to add a new procedure to the package (`upd_trans_type`) to update the transaction type. Here is the package altering script that you would need to execute:

```
create or replace package pkg_trans
is
        procedure upd_trans_amt
        (
                p_trans_id      vw_trans.trans_id%type,
                p_trans_amt     vw_trans.trans_amt%type
        );
        procedure upd_trans_type
        (
                p_trans_id      vw_trans.trans_id%type,
                p_trans_type    vw_trans.trans_type%type
        );
end;
/
create or replace package body pkg_trans
as
        procedure upd_trans_amt
        (
                p_trans_id      vw_trans.trans_id%type,
                p_trans_amt     vw_trans.trans_amt%type
        ) is
        begin
                update vw_trans
                set trans_amt = p_trans_amt
                where trans_id = p_trans_id;
        end;
        procedure upd_trans_type
        (
                p_trans_id      vw_trans.trans_id%type,
                p_trans_type    vw_trans.trans_type%type
        ) is
        begin
            update vw_trans
            set trans_type = p_trans_type
            where trans_id = p_trans_id;
        end;
end;
/
```

After altering the package, take time to examine the status of the objects.

```
OBJECT_TYPE          OBJECT_NAME                     STATUS
-------------------- ------------------------------- -------
VIEW                 VW_TRANS                        VALID
TABLE                TRANS                           VALID
PACKAGE BODY         PKG_TRANS                       VALID
PACKAGE              PKG_TRANS                       VALID
FUNCTION             ADJUST                          VALID
```

Everything is valid. (Please note, in pre-11g versions, you will find some objects invalidated, due to the absence of fine-grained dependency tracking). Even though the package was altered by adding a new procedure, the function ADJUST itself does not call that procedure and therefore doesn't need to be invalidated—a fact recognized by fine-grained dependency checking in 11g. As you can see, the fine-grained dependency model not only tracks the column references but components in the stored code as well.

Although Oracle 11g and above seems to take care of the invalidation issue automatically, be aware that it is not always so. Consider another case where you want to have a new procedure to update the store_id.

```
create or replace package pkg_trans
is
        procedure upd_store_id
        (
                p_trans_id      vw_trans.trans_id%type,
                p_store_id      vw_trans.store_id%type
        );
        procedure upd_trans_amt
        (
                p_trans_id      vw_trans.trans_id%type,
                p_trans_amt     vw_trans.trans_amt%type
        );
end;
/
create or replace package body pkg_trans
is
        procedure upd_store_id
        (
                p_trans_id      vw_trans.trans_id%type,
                p_store_id      vw_trans.store_id%type
        ) is
        begin
                update vw_trans
                set store_id = p_store_id
                where trans_id = p_trans_id;
        end;
        procedure upd_trans_amt
        (
                p_trans_id      vw_trans.trans_id%type,
                p_trans_amt     vw_trans.trans_amt%type
        ) is
        begin
                update vw_trans
                set trans_amt = p_trans_amt
                where trans_id = p_trans_id;
        end;
end;
/
```

Notice that the new procedure is inserted at the beginning of the package instead of at the end. If you check for the validity, you get the following:

```
SQL> select status from user_objects where object_name = 'ADJUST';
```

```
STATUS
-------
INVALID
```

Why was the function invalidated? Interestingly, had you placed that procedure at the end, you wouldn't have invalidated the function. The reason for this seemingly odd behavior is the placement of stubs in the parsed version of the package. Each function is represented in the package as a stub and the stubs are ordered in the way they are defined in the package. The dependent components reference the stub by their stub number. When you add a function or procedure at the end, the new component is given a new stub number; the stubs of the existing components are not disturbed, so the dependent objects are not invalidated. When you add the component at the top, the order of components inside the package changes, which affects the stub numbers of the existing components. Since the dependent components refer to the stub numbers, they need to be reparsed and are therefore invalidated immediately.

■ **Tip** To avoid invalidations in dependent objects when new code segments are added to the package, add new components such as functions and procedures to the end of a package specification and body—not in the middle. This will retain the stub numbering of existing components inside the package and will not invalidate its dependents.

I'll close the discussion on the dependency model with another very important property that should affect your coding. Dependency tracking checks for changes in columns. If a newly added column is not used, the dependent is not invalidated. For instance, consider the cases where the following constructs are used inside a stored code.

```
select * into ... from test where ...;
insert into test1 values (...);
```

Note that there are no column names. In the first case, the * implicitly selects all the columns. When you alter the table to add a column, the * implicitly refers to that new column, even if you do not use it in the code, and so it invalidates the stored code. In the second case, the insert does not specify a column list, so all the columns are assumed and addition of a new column in test1 will force the statement to check for the value for the new column, forcing the invalidation of the stored code. Therefore, you must avoid constructs like this. You should use named columns in the stored code.

Another cause of invalidation in this scenario is all-inclusive implicitly defined column lists. In their quest to write agile code, some developers use a declaration like this:

```
declare l_test1_rec test1%rowtype;
```

Since the column list is not named, all the columns of test1 are assumed. So when you add a column, it invalidates the variable l_test1_rec, which invalidates the stored code. Do not use declarations like this. Instead, use explicitly named columns such as the following:

```
l_trans_id      test1.trans_id%type;
l_trans_amt     test1.trans_amt%type;
```

In this way, if a new column is added, it will not affect any of the declared variables and will not invalidate that stored code. However, please understand a very important point before you make that leap: using %rowtype may make the maintenance of the code easier since you do not have to explicitly name the variables. On the other hand, doing so makes the code more vulnerable to invalidations. You should make the decision to go either way using your best judgment.

Synonyms in Dependency Chains

Most databases use synonyms, for good reasons. Instead of using a fully qualified name like *<SchemaName>.<TableName>*, it's always easier to create a synonym and use it instead. However, bear in mind that a synonym is yet another object in the dependency chain and affects the cascading invalidation. Suppose that synonym S1 is in the dependency chain, as shown here:

P2 → P1 → PACK1 → PACK2 → S1 → VW1 → T1

In almost all cases, synonyms do not break the chain; they simply pass on the invalidations from their referenced objects downstream, with one important exception. When you alter a synonym, you have two choices.

- *Drop and recreate:* You would issue drop synonym s1; create synonym s1 as …

- *Replace:* You would issue create or replace synonym s1 as …

The difference may seem trivial, but the first approach is a killer. When you drop a synonym, the downstream objects reference an invalid object. In the dependency chain, all the objects starting with PACK2 all the way to P2 will be invalidated. When you recreate the synonym, these objects will be automatically recompiled at their next invocation, but not without consuming some valuable CPU cycles and obtaining parse locks. The second approach does not invalidate any of the dependents. When you change a synonym, never drop and recreate it—replace it.

▨ **Note**   The OR REPLACE syntax was introduced in recent versions of Oracle. Some of your application scripts may still implement the older approach. You should actively seek and change such scripts, modifying them to use the newer CREATE OR REPLACE syntax.

Resource Locking

Changes are a fact of life. Applications do change in requirement and scope, forcing changes in stored code. The alteration of the stored code needs an exclusive lock. If any session is currently executing that object or another object that the changed object references, this exclusive lock will not be available. Let's examine this with an example table and a procedure that accesses this table:

```
create table test1 (col1 number, col2 number);

create or replace procedure p1
(
     p1_in in number,
     p2_in in number
) as
begin
     update test1 set col2 = p2_in where col1 = p1_in;
end;
/
```

Once created, execute the procedure. Do not exit from the session.

```
SQL> exec p1 (1,1)

PL/SQL procedure successfully completed.
```

On a different session, try to add a new column to the table.

```
SQL> alter table test1 add (col3 number);
```

The earlier update statement will have put a transactional lock on the row of the table. The lock would be present even if there is not a single row in the table test1. This lock will prevent the alteration of the table. In Oracle 10g, this will error immediately with:

```
alter table test1 add (col3 number)
*
ERROR at line 1:
ORA-00054: resource busy and acquire with NOWAIT specified
```

On Oracle 11g, the ALTER TABLE statement will not error out immediately; it will likely wait for a specified time. If you check what the session is waiting on, you should get results like the following:

```
SQL> select event from v$session where sid = <Sid>;

EVENT
----------------------
blocking txn id for DDL
```

This parameter ddl_lock_timeout is very handy in busy databases where the tables are being accessed by applications constantly so there is little or no downtime for the altering command to complete. Rather than just exiting immediately with the ORA-54 message, an ALTER TABLE statement will wait until it gets the lock. In the first session, if you issue a rollback or commit, which will end the transaction and effectively release the locks, the second session will get the lock on the table and will be able to alter the table. In the 10g case, the statement will have to be reissued.

Forcing Dependency in Triggers

Triggers are an integral part of any application code. Since they are in the domain of database, they are often considered outside of the application. Nothing can be farther from truth; triggers that support business functionality are application code and must be evaluated in the context of the overall application. Triggers are automatically executed and associated with certain events such as before insert or after alteration of table. When used properly, they offer an excellent extension to the functionality of the application not controlled by the user's action.

Best practices in code design suggests that you modularize your code (build small chunks of code that can be called multiple times instead of creating a monolithic code). This accomplishes a lot of things, such as readability, reusability of the code, ability to unit test, and much more. However, in the case of triggers, this strategy poses a unique problem. You can define multiple triggers on the table, but Oracle does not guarantee the execution order of the triggers. The triggers of the same type can be fired at any order. If they are truly independent of each other, it may not be a problem, but what if they do depend on the data and one trigger may update the data used by the other trigger? In that case, the order of execution is extremely important. If the data-changing trigger fires after the trigger that consumes that data, then the execution will not be as expected, resulting in potentially incorrect results. Let's examine that scenario with an example. Consider the following table named PAYMENTS:

```
Name              Null?    Type
--------------    -------- --------------
PAY_ID                     NUMBER(10)
CREDIT_CARD_NO             VARCHAR2(16)
AMOUNT                     NUMBER(13,2)
PAY_MODE                   VARCHAR2(1)
RISK_RATING                VARCHAR2(6)
FOLLOW_UP                  VARCHAR2(1)
```

Assume there is only one row.

```
SQL> select * from payments;

    PAY_ID CREDIT_CARD_NO    AMOUNT P RISK_R F
    ------ ---------------- ------ - ------ -
         1
```

The columns are all empty at first. The column RISK_RATING is self explanatory; it shows the type of risk of that particular payment being processed with valid values being LOW (payment amount less than 1,000), MEDIUM (between 1,001 and 10,000) and HIGH (more than 10,000). Payments with higher risks are meant to be followed up later by a manager. The company uses a standard logic in defining the risk. Since this risk rating is meant to be assigned automatically, a before update row trigger does the job well, as shown:

```
create or replace trigger tr_pay_risk_rating
before update
on payments
for each row
begin
        dbms_output.put_line ('This is tr_pay_risk_rating');
        if (:new.amount) < 1000 then
                :new.risk_rating := 'LOW';
        elsif (:new.amount < 10000) then
                if (:new.pay_mode ='K') then
                        :new.risk_rating := 'MEDIUM';
                else
                        :new.risk_rating := 'HIGH';
                end if;
```

```
        else
                :new.risk_rating := 'HIGH';
        end if;
end;
/
```

The high risk payments were meant to be followed up, but with high workload of managers, the company decides to follow up only certain types of high risk. The follow-up should occur for HIGH risk payments to be paid with a credit card or MEDIUM risk payments to be paid with cash. Also, credit cards from a specific bank (which is showed by the second to sixth digit of the number) are also to be followed up. A trigger is set up that automatically sets FOLLOW_UP column to Y under those conditions, as shown:

```
create or replace trigger tr_pay_follow_up
before update
on payments
for each row
begin
        dbms_output.put_line ('This is tr_pay_follow_up');
        if (
                (:new.risk_rating = 'HIGH' and :new.pay_mode = 'C')
                or (:new.risk_rating = 'MEDIUM' and :new.pay_mode = 'K')
                or (substr(:new.credit_card_no,2,5) = '23456')
        ) then
                :new.follow_up := 'Y';
        else
                :new.follow_up := 'N';
        end if;
end;

/
```

I have deliberately placed the dbms_output lines to show the execution of the triggers. After these two triggers are created, perform an update on the table.

```
update payments
set credit_card_no = '1234567890123456',
    amount = 100000,
    pay_mode = 'K';

This is tr_pay_follow_up

This is tr_pay_risk_rating

1 row updated.
```

After this, select from the table.

```
SQL> select * from payments;

    PAY_ID CREDIT_CARD_NO   AMOUNT P RISK_R F
    ------ ---------------- ------ - ------ -
         1 1234567890123456 100000 K HIGH   N
```

If you examine the above output, you will notice that the payment amount is more than 10,000—a condition for RISK_RATING to be HIGH. The trigger computed that condition and set the value correctly. The mode of payment is cash (PAY_MODE is set to "K") and the amount is 100,000 and the credit card number matches the pattern "23456"—all the conditions for the FOLLOW_UP to be "Y"; but instead it is "N". Did the trigger not fire? No, it did, as you saw in the output after the update statement "This is tr_pay_follow_up". If the trigger fired, why didn't it set the value properly?

The answer lies in the order in which trigger executed. Note the output after the update statement was issued. The first trigger to fire was tr_pay_follow_up; not tr_pay_risk_rating. When the trigger fired, the values of all the columns satisfied the condition for follow-up, but not the RISK_RATING, which was NULL. Therefore, the trigger didn't find the row to satisfy the condition for follow-up. After the other trigger fired, it properly set the RISK_RATING column, but by that time the previous trigger had already executed and would not have executed again. However, if the order of execution of triggers were reversed (the risk rating trigger followed by the follow-up trigger), the situation would have been as you would have expected.

This is a great example of how the order of trigger execution is vital to application logic. Clearly the present example would be considered a bug in the application code. What's worse, the scenario is not reproducible at will; sometimes the order will be as expected and other times will be reverse. If you have a large number of such triggers, the potential for bugs will be even higher.

You can address this issue with putting all the code inside a single pre-update row trigger to control the execution code. You can create separate procedures for each trigger logic and call them inside a single pre-update row trigger. This may work but is not advisable because you have one trigger. What if you want to suppress functionality of one of the triggers? If you had multiple triggers, you could just disable that trigger and enable when needed again.

In Oracle Database 11g Release 1, there is an elegant solution. You can specify the order of execution of triggers.

```
create or replace trigger tr_pay_follow_up
before update
on payments
for each row
follows tr_pay_risk_rating
begin
        dbms_output.put_line ('This is tr_pay_follow_up');
        if (
                (:new.risk_rating = 'HIGH' and :new.pay_mode = 'C')
                or (:new.risk_rating = 'MEDIUM' and :new.pay_mode = 'K')
                or (substr(:new.credit_card_no,2,5) = '23456')
        ) then
                :new.follow_up := 'Y';
        else
                :new.follow_up := 'N';
        end if;
end;
/
```

Note the clause "follows tr_pay_risk_rating," which specifies that the trigger should be executed after the risk rating trigger. Now you can guarantee the execution of the triggers: the risk rating trigger will fire first and then the follow-up trigger. With this new setup, if you re-execute the previous example, you will see the following:

… perform the same update as before …
This is tr_pay_risk_rating
This is tr_pay_follow_up

1 row updated.

SQL> select * from payments;

```
    PAY_ID CREDIT_CARD_NO    AMOUNT P RISK_R F
    ------ ---------------- ------ - ------ -
         1 1234567890123456 100000 C HIGH   Y
```

1 row selected.

The order of execution is now tr_pay_risk_rating and then tr_pay_follow_up— *guaranteed*. The first trigger set up the column values properly, which allowed the second trigger to compute the follow-up flag correctly. This functionality now allows you to build modular code that you can just turn on and off at will.

Creating Triggers Disabled Initially

Speaking of triggers, there is another issue that bites even the most experienced and careful developers. In many organizations, application changes such as new trigger code are deployed within a planned and approved "change window," which is usually a time considered to be least impacting for the application and all the dependent components are deployed together. Suppose you are creating a new trigger (not a change to an existing trigger) on a table. The application change is perfectly coordinated and you create the new trigger, like so:

```
create or replace trigger tr_u_r_test1
before update on test1
for each row
declare
    l_col1 number;
begin
    select col1 into l_col1 from test3 where col1 = :new.col1;
    if (l_col1 > 10000) then
        :new.col2 := :new.col2 * 2;
    end if;
end;
/
```

And it fails with this message:

```
Warning: Trigger created with compilation errors.

SQL> show error
Errors for TRIGGER TR_U_R_TEST1:
```

```
LINE/COL ERROR
-------- -------------------------------------------------------------------
4/2      PL/SQL: SQL Statement ignored
6/7      PL/SQL: ORA-00942: table or view does not exist
```

To your consternation, you find that there was a little pre-requisite missed—the user was not granted the select privileges on the table TEST3, so the trigger body was invalid. However, the trigger will fire for update statements since it is enabled. You can confirm that by checking the status of the trigger.

```
select status from user_triggers where trigger_name = 'TR_U_R_TEST1';
```

```
STATUS
--------
ENABLED
```

The fact that the trigger is enabled creates a very serious condition. Since this is an update trigger, and it is enabled, the update statements will fail on the table. Here is an example:

```
SQL> update test1 set col2 = 2;
update test1 set col2 = 2
        *
ERROR at line 1:
ORA-04098: trigger 'ARUP.TR_U_R_TEST1' is invalid and failed re-validation
```

Since the trigger is enabled it will be fired for each row updated but all the executions will fail since the code is invalid. This failure of execution causes an application outage. You can fix the outage immediately by either dropping the trigger or disabling it.

```
drop trigger tr_u_r_test1;
alter trigger tr_u_r_test1 disable;
```

However, in a busy system, you may not get the locks to so implement either solution, causing the outage to extend for a longer time. To address this issue, Oracle 11g has a better option; you can create the trigger initially disabled as shown below. Note the disable clause shown in bold.

```
create or replace trigger tr_u_r_test1
before update on test1
for each row
disable
declare
    l_col1 number;
begin
    select col1 into l_col1 from test3 where col1 = :new.col1;
    if (l_col1 > 10000) then
        :new.col2 := :new.col2 * 2;
    end if;
end;
```

After this trigger is created, if you check the status, it will be disabled. If the trigger does not compile due to missing objects or grants, it will cause any application issue since it will not be enabled. If the trigger didn't compile, you will know it immediately and be able to correct the problem by adding the referenced objects or granting necessary privileges. This way you will have all the necessary prerequisites before enabling the trigger. You can also use this functionality in a slightly different manner; you can create the trigger prior to the change window and enable it during the window using alter trigger … enable command.

Summary

Validation of dependent objects as a result of the change in the parent object is inevitable. In this chapter, you learned different techniques to reduce the number of invalidations. Let's summarize the key points to know to develop applications that have fewer chances of invalidations and create shortened dependency chains.

- Dependency chains show how others reference objects. The alteration of an object may render the validity of the dependent objects questionable. To resolve that potential, Oracle may mark them invalid, forcing a reparse later.

- When objects become invalidated, they may be manually recompiled to be valid. Objects will be forced into recompiling during runtime when some session invokes them.

- Compilation requires parse locks and CPU cycles, so it affects performance.

- In a RAC database, the invalidation and revalidation must occur in all instances. This causes increased inter-instance messaging and locking exacerbating the performance issue.

- Packages offer different types of dependency. Package bodies, not specifications, depend on the objects referenced within the code. Therefore, the specification does not get invalidated when the referenced objects are altered (unless the specification refers to the altered objects as well). The dependents of the package display the specification as the reference, not the body. Therefore, while changes to a referenced object may invalidate the body, the package specification may remain valid, causing no downstream invalidation.

- Use packages instead of standalone procedures and functions to shorten the dependency chains and reduce invalidations.

- When adding new procedures and functions to packages, always add to the end instead of in the middle or the top.

- Consider using views, not tables, inside the package, which will insulate the changes to the tables from the package and reduce invalidations.

- When altering synonyms, use CREATE OR REPLACE synonym syntax, not drop/create.

- Don't use constructs like select * or insert into <Table> values (…). Use column names explicitly to reduce implicit use of columns and increasing the possibility of invalidation.

- Avoid declarations referencing entire row, such as TableName%rowtype. Instead, use TableName.ColumnName%type.

- Use multiple triggers for different types of code. Establish the dependency and execution order by FOLLOWS clause.

- Always create a trigger as disabled and enable it only after it compiles fine.

- When altering an object that might be in use, instead of shutting down the application to get the lock, use the ddl_lock_timeout parameter to let the alter statement and wait for a suitable time.

All these recommendations are exactly that: *recommendations*, not gospel to be followed blindly. You must consider them carefully in the context of your specific scenario and weigh the pros and cons before actually implementing them. In this chapter, you learned how dependencies work, how invalidations occur, and how you can avoid them, thereby making your application highly available and increasing the performance of your application by reducing unnecessary work such as forced parsing.

Index

■W, X

■Y, Z

2103821R00272

Printed in Great Britain
by Amazon.co.uk, Ltd.,
Marston Gate.